THE GUPTA VIDYA

THE GOLDEN THREAD

THE GUPTA VIDYA

There is a road, steep and thorny, beset with perils of every kind—but yet a road: and it leads to the Heart of the Universe. I can tell you how to find Those who will show you the secret gateway that leads inward only. . . . For those who win onwards, there is reward past all telling: the power to bless and save humanity. For those who fail, there are other lives in which success may come.

HELENA PETROVNA BLAVATSKY
(discovered in her desk after her death
on May 8, 1891)

THE GUPTA VIDYA

VOLUME II

THE GOLDEN THREAD

RAGHAVAN NARASIMHAN IYER

TT

Theosophy Trust Books

Norfolk, VA

The Gupta Vidya
Volume II
The Golden Thread

by Raghavan Narasimhan Iyer

Library of Congress Control Number: 2019908542
ISBN: 978-1-7334650-1-4
10 9 8 7 6 5 4 3 2 1

Publisher's Cataloging-In-Publication Data
(Prepared by The Donohue Group, Inc.)

Names: Iyer, Raghavan, 1930-1995, author.
Title: The Gupta Vidya. Volume II, The golden thread / Raghavan
Narasimhan Iyer.
Other Titles: Golden thread
Description: First edition. | Norfolk, VA : Theosophy Trust Books, 2020.
| Previously published in Hermes, 1975-1989. | Includes bibliographical
references and index.
Identifiers: ISBN 9781733465014 | ISBN 9781733465038 (ebook)
Subjects: LCSH: Theosophy. | Spiritual life. | Religions. | Immortality. |
Ethics. | Consciousness.
Classification: LCC BP565.I97 G862 2020 (print) | LCC BP565.I97
(ebook) | DDC 299.934–dc23

Theosophy Trust Books
Norfolk, VA

First edition: June 20, 2020

Published and printed in the United States of America

Articles from *Hermes* may be found at https://www.theosophytrust.org

ACKNOWLEDGEMENTS

[Editor's note: the introductory materials were intended for all three volumes, and are reproduced in each volume for the reader's convenience.]

The arcane teachings in these three volumes on the Gupta Vidya were, almost entirely, delivered orally from 1949 to 1989 in India, England, Canada and the United States. The talks and answers to questions were taped and transcribed, edited and published in the journal *Hermes* (1975 - 1989), Concord Grove Press, 1407 Chapala Street, Santa Barbara. I am deeply grateful to all those who generously helped in the task of taping, transcribing, preliminary editing, proofing, composing and formatting, copy editing and printing.

I am especially indebted to Pico Iyer for his patient and superb editing, and to Elton Hall and Kirk Gradin for transferring them from the Verityper format to that of my own computer, whilst I alone am responsible for all errors and deficiencies in this work. Whatever is of value in these volumes I owe to the writings of H.P. Blavatsky, W.Q. Judge, D.K. Mavalankar, Claude St. Martin, Bhavani Shankar, Robert Crosbie and Krishna Prem, and to my Spiritual Teachers — Ramana Maharshi, B.P. Wadia, D.S. Sharma, Sarvepalli Radhakrishnan, S. Subramaniya Aiyer, Thangammal Gopalaswami Iyer, K. Swaminathan, Krishna Shastri, my parents L. Narasimhan and Lakshmi N. Iyer, and my wife Nandini.

I have also enormously benefitted over half a century from memorable conversations with honest agnostics and humane gnostics alike — Dr. J.N. Chubb of Elphinstone College, T.D. Weldon (my main Oxford Tutor), Dr. R.H. Thouless, Maude Hoffman, Hans Christofel, Christmas Humphreys, Claude Houghton, Clifford Bax, Gilbert Murray, Victor Gollancz, H.S.L. Polak, Friedrich Plank, Rabbi Rosen, Dr. John Smythies, James Laver, Lord Bertrand Russell, Bhikshu Sangharakshita, H.D. Lewis, Stephen Spender, Arne Naess, Arnold Toynbee, Julian

Huxley, David Astor, Rev. Michael Scott, Sir William Deakin, David Footman, James Joll, H.H. Price, Sir Alfred Ayer, Sir Patrick Strawson, Patrick Corbett, Geoffrey Hudson, John Plamenatz, Richard Crossman, Sir Isaiah Berlin, Guy Wint, Albert West, Pyarelal Nair, Lord Pethick-Lawrence, Viscount and Bronwen Astor, Vinoba Bhave, Fosco Maraini, Sir Richard Livingstone, Dr. Roberto Assigioli, the monk Sangye Tenzin, the Ashanti Chief in Ghana, Danilo Dolci, Bratako Ateko, Kudjo Mawudeku, Robert Hutchins, Herbert Schneider, Paul Wienpahl, Bishop James Pike, Caesar Chavez, Ian Stevenson, Svetoslav Roerich, Tenzin Gyatso (the 14th Dalai Lama), Periyavar (the late Kanchi Shankaracharya, 1894 - 1994), and Tangye Tenzin, the wise Abbot of Sera Je Monastery (Shigatze and Bylakuppe, Mysore).

This three-volume work on the *Gupta Vidya* is gratefully dedicated to The Venerable Lohan ("The Great Sacrifice"), The Maha Chohan (Arghyanath, the "Lord of Libations"), Agatsya Muni ("the Regent of Aryavarta"), Mahatma M. (Rishi Vishvamitra) and Mahatma K.H. ("Pitaguru"). They called it forth and for Them it was recorded.

March 10, 1995   R. N. I.

SHRI RAGHAVAN N. IYER

(March 10, 1930 – June 20, 1995)

He drew a circle that shut me out —
Heretic, rebel, a thing to flout.
But Love and I had the wit to win:
We drew a circle that took him in!

Edwin Markham

The spiritually penetrating essays in these three volumes were set forth for the expressed purpose of shedding the pristine light of universal Theosophy on the path of spiritual self-regeneration in the service of humanity. The Theosophical philosophy is predicated on the ageless truth that divine wisdom exists, and, most significantly, that wise beings exist who dynamically embody it in world history; that sages and seers still grace the globe and that they continually oversee the spiritual, mental, and physical evolution of man and nature. The secret Society of Sages that guides human progress periodically sends forth one of their own to sound afresh the Divine Philosophy and exemplify the spiritual life in all its richness and mystery. Such an enlightened spiritual teacher articulates eternal but forgotten truths in ingenious ways, adopting modalities that inspire the mind, release soul perception, and cut through the froth of history and the miasma of an age.

Shri Raghavan N. Iyer was a man of immense magnanimity and deep spiritual and intellectual genius. Born in Madras, India in 1930, he matriculated at the University of Bombay at the precocious age of fourteen and received his bachelor's degree in economics at age eighteen. Two years later he received the Chancellor's Gold Medal, earned his master's degree in Advanced Economics, and was selected as the Rhodes Scholar from India to Oxford University. At Oxford, he excelled in his academic studies and avidly participated in Oxford's rich social, political, and cultural life. During his undergraduate years, he eagerly joined a number of Oxford University clubs and societies. He was apparently so well-liked and respected that, in time, he was elected president of several prominent student organizations: the Oxford Social Studies Association, the Voltaire Society, and the Plotinus Society (which he also founded). His broader social sympathies and para-political concerns were served by joining and eventually becoming president of the Oxford University Peace Association and the Oxford Majlis Society (a debating society of Oxford students from South Asia that took up political issues). In 1954, he became president of the prestigious Oxford Union — perhaps the premiere debating society of his time. (Debates were usually spontaneous, witty, and packed full of appropriate references to recognizable historical figures in literature, politics, and society.) At year's end, he earned first-class honors in Philosophy, Politics, and Economics and later was awarded his master and doctorate degrees in Political Theory.

Shri Raghavan was an outstanding teacher of philosophy and politics throughout his public life. He assumed the mantle of teaching at the age of eighteen when he was appointed Fellow and Lecturer in Economics at Elphinstone College, University of Bombay. In 1956, he was appointed an Oxford don, giving tutorials in moral and political philosophy. In addition to teaching at Oxford, he lectured throughout Europe, America, and Africa, e.g., the University of Oslo in Norway (1958), the College of Europe in Belgium (1962), Erasmus Seminar in the Netherlands (1962), the University of Chicago in America (1963), and the University of Ghana in Legon (1964). His profound insights, sparkling intellectual clarity, mastery of different conceptual languages, and his infectious enthusiasm inspired thousands of students on different continents and earned him the deep respect of his contemporaries.

After accepting a professorship at the University of California (Santa Barbara) in 1965, he taught classes and seminars in political philosophy until his retirement at the age of fifty-six. His introductory classes and graduate seminars were legendary for their philosophical depth, theoretical openness, and visionary richness. His class topics were innovative and they attracted the curious, the committed, the idealist, the political realist, and the culturally disenfranchised. The most inspiring (and exacting) undergraduate courses were always enrolled to the maximum and lectures frequently ended with spontaneous standing ovations from the students. Those classes included: "Parapolitics and the City of Man", "Anarchist Thought", "Plato and the Polis", "The Dialectic from Plato to Marx", "Politics and Literature", "American Radicalism", and "The American Dream and the City of Man". His lectures were full of wit as well as wisdom and they unfailingly inspired students to cultivate an abiding confidence in themselves as learners and to become viable contributors to the emerging City of Man. His formal lectures and innumerable informal gatherings affected generations of students who later contributed to diverse fields of work, worship, and humanitarian service.

In addition to his vast and varied gifts as a teacher, Shri Raghavan Iyer was a devoted consultant and lecturer to various world organizations committed to some form of universal human betterment. While an Oxford don, he became a member of the Executive Committee for the World Association of World Federalists (The Hague) and likewise became a consultant and lecturer for the Friends International Centre (Kranj, Yugoslavia). In a similar spirit of rendering service, he became a consultant to OXFAM and accepted the temporary post of Director of Studies, UNESCO Conference on "Mutual Understanding Between the Orient and the Occident". He was also a member of The Club of Rome, The Reform Club, and The World Futures Studies Federation. In later years he became a contributing member of the Task Force appointed by U.S. President Jimmy Carter to develop "The Global 2000 Report for the President"—a call for Promethean initiatives to meet the most compelling needs of an emerging global civilization.

Over the arc of his extraordinary life, Shri Raghavan wrote numerous articles in diverse fields of thought as well as authored and edited many works that point toward an emerging global consciousness—replete with multiple challenges and stirring prospects. In 1965, he edited *The Glass Curtain between Asia and Europe*. This compilation of essays by internationally reputed historians contained a fascinating dialogue between Shri Raghavan and the world's most eminent historian at the time, Arnold Toynbee. They mutually explored Shri Raghavan's thesis that there exists an obscuring "glass curtain" between Asia and Europe that needs to be recognized and dealt with before there can be true intellectual and cultural understanding between East and West.

His most well-known and prominent books are *The Moral and Political Thought of Mahatma Gandhi* (1973) and *Parapolitics—Toward the City of Man* (1977). Each of these remarkable pioneering works is accessible to both the profound thinker and the serious inquirer, the erudite scholar and the dedicated student, the earnest seeker and the committed practitioner. Later, in 1983, he edited an extraordinary collection of spiritually inspiring readings entitled *The Jewel in the Lotus*—aptly characterized by Professor K. Swaminathan, a noted compiler of Gandhi's collected writings, as "a Universal Bible". In addition, Shri Raghavan edited and wrote luminous introductions for numerous sacred texts, including Hindu, Buddhist, Jain, Jewish, Christian, and Sufi teachings.

The deeper replenishing current of Shri Raghavan's life, however, flowed from the empyrean springs of *Theosophia*. He became a Theosophist at age ten when his father first took him to the United Lodge of Theosophists in Bombay. In time, he was introduced to the profound writings of H.P. Blavatsky and W.Q. Judge. Not long after entering the orbit of the Theosophical Movement, he made a sacred resolve to serve the Lodge of Mahatmas and increasingly assumed responsibility for forwarding the impulse of the worldwide Theosophical Cause of promoting universal brotherhood. For the rest of his life, all his efforts in the academic, social, political, and religious arenas were infused by his wholehearted devotion to the service of the Brotherhood of Bodhisattvas and to the enlightenment of the human race. This deeper, ever-present golden thread of meaning that wove together all his worldly activities became more apparent when he emigrated to America.

In 1965, Shri Raghavan moved with his wife and son to Santa Barbara, California. (His wife, Nandini, a brilliant Oxford don who received a First in Philosophy, Politics, and Economics at Oxford, went on to teach in both the Philosophy and Religious Studies departments at the University of California, Santa Barbara until her retirement. Pico, their only child, was born in Oxford in 1957. He later graduated from Oxford University and became a contributing writer to *Time* magazine and is now a noted author of international standing.) Once settled in California, Shri Raghavan and Nandini founded the United Lodge of Theosophists, Santa Barbara. Beginning informally in October of 1966, the Lodge grew from fourteen initial students to over a hundred active associates. Soon after its inaugural meeting on February 18, 1969 (the death anniversary of Shri Krishna), Lodge members were invited to give talks and, in time, to co-lead Theosophy School classes for the young. In addition to evolving various modalities of giving and receiving Theosophical instruction, Shri Raghavan and Nandini founded several ancillary institutions that further served the global aims of the worldwide Theosophical Movement.

One such ancillary institution is the Institute of World Culture in Santa Barbara. On July 4, 1976 — the bicentennial of the American Declaration of Independence — Shri Raghavan and Nandini co-initiated this educational non-profit organization. Its "Declaration of Interdependence" elucidates ten aims that are the visionary basis of all its intellectually and culturally enlightening programs and activities. The Institute of World Culture regularly hosts engaging seminars, forums, lectures, study circles, and film series. There is a wholesome blending of spiritual, intellectual, ethical, and cultural themes for focused thought and extensive discussion. The Institute has proved to be a culturally "consciousness expanding" experience for many and has, in its own way, contributed to a deeper appreciation of the often unsuspected power of classical and renaissance cultures to provide illuminating perspectives on a host of contemporary national and global issues.

As a forward-looking extension of his sacred obligation to serve the Theosophical Movement, Shri Raghavan founded, edited, and wrote for the golden journal *Hermes* (1975 – 1989). This wide-ranging spiritual journal was dedicated to the pristine sounding of Brahma Vach and to the spiritual regeneration of humanity. The profound articles found in *Hermes* span the spectrum of human thought from the metaphysical to the mystical, the ethical to the psychological, the spiritual to the material, the mythical to the historical. They convincingly reveal the subtle Theosophical foundations of all religions, philosophies, and sciences. They ingeniously address the chronic problems of the age and provide much needed "correctives to consciousness" in an age that tilts away from soul-saving and revitalizing ideals.

As repeatedly witnessed by close students, Shri Raghavan spoke at many different levels and freely interacted with each and all — regardless of race, creed, or condition. He exemplified — for the sake of the future — a multitude of Aquarian modalities and qualities. He was, in one sense, very Hindu: a true Brahmin — spiritual, cultured, brilliant, full of the graces that immediately remind one of ancient India and of golden ages long past. He was also very English: confident, highly educated, extremely literate, and at ease with statesmen, scientists, educators, and royalty. He was also very American: a true and fearless rebel, innovative, resourceful, visionary, and the eternal friend of the common man. But, beyond all this, he was in a much deeper sense the Universal Man, original, *sui generis* and timeless. His sympathies were always compassionately inclusive and his repeated emphasis — from first to last — was to "draw the larger circle" through universality of thought, the richness of imagination, the therapeutics of speech, and the magic of selfless action.

The wide-ranging arcane teachings in all three of these volumes were transcriptions of talks given between 1949 to 1989 in India, England, and the United States and were carefully edited by Shri Raghavan shortly before his death. When meditated upon and skillfully applied to the realm of self-chosen duties, they purify the mind, cleanse the heart, and give birth to men and women committed to creatively contributing to the universal civilization of tomorrow.

CONTENTS

ॐ

AUM

To contemplate these things is the privilege of the gods, and to do so is also the aspiration of the immortal soul of man generally, though only in a few cases is such aspiration realized.

PLATO

G UPTA VIDYA *is like an ancient Banyan tree.*
*Some come to sit in its shade, while others come
to exchange words and seek friends. Still others come to
pick fruit. Nature is generous.*

*Some come to sit in the presence of teachers to receive
instruction in the mighty power of real meditation, to
secure help in self-examination. All are welcome.*

*The antiquity and enormity of the tree are beyond the
capacity of any person in any period of history to enclose in a
definition or formulation.*

*Great Teachers point beyond themselves to that
which is beyond formulation, which is ineffable and
indefinable. They seek to make alive and to make real
for every man the priceless boon of learning truth.*

RAGHAVAN N. IYER

THE GUPTA VIDYA

The universe is even as a great temple.
CLAUDE DE ST. MARTIN

The central truths of Gupta Vidya are not derived from any ancient or modern sect but represent the accumulated wisdom of the ages, the unrecorded inheritance of humanity. Its vast scheme of cosmic and human evolution furnishes all true seekers with the symbolic alphabet necessary to interpret their recurrent visions as well as the universal framework and metaphysical vocabulary, drawn from many mystics and seers, which enable them to communicate their own intuitive perceptions. All authentic mystical writings are enriched by the alchemical flavour of theosophical thought. Gupta Vidya is an integrated system of fundamental verities taught by initiates and adepts across millennia. It is the *Philosophia Perennis*, the philosophy of human perfectibility, the science of spirituality and the religion of responsibility. It is the primeval fount of myriad religious systems as well as the hidden essence and esoteric wisdom of each. Its cosmology is known as *Brahma Vidya* and its noetic psychology is known as *Atma Vidya*. Man, an immortal monad, has been able to preserve this sacred heritage through the sacrificial efforts of enlightened and compassionate individuals, or Bodhisattvas, who constitute an ancient Brotherhood. They quietly assist in the ethical evolution and spiritual development of the whole of humanity. Gupta Vidya is Divine Wisdom, transmitted and verified over aeons by the sages who belong to this secret Brotherhood.

The supreme presupposition of Gupta Vidya is an eternal substance-principle postulated as the ineffable Ground of all being. It is called a substance-principle because it becomes increasingly substantial and differentiated on the plane of manifestation, while it essentially remains a homogeneous principle in abstract space and eternal duration. The perceived universe is a complex mirroring of this Unknown Source, all finite conceptions of which are necessarily incomplete. It is the Absolute Negation of all that exists. It is Be-ness or *Sat*, the Secondless Reality, the No-thing of ancient philosophy, the 'Boundless Lir', the Unknown Beginning of Celtic cosmogony. Compared with It, all manifestation is no more than an impermanent illusion or *maya*, a kaleidoscopic medium through which the one Reality shows itself in a series of reflections. Spirit and matter are the two facets of this indivisible principle which only seem to be separate during a vast period of cosmic manifestation. They radiate from this transcendent source, yet are not causally related to It, since neither quality nor mode may properly be ascribed to It. They appear periodically on the objective plane as the opposite poles of this Reality yet they are not inherently separate, but mutually coexist as spirit-matter. In manifestation this substratum differentiates itself into seven planes of increasing density, reaching towards the region of sense data. Everywhere the root essence of homogeneous substance is the same, transforming itself by minute degrees from the most ethereal to the most gross.

The seven planes of manifestation may be seen as condensations of rarefied matter and also as living streams of intelligences — primordial rays proceeding from an invisible Spiritual Sun. All modes of activity in the Universe are internally guided by powers and potencies arrayed in an almost endless series of hierarchies, each with its exact function and precise scope of action. They are called Dhyan Chohans in Tibetan cosmogony and bear many other titles in the rich panoply of religious traditions — Angels, Devas, Dhyani Buddhas, Gods, Elohim, etc. All these are transmitting agents of cosmic Law (*ṛta*) which guides the evolution of each atom on every plane in space, the hierarchies varying enormously in their respective degrees of creative consciousness and monadic intelligence. As an aggregate, this immense host of forces forms the manifesting Verbum of an unmanifest Presence, constituting simultaneously the active Mind of the cosmos and its immutable Law. The idea of myriad hierarchies of intelligences animating visible Nature is a vital key to understanding all true mysticism. Many flashes of intuitive perception reveal multitudes of radiant beings elaborating the interior architecture of matter. Great mystics show a reverential recognition of the Logos or Verbum, the Army of the Voice, operating behind the screen of surface events as the noumenal cause of natural phenomena. This involves deciphering the signs of these intelligent forces by following the traces of their effects. The natural world bears the signatures of a divine archetypal world. With proper keys to archaic symbolism, the true seeker can read these signatures and recover the lost knowledge which would restore a primeval state of gnosis equivalent to that of the Gods. The letters composing the Sanskrit language are the phenomenal expressions of these finer forces, and by understanding them one could discover the root vibration, the ineffable Word, reverberating throughout the sentient world of visible Nature.

The arcane teaching concerning the Great Chain of Being in the supernatural realm continually reappears in human history as the inexhaustible fountain-head of aesthetic expression, heroic action and mystic illumination. The diverse expressions of creativity in the arts, religion and philosophy stem from this common unseen source, and the search for its origin is the hallowed mission of many a mystic and artist. The problem of tracing particulars to universals is as crucial to art as to psychology. The sevenfold classification of man's inner constitution corresponds to seven cosmic planes of being. Man is truly a microcosm and miniature copy of the macrocosm. Like the macrocosm, the individual is divine in essence, a direct radiation from the central Spiritual Sun. As pure spirit, every human being needs the vestures through which life may be experienced on differentiated planes of existence, so that one can become fully conscious of individual immortality and one's indissoluble identity with the whole. Every person is a complete reflection of the universe, revealing oneself to oneself by means of seven differentiations. In one's deepest self, the individual is

Atman, the universal spirit which is mirrored in the luminous soul or *Buddhi.* The light of *Buddhi* is focussed through *Manas* or impersonal intellect, the source of human individuation. These three together constitute the imperishable fire in man, the immortal Triad that undertakes an immense pilgrimage through successive incarnations to emerge as an effortlessly self-conscious agent of the divine will, the Light of the Logos, Brahma Vach.

Below this overbrooding Triad is the volatile quaternary of principles drawn from the lower planes of cosmic matter: they are *kama,* the force of blind passion and chaotic desire shared by man with animal life; *prana,* the life-current energizing the whirling atoms on the objective plane of existence; the astral paradigmatic body *(linga sharira),* the original form around which the physical molecules shape themselves, and hence the model for the physical frame *(sthula sharira).* This quaternary of principles is evanescent and changeable, established for man's use at the time of incarnation and dissolved at death into its primary constituents on their corresponding planes. The real man, the higher Triad, recedes from the physical plane to await the next incarnation. The function of each of these sheaths differs from one individual to another according to the level of spiritual development of the incarnated soul. The astral body of the Adept is of a much higher degree of resilience and purity than that of the average man. In visionaries and mystics, the sheaths intervening between the spiritual man and the brain-mind are sufficiently transparent so that they can receive communications from the overbrooding Triad in a relatively lucid manner. Man is a compound being simultaneously experiencing two worlds, inner and outer. Each person's present life experience is but a minute portion of what was witnessed by the immortal individuality in previous incarnations. Thus if men and women assiduously search within themselves, they can recover a vast heritage of knowledge spanning aeons. These memories are locked in mansions of the soul which only ardent desire and strong discipline can penetrate.

Memory is integral to consciousness and since all matter is alive and conscious, all beings from cells to deities have memory of some type. In man, memory is generally divided into four categories: physical memory, remembrance, recollection and reminiscence. In remembrance, an idea impinges upon the mind from the past by free association; in recollection, the mind deliberately searches it out. Reminiscence, however, is of another order altogether. Called 'soul-memory', it links every human being to previous lives and assures each that he or she will live again. In principle, any man or woman may recover the knowledge gained in previous incarnations and maintain continuity with the *sutratman*, the thread-soul, the eternal witness to every incarnation. There are also types of memory which are indistinguishable from prophecy, since the more one progresses towards homogeneous and rarefied planes of existence, the more past, present and future collapse into eternal duration, within the boundless perspective of which an entire cycle of manifestation may be surveyed. Such was the level of insight reached by the great seers or rishis who recorded their findings in the Vedas and other great scriptures, thus transmitting the ancient *Gupta Vidya* or 'the Secret Doctrine', fitly taken as the title of H.P. Blavatsky's monumental modern exposition of theosophical thought. Some mystics have penetrated deeply into the realms of reminiscence, bringing back the fruits of knowledge in previous lives. Greater still is the ability to enter into former and more spiritual epochs of humanity and to make those visions come alive for those who had lost all but a faint intuition of a larger sense of self.

The source and destiny of the soul's inward life fundamentally involve the entire scope of evolution. Coeval with the manifestation of the seven worlds of the cosmic plenum is the re-emergence of beings who assume once more the evolutionary pilgrimage after an immense period of rest. The emanation of matter and spirit into the objective plane of existence is but half the cycle. Its return brings all beings and forms to the bosom of absolute darkness. The period of manifestation covering trillions of years is called a *manvantara* and the corresponding period of rest, called *pralaya*, lasts for an equal duration. They are the Days and Nights of Brahmā, which were reckoned with meticulous precision by the ancient Aryans. The whole span of the *manvantara* is governed by the law of periodicity which regulates rates of activity on all planes of being. This is sometimes spoken of as 'the Great Breath' which preserves the cosmos. The essence of life is motion, growth and expansion of awareness in every atom. Each atom is at its core a monad, an expression of the highest self *(Atman)* and its vesture is the spiritual soul *(Buddhi)*. Prior to the monad's emergence in the human family, it undergoes aeons of experience in the lower kingdoms of nature, developing by natural impulse (metempsychosis) until the latent thinking faculty of *Manas* is awakened by the sacrificial efforts of beings who have risen far above the human state in *manvantaras* past. They kindle the spark of self-consciousness, making the unconscious monad a true man *(Manushya)*, capable of thought, reflection and deliberate action. The soul embarks upon a long cycle of incarnations in human form to prepare itself for entry into still greater planes of existence.

The evolutionary tide on earth is regulated by the unerring hand of cyclic law. Man passes through a series of Rounds and Races which allows him to assimilate the knowledge of every plane of existence, from the most ethereal to the most material. Man's planetary evolution describes a spiral passing from spirit into matter and returning to spirit again with a wholly self-conscious mastery of the process. Each Round is a major evolutionary period lasting many millions of years. Each Race in turn witnesses the rise and fall of continents, civilizations and nations. An earlier Race than our own, the Lemurian, lived in an idyllic Golden Age, an epoch ruled by natural religion, universal fraternity, and spontaneous devotion to spiritual teachers. Many of the myths regarding an era of childlike purity and unsullied trust in humanity's early flowering preserve the flavour of this period. As man evolved more material vestures, *kama* or passion tainted his power of thought and inflamed his irrational tendencies. The nightmare tales of Atlantean sorcerers are the heavy heirloom of contemporary humanity. The destruction of Atlantis ushered in the Aryan race of our own epoch. The Indian sages who inaugurated this period are among the torchbearers for the humanity of our time. Intuitive mystics recognize the sacred role of ancient India as mother and preserver of the spiritual heritage of present humanity. The classical Indian scriptures resonate with the authentic voice of the Verbum, uncorrupted by time and human ignorance.

Pertinent to historical insight is the doctrine of the *yugas,* the cycle of four epochs through which every Race passes, the Golden, Silver, Bronze and Iron Ages. The *yugas* indicate a broad sweep of karmic activity at any point in the life of an individual or collection of individuals. The entire globe may not be undergoing the same age simultaneously nor may any one individual be necessarily in the same epoch as his social milieu. According to Hindu calculations, *Kali Yuga* began over 5,090 years ago and will last altogether for a total of 432,000 years. This dark age is characterized by widespread confusion of roles, inversion of ethical values and enormous suffering owing to spiritual blindness. Many have celebrated the myth of the Golden Age as extolling the plenitude of man's creative potential. The doctrine of the *yugas* is not deterministic. It merely suggests the relative levels of consciousness which most human beings tend to hold in common. Thus a Golden Age vibration can be inserted into an Iron Age to ameliorate the collective predicament of mankind. The Golden Age surrounded human beings as a primordial state of divine consciousness, but their own pride and ignorance precluded its recovery. In the wonder of childhood, in archaic myths, in the sporadic illuminations of great artists and in mystical visions, one may discern shimmering glimpses of the Golden Age of universal *eros,* the rightful original estate of humanity.

The progress of humanity in harmony with cyclic law is facilitated by a mature grasp of karma and rebirth. These twin doctrines of responsibility and hope unravel many of the riddles of life and Nature. They show that every person's life and character are the outcome of previous lives and thought patterns, that each one is his or her own judge and executioner, and that all rise or fall strictly by their own merits and misdeeds. Nothing is left to chance or accident in life but everything is under the governance of a universal law of ethical causation. Man is essentially a thinker, and all thoughts initiate causes that generate suffering or bliss. The immortal Triad endures the mistakes and follies of the turbulent quaternary until such time as it can assume its rightful stature and act freely in consonance with cosmic order and natural law. As man is constantly projecting a series of thoughts and images, individual responsibility is irrevocable. Each person is the centre of any disturbance of universal harmony and the ripples of effects must return to him. Thus the law of karma or justice signifies moral interdependence and human solidarity.

Karma must not be seen as a providential means of divine retribution but rather as a universal current touching those who bear the burden of its effects. This has been called the law of spiritual gravitation. The entire scope of man's affairs — his environment, friends, family, employment and the like — are all dictated by the needs of the soul. Karma works on the soul's behalf to provide those opportunities for knowledge and experience which would aid its progress. This concept could be expanded so as to encompass all connections with other human beings of even the most casual kind, seeing them as karmically ordained not for one's own progress but for the sake of those who struggle with the dire limitations of ignorance, poverty or despair. A deeply moving account of this trial is given in *The Hero in Man*, wherein, while walking among the wretched outcasts of Dublin, the author, George William Russell ('A.E.'), rejoices in the conviction that the benevolence he feels for each benighted soul will forge a spiritual bond through which he may help them in the future. Karma means a summons to the path of action and duty. As one cannot separate one's own karma from that of one's fellow-men, one may determine to devote one's life to the remission of the karmic burden of others.

At death the true Self or immortal Triad casts off the physical and astral bodies and is released from the thraldom of passions and desires. Its natural tropism to gravitate upwards allows it to enter the rarefied plane of consciousness where its thoughts are carried to culmination, clothed in a finer body suited to that sublime existence. This state, *devachan*, is a period of rest and assimilation between lives and the basis of the popular mythology of heaven. On the other hand, the lower quaternary languishes after death in *kamaloka*, the origin of theological dogmas concerning hell and purgatory. There it dissolves by degrees back into its primary elements at a rate determined by the cohesion given them by the narcissistic personality during life on earth. Inflamed passions and poisonous thoughts sustained for long periods of time endow this entity with a vivid, vicarious and ghoulish existence. This plane of consciousness, termed 'the Astral Light' by Eliphas Lévi, is intimately connected with the lives and thoughts of most of mankind. It is the vast slag-heap of Nature into which all selfish and evil thoughts are poured and then rebound back to pollute and contaminate human life on earth. This plane of carnalized thought tends to perpetuate the horrors of the Iron Age and condemn humanity to a state of spiritual darkness.

The crucial difference between individuals lies in whether they are enslaved by the Astral Light (the region of psyche) or whether they are capable of rising above it to a calm awareness of the wisdom and compassion latent in their higher nature, the realm of nous. Beyond the region of psychic action lies the pristine sphere of noetic awareness called *Akasha*, from which empyrean individuals could derive the inspiration needed to go forth and inaugurate a Golden Age by laying down the foundations of a regenerated civilization. Sages, past and present, saluted as Men of the Word (*Brahma Vach*), have accomplished the arduous transformation of their own natures, overcoming every vice and limitation and perfecting themselves in noetic ideation and sacrificial action. Mahatmas or Hierophants and Bodhisattvas renounce everything for the sake of suffering humanity. Solitary mystics on the ancient Bodhisattva path of service salute them as gurus, guides and preceptors and acknowledge their invisible presence as the *Guruparampara*, the sacred lineage behind their own modest labours for mankind. These wise beings are the noble trustees of the *Philosophia Perennis* and the compassionate teachers of the whole human family. The mystical pilgrimage of mankind is an authentic reflection of their ageless wisdom.

THE
GOLDEN THREAD

THE PHILOSOPHY OF
PERFECTION

The philosophy of perfection centres upon a constellation of important ideas which can be clarified by distinguishing between three levels of reflection. First are those considerations that turn upon the relativity of perfection as a concept in the realm of time and in the world of the visible. Secondly, there are other factors which focus upon what may be called the engine or motivating power which actually makes perfection not just a concept, but a driving force in human life and evolution. The elements in this engine — imagination, illumination and devotion — are involved in the problems of relativity intrinsic to the concept of perfection and require a philosophy or metaphysics to put in perspective. Thirdly, there are those transcendental virtues (*paramitas*) that refer to perfection in its deepest and highest aspect: perfection in spiritual wisdom. In *The Voice of the Silence* the Teacher speaks of "the great Perfections three." These are like three degrees in the attainment of spiritual wisdom.

To take the simplest level first, 'perfection' as a term is always relative. It is relative to a context, relative to standards set or recognized as relevant. It is also relative to expectations, and so to the dynamic and painful, contradictory and compelling patterns of human relationships. A great deal of misdirected energy goes into perfecting other people, coupled with a refusal to learn anything at all, let alone to be told anything by anyone else. This involves something tricky and even treacherous, which has a lot to do with perfectionism, fussiness and sheer bloody-mindedness. Such perfectionism, indeed, has given the very notion of perfection a bad name, making it static and tyrannical, and making the notion of perfectibility seem at best a fantasy myth in politics. No wonder, then, it is the prevailing fashion among right-wing thinkers to turn their noses against perfectibility; though few

Americans would have the courage to turn their noses directly against the Founding Fathers, they will readily turn their noses against their ideas — all in the name of being Americans. This has happened before. It happened in reference to Buddha. It happened in reference to Christ. It happened, to a lesser extent, in reference to earlier Teachers like Krishna and later Teachers like Pythagoras. It certainly happened a great deal in reference to Confucius, a fact central to the history of China.

If the word 'perfect' is used in a relative sense, it is most meaningful when talking about the perfection of a skill or a function. Everyone can understand a functional view of perfection: mastering a craft or a musical instrument, or else summoning a certain speed, smoothness or efficiency, as when one sits before a typewriter and aims at a certain standard of perfection. This idea, however, has been infected in the modern age with a spurious precision that arises entirely out of quantification. This approach is perfectly meaningful, though somewhat illusive, at the cosmic level, but when translated into machines it gives one a mechanistic view of robotic perfection. This can enormously oppress a whole nation, such as Japan, which has become the latest entrant in the appallingly perverse drift towards mechanization in the name of progress.

Such a mechanized and quantified notion of perfection, connected with the use of machines, may allow one to speak of perfectly smooth-running machines or perfect computers. But this notion has spread so far that some people have forgotten about the deeper organic meaning of perfection, as, for example, when it is applied to the human body. The human body is still a mystery, not only to medicine but also to modern man. If perfection has as much to do with resilience, resistance and abstention as with smoothness, if it involves not doing something as much as doing something, it becomes much more than a merely functional term. If the heart or any of the human organs persistently overdoes something, that is a sure sign not only of imperfection but of disease and death. In the body, perfection consists in doing only what is needed. This applies to the brain, with its vast complex of mostly untapped centres of electricity. It is true in reference to the heart and the entire nervous system. It is crucially true in reference to the cerebellum and the sympathetic and autonomic systems and their relation to the cerebrum and the conscious process of selection. There is something about the way the process of selection works that is balanced by a sense of limit — one only selects as much as one can handle. These considerations alone yield a concept of perfection much richer than what one would find in a purely functional notion grafted onto a mechanistic picture of robots.

Nonetheless, at the root of this limited and limiting idea of perfection is an idea that anyone, even a child, can understand, and is relevant to the very highest levels of spiritual perfection. It is the idea of an art. It is the idea of judicious use. It is most readily understandable in music. One may listen to several distinctive but 'perfect' renditions of a great piece of music. How can there be several different perfect versions of the same piece, each communicating something different, each transmitting something distinctively new? To understand this is to pay tribute to the inexhaustible depth of music and to the potential wealth of artistic genius. But it also refers to that complex relationship between human beings and instruments matured over a period of time which enables a person to use an instrument so as to hover trembling at the limits of what is audible, and, in pregnant moments of silence, to give a sense of the deeper unstated meaning of music.

This conception is much subtler than even the organic notion of perfectibility. It involves a rich conscious relationship between subject and object. This leads one to ask what is the metaphysical basis of a view of perfection which can accommodate myriad possible views, modes and instances — in function or form, in art or music, in a leaf or a flower — without limiting or exhausting the content of possibility. In short, perfection requires assumptions not only about what actually exists but also about what is possible. In other words, there is a dialectical relation between potential and actualization. To admit this capacity to actualize unknown

potential necessarily inserts a subjective element into the notion
of perfection. It is therefore totally absurd to say that a human
being can ever settle for an objective external view of what is
perfect. If ten imperfect men befriended a 'perfect' woman, each
would have to work out a very different relationship with her. Each
would also have to revise and rethink the notion of what is perfect.

Whenever one considers a relational notion of perfection,
which is to be experienced, assessed, tested, revised and rethought,
one must acknowledge the element of subjectivity. To take a simple
example, when one talks of a perfect meal, there is a good reason
why nothing tastes quite like what one's mother cooked long ago,
and nothing in turn tastes like what one's mother learnt from
her mother. And so it goes, from the accumulated wisdom of
cooking that is not transmissible through a recipe book. Cooking
becomes esoteric and can never be revealed; cooking becomes
exemplified. Here one is talking about one's own experience of
examples in the past, one's own attempt to relate them to
expectations and evolving standards, all of which affect one's
notion of perfection.

This much being clear, one is beginning to stand at the
threshold separating the empirical, the linguistic and the semantic
from the metaphysical. What, then, is the metaphysical basis of
perfection? An excellent example in modern thought is provided
by Leibniz, for whom there is something intrinsic in every
organism and therefore in every monadic atom in every being in
all the visible kingdoms. There is, in the monad, an entelechy, an
intrinsic propulsion towards realization and elaboration of all that
is already programmed in everything that is already potential.
Because the monad is not concrete, this has metaphysical
implications. The monad is not limited by reference to external
physical form, nor is it psychologically bounded in reference to
inward experience. It is philosophically similar to the theological
notion of the soul, which was tainted by dogmatism even in the
time of Leibniz, but which implies something abstract, having to
do with logical possibility, and therefore something that is
theoretically prior to the empirically given.

At the same time, what makes this conception metaphysically compelling is the notion of necessity attached to that which is theoretically and ontologically prior to what exists. This is a philosophical way of saying that human beings, as immortal souls, have already within themselves something which is deeper than an image, profounder than a concept, and more lasting than even an urge to perfection — something rooted in the nature of consciousness itself. Metaphysically, it concerns the relationship of the infinite richness of consciousness to the infinite variety of possible form. It does not lie in either separately, but is hidden in the relationship of consciousness to form. If this is the metaphysical basis of such a notion of perfection, it is equally important in practice. Every human being is searching for a sense of distinction between the real and the unreal, the ever-changing and the evanescent, the immortal and the mortal. Every human being is engaged in defining what is perfect and perfectible amidst conditions of limitation and imperfection.

This insight gains especial significance when seen in the light of a central metaphysical tenet of the philosophy of perfection in Gupta Vidya: namely, the proposition that all human beings are both perfect and imperfect, both immortal and mortal. Human beings are capable of a degree of creative vision and imagination in elaborating what is potentially possible. At the same time, the fullness of perfection far transcends the capacity of expression in words, in sketches or even in mathematical formulae. One can always draw a circle to circumscribe something in the mind, but there is much more that is implied in the blank space within and outside the circle. There is always a gap between what people are capable of conceiving and what people are actually capable of creating. There is a further gap between what they are capable of creating and what in fact they actually create. These two gaps are crucial to the philosophy of perfection.

Given the second gap in human life, much weight is given to intention. Where there is an intention to create for a noble and selfless purpose, a great deal can be overlooked in the realm of the created. Suppose that one person actually creates something better than another person, but in the first person the motivation is largely self-satisfaction, competition and self-indulgence, while in the second person the motive is charity, inspiration and gratitude. An objective observer looking at the two will notice a very real sense in which the more imperfect creation is actually a greater example of the richness of mental perfection. Ever since the last war, people have become used to having international exhibitions of children's paintings. Many people have come to see that in these often badly structured and crude paintings there shines a vitality, a dignity and a beauty that transcends many finished works of art. The trained eye sees in them an *eros* struggling to breakthrough.

Chinese and Japanese artists often held that one should never attempt anything without including incompleteness and imperfection, an emptiness that leaves room for further growth. To do otherwise is an insult to the viewer, a failure to leave room for the imagination. In that sense, the greater part of any actual creation is what it intimates about the future. Put in a paradoxical way, the less perfected something is, the more perfect it is. That which is less perfected opens the door to greater perfection.

Metaphysically, if every human being is both perfect and imperfect, there is a clear need for a much deeper explanation of the relation between spirit and matter, consciousness and form, *purusha* and *prakriti*. If one is perfect in consciousness, whilst imperfect in form, what, then, is human perfection? Human perfection must refer to the relationship between that which is mortal and that which is immortal, that which is finite and that which is inexhaustible. Clearly, one cannot work out such a doctrine of perfection without a doctrine of planes of consciousness and states of matter, with correspondences and consubstantiality between each plane of ideation and each state of matter. Therefore, the entire notion of perfection involves a cosmology. It also involves a complex system of teachings about the interactions between the finitizing tendency in Nature and in human consciousness and the transcendent elements that work through matter.

Thus one reaches the critical conclusion that one cannot know from the outside, in the realm of the mortal and the imperfect, what is really going on inside human beings. One has very little clue to the degrees of growth made by souls. Yet by watching the way a person sits, the way a person moves, the way a person chooses, one can see something about the relation between inner and outer. A crucial starting point, which provides a criterion of the spiritual quality of different cultures and collective notions of progress, goes back to a contribution of Pico della Mirandola at the time of the Renaissance: *human beings are so constituted that what is paradigmatic about being human is the possibility of exercising the power of choice.* This goes much further than any Aristotelian emphasis on reason or any conception of man as a rational animal capable of seeking happiness. Yet it is also diametrically opposite to the conventional Christian notion of man as an original sinner created by an omnipotent god. Man is that being who, alone in the universe, has both the prerogative and the predicament of exercising free choice. The extent to which a human being matures, develops and perfects the power of choice governs the extent to which he or she is able to bring down perfection into the realm of time, while at the same time recognizing the limits of what is possible in time. One cannot perfect the power of choice if one's concern is with anything less than the universal good. This insight goes all the way back to Plato. It comes through in Leibniz and it is implicit in Pico. If one is choosing in relation to a universal standard or the universal good, it is important to choose well. But it is also important not to expect that what one chooses will be more than a limited actualization of what is possible.

Take an example of effective choice. The average person has forty or fifty years between youth and old age in which to hold a job. One may, at high school and in the early years of university life, be spoilt by being able to switch constantly from course to course, by dropping out and coming back. Nonetheless, a point comes at which one has to choose to make the most of one's life vocationally, in terms of perfecting a skill and offering something useful to society. One stays with the job until ready to retire. Whatever the limitations of one's job, one makes the most of it, lending it meaning from outside, and bringing to it a moral quality that goes beyond the technical job description. One must make an art of one's life, of the way one discharges duties, grows as a human being, and continues to read, think and learn. At the same time, one must learn from errors and make adjustments, not only in one's psyche, but also in one's expectations, and above all in one's relationships, so that one comes to value fidelity. One must not see others as expendable in terms of one's erratic notions of unlimited satisfaction, but must stick with them. The moment one chooses a specific vocation — what Buddha called right livelihood — one must limit oneself.

The moment one begins to see the subtleties in the notion of perfection, one must prepare for a shock. Every human being defines himself or herself at the moment of birth by the way he or she pronounces the AUM. Human beings delude themselves over a lifetime, because they have in fact defined themselves by the sound they uttered at the moment of birth. The way that sound is uttered, the quality of it, the degree of detachment it represents, marks the degree of honest recognition of the limitations built into physical incarnation. It is a cry of universality, of enthusiasm and of gratitude to the mother. If this is not shock enough, one must also see that the sound uttered by human beings at the moment of death has consequences equally devastating to complacency. How many human beings are able to die with the same sound they began with as babies? If all babies begin life with the AUM, how many can die with it on their lips, not uttered in the same way as before, but uttered with wisdom, detachment and compassion? If one sees this connection between the moment of birth and the moment of death, one will understand something about continuity in life.

How little, then, is known about human beings from the outside, and how little do people know about themselves. There is no basis whatsoever for making any external judgements about the status of human souls, because all such notions can only be made from the outside. No wonder, then, that people caught up in empiricism and perfectionism reduce their assessments of human stature to false ideas about tall and short. Often people are imprisoned in totally false and unnecessary myths. It is so sad to think of whole nations wasting their energy trying to be taller. There must be something more inspiring to human life. Yet this is what happens when people will not be agnostic and calm, will not look within and be honest with themselves. Anxious to settle for an external criterion, they will usually go for a crude measure that tells nothing at all about the human condition. This is only possible because today, as never before, people are willing to divorce notions of perfection from ethical considerations. All the notions of perfection that sustained excellence in classical cultures for a long time had ethical foundations. In the most ancient civilizations, this went far beyond any notions of heaven and hell, salvation and damnation.

Once one has genuinely faced one's ignorance of perfection, one is entitled to ask what it is that will actually provide consciousness a means of sifting and selecting. How can one not only get to know, but get to know better? How can one learn to do better and sustain an incentive to grow, to perfect oneself beyond specific skills and beyond limiting lists of moral virtue? To answer these questions, one will have to look at all the ingredients involved in this process. The most important are illumination and imagination. Illumination is very rare. Each human being may have moments of illumination in deep sleep, certainly in meditation, but illumination is not something one can command. Nor is it something one can contrive or fool oneself about: it is something for which one has to prepare oneself. Imagination, on the other hand, is something everyone can start working with. The first step involves a good spring-cleaning job, as one cleans out the imagination, empties out all the rubbish put into it for years by television, the media and the visual bombardment of sensation. One should remove all limiting concepts of a perfectionist nature in regard to either the moral or the mental life, let alone the spiritual. One should also completely eradicate any lingering notion about whether perfected men are either bearded or beardless. *Yogins* may look like beggars. They may come as kings. They may come in whatever form suits them, for part of their whole purpose is to come in a form in which they are invisible. They are certainly not going to fulfil the requirements and expectations of those who are looking from outside.

In deep sleep, the immaculate imagination may recover the forgotten language of the soul. This may take the form of geometrical signs or more elaborate glyphs and symbols, but it can also take the form of powerful ideation. Above all, there is no richer food for the imagination than the magnificent portraits of Sages given in the sacred texts. Every day in his ashram throughout his adult life, Gandhi used the last nineteen verses in the second chapter of the *Bhagavad Gita,* the great section on the Self-Governed Sage. That one passage gives a basis for meditating about the perfected man, not in terms of anything external, but in terms of internal essence. Like a master musician who is not concerned with performing on stage, the Sage has perfected within himself his relationship to the instrument, to the vestures. One may read these great portraits in the *Gita* and make them come alive, just as millions of people around Southeast Asia have made come alive something that is intangible behind the Buddha statue. Such statues are all too often the subject of humour in Western drawing rooms, but to the poor peasant in Thailand they are everything. God, humanity and all the sages speak to him through the silence of that small stone statue. The gap in consciousness between this purity of imagination and the so-called sophistication of the polluted modern mind underscores the necessity of refining and redefining one's sense of imagination. When an island of pure thought is formed in waking meditation, it can link up with deep sleep, and the soul can become ready for illumination.

Full illumination requires complete mastery of the paradox of the manifest and the unmanifest, and supreme spiritual perfection requires effortless exemplification of the transcendental virtues "that transform the body into the Tree of Knowledge". Mystically, the three great Perfections are the three *kayas*, the three bodies of the perfected man. In Buddhist tradition they are the *dharmakaya*, the *sambhogakaya* and the *nirmanakaya*. Each represents a type of spiritual perfection. In the first case, spiritual perfection involves a long, deliberate and strenuous process of detachment through meditation upon emptiness, *shunyata*, and mastery of the ability to withdraw at will from one's astral form. At some point in some life, one attains absorption into the golden aura of the unmanifest Logos. This is a very high nirvanic state, equivalent to *moksha* or liberation in the Hindu tradition. It enables an individual to cut the chain of involuntary incarnations into a body in a world of suffering. But this emancipation is secured at the expense of cutting such beings off from any possibility of communication with ordinary suffering humanity. Those who take this *dharmakaya* vesture are absorbed into the most pristine state of matter that can be imagined. It is actually the state of matter that is the basis of *Adibuddha*, the ultimate Buddha-nature. Essentially, it is the basis of all perfected beings, but there are crucial differences in the ways that different kinds of perfected beings make use of that light-substance, *suddhasattva*. The *sambhogakaya* represents a second mode of spiritual perfection that is universally relevant to all manifested divine incarnations: Krishna is a paradigm of it. Wherever an exalted incarnation comes to give an indication of the divine graces and excellences possible for human beings, that is the *sambhogakaya*. Such a glorious being lives in the golden aura of the manifested Logos, whether he is called Christos, Krishna or by any other name.

The third type of spiritual perfection, designated as the *nirmanakaya*, is the specific goal represented by Gautama Buddha and the continuing work of the Brotherhood of Bodhisattvas, the Mahatmas who breathe solely for the sake of universal enlightenment. The *nirmanakaya* is a distinctive and extremely difficult kind of perfection. It involves perfection of the capacity to create out of the subtler vestures an astral form which is devoid of qualities. This alchemically regenerated form enables one to move anywhere invisibly and to assist human beings unknown to them. It also enables one consciously to take whatever body is necessary or available for the purpose of extending the work of universal enlightenment. Most Nirmanakayas are unseen, anonymous and disguised. One cannot discern them from outside, because they have chosen to come in ways in which they can perfect right livelihood and, at the same time, maximize the work they do in the realm of contemplation, ideation, true theurgy, healing and, above all, beneficent meditation.

The three types of spiritual perfection represented by the three *kayas* may be thought of in terms of different types of meditative discipline. The paradox is that going higher does not necessarily represent the attainment of a higher level of spiritual perfection. Going high and bringing down what one can for the sake of raising others is the highest perfection. Among the Mahatmas, therefore, there is no greater example of the perfect man than Gautama Buddha. Greatness among Mahatmas has to do with greatness in renunciation, greatness in control of temper, greatness in freedom from possessions, and greatness in total sacrifice for the sake of the least and the most tormented, so that they may re-enter the kingdom of divine selfhood. The whole challenge of the philosophy of perfection lies in one's potential, which is something less than one's conceivable perfection and more than one's actual perfection. It lies in the ratio of silence to speech, of patience to self-assertion, of surrender to imposition. The more one is non-violent, the more one is willing to yield to another. "Greater love hath no man than that he lay down his life for another" is one of the greatest mantrams of all times. Here is the authentic accent of that particular kind of spiritual perfection which is the highest and holiest in human evolution. It is much harder than everything else because it involves overcoming the ego, while at the same time remaining in a world which, as depicted in the Allegory of the Cave, remains a dungeon whose language is egotism.

Spiritual perfection requires extraordinary courage and patience. Continuity of consciousness is, therefore, the most meaningful way of looking at perfectibility. How much can one maintain a vibration through day and night? Through the days of the week? Through a month? Through the seasons between the winter solstice and the spring equinox, between the spring equinox and the summer solstice — not just through one year, but through seven years? Can one even imagine what it means to maintain a spiritual vibration until the last breath? If so, can one then begin to imagine what it is like to be able to keep appointments across future lives, not in the realm of fantasy, but in the realm of painful fact?

An extraordinary story is told of Ananda, the disciple of Buddha, who once turned aside an attractive young lady because she was totally unready for renunciation. Before she could curse him, he said, "One day, when no one else wants you, I will be there." Decades later, when she was a dying, rotten carcass in the streets, Ananda heard her cry and left the company of Buddha. He went many miles to reach her, and then, practically unknown even to her, washed her body, tended it, and helped her enter the Sangha before she died. What a different criterion of greatness this is from anything in modern times. The present is an age in which people cannot even be true in the evening to a promise made in the morning. Yet this sad fact only reinforces the therapeutic importance of considering examples of beings so great that they can keep appointments over decades and across lives.

The one thing one must never do is sell short the ideal of human perfection. All human beings are perfected gods in chains. But all human beings also have to go through the same arduous process before they can attain to a high degree of spiritual wakefulness, fidelity and control. Where individuals can remain true to a vibration, they must do so, showing the moral courage of those, like Thoreau, who listen to the beat of another drummer. Those who hear and heed the music of the spheres can rarely share it with others, because most people are totally caught in the noise of the age. To be able to remain with and among all those people, who are like lotuses suffocating in the mire, while at the same time giving hope and instruction to those rare flowers that are struggling to rise to the surface, is indeed a high degree of continuity of consciousness.

Unless one establishes oneself in what is universal, on the side of all beings and the future, one will irreversibly fall behind. The stakes for humanity have become extremely high, and the ultimacy of choice represented by the words of Jesus, "Whom choose ye this day?", has come to pass. It is truly the case that the Perfect Sage has no name and no form. He lives in the nameless, and he is formless. But the current of light-energy and good represented by such a being leaves one no choice except to be with it or to be tossed away by its force. Starting from small concepts and simple examples, one can see that the notion of perfectibility embraces something so much vaster than can ever be put into any categories. At the same time, it is a viable, living, relevant ideal for every human being, because each human being archetypally goes through the same stages, is involved in the same powers and faculties, and lives in a common field of space, time and energy. Every human being by day, and certainly in deep sleep at night, experiences something of the true meaning of the odyssey of the soul in its long and immemorial quest towards the perfecting of all humanity.

THE LANGUAGE
OF THE GODS

Out of the silence that is peace a resonant voice shall arise.
                                            Light on the Path

In the beginning was the Word," declare St. John and the Upanishads. All existence is a confluence of vibratory motions, from the cosmic to the atomic. Creative speech — Logos, Verbum, the Word — is sound impregnated with the potency of ideation. The primordial and sempiternal sound is like the quiet pulsation of the ocean's depths and the inaudible reverberation hidden within the gentle whisper of the breeze, the joyous dance of the elements and the 'still, sad music of humanity'. When the mind listens to the cacophony of seemingly discontinuous sounds, or speaks a transient tongue which corresponds to evanescent phenomena, it is turned away from its true Self out into the world. It perceives an array of discrete entities and separate existences, and constructs for itself an illusory identity. This is the fugitive psyche, the soul that is captive to a temporal succession of images, bound up with likes and dislikes. When the mind turns within, searches for the root of sound in the silence, it retreats and looks to its own ultimate origin. When it engages in deep meditation, it senses a continuity in duration which reflects an eternal wholeness.

Ancient philosophers and mystics held that through this inward turning the mind becomes an awakened nous, a noetic focus which renders universal truths intelligible in relation to everyday experience. In the apt words of G.W. Russell (A.E.),

The meditation they urged on us has been explained as 'the inexpressible yearning of the inner man to go out to the infinite'. But the Infinite we

would enter is living. It is the ultimate being of us.
Meditation is a fiery brooding on that majestical Self.
We imagine ourselves into Its vastness. We conceive
ourselves as mirroring Its infinitudes, as moving in all
things, as living in all beings, in earth, water, air, fire,
æther. We try to know as It knows, to live as It lives,
to be compassionate as It is compassionate. We
equal ourselves to It that we may understand It and
become It. . . . 'What a man thinks, that he is: that is
the old secret,' said the wise. We have imagined
ourselves into this pitiful dream of life. By imagination
and will we re-enter true being, becoming what we
conceive of.

The Candle of Vision

Whilst this vision brings its own proof to the spirit, we are
rightly conscious that criteria for knowing are necessary if the
mystical perspective is not to degenerate into mere epistemological
relativism. Knowledge-claims may be for many people what Plato
called true opinion, statements for which they can offer no
support outside received tradition or majority convention. For the
mystical philosopher, however, knowledge-claims must be
validated. Some claims to knowledge may be simply avowals
which do not tell us anything about the world or ourselves, but
merely report the subjective experiences of another. Other claims
to knowledge are pragmatic. Their apparent objectivity is
established if they are conclusions which all investigators are likely
to reach, or if they are expedient within the contexts to which
they are held. Such validation, of course, does not yield timeless
truths or any fundamental insight into the structure of the world
or the self. Knowledge-claims may also be justified as inferences
from other accepted statements, or if they at least do not
contradict such statements. As strict inferences, such statements
do not add to the sum or significance of knowledge, however
much they may spell out what is thought to be known already.
Often a statement is offered as true in the belief that it in some
way 'corresponds' to the facts. Since we commonly assume that

we know both the relevant facts and the meanings of statements, this view finds general, if uncritical, acceptance. But specific facts are not easily discerned or interpreted, and the general concept of a 'fact' is obscure, while many statements and even 'statement' are not unambiguous. It can be philosophically frustrating to make precise the notion of 'correspondence' without restricting it to familiar operations.

Our shared language is putatively divided between words which denote sense-objects and words which signify ratiocinative concepts. For the mystic who has experienced the harmonics of invisible nature and intimations of the fount of sound itself, such language seems woefully inadequate to the task of elucidation. A.E. wrote of his experience:

> The tinted air glowed before me with intelligible significance like a face, a voice. The visible world became like a tapestry blown and stirred by winds behind it. If it would but raise for an instant I knew I would be in Paradise. Every form of that tapestry appeared to be the work of gods. Every flower was a word, a thought. The grass was speech; the trees were speech; the waters were speech; the winds were speech.
>
> *Ibid.*

A.E. speaks in company with mystics throughout the ages, and cannot be understood by the simple application of a single criterion for knowledge-claims. We must look to the integrity of the seer and to our own authentic experience to discover whether we are warranted in ascribing truth and meaning to what he says. If in meditation one focusses the mind with laser-like precision upon one object, penetrating to its inmost and ineffable core, one is able to trace the roots of existence and simultaneously to unveil the origins of things, witnessing terraces of being from near perfect homogeneity to almost total heterogeneity. This process allows one to discern different levels of causality and intermediate orders of existence.

In his preface to *The Candle of Vision* A.E. warned the reader:

> When I am in my room looking upon the walls I have painted, I see there reflections of the personal life, but when I look through the windows I see a living nature and landscapes not painted by hands. So, too, when I meditate I feel in the images and thoughts which throng about me the reflections of personality, but there are also windows in the soul through which can be seen images created not by human but by the divine imagination. I have tried according to my capacity to report about the divine order and to discriminate between that which was self-begotten fantasy and that which came from a higher sphere.

Mystics find the sifting of the imagination a lonely task to which neither modern psychology nor philosophy give assistance. "I surmise," A.E. wrote, "from my reading of the psychologists who treat of this that they themselves were without this faculty and spoke of it as blind men who would fain draw although without vision." One untutored in geometry would be foolish to declare a theorem undemonstrated and more foolish still to pronounce geometry a superstition or aberration of the speculative mind. One must train the mind to comprehend the nature of axioms, rules of inference, geometrical operations and proofs before making judgements. This applies also to the cognitive content of mystical experience, as A.E. recognized:

> We rarely find philosophical writers referring to vision of their own, yet we take them as guides on our mental travelling, though in this world we all would prefer to have knowledge of earth and heaven through the eyes of a child rather than to know them only through the musings of one who was blind, even though his intellect was mighty as Kant's.
>
> *Ibid.*

No laboriously elaborated conventional wisdom can threaten the self-validating authority of direct experience, though unscrutinized experience can be misleading. To A.E.'s own question, "What certitude have you that these things you speak of are in any way related to a real world invisible to our eyes?" he replied that he could not fall back upon external authority, even that of other mystic seers. Rather,

> On that path, as an ancient scripture says, to whatsoever place one would travel that place one's own self becomes, and I must try first to uproot false ideas about memory, imagination and vision so that by pure reason people may be led out of error and be able to distinguish between that which arises in themselves and that which comes otherwise and which we surmise is a visitor from a far country.
>
> *Ibid.*

Freed from enslavement to a conventional picture of reality, reason and the self-willed expansion of the range of experience together warrant claims to knowledge for the mystic. His world is not reserved for a unique class of individuals who have special spiritual privileges. Meditation is a deliberative experience undertaken for the purpose of discovery without the burden of pre-established goals or results. What is discovered can then be subjected to reason. As A.E. frankly acknowledged, "being an artist and lover of visible beauty, I was often tempted from the highest meditation to contemplate, not divine being, but the mirage of forms." Neither the vision nor the layers of delusion are exclusive to him. There is nothing uncommon about such visions. It is in the interpretation of them that errors arise. The crucial test of mystical claims to knowledge lies for A.E. in our innate capacities for self-transformation as thinking beings.

> On the mystic path we create our own light, and
> at first we struggle blind and baffled, seeing nothing,

hearing nothing, unable to think, unable to imagine. We seem deserted by dream, vision or inspiration, and our meditation barren altogether. But let us persist for weeks or months, and sooner or later that stupor disappears. Our faculties readjust themselves, and do the work we will them to do. Never did they do their work so well. The dark caverns of the brain begin to grow luminous. We are creating our own light.

Ibid.

When this disciplined effort is made, we may share some inexplicable but recognizable flashes of resplendent insight. We may then readily acknowledge the long lineage of mystic seers and sages. Furthermore, we can distinguish clearly between the psychic images of personal consciousness and the universal noetic vision of mystical awareness. Claims to knowledge will gain a coherence forged by pure reason, a vital correspondence to a world unfolded in lucid insight, and timeless relevance to the spiritual nature of man. This prospect is universal because the authentic language in which it is always expressed is a distant echo of the Logos in the cosmos, the transcendent Word and the Soundless Sound. Man, the microcosmic mirror of the macrocosm, elaborates the archetypal patterns of sempiternity in time, patterns which are themselves a mystic presentment of the eternal and unknowable. The universe itself could be viewed as a soliloquy of Deity wherein Ain-Soph talks to Ain-Soph. The core of man's being is consubstantial with the root of nature. No bridge need be built between man and Deity save the bridge of awareness, constructed out of unfolding knowledge through meditation. The primordial Word is both primordial light and universal form. The language of the gods is the primary modulation of that light — "colours beyond the rainbow" and first figures. The Word resounds throughout the abstract medium which is space.

The *Akasha* of the Hindu philosophers is not a vacuum but rather a homogeneous and supple substance. It receives, transmits and echoes that first speech imprinted upon it, and as sound recrosses sound, a world composed of interlaced vibrations arises, assumes forms and eventually crystallizes in its grosser aspects into the world of ordinary experience. Mortal speech is a distant derivate of divine speech and must ultimately be traced back to the Word or Verbum. This arcane view of the origin of language is at variance with the theory that language is to be traced back to rudimentary conventions derived from pre-human onomatopoeia. We may discover a spiritual relation between sounds and the various powers, forms and colours, and the universe. The roots of human speech are the sound correspondences of powers which in their combination and interaction make up the universe. To trace the origin of language through the discovery of its fundamental structure is to outline the unfoldment of nature from its seed in the abstract Word. In human speech,

> Every root is charged with significance, being the symbol of a force which is itself the fountain of many energies, even as primordial being when manifested rolls itself out into numberless forms, states of energy and consciousness.
>
> *Ibid.*

A.E. proposed that the first root of language — A — is "the sound symbol for the self in man and Deity in the cosmos." Its equivalent in symbolic form is the colourless circle, whose centre is everywhere and whose circumference is nowhere, in the language of Pascal, Nicolas of Cusa and Hermes Trismegistus. "The old world," H.P. Blavatsky wrote, "consistent in its symbolism with its pantheistic intuitions, uniting the visible and invisible Infinitudes into one, represented Deity and its outward VEIL alike — by a circle." St. John states that "the Word was with God, and the Word was God." The second root — R — represents motion, the lines which generate heat — H — and gives rise to the triangle, symbol of life and transformation. As the root sounds proceed from the back of the throat (A) toward the closed lips (M), they represent the increasing involvement of Spirit in material

planes, the ultimate dissolution of voiced creation and the return
to stasis *(OO)*. The investigation of Indo-European or Aryan roots
uncovers abstract conceptions more than particular terms.

> We find for example comparatively few words, such
> as *bow, arrow* and *tent,* while there are a great many
> expressing abstract or reflective ideas, like *to shine, to
> fly, to know, to burn.*
>
> A.E., *The Speech of the Gods*

A.E.'s own vision and expression, his compassion and conduct,
brought word and deed together in a living example of more
divine and primordial speech which is the manifestation of the
Word against the background of eternal Silence.

The myth of Prometheus is a veiled version of ancient
accounts of cosmogenesis. It presupposes a perpetual struggle
between regeneration and regulation, between free thought and
orthodoxy, between spiritual and material creation. The higher
powers of solar intelligences are continually at war with the lesser
powers attached more intimately to form and stasis. They
incarnate into the lower regions to rescue man from his spiritual
inertia and bestow upon him the sacred prerogative of creative
ideation. Passivity induced by all systems of external authority is
contrasted with the autonomy of the individual and the integrity
of the unconditional and indefinable element in every soul. Each
man is an integral ray of Absolute Consciousness, simultaneously
allied with oneness and manyness. Man's task is to harmonize and
transcend the antipodes of his being, to contemplate that divine
Triad of mind, energy and matter exalted above itself and existing
in a unity. In Pythagorean language, such a being makes of the
Triad a Tetraktys, a triangle of cosmic force with a point in the
centre concentrating its focus in and through the enlightened
man. Such beings are complete symbols of the Self-Existent or
Solitary of Heaven in whom all qualities inhere and yet who are
committed solely to the ethical elevation of the human race.

The solar element in man is the true hero in the secret saga of history. It is the spiritual genius latent in every individual which, when stirred by the fires of wisdom, is able to reflect some facet of the Heavenly City, its true ancestral home. Patanjali postulated that the whole universe exists for the enlightenment of the human soul. Politics bears a similar relationship to man's immortal self. It is an imperfect means to a transcendental end, the repeated channelling of human energies for the enlightenment of the entire race. Its perfectibility is based upon its approximation to that celestial city of divine beings who are attuned to the silent music of the immortal soul. The earth is ensouled by a planetary spirit, a divine Logos honoured in the great religions and mythologies of mankind. Universal history, recorded in archaic symbols and myths, is the ceaseless activity of this moving spirit which manifests through avatars. They appear during critical epochs, intoning the accents of sacred speech, the language of the gods, incarnating the eternal resonance of Brahma Vach.

THE LIFE-GIVING STREAM

> *The Secret Doctrine is the accumulated Wisdom of the Ages, and its cosmogony alone is the most stupendous and elaborate system: e.g., even in the exotericism of the Puranas. But such is the mysterious power of occult symbolism, that the facts which have actually occupied countless generations of initiated seers and prophets to marshal, to set down and explain, in the bewildering series of evolutionary progress, are all recorded on a few pages of geometrical signs and glyphs. The flashing gaze of those seers has penetrated into the very kernel of matter, and recorded the soul of things there, where an ordinary profane, however learned, would have perceived but the external work of form.*
>
> The Secret Doctrine, i 272

The Secret Doctrine is directed to those who are devoutly seeking to bring about a fundamental transformation in consciousness. Early in the book H.P. Blavatsky states:

> 'When *Buddhi* absorbs our EGO-tism (destroys it) with all its *Vikaras*, Avalôkitêshvara becomes manifested to us, and Nirvana, or *Mukti*, is reached,' 'Mukti' being the same as Nirvana, *i.e.*, freedom from the trammels of 'Maya' or *illusion*. 'Bodhi' is likewise the name of a particular state of trance condition, called *Samadhi*, during which the subject reaches the culmination of spiritual knowledge.
>
> The Secret Doctrine, i xix

If *samadhi* and *nirvana* are exalted states of consciousness, evidently the Brotherhood of Bodhisattvas, the Society of Sages, the Lodge of Mahatmas continuously resides on this cosmic plane of supreme cognition. These self-luminous beings are everywhere and nowhere, with three main sanctuaries on this globe: one beyond the Himalayas, which has existed from the most ancient times; another in the Near East, which also goes back far beyond recorded history; and the third in South America. Yet, while there are these secret centres of initiation, access to the Brotherhood has nothing to do with physical nearness or distance. Mahatmas are essentially beings who ceaselessly function on unseen planes of ideation mirroring universal states of consciousness. Any individual anywhere who is universal in spirit, unsectarian in attitude, free from fixation upon place or time, who is truly devoted to universal good and human welfare, may come into the radius of influence of the Brotherhood of Bodhisattvas and their accredited agents in the world.

The Dedication of *The Secret Doctrine* strikes the self-validating keynote of universality:

> This Work I dedicate to all True Theosophists, in
> every Country, and of every Race, for they called it forth,
> and for them it was recorded.

In the Preface, the same keynote of universality is strongly stressed. The teachings of Theosophy are not confined to the ancient tetrad comprised by the Hindu, the Zoroastrian, the Chaldean and the Egyptian religions. Nor is it the exclusive possession of the more recent Buddhist, Islamic, Judaic and Christian faiths. The Secret Doctrine is the essence of all these. "Sprung from it in their origins, the various religious schemes are now made to merge back into their original element, out of which every mystery and dogma has grown, developed, and become materialised."

Owing to the fall of all religions through false claims and creedal dogmas, true seekers everywhere today are longing to find the pristine source of Divine Wisdom, pure and unsullied. Naturally, even among such earnest seekers there is the ever-present danger of materialization. This can be minimized through close attention to the critical distinction made in the *Bhagavad Gita* between the external attributes and the immaterial essence of the Self-Governed Sage. Those who have eyes will always be able to see and will also be able to know how to come closer to the Trans-Himalayan Brotherhood, which is not to be found by external means. It has monasteries and schools and systems of initiation in secret sanctuaries which cannot be readily discovered by travel and exploration. Even the individual seeker who is able, by undertaking a pilgrimage, to come closer to the Brotherhood, is led on by the intuition of the heart, by inner guidance, and not by maps or any adventitious aids.

H.P. Blavatsky once stated that a single journey to the East undertaken in the proper spirit will do more than all the books in the world. She herself conducted such a journey but she was intensely concerned with fundamental questions: 'Who, where, and what is God?' 'How can man's spirit prove God's spirit?' These were the burning questions in her heart to which she devoted years of thought and enquiry. Having already had the vision of her Guru, asking these questions, she re-enacted for the sake of the entire human race the archetypal quest for enlightenment. This is part of the ever-renewed sacrifice of every Rishi or Mahatma, or great Teacher. Inquirers who have sought the Brotherhood of Bodhisattvas through external means are easily misled. In the Aquarian Age, especially, no encouragement can be given to people who want some kind of external and verifiable means of speeding their own growth. True spiritual growth is wholly internal, and only its efflorescence may illumine the external world through wisdom in thought, word and deed. This is the fruition of continuous meditation, and therefore one must realize, as many an ancient seeker knew, that the sacred places of pilgrimage correspond to secret centres in the human constitution. For example, Prayag, the meeting-place of rivers, corresponds to a spiritual centre in every human being. The symbolism of a sacred pilgrimage conveys clues to the inner meaning of the teaching, intimating the inward ascent through which a human being comes closer to planes of consciousness involving higher centres within the human vestures. It is possible, through deep meditation, to enter the inmost sanctuary within the tabernacle of Isis, Shekinah, Sarasvati, Kwan Yin, Brahma Vach. An indispensable pre-requisite is true devotion to the *Ishtaguru*.

The word *Theosophia* goes back to Ammonius Saccas and earlier, and there has continued an unbroken line of shining witnesses in every part of the world — even where the mystery-fires were snuffed out long ago. This line may be discerned in a few Church Fathers like Origen and Clement of Alexandria, as well as in St. Augustine. It is clearly to be seen in the neo-Platonic thinkers, as in Pythagoras and Plato, and also among the pre-Socratics. From further back than Krishna and Buddha, the ancient Egyptians and Chaldeans, and continuing all the way through recorded history, it comes down again through the last seven centuries, starting with the First Impulsion of the modern Theosophical Movement given in the fourteenth century by Tsong-Kha-Pa, who came to resuscitate the Divine Wisdom. Every century thereafter a special effort was made by the Lodge of Mahatmas to awaken human awareness of the accessibility as well as the enduring existence of the Wisdom Religion. Thus, 'The true Theosophist belongs to no cult or sect, yet belongs to each and all'.

The Secret Doctrine of H.P. Blavatsky is an encyclopaedic and talismanic guide to that which is hidden in Nature, to the sacred scriptures of the world and to the ancient source of arcane knowledge. It points to the great range of diverse cultures of the recorded and unrecorded past, providing keys to many language systems, mythic maps, code languages in mystical texts, alchemical works and ancient catechisms, some of them orally transmitted or only partly transcribed and some dependent upon further commentaries that are not readily available. The two volumes encompass such a vast and varied range of material that if one were to spend one's entire life trying to follow up on every term and concept, on every school and system, one would find at the end of a lifetime that one would have to start all over again in future lives. This is truly a Himalayan pilgrimage.

Speaking of the great Transmitters of the Wisdom Religion, H.P. Blavatsky states:

> They were the authors of new forms and
> interpretations, while the truths upon which the latter

were based were as old as mankind. Selecting one or more of those grand verities — actualities visible only to the eye of the real Sage and Seer — out of the many orally revealed to man in the beginning, preserved and perpetuated in the *adyta* of the temples through initiation, during the MYSTERIES and by personal transmission — they revealed these truths to the masses. Thus every nation received in its turn some of the said truths, under the veil of its own local and special symbolism; which, as time went on, developed into a more or less philosophical cultus, a Pantheon in mythical disguise.

The Secret Doctrine, i xxxvi

In the process of transmission there is an inevitable dilution of the life-giving stream of the eternal Wisdom. Every sincere seeker must make an earnest effort to grasp what it would mean for these truths to be actualities visible only to the eye of the Sage and the Seer. For example, many Theosophists are vaguely familiar with the Sanskrit term *Mulaprakriti*, root-matter, which is also known by the English phrase 'primordial root-substance'. If one were to probe deeply into what is currently thought about matter, one would discern that already in contemporary physics the concept of matter is so subtle and recondite, so much an abstraction, that it has nothing to do with crude sensory conceptions of matter. If, through meditation upon the very idea of root-matter, one were to go even further, using several sections of *The Secret Doctrine* which throw light upon the philosophical problems connected with matter and forces, one could begin to comprehend what is meant by pure, noumenal matter. By experiencing even at a preliminary level that which would make the word *Mulaprakriti* sacred, one could become increasingly conscious of the ever-present cosmic sacrifice of which Shri Krishna spoke to Arjuna.

If the seeker is not living out of any concern with individual salvation, but only out of a deep desire for universal progress, then one can become a true devotee of Krishna. The Guru is depicted in the abstract portrait of the Self-Governed Sage given by Krishna. Persisting in true devotion to such a Guru, who will always be both an ideal and a fact, a veil and a presence, a person may experience subtle mutations in his vestures. The physical body changes considerably every seven years. The skin is completely renewed every seven years, and the lines on the hand change more slowly but surely. Micro-changes take place continually, affecting the blood and its circulation. The entire system renews itself so continuously that one is constantly involved in these alterations and changes. They apply not only to the gross astral that is called the physical body, but involve processes which are witnessed by and are relevant to the immortal soul. The way in which the soul sees and apprehends these processes can make a decisive difference to the whole of one's life. The common saying that "You are as young as you feel" is the mirroring of a profound truth when 'feel' is understood in terms of how one thinks and breathes. Spiritual rates of metabolic transmutation, change and transformation can be affected by the Guru who can see into the very essence of things, and deals directly with a facet of *Mulaprakriti* which is the substratum of *Akasha*. If one genuinely tries to work through correspondences, then although one may not directly understand the process, one can at some level appreciate it by analogy to the sense of lightening and refining of the physical instrument that comes with bathing. All human souls have some glimmer of awareness of noumenal states of matter, but to be able to put that knowledge to work needs meditation, continuity of consciousness and continuous concern. Typically, this quality of concentration and continuity will not be forthcoming except among those few who have such an overwhelming love for the human race, profound compassion for human suffering and pure joy in the presence of Divine Wisdom, that they would really wish to commit themselves totally and continuously to progressive self-refinement for the sake of all.

With deep concentration there is a distinct change in the quality of perception. The left eye and the right eye focus differently, not only on the physical plane, but also in ways that involve centres behind the eyes suggested in phrases like 'the mind's eye', 'the soul's eye' and what Krishna calls "the place between thine eyes". The eyes are the windows of the soul, and it is possible to unfold spiritual perception slowly, intermittently, but recognizably. The perception which unfolds is similar in kind, even though distant in degree, to the eye of the Sage and Seer. That is an eye for which there is no veil, an eye which can see into past, present and future though it does not see them as such but only an eternal Now. What is day to the Sage is night to the ordinary man, and what is day to the ordinary man is night, the night of ignorance, to the Sage. There is a radical difference in the perception of light and darkness, abstract and concrete, real and unreal, day and night, between the Sage or Seer and the seeker who is still fumbling and stumbling with sensory perceptions, with worldly desires, with carnal limitations, with a narrow sense of identity and personality, but who still wishes to go beyond. There is evidently a radical difference between the spiritual wisdom come alive in those who breathe it, and those who merely have it on hearsay. This is the oldest distinction in the world. In Shankara it is the distinction between *aparavidya* and *paravidya*, *parokshavidya* and *aparokshavidya*, indirect knowledge and direct awareness.

This is hinted at in the Preface, where the word 'revelation' is used, and in different places in the book where the idea of spiritual revelation or spiritual seership is elucidated. In the beginning we are told that:

> . . . the secet portions of the *'Dan'* or *'Jan-na'* (*'Dhyan'*) of Gautama's metaphysics — grand as they appear to one unacquainted with the tenets of the Wisdom Religion of antiquity — are but a very small portion of the whole. The Hindu Reformer limited his public teachings to the purely moral and physiological aspect of the Wisdom-Religion, to Ethics and MAN alone. Things 'unseen and incorporeal', the mystery of Being outside our terrestrial sphere, the great Teacher left entirely untouched in his public lectures, reserving

the hidden Truths for a select circle of his Arhats. The
latter received their Initiation at the famous Saptaparna
cave (the *Sattapanni* of Mahavansa) near Mount
Baibhâr.

The Secret Doctrine, i xx

And then we are told on the next page:

> How the pristine purity of these grand revelations
> was dealt with may be seen in studying some of the
> so-called 'esoteric' Buddhist schools of antiquity in their
> modern garb, not only in China and other Buddhist
> countries in general, but even in not a few schools
> =in Thibet, left to the care of uninitiated Lamas and
> Mongolian innovators.

Ibid., i xxi

In India, in China and Japan, in Siam and Burma, in Egypt
and Greece, in Chaldea and Mesopotamia, later in Rome and in
the Arab world and among the Jews, and in the modern age in
Europe and the United States of America, also in the last hundred
years in the Theosophical Movement, it is the same story of partial
understanding leading to misunderstanding, concretization
resulting in desecration. That is the karma of the transmission of
Divine Wisdom, because the uninitiated will, in the sense in which
Jesus spoke of casting pearls before swine, drag down the solar
teaching into the murky realm of lunar consciousness polluted
by profane sense-perceptions. This is profanation, but at the same
time, the immortal soul in those individuals may gain some food
for *sushupti* and for *devachan* if they still have some link with the
higher Triad. There would also be those who can get their mental
luggage ready for another life. One may never really know how
the process goes on from the outside, but one can understand
why something always had to be kept secret from every person
who is self-excluded from the sacred circle of initiates and
ascetics. There will always be such a sacred circle, just as there
will always be only a few who actually have climbed Himalayan

peaks. But there will be very, very many who are fascinated by the enterprise.

Those courageous souls who are truly drawn to spiritual mountain climbing will be struck by the *Stanzas of Dzyan*, the *sutratman* of the *Gupta Vidya*, which forms the basis of the volumes of *The Secret Doctrine*. These *Stanzas* are also included as an appendix to *The Voice of the Silence*, which is derived from the same ancient source. Through their help, it is possible "to reform oneself by meditation and knowledge", but for this to happen, everything depends upon the state of mind and consciousness in which one approaches them. Those who have found them helpful take the *Stanzas* and read them silently again and again. On the whole, reading them aloud would be unwise because one may activate lower psychical forces much faster than one has gained the ability to govern them. This is a hazard with many people because of the ratios of the noetic to psychic in their lives. It is always a good practice to read quietly and absorb ideas with the mind's eye so that one receives the teaching on deeper planes than merely through the astral senses. Because in the Aquarian Age the mind is very crucial, without some understanding no such activity could be truly helpful and it may even degenerate into quasi-religious pseudo-ritual. This one does not want to encourage, and there is a constant danger that people will be pulled back through their *skandhas* into one or another form of ritualistic salvationism.

The whole of *The Secret Doctrine* is a partial commentary on certain fragments of a few of many Stanzas, most of which are not given. If one understands all of these at some level, and tries to take a particular *Stanza*, making correlations between the *Transactions* and *The Secret Doctrine*, reading a paragraph and making a few notes, thinking deeply about it and meditating upon it, and then rereads the original *Stanza*, it would help. Clearly this is an exercise involving attention, effort, patience and calm. Anyone who has been so privileged as to have entered into the current of Divine Wisdom will have sensed that the *Stanzas of Dzyan* may be correctly intoned as the basis of noetic magic. This can only be done by initiates, a mantramic activity that is not publicized. Nevertheless, it is extremely potent and has a profound effect upon the entire globe and is solely undertaken for the benefit of all living beings.

If a person is very far from these Himalayan prospects, and has in fact gone wrong for a period of time, for a year, for three years, for ten years, for ten lives, yet would wish to begin again on the path of *anasakti*, selfless action, and seeks to reform his or her self by meditation and spiritual knowledge, and even hopes for a second birth, this is indeed possible. Not only is it possible, it is verily the true purpose in transmitting *The Voice of the Silence* and *The Secret Doctrine*.

The sacred teaching is for those who seek to become *dwijas*, twice-born, those who wish to be born again as in the Nazarene gospel, those who ardently aspire to be spiritually regenerated. But this must be the product of a patient, persistent and yet relatively unanxious reform of the self. Knowledge only becomes wisdom through meditation acting as the basis of realization. The more one meditates, the more one's knowledge becomes real. The more it becomes real, the more it acts upon one's life-atoms and the spiritual will, transforming the sense-organs and the body, altering and elevating one's whole life. It becomes the current of a living power made free in a human being, and is highly potent. *The Secret Doctrine* is for those who devoutly seek to become Men of Meditation. As a preparation, it is helpful to gain even a little spiritual knowledge, by Buddhic intuition, of the universal, hidden, archetypal, regenerating current of spiritual life-energy referred to as the living stream of wisdom. If one can get into the current, it is bound to make a change that will work slowly but infallibly. The proper use of *The Secret Doctrine* and *The Voice of the Silence* could be like unto the study of the Vedas or of the Gospels according to John or Thomas. Even if taken in small doses but on a regular basis, the way Nature does all things, much benefit can accrue. This is really the problem: Can people learn to grow as they have seen trees grow? A little bit done regularly is of inestimably more value than doing a lot one day and nothing for weeks.

Just because the study of *The Secret Doctrine* is so vast, it does not mean that one cannot gain some benefit even from taking a single phrase or a sentence from almost anywhere in the book. One can, as sincere effort will surely demonstrate. Sometimes people suppose that they cannot come any closer to *The Secret Doctrine* because they are unworthy, but this is a great mistake and a defamation of human dignity. Some people are always making an assumption that they 'belong' to themselves. This is philosophically baseless, since the mere fact that they can formulate such a claim does not in the least imply that either the body or mind is a possession of theirs. Of what is any person claiming to be the owner in this 'private ownership theory' of the vestures? It is an absurd form of ignorance. One must put oneself in a learning mood or posture, and one must forget about worthiness and unworthiness. Instead, one should thrill to enter the perennial stream of supernal knowledge rendered into a living current of spiritual cleansing of the mind and purification of the heart, acting as a solvent to the lower will, and releasing the higher energies, potencies and faculties of the human being. That is what is truly intended, and those who have intuited the intention from the Preface, perhaps even from its very first words — "The Author — the writer, rather . . ." — will enter the stream in such a way that their lives will never be the same again.

It is indeed a great shame that the golden opportunity is not taken by many more people. The reason usually is about the same, whatever the external excuses and explanations. It is a superficial entering of the stream that blocks a real entering of the stream. On the other hand, one who is afraid to enter the stream wastes this incarnation. Both of these are pointed out in *The Voice of the Silence*. Fear kills the will, leaving one paralyzed. Nothing may happen, but one will not get the golden karma, maybe for many lives, of coming any closer to such exalted teaching. Others, on the other hand, forget that the sacred teaching is for the whole of humanity, that it necessarily involves ascending planes of consciousness. Because of salvationist tendencies in previous lives, they take a Fundamentalist attitude towards *The Secret Doctrine*, supposing that through mere ritual repetition they will gain insight and find redemption. A person must, rather, choose a sentence for meditation, take a paragraph for reflection, select a page for reading as a preparation for reflection and meditation. If one has more time, and the energy and will are summoned after one's duties are done by nature and by man, one may read more for the sake of making a deep study in order to strengthen the quality of one's daily reflection and meditation.

One's whole attitude to what one can do every week is crucial. People are of differing capacities and temperaments and also have different ways of ordering their lives or of remaining disordered. It would be helpful if a person altogether avoided the 'hundred percent or nothing' approach, which is Atlantean and adolescent blackmail, saying, "Either I do it all or I do nothing," a sure sign of spiritual failure through pride and perversity. Just as chelas may recognize Adepts, it is only logical that Adepts can recognize failed chelas. Rather than become trapped in such foolish pride, one might cheerfully listen to the words of Gautama Buddha: "Drop by drop a jar of water is filled." Choose a sentence, take a paragraph, but use it during the week to prepare for the next week. The real point is to gain greater continuity of consciousness. The Secret Doctrine is the unbroken, uninterrupted Wisdom of Those with unbroken, uninterrupted consciousness for over eighteen million years. They are the Manushis who became the Sons of Yoga, and those Sons of Yoga became the Sons of Wisdom. They teach under the same rule that was central to all the ancient systems of Spiritual Teaching: If you take one step in the direction of the Teaching and the Teacher, the Teacher will take one step in your direction and help you to become more capable, through meditation and practice, of spiritual regeneration, maybe even a second birth, leading to further changes in lives to come.

> He who would hear the voice of Nada, the 'Soundless Sound', and comprehend it, he has to learn the nature of Dharana.
>
> *The Voice of the Silence*

THE HERMETIC METHOD

Are we the creators of our destiny, or are we the agents, unknowing, unwilling, or unwitting of a cosmic plan? To ask this is to attempt to understand the relations between the conscious, the unconscious, and the self conscious in all of us. To achieve universal self-consciousness is to dispel all illusions and to know no difference between oneself and the whole of Nature. It is to make the plan of nature the very framework of one's being and the deliberate basis of one's destiny. It is like floating on the ocean of life. That is difficult enough on the physical plane, but in relation to the whole of cosmic life it is extremely difficult for us to grasp. Because we are only partly conscious, we are also partly unconscious, and therefore liable to self-deception. In another way, we face the problem of protective illusions. No man could live if he did not have some protective illusion. Each must attach a somewhat exaggerated reality to something in order to live at all. To the extent that we have to do this, we are used by the plan, because the exaggeration is eventually going to be cut down. Growing up means the removal of the protection.

Ordinarily, men and women replace one kind of protective illusion by another kind of protective illusion, which means they are part of the process and cannot stand outside it. To that extent free will is an illusion. If the universe is mathematically just, there is an incredible intricacy to its complex systems dynamics and, in the sense which Spinoza understood, no man is free. As long as you are a particular being, mentally separate from the whole, you are not free. What you think is freedom amounts to being determined by likes, dislikes and impulses which you do not fully choose. This is true of all of us, but to the extent to which, unlike the kingdoms below man, we can adapt ourselves to the environment and also adapt the environment to us, we are Prometheans, we are gods, we are self-determining agents.

For millennia we have been brought up in the terrible habit

of dichotomous thinking, assuming that everything must be one thing or its opposite. Pythagoras actually discouraged people from even thinking in terms of the number 2. So much did the Sophists encourage it that Plato said the very method should be abandoned. In other words, when we ask whether we are creative or passive in relation to our own destiny, we should start by saying, "Yes, we are both," but then ask what it means to say we are either. What does it mean effectively for us — philosophically, or impersonally; psychologically, in the realm where we can relate it to our life; ethically, in relation to our problems; and also socially or collectively? Look at the men who make plans. As Robert Burns said:

> The best laid schemes o' mice an' men
> Gang aft a-gley.

In Tolstoy's *War and Peace* the most powerful men of history are still instruments. On the other hand, each of us should ask what it means to say that we create and choose, because we do take decisions which can make a tremendous difference. We have to understand to what extent we are beings who have got our heads above the waters of life and to what extent we are immersed in the process.

Even this measure is not constant or static. It is ever-changing, and hence there is growth. There is a danger of being drowned, but it is also possible for a person to come right out. This is a matter of degrees, however, and when we consider degrees of self-awareness in the highest sense, we are confronting something way beyond simple delusions and phenomenal relativities. We have to come clean and be confident enough to impose no petty prejudices or minor obsessions, to which the fullness of the universe is irrelevant, on our pathway. We have to do a preliminary therapy and cleanse ourselves before we are ready to accept the universe and before we are ready to enter the first portal.

But this, of course, recurs at a later level as well. The unavoidable trouble with so many paradigms of the Path is that they seem to suggest that the process is a linear movement. Even the analogy of climbing one mountain can be misleading. We have got to imagine a tremendous mountain range. We climb, we come down, we climb again. In other words, it is like a spiral. The problem will keep recurring. At any level, in attempting to maintain awareness, you run the risk of either seeing so much of the huge perspective that you don't notice particular things, or of so concentrating on the particular that you forget the whole perspective.

A beautiful example of this can be found in Japanese landscape paintings. It takes time to realize that the most important thing in the paintings is blank space and its relation to the mobile trees and blades of grass. But even more, the blank space is not only the blank space *in* the painting. It involves the relationship to the space in the room where the painting is hanging. When you really appreciate these incredible paintings, you can appreciate pure empty space. In other words, you can begin to understand perspectives on that of which you are aware. You can be aware, at one level, of the objects in the painting, or you can move to a distance and be aware only of relations, not of forms. If you come close, then you are aware of nothing. Or, you may move to another point where you become aware of empty space. The important thing, then, is mobility in awareness.

What is true of space is also true of time. To adapt Heraclitus to a contemporary example: you are not sitting for two successive moments in the same room. The moment you come in, you come into one kind of place, and an instant later it is a different kind of place. Where the universe is ever-changing, we are never for two moments in the same point, either in a spatial or a temporal sense. From this perspective there can be no recurrence. There is only flux because nothing is ever like anything else. But from another standpoint you could take the opposite point of view, for example, that of Parmenides and the Vedanta. You could say that all of these changes have no meaning. There is always a one changeless reality. But then, if you merely want to say, dogmatically, that there is one changeless reality, you cannot understand process.

The problem is how can you see both — that everything is ever changeless and that everything is so constantly changing that there are no two similars.

Plato called this the problem of the 'same and the other'. H.P. Blavatsky says that what Plato taught is what the Wisdom-Religion teaches, terming it objective idealism. It is not subjective idealism, which says the One is the Real, and it is not that kind of materialism or realism or atomism which says the Many are Real. Nor is it any fixed relation between the One and the Many. It is a dynamic participation, but involving degrees of participation of the One in the Many and the Many in the One. As examples in our everyday life, take eating for a person who is a gourmet, or the act of love for two people who are extraordinarily proud of each other. In either case you will see there is one sense in which each instance is unique, inimitable and irreproducible. There can be no recurrence. But in another sense, there is recurrence. In effect, we have to say that at the level of particulars there can never be recurrence except in principle, and not a recurrence in a literal way. But equally, in terms of ideas or matrices there is constancy, but a constancy that is relative. What is constant in one long period of time will itself change over a longer period of time. This becomes a problem of periods of manifestation. This, then, is why all questions about human destiny and choice merely show that in the end we have to learn the dialectic, the method of analogy and correspondence. However much the term dialectic, like every sacred word, is tortured and abused, it remains the sovereign method of maintaining a mobile relationship in reference to degrees of reality, knowledge, and truth.

Students of Theosophy are helped to do this and are thus prepared for true meditation by study of *The Secret Doctrine*. This study is literally what it says, a study of *The Secret Doctrine*, not merely of a book. The Secret Doctrine is in nature and it is in every one of us. Concerning the book *The Secret Doctrine*, unlike almost any other book of the modern age, one could assume that every word has been chosen with great care. It is also wise to assume that there are a lot of blinds and also a lot of aids. It is meant to speak authentically to the widest possible audience, but in that code language where each one determines what he can receive. In Shelley's words, "It talks according to the wit of its companions; and no more is heard than has been felt before. . . ." It uses many conceptual languages and speaks in terms of many myths. No one finds all of these immediately meaningful. There is also a catechism and a hidden mathematical logic to the book, but grasping them involves the reflection of *Buddhi,* or intuition, in *Manas,* the focus of ideation.

What this means for us, first of all, is not to read the book except when in a state of calm; secondly, not to read the book with any anxiety. Put as a paradox, we give it its importance by treating it casually. We can become familiar and friendly with the book and put ourselves in the position of the writer in trying to see why there is a certain framework. We can read the contents of both volumes and try to see not the details of the framework, but the method which is in the contents. It is the Hermetic method of coming from above below, the method of analogy and correspondence, of the same and the other. It is not taught in the modern age in schools, in universities, or in our society. It includes what we call deductive reasoning and has a place for experience, but excludes induction. It really goes beyond all such divisions. It is what used to be called in the East the archetypal dialectic, *Buddhi Yoga,* and was also taught by Pythagoras and Plato.

The Secret Doctrine, then, involves planes of consciousness, degrees of knowledge, stairways of reality, a series of super-impositions of pictures — like pictures created with certain photographic techniques where different forms and shapes assumed by the same object are simultaneously represented. One might say of the book, and this is a paradox, that, like everything cosmic, the more we study it, the more we learn how to study it. The more we read it, but with love, the more that is worthwhile will emerge. Particularly to be enjoyed are those statements in the book which are combinations of sounds that are mathematically precise. One day there will be men who will pronounce the Stanzas and perform magic. But that will be a very different kind of humanity. Today there are men who can enter into the deeper realm of the book, even though they don't know where they are in terms of ordinary conceptions of growth and progress. In other words, *The Secret Doctrine* is a book to take up again and again. We should read it up to that point where the mind is calm and not exhausted. Put it away, and preferably sleep, after one has read it. Let things happen.

Whichever method one chooses, one should not cling to it, because another method may be found that will seem more appropriate later on. This is why a simple chronological way of reading the book may not be suitable. On the other hand, too awe-inspired a reception of the Stanzas may not be appropriate either. Certainly the lower Manas cannot understand the book, and trying to 'fit it together' with other things for the sake of fitting is a waste of time.

A broad and simple statement of how to approach the book is to approach the mind of the author and to see that mind in relation to *Mahat,* the collective mind of nature, and to see that in oneself. Put in concrete terms, a point comes in any important book where you want to ask not "Do I understand?" — which is to start off too apologetically — but "If I were this author, why would I want to be saying this?" This may sound presumptuous, but it is a legitimate way of becoming attuned to the mind of the author. So one says, "If what is said in the Preface is true, and if these things happened to anyone in the particular kind of instruction to which H.P. Blavatsky refers in the Proem and the Preface, then what would be the point of doing this and that?" This is a means to unite or yoke through yoga one's mind with the mind of the author. The most important clue which gives away the code language of *The Secret Doctrine* is in the very first words. The book begins by saying "The author — the writer, rather." Right away the book tells you that its author is not any one person. It is a very enigmatic book.

In the practice of meditation for which *The Secret Doctrine* prepares us, we can see the method of the dialectic in the relationship between meditation with a seed and meditation without a seed. According to Patanjali, the oldest text on meditation, whichever seed you take, you must dissolve it. To take a simple example, in the ideal school of the future, children would start very early on to take a slate, make diagrams, and wipe them out; then make different diagrams and wipe them out as well. There should be a tremendous freedom in relation to the seed that one takes and a recognition that whichever seed is taken, it is for the purpose of obliterating the seed. It is attempting to go from form to the formless, but in the formless not to be reacting against a particular form. It is a matter of repeated and various modes, and what works for one person will not work for another. Probably it is better to choose as a seed that which makes you less emotional rather than more, and this each one has to decide individually. To the extent to which it does make one emotional and involves exaggeration or protective illusions, better that the emotions are positive rather than negative. As the Buddhist meditations teach, we can make corrections for our own particular needs, and we can do this empirically within the context of our prevailing understanding of our unfolding and evolving destiny.

Toronto
October 9, 1971

UNIVERSALITY
AND SECTARIANISM

Universality and sectarianism are of fundamental significance to all of us. They are interlinked with an intractable problem in relation to Nature, in relation to knowledge, and in relation to what we call Theosophia — the Wisdom of the Ages. They are also reflected in the enigmatic relationships between past, present and future, between all three and the Eternal, between the abstract and the concrete, the manifest and the unmanifest. In the Vedic hymns we have a supreme statement of affirmation combined simultaneously with a note of agnosticism. We find this tradition in all the great Teachers of Wisdom who truly came to formulate and also to intimate, knowing that formulation could become the enemy of the unformulated. They knew that, while in a Platonic sense Time is the moving image of eternity, there is another sense in which there is an unavoidable tension between the dreams, the ideas, the potentialities that lie within Eternity and the cycles that work themselves out with highs and lows, ups and downs, through all the vicissitudes of historical time.

The problem is cosmological and metaphysical. Philosophically, it becomes a problem of epistemology, of the relation between the knower and the known. Ethically, it becomes a problem of action, of the relation between the individual as an actor or agent and the world that is external to him, a problem of inner and outer. And, of course, if the Theosophical Movement in time is an integral part of a vaster history that extends far beyond the recorded annals of time, then the Theosophical Movement, in our historical sense, will participate in the age-old problem. This was a distinction that H.P. Blavatsky was extremely concerned to make. She made it in the very first article that she wrote, stating what Theosophy is, and she maintained this distinction till the end. Mystically, it is present in *The Voice of the*

Silence, sometimes illuminated in the footnotes that she prepared. She was asked by the Brotherhood to hint at the distinction between the psyche and the nous, the psychic and the noetic in man and in Nature. At the very end of her life she wrote her article on psychic and noetic action. All of this is deeply worth pondering upon, but it is something that each of us must do for himself, something on which there can be no formulated consensus among those who call themselves either Theosophists or students of Theosophy, least of all among formal organizations.

In a way the problem is acutely present on the political scene. It arises in the relation of world order to its materialization on the visible plane — the connection between the cosmopolis which is metaphysical and mystic, existing already for some though utterly irrelevant for others, and some kind of megalopolis which we would like to see emerge in the realm of political institutions. It is bound up with the problem of identity for individuals in all cultures and nations, of all races, of both sexes, of different age groups. It is involved in all the feuds of our time — those tensions which cannot be resolved merely by words, by gestures or symbols, and which cannot be resolved vicariously for the many by a few, however gifted or generous they may be as leaders of thought and opinion. It cannot be resolved for the laity by popes or bishops, swamis or lamas, self-styled or otherwise. It is a problem that is at the very core of every human being. We face the problem collectively, in all walks of life, as a problem of organizations.

Historically, it is the problem of why, at the very times and in the very places where the most ardent movements emerged in the name of the very greatest ideals, we find in those very places and springing therefrom in a subsequent period the most hideous nightmares — long shadows cast by large causes. We find this in all the syncretist movements in the nineteenth century, often succeeded by the most terrible forms of separatism. It is almost as if to speak of unity and universality, and to speak more often than one means it or more than it is possible to mean it, is to tempt the satan or the devil in every man and in collective humanity, and to invite more disorder, more division. This is an age-old story. This may well be the reason why some of the greatest students of even the recorded and over-written history of the West came to dismal, grim and pessimistic conclusions. This could be the reason why Gibbon said that history is a story of crimes, follies and misfortunes. This could be why Hegel, among philosophers, could assert that the only lesson men seem to learn from history is that they learn nothing from it.

In this larger context students of Theosophy cannot but be truly humble. There never was a suggestion, and there never could be, that by any act of association with any Theosophical organization, even by long years of study and involvement with Theosophical texts, even by long years of ethical and mystical training along Theosophical lines, that a person somehow has a privileged access to the Wisdom-Religion. No man can speak as its sole custodian or its ultimate authority. No man can claim that he is any different from other men. The very thought of separation becomes for him a wall, a barrier that will divide him both from other men and also, alas, sometimes unknown to him but often painfully so, separate him from the Great Custodians of the Wisdom-Religion. It is only appropriate, recognizing these limitations and the immensity of the fundamental problem of unravelling and using Theosophia in our lives, that we should turn beyond the nineteenth century, beyond the centenary cycle that began in 1875, to the Mahatmas of whom H.P. Blavatsky spoke and to the wider vision we can discern in the scriptures and the teachers of world history.

Over five thousand years ago Krishna, the enigmatic and mysterious Teacher who came at the beginning of Kali Yuga, both ended a cycle and struck a keynote for the long Dark Age into which humanity would be plunged. On the battlefield of Duty, *Kurukshetra*, which was *Dharmakshetra*, he made a beautiful and puzzling statement to Arjuna — who went through all the many vagaries and ambivalences of friendship and discipleship, and indeed at the end proved himself to have been a worthy friend and pupil of Krishna though not ready for initiation. After giving Arjuna the universal vision of the 'Divine Eye', Krishna said to

Arjuna: "But what, O Arjuna, hast thou to do with so much knowledge as this? I established this whole universe with a single portion of myself, and remain separate." This statement partakes of that deeply puzzling relation between the transcendent and the immanent in all subsequent theologies and concepts of the Godhead. It is dramatically put forward here in a manner that seems to be personified and yet has the curious obscurity of an impersonal cosmic enigma. There is a world and yet there is no world. The world has a mind and a Logos, and yet it does not. There is meaning to the world and yet there is absurdity to it. There is a supreme concern and compassion in the world flowing from whatever preceded it, whatever sustains and nourishes it, whatever destroys and recreates it. At the same time there is a supreme detachment that may sound to us almost like cold indifference.

While it is a classical stance, the importance of the statement is not merely what it says about Krishna. Like everything else that a great Teacher does, it is meant to release in Arjuna authentic representations of an archetypal stance. Whatever part he chose or course of action he took, it was possible for Arjuna to have unconditional help from Krishna. It was also possible for him — in relation to his world — both to be involved and to stand outside it. This central message of that Great Teacher became a clue for ancient Brahmins who were torn between deploring the end of what looked like a Golden Age in comparison to what was emerging, and a deep concern to preserve and maintain something in the new age. It became a keynote pointing to a new modulus of growth, a principle of self-reliance not merely grounded in individual human nature but also serving as a basic pattern for social structures.

It was a very difficult lesson, hardly capable of being absorbed and assimilated by those who conservatively became attached to the existing and subsequent representations of an ideal, classical social order. At the same time, there was an awareness that the lesson could be grasped in principle by any man, especially when he had really got into a series of messes, when he had been betrayed on the basis of the trust he had put in fathers and teachers who failed him, when he was involved in all those acts of betrayal that are a part of the human inheritance. It would still be possible for him to say, "I am not abandoned," or "I do not have to insult the integrity of the universe, because if there is meaning, divinity and dignity to the world and in my life, it is always possible for me to claim it. This is my privilege. In order to be a man by self-assertion in the deepest sense, by self-definition, I shall declare my destiny as one who is proud to inhabit a human form." Hence in art, in literature and in traditions of mystical training, the celebration of the privilege of birth in a human form. It became part of the recognition that every man is given in trust that which he did not make — a potential temple in which there is an indwelling god — where Krishna is closer to each one of us than anyone else outside.

The way to that Krishna within requires a transformation and a humbling of the insecure, weak and personal self, representative of all the conflicting doubts of Arjuna. This self that wants to be loved, that wants guarantees of salvation, has got to be abandoned, to yield. Arjuna is ready for the universal vision only when he reaches that point where he ceases fault-finding and Krishna is able to say to him: "Unto thee who findeth no fault, I shall now make known this most mysterious knowledge." In all human relationships there must be a certain magical quality of trust — between mother and child, between teacher and pupil — though this is more easily seen in areas that appear mystically or morally neutral, like music, than in our ordinary encounters in society and the system. Unless there is that spontaneous ceasing of a sense of difference there will not be the possibility of the magic, the magic of pregnancy which will be fruitful, which would culminate in the birth of something meaningful and joyous — the birth of Wisdom.

We have, then, five thousand years ago, an archetypal statement of the relation between the whole and the part, the unmanifest and the manifest, the transcendent and the immanent. Krishna is both. He is the cosmic Krishna — more a force than a person, not to be understood in ordinary terms — and he is also a historical personage. The same tradition, but in another mode, is enunciated again two thousand five hundred years ago, in the coming of Gautama Buddha. While he ridiculed the claims of any men to be the exclusive heirs, to be the custodians, the trustees in Time, of the eternal revelation, the *Sanatana Dharma*, he at the same time redefined the very notion of the Eternal Religion. The *Sanatana Dharma*, he said, is the religion which teaches that hatred ceaseth not by hatred, but by love. It is only the person exercising the extraordinarily and increasingly elusive skill of being able to draw the larger circle, of resolving and reconciling by going beyond, without getting caught in confrontations and dichotomies, who can speak authentically about the Eternal Religion.

There is an Eternal Religion written in the very hearts of men that is reinforced by the most natural modes of transmission from the old to young, from teacher to pupil, from mother to child. There are these intimations in the hearts of all human beings. There are certain things that no one can be told or need be told, because if he does not know them already, telling will never be able to instruct. These fundamental truths are not merely felt. They can also be known, but this involves conceptions of knowing and of knowledge that are remote from our time because they presuppose the dissolution of the very separation between the knower and the known. You can truly know these fundamental truths only when they cease to be external and become the very breath of your life and basis of your being. Then they set the context or perspective in which everything else may be known and identified in a more specific sense. Unless we could know something — and this would require a particular kind of meditation — about abstract, absolute, unmanifest Space, all statements that are spatial in context would have a disproportionate significance. In affirming they would also be denying. In the truth they tell they would also be lying. As with Space, so too with Time. Unless we could recover a sense of an unconditioned reality reflected in an eternal and perpetual process that far transcends all limited conceptions of times that have a beginning and an end, there would be no way by which we could emancipate ourselves from the tyranny of beginnings and endings, no way by which immortality could become not merely a right or an ideal but a fact for human beings.

Similarly, with Consciousness and Motion. Unless we could visualize unconditioned consciousness we would always be liable to be caught in the conditionalities of manifested consciousness. We would be involved in illusions. How would we know this? Because every time we were involved in that which is conditioned, we would pretend that it is not and exaggerate its value. This becomes the root of what we call the problem of the ego — the problem of the shadowy self that pretends to be that which it can never be. Growing from childhood like a spoilt child, it becomes a terrible tyrant who displaces from the central throne the inner ruler, the unknown god, the Krishna within, and actually becomes the enemy, the satan. Until a person could recognize this within himself, there would be no solution to the human problem. But metaphysically he could never recognize it unless there were in that shadow a vulnerable point, a connection between that lower self and the unconditioned.

Hence the enormous significance of the assertion by Buddha:

> Ho! ye who suffer! know
>
> Ye suffer from yourselves. None else compels,
>   None other holds you that ye live and die,
> And whirl upon the wheel, and hug and kiss
>   Its spokes of agony,
>
> Its tire of tears, its nave of nothingness.
> *The Light of Asia*   EDWIN ARNOLD

You are free, but you can only assert that freedom by exercising it, and you could only exercise that freedom authentically by becoming and behaving like a man who is in awe of no one, afraid of nothing. Any other conception of human dignity or of human equality has a compensatory value. It strikes a false note. It cannot carry the certification of the absolute assurance with which Krishna speaks of immortality in the second chapter of the *Gita,* the absolute assurance with which Buddha speaks of the possibility for every man of becoming a Buddha, or the like assurance he displays at the end of his life in making light of all distinctions — between Buddhas, Bodhisattvas and hierarchies — that people try to impose upon One Universal Life.

We find the same principle in subsequent teachings. We find it in the elusive magic of the relationship of Pythagoras to his own School. He insisted upon a certain kind of acceptance by all, of their individual unimportance in relation to the collective, while at the same time he found the need for taking upon himself responsibility. In his life this meant his assumption of all ascriptions of credit. This was done to disallow anyone from corrupting the common core. He also tried to make men see it mathematically, to make men understand the supreme sovereign importance of limit, which they would better understand in the architecture of the world and of all creativity when they already had some sense of the unlimited, the illimitable. Zero must be seen and understood before we can appreciate the number series and the distinction between odd and even numbers.

Similarly, it is found in the life of Jesus, the most dramatic and tragic of incarnations in the recorded history that we have so over-celebrated and are now trying to get away from in what we call the Christian era. This extraordinary Initiate, in his own direct relations with those around him, was able to carry conviction about the indwelling Christos in every man. He made each feel much better and, indeed, a participant in the glorification of the Kingdom of God on earth. At the same time he made each one aware that nobody, not even himself, could be any more than merely a pointer to That which does not come into the world, which is not in the realm of appearances, That which will come again but which in one sense never began and never can be seen or shown in time. Understanding of this enigma underwent a complex subsequent development, which came to a certain culmination crucial to history in St. Augustine, concerning the relation between the unmanifest and the manifest, the tension between the Platonic element in Christianity and the more narrowly materialistic aspects of both Hellenic and Hebraic thought, for various reasons known only to a few who were the custodians of the other and unspoken side of both.

It is a very complex story, but knowing its subtle details is not relevant here. We do know it writ large in history in the name of the Prince of Peace. Untold bloodshed and violence have been dropped upon the human sea in the name of the meekest of men, that paradigm of saintly Initiates and Teachers who went to preach the gospel of universal love and goodwill. There emerged the most monstrously narrow and shallow claims to a historic and physical uniqueness, which people are now trying somehow to rationalize. There is something in the human mind that is insulted, the subtler the apologetics. There is also something which makes one feel "I've been that way before." Is there, then, a sense in which all of us — from wherever we come, whatever tradition we inherit in this life, whatever memories we bear from our possible previous lives — come into the Theosophical Movement in the hope of a transubstantiation that will make us free? But only as we grow older do we see the scars and the wounds in our psyche. We can see in each other, and more painfully in ourselves, mirror images of the fundamentalist, of the latitudinarian, of every kind of heretical denomination to be found in the Christian tradition or in all of the religious schools.

We find them even in that most crucial of arenas, the very relationship of a man, who calls himself a student of Theosophy, to Theosophy itself; the relationship of the seeker to the wisdom he seeks; the relationship of a man, who is a potential disciple of a Brotherhood of Bodhisattvas, to that Brotherhood itself. Perhaps more caricature, more ridicule, more martyrdom was psychologically experienced in the modern age by the great Teachers of Theosophy than in past ages, even though endured at a level of humorous compassion. Those Beings took the extraordinarily bold and unprecedented decision to make known publicly what was always guarded secretly — their very existence and accessibility in time to any man. Yet They themselves came to be appropriated both by individuals who tried to claim special relationships and treated Them like personal gods or household idols, and by those who transcendentalized Them out of existence.

We are dealing with a fact of human consciousness. In love, in family life, in scholarship, in the quest for truth, in the pursuit of skills in music or art — anyone may understand the profound importance of continuity of consciousness, of being true to an ideal despite one's forgetfulness and one's limitations. Surely in this realm too, it is evident that the world of the future which Theosophists wish to frame will be determined by what dominates their consciousness twenty-four hours a day and seven days of the week, as much as by the wisdom and the compassion, the energy and the ideation of Adepts. Now, when all earlier judgments which at first appeared so Olympian have subsequently proven absurd in regard to great Teachers — small men trying to size up greater Beings and put them in a Pantheon — are we going to try to have a true assessment, a correct scholarly estimate of H.P. Blavatsky? We are liable to the same error on which a whole tragic novel was written by Hermann Hesse — *The Journey to the East.* Is it not like asking, "How do I know that the Fraternity exists?" when in the very asking of that question one is defining oneself: "Because my life is meaningless, I may think the universe is meaningless. Scriptures are empty and do not speak, but let me be careful." We may fall into the trap but how long do we stay in it? Do we give ourselves a chance to come out of it? Or do we box the compass and become unwitting partners in our own self-destruction? This is a fateful question bound up with the problem of survival — psychological survival for men and women today at all levels of the contemporary revolution.

The only persons who can psychologically accommodate themselves to the kind of world we live in and which is emerging are those who can authentically inherit the whole of human history, even though most of it is unknown to us. Which of us can say: "Everything human is deeply relevant and meaningful to me, and where I cannot know, at least I will not condemn. Even if I cannot understand the myths of particular peoples, the scriptures of other times, the languages, the cultures, the folk ways of other men which may be strange to me, let me not mock, let me not make a great thing of my pathetic ignorance. Let me be silent. Let me be open. Let me in some way that is natural to me show that I too can acclimatize myself to the more rarefied altitudes of world citizenship that are authentic, that are more than mere assertions of goodwill, but are filled with a positive enjoyment and exaltation at every kind of human endeavour, every form of excellence as well as positive appreciation for every kind of struggle and compassion for every kind of failure."

Unless a man can do this, can he even survive into the future? There are those who are afraid they cannot, who therefore want to write about the end of history, but only find themselves unable to communicate with others who, though young, weak-willed, lazy, lonely, spoilt and everything else, still know something else — that they are not going to play that game. They do not want sophistication at that price. They do not want packaged Great Books from whichever university. They can see through that. They at least want to be able to feel that inwardly they can extend a hand to the wretched of the earth, that they can understand what it means to take one's place in the great galaxy of mankind's history. Minimally, they are willing to stand in the backstage of the theatre on which world history is being played.

This is a crucial question. For some it may seem that the world 'outside' has very little relevance to the Theosophical Movement as it was constituted in 1875. To others it might seem exactly the opposite. It may well be that in the world outside more has been gained and more is at stake that involves Theosophical issues than we shall ever be able to recognize within the narrower groups and organizations that are called Theosophical. Stranger things have happened in the history of humanity. Today there are souls outside the countries where Krishna taught and the Buddha preached to whom Krishna and the Buddha are more meaningful than they are to those who might claim a kind of inherited relationship to them purely because of race or pride of birth, but who cannot sustain that relationship or be credible in it. Equally, there may be those who do not call themselves Theosophists but who may better understand what is at the core, what is at stake, in the great drama of coming events.

H.P. Blavatsky, of course, wrote about this. In her letter to the Archbishop of Canterbury she pointed out that there were many people calling themselves Christian who simply did not find it convenient or possible to speak frankly but who knew more than the subtlest and even seemingly generous liberal flights of the theologians. Something more was at stake which has now increasingly come to the fore. The man in the pew might for many reasons have gone along with what came from the pulpit, but inwardly he was asking himself questions and making distinctions. There are people all over the world, of whatever race or religion, or totally uprooted in every feasible cultural and social sense, who understand intuitively authentic affirmations of universal needs, of universal propositions that are fundamental, of universal compassion and charity. A Yevtushenko could understand and celebrate a Martin Luther King more than his own compatriots. It is possible for men in far places to identify with those forerunners, few and far between, of the authentic language of the human race. To take a magnificent phrase of Stringfellow Barr, "Let us join the human race." Anyone can join the human race. There are many young people who are afraid to be joiners, no doubt for a variety of reasons, some of whom are seekers, and seekers who perhaps need more help than they know. But there is also a sense in which whatever one joins that is universal will not limit one's capacity to communicate with or reach out to anything outside.

These are curious, inchoate, compelling and sometimes contradictory demands upon the human sea. Does Theosophy, in its primordial statement by H.P. Blavatsky, show an awareness of all of this? Surely the only way to know is by reading what she said. In her articles she gave many definitions, and that was always typical of her. She constantly varied, like an Indian musician, the manner in which she expressed herself. She was a dialectician. She did not want people to get fixated on particular formulations, and she varied them so much that only years of commitment allow one to recognize the immense inner consistency of her work, the pointing to That which is beyond, to which all forms of music point — That which is the Soundless, the music of the spheres. We find this in her writings, archetypally, again and again. One has to read every word carefully, which is difficult, because most of us have lost that habit, and some of us have never learnt it. But if we are going to value the privilege of reading her, then surely we should assume she meant the words that she used. It takes years before one comes to see, given the limitations of language, the multi-dimensional nature of what she is saying.

In the article "What is Theosophy?" she declares: "With every man that is earnestly searching in his own way after a knowledge of the Divine Principle, of man's relation to it" — not his own, but *man's* relation to it — "and Nature's manifestation of it, Theosophy is allied." If Theosophy is allied with such, then it is less so with any man who is not earnestly searching but merely claiming second-hand knowledge of that symbol or token of the Divine Principle to which he wishes to pay allegiance or by which he wishes to be saved. It is less allied with those men who are more concerned with being left out, or with their own relationship to the universe than they are with the relationship of all men or of man as a species to the universe. It is less allied to those who think that Theosophy is only to be found in the written word or in so-called great examples of art and music, but who cannot read it in the heavens every night, read it in their dawn meditation — in that which is so profound and yet so unmanifest — where everything is covered and hidden, but everything is expressed. Everything is a veil upon that which is yet to be found.

Growth is invisible. It is under the soil. Yet the visible is an immense representation of the diversity and the variety sustained by a central unity in growth, the one in the many. The relation between the abstract and the concrete can be seen and shown in any child or in any tree. People refuse to recognize, however, that there is any connection between all of that and themselves, and are more concerned to come to a correct judgment in regard to which book will help them or how they should regard H.P. Blavatsky. They are fortunate whose innocence and ignorance protect them from childhood and make them feel that with Teachers of Wisdom, whoever they be, there is no such thing as half-hearted commitment. You either commit yourself a hundred percent, or you do not bother about it.

Religion does not have to do with making claims or with reconciling them, but with transcending everything that divides men. All of us must come to know for ourselves — and each one can only speak for himself — that if we are going to be serious about committing ourselves to the study, the practice and above all, the service, of the wisdom in *The Secret Doctrine* and *The Voice of the Silence*, then that commitment must be complete at some level. It must be unconditional at the very core, even though we may participate as fallible and personal beings in ups and downs, the vagaries of the implications of that commitment. Each must choose a particular way, and each one must choose his own, but let there be no doubt that we can ever come any closer to the Wisdom without an immense gratitude, a profound unqualified reverence for the Teachers.

"From the Teachings to the Teacher" can have meaning as a motto only if we understand that with the Teachers there is no dilly-dallying, no game-playing. This is as old as the wisdom of mankind, as old as all the Orders and goes beyond the Orders in the East. Whenever H.P. Blavatsky speaks of her Teachers, it is with a reverence that exalts her with a beauty, a feeling, an *eros* that is magical. When she spoke at the end of her life about herself, the only claim she made, and was rightfully insistent upon making, was that "Never for one moment have I denied or doubted Him, my Teacher." She invoked the servant in *As You Like It*, to illustrate her point. She quoted the statement: "Master, go on; and I will follow thee to the last gasp, with truth and loyalty." Anyone reading this should know that it is real, that it is a hallmark of the true Teacher. You can tell it at any time. But he should also know that he is in no position to make an assessment of her, but simply to desire to learn at her feet, and to look where she pointed — to Those beyond her, to the Path of which she spoke. Whoever is able to take such a decision with a natural simplicity will find that it makes all the difference to their own particular life. What some few do as naturally as breathing they will also find, in their lives, has been possible for other rare individuals in every part of the world. These men and women are not *lusus naturae* or accidents, and can never be explained empirically. They are awakened souls, incarnating the vested wisdom of the maturity of the past in the context of the present, pointing to the future. They are the true Theosophists of whom H.P. Blavatsky spoke, Theosophists who are the friends of all living beings.

This is not to deny that any one of us can self-consciously recover an authentic universality, remain within and yet refuse to be enclosed within the sectarianism of every single person, whether on the religious, the political, the social or even the Theosophical plane. Of course *something* can be done about it. That was why H.P. Blavatsky came. To do *everything* about it is to prepare oneself for the Path, for discipleship, for initiation. She pointed out that it was the Buddha who decided — for no one else could take that decision — that in a humanity that was old in the Dark Ages, the rules could not be relaxed, but the access to the Mysteries could be increased for all. Hence many new and subtle guises of the age-old relationship most connected with the sacred — that between the esoteric and the exoteric — will be available. Anyone may wish to become a companion of the Brotherhood of Initiates. Everyone in life may go through many initiations on many planes in many forms. But if he is sensitive and delicate, and in this is authentic and concerned with the sacred, he is going to be suspicious of people who talk about it out of season, people who call attention to it. He is going to be as embarrassed as any man would be in speaking too openly about parents he loves or about those closest to him, to those for whom it may mean nothing. He knows better than that. Of course this has been done in the name of religion. It is the standard compensatory device offered, but it never worked. It did not work for the Brahmins, nor did it work in any single religion, whether for the Jews, the Egyptians, or Christians; and it is not going to work for Theosophists today. But that does not mean that men should be caught in the dichotomy between saying, "Oh, the sacred doesn't exist," and on the other hand, becoming insanely anxious about it.

There is always a middle way. It is always possible for a person to gain access into the most exalted chambers of initiation, to take his place in various sanctuaries, even in this day and age, anywhere in this world. But whoever he be, he can only do that by taking vows, assuming trials with a certain courage, with a certain detachment, with an authentic compassion to do it only for the sake of the whole, and with a deliberate decision to be utterly uninvolved in worry, let alone waste of energy, on behalf of his own salvation. This requires a break with the salvationism that may have been part and parcel of the Piscean Age, but will have no place in the future. W.Q. Judge wrote of that future moment when "powers will be needed and pretensions will go for naught". That was perhaps true even in his own day for a few. Today it is true at all levels. Above all, no one can make or unmake the invisible degrees to which souls belong, nor can they easily be known because those who know will never tell, and those who tell, by definition, do not know. In regard to the invisible, spiritual stature of any human being, those who truly know are pledged to eternal secrecy, and those who are outside can never know by definition. This is analogous to the Wittgensteinian affirmation in regard to immortality, as well as to the Shavian aphorism comparing marriage and freemasonry.

There is a sense in which self-definition or self-validation becomes an authentic key towards a great universality. It opens doors and we can test it in terms of our capacity to come closer to, communicate with, and become credible to more and more human beings wherever they be, whatever their language, their upbringing, their external labours. It does not happen automatically with a Constitution, even where that Constitution had behind it the benediction of Adepts, such as that of the United States of America. Canada may be fortunate to know that while America aimed higher than any historical society, it failed so greatly too, that now the aim and the failure have both to be reckoned with. The time may yet come when Theosophia alone, in the broad and the deep sense, could provide the only metaphysical basis for the U.S.A., for Canada, or for any vast experiment that is, like the Greek *polis,* a microcosm of mankind. There is enough in Theosophy to be relevant by translation and application to every single problem.

When H.P. Blavatsky speaks of the universal solvent of *Akasa* and the true philosopher's stone, if one is very serious one is either going to find out something about them or one is going to say, "Well, there is something I don't know." Alas, there will be many who will never even notice the deadly earnestness with which such profound matters were spoken of in *The Secret Doctrine.* Many of the greatest minds of the age are looking for the equivalent to $E=mc^2$ which will apply to a variety of fields. They seek a philosopher's stone. Leading men in various fields of thought know enough now to realize that there is something more that could not be known by the existing methodologies and presuppositions. They are not concerned with which book you find it in. They seek to know individuals, multi-lingual in a conceptual sense, who can help. They also sense that someone who really knew would not help them unless they deserved it, unless there is a reasonable likelihood that they will not misuse the help. The universal solvent and the elixir of life are realities and not metaphorical expressions. Why, then, do we who inherit so much tend to narrow the universe and put it in a little box, instead of mirroring the universe in a grain of sand and seeing it there mirrored? Instead of doing that of which the poets and the mystics speak, why do we try to behave like those individuals who, when the Bodhisattva in the guise of an elephant came striding majestically, simply clung to their particular metaphorical planks of salvation which the compassionate elephant swept aside on its way.

Adepts, Mahatmas, and Universal Beings are not here to consolidate anyone's pet ideas, pet likes and dislikes, but watch over those who can appreciate and enjoy what is involved in the gait of a noble elephant, who will accept it like children, who will cling to nothing. Yet many people, because of fears that are understandable enough, want to save something and therefore there is sectarianism. Coleridge put the problem very well in regard to Christianity, but it is true equally in regard to Theosophy. He who loves Christianity more than every other religion will love his own sect more than every other sect, and in the end love himself best of all. There is a logical and psychological connection between egocentricity and claims on behalf of the uniqueness of institutions or of formulations. This much is by now clear in relation to each other's orthodoxies and isms, and every man is desperately wanting to get out of the problem within himself in some way. But there is no technique. Authentic solutions involve a redefinition of self, a breakthrough — from the realm of *kama manas*, the psychic self, with its elaborate and boring history of likes and dislikes, fears and personal memories — to the sphere of the noetic with its golden moments of freedom of awareness, which every human soul has and which may be threaded together on a single strand.

So the problem again becomes one of sifting and of recovering continuity of consciousness. When a person is able to do these things, he can rise to those planes of consciousness where the great universal archetypal ideas are ever-present. He will also have a due wisdom in rendering them into the language and the form that is best suited to meet human need and to serve the circumstances of people's space and time. Since he would see every human being as a mirror of the whole of humanity, he would not think statistically about humanity, but know that each individual is infinitely important. He would, in other words, become an apprentice in the art of the dialectic so magnificently exemplified by the Buddha, who said different things to different individuals because he knew that the Teaching was multi-dimensional. Something of what he did under trees and on the great dusty pathways of a vast, teeming, and torrid country, of which we have images in fables, myths and legends that as much conceal as reveal what really happened, could well be true now in another form. In the old days wisdom was veiled by various devices — cryptic devices, codes, cyphers, glyphs, symbols — but also by saying too little. In our time wisdom is veiled by seeming to say too much. There is a luminous nature in *The Secret Doctrine* enabling an incredible concealment which the intuitive student can gradually learn to enjoy. The most ineluctable forms of priceless magic and incantatory mantramic teaching reside within the foliage of references that connect at many points with the complicated and many-sided story of the soul of man.

That, then, is our heritage. It is universal not merely in an abstract sense. It has amazing diversity, and the variety is infinite, as is the wonderment of the Theosophical enterprise. But the point is not whether a person goes this far or adopts that way, but whether at any level he is able to develop the fruit of his study and meditation into an authentic capacity to draw the larger circle. We should truly try to put ourselves in a proper mental relationship — for some of us this may come naturally, for others this may be a strain, but every man could attempt it — to the Brotherhood, to the Mahatmas, to Beings like H.P. Blavatsky. We should see her in a long lineage of Teachers and do the same in regard to one or all the Teachers. We may choose any as our particular *Ishtaguru*. If we could really do this, then it would truly be possible to become capable of negating those thought-forms that become divisive sources of human suspicion. It would become possible to make that extraordinarily elusive linkage between the eternal and the momentary but timely, the appropriate and the relevant, the abstract and the concrete — the dynamic relationship implicit in the divine dialectic.

This is challenging because synonymous with living. But when a person does it with the help of the knowledge that he gains from Theosophical Teachers, it is living dangerously. It is living with a new self-consciousness, living with increased pain and anguish on behalf of human beings, living with great heightening of joy that may make one manic at times with regard to the Divine Dance of the whole of life and of history. That is why people today and in the future are really going to make Theosophia important in their lives, especially the young, the lost and the rootless. It is a whole way of life. It is too late for the equivalent of going to churches on Sundays, synagogues on Saturdays, mosques on Fridays, temples on Mondays, and so on. It is too late to find the equivalent of all the elaborate complexities of human attitudes towards the Vedas or the Bible in our attitudes towards Theosophical texts. It is the all or nothing attitude that could be dangerous on the plane of the mind but is, for many, part of the historical compulsion of our time.

Therefore, as the Maha Chohan stated in his letter, unless Theosophy can be shown to be relevant to the most crucial problems that affect mankind as a whole, and involve ultimate questions in regard to the very struggle for existence and the meaning of life, Theosophy will not be relevant. The Fraternity will have nothing to do with it. Perish the thought, says He, rather than that They should have anything to do with anything that evades the crucial issue — the full demands of universal brotherhood in thought, feeling, word and deed. So They have spoken. They have spoken in terms of the immensity of the challenge. The Theosophical Movement of the nineteenth century, like the Constitution of the United States, is an educational phenomenon where the invisible Founding Fathers knew that it might take a hundred years for people both to see that it is not easy and that while it looks irrelevant, it had better be made relevant. This may take the coming hundred years for those individuals who really are alive to the problems of our time and worthy of the enormous privilege of the inheritance that they have as students of Theosophy. They must at the same time have the proper posture in regard to the Fraternity of Teachers who are invisible, but who could become more real than anything else, according to a person's degree of development. Anyone could come to see in the future a new relevance, a new magic, a new significance to the work of H.P. Blavatsky and her predecessors.

Therefore, as the 1975 cycle unfolds, we must become less apologetic in every sense on behalf of, or about, any aspect of the Teachings, and we need be less concerned with claims. But at the same time we have to be immensely and actively concerned with the effective embodiment and translation of Theosophical ideas and principles that can be seeds for meditation, because the pioneers of the future want to learn about meditation. If they cannot learn it under a banyan tree, they are willing to learn it in a café. But they seriously want to learn about it. Of course, there are many mistakes that they could make. How could we be of any help unless we ourselves have attempted it enough to be humble about ourselves, while at the same time remaining proud about the undertaking? One might say that the Theosophist of the coming cycle will be the kind of person who will show himself not merely by his acts, but by the whole of his mental attitude to other beings, from the most exalted to the most wretched. He will show that it is more important to travel than to arrive; that there is a difference between perfection and perfectibility; that it is true, as Samuel Butler wrote, that everything matters more than we think it does, and at the same time nothing matters so much as we think. It is true that to become a Buddha is impossibly difficult, but it is equally true that it could be said of every man "Look inward: thou art Buddha."

Theosophy must be both as elusive as the empyrean of the most universal kinds of space, time, motion and matter, and as close to home and as real as our daily breathing. It must be relevant to our every problem. This will be eternally enigmatic. In a Platonic sense this could never be taught, could never be learned, but could only be developed by a series of intimations — efforts at living by these ideas — so that the whole world becomes for every one of us, as it became for Arjuna, a *Kurukshetra*, a theatre of trial, a tremendous drama in which the stakes are high. But the stakes are not high for us as separate beings who are going to be individually saved or damned. They are high for us all collectively, even at a time in which there is a great deal of absurdity. We must learn to become the psychological equivalents of those who can ascend and descend into the depths like divers, adapting ourselves to different altitudes and perspectives, becoming flexible and multi-dimensional. And we must do this with a certain panache, but in every case as the result of honest striving, and with compassion, with laughter and love. This is existentially to show what it means in our time to be a true Theosophist, and anyone who wishes to do this might well reflect upon the timeless injunction of Mahatma K.H.: *"If you wish to know us, study our philosophy. If you wish to serve us, serve our Humanity."*

October 8, 1971   *Presidential Address*
Toronto, Canada   North American Theosophical Convention

THE DAWNING OF WISDOM

*'What is it that ever is?' 'Space, the eternal Anupadaka.'
'What is it that ever was?' 'The Germ in the Root.' 'What
is it that is ever coming and going?' 'The Great Breath.'
'Then, there are three Eternals?' 'No, the three are one. That
which ever is is one, that which ever was is one, that which
is ever being and becoming is also one: and this is Space.'*

*'Explain, oh Lanoo (disciple).' — 'The One is an
unbroken Circle (ring) with no circumference, for it is
nowhere and everywhere; the One is the boundless plane of
the Circle, manifesting a diameter only during the
manvantaric periods; the One is the indivisible point found
nowhere, perceived everywhere during those periods; it is the
Vertical and the Horizontal, the Father and the Mother, the
summit and base of the Father, the two extremities of the
Mother, reaching in reality nowhere, for the One is the Ring
as also the rings that are within that Ring. Light in darkness
and darkness in light: the "Breath which is eternal." It
proceeds from without inwardly, when it is everywhere, and
from within outwardly, when it is nowhere — (i.e., maya, one
of the centres). It expands and contracts (exhalation and
inhalation).'*

The Secret Doctrine, i 11-12

The metaphysical connection between spiritual knowledge and material manifestation is conveyed in the Proem to *The Secret Doctrine* through illustrations from an archaic palm leaf manuscript, ancient beyond reckoning and impermeable to all the elements. On the first leaf of the manuscript there is an immaculate white disk within a dark background. On the second, the immaculate white disk remains on the dark background, but with a central point. The first diagram represents a state which is before the awakening of any universe. It is Cosmos in Eternity, the Ideal Cosmos which is veiled within Ideal Space and endures throughout Ideal Time, or Eternity. It is the Germ in the Root lying within *Anupadaka*, parentless, boundless Space. It is that which ever was, whilst the Great Breath is ever coming and going and Space ever exists. These three are all One in the dawn of differentiation. This pristine state is mirrored in the rising of Venus as Lucifer, the depth of silence which inaugurates each day, analogous to the dawn of a *manvantara*. The dawn of differentiation must be seen in relation to the one circle which is divine unity. The circumference, which is not a fixed line but a metaphysical, fluctuating boundary, is the All-Presence that sets limits upon an entire period of manifestation. The plane of that circle is the universal soul, the *Anima Mundi, Alaya*, the *Paramatman*, and every human being is an immortal ray of that ineffable Light.

Divine Wisdom is at the hidden core of all manifestation, and hence one cannot possibly understand nature without seeing it as intelligent, as innately a manifestation of divine Reason. Man as part of Nature is richly endowed with creative faculties that are analogous on planes of consciousness with powers and forces in Nature. Every human being is ensouled by individuated *Manas*, which affords, through the sum of states of consciousness, an initial representation of Universal Mind, in which Divine Thought is potentially ever present. It is the sacred teaching of Krishna and Buddha, Pythagoras and Plato, Christ and Confucius and a galaxy of Teachers throughout history and before recorded history, that every human being is inwardly and inherently capable of spiritual vision. Each person may embrace the whole of manifestation, for the immortal soul is capable of standing outside time, transcending the boundaries of manifestation, reaching beyond the visible universe. Through contemplation, one can come to the very core of one's being and become attuned to the invisible ideal universe in the realm of Divine Thought. This teaching implies that all possible knowledge available in principle to any human mind is enshrined in the totality of things. The totality may be compared to the face of the disk, set against the limitless background, symbolizing the fact that myriad universes in all periods of manifestation do not exhaust the potential of the realm of BE-NESS or Non-Being.

Each world is an extraordinary mirror of the whole. It is vast, massive, but it is still a fragment, yet within that massive fragment each human being is like a microscopic drop within a cosmic ocean. Within every drop there is the same quintessential life, light and wisdom or energy found in the entire ocean. It is possible for the individual human being self-consciously to become united with the One that is secondless, and from a reflection of which emanates the entire universe during a *Mahamanvantara*. As the Mahatmas teach, "The whole of Nature lies before you, take what you can." Nature is the repository of far more knowledge than human beings are willing or ready to use. Fortunately, it is now widely recognized that human beings use only a minute fraction of the potential energy of the brain. They not only live well within their means, but also live far below their needs. When it comes to creative ideation, human beings are extremely bankrupt, or unduly thrifty.

If pioneering individuals could learn to partake of the generous teaching of *The Secret Doctrine*, making it the basis of their ideation, they would increase the proportion of their available mental energy. They could become more wide awake and more attentive to the secret wisdom and the compassionate purposes of invisible Nature. By using the teaching they could grasp the hidden logic of the Logos in manifestation. They could come to see in every dawn meditation an archetypal sequence of states of consciousness partly corresponding to the subtle stages of differentiation of the noumenal light in darkness. The phases of dawn meditation correspond to the stages of the dawn of manifestation. Those who make meditation a regular practice come closer to those beings who eternally are awake, the Watchers in the Night of non-manifestation, the Self-Governed Sages, the Mahatmas and the Rishis, who are on a plane that is far removed from that of mundane concerns. The moment of choice has come for many individuals, who must either endure the atrophy of their faculties or become attentive to these immense possibilities. One can begin to use intuition to come closer to the concealed plan, not of every future cosmogony, but to the vast design that is deeply relevant to human evolution. Intuition rapidly soars above the tardy processes of ratiocinative thought. The quickest minds are too slow compared to the speed of the laser beam of the light of intuition, the light of Hermes. Hermes-Mercury takes the slowest minds and gives to them self-training through meditation, so that *Buddhi* may be activated from a germ and surely develop into that pure light of intuition which is the essential basis of all knowledge.

Any real awakening of the Buddhic light is inevitably connected with the breathing — spiritual, mental and heart breathing, as well as the physical breathing — of every human being. The profound Catechism in the Proem, in setting forth the cosmic nature of breath, distinguishes between two archetypal modes in all manifestation. The Great Breath either proceeds from without inwardly when it is everywhere, or from within outwardly when it is nowhere. This may be understood in relation to human nature by considering the cosmic origins of the quintessentially human faculty of *Manas*:

> Whatever the views of physical Science upon the subject, Occult Science has been teaching for ages that A'kasa — of which Ether is the grossest form — the fifth universal Cosmic Principle (to which corresponds and from which proceeds human Manas) is, cosmically, a radiant, cool, diathermanous plastic matter, creative in its physical nature, correlative in its grossest aspects and portions, immutable in its higher principles. In the former condition it is called the Sub-Root; and in conjunction with radiant heat, it recalls 'dead worlds to life.' In its higher aspect it is the Soul of the World; in its lower — the DESTROYER.
>
> *The Secret Doctrine*, i 13

If, while breathing, one thinks of the One Source of the One Light, this will alter the quality of breathing by taking the grosser exhalation and using it to destroy that which needs to be destroyed, simultaneously taking the subtler inhalation and using it to rejuvenate. What has become dormant or is dying in one's subtler thought-forms will be called back to life. This is just the initial step. Next, a pause, or retention, between inhalation and exhalation is introduced to make it a three-in-one, corresponding to the macrocosmic Breath:

> *Hiranyagarbha, Hari,* and *Sankara* — the three hypostases of the manifesting 'Spirit of the Supreme Spirit' (by which title Prithivi — the Earth — greets Vishnu in his first Avatar) — are the purely metaphysical abstract qualities of formation, preservation, and destruction, and are the three divine Avasthas (lit. hypostases) of that which 'does not perish with created things' (or Achyuta, a name of Vishnu).
>
> *Ibid.,* i 18-19

Of the three, inhalation, retention and exhalation, the middle would be the most crucial because it will enable one to slow down and suspend inhalation and exhalation, keeping them from becoming chaotic and spasmodic. When one has begun to do this, one will soon find that it cannot really be done on a continuous basis without working causally upon one's mental breathing. This means that when a thought is going out and before a thought rushes in, one must pause. This is a most precise and radical mode of 'deliberation'. It may be put in the form of a simple injunction: *Think before you speak.* If one really thinks before speaking, if one thinks before choosing a line of action, it will certainly steady the mental breathing and thereby steady the mind. This is truly helpful to others because, as one gains a measure of serenity or stillness, one can become a source of benediction to those who come into one's sphere of influence.

The implications of this ancient teaching for the distant future are suggested in a statement following the Catechism, indicating that there are seven cosmic elements. Four of them are physical, and the fifth, which may provisionally be called aether, is a semi-material aspect of *Akasha* corresponding to *Manas* and critical to the relationship of thought and breathing, as well as to the further incarnation of *Manas.* Those who have refined their sense-perceptions will show this by the way they handle all objects, through the manner in which they eat, breathe, listen and watch. During World War II, resisters like Sartre recognized that something they had always taken for granted, the privilege of thinking, became very precious because of the Gestapo. Solzhenitsyn states in *The First Circle* that when prisoners find that everything has been taken away from them, they suddenly experience freedom, the sheer joy of thinking. Many people would rather not think but merely emote, cerebrate and react passively. Once one develops a taste for such mindless activity, deep thinking becomes painful. It is like having one's teeth ground, since it will break down the incrustations of half-chewed and half-dead ideas that have settled down like a crust. Thinking forces these to be broken up because they have got to be eliminated. How much this will have to be done will depend upon the degree of damage already done by the crust. The mind can be always revivified by turning to seminal ideas which, like the rain on parched soil, will quicken germs of living seeds of regenerative truths. The plant of *Manas* will begin to take root. Long before it becomes a tree, it will release the fire of creative thought, making it a thrill to create by the power of ideation. Those who begin to do this are going to find that they are also tapping a subtler realm of matter. One cannot separate thought from matter, subject from object. To really think is to tap subtler life-atoms in one's vestures, and that means also to become more receptive and attentive to subtler life-atoms in visible forms, prepared to design new structures. This is necessary for *Manas* to incarnate further.

H.P. Blavatsky said in the nineteenth century that the Aquarian Age will bring about a lot of psychological disturbances. These arise in the vestures because of the unwillingness to let go of what is dead or dying. Many human beings have a morbid love of decay and are threatened by the Ray, terrified of living seeds. They are so fond of the husk that they have forgotten what the germ is like. The husk of indigestible, decaying ideas prevents the living wheat germ of spiritual ideas from giving birth to new thought-forms. Individuals who cannot do this now will have to do it by the end of the Fourth Round, because the great moment of choice must come finally in the Fifth. This is far in the future, but even the highest two elements, the sixth and the seventh, which are now far beyond the range of human perception, will be sensed during the Sixth and Seventh Races of this Round, though they will not become known to all until the Sixth and Seventh Rounds. They will be aroused partially and by anticipation in the Sixth and Seventh Sub-Races of the Fifth Root Race. Those of the Fifth Sub-Race who are touched by the current of the Sixth Sub-Race with the help of Teachers using the seventh principle, the *Atman,* will be able to germinate living seeds of creative thought. This will enable them to serve in future civilizations in those arenas where the seed-bearers, the vanguard of human growth, will be vitally active. Those who cannot keep pace will incarnate in those portions of the earth where slower moving structures carry on the work of evolution. Evolution takes care of everyone. There is a joy and a thrill in activating *Manas,* the power of abstract ideation, with the help of seminal spiritual ideas and laying down fertile seeds of self-regenerating modes of thought and patterns of living.

The Third Root Race was characterized by an effortless sense of universal unity and brotherhood. The whole of humanity was of one lip, one language, one religion, one race and this was the Golden Age, though there have also been minor golden ages. For the mystic the golden age is ever present. The golden age for the whole of humanity would correspond to the dawn of differentiation, the descent of the gods and the awakening of the fire of self-consciousness.

> 'Fire and Flame destroy the body of an Arhat, their essence makes him immortal.' *(Bodhi-mur, Book II.)* 'The knowledge of the absolute Spirit, like the effulgence of the sun, or like heat in fire, is naught else than the absolute Essence itself,' says Shankaracharya. IT — is 'the Spirit of the Fire,' not fire itself; therefore, 'the attributes of the latter, heat or flame, are not the attributes of the Spirit, but of that of which that Spirit is the unconscious cause.'
>
> *The Secret Doctrine,* i 6

The Spirit gave birth to self-consciousness in the Third Root Race in a paradisaic state characterized by Plato in *The Statesman* as the Age of Kronos. Since that was an epoch of human solidarity and universal brotherhood, it is hardly surprising that it was marked by effortless devotion.

Devotion is the highest of human qualities. Devotion sustains the universe through that mysterious and irresistible force of mother love, which no psychologist, no misanthrope, has yet been able to destroy. The human babe, unlike animal offspring, is very vulnerable; it will not survive without solicitude. The infant is vulnerable especially in that tender spot on the head which should not be touched. The protective power of mother love makes human evolution possible. It also provides proof, if proof were needed, that devotion is the most natural human quality. Those people who find mental prostration or devotion unnatural are themselves unnatural. Love of parents and of children, love of brothers and sisters, respect for elders, devotion to teachers: this is what is natural. Anything else is unnatural and will be wiped out because there is no room for it in human evolution. H.P. Blavatsky states in *The Secret Doctrine* that the Hindu heart is the most devoted, and also that the Hindu mind is the most metaphysical, readily able to visualize the abstract. To contemplate the abstract and also cherish the deepest feelings is indeed to approximate the paradigm of the Golden Age of the Third Root Race when the fire of self-consciousness was lit. These excellences are essential to the humanity of the future, the civilization of tomorrow. The Theosophical Movement, under the guidance of the Brotherhood of Bodhisattvas, offers every human being the golden opportunity to develop the devotional heart and to engage in the meditation of the abstract mind that is capable of lighting the fire of self-consciousness. The Bodhisattvas ceaselessly sacrifice so that every soul may make the effort to come out of the cold gloom of sick egotistic fear for its own salvation, become free from obsession with the shadow caused by self-hatred, and enter the light of the Spiritual Sun.

If the potency of the Third Root Race vibration were used

in concert with *Manas*, the active power of the Fifth Root Race, and the latter became the servant of spiritual intuition, a very fruitful combination would result, whereby the Sixth corresponding to the Third through the Fifth is able to alchemize the Fourth. What is fundamental is what is beyond every series, the Self-existent, the Seventh, which gives life-energy to the First, the temple of the Divine, wherein lies the holy of holies. Deep reflection upon these themes can be enriched by meditation upon the basic symbols taken from the ancient palm leaf manuscript: the plain disk, the disk with the point, the disk with the diameter and the disk with the cross. The mundane cross marks the point where humanity reached the Third Root Race. In the Fourth Race it became the cross without the circle, although among the spiritually wise the loss of the Divine Eye implicit in this separation did not occur.

The Egyptian *Tau* cross, which later became the sign of Venus and also the swastika, Thor's hammer or the Hermetic cross, is a most profound symbol. Originally it was the Jaina cross, the swastika within a circle or Thor's hammer within a circle, called the *Tau*. In meditating upon these sacred glyphs, the third *Stanza* would be most helpful. The difference between the first *Stanza*, the state of the One All during non-manifestation, and the second — which is almost indistinguishable from the first except to the most intuitive — would be like the difference between the first and the second months of pregnancy. The third *Stanza* depicts the reawakening of the universe to life after *pralaya*. After each terrestrial dawn every morning, there is a reawakening of the universe, a new birth or micro-*manvantara*. Each night is like the Night of non-manifestation, a micro-*pralaya,* to be inevitably followed by the reawakening to life of the universe of monads. The third *Stanza* refers to the emergence of Monads from their state of absorption within the One. Analogically on earth, human Monads would be absorbed within the One in *sushupti* during sleep. The first stage is analogous to the seventh, which is why the Self-Governed Sage is sometimes compared to a newborn babe. But whereas the babe utters the *Aum* and then forgets it, the Sage ever remains in the *Aum.*

The term 'Monad' may apply equally to the vastest solar system or to the tiniest atom. The most self-conscious Monads enjoy fellowship with the entire solar system, with all other Monads as well as with the tiniest atoms. When the sage is teaching disciples, he is not addressing them as personalities, but is adjusting their life-atoms and affecting their *sushupti.* He is not talking to the lower mind, but pushing it out, freeing the higher mind in its descent. He is awakening the *Buddhi.* The difference between the Third Root Race and the Fifth is that the former intuitively knew this to be true. In the Aquarian Age, which has entered its second degree, Fifth Race laggards can self-consciously re-enact what was intuitively known by all in the Third Root Race. Self-consciously they could come together and learn from the Teachings of Sages, thereby altering their modes of breathing and becoming a help rather than a hindrance, not only to each other, but also to all living beings on earth.

ATMA VIDYA

*Just as milliards of bright sparks dance on the waters
of an ocean above which one and the same moon is shining,
so our evanescent personalities — the illusive envelopes of
the immortal* MONAD-EGO — *twinkle and dance on the
waves of Maya. They last and appear, as the thousands of
sparks produced by the moon-beams, only so long as the
Queen of the Night radiates her lustre on the running waters
of life: the period of a Manvantara; and then they disappear,
the beams — symbols of our eternal Spiritual Egos — alone
surviving, re-merged in, and being, as they were before, one
with the Mother-Source.*

The Secret Doctrine, i 237

L ate in the nineteenth century the Maha Chohan spoke of
the great dual principles, right and wrong, good and evil,
liberty and despotism, pain and pleasure, egotism and
altruism. Pointing to the degraded moral condition of the world
and particularly of its so-called civilized races, he declared that
this sad plight is *prima facie* evidence of religious and philosophic
bankruptcy. The intervening century, with its virtually unrelieved
record of bloodshed and cruelty, should have clearly demonstrated
that the dark forces of superstition — disguised as nationalism,
ideology and racism — and materialism, with its sterile promise
of technocratic utopias, obscure the pathway to adequate
explanations and effective solutions to fundamental problems.
Insoluble though these may appear, and although the world may
seem to be locked in its "mad career towards the unknown",
especially to those who are dazed and numbed by the spectacle,
this is a time of immense opportunities for courageous individuals
who aspire to constitute themselves as creative pioneers of the
civilization of the future. As in the classic *Tale of Two Cities*, it is
the best of times and the worst of times. For each person today
the critical difference turns upon whether one chooses the

standpoint of Shamballa or that of Myalba. Either one learns to trace the eternal beam of the spiritual Ego back to its invisible seat in the Atmic Sun, and thereby perceives the sacred and sacrificial purpose of personal existence — twinkling and dancing on the running waters of life — or one is swept away in the stormy sea of human life. Whilst every perceptive person must develop the Manasic determination and Buddhic insight to attain reunion with the Divine Monad, all souls must fully insert themselves into the mighty currents of cosmic and human evolution.

Over five thousand years ago, Krishna gave the profound and potent teaching that all the pairs of opposites are relative to each other. From the standpoint of abstract and absolute Unity, the entire world is seen as an interplay and interpenetration of various grades and degrees of light and shadow. What is stated archetypally in the *Bhagavad Gita* in terms of light and dark is also pertinent to all the dualities of physical, psychic and mental existence. This applies not only to sensuous states of matter and correlative states of consciousness, but also to consciousness and matter on all the seven planes. Hence, one may speak of sound and silence, light and darkness, existing entirely outside the average range and sector of rates of vibration apprehended by ordinary sensation. Unfortunately, most people are far from fully using even their physical senses. Consider the human eye. It is an extraordinary instrument, a divine gift, capable of seeing objects but a few inches away and also able to view the distant stars and galaxies. This tremendous elasticity of the human power of vision intimates what the mystics speak of as spiritual vision and the spiritual eye. It is as a seer and perceiver that each human being is a truly self-conscious, Manasic being capable of infinite extension of the power of vision from the highest transcendental realms to the most concrete regions of sensuous existence. Therefore, the first step in metapsychology, the effective transcendence of the pairs of opposites, is to cognize the immanent reality of the immortal soul, the Atma-Buddhic Monad.

The psyche is merely the projected ray of the divine Monad.

As the Monad functions on a plane of space and time removed from that which is customarily apprehended by the psyche, the Monad is only partially incarnated. If it were not incarnated at all, human existence would be impossible. One might visualize *Atma-Buddhi-Manas* being above one's head, with a pristine ray of light — which would be *Buddhi* — entering the head and passing through the brain, through the spinal cord and down to the feet. This would be a graphic way of representing the metaphysical truth that the human being is overbrooded from head to toe by the imperishable Monad. The Fohatic current pictured as passing into the body from above would be the radiation of *Manas*. This downward current of reflected *Manas* mingles with the mixed energy-currents flowing through the astral vesture. Just as blood circulates in the physical body, there are electric and magnetic currents flowing in the *linga sarira*. These astral currents are insipid in comparison to the intense levels of energy generated by pure manasic ideation. *Manas* may be understood as the essential ability to separate oneself, through self- consciousness, from the hooking-points in the astral vesture. The process of regaining access to the higher energy fields of the Monad is accomplished through abstraction, withdrawal and detachment from the field of the self-cancelling pairs of opposites on the plane of the senses.

When in meditation one assumes the standpoint of the *Mahat-Atman,* the spectator without a spectacle, one shuts out the light of the illusory physical world with all its seemingly separate subjects and objects. When these recede into the darkness of the Void, one may picture a point. That point can be transformed into a triangle, analogous to the cosmic Monad, which then expands continuously and scatters triadic sparks which scintillate throughout the invisible universe. These sparks, streaming forth like rays from a single source, may be seen to be reflected in the underworld of dense matter, the dungeon or cave of terrestrial existence, wherein they seem to be like sun sparks scattered through the leaves of a tree. Between the billions upon billions of leaves of the World Tree, there are scattered myriads of sparks of brilliant light. These points of illumination are the noetic intimations to be found in every religion, philosophy and science, every civilization and culture, of the divine inheritance of humanity. Scattered throughout the great gallery of nature and scintillating in what Shakespeare called "the book and volume of my brain", they are but a partial screening and panoramic reflection of the electromagnetic activity of the cosmic brain. Great as is this central source of cosmic illumination which enormously surpasses human conception, it is still minute in comparison to the transcendental sources of noumenal light that are hidden in the Divine Darkness beyond the infinite Kosmos.

Given this possibility of initially apprehending the vital relationship between human existence and the infinite universe, one may begin to comprehend Universal Good (the *Agathon*) in terms of the sacrificial circulation and return of the life essence to its invisible source, continually sifting what is needed by the immortal Monad and casting off the rest for appropriate redistribution amongst the lower kingdoms of nature. Evil is that which consolidates and which refuses to acknowledge the source. In terms of the relativity of opposites, evil is that which obscures the light, whilst good is that which transmits the light. The highest good is self-luminous. Light and obscuration exist at many different levels and in a great variety of modes. For example, one might simply pass one's hand in front of a candle, blocking its light. Or one might observe an eclipse of the sun or of the moon. During an eclipse, as astronomers know, nothing really happens. It is only because of the relative positions of the sun, earth and moon from the standpoint of the observer that there appears to be an eclipse. It is all mayavic. The relative modes of movement of the observer and the objects create the appearance of obscuration. Similarly, an eclipse of the sun or of the moon may seem good or evil, depending upon one's perspective and point of view. H.P. Blavatsky pointed out that if the homogeneity of the one Absolute is accepted, then one must also accept in the realm of the heterogeneous that good and evil are twin off shoots of the same trunk of the Tree of Being. If one does not accept this, then one is committed to the absurdity of believing in two eternal absolutes.

> Indeed, evil is but an antagonizing blind force in nature; it is *reaction, opposition,* and *contrast,* — evil for some, good for others. There is no *malum in se*: only the shadow of light, without which light could have no existence, even in our perceptions. . . . There would be no *life* possible (in the *Mayavic* sense) without *Death,* nor regeneration and reconstruction without destruction. . . . On the manifested planes, one equilibrates the other.
>
> *The Secret Doctrine,* i 413-414

For a truly fundamental understanding of good and evil, along with all the other pairs of objective opposites, one must turn to the quintessential distinction between the manifest and the unmanifest. This distinction is a modern formulation of that drawn by Shankaracharya between the Real and the unreal. Given the relationship between the good and inward acknowledgement of the source of illumination, it is significant that Shankaracharya, when expounding the Teaching concerning the Real and the unreal, invokes the Upanishadic sages and their revelation of the Path leading from death to immortality. As Shankaracharya explicitly states, there can be no realization of the *Atman* and its unity with *Brahman* apart from a reverential and grateful recognition of predecessors and preceptors. It is only when one realizes the true meaning of the posture of authentic humility, assumed by even so great an Initiate as Shankaracharya in relation to the ancient Rishis, that one may begin to understand the unwisdom of the modern age. The ingratitude of latter-day Europeans towards Islamic scholars who transmitted the teachings of the classical world, the earlier ingratitude of Christian theologians towards the children of Israel, and the even earlier instances of ingratitude between Greece and Egypt, between Egypt and Chaldea, between Chaldea and India, and between Brahmins and the Buddha, have all left a heavy burden of unacknowledged debts which contribute to the moral bankruptcy of the modern age. The sad consequences of this spiritual ingratitude are to be discerned in the moral blindness of contemporary society, in the restrictiveness of its range of vision, so that the succession of events is seen as a random series of amoral happenings.

As long as the inward spiritual senses of man — *Buddhi* and *Manas* — remain obscured, karma must appear mayavic in the realm of physical space and time, whilst life itself seems to be largely meaningless. Real meaning in human life can only be regained by lifting the horizon of consciousness above the level of secondary causes and effects. This can only be done by rising to the Causeless Cause, *Nada Brahman*, the Light and Sound of the Logos identical with the Wisdom Religion (*Brahma Vach*), even beyond the Soundless Sound. The Soundless Sound is rather like a serene ripple upon the boundless ocean of space. It is sacred because in its boundlessness it reverberates to the silent breathing of That, which is beyond all categories of space, time, causality and motion, and which transcends all incarnated conceptions of the true and the false, of good and evil, the meretricious and the plausible, the beautiful and the ugly. The arduous ascent from the manifest to the unmanifest, from the unreal to the Real, cannot take place without the aid and guidance of the Guru, and hence it is taught that outside the portals of Initiation the wings of ratiocinative thought must forever remain clipped. "Thus far and no further" is the story of human endeavour. Human beings live on tiny hillocks in space and time in comparison with the mighty Himalayas where Masters of Meditation reside, or with Mount Kailaś, the abode of Shiva, the *Maha Yogin*. Nonetheless, there is an imperfect analogy between every tiny hill and the Himalayas, and any increment of detached calm and meditative elevation that an individual can achieve is helpful in attempting to go beyond all concretizations and constant thraldom to the pairs of opposites. Each genuine effort towards meditation undertaken in a spirit of devotion and sacrificial service can aid in the discovery of the *sanctum sanctorum* in the temple of the human form, hidden in the depths of the spiritual heart.

The complex human form represents a matrix of polarities and interconnections, all of which are subordinated to the overbrooding *Atman* which is beyond all polarity or hint of heterogeneity. Just as there is a north and south pole to the earth, there is also a north and south pole to the body. There is also a polarity of the astral vesture and, most important a polarity of the mind *(manomaya kosha)*. At one level the reflective *Manas* stands as a moon towards the sun above it, whilst at another level higher *Manas* stands as the sun in relation to lower *Manas* or the lunar mind. Good is that which is pleasing to the Krishna-Ishwara within. In the heart of every human being there is a ray of Krishna, programming the possibilities for that soul during incarnated existence and for its participation in all the three worlds. There is no being in any of the worlds which entirely lacks the possibility of entering into the realm of light, and not a single person can wholly avoid participation in the darkness of *moha*, delusion, of *maya*, illusion, and of *kama, krodha* and *loba*, desire, anger and greed. This is represented in Buddhist iconography by elaborate *tankas* which display the vast array of archetypal and collective human faults surrounding samsaric existence. Early in the *Gita*, Krishna speaks of the omnipresent obscuring power of *rajo-gunam*, the common enemy of humanity, that which leads the best of persons to lose their firm foothold in the realm of the Divine. This progenitor of evil operates upon the mind which, as a dynamic field, may be seen to manifest a positive and negative polarity, together with a third intermediate factor. By placing *rajas* on one side and *tamas* on the other, with *sattva* in the middle, like the central column in the Kabalistic tree of life, one may picture everything below a certain plane as a continual alternation of *rajas* and *tamas*, activity and inertia. But this cannot take place without a nodal equilibrium point in between, which is called a *laya* centre, a motionless point.

If one considers a child's top spinning on the ground, there must be a motionless point where the spindle of the top touches the ground and also a motionless point at the crown of the spinning top. These two points, however, only exist because one has already assumed the reality of the spinning top, but, as Shankaracharya teaches, such reification of objective forms is merely a superimposition. Ultimately there is nothing 'going on.' There is only the mayavic appearance of the spinning top. Similarly, in the region of appearances there seems to be a great deal going on in the periodic alternations and movements of the polarities within the human principles as they revolve and rotate in and around *laya* centres in the human constitution. In contrast to this complicated and chaotic realm of events, every human being experiences in deep sleep a state of consciousness which is simply not remembered in terms of the succession of so-called events. Ordinarily, because they are so immersed in the outward flux of temporal events, human beings find it exceedingly difficult to recall or recover the state of consciousness they experienced in deep sleep, and it seems to be a blank. It is, therefore, a helpful preliminary discipline and a salutary spiritual practice to prepare oneself for sleep each night by meditation, by study of sacred texts and by directing the mind deliberately and self-consciously towards the unmanifest. Here one can test oneself by seeing whether the last thought one ponders, however briefly, before passing into sleep can be made the first thought that one entertains upon returning from sleep to wakefulness.

In this effort to reverse the polarity of the mind, changing it from involvement with concrete manifest particulars to immersion in the unmanifest universal *Atman,* the attention should not cling to the content of particular thoughts. All thoughts are relative. They are affected by the peculiar condition of one's physical and astral bodies as well as by the state and subprinciples of one's personal and higher mind. Hence it is helpful to pursue the path of negation embodied in the mantram 'Neti, neti.' One can deliberately affirm that one is not the body or brain, not one's likes or dislikes, not one's friends or so-called enemies, not the various sense-perceptions, and not one's lower mind or *kama manas.* One should not merely say these things to oneself but actually think them, withdrawing consciousness from each successive element and voiding a series of connections with form.

In a sense, this is like switching off a series of lights. Here technology mirrors what is possible in consciousness — the actual process of disengaging from the astral form through the power of self-consciousness. Through this withdrawal from the transitory connections one has apparently established with the lower principles, one can ascend through them, but this must be done calmly whilst wide awake.

One must familiarize oneself with this internal mountain climbing because otherwise one is liable to get hurt, to stumble and fall, and then it will become very difficult to pick oneself up and begin the ascent again. It is, naturally, unavoidable that over eighteen million years almost everyone has become dizzy and fallen repeatedly. This gives an important clue to the corruption of consciousness that takes place through rationalization and myriad excuses for spiritual failure. This is the fertile source of evil. The moment one rationalizes and justifies one's failings, one is spiritually stymied during that incarnation. But if one is willing to let go of pride and see things for what they are, recognizing the agencies at play, then one may take full responsibility for oneself and for the entire kingdom of elemental beings that constitute one's vestures. One must be willing to take responsibility for what happened over millions of years and also for the strong likelihood that one has taken spiritual vows in past lives. This must necessarily have great consequences for oneself, particularly if one is so privileged as to contact the Teachings of the Mahatmas in this life. The more deeply one thinks about this, the more clearly one will come to understand that one's life up to the present time and indeed every day that one lives is largely a re-enactment of everything that one has done over past lives.

Once one begins to initiate the process of Manasic withdrawal, one will rapidly discover that much of the cacophony and noise of the outer world is a pathetic and perverse degradation of the sacred. This lack of silence, which is equivalent to a loss of reverence for the sacred power of speech, is the result of human beings attempting to run away from their own karma. Inevitably it leads to a desecration of the earth and of nature and the arousing of hosts of angry elementals which congregate in every wasteland abandoned by human failures. Like the *djinn* of the desert that hover above the sites of buried cities, they inspire nervousness and fear in all those who pass by. The desire for revenge in the elementals is so intense because the devastation of the earth through the misuse of human powers has gone on for so long and has not been acknowledged or corrected. In response to this agitation many people develop a kind of a death-wish because their lives are devoid of meaning and they themselves have become empty vessels. Being afraid of death, whilst not knowing how to live, they end up game-playing, producing more noise and further obscuring the light of spirit. In the face of this restlessness and ennui, one must learn to preserve silence whilst coolly performing one's duty.

One must learn to set a good example by concentrating upon one's work, by exemplifying calm concentration, and by generating a true spirit of friendliness rooted in the depths of one's heart. One should render help when possible and also point out the source for further help. Through the grace of compassion one must remove the dryness and stiffness of one's own nature, but one should not become engrossed in compensatory reaching out to others which is only a mask for inadequate meditation. One must learn to restore a deeper spiritual breathing in one's mind and in one's actions. Generally in the realm of speech and conduct, "less is more" is the mantram that one needs to apply. "Bigger is always better" is an Atlantean mode of thought which is enraptured by excess and sheer bulk and considerations of quantity rather than quality. It is impossible to avoid the world of illusion, but one should learn to practise self-chosen ascetic disciplines lest one become a slave to the stomach, or subject to all forms of physiological, psychological, mental and spiritual indigestion, through lack of proper assimilation.

What may be seen from one side as an ascetic withdrawal from noisy and habitual involvement in the pairs of opposites on the psychological and sensory planes may be seen from the other side as learning the magical enactment of the AUM. The *Uttara*

Gita hints that just as there is an archetypal polarity between the spiritual, immovable mind and the sensuous, movable mind, there is also a vital difference between noisy, uttered speech and the sacred and silent power of noiseless speech which invokes Sarasvati-Vach. The text also depicts the operation of the various vital winds or breaths passing as currents through the human form in their relation to the seven senses spoken of as priests or *hotris*. In essence, every action has sacrificial import and meaning but this can only be properly grasped when one abandons all concretized and exteriorized theories of value and adopts the cosmic perspective of universal sacrifice — *Adhiyajna*. Owing to mechanistic and instrumental theories of value, which are the bane of all institutions and societies, a false dichotomy arises between creators and consumers of value. In truth, human beings need to learn that all must equally share in universal modes of sacrifice.

Whilst individuals will vary in the roles and degrees through which they participate in sacrifice, each can strengthen his or her own sense of the sacred in every duty performed. Each must harmonize and modulate the rates of mental breathing by adjusting the ratio of the unmanifest to the manifest in everyday consciousness. At a minimum, everyone must try. This is a take-it-or-leave-it proposition with regard to the life of the sacred. The amount of progress made is much less important than the regularity and persistence of the effort. As in the Buddhist metaphor of the filling of the jar, what is most important is that drops of clean water actually fall into the jar. As one collects in one's vessel what *The Voice of the Silence* calls "Heaven's dew drops", the Real will displace the unreal and one will become prepared for the time when "night cometh and no man shall work". It is self-evident that one can only come to experience the waters of compassion through enacting the Word with the motivation of selfless love towards all, even those who are ensnared in their own failures. There must be no desire to discover some Noah's Ark of salvation for oneself but rather a willingness to use every opportunity in life to be a messenger of goodwill and a witness to the wisdom one has received freely from within. If one would not be caught in the mad rush of those who are like the gathering swine in the New Testament, one must understand that every golden moment of new beginnings for oneself must be self-consciously transformed into a deepened spirit of dedication to the welfare of all, *Lokasangraha*.

As one patiently perseveres in 'the divine discipline' of enacting the AUM in deeds, one may receive timely intimations of the vast perspective of the Army of the Voice, the Host of the Logos. Remaining above the plane of immanent, relative polarities, they see the essential core of everything. They are *Tattvajnanis* — those who see the essence of each of the *tattvas*. They are *Brahmajnanis* — those who see *Brahman* in every atom and being. They are *Atmajnanis* — those who see by the light of the manifested Logos, sometimes called Ishwara, and its mirroring in *Atman*, although one cannot separate the two. Terms like 'mirroring' and even 'light' can be misleading when referring to a plane of primordial matter or homogeneity wherein there is hardly any difference between subjectivity and objectivity. Having awakened the three highest centres of human consciousness, and also attuned the corresponding states to the three *arupa* planes in the Kosmos, they have become Masters of *Atma Vidya*. Having realized the mystic bond of Being and Non-Being within the depths of their own unmanifest Self, they stand as luminous witnesses to the nobility and promise of human endeavour. Established within the circle of boundless light, they are able to perceive the metaphysical origins of human suffering and strife. H.P. Blavatsky depicts the impersonal nature of the problem:

> In human nature, evil denotes only the polarity of matter and Spirit, a struggle for life between the two manifested Principles in Space and Time, which principles are one *per se*, inasmuch as they are rooted in the Absolute. In Kosmos, the equilibrium must be preserved. The operations of the two contraries produce harmony, like the centripetal and centrifugal forces,

which are necessary to each other — mutually
inter-dependent — 'in order that both should live.' If
one is arrested, the action of the other will become
immediately self-destructive.

Ibid., i 416

The Silent Watchers, awake during periods of *pralaya,* having
transcended the primal pair of *pralaya* and *manvantara,* through
a process of partial descent and incarnation under karmic
law participate in the vast round of human existence. With
mathematical precision they are able to determine precisely
which elements in human volition and consciousness
are operative at any given time and the exact nature of the
evolutionary task before humanity in any given period.
Every human being, whether consciously or unconsciously, is
performing the evolutionary task inherently necessary owing to
the sevenfold constitution of man and the earth. For human
beings in the Fourth Round, the aim is to become self-
determining and self-conscious in relation to the evolutionary
process. True self-consciousness cannot be awakened through any
exterior means but only through establishing the true posture of
inner devotion to the Guru. The Guru alone can kindle that inner
light which can quicken in every human being the powers of
higher self-consciousness. The degree of self- consciousness
attained by any individual will be a product both of the intensity
of devotion and the starting-point in any given life. Hence there
is a vast variety of degrees of intelligence, self-determination and
energy displayed by particular human beings.

The integral relation between *Guru Yoga* and *Atma Vidya,*
which must be realized by the human Ego, is embodied in the
Hermetic maxim that the Guru is Spiritual Fire.

Unless the Ego takes refuge in the Atman, the
ALL-SPIRIT, and merges entirely into the essence thereof,
the personal Ego may goad it to the bitter end. . . .
Uproot the plant and transfer it to a piece of soil where
the sunbeam cannot reach it, and the latter will not

follow it. So with the Atman: unless the higher Self or
EGO gravitates towards its Sun — the Monad — the
lower *Ego*, or *personal* Self, will have the upper hand in
every case. . . . Metaphysically, or on the psychic and
spiritual plane, it is equally true that the Atman alone
warms the inner man; *i.e.*, it enlightens it with the ray
of divine life and alone is able to impart to the inner
man, or the reincarnating Ego, its immortality.

Ibid., ii 109-110

In each succeeding Round, the degree of incarnation of the
Atman and the corresponding degrees of human perfection and
karmic responsibility increase. With the advent of the Fifth Round,
human beings will be held fully responsible for their descents
from sphere to sphere, and those who are unable to fulfil this
responsibility will not be able to accomplish the transition from
the Fourth to the Fifth Rounds. Unable to fulfil the evolutionary
programme, they will not be able to incarnate in future Rounds,
and their shells will be incinerated by nature. Hence in the Fourth
Round great courage is needed. Without it one is going to be afraid
of the abyss, but there is no reason to be afraid because every
human being is of a divine degree and can cooperate with the
upward movement. Those who have become perfected in Buddhi-
Manasic responsibility during the Fourth Round and have become
capable of universal cognition and become great in the power of
sacrifice will prepare over millions of years for the descent of a
still more perfect and intellectual race. Whilst the full fruition of
this race lies in the far distant future, the turning-point has already
been reached with regard to its karmic inception. This is due to
the extremely abnormal condition of humanity produced and
perpetuated by the misuse and atrophy of spiritual powers during
the Fourth Round. This condition was characterized in the last
century by H.P. Blavatsky:

. . . the selfishness of the *personality* has so strongly
infected the real *inner* man with its lethal *virus*, that the
upward attraction has lost all its power on the thinking

reasonable man. In sober truth, vice and wickedness are
an *abnormal, unnatural* manifestation, at this period of
our human evolution — at least they ought to be so.
The fact that mankind was never more selfish and
vicious than it is now, civilized nations having succeeded
in making of the first an ethical characteristic, of the
second an art, is an additional proof of the exceptional
nature of the phenomenon.

Ibid., ii 110

The aftermath of two world wars and the slaughter of
millions of people in this century have not brought humanity any
closer to peace on earth and the reign of justice. Viewing humanity
through the eyes of compassion and seeing the tragedy of human
misery everywhere, one cannot help but notice the victims of
injustice. To let them hear the Law, whilst at the same time the
Law must take its course, would take something much stronger
than was even imaginable in the time of Buddha and Christ. It
would need something golden and generous and divine and free,
such as in the time of Krishna or as sung by Shelley, but at the
same time it would need the immense preparation that comes
from the silent work of all the sages and rishis who know that
human beings could only become truly human through
meditation. Thus a time will come, though not in this century,
when there will be men of meditation and exemplars of
compassion in every part of the globe. In order to protect and
promote the interests of the humanity of the future and to wipe
out the humbug of the ages, the pristine avataric descent of the
Aquarian cycle has been accompanied by a tremendous
acceleration in the programme of evolution. The misuse of the
human form had to be halted. All over the world this is sensed,
and although there are those who, as Shakespeare put it, "squeak
and gibber in the streets," there is a resonant feeling of joy amongst
the greater portion of humanity which recognizes what has
already begun to take root.

The meaning of the sounding of the keynote of the 1975
Cycle in relation to the great globe itself can only be understood

in terms of the relation of the Logos, of Avalokitesvara, to the descent of *Atman* in the human race in its entirety. In the last century Mahatma M. gave a clue to the mystery when he said, "We have *yet some Avatars* left to us on earth." As it was in the past, it is now and it always shall be that the entire sacred tribe of Initiates serves Dakshinamurti, the Initiator of Initiates. For over eighteen million years they have been the faithful witnesses to the mysterious bond between the Ever-Living Human Banyan, the fiery Dragon of Light, Fire and Flame, and the seventh principle in the Cosmos which extends beyond all the manifested cycles of galaxies. Those who seek intimations of the meaning of the end of the old habits, modes and orders and of the auspicious birth of the new, which is the oldest of the old, should meditate deeply upon these words of Pymander:

> The Light is me, I am the Nous (the mind or Manu), I am thy God, and I am far older than the human principle which escapes from the shadow (*'Darkness,'* or the concealed Deity). I am the germ of thought, the resplendent *Word,* the *Son* of God. All that thus sees and hears in thee is the *Verbum* of the Master, it is the Thought *(Mahat)* which is God, the Father.
>
> *Ibid.,* i 74

THE INHERITANCE
OF HUMANITY

In exoteric knowledge there is always a gap between an essentially external view of historical events and a rationally contrived metaphysics or an individualistic conception of an inner spiritual life. It is this gap that is closed in *The Secret Doctrine*. Here we find no tension between the transcendental and the temporal, and no frustrating hiatus between the notions of 'is', 'ought', 'can', and 'must' in ethical thought. We are invited to consider our individual potentialities and limitations in terms of a common human nature that is continuously alterable and finally perfectible under laws of cosmic evolution that are reflected in the universal history of mankind, extending into a remote but recoverable antiquity. If we do not yet know our own far-flung potentialities, or understand our human limitations in a reflective temper, this is because we are not really aware of our immense collective inheritance, nor do we see why, in the course of a long involution into matter, this inheritance became inaccessible to our materializing minds.

H.P. Blavatsky pointed to the primeval revelation granted to the ancestors of the whole race of mankind. The Wisdom-Religion is the inheritance of humanity, not of any privileged race or nation. Its truths are as old as thinking man, actualities visible only to the eye of the real Sage and Seer, and orally revealed to man and preserved in the *adyta* or temples through initiation. "Thus every nation received in its turn some of the said truths, under the veil of its own local and special symbolism; which, as time went on, developed into a more or less philosophical cultus, a Pantheon in mythical disguises." We are enabled by *The Secret Doctrine* to raise our sights from the local and the heterogeneous to the universal and the homogeneous, to deepen our insight by piercing the veil rather than by exchanging one veil of symbolism for another. We are helped to withdraw our consciousness from the external precipitations and materializations in recorded History (or historical time) into our inmost recesses, at least to the *karana sharira* (the sheath of subtle, luminous, noumenal or causal substance), which may bring into view our 'soul-memories' of a past human evolution, helping us to stand outside history, as it were. When this is achieved, we shall be able to open and direct the Eye of Dangma (intimately connected with the third eye now lost to man) toward the essence of things in which no *maya* can have any influence.

In this way, in time, the mind may become free of the partisan perspective of individual *skandhas* and locus in space and time — taking a wider, deeper, and nobler view of the human inheritance than any extant in the modern world; grasping through a study of likes and dislikes the reasons for the hold of a particular and complex set of *skandhas* over man's kama-manasic rationalizations; appreciating and accepting the relentless course of the workings of Karma-Nemesis in the lives of individuals, races, and nations; developing patience with the limitations of ourselves and of others, and finding a detachment from the delusions of cultural egotism everywhere that can only come from a cyclical (rather than a unilinear) view of historical evolution; seeing the continuity in recorded history as a mirroring of the continuity of individual and collective action on the plane of conflict among personalities with their rival but short-sighted notions of want, need, and interest; recognizing that the facts of recorded history are effects in relation to the crucial causal chains generated in prehistory during the earlier Races; regarding the episodic experiences of partial collectivities in history as the cruder shadowings of archetypal patterns of cosmic involution and human evolution depicted in primordial myths and legends, and recorded in the secret history of occult tribulations in antiquity; and, finally, studying our own psychological make-up and the development of earlier Races in the present and earlier Rounds.

This is a tremendous undertaking. H.P. Blavatsky's genius and method made it a possibility for a wider range of human beings on this planet than ever before. She spoke to each and all, awakening the deepest memories and dormant perceptions of receptive souls.

The consciousness of human beings is, for the greater part and most of the time, intensely bound up with their personalities conditioned by the influences of this life. Men are all too apt to externalize their internal defects (inherent in their lower *upadhis* and their habitual use of them) and project them upon their own race or family or nation or some other. Further, because of the 'need' of the personality to 'belong,' while evading confrontation with its individuality (which must stand on its own and shine by its own light), human beings tend to make sectarian claims on behalf of the group with which they are identified by birth — or by a choice which is more emotional than rational — and thus are caught up in those materializations of thought and feelings that constitute the degradation of every group, religion, and nation. These identifications reinforce false identity, false alibis, narrow attachments, and aversions, by invoking the apologetics and distortions of "cunningly made-up History." They lead men to deny their debts to remote ancestors or their own share in the iniquities of the past and the injustices of the present. Also, they look outside themselves at fragmentary and distorting portions of history that obscure the continuity and interdependence of the past endeavors and failures of mankind. Caught up especially in the current doctrines and fashionable slogans, they see the past largely in terms flattering to their present predicament. Reacting rebelliously against received notions is not much better, and far from the same as achieving a true objectivity.

The proper use of history enables us to internalize all external defects and excrescences in our own immense past as Egos, thus assuming instead of evading responsibility; to look at all historical epochs and sectarian claims and human achievements from the standpoint of the needs of the soul and of spiritual growth; to reflect upon the ancient war in the Fourth Race between the Sons of Light and the Sons of Darkness — a war in which we were all involved and which has left its marks and effects, not only upon history and human institutions, but also upon our psychic natures and our very capacity for reading historical lessons. We now use language in an inverted manner and pervert the vocabulary of soul-life to serve the egotistic purposes of the lower *manas*. But we must gradually learn to see that the mental habit of regarding everything unpleasant in our collective and individual lives as unjust or fortuitous merely traps us in time and makes us lose touch with reality. Nature does not move by fits and starts, and there are no 'accidents' in history or in our lives; what we cannot comprehend is not intrinsically inexplicable. The more we universalize our thinking and free our feelings from personal bias, and the more we contemplate the vast perspective of cosmic evolution and of prehistory, the more we can at least partially unravel the tangled skeins of collective Karma and cyclical manifestations of phenomena. These latter are mirrored in our own psychological tendencies. In short, human beings usually read and write history in ways that reinforce their own egotistic sense of uniqueness and separateness. To learn lessons correctly from the laws of evolution and the facts of the mental history of mankind is truly humbling to lower Manas and inspiring to higher Manas. The dignity of the human soul requires us to look for explanations, not excuses, for our limitations, to seek a heightening rather than a drugging of our sense of responsibility. The Mahatmas see human history (as an integral part of cosmic evolution) from the vantage-point of "the sacred Science of the Past", the birth and evolution of which are lost in the very night of time. The primary source of this Science is the secret annals, preserved in lost and hidden libraries known only to the Lodge of Adepts. The noumenal patterns underlying the events thus recorded are also enshrined in the Akashic records known to Initiates and dimly glimpsed by highly intuitive men on earth. A third source, accessible to humanity but comprehensible only to students of the Wisdom-Religion, is what H.P. Blavatsky called the "memoirs of Humanity", the myths and legends of all nations, especially conveyed under a veil of subtle symbolism and sustained allegory in the Puranas of the original Aryan Race. The first of these sources is not only unknown but even ruled out of court by the exoteric pedants, the ethnocentric scholars who produce fragmentary history in the framework of a jumbled, foreshortened chronology. The second of these sources cannot be tapped by those who have recourse merely to the fallible method of induction from bits of material 'evidence' on the grossest plane of the astral light, extending over the psycho-physical 'shells' of past events. The third source became effectively available only after publication of *The Secret Doctrine*, affording the necessary keys. Indeed, no scholar could write a philosophy of history that could compare in scope and universality and timelessness with the account of cosmogenesis and anthropogenesis given by an Initiate of the stature of H.P. Blavatsky.

Esoteric history, unlike that of modern scholars (among whom hardly one or two like Toynbee even imperfectly echo the ancient teachings regarding the universal operation of cyclic law), presupposes "the law of parallel history and races". The historian, according to Ranke, must view all epochs with an equal eye, but no scholar has risen to the level of objectivity and universality implicit in the statement: "Humanity is the child of cyclic Destiny, and *not one of its Units* can escape its unconscious mission, or get rid of the burden of its cooperative work with nature." The deliberate furtherance of this task, in the context of a definite global vision and long-term plan, is a crucial part of the programme to be progressively unfolded during the 1975 cycle.

"BY THEIR FRUITS . . ."

This mergence of the Jivanmukta into Ishwara may be likened to what may happen in the case of the sun when a comet falls upon it; there is in the case of the sun an accession of heat and light; so also, whenever any particular individual reaches the highest state of spiritual culture, develops in himself all the virtues that alone entitle him to a union with Ishwara and finally unites his soul with Ishwara, there is, as it were, a sort of reaction emanating from Ishwara for the good of humanity; and in particular cases an impulse is generated in Ishwara to incarnate for the good of humanity. This is the highest consummation of human aspiration and endeavour.

BHAVANI SHANKAR

Shankaracharya, in *Self-Knowledge* and *The Crest Jewel of Wisdom*, provides a wealth of instruction about meditation and particularly the relation between *viveka* or discrimination and *vairagya* or detachment. Anyone attempting to apply these teachings will find that it is difficult, but he will also learn that it is exhilarating. If thoughtful he will conclude that, by definition, there could not be any fixed technique of meditation upon the transcendent. Technique is as particularized a notion as one can imagine, a mechanistic term. A *techne* or skill has rules and can be reproduced. On the other hand, that which is transcendental cannot be reproduced. It does not manifest, and it is beyond everything that exists, so there can be no technique for meditation upon it.

Another way of putting it, an older way and perhaps less misleading, is that of the Dalai Lama in his book *My Land and My People*, where in a few pages he explains that the teaching of Buddha concerns both wisdom and method. They go together. Wisdom is meaningless to us unless there is a method. But the method itself cannot be understood unless in relation to wisdom.

He says that there is a distinction to be made between absolute truth and relative truth. In other words, wisdom is your relationship to knowledge, and that relationship involves the means you employ. It is skill in the use of what we call knowledge, but skill that is neither rigid nor final in its modes of embodiment. There is a natural allowance for growth in oneself and within others.

In this arena of inner growth, he who really knows does not tell, partly because he knows that what is essential cannot be told, in the Socratic sense in which wisdom and virtue could never be taught. But partly also he chooses not to tell when telling is of no help. Buddha, the Master of skillful means, said that whichever way you go — telling little, telling much, or keeping quiet — in every case you have created karma. There were times when Buddha said nothing. There were times when he said a great deal merely by telling a fairy story but saying through it much more than is ordinarily possible. There were times when he said very little, and even this sometimes became a bone of contention among disciples. We are dealing with the karma involved in human encounters, and this karma must not be physicalized and only understood literally and exoterically. That is our whole tragedy. We have a physical conception of telling and of silence, but that is because we still have not understood that the real battle is going on between that subtle and rarefied plane of consciousness where the true suns are, and that boisterous plane of consciousness which is the astral light, where there is an immense array of inverted shadows and images.

Words like 'telling', 'knowing' and 'being silent' have to do with inner postures. As long as we seek *external* representations of the *inner* postures of the spiritual life, the spiritual life is not for us in this incarnation, and perhaps just as well. Maybe this is where humanity has grown up. There is now no need for mollycoddling. There is no need for giving in to the residual and tragic arrogance of those who are on the verge of annihilation, by pandering to them, yielding external tokens, or performing external signs. In this Aquarian age, spiritual life is in the mind, and people have got to be much more willing to assume full responsibility for all their choices. The reading of the signs requires a deeper knowledge, or a tougher kind of integrity. The only honest position for anyone is that, given whatever one thing he really knows in his life, in terms of that he is entitled, in E.M. Forster's phrase, "to connect" — to connect with what is told and what is not told. People are brought up in India, and indeed all over the East, to know from early on that what the eyes are saying is important, what the physical gestures are saying is important, and that ominous or peaceful silences bear meanings of many kinds. Brought up in the rich and complex poetry of silence, gesture and speech through all the seven apertures of the human face, there is no such problem as between knowing in one particular sense and telling in one particular sense.

A lot of the subtlety has gone out of our lives, probably all over the world, but nonetheless we must recognize that wisdom always implies an immense, incredible flexibility of method. Let us not play games, least of all adopt sick and self-destructive attitudes, where in the name of belittling ourselves we insidiously belittle our Teachers. What this really comes to is bargaining and even blackmail, and these never helped anyone. On the other hand, let us genuinely be grateful for whatever we receive at all levels. It is part of the meaning of the *Guruparampara* chain that if one were smart enough to be benefitted at some level and to be ever grateful to the person who first taught one the alphabet, then one is more likely to make good use of Teachers in higher realms. We are dealing with something archetypal in which our whole lives are involved, but in which each one will be unique in his or her response.

Conversely, there is nothing predictably easy about the emergence, appearance, decisions, masks and modes of any spiritual Teacher. To assume that would be to limit the Fraternity or to imagine that an organization or some individuals could make captive or bind him. The moment such a being becomes captive, as Plato pointed out in *The Republic*, his withdrawal or his failure is inevitable. He will be free. And what he is really doing would be known only to him. What is important is to know that existentially he will point beyond himself to the Tathagatas. It is a hard lesson for the world — especially in a worn-out West that is still fighting the Middle Ages — that *a true Master is a true servant.* The reason why we find it difficult, even in our everyday language, to understand what is involved in being a Master is because we have ceased to understand what is it to be a true servant. When we can restore the full meaning and the grandeur to the notion of a true and totally reliable servant, only then will we understand what is it to be a Master of Wisdom and Method. Who are the Masters? They are the Servants of mankind. Who, then, must be their agents? Those who exemplify the art of service, who are unquestioning, total, and absolute in their obedience to their Gurus.

Apparently, as H.P. Blavatsky stressed, this turns out to be more difficult for many people in the post-Aristotelian age in the modern West than it appears at first sight. Can obedience be combined with a tremendous courage? Can a lion be a lamb as well? Nothing is impossible for human beings when they master the art of acting from within without, from above below. The process could never be successfully reversed. On sacred matters can one say anything definite? If one can, what should he say, or indeed what would be the point of so saying? But all of this must show itself by its fruits. Surely in regard to the latest of Teachers and their servants it would be true, as it was true of the oldest of Teachers who came to what we call the West, but who really came to the whole world from the East: "By their fruits they shall be judged." Surely it could be said of any teacher what was true of the paradigm of all Teachers, Gautama Buddha: he was a spiritual Teacher in that he gave lasting confidence to everyone else. Yet he did it in a way that was inimitable, in a manner that baffles analysis and defies imitation. Or we could even say that every true teacher must have something in common with Krishna, the planetary spirit who overbroods all Teachers, in that Krishna was always an enigma to everyone around him. It took Arjuna ten chapters to put right his relationship with Krishna, to whom he said, "I took you for a friend, I sported with you." In other words, he tried to put him in a box. In the second chapter of the *Bhagavad Gita*, when Arjuna asked him to describe the characteristics of a wise man, Krishna did not say, "Look at me." Krishna gave the most magnificent impersonal portrait. So surely then it is only on the basis of the invisible thirty-two psychological marks of the true Teacher that recognition and direct benefit are possible.

No Teacher can be separated from other Teachers, and when we consider the broader import of spiritual instruction we are really talking about a fundamental renaissance, heralding the civilization of the future. Those who feel they have found clues within themselves should treasure them. Those who want to help should perpetually prepare themselves. Certainly, no one need waste time and energy in speculating about it because this is not a matter which could be a fit subject for opinion or speculation. To put it in a more positive way, anyone's opinion is as good for him as anyone else's, because in the end it is his life; he has to decide. Many are called but few are chosen. But anyone could decide at any point to do the best he can in relation to the best he knows. In the talismanic words of Mahatma K.H., "He who does the best he can and knows how, does enough for us." Anyone who does the best he can and knows how can do enough for the Messenger of the Fraternity, and indeed thereby himself become a messenger, in a sense. He becomes a teacher because he has shown what it is to be a servant.

So then it gets back to oneself. What can one do to prepare oneself? What can one do to be a worthy servant available at the right time to do that which benefits oneself on one's Path, but which has meaning in relation to a much vaster vision and plan that can be seen with the mind's eye? Though it is hidden, it can be seen to be partly manifest, even before it happens. What is there at this very time which is crucial in enabling us to be ready to be at hand in the future? This is the classic chela-like attitude that anyone can take, but it does not mean going here or there. It requires that wherever one is, one is willing to be wholly available. There is a protective blindness in regard to the future, a protective blindness in one part of our nature. In another part of our nature we know. It is said in the oldest traditions of humanity that the future is very dangerous knowledge. The future is a closed book at all times through the compassion of the universe, and in another sense through the inability of individuals to be ready to bear the knowledge. A Teacher once said that unless a person is so made up, or so ready in his total makeup, that nothing in the future will frighten him and nothing in the future will make him elated, he will not be ready to know what is in the future. That is surely as true now as always in regard to unveiling the future. Shaw's remark about freemasonry and marriages applies even more to the code-language of Adepts — those who are outside will never know, and those who are within are pledged to eternal secrecy.

Behind all the rhythms of nature that are perceptible to us there are other rhythms that we impose. And behind these there is a kind of chaos in which there is another rhythm that is very mysterious. The Monad has no resting place. It is on a pilgrimage where it is ceaselessly changing conditions. There is no refuge, because if there were refuge for the Monad, it would no longer be involved in evolution. In that sense, one might say, surely at the end of evolution there must be a resting place. Whether there is or not, for a Monad that comes voluntarily into the process there is no resting place, in a more poignant sense. Above all, for the Son of Man who comes to bear a certain cross, there is no resting place in that he chooses a destiny within the framework of universal consciousness. We should reflect deeply on that extraordinary passage in *The Secret Doctrine* where we are told that in regard to the great cycle or circle of necessity, in the end the only choice is between being a volunteer in the iniquitous course and being involuntarily propelled into it. As Simone Weil said, you either choose suffering, or suffering chooses you. As Subba Row understood, the Logos chooses the Avatar who allows himself to be so chosen. This para-historical paradox is pivotal to the destiny of mankind in the culminating decades of this century.

Toronto
October 9, 1971

THE GOLDEN THREAD

The Theosophical Society was founded in 1875 in New York with three objects, the first of which was the formation of a nucleus of Universal Brotherhood. The second object was the comparative study of religions, sciences and philosophies, ancient and modern, so that all men and women, including Americans, might come to salute every true witness in a long, largely unknown but unbroken history of accumulated wisdom. *Isis Unveiled* taught the perennial philosophy (*Philosophia Perennis*) and invited its true students to find Ariadne's thread, a golden thread hidden behind the veil of form and symbol, in every great tradition of thought, philosophy, religious aspiration and myth. It is the very basis of real science, and it is the forgotten inspiration behind the founding of the Royal Society as well as much of the significant work of men like Edison, a Fellow of the Theosophical Society, and some other scientists influenced by the wisdom of *The Secret Doctrine*.

When we consider the efforts of sincere Theosophists to apply this philosophy to their lives, in accordance with the third object of the Theosophical Society, we must think of those moments which are the first concern of any person of any age seeking to find meaning within the flux of experiences: the moment of birth and the moment of death. We can also think of the line that threads these moments. Each of us discovers this entirely for oneself, exercising the supreme prerogative of a human being, the privilege of self-reflective consciousness, the gift of the gods, the Dhyanis and Manasaputras, seeking out what in one's whole life was most quintessentially sacred. We live in a society wherein fragmentation of consciousness is widespread and confusion prevails. In such times of trouble, students of *Theosophia* or Brahma Vach are wise in following the advice given by Merlin to Arthur: "*Go back to the original moment.*"

Beginnings are important, endings are inevitable and change is constant in a universe of ceaseless transformation. The wheel revolves constantly faster in the Age of Iron, and everything changes so rapidly that irrelevant analyses and outmoded diagnoses crowd the scene. The wise recognize the timeless truth of the teachings of Lord Krishna: that a person is wise to meditate upon birth, death, decay, sickness and error. This is the most ancient wisdom, and it is as fresh today as it was over five thousand years ago, thanks to the sacrificial ideation of the mighty Brotherhood of silent Teachers who worship the Nameless and Ineffable. They work in perfect harmony through willing and cheerful obedience to the Maha Chohan, who wanted a Brotherhood of Humanity to be initiated and knew that it would not happen at once, but that the line must and would be kept unbroken. In all theosophical assemblies and associations there are those self-determining agents who are self-elected to serve as the compassionate custodians of the living tradition of the primordial teaching of Gupta Vidya for the sake of all.

Gupta Vidya is like an ancient Banyan tree. Some come to sit in its shade, while others come to exchange words and seek friends. Still others come to pick fruit. Nature is generous. Some come to sit in the presence of teachers to receive instruction in the mighty power of real meditation, to secure help in self-examination. All are welcome. The antiquity and enormity of the tree are beyond the capacity of any person in any period of history to enclose in a definition or formulation. Great Teachers point beyond themselves to that which is beyond formulation, which is ineffable and indefinable. They seek to make alive and to make real for every man the priceless boon of learning truth spoken of in *The Voice of the Silence*.

Pythagoras, around 530 B.C., with the prescience of a man who had prepared himself through twenty-two years of training in the Egyptian Mysteries, came to the small town of Krotona. He spent twenty years there laying the foundations of a school and a college for the sake of establishing in the Near East, and in what subsequently became the western world, science (symbolized by the Pythagorean sphere), religion (symbolized by the Tetraktys), and philosophy (a term that he devised). When asked, "Are you a wise man?" he said, "I am a man who is in love with wisdom, a philosopher, *(philosophos)*." Any man who loves — like a child, like a teenager, like all human beings — but loves with a wisdom sufficient to care for love itself, to treasure it, and to prize it, becomes like the blooming lotus. So he exercises the privilege and the right extended to every human being. Independent of authorities and experts, independent of the clash of rival and changing fashions, fads, isms, sects and systems, he or she may exercise the privilege of becoming a true philosopher, of reflecting upon the long journey. Every person is a nomad. The journey begins we know not where. It leads we know not whither. In a world which is like a stage, in which all the players are pilgrims, the pilgrimage is the thing. What is unique, precious and private to each one can only be partly known or shared imperfectly with even the closest friends. *Light on the Path* teaches that no man is our enemy, no man is our friend, but that all alike are our teachers. Our enemy is a mystery, a problem that must be solved even though it take ages. Our friend is an extension of ourself, a riddle hard to read. Only one thing is even more difficult to know, and that is one's own self. Not until the bonds of personality — the mask under which all souls masquerade — is loosened, shall that Self be truly known.

Hence the great cry of the ancients, "Know thyself", and the sacred teaching in relation to self-knowledge and self-reference: that they involve and include a real love of wisdom — unmanifest and manifested, in books and brooks, in stones and in trees, and everywhere for those who have eyes to see, and ears to listen. One of the Mahatmas spoke of music as the most abstract of the arts and mathematics as the most abstract of the sciences. Pythagoras was concerned with both music and mathematics. He fused in himself active and passive contemplation. This is the subject of a conversation in *The Merchant of Venice* between the newly-wed Lorenzo and Jessica, where Jessica experiences what Lorenzo formulates. It is Lorenzo who says that the man who has no music in his soul is fit for stratagems and spoils.

We are very fortunate to have had from the beginning of the Theosophical Society a great plan laid down in the historic letter of the Maha Chohan in 1881. He spoke of the Theosophical Society as the cornerstone, the foundation of the future religions of humanity. There is a grandeur, a magnitude, a magnificence and a breadth of love and compassion in that sacred document which few students of Gupta Vidya can remotely hope to emulate, but which every man or woman is invited to attempt to honour in daily life. H.P. Blavatsky said that we must honour every truth by its use, and that this is the archetypal ritual of any theosophical society. When we ponder the memorable statements of the Great Master, we discover that the great plan laid down was not irrelevant then, never has been irrelevant since, nor could it ever be. Today it rings with a freshness and a contemporary relevance — especially in its reference to the struggle for existence. It is a magnanimous letter, helpful to any of us at this point of time in relation to our fellow human beings.

Each of us is potentially perfect, but each of us is like an iceberg and a mystery to himself and to everyone else. Each of us knows several texts and tomes of mystical philosophy. When so much is known, to so little avail, clearly then what we are faced with requires more than the knowledge of the discursive mind. It involves more than what we, as inheritors of the methods and modes of Aristotle and Bacon, regard as head-learning. We need soul-wisdom. Here we might well think of simple people walking the streets with waiting, wanting lips. Some are very old, some of them so poor in the wealth of the world that they only have what Lord Buddha called the greatest wealth — contentment. This is the simple soul's golden thread. Have some of us lost that simplicity, being so overburdened with our divine discontent which sometimes takes less than human forms? Have we overlooked perhaps the importance of that which is so obvious — a measure of contentment?

We are Promethean beings. We have gaps between our limitations and our potentialities. Every one of us knows that one might have been much more than what one actually is or what one can show on the surface. In modern society the surface has become excessively important. Appearances are lies, but we are caught in the *Mahamaya* of these lies, which then become deep delusions. Gautama Buddha taught that each person makes his or her own prison and that within ourselves deliverance must be sought. No one can be saved in isolation, and yet no one can be saved by another. In fact, the very notion of 'saving' needs re-thinking. We are taught in *The Voice of the Silence* that salvation for one person has no meaning apart from the salvation of the whole of mankind and all living beings. The Maha Chohan spoke of mystical Christianity, of the mystical in every religion, and of *self*-redemption through one's own seventh principle, the liberated *paramatma*. Etymologically, it is this which ceaselessly moves and which in its movement is the source of light, and life, and joy.

If a person asks, "How can we see the golden thread in relation to God, Law and Man?", we might say that God is formless, beyond colours and sounds, yet immanent in all of them. God is to be found in each of the colours of the spectrum, which are in turn puzzles in themselves. They hide subtler hues which may only be seen by those who have the appropriate senses developed and controlled on the planes where alone those senses operate. But all can salute TAT, that which is like the one white colourless light, like the sacred white in rice or in the semen which gives birth to a human body within a holy receptacle. Every human being can understand that which is in the heavens, even if only in the realm of appearances, well enough to realize that there will always be some contrapuntal tension between solar wisdom — Mercury close to the Sun — and the moon that waxes and wanes. Every human being finds that he participates in this waxing and waning, albeit not self-consciously enough since his knowledge of cyclic law is limited, his capacity to use it is less, and he usually forgets to look at the heavens. Gupta Vidya appeals to no less an authority than the authority of the heavens, the universal wisdom from which all religions, sciences and philosophies sprang. The greatest founders of all faiths spoke in accents of great awe before That which could not be spoken about.

This profound message is relevant to seeking the golden thread that binds all monadic minds in the great universal pilgrimage, and to looking for that common storehouse in *Akasha* wherein lies the universal solvent which no man can use unless he wishes to use it for all. In seeking the larger good, a man is able to insert his own good into the good of all, *lokasangraha*. Every man is entitled to be concerned, directly and squarely, with his own good. But his good is only supportable by the law of the universe when it is compatible with universal good. We do not fully know this. Therefore, to the extent to which either we do not know — or knowing, forget it — we have to look for clues. These clues are in the process of life, in Nature and in the working of *prana*. When the force of this good comes from outside, it seems like karma or fate, but when we understand it and it works within, it is always seen as our very best friend.

The Golden Thread that binds the cosmos is unveiled only in partial ways. Arising in the realm of the unmanifest, it participates in the Light of the Logos, *Daiviprakriti*, which is like a veil upon the Absolute. The Absolute is beyond all relativities or absolutizations of the relative, and, in the words of the *Mandukya Upanishad*, is "unthinkable and unspeakable". But if it is unthinkable and unspeakable, can men recognize it in each other? Can souls greet each other with an inward thought and an authentic reference to the absolute centre of a boundless circle within the consciousness of another soul inhabiting that holy temple we call the human body? Is this possible for a human being, in the midst of the primary activities of life, in one's respect for one's parents, in one's respect for one's husband or wife, ex-husband or ex-wife, future husband or future wife? Is it possible, in relation to one's own children and the children of others, to remember, where it counts and where it hurts, but where it matters most, that all are children, all are old souls, all are fallen gods, all are pilgrims who have made mistakes, but who deserve a chance to become self-conscious in relation to spiritual survival. Theosophy, warned the Maha Chohan, is for all, not for a few.

The story of the Theosophical Movement and of every group

that came together in the name of the Wisdom-Religion, is that each fell below the grandeur of the universality and catholicity of the primordial and eternal revelation which remains always in the hands of its great and mighty custodians. Though its breadth is boundless, its height is relevant throughout history and in every religion. It is relevant to every soul because every soul is entitled to seek and to become worthy of relationship with those beings of spiritual stature whom we revere as real Teachers. They cannot be known by external marks. Buddha's thirty-two marks were always invisible, and as Kali Yuga proceeds, it is only from within without that anything worthwhile may be known. All else is a kind of tomfoolery, a concession to Wall Street and Madison Avenue which the Brotherhood has never made and does not now propose to make. "Are not our beards grown?" wrote one of Them. Humanity is mature to a point where it must observe with a wise eye, with a loving heart, and with a compassion that thrills and pulses with the heart of every human being. The Theosophical Movement is for all. The contented simple man who walks the valley of life with very little, and yet smiles and laughs, is one of the teachers of the Theosophical Movement.

The Wisdom-Religion *(Bodhi Dharma)* is everywhere, it assumes strange and manifold guises, but it is always sacrificial. Self-reliance is not to be thrown at others like a weapon, but rather, to be gently exemplified through love. Appeals to lesser authorities are mutually destructive, cancelled by the boundless authority of the universe, with which every person is directly linked without need of intermediary. Every soul has its own access to God, as was known by the Puritans who spoke of the civil war within the breast of every human being. When we think of the very idea of God, we know that we have to negate and negate. We must negate until we begin to recognize the relevance of *No-thing* to *everything*. To see this in Nature with the mind's eye takes time, but once seen, it is the Golden Thread. It shows itself in human affairs as partial representations of the mighty workings of the great wheel of the Law, which is no protector of the illusions of classes, groups, or nations, but which can ultimately be understood by all.

A person may seek the Golden Thread that binds all religions, sciences and philosophies, and yet never be wholly successful unless he becomes a universal man, a Renaissance man, a man of all cultures. This is a task that is coeval with a whole lifetime. It would be good to begin it in childhood. It is never too late to start, but once started, it is not easy to pursue. Above all, it must be sustained with continuity of consciousness if we are to unravel the mystery of mysteries, the mystery of individuality. Who am I? Am I this or that? Am I the person who can be identified in terms of fears and hopes? Am I to be known by my likes and dislikes? Am I the person who masquerades behind a physical form of a certain age and sex, with advantages and disadvantages inherited from a whole line of remote ancestors? We know that over a thousand years every person has had a million ancestors. If a million ancestors have entered into the making of each human being, surely in the complex maze of psycho-physical ancestry there is no clue comparable to the Ariadne's thread that Theseus used to escape the labyrinth.

Each of us is a labyrinth of complexity today. Everything is in print, but there is scarcely enough time to read or enjoy anything. We suffer from such a surfeit that it is tempting to become nominalists. Yet we know better than that, because we know that refinement of the soul and the culture of the man of the future have nothing to do with class. Therefore, Theosophy can speak to souls of all sorts. It cannot be identified with the aristocracy, though H.P. Blavatsky helped them in the nineteenth century. It cannot be identified with the so-called working class, though it benefited through the laying of the foundations of Theosophical socialism. Annie Besant founded the first trade union for girls in England, while B.P. Wadia founded the first trade union in India. Theosophists who must work in different ways must above all learn to respect diversity. We cannot have a secular fundamentalism wherein each one claims that his or hers is the only diet, the only way. This merely creates more walls that divide humanity. Each must enjoy his own mode and make his own changes. A Theosophist who learns to set out on his own as an individual cannot make concessions to the conformities of a culture that is now dying. Its death throes, as well as its labour pains, are already evident everywhere. The young, with their hungers, sense that something is changing and that something has got to change. Sometimes, even though they love their parents, they cannot outwardly express their respect. In turn, sometimes parents love children so much that they cannot communicate to them the difficulty of the human enterprise. Many a soul knows at some level that God is not mocked, that, "As ye sow, so shall ye also reap." Nature is a great Teacher. No one can teach this to another except by the power of love and the force of example.

The modes of the future will require giving paramount emphasis to that greatest gift possessed by every human being — the most divine gift in the hands of man, treasured in the oral traditions of the past — the gift of sounding the Logos within the frame of the human body. It is the gift of making sound, of speech, of articulation. Appropriate articulation, with intrinsic negations, touches that which transcends all verbalization and is beyond verbal expression, that which must always baffle analysis and defy imitation. If we do not appreciate and respond to these opportunities in relation to self-discovery, it is because of the game of externalization, which people play when they come together in a variety of roles and contexts. We are all violating so constantly the most sacred commandment of the Master Jesus, "Judge not, lest ye be judged," that we are not even aware of it. Ceaseless judgment of other human beings — in small towns, in large cities, and in villages — pursued with loveless intransigence in small companionships and groups, makes us think that there is much we all have yet to do if our divine gifts are to become the basis of permanent well-being. What can we do — but not 'do' in the sense in which 'doing' is usually understood in a society which runs around too much? Can we feel what is in the hearts of the young? Of those who are aging? Can we draw larger circles? Can we learn to come together not to analyze why we cannot cooperate but to forget ourselves and to see beyond ourselves? In simple ways, can we accommodate human foibles for the sake of enhancing the good of all?

The good of all is the key to the Golden Thread. No wonder Plato, the distant disciple of Pythagoras, taught that the best subject for meditation is the universal Good — *tò 'agathón*. He who wishes to meditate on the universal Sun, the source of life and light, is invited to dwell on the sacred mantram, the Gayatri:

Aum bhūr bhuvaḥ svaḥ
tatsaviturvareṇyam bhargo devasya dhīmahi
dhiyo yo naḥ prachodayāt. Om.

Let us adore the supremacy of that divine sun who illuminates all, from whom all proceed, to whom all must return, whom we invoke to direct our understandings aright in our progress towards his holy seat.

Anyone who wishes to meditate upon the Spiritual Sun must see beyond the planets, beyond the diversity of the myriads of galaxies, to the midnight sun in the darkness of the firmament. He must see the hidden Sun as the source of one flame from which shoots a ray of light that kindles every spark in every atom. It is that which is differentiated into innumerable Monads and is the only line that persists through its reflection within the human being. Therefore, this is the thread upon which hang like pearls all the personalities of human beings over an immensity of lives in the long journey already extending over some eighteen million years of human existence on this planet.

Every human being has played every role from Puck to Prospero. There is hardly a person who has not held the burden of kingly office. There is no human being who has not known the iniquity of poverty and deprivation. Thoreau understood this when he said that he was in Judea once, in Greece, in Egypt, everywhere. Whitman knew this and sang of it with love in his heart in the *Song of the Open Road* so that we may all become compassionaters, brothers and lovers of all men, nations and races. It is a teaching sung throughout the short history of this Republic. Theosophy is an integral part of the inheritance of the American Republic, originally conceived as a Republic of Conscience.

It has been forgotten. Individuals, sects, ethnic groups, political parties and coteries of every sort have tried to limit America. Some have tried to say that this is a three-religion country, and that each American has to choose between being a Catholic, a Protestant, or a Jew. Now, there is a great deal to learn from the Jewish tradition. It speaks of justice. It speaks of the joy of God when a man and woman come together. It is linked up with the honesty of the psychiatric tradition. Every human being is an honorary wandering Jew. But every human being can also learn from the Catholic tradition, in terms of its current emphasis upon simple decency and the beauty of simple things that can be made sacramental. Just as every boy who is born Jewish has the right of choosing to be as Jewish as he pleases, so too every Catholic boy or girl must choose his or her own ways of making moments in daily life sacramental. Also, we are all Protestants because we are all protesting against the views of authority. This was at the very basis of the inspiration of the Constitution. It is imperfect, but it is too late merely to condemn the Protestant tradition. Perhaps it is not three cheers, but it is surely at least two, for the Protestant ethic. It came with the Reformation as a part of the work of Tsong-Kha-Pa and the Brotherhood for the sake of a spiritual reformation within Christianity, comparable to a concurrent spiritual reformation within Hinduism and Buddhism and earlier work within the Catholic church. The last Adept actually to work within the church was Nicolas of Cusa.

No religion or institution is exempt from the all-seeing gaze of Migmar, whose eye sweeps over slumbering Earth. Every sincere human being who seeks to become a true disciple of the divine discipline of the Wisdom-Religion has the protective aura of the hand of Lhagpa over his head. When things go wrong we cannot blame our Teachers. Accepting or assuming our own limitations, we must not limit the Brotherhood. Men have often limited and crucified those the Brotherhood sent. They did it again in a subtle psychological way in the nineteenth century. They will surely attempt to do it in this century and in the future, but will always fail because a great galaxy of Beings is involved, with a carefully designed plan providing lines of retreat to one and all. It was only Buddha who could take the vital decision in Kali Yuga, where all souls have failed and no one can condemn another as a sinner, that although the rules cannot be changed (since occult laws are inviolable), nonetheless access could be made easier for more souls in every part of the world to the secret wisdom of its Mystery Temples. The key always lies within. Tom Paine was prophetic when he anticipated the religion of the future as a trimming away of all the excrescences upon the original substratum. In the beginning was the Word, the Verbum. Because Theosophy is ultimately beyond names, the Wisdom-Religion or *Bodhi Dharma* was known by many names at all times. Today, the immensity and magnificence of the Wisdom-Religion is a Golden Thread of protection for any person who wishes to make credible contributions to the future or who wishes to come out and become separate from the cycles of the past which must run their course.

The Golden Thread binds the various centres within the human constitution. In every human being the *sutratman*, the thread-soul, is *sutratma buddhi*. It is reflected in an innate sense of intuitive recognition, decency, fairness, kindness and minimum self-transcendence. In our culture minima have become profoundly important. They will be the foundations for the maxima of the future. Anyone who has contacted the Path of the Wisdom-Religion can, at the minimum, grasp the simple message, a reminder of what everyone already knows, that it is possible at *this* moment to make a difference to the moment of death. There is the injunction of *The Voice of the Silence*:

'Great Sifter' is the name of the 'Heart Doctrine',
O Disciple.

> The wheel of the Good Law moves swiftly on. It
> grinds by night and day. The worthless husks it drives
> from out the golden grain, the refuse from the flour.

Every soul can sift from experience what is worth saving from what cannot be taken or must later be discarded. This was part of the training of the disciples of Pythagoras. It is part of the American Dream. Every human being can, with psychological as well as social mobility, rearrange his or her critical luggage in the realm of the mind. This has to do with chains of self-reproductive thought, which cannot be stilled suddenly by a dramatic attempt at meditation. Meditation involves the hindering of hindrances. Patanjali's *Yoga Sutra* defines meditation as the hindering of the modifications of the thinking principle. Each must do this in his or her own way. In the old traditions of Tibet, where all the various schools of Buddhism respected each other and tolerance and civility were shown between the different orders, the distinctive teaching of the Gelukpa Yellow Cap tradition was that the best thing to meditate upon is meditation.

The Golden Thread eludes us when we try too hard to think about it. At the same time, when we do make the attempt we must think seriously about what it is and what it is not. The Golden Thread cannot be discerned in the realm of the physical body which lives through food — the *annamaya kosha*, the lowest, grossest sheath. The Golden Thread cannot be discerned in the *pranamaya kosha*, the sheath in which the lower currents of energy circulate. The Golden Thread is not to be picked up from those portions of the *manomaya kosha* which are made up of thought-patterns that come from outside and that do not originate from above. The Golden Thread can be picked up in that aspect of the *manomaya* sheath which negates externals and seeks the sheath of Atman, the *vignanamaya kosha*, having to do with *vignam*, discrimination or *Buddhi*.

The Golden Thread can only be genuinely picked up in the realm of discriminative insight, available to every person. When it is picked up, then one must seek by negation to become self-conscious in one's awareness of continuity of consciousness. Thereby, *manas* itself can shine and then in turn illuminate the *sutratma* thread which is *sutratma buddhi*. This, then, can become *manas sutratman*. Every human being is a unit ray reflecting the light of the Logos. It is the light with which every person was born, according to the gospel of St. John, and with which one may become resplendent in its fullness. It may be found by all who choose the heroic steps outlined in the *Book of the Golden Precepts*:

> Shun ignorance, and likewise shun illusion. Avert thy face from world deceptions: mistrust thy senses; they are false. But within thy body — the shrine of thy sensations — seek in the Impersonal for the 'Eternal Man'; and having sought him out, look inward: thou art Buddha.

Ojai
April 25, 1972

THE
GURUPARAMPARA

JNANA YAJNA

For the good man 'tis most glorious and good and profitable to happiness of life, aye, and most excellently fit, to do sacrifice and be ever in communion with heaven through prayer and offerings and all manner of worship.
The Athenian Stranger   PLATO

During the primeval dawn of human evolution, the whole of humanity was suffused with a spontaneous devotion to Gurus and Preceptors, to the golden chain of transmission of the Guruparampara, a galaxy of known and unknown teachers. Simultaneously, all found no pain but a pure pleasure in the performance of the daily duties of life, revealing an intimate connection between devotion and duty. The conception of such a humanity differs totally from our own. It is like a Golden Age far removed from our time, because for many centuries we have engendered, with extraordinary violence and pertinacity, the falsehood of a separate identity for each human being, supposedly gestated at birth and terminated at death. People tend not to think about death and live as if they have a kind of invulnerability. But they blunder through without any knowledge of who they are, and find themselves oppressed by a sense of inward confusion, which only allows them to speak and think in terms of comparison and contrast. They are driven by their dwarfed conceptions of success and failure and are trapped in differentiated consciousness based on unending comparison and contrast. At the same time, this consciousness assumes an apparent stability not intrinsic to it, but involving a shutting out of the archetypal moments of birth and death. In time, this means forgetfulness, an indifference to the primary facts that apply to all humanity — that there is a great continuity to the human pilgrimage, that death is followed by rebirth, that this is true not only for particular souls but also that there is a continuous passage from generation to generation.

The whole process is so vast that the moment we try to limit it, in terms of crude conceptions of duty or obligation, we also feel that any personal devotion we show is gratuitous. Captivated by personal differentiated consciousness, we live under the sway of the specious idea that the universe is for one's own private benefit and that each one is favouring the world, favouring other human beings, by an egocentric stance, by supererogatory acts, and that if one is devoted one has set up some kind of claim upon the object of devotion. All of this thinking is distorted, inverted, and perverted, bound up with the descent of consciousness into matter. At a certain point of material density and fragmentation of consciousness, the pale reflection of the unmanifest light of the Immortal Triad assumes a false centrality. This would be like a shift from the self-luminous centre of a circle to a lit-up region which only seems luminous by contrast with the shadow around. The latter is the spurious ego, the limited personal consciousness. Given this condition, every human being can, at one level, understand that there is something very beautiful and elevating, something extremely authentic, in poetic accounts of a Golden Age of primordial humanity, when human beings moved naturally and related to each other beautifully. They were spontaneously held together by an effortless sense of moral and spiritual solidarity with the whole of nature, with those before and those yet to come, and above all, with their great Teachers. Though we can resonate with such an Age, we also know that if we have to ask questions about it, we already presuppose that it is estranged from us.

What good, then, can come of talking about devotion for a person who has become totally convinced that he has no capacity for any feeling, any devotion for anyone else? Who is that person? A cerebral machine, chatting away, insecure, confused yet making judgments? Is that the whole of that person? But if he has assumed this is all he or anyone else is, how can talking about devotion make a difference? Suppose such a person were told that there are great beings like Krishna and the Buddha, hosts of hierophants who are seated in meditation and constantly engaged in ideation upon universal good, who have so vast a perspective of endless time, boundless space and ceaseless motion, that they can see the rises and falls of civilizations and epochs in perspective. Suppose he were told that they can see the antics of human beings in much smaller spans of time and space with unwavering compassion, and also that they can see the root illusion. These beings are involved in universal welfare and uplifting the whole of humanity. Any human being who can vibrate in mind, heart and self to the tune of the great universal impulse of these mighty beings, may serve as a focal point through whom some mitigation of human misery and some elevation of consciousness is possible.

To the sick, as in the time of Jesus, the idea of a super-healthy human being does not speak. Similarly, how can a person completely incapable of ordinary feelings grasp the idea of such noble beings? Unconsciously that person has been ceaselessly worshipping at the altar of the material self — and not even doing a very good job at it, not even being constant in devotion to his own personal self — inattentive, afraid, fickle, confused. With the lunar shadow as his only focus, how can such a person comprehend the light of the Spiritual Sun? How can such a person grasp the perspective of Mahatmas? But then, even if the person cannot comprehend those beyond him, can he still apprehend something that is at once universal and archetypal, which is found throughout the animal kingdom in the love and protection shown by animals for the young, which is found in the human kingdom between mothers and children? Even with all the corruption of modern modes and relationships, we still find this pulse of decency, warmth and kindness, a dauntless trust that is in the human heart. Surely a person should be able to reawaken that which now has been buried and obscured but which was once strong and secure. This is the point at which a person can benefit from the teaching of *Jnana Yajna* — Wisdom-sacrifice.

Lord Krishna came at a time when he knew that humanity could not go back and restore its child-state without any effort. But on the other hand, he also knew that human beings were going to be enormously vulnerable to self-righteous merchants of the moral language who narrow and limit conceptions of duty and morality by institutionalizing them, and thereby bind human beings through fear to mere externalities of conduct. Therefore an alternative had to be shown. Being magnificently generous, Krishna speaks at the widest cosmic level of how the Logos functions out of only a small portion of itself and yet remains totally uninvolved. It is like the boundless ocean on the surface of which there are many ships, and in which there are many aquatic creatures, though the depths of that boundless ocean remain still. The whole world may be seen from the standpoint of the Logos, which is essentially incapable of incarnating and manifesting within the limitations of differentiated matter. The Logos can only overbrood. This overbrooding is joyous, producing myriad kaleidoscopic reflections within which various creatures get caught. Krishna gives the great standpoint, the divine perspective, which is all sacrifice. That is the critical relationship between the unmanifest and the manifest, because if the unmanifest can never be fully manifested, how can the manifest ever be linked to the unmanifest? There is always in everything that is manifest, behind the form, behind the façade, a deathless core of the very same nature and of the very same essence as that which is unmanifest. Where a human being can, by the power of thought, bring this to the centre of individual consciousness, it is possible to consecrate. It is possible to act as if each day corresponds to the Day of an entire universe, or to a lifetime. It is possible to act in each relationship as if it were a supreme expression of the very highest relationships between teacher and pupil or mother and child. It is possible to act in a small space as if there is the possibility of an architecture and rearrangement which can have analogues to the grand arrangements of solar systems and galaxies.

This is the great gift of creative, constructive imagination without illusion. What makes it Wisdom-sacrifice is that one trains personal consciousness — the chattering mind, the divided and wandering heart, the restless hands — one centres all of these energies around a single pivotal idea, having no expectations. If an ordinary human being had no expectations whatsoever, the person would die simply because typically a person lives on the basis of some confused and vague expectations in regard to tomorrow, next year and the future. Deny a human being all expectations, all claims and personal consciousness usually will collapse. Of course this cannot be done from the outside. The shock would be too great. But human beings can administer the medicine to themselves progressively and gradually. Merely look at the years already lived and see how many expectations have been built up. Either you dare not look back at them and how they were falsified — which means there is a cowardliness, a lie in your very soul — or you have replaced them so fast by other expectations that you are caught in a web of externalizing expectations. To initiate a breakthrough you can earnestly think, "Supposing I have only one day more to live; supposing everything that I have is taken away from me; supposing I can rely on nothing and expect nothing. What would be the meaning of joy, the dignity of grief?"

At that point, if a person thinks of Sri Krishna, of the unthanked Mahatmas and Adepts, and thinks of them not as distant from the human scene but as the ever-present causal force behind the shadow play of history, then he finds an incredible strength in that thought, a strength in consciousness but without a solidification of the object of consciousness. One can act with a freedom that is ultimately rooted in total actionlessness, like the supreme light of the *Atman* which is in eternal motion but which is not involved in what we call motion, refracted by differentiated matter. At the same time, one can live as if each act is supremely important, sublimely sacred. The person who really comes to think this out trains himself in this mode of thinking, feeling, breathing, acting and living and can in time gain a new lightness and economy, a fresh conception of real necessity, but above all a fundamental conception of identity — merely as one of manifold unseen and unknown instruments of the one Logos.

This is the great teaching of *Jnana Yajna* which, stated in this way, looks difficult, but is at the same time at some level accessible

to each. It is a teaching so sacred that it is veiled in the *Gita* —
hidden when it is given in the fourth chapter and again at the
very end of the eighteenth chapter. It is a teaching which, if fully
grasped, is the gateway to freedom and will enable one to become
karmaless, to avoid becoming caught through the mind in the
intertwining chains of karma. Clearly, karmalessness was not
possible for early humanity, but it had all the ingredients of the
quality which must belong to the mature person of the present
when adopting the standpoint of those pioneers of the future who
act self-consciously with a universal perspective and without
residue, without becoming involved in the externalities or, as
Gaudapada taught, without leaving any footprints.

The difficulty of this can be appreciated when we recall that
in the fourth chapter of the *Gita* Krishna says that there are some
who sacrifice the in-breathing and the out-breathing, while others
chant the texts, and still others actually surrender themselves. All
these sacrifices arise out of action. They arise out of the non-self
and retain the illusion of an agent. In every one of these sacrifices
we can distinguish archetypally five elements. There is that which
is the oblation offered in sacrifice. There is the fire into which it
is offered. There is the instrument — a ladle or whatever — with
the help of which the offering is placed in the fire. Then there is
the agent, the 'I,' the person who says, "I am performing the
sacrifice." There is the object of the sacrifice. All of these exist at
one level in a universe of differentiated matter, constituted of
innumerable beings that are ever at work and interacting in
ceaseless motion. There is the interplay of subject and object, the
deceptive contrast between light and shadow. There are separate
objects and a background. All of this is maya, the projective yet
veiling power of the Logos, of the Ishwara, of Krishna.

A human being does not have to project or be taken in by
the veiling. It is possible for him to stand apart from roles, from
sounds and sights, and to see through and beyond the seeming
separation of objects. To take a simple example, we have artificial
light, and by it we see and focus. We see many colours, a room,
separate people. If we turn all the lights off, some people will be

uncomfortable. Suddenly we no more see objects, selves, colours, contrasts, but we can then experience the breathing and pulsation of human beings. Paradoxically, we would have a greater sense of what it is to be human when all lights are turned off, when we can sense the collective breath of so many human beings, than when in an illuminated room we see faces, contrasts, colours, and all the differentia of the external plane.

This is true of every archetypal mode of sacrifice rooted in action. It is mayavic. Wisdom-sacrifice begins with the recognition that all of these are mere epiphenomena, only appearances cast upon the one *Brahman*, the ever-expansive, immeasurable force, essence, spirit, primordial matter — call it what you will because no distinctions apply at that level. That boundless existence, *Brahman*, the Supreme Spirit, is the offering; *Brahman* is the fire; *Brahman* is the mode of making the offering; *Brahman* is each of us and the person making the offering; *Brahman* is the object of the sacrifice. If *Brahman* is *all* these, why become focused upon specific differentia?

We all have experience of this when we witness a noble piece of music performed by a superb orchestra, or when we watch a moving play with the most highly synchronized and dedicated actors. As Shakespeare said, "The play's the thing." There is a sense of something beyond all the details, the incidents, the scenery and the individual actors. There is an intricate interplay that points beyond itself. But we try to reconstruct — and that often happens, alas, because it is one of the futile tendencies of human beings — instead of keeping very quiet and assimilating a deep experience in music or in drama. We are tempted to share it with someone else, and in the telling, we distort, fragment and emphasize contrasts. When one gets to the extreme condition of those congenital critics who are compelled to do this habitually, a sad destruction takes place. The person who does this propagates a distortion. His life is truly "a tale told by an idiot, full of sound and fury, signifying nothing." How much did such a human being add to the sum-total of good when he breathed his last? What difference did his life make to other human lives, to the relief of human pain, to the liberation of human minds, to the enlightenment of human hearts?

We have to recover the sense of the transcendental, unmanifest One. We have to reach again and again to that which is above the head, that which is without any parts or attributes, that light which can never be mirrored except in *Buddhi*, the only part of a human being that is capable of mirroring *Atman*. *Buddhi* is usually wholly latent, but if *Buddhi* mirrors *Atman* there is an infallible result, a decisiveness and assurance which nothing else can give. *Nischaya* is the word in Sanskrit, meaning 'without any shadow.' When a person, in the depths of meditation, out of the very finest ineffable feeling, touches that pure vessel of the *Atman* in the inmost brain, a perfect mirror of the colourless omnipresent light, there arises an assurance and certainty which is constant and can never be destroyed. Equally, it can never be shared or verbalized though it becomes the constant, central fact of life. This is irreversible. Even though a person has made many mistakes over many years — wasted words, harsh sounds, violent speech, empty words — even though a great deal of karma has been generated, all of which will have to be rendered in full account in future lives, nevertheless, if one truly touches the inmost core of the soundless sound and achieves that supreme sense of decisiveness, clarity, confidence, and calm, then it is possible to negate and counteract a lot of the karma produced in the past.

Wisdom-sacrifice is the mode of creative speech in silence, meditating upon the soundless sound, where there is no attachment, no involvement, and one does not participate in lesser emanations. The Pythagorean *Monas*, like the human triad, emanates out of the total darkness, initiating a universe, and withdraws forever after into the darkness. Human beings can initiate in that spirit, can come out of the vast silence of contemplation to begin something and let a whole series follow while withdrawing totally. They thus exemplify the archetypal stance of the Bodhisattvas. The very fact that we can think about such ideas, understand and appreciate them, means there is that in us which, though fearful of death, is willing to cooperate now with the consciousness which after death will witness the separation of the principles, and take stock of a lifetime to prepare itself for the karma of the future. It is possible to cooperate in waking life with that perception which, in deep sleep, represents an unbroken, undivided consciousness. Then there is no limitation of space, time or energy in one's perspective and understanding of humanity and the universal good, and one can insert oneself into the whole.

Anyone who can, as a result of deep meditation, start with small beginnings and try to utter a word to help or heal another human being, or who can stay in a period of silence for the sake of some larger purpose of benefit to humanity, can come to know what it is to initiate. To gain the power of the Initiator, one must both specialize and concentrate magnetism and be attentive enough to apply a thought with such controlled precision and perfect timing to the needs of another human being, that one can make a permanent change for the good in that person's life. In the light of Wisdom-sacrifice, *Jnana Yajna*, good and bad are merely relative appellations from the standpoint of differentiated consciousness in time and space. We grow over a lifetime in making finer and finer discriminations because the cruder relativities with which we live prevent us from understanding a great deal of human life. If this is true of the world around us, it is also true of ourselves.

This has been put in the form of a story about the three *gunas* — *sattva, rajas* and *tamas* — all of whom are compared to impostors who accost a man in the jungle. We are told that *tamas* is the one who assaults the victim for the immediate purpose of robbery, *rajas* is the one who binds him up for the purpose of making the proper kill, and *sattva* is the one who releases the person, can take him to the edge of the forest but cannot go any further. *Sattva* is afraid of what is outside the forest. He is also a thief, but his theft is through goodness. It is an attempted theft of that illimitable light of the spirit which can never be captured or translated into attributes.

A person must see all his limitations and weaknesses as

shadows of certain qualities which are the painstaking results of karmic good works in previous lives, but which still are bonds, because they become ways in which one defines oneself. *Sattva* involves one as a personal self in imagining that one is better than others, in imagining that one is separate from the beast and the most wretched. It also is fundamentally unable to rise to the level of the compassion of Krishna, who can see in all the same diffused light throughout the great masquerade of maya, but who also perceives the many degrees of enslavement to the masquerade which can only be overcome during a long period of time. He says to Arjuna that though Arjuna is grieving for all these people, they are better off gone. They cannot in their present incarnation emancipate themselves from their lifelong qualities, but they can in the future. In an unlimited universe there is hope for all, but in any limited period of time everybody cannot progress equally or to the same extent. To understand this is common sense. It is part of the mathematics of the universe. But to use that understanding with wisdom and compassion means we must not become excited about beginnings and endings or about when and where such and such happened to whom. We must not be caught up in all of this because this is the very framework that binds, especially when it is cloaked in one's better qualities. The light of the *prajnagarbha* — the *Atman* beyond and above all the *gunas* and qualities — is a wisdom that is essentially unmanifest and is the perpetual motion which is pure motionless self-existence.

We need to say to the personal conditioned self, "Even though you are incapable of appreciating the grandeur of the cosmic sacrifice, I, that Self which knows that you are incapable, take you and throw you into the cosmic fire." Now this can be treated ironically but it is also profoundly sacred. It is what H.P. Blavatsky termed 'will-prayer.' At any given time we do not know what more we are capable of tomorrow, but there is no reason for us, equally, to exaggerate the facts as they are. Even more important than either our changing perspective of tomorrow's possibilities or our present view of today's actualities, is our need to see beyond ourselves altogether. We must lift ourselves from the egotism of the shadow to the egoity of that which looks towards the light and which at some point is absorbed in its selfless expansive wonderment at the one supreme, single light of spirit. If this is what we are required to do, we have got to give up any sense of identity. It is more difficult to give up a sense of identity when it is bound up with good qualities, with our spiritual assets and whatever we have worked towards for so long. All of these have got to go. One has to train oneself to be established in a state of mind with no expectations. Without expectations we are less liable to distort and obscure what is going on, because what is going on manifests on many levels. What is going on involves maya. Though this maya veils and we add to maya by projecting and fantasizing, it is also possible to use maya to reveal what is relevant and what is at the very core.

This therapeutic art involves training, and it cannot come if one is either blinded by the film of one's own goodness or the nightmare of one's own badness. One must see a whole universe of myriads of selves and monads, and the saga of humanity as a vast, essentially untold and unfinished story. At any given moment what is unmanifest is most important and what people are feeling deep down is more important than what they say. What they are unable to think in the language that they use, and which somehow negates their thoughts even if it only makes them tired and go to sleep, still comes closer to the ground of being as the field of abstract potential. Coming to see it as a living realm of awareness is to function on the truly causal plane. We may thus come closer to those beings who initiate potent and beneficent causes upon the human scene. We might even make that difference to the soul of another human being which may not show for many future lives, but which could eventually be crucial.

We do not know all the arithmetic — how it all adds up, how it interconnects — but we prevent ourselves from knowing a great deal that we could know by imposing expectations, by over-analysis, but above all by a false dramatization of our personal egos. If we can *let go* of all of these, and if we can look beyond and behind the shadow play of personal selves, we can see in the divine dark the mighty manifestation of the great hosts represented by Krishna, the Logos, the Christos. We can see this in ourselves, even if the only way we can see it in ourselves is by making it a point. Before we can make it a point, we have to reduce our composite astral form to a cipher. We have to void the very language and categories of the personal self. An ancient scripture teaches that any feeling of like or dislike reinforces, expands, aggravates that shadow. Pandit Bhavani Shankar suggests that when one enters the spiritual path and reaches the *karana sharira*, one reads therein the archetypal origins of like and dislike. They are much more difficult to understand than their materialized manifestations. Attraction towards existence and aversion from non-existence bind the individuality itself. Their personal reflection is a pseudo-attraction and a pseudo-repulsion that maximizes the elemental interaction of the shadow. This has to be cut at the root. One has to go beyond 'history' to see all events as participating in a common medium, all beginnings and endings as existing merely in the region of form. One has to gain that unbroken consciousness which does not participate in succession, in simultaneity, in contrast or comparison. One of the necessary steps to get to this stage is to see beyond the deceptive contrasts of good and evil as pictured by the personal self. One must become so humble before universal welfare that one can only say one does not know what is the supreme criterion of the sum-total of human good, of the optimal use of everything.

This perspective is radically different from our ordinary way of looking at the world, where we have elaborated our childhood fears and traumas and created notions of success and failure which have bound us. We must get away from this altogether, voiding it in our consciousness. In the beginning you have to reach, even if you cannot go beyond, that point where in the very act of reaching you render obeisance — in the words of the *Gita*, a long prostration — devoted service to those Mahatmas who embody *par excellence* the *yajna* of *Jnana Yoga*. If you do the best you can, and lose yourself in the adoration of those who do so much more, a sort of healing takes place. There is a progressive dissolution of the personal self and a gradual atrophy or dying out of *ahankara,* the 'I'-making faculty.

It will take time for this process to work itself out fully, because every now and again you will be tempted, like a miser counting his coins, to count your blessings in terms of some plausible story of your progress over a period of seven years, over a lifetime, over the remaining length of time until the moment of death, linking this up to some notion of before and after. The moment you start to dwell on such thoughts, you have short-circuited the process. You have restored egotistic concern. Therefore, you will have to make the voiding of self a whole way of living that applies to everything. Initially you can apply it to one thing, two things, more things. If you can link it up to the most elementary necessities of life like waking up, going to sleep, eating and bathing — if you can link it up to these archetypal activities whereby you are discharging debts on the lower planes of consciousness — and you can do this with an awareness of the cosmic host — then in time you can make a decisive difference. In due course you can actually create out of the very ashes of your former sense of being, from a germ and an embryonic seed, a new vesture or *rupa,* a supple astral form saturated with the sacrificial energy of steadfast devotion. Its tropism will naturally help it to turn towards the holy *Hiranyagarbha,* the golden vesture of Krishna and Buddha. Mahatmas are continually engaged in giving a forward impulse to human evolution, without any attachments to the relativities and partialities of the perceptions of beings bound upon the great wheel of change.

Wisdom-sacrifice begins where one is, but its end is beyond one's capacity to reckon or conceive. It resembles Jacob's ladder. It is the *Ahavaniya* of the Vedas, the great sacrificial ladder, the golden chain of the Guruparampara. It is like fire which must arise for each as a spark at some point, but which can become a leaping flame bursting the boundaries of all our maps of manifested existence. Hence it is called the fire of knowledge, the sovereign purifier. There is something about fire that is non-discriminatory. It is involved in a relentless process of purgation. Self-conscious participation in the cosmic fire of universal sacrifice is the great privilege offered in an initiatory mode by Krishna to Arjuna, and to all those disciples who could use the sacred teaching for the sake of adding to the sum of universal good.

THE FLUTE OF KRISHNA

*Hear, O son of Pritha, how with heart fixed on me,
practising meditation, and taking me as thy refuge, thou
shalt know me completely.*

SHRI KRISHNA

Any person who seeks the supernal radiance of the Invisible Sun, the ceaseless vibration of the Logos ensouling the Fraternity of Enlightened Seers, must abide at all times with heart fixed upon the object of his devotion. He must be worthy of that total devotion, continually practising meditation, returning his mind whenever possible to its favourite subject of contemplation, the one Guru that he has chosen, the embodiment of the Logos that is the noumenal force behind the whole of life. Only then can he truly say that he has found the Krishna-Christos within himself. Only then does he activate and arouse, by his realization of the Logos in the cosmos, the spirit which moves and animates every single atom and molecule, endowing each with that vortical motion which maintains it for a time in the world of manifestation, thereby enabling it to have life in a form under law. To do this he must take Krishna as his refuge. He must have total trust and faith in the chosen one, the *Ishtaguru.*

In every case he has chosen Krishna. Suppose he was a very sincere disciple, for example, like John, deeply devoted, when writing the Gospel, to the memory of Jesus, Christ will write for him. Everyone is provided for, everyone is protected, everyone is helped. But those alone who embody Krishna's precepts will know Him completely. They alone will be instructed fully in this knowledge and in this realization, having learned which, there remains nothing else to be known. Clearly, this is an unattainable ideal for the average person in our time and in our culture. He cannot possibly expect suddenly to achieve that continuity of consciousness, that ceaseless contemplation, that total devotion, and above all, that unwavering and absolute allegiance to the one shelter and source chosen. He will not attain to this knowledge in this lifetime. He will not hear the pure strains of the flute of Krishna.

Nonetheless, there is hope for every human being. Every human being does in some moments experience the simple joys of daily life known to the great masses of mankind. No wonder that Krishna, the eighth Avatar of Vishnu, is the favoured incarnation among the common folk in India. No wonder the *Bhagavad Gita* spoke so powerfully to Thoreau and Bellamy in America, to Wilkins and Warren Hastings among the early Englishmen in India, and to Schlegel and Goethe and many others in Germany. No wonder, then, all over the world men have sat at the lotus feet of the Teacher, in any form, for the sake of true help. Anyone who has ever leafed through the sacred pages of the Song of the Lord has benefited, whether he turns to the translation by William Quan Judge which is mantramic, or the translation by Christopher Isherwood which is poetic and beautiful, or the many other translations that have been composed over the last century. Even more richly blessed are those who have been privileged to study that magnificent, unexcelled and supremely illuminating commentary recorded by Shankaracharya for those who are ready for the deeper mysteries of the *Gita*.

Whoever ponders the *Gita* over a long period of time is deeply stirred. It is sadly significant that Mahatma Gandhi, as also his assassin, appealed to the same scripture. He who died by the bullet of Godse revered the *Gita* as his mother, and he who slew Gandhi had deluded himself into thinking that he was obeying the injunctions of the *Gita*. In general, there is a very real sense in which a dedicated few hear Krishna's flute in tones that are sublimely different from the modes in which many others hear it. As long as there are as many ways to God as the breaths of the children of men — in the words of the *Koran* — while at the same time each man is lit up by the same light, so long will each choose his own path according to his own state of consciousness, his wants, his intentions and his goals. Everyone is included in the benediction of Krishna, in accordance with the karma of his 'line of life's meditation.'

This is a difficult doctrine to understand. There are no distinctions in it between the saved and the damned. In this doctrine the only elect are those who are self-elected, in the manner of Krishna, by the profundity of their overwhelming concern and continual sacrifice. Those who comprehend *Adhiyajna*, the supreme sacrifice, share in its celebration. Everyone must, in his own way, find the Logos within and light up the lamp of true spiritual discernment. In this fundamental sense, all human beings are provided for and the important thing for anyone is not where he is but how he can do better.

All beginnings are seminal and are immensely significant. If a person really wishes to listen to the sound of the divine flute, he must understand the dialogue within his own consciousness which is like the interplay between flute and harp in the great concerto of Mozart. It occurs between the divine promptings within himself and the less rhythmic breathing of his lower self. Through it, he can become self-consciously capable of appreciating the flute. Among people who go to a concert there are those who are merely awed by what takes place. There are those who have some understanding of the music that is played. Others have some knowledge of the skill involved in using instruments and the immense deliberation and meditation behind masters of music in manifestation. Then there are those very few individuals who intensely love the music and, in Eliot's phrase, have heard it so deeply that it is not heard at all, who have become the music while the music lasts. They love the musicians so much that they are one with them, going beyond all the cacophony of inaudible sounds in the heads of the members of the audience. The function of the greatest music is in pointing to that which is unuttered on the physical plane, but which is a ceaseless utterance in eternity. Any man who hears the rumbling of a thunder cloud, the roar of the ocean, or the rush of the winds above a holy place, is truly blessed, because of the sacred undertaking to which the whole of nature has been consecrated under Karma. Anyone who goes anywhere and is responsive to the F-note of nature — the keynote of Beethoven's Pastoral Symphony — the one sound into which all sounds are resolved, even if he hears it only in the still hours of dawn, hears the song of the flute. Anyone who then consecrates himself to the service of the unity of all men and women, has chosen a great undertaking. He feels the pulse of light, the 'core of the unuttered' — in the words of Shelley. With Wordsworth, he hears the "still, sad music of humanity." And, hearing these, he may also, in favoured moments, in the season of spring, hear the nightingale "warbling its native woodnotes wild." We might say that the message and meaning of the incarnation of Krishna, over five thousand and ninety-three years ago, was to bring into the lives of men the beauty, the vital relevance and the abundant hope of the eternal rhythm of the cosmos.

There is a critical sense in which our ability to hear the flute is a function of our receptivity, and receptivity requires spiritual knowledge. The Heart Doctrine springs from the heart and lights up the mind. It also involves all aspects of our lives. If, with our whole being, whether intermittently or continuously, we can sift within the stillness and solitude of our inmost calm, only then can we feel the presence, hear the sound, and share the divine joy of the dance of the Logos. A person is deeply fortunate to have earned the opportunity to make such a consecration and, through devotion, to move in the mighty current of meditation sustained by those who are the perpetual servants of the Logos.

Tragically, most men do not grasp the universal significance of the benediction of Krishna and mistake the great magnanimity of the cosmos for an endorsement of their personal misconceptions and partial insights. But even they are provided for. Those who worship the lesser gods choose terrestrial things. They chase after shadows. They pursue secondary emanations. Some worship money, which comes from the elementals who preside over money, compounded out of the thought-elementals of all human beings focused upon the precious metals. They obtain what they crave. Some extol the pleasures of the body and think they seek Venus Aphrodite. They cling to secondary emanations, evanescent pleasures, for the sake of forgetfulness and momentary extinction. They also secure the object of their quest. Some woo the promiscuous goddess of fame, who courts different men and women on diverse occasions. They gain their object one way or the other, if not in this life, then in some future incarnation. Everyone in the progress of time receives such objects of imperfect devotion. Some are truly fortunate, under karma, to be prevented from securing the objects of their devotion in this life because in previous lives they took a decision that they do not want them again, however tempting they appeared. What comes to the personality as a setback is a bonus from the past, a current from the Higher Self which protects. Thereby they are saved from endless repetitions and compulsive re-enactments of the mistakes of previous lives.

There are also those who, with simplicity, propitiate by means of mantrams, chanting in the streets. They do not know what they really want. At some level they love Krishna. At another level, they wish to reach out to other human beings. Though all of this is sincerely meant, they often mistake the chanting, the dining together, and various monastic practices for some kind of short cut to Krishna. This mistake is only possible if one does not study the *Bhagavad Gita*. Alas, there are also teachers who are very earnest but who, because of their own limitations, underestimate other human beings and say that there can be a substitute for *dhyana*, meditation upon the living words of Krishna. There is none. No man can fully comprehend the *Bhagavad Gita* the first time he reads it, nor indeed, even if he reads it every day for the whole of his life. There are Hindus who merely take one stanza and chant it endlessly. This helps, though it cannot substitute for a study of all eighteen chapters. People often turn to the *Gita* only in times of distress. They get solace, but it is transitory. There are others who learn the whole of the *Bhagavad Gita* by heart in Sanskrit and intone it repeatedly. This may help as well, depending upon their state of consciousness. If they are thinking only of themselves, they have thereby blocked the inner channel to the divine flame concealed within and they cannot light the lamp of the heart. They cannot erect the throne upon which alone Krishna can preside with regal glory. There are still others who invoke Krishna at festivals, for the sake of getting a child, or for the sake of the means of livelihood that will enable the family to go through another year in times of trouble. There are those who invoke Krishna for the sake of consecrating the simple little book children use in learning the alphabet. There are those who at certain times of the year exchange gifts for the sake of bringing a little joy into the hearts of each other. Innumerable are the ways in which human beings seek to become worthy of a relationship with Krishna, the Divine Lover, the eternal darling of every *gopi*, the supreme guardian of each devotee.

During the sad prelude to the Mahabharata war, every effort had been made by Krishna, by myriad devices, to avoid a carnage that became increasingly inevitable. This was due to the demonic will of one man — Duryodhana — and the weaknesses, compromises and corruptions of other men, coupled with the fear of taking decisions which could avoid what many knew would be a catastrophe. When all attempts failed, Krishna made a speech in the court of the blind King Dhritarashtra, father of all the sons who were now going to be arrayed on two sides in the arena of confrontation. Krishna was known as a child as a prankster and as a young man as a flute player who charmed the milkmaids. In his manhood he was first involved in the slaying of demons, but also advised the court of King Dhritarashtra. At the critical point, he came to the king and said, in one of the greatest speeches in the Mahabharata, "For the sake of a village, an individual may have to be sacrificed; for the sake of a nation, a village; for the sake of the world, a nation; for the sake of the universe, a world." The whole must prevail, not the part. Then he appealed to the blind king to avoid the horrors of war. He said, "Bind that man." For the sake of the demonic will, the insatiable insecurity, the endless egotism of one man who was sick, so many people could not suffer. It became clear to the whole court that this was not idle talk, but the king himself was too weak, too exhausted, to be able to take such a painful decision at that moment. A definite choice would have been impossible for him, given his habit of shilly-shallying. Krishna, knowing that the battle was unavoidable, went to Duryodhana and asked him to choose between himself and his finely trained warriors. Duryodhana scowled and said, "I can use all these people, but what can I do with you, one person? What can you do that is crucial?" So he chose the armies. Krishna went to each and every person and said, "You can have one gift, but only one. Choose what you want and you shall have it." And, of course, many only chose some paltry and ephemeral object of sense-desire from the great marketplace of the world. Arjuna alone was left with the option of either choosing or not choosing, accepting or not accepting, Krishna as his sole companion. Arjuna chose Krishna as his charioteer without really knowing why. Hence the questions raised by him in the *Bhagavad Gita*. Arjuna was so filled with doubt that he simply could not understand the implications of his choice or the meaning of the war until, in the ninth chapter, Krishna addressed him, saying, "Unto thee who findeth no fault, I shall now make known this most mysterious wisdom." Krishna then gave to Arjuna a vision of the universal mystery because Arjuna had become unconditional in his devotion.

Krishna does not do this for everyone, but because he excludes none and loves each and all, he can give each one something. Therefore, we are told, "Those who devote themselves to the gods go to the gods; the worshippers of the *pitris* go to the *pitris*; those who worship the evil spirits go to them, and my worshippers come to me." He says of those who worship him silently and secretly, as the Self of all creatures and manifested in any form and no form, as well as in the form of their chosen precepts, that they, "knowing me to be the *Adhibhuta*, the *Adhidaivata* and the *Adhiyajna*, know me also at the time of death."

So inexhaustible is the joy of the *Gita*, that any person, even late in life or after many tragic failures along the path, may turn to it and hear the regenerating rhythms and authentic accents of universal Wisdom. Even if a person were to see that his whole life was meaningless and without importance to a single living being, still, in making his obeisance to Krishna, he will find that he is not excluded from the boundless generosity of the Logos. Divine men, like Krishna and Buddha, and those of their tribe — the race of deathless kings, perfected beings, immortals from the Isle of the Blessed who move among men in many disguises — can help each and every man according to the manner of his devotion. "In whatever way," says Krishna, "men worship me, in that way shall I assist them." The flute of Krishna sings of unconditional love and infallible help. The limits are only set by those who ask in relation to what they are ready to receive. This is the priceless teaching, replete with boundless joy and timeless relevance for every honest and humble seeker, for each blessed devotee.

BUDDHI YOGA
AND SVADHARMA

Whosoever knoweth me to be the mighty Ruler of the universe and without birth or beginning, he among men, undeluded, shall be liberated from all his sins. Subtle perception, spiritual knowledge, right judgement, patience, truth, self-mastery; pleasure and pain, prosperity and adversity; birth and death, danger and security, fear and equanimity, satisfaction, restraint of body and mind, alms-giving, inoffensiveness, zeal and glory and ignominy, all these the various dispositions of creatures come from me. So in former days the seven great Sages and the four Manus who are of my nature were born of my mind, and from them sprang this world. He who knoweth perfectly this permanence and mystic faculty of mine becometh without doubt possessed of unshaken faith. I am the origin of all; all things proceed from me; believing me to be thus, the wise gifted with spiritual wisdom worship me; their very hearts and minds are in me; enlightening one another and constantly speaking of me, they are full of enjoyment and satisfaction. To them thus always devoted to me, who worship me with love, I give that mental devotion (Buddhi Yoga) *by which they come to me. For them do I out of my compassion, standing within their hearts, destroy the darkness which springs from ignorance by the brilliant lamp of spiritual discernment.*

Bhagavad Gita, X

Lord Krishna represents the universality and versatility of boundless joy *(ananda)* and the unconditional love at the core of cosmic and human evolution. Wherever thought has struggled to be free, wherever the human heart has opened itself to the invisible Spiritual Sun, and wherever even a drop of wisdom has been awakened through suffering and pain, courage and persistence, there you will find the immortal Spirit, the sovereign power of the omnipresent *Purusha.* All the Rishis and Mahatmas reside within the universal form *(brahmanda)* of Vishnu-Narayana-Krishna. In saluting them, one experiences a sense of the timeless, a transcendence that reaches beyond all limits, frontiers and boundaries of manifestation. One may greet the Supreme in the midnight sun, in the dawn of Venus, at midday or in the gathering dusk — the time of memory or the time of reverie. And one must always reach out towards that Divine Darkness which is prior to all worlds and beyond all forms. Myriads upon myriads of worlds of billions of beings arise from that Divine Darkness and reside in the unmanifest light of the invisible form of Vishnu-Narayana.

That light neither rises nor sets, neither waxes nor wanes. It is the same light which, in the words of the Gospel according to John, irradiates every soul that comes into this world. It is the light to be found in the sound of the AUM, uttered, however imperfectly, by every baby at birth. It is the light that descends upon every human being at the moment of death, when he or she stands ready to cast off the external garments of this world and return to the inmost vesture, the *karana sharira,* and come closer to the *Atman.* It is also the light-vibration of the ever-present Brahma Vach that pulsates throughout the cosmos, maintained in motion by mighty men of meditation, Dhyanis, Rishis, Mahatmas, Buddhas and Bodhisattvas. All human beings can return, again and again, to sit at the feet of Lord Krishna and so learn how to brighten their lives and awaken compassion in their hearts.

Every pilgrim soul who seeks to increase skill in action for the sake of increasing his or her capacity to add even a little to the sum of human good can benefit from the Teachings of Lord Krishna in the *Bhagavad Gita.* Taken as a whole, the *Gita* is a treatise on yoga, the kingly science, of the individual soul's union with the universal Self. That union is, ontologically, ever existent. But because of the maya of manifestation and the descent of consciousness through vestures which seem to create a world of many selves and many forms, the human mind becomes alienated from the true inmost Self in which Ishvara resides. It becomes confined within time and space, within past, present and future, and it must struggle to overcome these illusions. Thus the whole of the *Gita* is a summons and challenge to engage in that righteous warfare which every human soul must undertake. In the eighteenth chapter of the Gita, Lord Krishna declares that if one will not voluntarily choose to engage in this righteous war, karmic necessity will compel one to do so. The wise are those who cooperate with cosmic necessity, with their own divine destiny, with their own sacrosanct duty or *svadharma*. The wisest are those who choose as firmly and as early as possible, making an irreversible and unconditional commitment, in the gracious manner and generous spirit of Lord Krishna. Without doubt or hesitation, they choose His path, His teaching and His prescribed mode of skill in action.

In the second chapter of the *Gita*, Krishna begins by affirming to Arjuna the eternal existence of one indivisible, inconsumable, inexhaustible Source of all life, light and energy. Having dispelled the danger that Arjuna would abandon through fear the righteous battle and his *svadharma*, Krishna presents before Arjuna the talismanic teaching of *Buddhi Yoga*:

> Yet the performance of works is by far inferior to mental devotion (*Buddhi Yoga*), O despiser of wealth. Seek an asylum, then, in this mental devotion, which is knowledge; for the miserable and unhappy are those whose impulse to action is found in its reward. But he who by means of yoga is mentally devoted dismisses alike successful and unsuccessful results, being beyond them; yoga is skill in the performance of actions: therefore do thou aspire to this devotion. For those who are thus united to knowledge and devoted, who have renounced all reward for their actions, meet no rebirth in this life, and go to that eternal blissful abode which is free from all disease and untouched by troubles.
>
> *Ibid.*, II

Buddhi Yoga requires a fixity and steadfastness in intuitive intelligent intelligent determination which is superior to *Karma Yoga,* the yoga of works, as a means of gaining enlightenment. It involves an eye capable of recognizing essentials, which, once awakened, will give a decisiveness without wavering or wandering. Through this resolute intellect, one's actions may become shadowless — *nischaya.* Even though one may be obscured, as a member of the human family participating in the world's pain, ignorance and turbulence, nonetheless one inwardly preserves the dignity of the power of choice. It is, therefore, possible to touch within oneself that level of absolute resolve which ensures that something essential will never be abandoned, or diluted or doubted, never weakened by careless speech nor lost in the chaos of compulsive acts, but always protected from discursive and dissecting Manasic reasoning. Every human being enjoys such moments of assurance. Otherwise it would not be possible to survive. Even fools and knaves have a few moments of *sushupti* at night inspiring them to awaken in the morning to greet another day. Were it not for this abiding sense of assurance about one's minimum dignity within the core of one's being, one could not go on.

This sense of one's distinct place in the total scheme of things is what Spinoza called the *conatus,* the urge or will to sustain rational and spiritual self-preservation. This is not merely an intellectual notion, but a biological fact. When a person begins to approach death, the *anahata* vibration in the spiritual heart ceases to sound in the *linga sharira.* The Sage or Seer can recognize this cessation of sound and a subtle alteration in the rate of breathing several months before the time of physical death. Throughout this period, the human being is engaged in a protracted review of the whole of his or her life, a review which is too often chaotic and confused, a jumble of recent memories and childhood events. Only at the time of separation from the physical body is the soul enabled to view in an orderly and rapid manner the entire film of an entire life. In the final preparation for this there is an ebbing of the connection between the sound vibration in the spiritual heart and the *karana sharira* and the vibration in the *linga sharira*, and therefore also in the *sthula sharira*. Once this ebbing begins, the person has begun to withdraw or die.

The sense of resolve and human dignity is so weak in human beings today that vast numbers, in the phrase of T.S. Eliot, are only "living and partly living". They have become so disgusted with the world, so confused about the events of our times and the precipitous decline of humane values throughout the globe, that they are hardly incarnated. They are mostly asleep or sleep-walking, drowsy or passive, or they mechanically go about their duties. They maintain none of that minimal wakefulness that is found in many a humble villager who, through desperation and poverty, maintains intact the light in the eyes, the light of *Manas* and human self-awareness. Paradoxically, one can sometimes sense the ray and radiance of pure consciousness in the most desperate and despised of human beings, whilst others have, alas, been educated beyond their capacity to make use of their knowledge. Between the head and the heart there is a terrible chasm, or even a battle. Many tend to be lost and therefore they live and partly live. It is as if the will to live, the *conatus*, has weakened; nothing remains but an automatism of habit and the power of cohesion in the *skandhas*. This is the pitiable condition referred to by Lord Krishna when he speaks of those who are wedded to the fruits of action. The plight of those who have conditioned themselves only to act for the sake of results is an indictment of modern education in Kali Yuga. The Iron Age arms too many people to live only in terms of what is perceptible, measurable and tangible. Having reduced all to the terms of a utilitarian consciousness, they come to view their fellow human beings in a crude Lockean fashion: "Every human being is a threat to you, unless you can join interests with him." If a person is neither a threat nor an accomplice in some selfish interest, he is a stranger. Today vast numbers of human beings live in cities of strangers. They live alone amidst humanity, unloved, with no sense of warmth. Such is the tragic condition of 'modern man'.

Over five thousand years ago Lord Krishna anticipated this condition of *varnashankar*, the confusion of castes. Although it will increase and proceed throughout the entirety of Kali Yuga, it will also provide an opportunity for those who engage consciously and voluntarily in a discipline of intuitive determination, *Buddhi Yoga*. Human beings who are yoked to *Buddhi* are lifelong exemplars of *Buddhi Yoga*. Preferably before the age of seven, and in rare cases even before the age of three, they have permanently married themselves to the Light of the Logos within the secret spiritual heart. Having so early betrothed themselves and permanently married themselves to the Lord within, they go through the obligations of life with ease, without much expectation, but with a certain lightness and skillfulness in the performance of duty. They do what is needed for their parents and grandparents. They do not despise those who claim to be their rivals or enemies. They do not become too attached to their own siblings, and see themselves as essentially no different from the other children they encounter from poorer families, from humbler circumstances, or even from rich and unhappy families. All of them they recognize as a part of one sacred family.

Between the ages of seven and fourteen, having already secretly betrothed themselves to this inner core of the Ishvara within, they become quite ready to engage in the duties of the *grihastha ashrama*. At the same time, they have cultivated that skill in self-education which will last all through the *grihastha ashrama* and take them into the third *ashrama*. Even if they cannot retreat into the solitude of forests, mountains or caves, but remain in the midst of society, they will be like wanderers or *parivrajakas*, preparing themselves for the fourth *ashrama*. They will always be one step ahead of the stages of life. By the age of twenty-one they will have sharpened their powers of reason and by the age of twenty-eight they will have developed sufficient Buddhic insight to be able to synthesize and select. So they are able to let go of what is irrelevant and inessential. They can follow the teaching of Buddha: "O Bhikshu, lighten the boat if you will cross to the other shore." While others who are less wise are engaged in amassing and accumulating, they learn to lighten their claims upon the world and their demands upon others. By lightening their expectations from institutions, their hopes and fantasies in relation either to the opposite sex or in relation to children or parents, they become capable of looking with eyes of wonder each day for what is unexpected. They begin to perceive the unwritten poetry of human life and the silent drama of human existence. Thus they become witnesses to the divine dialectic ceaselessly at work.

Such souls are fortunate, for they have chosen to become yoked to *Buddhi*. Having established true continuity of consciousness in youth, by the age of thirty-five they have already started withdrawing. At the moment of death, whether it come early or late, they are able to engage in a conscious process of withdrawal, maintaining intact the potency of the AUM. In life they have not merely learnt to meditate upon the AUM, but also to enact it. They have learnt the art of will-prayer and gained the ability to act in any and every situation for the good of others, without expectation of reward. They have learnt to cast their actions, like offerings, into the ocean of universal sacrifice in the spirit of the AUM. Thus they are able to experience the AUM, whether in the silence that precedes the dawn or in the noisy rush and din of cities. Even in the cacophony and cries of human pain they hear the AUM. It cries out to them in all of Nature's voices. So they maintain continually an awareness of the AUM, and well before the moment of death they are able to receive the help that will enable them to follow a life of *svadharma* and *Buddhi Yoga* in their future incarnations.

Having given Arjuna preliminary instruction in *Buddhi Yoga* in chapter two of the *Gita*, Krishna conveys in chapter four the correct mental posture of the disciple. He depicts that divine *bhakti* which is the prerequisite for *jnana* and also the true spirit of *Karma Yoga*, because they all fuse into a sacred current of consciousness.

Seek this wisdom by doing service, by strong search,
by questions, and by humility; the wise who see the

truth will communicate it unto thee, and knowing
which thou shalt never again fall into error, O son of
Bharata. By this knowledge thou shalt see all things and
creatures whatsoever in thyself and then in me.

Ibid., IV

In this depiction of the perfect posture of the chela, Krishna
stresses the humility of the wise and the silence of the strong,
virtues of the Sage whose portrait was given in the second chapter
of the *Gita.* Having conveyed this ideal posture, Krishna proceeds
in the seventh chapter to present *Buddhi* as an element in cosmic
manifestation. Here he goes beyond the teachings of the Sankhya
School, which holds that *Buddhi* is a kind of radiant matter or
substance present throughout all Nature. Krishna affirms *Buddhi*
as wisdom itself and inseparable from himself, something that
no human being can develop except by the grace of the Lord.

In all creatures I am the life, and the power of
concentration in those whose minds are on the spirit.
Know me, O son of Pritha, as the eternal seed of all
creatures. I am the wisdom *(Buddhi)* of the wise and
the strength *(tejas)* of the strong.

Ibid., VII

To understand this a human being must be able to insert
himself or herself into the whole of humanity, recognizing that
there is a cosmic force working in human evolution. This is
Mahabuddhi, connected with *Mahat* and *Akasha,* the Alkahest of
the hierophants and magicians. It is the universal solvent and the
elixir of life. It is the basis of self-conscious immortality and self-
conscious transmutation of the *linga sharira* and the *sthula sharira.*
It is the Light of the Logos. All expressions of intelligence —
whether latent, partial or highly specialized, whether precise,
diffused or merely potential, whether in a dog or an Adept —
are drops in one universal shoreless ocean of cosmic *Buddhi.*
Therefore, no human being can develop *Buddhi Yoga* on the basis
of individualistic conceptions of progress. One cannot simply say

to oneself that because one has seen through one's illusions, one is now going to become an apprentice in *Buddhi Yoga*. To say that is to misapprehend the nature of the quest. All forms of yoga require, at some level, what M.K. Gandhi called *anashakti*, egolessness; this is supremely true in *Buddhi Yoga*.

In the practice of spiritual archery one must forget oneself. One can do this meaningfully only if, at the same time, one remains spiritually awake. One must become intensely conscious of one's kinship with all of creation, capable of enjoying its beauty and intelligence without any sense of 'mine' or 'thine'. Wherever there is a display of wisdom, one must salute it. Wherever one finds an exhibition of that true common sense which is helpful in the speech of any human being, one must acknowledge and greet it. This does not mean merely saying *"Namaste"* outwardly, but inwardly bowing down, prostrating oneself before others. At night, before falling asleep, one must count all the benefactors and teachers that one met during the day. No matter how they are disguised, you must be so taken up in rejoicing that you have learnt from other human beings that you have no time to complain of injustice or to become discontented, let alone contentious and cantankerous. In the *Uttara Gita*, long after the Mahabharata War had ended, Krishna told Arjuna that every time one speaks unnecessarily or falsely, one's astral shadow lengthens. If one speaks unwisely, harshly or without thought and deliberation, one expands and fattens the *linga sharira*. One creates a smoky obscuration of the power of *tejas*, the light within the spiritual heart. The true *yogin* does the opposite, becoming very conscious and deliberate in the exercise of mental and therefore uttered speech. He learns the art of what D.K. Mavalankar calls self-attenuation. Through this stripping away of inessentials, one becomes capable of maximizing one's every use of life-energy.

Paradoxically, one cannot acquire this self-mastery without recognizing that one cannot do it on one's own. Therefore, Krishna teaches that the power of universal *Buddhi* is an omnipresent essence. Krishna is the radiance in all that is radiant and the intelligence in all the intelligences in the universe. Thus it is only by Krishna's gift that one can arouse that power of devotion which brings the disciple to him. This ultimate paradox, which can be understood in relation to music and love, is vital to spiritual life. It is not only that one must strive and try; a moment comes when one is so absorbed in the object of the quest that one feels the magnetic attraction of that which one seeks. Therefore, the more one enjoys being drawn towards the Lord, the more one can recognize and receive His gift of *Buddhi Yoga*. To prepare oneself to use the gift of the Lord, one must, as the second chapter of the *Gita* teaches, become a spiritual archer, skilled in the art of action. One must become perfected in the precise performance of one's self-chosen duty or *svadharma*. Initially, when Krishna uses the term *svadharma* in the second chapter of the *Gita*, he uses it in relation to the duties of birth, of calling and of caste. He chides Arjuna for forsaking the *svadharma* of a Kshatriya. He suggests that if one does not fulfil one's own obligations, chosen and accepted over lifetimes, and if one does not come to terms with the limits, possibilities and opportunities of one's birth, one is moving in the wrong direction and will accrue much evil. Even this initial definition of *svadharma* in terms of one's starting-point in life is much more than a reference to mere occupation and caste.

In the early years of life, most human beings have so little meaningful choice with regard to circumstances that it is difficult to talk credibly of freedom at an early age. Nonetheless, there is for every human being a clear opportunity to accept or not accept that which one cannot alter. In that context, one may be said to choose one's *svadharma*. The concept of choosing that which one cannot change is not fatalism. Rather, it is a critical assessment in consciousness of those elements in one's life which are innate. In the very act of understanding and in the attempt to give meaning to these initial parameters, one must develop and apply some understanding of the karmic field. Moreover, by understanding the karmic tendencies in one's own constitution and confronting one's likes and dislikes, one may come to sense something about one's lower nature and gain some understanding of one's possible behaviour in other lives. Thus, one will recognize that in one's family, for all its obvious limitations, there may be many opportunities for enjoyment and for learning. All true soul-education is an unfoldment through worship and affection, and it is open to every human being to make all life a celebration of learning.

If one really wishes, through the power of worship coupled with affection, to become skilled in the performance of duties, one must recognize that there are those who have gone beyond the initial stages of *Buddhi Yoga*. They have become constant in the power of *Jnana Yoga*, men and women of ceaseless meditation and contemplation. They are the Buddhas and Bodhisattvas of ceaseless contemplation, constantly ideating and thereby sustaining the possibility of human aspiration. They are able to do this through their conscious choice of mental solitude and their freedom from attraction and repulsion. Above all, they exemplify perfection of mental devotion. They have become supremely steadfast, like the immovable Himalayas. They are rock-like in their strength of *tapas, bhakti* and *dhyana*. Krishna repeatedly gives encouragement to all beginners making their first tentative steps on the path by urging them to discern in themselves something in common with the highest beings who have ever existed. He offers to Arjuna a living portrait, in potent words, of the true Sage. Whilst it is difficult for modern man to understand, there are in fact many more sages, *munis* and *yogins* than guessed by human beings incarnated on earth. Whilst there are billions upon billions of human beings, there are also galaxies of adepts and Bodhisattvas. Whilst they are invisible to the physical senses, they nonetheless exist and they all have their roles in the task of cosmic and human evolution.

To become capable of recognizing them and saluting them means that it is possible to gain some light with regard to one's own *svadharma*. Hence, Krishna affirms that it is even better to die in one's own *svadharma* than to be concerned with the duty of another. Even if little is going to change significantly in one's life, the acquisition of wisdom always remains possible and worthwhile. It is a useful mental exercise just to imagine that one is going to die in exactly one's present situation. Then, without giving any room to fantasy and expectation, one must understand how, through this acceptance of immediate *svadharma*, one may strengthen the power of mental devotion or *Buddhi Yoga*. Growth in the power of sacrifice or *Jnana Yajna* is always possible in every circumstance. But that growth requires a turning away from the region of separative consciousness towards the realm of the united hosts of perfected performers of yoga who reside within the universal form of Krishna.

To begin to apprehend this is to begin to prepare for the opening of the Wisdom-Eye, a process that is beatified by the realization of the universal vision given to Arjuna by Krishna in the eleventh chapter of the *Gita*. At the end of that vision Krishna makes a statement which is the foundation of all self-conscious transcendence: "I established this whole universe with a single portion of myself, and remain separate." Here Krishna is the paradigm of the Pythagorean spectator, the *Kutastha*, he who is aloof and apart from all manifestation. He is the fount of those great Dhyanis who descend in the dawn of manifestation, knowing its limits and uninvolved while performing their tasks in manifestation. Maintaining their continuity of consciousness and self-transcendence in the Logos, they remain free from the hypnotic spell of *Mahamaya*. What is exemplified by Dhyanis in the dawn of manifestation is repeatedly re-enacted in the course of human evolution when human beings, by the power of *vairagya* — true dispassion established by the power of a vow of fixed determination — are able to generate a continuous current of Buddhic insight. Establishing and maintaining this current, testing it in action and correcting themselves by it, individuals may become constant witnesses to the truth. After a while, their minds become so firmly yoked to Buddhic discrimination that it becomes as natural as breathing. In many Buddhist schools and sanctuaries, particularly in the Hinayana tradition, neophytes are taught to observe their breathing. When coupled with the

Mahayana refinement of motive, this can serve as the enduring basis of bare mindfulness and pure attention.

Vinoba Bhave sums up the whole teaching of *svadharma* in the *Gita* in terms of the concept of *chittashuddhi* — purity of consciousness. All human beings, even in Kali Yuga, and even surrounded by pollutions, are capable of mental purification. All are capable of maintaining unbroken and intact a stream of pure consciousness, but this requires spiritual food. One must learn to devise one's own rituals and sacrifices, to treat one's body as a temple in which one will greet and bathe in the Light of the Logos. One must learn to consecrate one's own vesture, becoming wholehearted, uncalculating and without expectation in one's relationship with Krishna. When through self-consecration *bhakti* and *buddhi* come together, *jnana* is released. From *jnana* one may eventually rise to *dhyana*, ceaseless contemplation. Then it is possible to return to *svadharma* and understand it in the salvific sense expressed by Krishna in the eighteenth chapter of the *Gita*. There Krishna puts *svadharma* in terms of a universal formula, independent of birth, of early circumstances, of vocation and calling. It is the art of discovering one's true nature, and therefore becoming creative in one's capacity for self-expression.

Each human being is an original, and each act is unique. Out of enjoyment of the cosmic *lila* and out of veneration for the universal form and omnipresent light of Krishna, a human being can become unrestricted and spontaneous in enacting and delivering *svadharma*. There is a great joy in this and such *ananda* is so all-absorbing that there is no time to interfere with other people or to criticize them. There is no distraction in relation to the demands of *dharma*. Instead, there is full concentration on becoming a servant and instrument of the universal Logos in the cosmos, the God in man, Krishna in the heart.

> With thy heart place all thy works on me, prefer me to all else, exercise mental devotion (*Buddhi Yoga*) continually, and think constantly of me. By so doing thou shalt by my divine favour surmount every

difficulty which surroundeth thee; but if from pride thou wilt not listen to my words, thou shalt un-doubtedly be lost. And if, indulging self-confidence, thou sayest 'I will not fight', such a determination will prove itself vain, for the principles of thy nature will impel thee to engage. Being bound by all past karma to thy natural duties, thou, O son of Kunti, wilt involuntarily do from necessity that which in thy folly thou wouldst not do. There dwelleth in the heart of every creature, O Arjuna, the Master —Ishvara — who by his magic power causeth all things and creatures to revolve mounted upon the universal wheel of time. Take sanctuary with him alone, O son of Bharata, with all thy soul; by his grace thou shalt obtain supreme happiness, the eternal place.

Ibid., XVIII

To become a true votary of *Buddhi Yoga* through the performance of *svadharma* is to become ready to serve the divine will of the *Atman,* the workings of the Logos and the Avatar behind all the turbulent sifting and chaos of the historical process. The *Buddhi Yogin* recognizes the intimations of the divine dialectic in maturing human beings, mellowing minds and hearts, broadening and expanding their quintessential humanity. Cooperating with the Light of the Logos within, they are able to rediscover the germ of purity of consciousness and thereby enter the family of the wise, the fraternity who know all of this and exemplify it ceaselessly. The true hallmark of these Rishis and Mahatmas is the power of devotion and adoration. They are constant in adoration of Krishna, His *lila,* His wisdom, the joy of His dance, the beauty of His unconditionality. They understand from within themselves the way in which Krishna may be seen in Arjuna, in Arjuna's aspiration to reach up to Krishna, and also in Krishna's enjoyment of the seeming separation of himself from himself in Arjuna. This is the mysterious art of the universal diffusion of the one Light, the problem of the One and the many, and the participation of the many in the One. Through *Buddhi*

Yoga, bhakti and *svadharma* there can be a self- conscious return
to the One, but only on behalf of the many. This is the sacred
teaching of Lord Krishna in the *Bhagavad Gita*, given to sustain
humanity throughout Kali Yuga. All may benefit from the
teaching, returning to it again and again, using it in individual
ways, enjoying and appreciating its beauty. Those who are
perceptive and appreciate this great gift will make resolute vows
to be steadfast in maintaining unbroken a sacred relationship with
the Teaching and its great Giver.

SHIVA AND SELF-REGENERATION

There is neither teacher nor teaching, learner nor learning, neither thou nor I, nor this empirical universe; I am universal self-consciousness, the reality which is untinctured by any modification. I am the secondless, supreme and attributeless Bliss of Shiva.

SHRI SHANKARACHARYA

S hiva is the supreme principle of potent ideation and constructive imagination, bridging the unconditioned and the conditioned, the unlimited and the limited, the boundless and what is bounded in the realm of time. Shiva represents a noumenal intelligence ceaselessly at work in the life process through all the elemental, mineral, vegetable and animal kingdoms of Nature. Shiva is also accessible to each and every human being, not only the highest and the holiest, but also the most sinful and depraved whenever they have a flash of true repentance. The mundane realm, of course, is that wherein most human beings encounter a host of difficulties, because they cannot connect disparate elements of fleeting experience or else are victims of false connections that bombard them from outside. Human beings must resolve to stand on their own. They need to wake up to the fact that each is alone in this world, that in the end each is the custodian of his or her own hopes and promises, and that each is the only agent able to make a radical change in his or her own kingdom. This is not a task that can be transferred to any other agent.

A person who comes to understand this is ready to contemplate Shiva as a *yogin*, as the archetypal Man of Renunciation, as the paradigm of the pilgrim soul who has been through every possible experience of every possible human being.

But Shiva can also be seen constantly at work destroying the froth of complacent illusion through disintegration. Shiva represents the universal frustration of all the foolish and faulty plans of deluded souls. In other words, Shiva epitomizes the insight that most of human history is based upon a terrible expenditure of emotion, an attempt to force upon this world schemes which must inevitably be frustrated because they are based upon the lie of separateness and cannot be supported by the cosmos. Beyond the lower realms of Nature and beyond the human realm, Shiva is the living metaphysical link between the unmanifest and the manifest Logos.

Since most problems arise in the middle or human realm, wherein individuals must learn to take a stand, Shiva is initially most relevant as the archetype of every seeker on earth. There is a specific point at which individuals are ready to take stock of the sum total of their experiences and to cut through the compulsive succession of dreamy, illusionary experiences. For the individual at this crossroad, Shiva becomes the paradigm of the perfect human being who is fully self-conscious. Within all the traumas and tragedies of human beings there lies latent the seed of self-awareness which enables an individual — whether in a future life, or at the moment of death, or many years later in this life — to cut through the froth. Shiva represents the pristine seed of a new beginning rooted in the Truth that makes one fearless. This signifies a new kind of courage — to see all the phases of life together and to cut through the process of *samsara*.

Unfortunately, too many human beings are ready to renounce only after they have been burnt out by their previous refusals to renounce and by the enormous burden of their exaggerated and ever-growing attachments. There is, therefore, a certain sadness in the eyes of a person who starts the climb towards the mountains, often at an advanced age, in the hope that at least his few remaining years may not be wasted in delusion. When one renounces separateness, one's life opens itself up to all human lives, to the enormity and vast Himalayan scope of the human pilgrimage, encompassing not only friends and relatives, but all human beings — strangers in the city, strangers in the streets, millions upon millions of persons who live and toil in extreme conditions of deprivation and desolation. Everywhere human beings are caught up without meaning in a life that is extremely hard economically or enormously wasteful in its focus upon providing for the passing fancies and endless consumption of other human beings. Everywhere there is the pain of emptiness, of fatigue, excess and self-indulgence. But there is also the pain of actual deprivation and the pain of loneliness.

The challenge of Shiva today is to learn to relate to all these beings. What has always been true has now come much more to a head. Many human beings are living lives of utter waste, yet the very impulse that gives one the courage to go back to sleep after a trying day can become something more. It can become the courage to renounce the whole concept of the self bound up with memories and frustrations. It can quicken a sense of a larger self, a sense of involvement in the self of all humanity, and a concern for the wider horizon of human consciousness transcending the visible, the partial and the transitory.

In that fearless willingness to renounce, such a person has not only the actual inspiration of Shiva as an ideal or object — whether as a *linga*, or a statue, or as the author of certain texts, or as the supreme god Maheshvara who presides over and transcends the process of creation — but also as an actual hierophantic *yogin*. In Gupta Vidya, Shiva is Dakshinamurti, the Initiator of Initiates, responsible for the Mysteries in the Third, Fourth and Fifth Root-Races. Shiva was involved in all the triumphs and travails of the human race going back to Atlantean times, and Shiva will also be involved in all the heroic struggles of human beings for millions of years into the future, until the emergence of the Sixth Race. It is as if all the knowledge of all human souls in their desperate gropings towards the Mysteries is engraved within his sphinx-like face. He is the silent witness to their terrible failures. At the same time, he also bears shining witness to the vital hint of hope that all may one day begin anew and make a fresher, cleaner, better start.

Shiva, then, has a universal meaning, whether one has explicitly heard or thought much about him or not. No human being who experiences suffering and deep disappointment, no one who is frightened by what lies ahead when death draws near or who deeply reflects upon the suffering of humanity can help but see that something new is needed to understand the human predicament. Something is needed which involves going within, and it comes from silence rather than speech, from brooding rather than verbalizing. It involves thinking deeply and with total honesty about oneself, acknowledging every tendency of prevarication, doubt, procrastination, contradiction, ambivalence, ill will, envy, jealousy, hatred, pride and vulnerability. The willingness to enter into the dungeon within the psyche in which these demons exist, and the strength to come out of it courageously, vindicate Shiva. Shiva represents the assured capacity to reduce delusions to ashes. The fire of spiritual perception and objective honesty, the light of pure *Manas,* can burn out psychic dross which is powerful only because of a misplaced allegiance to a false persona. This is a long and painful process of purification. It takes years and lives to complete. If it is a true beginning, however, it will have the benediction of all those who have made similar beginnings and who have attained to some level of success on the side of that which is strong in the human race.

What characterizes wise beings, Initiates, Teachers and Mahatmas is the unconditional faith they can place in every single human being, against all odds, despite the past and whatever the record. This is not faith in something merely potential, but faith in that which is omnipresent, sacred and indestructible. It is like a cry to the divine and an affirmation of willingness to persist, to be tested, to sift and select ever more clearly and wisely. Such a faith implies increasing silence, with less propensity to manifest in the coming years, so that one begins to take on the burden of living with more deliberation and more dignity. This resolve and the very desire to make it, as well as the willingness to persist in it, draw upon that which Shiva represents. Rather than being a negative view of human despair, it is a fearless recognition of the myriads of forgotten instances of extraordinary redemption. Something Christ-like and Buddha-like has happened again and again among millions of human beings, and yet it has been accompanied by a colossal sense of waste, suffering and frustration caused by false consolidation of the ego. All this involves vast magnitudes. To talk of Shiva is thus to get beyond a narrow focus upon one's own horizon and to take one's own place within the larger whole. This is not something vague. It requires hard work, the effort of thinking through the problem and beginning to look at all beings in a different way.

While many of the obstacles that emerge are the familiar ones, they appear in different forms. One of them provides a clue to the subtle connection between love and asceticism. Shiva represents that strength which results from voluntary self-control carried to its highest point, where it becomes effortless and full of joy. As the paradigm of *yogins*, Shiva is often depicted as besmeared with ashes, carrying a necklace of skulls. This signifies a clarity of vision in which there is no truck with human fantasy, desire or ambition. It represents a courageous recognition of the underground in which most human beings live. This terrible Hades exists owing to the ugliness of human presumption. While there is so much of this everywhere and everyone can see it in themselves, nonetheless, something else that transcends understanding is involved in this perception. A kind of veiling has taken place. One could not see all this ugliness if one were not more than the sum total of all that is repellent, if there were not a seed of Platonic divine discontent moving one constantly towards an ineffable beauty. Shiva stands outside time. He carries in his right hand the drum, which represents the cyclic beat of time, but he himself is beyond time. Even the iconography and mythology of Shiva are amongst the oldest that exist. They precede all known religions and go back at least five to seven thousand years, to ancient coins and seals. They are part of the prehistoric folk memory of mankind. Shiva always has to do with the truth of the human condition, the truth of human failure, the truth of human persistence, and especially the truth of the possibility of human redemption which can only come with freedom from illusion.

Certainly, the effortless asceticism of Shiva was an ideal beyond all possibility for Parvati. As a young girl, totally devoted to Shiva and feeling totally unworthy of him, she nonetheless wanted to give her whole life to Shiva and to receive his guidance and love. Therefore, Parvati went into a tremendous *tapas* lasting thousands of years. It is quite overwhelming to think of so great a preparation — strengthening, purging, purifying oneself — but people have done these things and done them life alter life, thus earning proximity to the great hierophants of the human race. Parvati, propelled by one-pointedness and unconditionality of love, was able to penetrate the veil of Shiva's totally impervious, impartial and cold-seeming impersonality. She was able to touch that in Shiva which knew all along that she had to go through the fire of purgation and trial. Then he could expound to her the most magnificent mystical truths about initiation, reveal to her the magic that is possible in human life, in terms of fundamental philosophical and metaphysical principles, so that she herself came to be revered as a custodian of the Mysteries, invoked like Kwan-Yin for her boundless compassion. She is on everyone's side, and she is immensely resourceful in showing how the door can open for every single being. At the same time, however, she has no illusions, and sees to the core of every human heart.

The essential meaning of the story of Shiva and Parvati involves the hidden heart of the cosmos, the secret heart of humanity and the infinite depths within one's own immortal heart. No education in terms of the imperfect, tortuous and complicating mind has anything to do with true concentration and understanding. Many an athlete learns to concentrate better than a person burdened by words and concepts that have nothing to do with the power of ideation. When the soul's true power of understanding is aroused, it can take wings and remain in a state of deep abstraction for hours, days or even months, visualizing that which must ultimately represent the incarnation of universal

Good. Genuine training in this direction can begin with the exercise of thinking outward through a series of concentric and expanding circles. It is not easy to expand one's horizon to include all visible human beings on earth today, much less to include all human beings. Yet to understand the heart of humanity, one must enlarge one's vision to encompass all human souls that are disembodied. This includes all those who died in recent centuries, leaving their shells in *kamaloka,* as well as all those who died earlier and who are in various stages of *devachan,* ranging from hundreds to thousands of years in duration, and who wake up at different times and come as babies onto the earthly scene, becoming involved in different parts of the world, in different families, as puzzled strangers. To think consciously of all human souls in this enigmatic way is to bring one's mind closer to the perspective of Shiva, for Shiva sees all humanity at once.

In principle, it is possible for a perfected being with such an infinite horizon to be an ideal for imperfect human beings only if we presuppose that all souls can free themselves from captivity to images, captivity to the present and, above all, captivity to the froth that surrounds their conceptions of perfected beings. Even though there may be something precious and noble at the root of one's conception of Shamballa, El Dorado or the Golden Age, psychic excitement is generated the moment one materializes it. This excess produces a plethora of escapist tendencies which result in pathetic and irresponsible human beings who cannot do the most elementary things like sitting, reading or writing. Victims of their own fantasy, they want to escape but find there is nowhere to go. The entire delusion is based upon a lie that is fed by popular literature and movies from which a few make a lot of money trafficking in human illusion. It invades the psyche of millions of human beings, so that they hardly begin to live or to take any responsibility for their lives. Instead of maturing, they are retarded, pushed towards the doom of nihilism. What provides the pressure behind all this is the toughest peer pressure of all, which comes out of *kamaloka.* One may think that it comes from contemporaries, but in fact it comes from *kamaloka* as the raucous cries of those on the verge of annihilation. They are bitter because they were self-righteous before, and even now have no humility or honesty, but curse and curse with unmitigated fury. With their evil-eyed cocksureness about human weakness, they are convinced that there will be more and more hosts of victims coming out of this world who are going to be taken in, trapped in the sacred name of freedom which is misused, and reduced to a condition that is a prelude to disintegration.

Think, then, of the compassion involved in a being who must know all of this. Looking at the world, Shiva can immediately see its pure potential in the golden embryo of every baby. At the same time, seeing the way so many live and the karma they are creating, he can also see them tortured. This torture is psychological. Though artists may sometimes render it in graphic images or poets like Dante may convey it through metaphors of fire and ice, it is in reality terrible mental self-torture. Once set into motion by one's actions, it is inevitable, because all the life-atoms one has ever misused come back to render one completely coiled, impotent and powerless. No amount of cries for forgiveness can cancel the karma. So much toughness is needed by beings who would take all this into account that one is speaking of a perspective far removed from all but the very greatest of human hearts. Only a Buddha or Shakespeare or Jesus could truly begin to understand the immensity of the human condition, the immensity of the human tragedy and the immensity of the cost of illusion. That is why Shiva is so often shown in a terrible form, dancing in the crematorium, garlanded with skulls. He has seen it all, and he has seen through it all. He has seen all the fake *yogins* and pseudo-fakirs, and has also seen the sadder victims, who never learnt how to think for themselves or how to use imagination, speech and self-command to initiate a current for the general good.

As one expands awareness of humanity through ever-increasing concentric circles, in a mythic and mystical sense one is going to enter Hades. One is going to confront the torment of millions of human souls who are snuffed out like candles. This is true whether one considers human beings presently incarnated

on the earth — which looked like a necropolis to some in the
Victorian Age and is still the same — or whether one begins to
be aware of human beings in the invisible realms. The difference
between the invisible world and the physical plane is little indeed.
To be able to see all this and still believe that there is meaning to
it, that everything is totally just and exactly what it is because of
long chains of causation going back over hundreds of lives and
thousands of years, and yet refuse to condemn a single soul,
requires extraordinary courage. No wonder, then, it is impossible
to convey such an experience. It requires the wisdom of Hermes
to assimilate such a perspective, but that wisdom is not only for
the living. It is for the future, when Initiates will come into this
world disguised and disseminate the self-regenerating modes of
new social structures.

Something of this vast perspective can be glimpsed by
looking into the Puranas. Even if one reads just a few passages
from the many volumes of the *Shiva Purana*, one will be amazed
at its scope. The perspective is inclusive of all gods, all Rishis, all
classes of souls. To begin to get a sense of this is to begin to awaken
from the utter absurdity of pseudo-knowledge and gross over-
generalization. It takes courage to recognize that one knows too
little of the human condition and still less of universal good.
Yet one can nonetheless find the strength to enter a series of self-
regenerative meditations. That is what Shiva represents and it is
what Buddha did archetypally. It is what all great beings have
done in the past, and it can be done again at any time by anyone
who is ready to go into the deepest series of meditations. If one
cannot do it indefinitely and sustain it, one can make small
beginnings, using a week or a month, taking advantage of the
cycles of the sun and the moon, and especially times such as
Shivaratri, the vigil night of Shiva. Such times should be used for
spiritual self-regeneration on behalf of the humanity of the future.
One may prepare by spending several days living quietly but
remaining wide awake, sleeping less than normal and eating less.
One could use the time to think about the universal human
condition and one's own life in that context. Courage is needed

for this kind of extended meditation, because once one has begun it, one cannot get out of it. Yet one is glad at certain times to enter a deeper meditation which is even more detached and in which one can tap an even profounder realm of calmness. Then one can empty out everything that comes out of this conditioned world — touch and taste, the waters, the sky, the fire, the flame, the aether, the fire mist, even the most ethereal vesture which is ever invisible behind the cosmos.

At this point, Shiva becomes a link between *Parabrahm* and Ishvara. Shiva, indeed, is in another part of himself Vishnu, and in yet another part Brahmā. These are all words for a single host under a single, supreme Logos. When Shiva has, so to speak, a foot in *Parabrahm*, Shiva has gone to sleep. This is the immovable Shiva, totally indifferent to clime and change, unaffected by earthquakes, cataclysms and geological changes. Untouched by everything, he is the immovable rock, the eternal pillar of light, one with *Parabrahm*, the divine ground in the Divine Darkness. Shiva is also connected to Ishvara, the creative Logos, but Shiva knows that even something so overwhelmingly glorious as Ishvara is only an appearance and a veil. It may last for billions of years, but still that is nothing for Shiva, merely a matter of a few days, according to the old books. What for a human being is a full lifetime is like a moment for Manu, and what is a lifetime for Manu is like a day for Vishnu. But what is like a lifetime for Vishnu is only a day for Shiva. The same immensity of perspective is found in the *Yoga Vasishtha,* particularly in the discourse of Bhusunda to the Sage Vasishtha. Bhusunda is only another name for the immovable Shiva, the Witness of all cycles and vast epochs of manifestation, myriads of worlds and galaxies. This reaches beyond the solar system and what are called stars and constellations in the myths connecting Shiva with Dhruva or Rohini.

This level of contemplation is so timeless and boundless, and at the same time so subtle and mobile, that it is often symbolized by Shiva as the dancing wanderer or beggar who travels in rags and who can be in any and every situation. This perspective is so extraordinary that it is no wonder all the old pictures of Rishis and Mahatmas show them ceaselessly bowing down to Shiva, prostrating before him. They who do so much for humanity over millions of years are in a state of total awe before the immensity of the boundless mental horizon of Shiva. It is mysterious and magical that something so vast and remote is accessible to each and all, and that it can help to regenerate oneself. To earn this help, one must try to burst the boundaries of one's mental and conceptual maps, transcend the luggage picked up along the way through various religions. In talking of Shiva, one is talking of that before which one has to stand speechless because it is so overwhelming. It is like trying daily to look at the sky in order to see one belt of light through all the myriads of stars, and then to go beyond that to an even deeper darkness. This challenge — open only to the mind which is wakeful, courageous and willing to dare — has to do with the ancient Mysteries, which Newton called a pristine science. One cannot go far in learning without recognizing one's place in relation to those who have gone before, those who stand as Teachers and elder brothers. Ultimately, one cannot do this without earning the privilege of entering through meditation into a state of consciousness wherein one can sit and prostrate before the *Ishtaguru*. Only the *Ishtaguru* can light up those centres in human consciousness where one can experience and at the same time accommodate incredible flashes of recognition, seeing one's connection with every being on earth.

There are initiations upon initiations, and Shiva is portrayed as the Initiator of Initiates. As Dakshinamurti, he is depicted in many temples, especially in South India, as a Sage seated cross-legged. He becomes the Teacher, the Initiator of Initiates; the *yogins* he is teaching are the highest human beings in evolution. Yet so great is their overwhelming love for their fellow beings that they sit together like brothers ready to make a new start. Seated in contemplation, Shiva assumes a very specific posture which represents mental and spiritual heroism. This heroism has nothing to do with external conceptions, but involves going into the most arcane recesses of humanity and plumbing to the depths the secret storehouses of all the human race. An extraordinary form of courage is needed for this. Hence, many are called but few are chosen. And of the few that are chosen, few indeed go all the way to complete enlightenment. This is why, as Buddha taught, there can never be more than one such being active in any system at any given time.

Shiva encompasses levels upon levels of consciousness which go far beyond everything one has ever learnt or anything one has ever thought. All this is merely a foot-rule too paltry to measure what is so immense. That is why Mount Kailas̍ is an appropriate symbol of the abode of Shiva. It is not the postal address of the hierophants, but rather a sacred representation on earth, amidst the mightiest mountains and snow-capped peaks, of innumerable secrets and hidden storehouses. Behind the pure virgin white snow, all that is good in humanity is preserved, all that is lofty, all that is elevating, all that comes down to the present from the time man became a thinking being through the lighting up of self-consciousness eighteen and three-quarter million years ago. Every noble thought, everything that is inspirational, altruistic and benevolent is recorded. The beautiful flora and fauna of Mount Kailas̍ are such as one can see nowhere else on earth. They are literally beyond the capacity of biologists to understand or analyse. Mount Kailas̍ is a place where the sheer wealth of Nature's material expression mirrors the inexhaustible potentials of the invisible world. But what are inaccessible potentials in the present age were actualities once, and remain so now for those who know. One day they will again become actualities for the humanities of the future. Within so vast a perspective, it can become as natural as breathing to take one's place in the human family, to do that for which one can respect oneself, without props but with the right reminders. One can face past mistakes and be willing to go into the uttermost contrition. One can also release a resolve, in the name of the Guru, with the Grace of Shiva and all the hierophants of humanity, and so move towards a better position at the moment of death, from which one may return to relieve human misery and ignorance, planting seeds for the enlightenment of future humanity.

CHOOSING THE TAO

Look, it cannot be seen — it is beyond form.
Listen, it cannot be heard — it is beyond sound.
Grasp, it cannot be held — it is intangible.
These three are indefinable;
Therefore they are joined in one.

LAO TZU

Inflexibility of modes cripples our contemporary institutions. Inertia of thought dulls our mental faculties, whilst insensitivity of moral perception weakens the will-power to realize good resolutions. It is conspicuously difficult for the brain-mind, faintly mirroring the chaotic flux of sense-impressions, to sift essential meaning from the monotonous succession of trivia. The *Tao Teh Ching* invites us to withdraw the mind from the cacophony of the world, to liberate the heart from the jungle fever of the passions. Above all, it counsels us to renounce our constricting conceptions of ourselves. These merely echo fleeting externalities extolled by the fickle opinions of the Epimethean crowd, which is sadly captive to crude conceptions of success and failure, status and reward. All such shallow distinctions are entrenched in the feudal shibboleths and the *petit-bourgeois* vocabulary of a commercial culture. They are entangling weeds of pain, sprouting in the parched soil of cavernous delusion, choking the living germs of human encounter. Flexibility is elusive without some degree of detachment. Until a person attains to a mature indifference to the illusory objects of desire and the volatile pairs of opposites, he cannot be truly practical. He cannot become sufficiently plastic in mind, resilient in imagination, creative in sentiment and speech, to enjoy the divine estate to which every human being is heir. To become constructively flexible requires a preliminary purification of the passions, a thorough cleansing of the mind, a deliberate sorting out of the chaos that bewilders one's shadowy self. In seeking to do this, one may initially be restless, anxious and devoid of calm.

One must face the perilous paradox set forth in the ancient mystical texts: the beginning foreshadows the end, the end inheres in the beginning. Without a valiant attempt to negate the world and to void one's very conception of oneself, it is not feasible to take the first critical step on the Path to Enlightenment. Many are called, but few constitute themselves as truly chosen to become sincere and credible servants of the whole of mankind. Nevertheless, many thinking beings have already reached a point of maturation from which they can see through the negative, contradictory and melodramatic valuations of the necropolis. This is a moment in history when Time itself seems to have stopped. Most people know too well that behind the futile exaggerations and false claims of external institutions and structures, there is an emptiness and hollowness, an unfathomable void. At a time of poignant and ever-increasing distance between human beings, there is a danger that aggression and desperation will enter even into the spiritual quest, thereby closing the door to spiritual awakening for myriad lives. This awful if unintended tragedy can be remedied only by courage and toughness in braving mental agony. Divine manliness consists in becoming heroic when it counts and where it hurts, in sacrificing every puny conception of selfhood. Everyone not only glimpses the fundamental truths known to poets, philosophers and sages, but hears them now on the lips of millions of messengers on earth.

The present historical moment offers a golden opportunity to learn from the wisdom of the Tao. For many centuries men contemplated the Tao, though no one in China would have claimed to comprehend it. The first commentary was written in the middle of the second century before Christ, perhaps about four centuries and a half after the appearance of the great Master, Lao Tzu. From birth Lao Tzu was greeted as an old man because he began by showing a mellow awareness of the teaching, and was apparently known by more than one name. Among his closest disciples the most influential was Confucius, in whose memory

elaborate rituals emerged over millennia which eventually became
frozen into stylized play-acting, with massive pride masked by
self-mockery, a tradition of hypocrisy which terminated in a total
disruption of the old order. A fearless Mandarin hinted fifty years
ago that what China needed then was not more gentlemen but
more prisons for its corrupt politicians. The anger of the masses
was directed against endless game-playing in the name of the
Confucian *Analects*. This is a predictable part of the recurring story
of mankind.

The Tao can only be attained by the human being who
approaches the Tao through the Tao. One must become the Tao.
One must meditate ceaselessly upon the Tao while seeming to be
engrossed in the daily round and common task. One must find
the secret sanctuary of inner peace and repose within it from dawn
through dusk to midnight, while retaining calm continuity of
contemplation in the soul's shrine through the sleep of the night
and even amidst dislocating dreams. The process of self-surrender
takes time because it can only become continuous and constant
when it flows from within without, from above below. The Tao
is the motionless centre of all the wheels of cyclic change. It is
the centre which is everywhere, in every point of space, in every
moment of time. Yet no boundaries can ever be drawn to contain
it. Everything participates in the illusion of birth and in the inertia
of systems that hide the simultaneous disintegration and decay
known among men and women as sickness, error, suffering and
death. The Tao teaches that in no single thing will be found any
freedom or exemption from the eternal process of ceaseless change
behind the shadow-play of colours, forms and events. Everything
that has a beginning in time and space must have a limit in space
and an end in time.

Everyone must necessarily seek the Tao within oneself. Each
must seek that which is consubstantial with the Tao that is before
all things. Words like 'before' and 'behind', 'below' and 'above',
can only be relevant to the seeming reflections of the Tao. The
Tao is formless form, the primordial pure substance prior to all
differentiation, and it is accessible to all human beings as the one

and only Source of eternal energy streaming forth in limitless light from the Invisible Sun. It is hidden within what seems to be darkness but is in truth absolute light. It is ever bestowing nourishment and sustenance, shedding light and yielding the vital power of hidden growth. The causal principle of true growth is necessarily invisible to the naked eye. If one is to come to understand how the transcendent Tao is in oneself, or how one can come closer to the Tao within, one must calmly ask how one's false mind and fictitious barriers — self-created, self-maintained, self-imposed limitations — may be pierced by the light of pure awareness. One may become the Tao more and more consciously yet effortlessly, starting from small beginnings, and patiently allowing for gradual, silent growth.

All growth is invisible. No one can see or measure the growth of a baby or a little child from moment to moment. No one can mark by visible and external tokens the point of transition from childhood to youth. No one can put a date on the boundary between youth and manhood. These divisions are arbitrary and relative. When a person remains constant in his cool awareness of the utter relativity of all of these false and over-valued distinctions, he comes to understand that there is nothing dead and nothing alive. He is no less and no more than the Tao, and so is everyone else. The divisions and distinctions in consciousness arising from sense-objects, through words and by images, are a smoke-screen that obscures, limits and distorts reality. The supreme, carefree joy of non-striving that flows from the omnipresent light can no more be conveyed by one to another than the taste of water can be described to someone who has never drunk a drop. No truly meaningful experience can be communicated to another except in terms of his own modes of living.

The wisest disciples, teachers and sages learn from the Tao all the time. The Tao is not a book. The Tao is not a scripture. The Tao was not given by any one person for the first time to other people. It is everywhere and nowhere. It is what some call God, what others designate as the One Reality, and what still others salute merely by saying "I do not know." To the extent to which men do not understand the Tao, instead of their choosing the Tao, the Tao seems to use them. A great deal of what is often called choosing is an illusion. No one chooses except by the power of the Tao. No one chooses thoughts except by a self-conscious comprehension of what is behind the energy of the Tao. No one can be a knower of the Tao, a true Taoist, without becoming a skilled craftsman of *Akasha,* a silent magician of the Alkahest, a self-conscious channel for the universal divine flame which, in its boundless, colourless, intangible, soundless and inexhaustible energy, may be used only for the sake of all. Only these universal, deathless, eternal verities may become living germs in the emerging matrix of the awakening mind of the age of Aquarius, a current of consciousness that flows into the future.

Following the ever-young example of the Ancient of Days each and every person today may focus his mind upon the eternal relevance of the ever-flexible and never-caring Tao:

> Under heaven all can see beauty as beauty only because there is ugliness. All can know good as good only because there is evil.
>
> *Tao Te Ching,* 2

How can one be flexible if one is fiercely attached to any external forms of good and of evil? *There is the same mutual relation between existence and non-existence in respect to creation as there is between striving and spontaneity, effort and ease in respect to accomplishment.* What is easy for one person is hard for another; what is easy for the same person at any time was hard once; and what is difficult now might become easy in the future. Fumbling with the strings of a musical instrument may be rather painful in the long period of apprenticeship, yet all can find supreme enjoyment in listening at any time to a great master of music who plays his enchanted instrument with lightness and versatile adeptship. The seeker who is patient and persistent, like the good gardener who plants the seed but does not examine it daily to gauge its growth, does no more than is needed, giving Nature time to do its own alchemical work.

How, then, can one contrive a hard-and-fast distinction between effort and ease in the many modes of human striving? Furthermore, is there any reason for preference between one person and another in human excellence? Not from the serene standpoint of the Sage. Those who enjoy good music do not feel threatened every time they listen to a great musician, but merge their selves into the motion of the music. There is that which every human being knows and yet forgets, though if one chooses one may remind oneself. A person always knows that what helped one to walk as a child may also help one to maintain oneself in a world of turmoil. Through the archetypal logic of non-action in activity, he can move away from the *turba* and the tumult of the crowd, and discover an inner peace through deliberate but casual control in the midst of spontaneous activity. *The same mutual relation exists between long and short in respect to form, as between high and low in respect to pitch.* What seem to be precipitous mountains in one country might be seen as hilly ranges in a distant land. The Alps are unquestionably beautiful, but, as Byron suggested, there are beauties in Derbyshire which are no less enjoyable than the Alps. The Sierras may be more inviting than the forbidding Himalayas. Each can make the most of what he finds where he can find it, between treble and bass on the scale of musical pitch, between before and after in the contest of priorities. There are no seniors and juniors among human souls — all alike are pilgrims on multitudinous pathways to enlightenment. All souls have participated variously in the immense pilgrimage extending through and beyond successive millennia. *The Voice of the Silence* teaches: "Such are the falls and rises of the Karmic Law in nature." He who was a prince is a beggar now, Buddha taught, and he who is exalted today may tomorrow "wander earth in rags."

In the eyes of the Sage, all temporal distinctions are absurd not only because they are foreshortened in time but also because they pretend to an ultimacy which cannot be upheld except by coercion. No one who has not conquered the will to coerce could freely practise the art of Wu-Wei even in everyday encounters. The Tao is the ontological basis of the archetypal teaching of non-violence, non-retaliation and true benevolence. Nature is not partial, partisan or sentimentally benevolent. This is known to the Sage, who fuses wisdom in action with compassion.

> Heaven and earth are ruthless;
> They see the ten thousand things as dummies.
> The wise are ruthless;
> They see the people as dummies.
>
> *Tao Te Ching, 5*

From a superficial standpoint, it looks as if God is the chief conspirator, but there is no arbitrary theism in the vision of Tao. The inscrutable mathematics of cosmic balance needs nothing like what Hegel called the cunning of history to upset the best-laid plans of mice and men. From a broader perspective, it seems as if what appears bad in the beginning turns out in time for the better, even for the best. The Good Law ever moves inexorably towards righteousness. The Sage is not benevolent to personal claims. He treats all with a light inexorability. From an external locus in the realm of changing appearances, nothing that is true could ever be said or could even be found. It is only by the inner light that a person becomes a disciple of the Tao, and in the progress of time may even become a friend of the Tao with the help of those who are the Masters of the Tao.

In China reverence for the primordial Divine Instructors of mankind eventually degenerated into empty rituals of ancestor worship. As with ancient Chinese civilization, so also with classical Indian culture there was a progressive diffusion and inward loss of meaning. In ancient India there was a solemn kindling of the sacrificial fire, and every sacred word and ritual act were offered at the altar of the Prajapatis, the Kumaras, the Rishis, the Agnishwatha Pitris or Solar Fathers. In time such practices were reduced to ritual propitiation of the dead for fear of consequences. The weaker souls who participated in that ritualization in China and India are no different from those who incarnated in European and American bodies. Immigrants came in succeeding waves from different parts of the world to the American continent not only for the sake of their own future, but also, under Karma, as pathfinders of the future of mankind. That which caused violence and deception in the past must return, but cyclical justice will also bring back gentleness and truth and beauty in the nobler ancestors. No human being is without ancestors of whom one could be proud. Over a thousand years every man and woman has had a million ancestors. Nothing that was accomplished by a million people over a thousand years is irrelevant to any person. Everyone has a lineage that ultimately traces one back to the Divine Instructors of the human family. Everyone has kinship to those who are the Friends of all beings and who forever abide as Silent Watchers in the night, guarding orphan humanity.

There is not a person who could not at any time enter his inmost sanctuary and so come closer to the Krishna-Christos within. "Where two or three are gathered in my name, there I am present." Those potent words of promise, uttered as a benediction by the Avatars, were not meant only for a chosen few or for any particular tribe. It is possible at any time for any human being to invoke and invite the sacred presences of any of the divine Teachers. They are not in any one place or epoch — they are always here, there and everywhere. One cannot say of enlightened beings that physical proximity in space and time determines the nearness or closeness of their sphere of divine radiance. By the strength of mind and the spiritual will released through true sacrifice, one may consecrate the altar within the secret heart and kindle the sacrificial fire, thereby becoming worthy of the living benediction of those who are ancestral in a spiritual sense, who are ageless and parentless, *Anupadaka*. Enlightened Sages are eternally in unison with the supernal light of *Shekinah*, the perennial wisdom of *Svabhavat*, the ceaseless ideation of *Svayambhu* or Self-Existent, the absoluteness of the Tao.

The Tao antecedes all ancestors by reaching out to that which was before everything and yet which has no beginning, which ever exists and embraces every moment and the myriad beings who are sustained by its inexhaustible strength. It reaches beyond name and utterance, colour and form. It is the Soundless Sound, the divine intonation, the *Svabhavat* which cannot be aroused except by those who enter the light and become one with its unending compassion. Its potency is limitless. It can heal the sick and raise the dead. It is that light which never shone on land or sea, yet lighteth every man that cometh into the world. If any sincere seeker wishes to invoke that primordial light which is parentless, *Anupadaka*, he must create an oasis of calm within the mind, a haven of peace within the heart, a diffused quiescence in the whole of his being. He cannot do this all at once, but must, as Krishna teaches, adopt the strategy of recurrent exercise *(abhyasa)* in a spirit of disinterestedness *(vairagya)*. In the course of time he will build his bridge, his mental pathway to the light of *Atman* in the lamp of *Buddhi*. For any human being there is nothing more beneficent than, by concentrating upon that which corresponds to the throat, opening up the devotional channel within his wandering mind between his heart-light and the star overhead.

All Avatars are apparent manifestations of *Mahapurusha*, while every Enlightened Being is an eternal branch of the ever-living Banyan, the Tree of Immortals. By invoking in consciousness with a proper reverence taught by the Tao, every true devotee may enter the radiant sphere of the spiritually wise and transmit to others the sweetness and light of the Tao. Every child experimenting with a palette of colours discovers rapidly that there are not only the seven prismatic hues but also many shades, tones and blends, that unforeseen combinations are possible by an adroit mixing of colours. It also learns through fumbling beginnings at mixing pigments for the sake of painting a landscape that mistakes and false starts must be endured. There is not a child that starts to paint who does not take many distracting bypaths, and sometimes fiercely assumes the posture of Shiva, destroying its own work. Sometimes it adopts the posture of Vishnu, thinking, "I am pleased." At other times it assumes the posture of Brahmā and attempts something new and original. All human beings as creative agents participate in the myriad scatterings and subtle hues of the prismatic seven.

Every human being in some life chooses the Tao, the pristine light which is colourless and beyond the differentiation of hues. Each of the great religions — originally a pure ray pointing to the One Light — in time produces tints that anathematize other people, thus resulting in walls of separation. This repeatedly arises because, as people no longer have access to the colourless light, they fall off the line of direction along the ray of their immortal individuality pointing towards the One that transcends all and yet is immanent in all. Sectarians thus speciously identify the pristine light with the *namarupa* of its reflected ray. They proclaim that all is contained in this particular book or that special scroll. But All is in every sacred book, is in the book of Nature. It is inscribed in every atom, and is in the pinpoint of light within every human eye. Men and women limit the inexhaustible richness of the All through fear, which kills the will and stays all progress. This is sad, and it arises because they become unbalanced. Either they have aggressively sought a selfish end or — when this went wrong — they retreated into some inversion and christened it by profane names such as cynicism, liberalism, this or that ism, protecting an insupportable illusion.

The harmony of the Tao is ever alive because it allows for endless change while at the same time ceaselessly balancing out. This is graphically represented in the familiar symbol of *yin* and *yang* within the invisible circle of Tao. When a person watches a slowly revolving wheel, studying the spokes, he will begin to understand the great wheel on which all beings revolve and in which all are involved. Those who cling to the circumference feel most the motion of the wheel. Those who cling to the spokes, the colours and the tints, find they do not have any sense of the subtler rhythm. The cyclic spin of the smaller wheel moves faster, so rapidly that it seems to be motionless. It has a centre which is an invisible, mathematical point. This may seem to be a mental abstraction and logical construction, but it is known on a subtler plane of homogeneous matter in a serene mental state of purified consciousness. Such centres could be consciously activated, thereby becoming gyroscopic in their power to awaken potential energies lying everywhere.

Every person may consciously choose to return to the central source, the pure light-energy of the motionless Tao without a name. This does not mean one should cease breathing. That would be a hasty reading of the Tao because one cannot live without breathing in and breathing out, and in this rhythmic activity one participates in the Tao, the Mother of Ten Thousand Things. When people are running or rushing they do not breathe rhythmically, but needlessly distort the rhythm. It is always possible to balance the chaotic breathing and the disorderly motions of daily life by providing spaces within the passage of time for a self-conscious return to the inner stillness, the serenity of meditation whereby one may renew oneself. Nature provides priceless opportunities for daily regeneration, and the Tao is experienced each night by every human being in deep, dreamless sleep. The Tao could also be known during waking life by the vigilant and contented person who practises deliberate mental withdrawal, self-surrender and non-violent action. The true seeker may heed the talismanic counsel of the Sage:

> In meditation, go deep in the heart.
> In dealing with others, be gentle and kind.
> In work, be diligent.
> In action, watch the timing.

THE DIAMOND SUTRA

In *The Voice of the Silence* we are told that the aspirant on the Secret Path must come to see the voidness of the seeming full, the fullness of the seeming void. At a first glance, this injunction seems to say no more than Samuel Butler's statement in his *Notebooks* that everything matters more than we think it does and at the same time nothing matters as much as we think it does. In fact, however, the student of Gupta Vidya soon finds in his attempt to practise his self-chosen discipline, that impersonality, detachment and discrimination are profounder concepts and more elusive virtues than he had thought at the threshold of systematic study. *Ahankara* or egotism is so deep-seated and so pervasive that the very struggle to overcome it seems to facilitate its expression in newer and subtler forms. Similarly, the continual effort to free ourselves from personal preconceptions in our perceptions of the realities around us and in our relationships seems to engender new and unnoticed presuppositions, fresh and unseen barriers to understanding. In order to see the central problem of the spiritual life more clearly, it would be worth while to ponder over the Mahayana classic, known as the *Diamond Cutter* or the *Diamond Sutra*.

The *Vajrachchedika* (Diamond Cutter) is a small Sanskrit text belonging to the *Maha-Prajnaparamita* (Perfection of Transcendental Wisdom). It has been suggested that this text was first transmitted by Nagarjuna who lived in the second century, but this has been denied by some scholars who have declared it to be written down only in the fourth century. It is, however, definitely known that this subtle and profound discourse was first translated into Chinese by Kumarajiva about 400 C.E. and has been subsequently rendered into Chinese and more recently into English by several scholars. Although the supreme doctrine of Voidness is now accessible to all truth-seekers, it remains essentially esoteric and difficult to comprehend. Mere head-learning will not enable us to grasp the Heart-Doctrine, and the *Diamond Sutra* stresses that the state of transcendence over all conditioned consciousness cannot be visualized by purely intellectual means or in terms of categories applicable to our common modes of awareness.

The first and last requirement for the attainment of spiritual wisdom is to rid our consciousness and our conduct of our continual obsession with the idea of an ego-entity, a personality, the dire heresy of separateness and the derivative notions of individual progress, personal salvation and self-realization. In order to hinder the hindrances to ego-free meditation and awareness, the mind should be kept independent of any thoughts which arise within it; for, as long as the mind depends upon anything, it has no sure haven. We are urged not to become passive or nihilistic but rather to make our Manasic consciousness more universal and eventually *Mahat*-mic by freeing it from the compulsions, obsessions and tortuous rationalizations of kamamanasic activity. This means in practice that we must become increasingly aware of the extent to which every single thought, feeling and judgment is conditioned by the limited context in which we experience it. The wider and more universal and more enduring the context, the easier it should be for us to prevent ourselves from becoming dependent upon and attached to it.

This requires regular meditation but also the adoption of an attitude of relaxed and well-meaning impersonality in all our activities and relationships. The more we do this, the more meaningful it becomes for us to consider, in any particular context of a personal thought or reaction, how a Mahatma or a Bodhisattva would react or view the matter in the same context. It is no doubt extremely difficult for our Manasic consciousness to adopt or even to visualize a Buddhic standpoint in any given situation, but this is precisely the object of our training and our daily discipline. We are told that if a Bodhisattva cherishes, even to the slightest extent, the idea of an ego-entity or personality, he is consequently not a Bodhisattva.

In the practice of this yoga, there must be, as the *Diamond Sutra* and the *Bhagavad Gita* make clear, no mental or emotional attachment to the results of our actions. In this system of yoga, the *Gita* points out, no effort is lost and even a little of this practice delivers a man from great risk. The *Diamond Sutra* warns us against even charitable acts performed with a view to attaining a spiritual benefit. A student of Gupta Vidya must not give of his time, money and energy with any thought of personal result or recognition or even because he is urged to do so, but it must become second nature for him to do so in view of the fact that he has initially accepted that all his obligations are wholly self-determined. It is paradoxically true that the assumption of full personal responsibility is the beginning of impersonality, for by ceasing to concern ourselves with the responsibilities of others we are ready to see that all our freely self-chosen responsibilities flow solely from the potency and will-energy of the Higher Self or the Divine Triad which belongs to all and therefore to none.

In the *Diamond Sutra* the Buddha denies the reality of all predictable things, of the individual self as of all changing appearances, likewise of merit and demerit, even of liberation and non-liberation. In the ultimate analysis, no differentiation is at all possible between the primordially undifferentiated and the differentiated cosmos. However we conceive the idea of the One Reality or of transcendental wisdom, it is no more than a mental concept, "merely a name." If we make a hard-and-fast distinction between *nirvana* and *samsara*, the Goal and the Way, we fail to see that they are, for the mind of man, merely the ultimate pair of opposites, no less unreal than all lesser pairs of opposites, like ego and non-ego. Only on the plane of the unconditioned consciousness, which is beyond all pairs of opposites and all dichotomous thinking, do we realize the Truth because we become IT.

Similarly, it would be a mistake for us to become concerned about our present incarnation in relation to past and future lives. It is no doubt useful to reflect upon the workings of Karma in relation to our present or any other personality, but we must gain the "higher carelessness" that is based upon the awareness that "there is no passing away nor coming into existence." Again, we must not become self-conscious about helping in the liberation of all beings, for this thought is itself illusory in so far as it fails to take note of the fact that the notions of being and of liberation are purely relative. Above all, we must see that the attaining of Buddhahood is not the attaining of anything, but only the realization of what is eternally and indestructibly potential in every living creature. The Buddha and the non-Buddha are not different in kind; a Buddha knows and the non-Buddha does not know that he, like everyone else, is a Buddha. On attaining Buddhahood, nothing is either lost or gained; "look inward, thou *art* Buddha."

The continual stress of the *Diamond Sutra* is upon the attainment of true impersonality, the performance of every activity, including charity, without any attachment to appearances. It is necessary for us to persevere one-pointedly in this instruction. Another lesson in the *Sutra* for students of Gupta Vidya is the assertion that the Tathagatas, the Masters of Wisdom and of Compassion, cannot be recognized by any material characteristic. As long as we are concerned with personal and material characteristics, we remain deluded. Nor should we cling to particular formulations of the truth; so long as the mind is attached even to the teaching of the Good Law, it will cherish the idea of 'I' and 'Other.' In order to enter the stream and become a *srotapatti*, the disciple must pay no regard to form, sound, odour, taste, touch or any quality. A Bodhisattva is one who has developed a pure, lucid mind, not depending upon sound, flavour, touch, odour or any quality.

The Tathagata is He who declares that which is true, that which is fundamental, that which is ultimate. A disciple who practises charity with a mind attached to formal notions is like unto a man groping sightless in the gloom, but a Bodhisattva who practices charity with a mind detached from any formal notions is like unto a man with open eyes in the radiant glory of the morning, to whom all kinds of objects are clearly visible. Thus, by perceiving the voidness of the seeming full, he participates in the fullness of the seeming void. The Tathagata is a signification implying all formulas for the attainment of

Enlightenment and he is beyond them all. He is wholly devoid of any conception of separate selfhood and cannot be identified with any sect or any particular formulation of doctrine. He understands the manifold modes of mind of all living beings, like the Krishna of the 10th and 11th chapters of the *Gita*. All Bodhisattvas are insentient as to the rewards of Merit. "Because TATHAGATA has neither whence nor whither, therefore is He called Tathagata." Buddha tells Subhuti:

> Who sees Me by form,
> Who seeks Me in sound,
> Perverted are his footsteps upon the Way;
> For he cannot perceive the Tathagata.

The *Diamond Sutra* has sometimes been misunderstood to be a plea for a world-denying and inert standpoint. It was actually meant as a dynamite to the complacency of formal believers and self-righteous coteries. At the time when the *Sutra* was written down, there were many Buddhists who had become as smug and yet as anxious for personal advancement in spiritual life as the Brahmins to whom the Buddha came with a profoundly relevant message. Students of Gupta Vidya, too, fall prey to the cosiness of complacency and the curse of anxiety. The message of the *Diamond Sutra* has been reiterated with pertinent clarity by W.Q. Judge and Robert Crosbie in their letters to those who came to them for counsel.

Though we are not separate from anything, we are surrounded by appearances that seem to make us separate, and we are urged by W.Q. Judge to proceed to state and accept mentally that we are all these illusions. If we are anxious, we raise a barrier against progress, by perturbation and straining harshly. No matter where we are, the same spirit pervades all and is accessible. "What need, then, to change places?" Again, we are told: "Now, then, is there not many a cubic inch of your own body which is entitled to know and to be the Truth in greater measure than now? And yet you grieve for the ignorance of so many other human beings!" "Resignation", we are told, "is the sure, true, and royal road." "The lesson intended by the Karma of your present life is *the higher patience. . . .* Insist on carelessness. Assert to yourself that it is not of the slightest consequence what you were yesterday, but in every moment strive for that moment; the results will follow of themselves." The higher carelessness that we are asked to cultivate is in reality a calm reliance on the law, and a doing of our own duty, checking ourselves by a periodic examination and purification of our motives. As we begin to rely on the Higher Self — the Buddha-nature — new ideals and thought-forms will drive out the old ones, as this is the eternal process.

Similarly, Robert Crosbie warns against the danger of thinking too much of oneself, one's present conditions and prospects. We have to acquire greater control over our thoughts, the power of direction, the exercise of deliberation at all times. "Get the point of view of the One who is doing the leading and hold to it." No one can clear another's sight. "We try to free *ourselves* from *something.* Is not this the attitude of separateness?" We forget that "The One *sees* All." We have power over nothing but the "is". "We" are the One Self and there is nothing but the One Self. Masters cannot interfere with Karma. The Egoic perceptions on this plane are limited by all personal claims. "Impersonality isn't talking; it isn't silence; it isn't insinuation; it isn't repulsion; it isn't negation. It means becoming less doctrinal and more *human.*" Is that not the central message of the *Diamond Sutra?*

It is not the individual and determined purpose of attaining Nirvana — the culmination of all knowledge and absolute wisdom, which is after all only an exalted and glorious selfishness — but the self-sacrificing pursuit of the best means to lead on the right path our neighbour, to cause to benefit by it as many of our fellow creatures as we possibly can, which constitutes the true Theosophist.

THE MAHA CHOHAN

THE CREST JEWEL

To affirm is to deny. It is obvious that we do this always, but we periodically forget because of narrowing our focus to what we affirm in the language of perceived objects and in terms of the illusive independent existence of a particular set of subjects who see those objects. We fashion a pseudo-system. The universe is boundless, birthless and partless. Both within and beyond visible space and in eternal motion within endless duration, going through apparent vicissitudes like the waxing and waning of the moon or the rise and fall of the tides, through cyclical and cosmically precise changes, human beings have the privilege of exercising the deific power of creative imagination. At the highest level conceivable to a finite mind caught up within the prison of the personality, imagination is ceaselessly enjoying the universe, for example, the play of light and shade upon the green leaves of summer. If we say that there is also continuous negation, we are correct because chlorophyll is gradually negated, and thereby the leaves turn yellow. Thus we know that spring and summer must be followed by autumn. Human beings, however, sometimes forsake these primal facts because they prefer convenient fictions which involve false affirmations.

There is the false affirmation that a whole lot of bodies are in existence today. Do the bodies say so, and if so, how do they know? Apparently they are supposed to have minds, but what is a mind and what is the evidence that bodies have minds? We entertain opinions about these matters, but are opinions the same as ideas and are ideas the efflux of fluctuating moods? Is that the same as thinking, the activity of a Thoreau in the woods and an Emerson in his study? Questions of this kind are deeply troublesome and difficult. Therefore, Sri Shankaracharya states that before you can begin to deserve the Crest Jewel, which is in the crest above the forehead of the human body, the regal gem of pure discernment and spiritual wakefulness, and before you can benefit by it in the three states of consciousness — waking, dreaming and dreamlessness — you must recognize that at the root you have made a false identification. Without knowing it, you have engaged in falsehoods to which you were invulnerable before you learned to walk, before you learned to identify with the body that stumbles and before you learned to talk, to repeat sounds associated by other people with sense-objects. You started to slip into a stupor, and began to live an increasingly unreal existence, mostly reinforcing your sense of unreality but insisting it was the only reality — thereby showing that it was not real to you — against other people's conceptions of reality. Therefore, that compassionate teacher Sri Shankaracharya states that we must get to the root and core of illusion.

What is the root? We are told that the Crest Jewel is that which causes all our problems but which also is their cure. The Crest Jewel represents the fundamental affirmation that two habitual negatives make a higher-order affirmation. On the one hand, there is a false negation in the notion of reality attached to the apparent freedom of all seemingly separate subjects, and the resulting glamour of the false shadow-play created by supposedly separate selves. On the other hand, there is also the notion of a plurality of separate objects, constituting a false negation of the one homogeneous substance or root-matter which is of the quality of pure primordial light and remains undivided and untransformed. All the various collocations of atoms, in seemingly fortuitous movement, whirl and revolve around invisible centres which are seemingly separate points in one homogeneous universal region, giving rise to the falsehood that there are separate objects. These two false negations have been marked out in the great teaching of the Guru.

Sri Shankara begins the text by saying there are three things extremely difficult to have. One is manhood. The second is the longing for liberation. The third is access to Masters. Without the second the third is impossible and the first is useless. If one wants access to Masters, one has to long sufficiently for liberation. One has to want sufficiently, with the whole of one's being, to become free from the massive burden of inane repetitions that we call life and the impossibility of making it meaningful with the help of borrowed, lifeless and bloodless categories that wear masks and don caps and engage in a perpetual pantomime play called living. Shankara says that there is nothing new under the sun, that it is all the same old story. One might say it began with thinking man, but it really began when man stopped thinking. As a result, a huge rigmarole emerged which men then packaged and called recorded history.

History represents in recent centuries a harsh but also a necessary negation of the absurdities, errors and illusions of the past. When that happens with so many minds, when so many wills are blunted, hearts hurt and human beings lamed and crippled, suddenly we know that springtime is near. The Golden Age is next door. Suddenly we realize what we always might have known — that there are children in this world, that other people exist, that while ten men are gloomy there are another hundred who are happy. Those who are engrossed in being happy do not go around certifying their happiness to the gloomy. The gloomy want certainty, but there is no certitude to be attained anywhere in the realm of differentiation. This is a philosophical truth which everyone knew as a little child. The intuitive negation of childhood, a beautiful sharing with no 'mine' and 'thine', was followed by cruel adolescent affirmations which are intensely ugly especially to others and sometimes to oneself. Then came the prolonged adolescence of those who are petrified that they might actually have to assume minimal responsibilities. But when men will not negate, Nature negates. Nature's power of negation is vaster than the collective power of negation of history, and both seem more awesome and decisive than the capacity of an individual to negate. Against this, however, we have the tremendous affirmation through the supreme negation of Sri Shankaracharya.

The individual who knows that at the root is the persisting illusion of separateness, is vaster than the universe, and can dissolve it instantly by breaking down at will the baseless, insubstantial fabric of his imagination. Anyone who can do that has begun to

wake up. There are people who will not wake up voluntarily
because they repeatedly fell asleep during eighteen million years
and are now frightened to settle accounts. They are themselves
negated by suffering which comes as healing compassion, and are
negated by others in the course of intolerable inhuman encounter.
Self-negation is shown by the timeless religion of responsibility
and the hidden science of divine wisdom. The invisible sun in
every man as the *Atman,* the spectator, ever radiates endless energy
for the sake of all. According to this teaching, darkness is prior to
what we call light; glamour or unwisdom is beginningless. It is
what the ancients called Chaos, Gaia, or *Mahamaya.* There is a
chaos prior to any cosmos. There are many myriads of systems,
galaxies and galactic clusters in the vast spaces of the heavens, but
if there were no primordial chaos one would be forever trapped
within the same universe. Before Adam was Chaos, the primordial
matter, in which is hidden the light that is the soundless sound.
In the beginning was the Word. Primordial chaos is necessary for
the universe, but whether we think it necessary or not, we have
no choice. We are caught. We can get out, because we have in us
the light that was hidden in the darkness, which lighteth up every
man who comes into the world.

The *Crest Jewel of Wisdom* speaks only to those who are
prepared to negate the world of appearances:

> Gaining at length human life, hard to win, and
> manhood, and an understanding of the revealed
> teachings, he who strives not for liberation in the Divine
> Self, deluded in heart, self-destroying, slays himself
> through grasping at the unreal. Who, then, is the very
> self of folly but he who, deluded, follows selfish
> purposes, after he had gained a human body and
> manhood hard to win? Even though they recite the
> scriptures, and sacrifice to the gods, and fulfil all works,
> and worship the divinities — without awakening to the
> unity of the Divine Self, liberation is not attained even
> in a hundred aeons.

From the standpoint of the Sage, the innumerable ways in which human beings are enmeshed in the *Mahamaya* are not very interesting. The Sage can recognize anyone who is fully awake behind a semi-sleepy projection. Those who really want to emerge from behind the false personal mask will receive what they deserve in mathematically exact proportion. This is a truth about consciousness on all planes. One must deserve to go beyond all the external forms and modes and, through the eternal soul-memory now awakened of the soundless sound behind the great vibrations of the universe, to light up in the lower mind a self-conscious reflection of the invisible sun that overbroods the egg.

Albert Einstein said there are no hitching posts in the universe. There are no boundaries except arbitrary and conventional ones assigned by human beings who happen to think that they occupy a fixed point of space and time, when in fact space is curved and time is relative. They do not understand the inner meaning of spatial coordinates and of clocktime. Although there are no hitching posts, there are innumerable hooking points. When people really begin to enjoy the thought that at any point of space-time they could break out of the boundedness of the universe, they can experience through self-knowledge what they have forgotten. The ancients taught that God is a circle with its centre everywhere and circumference nowhere. Human beings can find in the inmost depths of abstract meditation an active centre of intense, motionless, joyous consciousness. Abiding in universal welfare and doing nothing, as beings of light they enjoy pure unmoving spiritual will in, through and independently of, all material vestures. Even if we somewhat understand all of this, it is still very difficult to light the lamp of discernment. The moment we think, "Let me do this," "May I be that," we only create karma and imprison ourselves. But the moment we say, "Let me begin," and also recognize that there is a chaos we cannot explain and that there are no hitching posts, then we begin like true pilgrims to walk along the Path. It leads to invisible summits lost in glorious Nirvanic light which may be glimpsed from foothills and mountains arduously climbed in cheerful enjoyment, although one is aware of the many pitfalls on the way. The only hooking points are found within. They form the seven-knotted bamboo staff of the ascetic. If you were a montagnard you would cherish the serene strength of the individual and know what the communards forget, that communities are doomed to fail from the start when men are afraid to be alone. At the same time, if a human being in distress came for help, the montagnard will take care of him and then return to solitude.

The soul is ensnared through the power of misidentification in the chaos of primordial matter. If we enjoy narcissistically the illusions of the ever-changing reflective soul, then we forget the light of divine discernment, the Sleeping Beauty in the castle. She can only be awakened by Prince Charming, the androgynous *Manas*, the power of noetic thought, ideation and imagination. Real thinking has a self-sustaining quality determined by the grasp, the vision, the scope and the strength of the universal ideas that provide mental nourishment. When one truly begins to walk the inner Path, one does not need any reference point in external space and time, and can see the moment of birth as if it were this morning's dawn and can see the moment of death as if it were this evening's twilight. Thousands of previous lives seem like twinkling stars in the sky.

The real Gurus who truly know teach just by being themselves. They are self-existing, self-manifesting embodiments of the wisdom of compassion, crowned with the Crest Jewel of pure insight. Their very existence is testimony. Shankara spoke to disciples who were already free from the delusion of the *personal* 'I' but who were stuck in the illusion of the *individual* 'I.' His teaching is not about the hereafter, not about the now and then, not about the always and everywhere, but about That. The supreme affirmation is TAT TVAM ASI — 'That Thou Art.' That is the oldest teaching which Shankara explained by reference to reason, to experience, to states of consciousness, to vestures of matter in the fivefold classification, and also by references to madmen, *yogins* and free men. Universal self-awareness is the potential privilege and birthright of every human being, but no one can attain to it except by fulfilling the qualifications, embodying the conditions that approximate the posture and the position of a true learner.

The Crest Jewel could be in your hands. Use it, Shankara says, because by use you make it sufficiently your own to recognize that the greatest lies are 'I' and 'thou.' All amounts to an 'it' and 'it' equals THAT. THAT equals zero. Your sphere becomes luminous when you wholly adopt the standpoint of the Logos in the cosmos, God in man, and then enjoy the universe through every pair of eyes. Heal yourself, and others through yourself, by luminous thoughts and adamantine compassion.

PYTHAGORAS
AND HIS SCHOOL

Pythagoras was revered in India as Pitar Guru, Father and Teacher, and as Yavanacharya, the Ionian philosopher. He was known by other names in ancient Egypt where he spent twenty years in preparation before, at the age of fifty-six, he founded the School at Crotona in Magna Graecia, with great deliberation and in accord with the wisdom and the vision of the mighty Brotherhood he represented. He taught an entire emerging community, seeking four hundred pure souls who might constitute a small brotherhood for the sake of making that *polis* a city of souls in search of wisdom in harmony with the larger fellowship of man. His School was based upon the most stringent rules for admission, including a probation lasting five years and a requirement of total silence in the presence of those in the assembly who had been longer in the school. He initiated those who had passed all the preliminary trials, making themselves channels for the divine fount of omniscience, towards which he always pointed and upon which he enjoined an absolute, reverential silence.

For Pythagoras, philosophy was a purgation of the mind and emotions so that the pure light of the immortal soul may freely shine through the limited vestures common to all men. The purification must begin by preparatory reverence; becoming truly worthy of relationship, through silent worship of the immortal Gods, with the transcendental order which holds everything in the universe in a divine harmony. This order could be seen in the heavens and be studied with the help of geometry and mathematics of the most archetypal form. Through the honouring of heroes and peers, profound reverence may emerge for the whole of life when seen in the context of a vast universe. Pythagoras was the first to use the word 'cosmos'. The universe is a cosmos, not a chaos. It represents the majesty of a vast intelligible ordering of immense magnitudes through the application of an overbrooding architectonic principle in a rounded but boundless perspective. It is bounded in time and space but unbounded in its peripheral transition to the realm of the potential.

Apprehending this, a person begins to deepen his or her feeling for the mystery of life and all the multitudinous forms of matter, and thereby comes to have a true and rectified respect for those forces that are ceaselessly at work, even in the simplest acts such as the handling of objects. The person who is thus prepared would naturally honour the noble heroes, the forerunners of every race and every civilization who, though they are imperfect individuals, are yet capable of elevating the moral tone of human culture. Throughout history their name is legion. Anyone who has thought about these matters fosters a view of human nature that is enormously expansive, and comes to see human beings in terms of opportunities, not limitations, in terms of powers and possibilities rather than handicaps. Then, according to the Pythagorean teaching in the *Golden Verses,* any person can come to show fearlessness in relation to fate, having already acquired a mature self-respect that is rooted in an understanding and a reverence for all of life.

Self-respect means here very much more than in current usage and in our ordinary languages. It is the key to what is said in the *Golden Verses* about proper self-examination, which is an activity very different from offering a confessional before a priest, or going to a psychiatrist and having oneself analysed, or engaging in one or another form of tedious, furtive and repressive discussion of the shadow. In the Pythagorean teaching, the shadow cannot understand itself. The shadow is void of the very possibility of self-knowledge. Real understanding can come solely through the light of self-awareness which is inherent in every human being. The light of understanding can dispel the shadow of the personality only when, in lunar consciousness, a fruitful connection is made — metaphorically withdrawing to Metapontum where Pythagoras passed away, some say around the age of a hundred. Having built a bridge in personal consciousness towards the latent potential self, one sees that in this larger selfhood there are no differences between oneself and every other human being and also the inner light and essence of anything and everything. The same luminous essence is to be found in a piece of paper, a table, a stone, in each single atom in space, in every animal form, in each vegetable and mineral, and the same is also to be found in every constituent of that vast and complex universe that we call the human body. The same is also to be found in each thought-form entering into and leaving the human mind through its affinity with appropriate centres of excitation in the brain, or when self-consciously drawn from an abundant cosmic storehouse.

All who want to come closer to the spirit of the *Golden Verses* must prepare and purge themselves as Pythagoras taught, thereby coming to be known as a trainer of souls. When human beings seek to learn, in the privacy and solitude of their own solemn undertaking, the serious business of truly elevating a human life, they must begin to ask questions about themselves: "Who am I?" "What am I?" "Why did I do this then?" "Do I always say what I intend?" "Did I think before I acted this morning, and what do I now think I am supposed to do tomorrow, next week, next year?" It is significant that the only phrase occurring twice in the *Golden Verses* is: *Think before you act.* It is precisely because human beings with the best intentions in the world, with access to the profoundest ideas and sharing the noblest of feelings, are not able to deliver themselves in public life with the dignity of divine monads, that they need to give themselves a chance, by making time within the space of every day for looking back in review. By continually reflecting the standpoint of the immortal Self, they will surely come to understand others and increase their real confidence through recognizing what is good in themselves; this in turn gives the courage to notice what in themselves is left-handed and must be discarded.

It is well known, though little understood, that in the Pythagorean School the psychological disciplines were joined to the study of mathematics. If one really wanted to understand this, one would be well advised to meditate deeply upon the Pythagorean Triad and the Tetrad. When one truly does so, one will find that the mystery deepens further, because what is esoteric and what is exoteric are relative. What is hidden to one is not unknown to another. What is hidden at one time is not inaccessible at another time. Unfortunately, many people are victims of an Aristotelian-Baconian view of knowledge where thoughts are seen as bits of information transmitted from the outside and impressed upon the brain, itself misconstrued as a kind of *tabula rasa*. In contemporary culture many people erroneously believe that true knowledge has got to do with the information revolution, and hence all that is needed is to find proper ways of giving access to information to each and all. In the School of Pythagoras, if people sought to know the Mysteries, they were fairly and squarely told what were the rules that must be respected. These time-honoured rules have always been observed. Great Teachers make fresh applications of these enduring rules according to the exigencies of the age in strict obedience to the Fraternity on behalf of which they act, and of which they are faithful members.

In teaching the divine wisdom relevant to his time, Pythagoras, the great Master, followed very strict rules. In one mythic version the story is told of how this was done. If individuals sought admission into the School, having already found inspiration in daily life from the ethical teaching of the *Golden Verses*, then they were invited to put themselves through a preliminary set of freely chosen and strictly administered tests. One of these required that the candidate be conducted to some secluded place and left with bread and water. He was requested to remain there for a night and to think intently upon a single symbol such as the triangle. Having prepared properly and taken whatever steps were needed to gain calmness, the candidate then set down ideas on the subject in relation to the whole of life. The following morning, the candidate was invited to the assembly of those who had already passed through these stages and asked by Pythagoras, who presided, to convey his observations to the entire group. A common practice during those days was that various members of the assembly were instructed to make it difficult for the candidate to state what he had to say by ridiculing his ideas. Naturally, a new candidate was liable to be nervous though the assembly was really on his side, yet nonetheless no concessions were made to his limitations, ambiguities and mixtures of motive. This was for his own good. Unless one could maintain one's composure under these circumstances, it was clear that life in the School would prove too much for a candidate who was unduly sensitive to criticism. Something of this ancient tradition still persists, for example in Holland and Germany at the time of the defense of dissertations, although without the compassionate purport of the trial the ceremony becomes censorious and even absurd.

What was crucial for Pythagoras was the authenticity of self-knowledge in relation to the application for the sake of other men of the holy and sacred teaching in relation to the divine Triad. The Triad itself could not be comprehended except in relation to the Point. The Point could not be grasped except as a One in relation to the Duad. The Monad and the Duad could not be understood completely unless they were also seen in terms of the Triad. And so the number series proceeds. Underlying it is the difficult problem which has to do with form, the meaning of the Pythagorean Square. If all of these are to be put together, something is involved which is rather like squaring the circle, securing the elixir of life, the key to the Mysteries of life and death. Pythagoras taught that unless the Mysteries are found within oneself, they cannot speak to one. All must make their own experiments with truth. They must make their own exercises in the calming of the passions, the controlling of the mind, the concentration of the thinking principle, and above all, the purgation and purification of their motives, intentions, feelings, likes and dislikes. This must be done for the sake of fusing the whole of one's being into an overriding thought-feeling, one keynote vibration which becomes a sacred *verbum*, moving and animating the entire manifested self. All human beings have a unique and privileged access to the *verbum* within the sanctuary of their own consciousness in deep sleep, in daily meditation, in waking life, in golden moments, but, above all, when they begin to enter into a current of continuous thought and meditation upon the holiest of all subjects, which has to do with the *fons et origo* of all living things and beings. When they do this, then they will begin to understand the Tetraktys or sacred Quaternion, the Number of numbers.

Intuitive individuals will come to see that all these numbers point towards five, the Pythagorean pentagon, and six, which was used later in the Kabbalah but for Pythagoras was a six-pointed star where there was an eagle at the top and a bull and a lion below the face of a man. They will also begin to sense something about the significance of seven as the basic principle of division of not only colours and sounds, but of all manifestation. The seven in turn cannot be understood without the eight and Pythagoras taught how harmony may be produced when tuning the high and the low notes in the octave, thereby laying the basis for many of the theories and teachings that have come down through musical traditions. What he illustrated in music could also be applied to medicine, which means we cannot leave out the number nine. Nine has great meaning as three sets of three, but it also spells the ending of all things — incompletion. The wise take this into account in advance, thereby preserving the inviolable image of what since Pythagoras has come to be called the perfect number — ten — without seeking for its exact visual replica on earth. What is hidden in the Triad has been glimpsed by great architects, sculptors and craftsmen. The Chinese, when creating vases, abstained from making them perfectly symmetrical. Contemporary architects like Jacobsen after conceiving a fine building do not care to come to the opening ceremony as they are absorbed in the designing of the next. Truly creative minds have known that there is a joy in creativity which is constricted and cancelled by attachment to results. The criteria of the world which accommodate the concerns of the mediocre also act as a brake upon the ascent to those levels of excellence which are relevant to all cultures. In the Pythagorean tradition, a proper answer to any question about the Mysteries must throw one back upon oneself so that each will do his own meditation and reflection upon the Tetrad as well as the Tetraktys.

The vital essence of the Pythagorean teaching was to encourage the emergence of whole men and women. They cannot be manufactured, but must truly create themselves. Great Teachers assist in the self-production of whole human beings by making a holistic teaching come alive. Pythagoras was an originator of true science, religion and philosophy in the Near Eastern cycle which he initiated. The teaching of Pythagoras was also that of Buddha and later on of Shankara. Two thousand five hundred years ago Buddha taught his disciples first to become *shravakas*, listeners. When they had spent a sufficient time in listening and learning, as in the earlier Hindu tradition with its emphasis upon *brahmacharya*, a period of probation, then they could become *sramanas*, men of action. We find this also in the Pythagorean tradition, where neophytes are *acousticoi*, those who listen. This has reference not to something mechanical or rigid and therefore false, but to a balanced training in the art of perfecting through wisdom the conservation of energy. The purification of thought, the calming and harmonizing of feelings, was undertaken for the sake of the appropriate manifestation of the Inner Self through proper speech and fitting conduct.

Pythagoras taught a threefold division of humankind and a threefold division of desire. All men may be compared to people who attend a festival. There are those who are motivated by the love of gain and who go to buy and sell. There are those motivated by the love of honour and they go to compete with and emulate each other in attaining standards of excellence. Then there are those who are concerned with neither gain nor glory because they have either worn out these toys or thought through these illusions, or they are born with a natural indifference to them. Such are wholly concerned with the love of wisdom. Lovers of wisdom may be compared to those who at festivals are like spectators, not participating but at the same time not making external judgements, not buying and selling, not comparing and contrasting, but merely learning what is common to all men, learning something about the noble art of living. They do not do what is unnecessary. They try to find out what is intimated behind the forms in the vaster human drama in which all the world is a stage and men and women merely players. The play is the thing. Quiet attention is the beginning of the way to wisdom in the Pythagorean tradition.

Reincarnation, the philosophy of palingenesis, is also fundamental. Every human being has been involved as a spectator in a variety of spectacles, has played a multiple diversity of roles. In this perspective, all learning is recollection, and much of what is seen is the restoration of Soul-memory. What people think is new is mostly a recollection from where and whence they know naught, but which nonetheless acts as a divine prompting within them and sometimes saves them, in times of trouble and of trial, from making mistakes which would propel them further back than when they made them before, because by now they should have learnt something. The School which Pythagoras founded was one in which every kind of learning could be pursued, not for the purpose of integrating the isms and the sects of the time, but rather for coming down, from above below, so as to be able to see the synthesizing principles, in *theoria* and *praxis,* contemplation and conduct.

After the passing of Pythagoras, the pupils of his School separated out. Schisms ensued between the so-called scientific people, who spent their time making claims, arguing and attacking each other, and those who initially espoused simple enthusiasms and were mocked by the others. The latter were left solely with their disarming trust, faith and devotion, which helped to continue the transmission of the tradition. All of this was known in advance by that wise Promethean called Pythagoras. He wanted separation and self-selection to take place not only among the many who were influenced, but equally among the few who were experiencing the rigours of training, those who had the moral fibre to endure the extremely difficult ascent to wisdom. The claim that the path is easy is the facile excuse of those who do not truly intend to make the ascent, because they have failed many times before and are inwardly so terrified of failure before they start that they would rather not risk even the first test.

There is much protection in the time-tested moral codes of every true community of seekers. This is suggested in the proverbs and the folklore of all societies. Pythagoras taught that there must be an inward quiescence of the soul, a stilling of the mind in which the true receptivity of the heart can enable real learning to take place. A person concentrating while learning carpentry, or while training for athletics, is quiet. Individuals who concentrate while preparing and studying for anything are quiet. Could any less be required of a person who would study and persevere while seeking the divine science of the dialectic, as Hierocles called the Pythagorean teaching? The art of free ascent of the soul towards the upper realms, indicated in the concluding words of the *Golden Verses*, is portrayed as the unveiling of latent perceptions of realities that are hidden. Anyone who is in earnest must give Nature time to speak. It is only upon the serene surface of the unruffled mind that the visions gathered from the invisible may find true and proper representation.

In ancient India, classical Greece and in early America it was well understood that without veneration for forefathers, nothing worthwhile can happen to a human being, a group or a society. This tradition was partly preserved under the influence of the Theosophical Movement in the nineteenth century and the subsequent short-lived Platonic renaissance in a variety of fraternities and movements. Some are still doing well, but most other fraternities, which took Pythagorean rules and adapted them for the purpose of self-discipline, true friendship and self-respect, are not in the same position. While many have closed down, there are others that have held on though they lost the original impulse. There are also those few which have remained, and unknown to the many, have tried to be true to the original impulse. In some cases the impulse goes back not merely to the time of Benjamin Franklin or to the original societies of Philadelphia started at the time of the signing of the Declaration, but even earlier. As Burke suggested, any generation which fails to show respect to its ancestors will deserve nothing of posterity. Those who show little respect to those who have gone before them — their parents, grandparents, teachers and their teachers' teachers — will be repudiated in turn by their children. The law of Karma does not discriminate between persons, societies and generations.

The question came up among the early Pythagoreans, regarding the injunction to honour one's parents: What is one to do if one's parents are unworthy? The answer given at the time by wise Pythagoreans was: First ask yourself whether you really have paid sufficient homage to the immortal gods, to the heroes of all time, and to the earth's good geniuses. If you have done all of these, then you are entitled to ask whether you should show honour to your parents. But you will find, if you have observed all that is prior, that you will always find some reason to honour your parents while at the same time you do not have to blindly follow their ways. That is because, as the later *Golden Verses* stress, all people must think for themselves. Each must make up his own mind and choose his own way. This does not require any recommendation or advertisement in our time. It is part of our very constitution. It was also the deathbed utterance of Buddha. This is the oldest teaching, and it is common sense. There is hardly a human being who does not know it.

Human beings forget. All selfishness is rooted, Pythagoras felt, in thoughtlessness. It is hardly ever the case, even in the age of inversion, that people deliberately intend consistent and systematic inversion of reverence to the immortal gods, even though they may not know what that means, or to the heroes even though they may have demythologized them. They do not deliberately intend to flout the law taught by an Initiate a long time ago: "God is not mocked; as ye sow, so shall ye also reap." Every man knows all of these things. Why then did Schweitzer put so much emphasis upon reverence for life? He knew that if something is worth doing, it is worth emphasizing, because men think they know it, but act as though they never did. Men forget and therefore in the Pythagorean doctrine of *anamnesis,* as in the

Platonic teaching, everything has to do with remembering and forgetting. All human souls, when they have drunk of Lethe's waters, have become identified with forms and come under the influence of the lower languages transmitted to them by the world through their relatives and those near to them. They forget, and as they forget, the babies that stare and smile and greet the world in mystic wonder, in a very short time, in the process of learning how to toddle, to stand straight and to move, become confused in noticing the scorn and the scepticism, the cynicism and the distrust, the self-hatred that is all around. And by the time children are ready for the precious time of puberty, they have received no inspiration or help in learning to handle the sheer joy of using eros under the control of a calm and cool head. They are completely at war with others and with themselves.

We live in the age of Zeus, wherein it is difficult to understand the greatness, let alone the inner meaning, of the Pythagorean invocation of Brihaspati, Jupiter or Zeus — he who knows and can show the genius of every living being. Honour and reverence involve something more than the ordinary understanding of these words. They require what Pythagoras teaches in the closing stanzas of the *Golden Verses*, which collectively were called *Heiros Logos*, the Sacred Discourse. Pythagoras taught that discrimination and discernment are needed. One must learn not just to make distinctions but to show discrimination, to recognize nuances, sub-tones, sub-colours, shades of meaning, to recognize the immense diversity of forms of life but also to see the ordering and the structure under which they could be understood. It is necessary to recognize similars, notice opposites, identify counterfeits, cherish intimations, but above all, to see the continuity and the connection between all of these. Then it will be possible, when hearing opinions, to discriminate among them and to go for the good and the gold in all, even in the most foolish observations. One can learn and note down what is of value in anything and everything that one comes across. But if one comes across a lot that is not worth entering into a notebook, one can let it go and remain calm in the presence of its utterance. All of this points to a conception of manhood, a magnitude of self-possession which combines with compassion and love, magnanimity as well as prudence, and which is truly rare in any age, but wholly admirable in our epoch.

Pythagoras especially commends prudence, not cunning or what the world calls shrewdness, but the insight of wisdom in relation to the lunar realm, a region in which everything that begins will change and pass away. If one does not remember this, one cannot be prudent. To be imprudent is to be over-attached. Desires are of three kinds. There are those desires which when they first arise are ill-fitting, inauspicious, and will do no good from the very start. Often such desires are longings to do the impossible. If a person, before being able to walk the Sierras, wants to climb Everest next week, it is an ill-timed and inauspicious desire. A wise friend might urge him to go and find out what in fact he needs to know, that such learning could be very unpleasant. The second kind of desire is not inauspicious to start with, but makes sense, like the desire to finish something which one has begun, whatever it be, whether it has got to do with school or job or family. Yet herein lies the danger, of an immense inflation of that desire so that it becomes an obsession. It may become a virulent, over-mastering force, so that the person who has it is a slave and no longer a free human being. This kind of desire is not wholly bad, but it has got to be trimmed. The vehemence has got to be taken out of it until it runs like cool waters, consonant with the ocean of life into which it must eventually empty itself. Thirdly, there are desires which, though not unfitting to start with and though not vehement, become inappropriate in expression. A person might have a legitimate desire and a sense of proportion about it but not know how to express it appropriately, and hence become the frequent victim of bad timing. Bad timing is like bad faith, betokening a lack of total commitment and engagement in one's own project, to use Sartrean language. One is never quite there when needed but is always just that bit ill-timed. After a point one gathers around oneself elemental forces that become an ill-omened angel of misfortune.

When Pythagoras spoke of prudence and magnanimity, he gave a critical test. One is becoming a man when there is an increase in one's magnanimity. This teaching was so telling that even after Plato, with the decline of the Academy, Aristotle thought it fit to base his conception of the ideal man upon the quality of magnanimity. Every human being has access to magnanimity, but it cannot be secured instantly if one is mean, niggardly, fearful, selfish or contemptuous. Magnanimity is only released in the mind by large ideas and great visions. In the heart it is released only by a tremendous compassion for the sick and the suffering.

Pythagoras knew what was then to be judiciously chosen as a foundation stone for the culture of the future. At present when modern culture is nearly dying and giving a great howl while doing so — but barely concealing a rather pathetic whimper — and another culture has already begun to come into birth as the invisible dips into the visible, the Pythagorean teaching cannot now mean a mere return to the forms once given in Magna Graecia. It must be seen and meditated upon as the seed of self-regenerating institutions and the culture and etiquette of the soul. When the soul becomes established firmly like a statue motionless in mind, while at the same time entertaining the vast universe of thoughts, the whole is fixed immovably in contemplation, showing beauty of soul, beauty of mind, beauty of heart, beauty in every direction and every dimension. It thereby makes it possible for more and more human beings, with their imperfections, to come out of the multitudes for the sake of all and for the sake of self-transformation and self-actualization, culminating in self-transcendence.

Preparations are crucial for the Pythagorean school of the future. Anyone who studies the *Golden Verses* of Pythagoras, in any translation or edition, and seeks by reflecting upon them to draw some inspiration, can release a vital energy in inward consciousness which is causal in relation to the external realm of effects. Those who do this could constitute themselves as beings who come closer in spirit, thought and feeling to the inmost, ever-unmanifest Presence. In the days of Pythagoras many people knew that they knew him not. No great teacher ever incarnates or manifests except in proper conditions, and these are always hidden and always involve a few. When necessary he will manifest any relevant part of himself. Pythagoras spent a long time — twenty-two years — studying the Egyptian Mysteries, taking a projection of himself and letting it share all the ailments of the age. When he was ready to begin his work, he allowed people to see veiled appearances and partial expressions. His unmanifest and invisible Self, by its very nature (for those who apprehend the Golden Egg), can never be seen except by the light of the eye when the golden thread which is in every human being has been extended. This requires *Buddhi*. One who reads the *Golden Verses* in this reverential spirit can come closer to the Divine Being who was their wise author and gain inspiration which would be invaluable in times of trouble.

DE RERUM NATURA

Natura non facit saltum.

Although Lucretius, the follower of Epicurus, has sometimes been invoked by modern sceptics and scientific materialists, he was much in advance of those dogmatic scientists today who make extravagant materialistic claims on the basis of atomic physics. The atomism of Lucretius, like that of Kanada in India, has affinities with aspects of Theosophical teaching and was based upon presuppositions that are similar to elements in Buddhist thought. Of course, Lucretius cannot be taken as an early Theosophist, but almost no western philosopher and metaphysician, according to H.P. Blavatsky, succeeded in echoing more than a portion of the Secret Doctrine and sometimes in a distorted manner. Similarly, none of the six schools of Indian philosophy is more than an approximation to one facet of the Gupta Vidya.

Lucretius was a Roman noble who died about 55 B.C.E, supposedly the victim of a love potion. Next to nothing is known about the events of his life, but he has been celebrated as a poet's poet and is chiefly remembered for his *De Rerum Natura,* a didactic philosophical poem of over 7000 lines on 'The Nature of Things'. The central belief that lies at the heart of this poem is that the universe is ruled by wholly natural laws and that mankind is free to work out its own destiny, undisturbed by any supernal guidance. Lucretius was scathing in his scorn of superstition, but he showed a passionate fidelity to all sentient life and especially to the human race, and his insight into the grandeur of nature was profound. He was concerned to liberate men from fear, particularly the fear of death. He pictured the early terrors of mankind in the presence of the great unknown forces of the heavens. In Lucretian philosophy the conquest of death was to be achieved not by denying its powers but by a frank recognition of its certainty and its endlessness. Virgil referred to this aspect of Lucretius's teaching:

> Happy was he who, learn'd in Nature's law,
> Trampled on mortal fears, and could deride
> The pitiless fate that fills men's hearts with awe,
> The din of Death's insatiable tide.

The inability of Lucretius to conceive of the possibility of the survival of the death of the body by a disembodied entity using subtler vestures must be seen in the context of his general picture of the universe. He stressed the Second Fundamental Proposition of *The Secret Doctrine* and partly grasped the Third Fundamental and even portions of the First Fundamental, but it is not surprising that in his strong reaction to the superstitions taught in the name of religion he should not have come to a clear vision of the Three Fundamentals in their essential interdependence.

The main object of Lucretius was to show that life and matter are parts of the same order of things and that the soul of man results from the same general process as that which results in all other phenomena — in the body of man, in the flowers, the seas, the mountains, in the whole frame of the earth and in all the suns and stars. He regarded the earth and the system to which it belonged as but an infinitesimal portion of a universe of similar systems scattered through endless space, which always have been forming themselves, surviving and then decomposing in an endless process. The whole of this limitless universe, "which decomposes but to recompose," consists, in his view, of atoms aggregated in various forms. Nothing exists beyond space and the atoms and the laws in accordance with which the atoms exist. Consciousness, life, soul, whether in man or in animals, represent merely an atomic tissue of an exceptionally subtle kind. The atoms throughout infinite time make an infinite variety of combinations, but those alone have persisted which were fit to persist, the others resolving presently into their component parts.

Men and animals are forms of life that have been fit to live out of the innumerable forms that have appeared and perished because they have not been fit. The universe is not the miraculous creation of any deity, and if any deities exist they emerge from the nature of things just as man does and are not personally concerned with his actions. Men in general, Lucretius says, labour under the horrible belief that they are born under the wrath of God, or of the gods, and that these monstrous powers have called them into life only in order that, after death, they may torment them in hell for ever. Here is really the root of all human sadness and slavery. If men rid themselves of this baseless fear fed by fancy, the aching of their hearts will cease; they will rise up and be free. At other times Lucretius recognized that there is in man's self the same source of restlessness, discontent and sorrow that characterizes all life, even if all fear of hell and of the anger of the gods be done away with. Self is the secret malady of man — for ever unsatisfied, for ever ill at ease.

Lucretius began his poem with an invocation to Venus, the symbol of the creative energy of Nature,

> Since every living form through thee has birth,
> That breathes, and grows, and gazes on the sun! . . .
> All hearts with fond desire thou wakenest,
> Race after race, to propagate their kind.
> And, since all nature owns thy single sway,
> Nor, save through thee, can aught be born or blest
> With light divine, aught fair and lovely grow,
> Thy favour would I win, ere I essay
> Life's natural laws in stately song to trace.

This invocation may be regarded today merely as a poetic convention, but it is consonant with the spirit of the entire poem in which Lucretius puts forward some of the scientific truths of the ancient Wisdom-Religion. He speaks of the curse of superstition and refers to the fantasies that men have made of the gods as agencies capriciously intervening in human affairs; but he does not deny that gods exist or that natural forces may be personified as gods. The important thing is that there are "primordial substances" which "proclaim wherefrom, by nature's laws, each life upsprings, and thereunto returns dissolved in dust." He calls these the "seeds of things" or "first bodies," since they first gave birth to all.

> Albeit each primal body moveth fleet,
> Still seems the mass in perfect calm to bide,
> Save where some single shape its place doth change;
> For the elemental nature hath its seat
> Where sense can reach not, and itself unseen
> Must needs withdraw its motions from our gaze.

There are some memorable passages in *De Rerum Natura* on the motion of atoms, the boundlessness of the universe, the world's decay, the eternal rest, the secrets of the dead, the fantasies of colour, the humanizing of mankind and the worship of the gods. The universe is an ocean of floating elementals, clashing and combining in endless procession. We do not know their number, but "we know them in each kind, the first-beginning whence all forms proceed." Those elementals which are fertile, creative and life-dealing survive, while those which are sterile, destructive and death-dealing are eventually destroyed.

> So balanced is the elemental strife,
> From time eternal waged unendingly;
> Now here, now there, upsprings victorious life;
> Then sinks back vanquished.

Death results in the dispersion of elementals rather than in the total destruction of bodies. Forms disappear but the atoms remain. These atoms or primal bodies are devoid of "fleeting properties," the secondary qualities of sensation, colour, etc., which are produced by various combinations, the atoms of which

> So shift their semblance and their hues reverse,
> Sensation win and instant lose again,

> That this alone it profits us to learn —
> How they be grouped and how distributed,
> What motions they impart, what take in turn.

Men must meditate upon rather than marvel at the flux and renewal in the universe. Just as space stretches free beyond the world's wide bulwarks, so too thought projects us in unfettered flight when we contemplate the boundlessness of space.

> First, then, this truth I teach: how wide soe'er
> Outspreads the universe, above, below,
> No bound is: so the very facts declare
> And the clear-shining nature of the deep.
> Wherefore against all reason doth it seem
> That while toward every side yawns infinite space,
> And atoms in unnumbered numbers hurled
> Through myriad ways in endless motion sweep,
> The sole created thing is this our world.

Lucretius went on to derive from this first truth the further truth that "naught subsists alone, no creature sole is born, nor thriveth sole, but each hath kinship in some populous race." Land and sky, sun, moon and sea are parts of a great whole and all things that live must die. As in the celebrated Rig-Vedic hymn, Lucretius asks:

> Who would command the immeasurable, who dare
> To grasp the ponderous reins of the abyss?

Then comes the passage about the world's decay. "This wondrous world itself, its great walls riven by force of slow decay, shall crumbling fall." Men may curse the flight of time and pine for a past age of prosperous piety, when easier life in narrower bounds was theirs, but they must come to face the fact that all things, step by step, decline. The death of things and forms should not concern us because our sensory mind is itself mortal and cannot survive the death of the body. Even if the disembodied mind or soul were haunted by sense-memories and by conscious thought, this cannot mean anything to those who are still in an embodied state. Similarly, our past lives need not concern us as long as we do not remember them.

> Nor yet if time our scattered dust re-blend,
> And after death upbuild the flesh again,
> Yea, and our light of life arise re-lit,
> Can such new birth concern the self one whit,
> When once dark death has severed memory's chain.
> Naught reck we, then, our lives lived in the past,
> Nor for their sorrows feel one pang of pain.

In real death there can be no self to mourn the absence of another self or to stand and weep at death's indignity. Death is sleep and rest and there is no cause for dread. "By what false love of life are we misled?"

Lucretius recognized the existence of *simulacra,* phantom forms thrown off from the surfaces of things. These forms are of various hues and seem to sway, tinged with each dancing colour, and change anew their ever-shifting shape. The subtle nature of the gods is, however, hidden from bodily sense, intangible and inaccessible to human thought.

> For naught can touch save what is tangible:
> So in no mortal mansions must they dwell
> Like ours, but subtler, as their beings are.

While men aspire to longer life and their hearts are bound by fond affection to the earth, the gods are unborn, impersonal and, having no taste for embodied life, can feel no death. The gods had a creative function assigned to them by the laws of nature.

> How could they learn the all-generative force
> Of first-beginnings variously combined,

Had not great Nature's self the type designed;
For many in number, driven in many a way
From time eternal on their headlong course,
Impelled by their own weight were the atoms
hurled,
For ever striving to unite and find
The power to build new forms with life endued.

Lucretius taught that this universe and all in it are ever changing in a process of continuous evolution.

For time makes mutable the whole world's mass,
Which on from phase to phase must ever range;
Naught keeps its native likeness; all things pass,
All things by Nature's law must shift and change.
See, one in slow decrepitude decays,
Another leaps to light from mean estate;
So time the texture of the world repairs,
And Earth moves forward still from phase to phase.

The early races, he believed, were of massive mould and led a wandering life, uninstructed as yet in the use of the plough or the arts of cultivation, or even in the kindling of fire, unaware of the common good and unchecked by fixed laws and covenants. Gradually mankind in its infancy became humanized, subdued by the power of love, united by growing bonds of friendliness, and learning with stammering speech and gestures to express the belief that it is right to reverence the weak. These men soon came to have sight of the marvelous majesty of the gods, but they conceived of them in their own image of man and became fatalistic and helpless.

Lucretius evidently had partial glimpses of some of the basic truths of the *Philosophia Perennis*. *The Secret Doctrine* commends the doctrine of Leucippus and Democritus that Space is filled eternally with atoms actuated by ceaseless motion, the latter generating in course of time, when those atoms aggregated, rotatory motion, through mutual collisions producing lateral movements. "Epicurus and Lucretius taught the same, only adding to the lateral motion of the atoms the idea of affinity — an occult teaching." Real science is not materialistic as is shown by the recognition, by the earliest atomists in Europe, of supersensuous entities or gods. In the section on the elements and the atoms, *The Secret Doctrine* teaches:

> Modern physics, while borrowing from the ancients their atomic theory, forgot one point, the most important of the doctrine; hence they got only the husks and will never be able to get at the kernel. They left behind, in the adoption of physical atoms, the suggestive fact that from Anaxagoras down to Epicurus, the Roman Lucretius, and finally even to Galileo, all those Philosophers believed more or less in ANIMATED atoms, not in invisible specks of so-called 'brute' matter. Rotatory motion was generated, in their views, by larger (read, more divine and pure) atoms forcing downwards other atoms; the lighter ones being thrust simultaneously upward. The esoteric meaning of this is the ever cyclic curve downward and upward of differentiated elements through intercyclic phases of existence, until each reaches again its starting point or birthplace. The idea was metaphysical as well as physical; the hidden interpretation embracing 'gods' or souls, in the shape of atoms, as the causes of all the effects produced on Earth by the secretions from the divine bodies. No ancient philosopher, not even the Jewish Kabalists, ever dissociated Spirit from matter or vice versâ . . . Atoms and Souls having been synonymous in the language of the Initiates.
>
> *The Secret Doctrine*, i 567-8

Lucretius, then, was not the crude materialist he has often been made out but a philosopher whose notion of matter was subtler than that of modern scientists and included in it what theologians have ascribed to spirit.

Gupta Vidya teaches clearly that all the cosmic and terrestrial elements, capable of generating within themselves a concatenation of causes and effects, are animated by intelligence.

> Occultism does not deny the certainty of the mechanical origin of the Universe; it only claims the absolute necessity of mechanicians of some sort behind those Elements (or *within*) — a dogma with us. It is not the fortuitous assistance of the atoms of Lucretius, who himself knew better, that built the Kosmos and all in it. Nature herself contradicts such a theory.

It would be wrong to regard Lucretius as an atheist in the modern sense as he did, like his teacher Epicurus, believe in gods while also pointing out that the misunderstanding of their natures and functions had given rise to superstition and fear. Lucretius did exaggerate the extent to which primitive humanity was more miserable than present-day humanity. But he was entirely Theosophical in his concern to rid mankind of its nightmarish dependence upon anthropomorphic conceptions of deity. "The God of the Theologians," said Mahatma K.H.,

> is simply an imaginary power, *un loup garou* as d'Holbach expressed it — a power which has never yet manifested itself. Our chief aim is to deliver humanity of this nightmare, to teach man virtue for its own sake, and to walk in life relying on himself instead of leaning on a theological crutch, that for countless ages was the direct cause of nearly all human misery. . . . When we speak of our One Life we also say that it penetrates, nay is the essence of every atom of matter; and that therefore it not only has correspondence with matter but has all its properties likewise, etc. — hence *is* material, is *matter itself.*

We are also taught that it is motion that governs the laws of nature and that "wherever there is life and being, and in however much spiritualized a form, there is no room for moral government, much less for a moral Governor — a Being which at the same time has no form nor occupies space!"

Theosophical literature thus helps to throw light on the teachings of Lucretius and also to see beyond his denial of the immortal individuality of man. Even on this matter Lucretius was ambiguous rather than dogmatic and nihilistic. He urged men not to propitiate the gods or to fear the torments of hell but to "learn the nature of things; since what is at issue is the state not of one hour but of that eternity in which the whole age of mortals — whatsoever may remain of it — after death must continue." In his emphasis upon perpetual motion, the boundlessness of space and the cycle of mortality governing myriads of universes, the continual activity of atoms regulated by laws of affinity and dispersion the subtle forms of the gods who function on their own plane, the cosmic dance of the elementals, the need for men to meditate upon the nature of things and the sickness of selfhood, Lucretius showed an acute awareness of some of the axioms of Gupta Vidya and the *Philosophia Perennis*.

What is commonly understood by the word 'Spirit' then is nothing but that highly etherealized form of matter which we with our finite senses cannot comprehend. But it is still matter in as much as it is still something and liable to be grosser. . . . The one Infinite Agglomeration of matter is in some of its modes becoming more and more sublimated. The Circle is ever turning its round. Nothing goes out of that Circle. Everything is kept within its bounds by the action of the Centripetal and the Centrifugal Forces. The forms are changing but the Inner *substance remains the same.*

DAMODAR K. MAVALANKAR

THE GOSPEL
ACCORDING TO ST. JOHN

> *Let us beware of creating a darkness at noonday for*
> *ourselves by gazing, so to say, direct at the sun . . . , as though*
> *we could hope to attain adequate vision and perception of*
> *Wisdom with mortal eyes. It will be the safer course to turn*
> *our gaze on an image of the object of our quest.*
>
> PLATO

Every year more than three hundred and fifty Catholic and Protestant sects observe Easter Sunday, celebrating the Resurrection of Jesus, the Son of God who called himself the Son of Man. So too do the Russian and Greek Orthodox churches, but on a separate calendar. Such is the schism between East and West within Christendom regarding this day, which always falls on the ancient Sabbath, once consecrated to the Invisible Sun, the sole source of all life, light and energy. If we wish to understand the permanent possibility of spiritual resurrection taught by the Man of Sorrows, we must come to see both the man and his teaching from the pristine perspective of Brahma Vach, the timeless oral utterance behind and beyond all religions, philosophies and sciences throughout the long history of mankind.

The Gospel According to St. John is the only canonical gospel with a metaphysical instead of an historical preamble. We are referred to that which was in the beginning. In the New English Bible, the recent revision of the authorized version produced for the court of King James, we are told: "Before all things were made was the Word." In the immemorial, majestic and poetic English of the King James version, *In the beginning was the Word and the Word was with God, and the Word was God.* This is a *bija sutra,* a seminal maxim, marking the inception of the first of twenty-one chapters of the gospel, and conveying the sum and substance of the message of Jesus. John, according to Josephus, was at one time an Essene and his account accords closely with the Qumran Manual of Discipline. The gospel attributed to John derives from the same oral tradition as the Synoptics, but it shows strong connections with the Pauline epistles as well as with the Jewish apocalyptic tradition. It is much more a mystical treatise than a biographical narrative.

The Godhead is *unthinkable* and *unspeakable*, extending boundlessly beyond the range and reach of thought. There is no supreme Father figure in the universe. In the beginning was the Word, the Verbum, the *Shabdabrahman*, the eternal radiance that is like a veil upon the attributeless Absolute. If all things derive, as St. John explains, from that One Source, then all beings and all the sons of men are forever included. Metaphysically, every human being has more than one father, though on the physical plane each has only one. Over ten thousand years, everyone has had more ancestors than there are souls presently incarnated on earth. Each one participates in the ancestry of all mankind. While always true, this is more evident in a nation with mixed ancestries. Therefore it is appropriate here that we think of him who preached before Jesus, Buddha, who taught that we ask not of a man's descent but of his conduct. *By their fruits they shall be known,* say the gospels.

There is another meaning of the 'Father' which is relevant to the opportunity open to every human being to take a decision to devote his or her entire life to the service of the entire human family. The ancient Jews held that from the illimitable *Ain-Soph* there came a reflection, which could never be more than a partial participation in that illimitable light which transcends manifestation. This reflection exists in the world as archetypal humanity — Adam Kadmon. Every human being belongs to one single humanity, and that collectivity stands in relation to the *Ain-Soph* as any one human being to his or her own father. It is no wonder that Pythagoras — *Pitar Guru*, 'father and teacher', as he was known among the ancient Hindus — came to Krotona to sound the keynote of a long cycle now being reaffirmed for an equally long period in the future. He taught his disciples to honour their father and their mother, and to take a sacred oath to the Holy Fathers of the human race, the 'Ancestors of the Arhats.'

We are told in the fourth Stanza of *Dzyan* that the Fathers are the Sons of Fire, descended from a primordial host of Logoi. They are self-existing rays streaming forth from a single, central, universal Mahatic fire which is within the cosmic egg, just as differentiated matter is outside and around it. There are seven sub-divisions within Mahat — the cosmic mind, as it was called by the Greeks — as well as seven dimensions of matter outside the egg, giving a total of fourteen planes, fourteen worlds. Where we are told by John that Jesus said, *In my Father's house are many mansions*, H.P. Blavatsky states that this refers to the seven mansions of the central Logos, supremely revered in all religions as the Solar Creative Fire. Any human being who has a true wakefulness and thereby a sincere spirit of obeisance to the divine demiurgic intelligence in the universe, of which he is a trustee even while encased within the lethargic carcass of matter, can show that he is a man to the extent to which he exhibits divine manliness through profound gratitude, a constant recognition and continual awareness of the One Source. All the great Teachers of humanity point to a single source beyond themselves. Many are called but few are chosen by self-election. Spiritual Teachers always point upwards for each and every man and woman alive, not for just a few. They work not only in the visible realm for those immediately before them, but, as John reminds us, they come from above and work for all. They continually think of and love every being that lives and breathes, mirroring "the One that breathes breathless" in ceaseless contemplation, overbrooding the Golden Egg of the universe, the *Hiranyagarbha*.

Such beautiful ideas enshrined in magnificent myths are provocative to the ratiocinative mind and suggestive to the latent divine discernment of Buddhic intuition. The only way anyone can come closer to the Father in Heaven, let alone come closer to

Him on earth Who is as He is in Heaven, is by that light to which John refers in the first chapter of the Gospel. It is the light that lighteth every man who cometh into the world, which the darkness comprehendeth not. Human beings are involved in the darkness of illusion, of self-forgetfulness, and forgetfulness of their divine ancestry. The whole of humanity may be regarded as a garden of gods but all men and women are fallen angels or gods tarnished by forgetfulness of their true eternal and universal mission. Every man or woman is born for a purpose. Every person has a divine destiny. Every individual has a unique contribution to make, to enrich the lives of others, but no one can say what this is for anyone else. Each one has to find it, first by arousing and kindling and then by sustaining and nourishing the little lamp within the heart. There alone may be lit the true Akashic fire upon the altar in the hidden temple of the God which lives and breathes within. This is the sacred fire of true awareness which enables a man to come closer to the one universal divine consciousness which, in its very brooding upon manifestation, is the father-spirit. In the realm of matter it may be compared to the wind that bloweth where it listeth. Any human being could become a self-conscious and living instrument of that universal divine consciousness of which he, as much as every other man or woman, is an effulgent ray.

This view of man is totally different from that which has, alas, been preached in the name of Jesus. Origen spoke of the constant crucifixion of Jesus, declaring that there is not a day on earth when he is not reviled. But equally there is not a time when others do not speak of him with awe. He came with a divine protection provided by a secret bond which he never revealed except by indirect intonation. Whenever the Logos becomes flesh, there is sacred testimony to the Great Sacrifice and the Great Renunciation — of all Avatars, all Divine Incarnations. This Brotherhood of Blessed Teachers is ever behind every attempt to enlighten human minds, to summon the latent love in human hearts for all humanity, to fan the sparks of true compassion in human beings into the fires of Initiation. The mark of the Avatar is that in him the Paraclete, the Spirit of Eternal Truth, manifests so that even the blind may see, the deaf may hear, the lame may walk, the unregenerate may gain confidence in the possibility and the promise of Self-redemption.

In one of the most beautiful passages penned on this subject, the profound essay entitled "The Roots of Ritualism in Church and Masonry," published in 1889, H.P. Blavatsky declared:

> Most of us believe in the survival of the Spiritual Ego, in Planetary Spirits and *Nirmanakayas*, those great Adepts of the past ages, who, renouncing their right to Nirvana, remain in our spheres of being, not as 'spirits' but as complete spiritual human Beings. Save their corporeal, visible envelope, which they leave behind, they remain as they were, in order to help poor humanity, as far as can be done without sinning against Karmic Law. This is the 'Great Renunciation', indeed; an incessant, conscious self-sacrifice throughout aeons and ages till that day when the eyes of blind mankind will open and, instead of the few, *all* will see the universal truth. These Beings may well be regarded as God and Gods — if they would but allow the fire in our hearts, at the thought of that purest of all sacrifices, to be fanned into the flame of adoration, or the smallest altar in their honour. But they will not. Verily, 'the secret heart is fair Devotion's (only) temple', and any other, in this case, would be no better than profane ostentation.

Let a man be without external show such as the Pharisees favoured, without inscriptions such as the Scribes specialized in, and without arrogant and ignorant self-destructive denial such as that of the Sadducees. Such a man, whether he be of any religion or none, of whatever race or nation or creed, once he recognizes the existence of a Fraternity of Divine Beings, a Brotherhood of Buddhas, Bodhisattvas and Christs, an Invisible Church (in St. Augustine's phrase) of living human beings ever ready to help any honest and sincere seeker, he will thereafter cherish the discovery within himself. He will guard it with great reticence and grateful reverence, scarcely speaking of his feeling to strangers or even to friends. When he can do this and maintain it, and above all, as John says in the Gospel, be true to it and live by it, then he may make it for himself, as Jesus taught, the way, the truth and the light. While he may not be self-manifested as the Logos came to be through Jesus — the Son of God become the Son of Man — he could still sustain and protect himself in times of trial. No man dare ask for more. No man could do with less.

Jesus knew that his own time of trial had come — the time for the consummation of his vision — on the Day of Passover. Philo Judaeus, who was an Aquarian in the Age of Pisces, gave an intellectual interpretation to what other men saw literally, pointing out that the spiritual passover had to do with passing over earthly passions. Jesus, when he knew the hour had come for the completion of his work and the glorification of his father to whom he ever clung, withdrew with the few into the Garden of Gethsemane. He did not choose them, he said. They chose him. He withdrew with them and there they all used the time for true prayer to the God within. Jesus had taught, *Go into thy closet and pray to thy father who is in secret,* and that *The Kingdom of God is within you.* This was the mode of prayer which he revealed and exemplified to those who were ready for initiation into the Mysteries. Many tried but only few stayed with it. Even among those few there was a Peter, who would thrice deny Jesus. There was the traitor, Judas, who had already left the last supper that evening, having been told, *That thou doest, do quickly.* Some among the faithful spent their time in purification. Were they, at that point, engaged in self-purification for their own benefit? What had Jesus taught them? Could one man separate himself from any other? He had told those who wanted to stone the adulteress, *Let him who is without sin cast the first stone.* He had told them not to judge anyone else, but to wait for true judgment. Because they had received a sublime privilege, about which other men subsequently argued for centuries and produced myriad heresies and sects, in their case the judgment involved their compassionate concern to do the sacred Work of the Father for the sake of all. The Garden of Gethsemane is always here. It is a place very different from the Wailing Wall where people gnash their teeth and weep for themselves or their tribal ancestors. The Garden of Gethsemane is wherever on earth men and women want to cleanse themselves for the sake of being more humane in their relations with others.

Nor was the crucifixion only true of Jesus and those two thieves, one of whom wanted to have a miracle on his behalf while the other accepted the justice of the law of the day, receiving punishment for offenses that he acknowledged openly. Every man participates in that crucifixion. This much may be learnt from the great mystics and inspired poets across two thousand years. Christos is being daily, hourly, every moment crucified within the cross of every human being. There are too few on earth who are living up to the highest possibility of god-like wisdom, love and compassion, let alone who can say that in them the spirit of Truth, the Paraclete, manifests. Who has the courage to chase the money-changers of petty thoughts and paltry desires from the Temple of the universal Spirit, not through hatred of the money-changers, but through a love in his heart for the Restoration of the Temple? Who has the courage to say openly what all men recognize inwardly when convenient, or when drunk, or when among friends whom they think they trust? Who is truly a man? How many men are there heroically suffering? Not only do we know that God is not mocked and that as we sow, so shall we reap, but we also realize that the Garden of Gethsemane is difficult to reach. Nonetheless, it may be sought by any and every person who wants to avoid the dire tragedy of self-annihilation. Indeed, there are many such people all around who barely survive from day to day because of their own self-hatred, self-contempt and despair, and who tremble on the brink of moral death. We live in terribly tragic times, and therefore there is no one who cannot afford to take a little pause for the sake of making the burden of one's presence easier for one's wife or husband, for one's children, or for one's neighbours. Each needs a time of re-examination, a time for true repentance, a time for Christ-like resolve. The Garden of Gethsemane is present wherever there is genuineness, determination and honesty. Above all, it is where there is the joyous recognition that, quite apart from yesterday and tomorrow, right now a person can create so strong a current of thought that it radically affects the future. He could begin now, and acquire in time a self-sustaining momentum. But this cannot be done without overcoming the karmic gravity of all the self- destructive murders of human beings that he has participated in on the plane of thought, on the plane of feeling, especially on the plane of words, and also, indirectly, on the plane of outward action.

If the Garden of Gethsemane did not exist, no persecuting Saul could ever become a Paul. Such is the great hope and the glad tiding. As Origen said, Saul had to be killed before Paul could be born. St. Francis who was a simple crusader had to die before the Saint of Assisi could be born. Because all men have free will, no man can transform himself without honest and sincere effort. Hence, after setting out the nature of the Gods, the Fathers of the human race, H.P. Blavatsky spoke of the conditions of probation of incarnated souls seeking resurrection:

> . . . every true Theosophist holds that the divine HIGHER SELF of every mortal man is of the same essence as the essence of these Gods. Being, moreover, endowed with free-will, hence having, more than they, responsibility, we regard the incarnated EGO as far superior to, if not more divine than, any spiritual INTELLIGENCE *still awaiting incarnation.* Philosophically, the reason for this is obvious, and every metaphysician of the Eastern school will understand it. The incarnated EGO has odds against it which do not exist in the case of a pure divine Essence unconnected with matter; the latter has no personal merit, whereas the former is on his way to final perfection through the trials of existence, of pain and suffering.

It is up to each one to decide whether to make this suffering constructive, these trials meaningful, these tribulations a golden opportunity for self-transformation and spiritual resurrection.

If this decision is not made voluntarily during life, it is thrust upon each ego at death. Every human being has to pass at the moment of death, according to the wisdom of the ancients, to a purgatorial condition in which there is a separation of the immortal individuality. It is like a light which is imprisoned during waking life, a life which is a form of sleep within the serpent coils of matter. This god within is clouded over by the fog of fear, superstition and confusion, and all but the pure in heart obscure the inner light by their demonic deceits and their ignorant denial of the true heart. Every human being needs to cast out this shadow, just as he would throw away an old garment, says Krishna, or just as he would dump into a junkyard an utterly unredeemable vehicle. Any and every human being has to do the same on the psychological plane. Each is in the same position. He has to discard the remnants, but the period for this varies according to each person. This involves what is called 'the mathematics of the soul.' Figures are given to those with ears to hear, and there is a great deal of detailed application to be made.

Was Jesus exempt from this? He wanted no exception. He had taken the cross. He had become one with other men, constantly taking on their limitations, exchanging his finer life-atoms for their gross life-atoms — the concealed thoughts, the unconscious hostilities, the chaotic feelings, the ambivalences, the ambiguities, the limitations of all. He once said, *My virtue has gone out of me,* when the hem of his garment was touched by a woman seeking help, but does this mean that he was exposed only when he physically encountered other human beings? *The Gospel According to John* makes it crisply clear, since it is the most mystical and today the most meaningful of the four gospels, that this was taking place all the time. It not only applies to Jesus. It takes place all the time for every person, often unknown to oneself. But when it is fully self-conscious, the pain is greater, such as when a magnanimous Adept makes a direct descent from his true divine estate, leaving behind his finest elements, like Surya the sun in the myth who cuts off his lustre for the sake of entering into a marriage with Sanjna, coming into the world, and taking on the limitations of all. The Initiator needs the three days in the tomb, but these three days are metaphorical. They refer to what is known in the East as a necessary gestation state when the transformation could be made more smoothly from the discarded vehicle which had been crucified.

People tend to fasten upon the wounds and the blood, even though, as Titian's painting portrays clearly, the tragedy of Jesus was not in the bleeding wounds but in the ignorance and self-limitation of the disciples. He had promised redemption to anyone and everyone who was true to him, which meant, he said, to love each other. He had washed the feet of the disciples, drawn them together, given them every opportunity so that they would do the same for each other. He told them that they need only follow this one commandment. We know how difficult it is for most people today to love one another, to work together, to pull together, to cooperate and not compete, to add and not subtract, to multiply and serve, not divide and rule. This seems very difficult especially in a hypocritical society filled with deceit and lies. What are children to say when their parents ask them to tell the truth and they find themselves surrounded by so many lies? In the current cycle the challenge is most pointed and poignant. More honesty is needed, more courage, more toughness — this time for the sake of all mankind. One cannot leave it to a future moment for some pundits in theological apologetics and theosophical hermeneutics to say this cycle was only for some chosen people. Every single part of the world has to be included and involved.

The teaching of Jesus was a hallowed communication of insights, a series of sacred glimpses, rather than a codification of doctrine. He presented not a *summa theologica* or *ethica,* but the seminal basis from which an endless series of *summae* could be conceived. He initiated a spiritual current of sacred dialogue, individual exploration and communal experiment in the quest for divine wisdom. He taught the beauty of acquiescence and the dignity of acceptance of suffering — a mode appropriate to the Piscean Age. He showed salvation through love, sacrifice and faith — of the regenerated psyche that cleaves to the light of nous. He excelled in being all things to all men while remaining utterly true to himself and to his 'Father in Heaven.' He showed a higher respect for the Temple than its own custodians. At the same time he came to found a new kind of kingdom and to bring a message of joy and hope. He came to bear witness to the Kingdom of Heaven during life's probationary ordeal on earth. He vivified by his own luminous sacrifice the universal human possibility of divine self-consecration, the beauty of beatific devotion to the Transcendental Source of Divine Wisdom — the Word Made Flesh celebrating the Verbum In the Beginning.

Above all, there was the central paradox that his mission had to be vindicated by its failure, causing bewilderment among many of his disciples, while intuitively understood only by the very few who were pure in heart and strong in devotion, blessed by the vision of the Ascension. After three days in the tomb, Jesus, in the guise of a gardener, said to a poor, disconsolate Mary Magdalene, *Mary!* At once she looked back because she recognized the voice, and she said, *Rabboni* — "My Master" — and fell at his feet. Then he said, *Touch me not.* Here is a clue to his three days in the tomb. The work of permanent transmutation of life-atoms, of transfiguration of vehicles, was virtually complete. He then said, *Go to my brethren, and say unto them, I ascend unto my Father and your Father; and to my God and your God.* Subsequently he appeared three times to his disciples.

Jesus gave the greatest possible confidence to all his disciples by ever paying them the most sacred compliment, telling them that they were children of God. But, still, if a person thinks that he is nothing, or thinks that he is the greatest sinner on earth, how can the compassion and praise of Jesus have meaning for him? Each person has to begin to see himself undramatically as one of many sinners and say, "My sins are no different from those of anyone else." The flesh is weak but *pneuma*, the spirit, is willing. And *pneuma* has to do with breath. The whole of *The Gospel*

According to John is saturated with the elixir of the breathing-in and breathing-out by Jesus of the life-infusing current that gives every man a credible faith in his promise and possibility, and, above all, a living awareness of his immortality, which he can self-consciously realize when freed from mis-identification with his mortal frame.

The possibility of resurrection has to do with identification and mis-identification. This is the issue not for just a few but for all human beings who, in forgetfulness, tend to think that they are what their enemies think, or that they are what their friends want them to be. At one time men talked of the *Imago Dei*. We now live in a society that constantly deals in diabolical images and the cynical corruption of image-making, a nefarious practice unfamiliar in simpler societies which still enjoy innocent psychic health. Even more, people now engage in image-crippling — the most heinous of crimes. At one time men did it openly, with misguided courage. They pulled down statues and defaced idols. They paid for it and are still paying. Perhaps those people were reborn in this society. That is sad because they are condemning themselves to something worse than hell — not only the hell of loneliness and despair — but much worse. The light is going out for many a human being. The Mahatmas have always been with us. They have always abundantly sent forth benedictory vibrations. They are here on earth where they have always had their asylums and their ashrams. Under cyclic law they are able to use precisely prepared forums and opportunities to re-erect or resurrect the mystery temples of the future. Thus, at this time, everybody is stirred up by the crucial issue of identity — which involves the choice between the living and the dead, between entelechy and self-destruction.

The central problem in *The Gospel According to John*, which Paul had to confront in giving his sermon on the resurrection, has to do with life and with death. What is life for one man is not life to another. Every man or woman today has to raise the question, "What does it mean for me to be alive, to breathe, to live for the sake of others, to live within the law which protects all but no one in particular?" Whoever truly identifies with the limitless and unconditional love of Jesus and with the secret work of Jesus which he veiled in wordless silence, is lit up. Being lit up, one is able to see the divine Buddha-nature, the light vesture of Buddha. The disciples in the days of Buddha, and so again in the days of Jesus, were able to see the divine raiment made of the most homogeneous pure essence of universal *Buddhi*. Immaculately conceived and unbegotten, it is *Daiviprakriti*, the Light of the Logos. Every man at all times has such a garment, but it is covered over. Therefore, each must sift and select the gold from the dross. The more a person does this truly and honestly, the more the events of what we call life can add up before the moment of death. They can have a beneficent impact upon the mood and the state of mind in which one departs. A person who is wise in this generation will so prepare his meditation that at the moment of death he may read or have read out those passages in the *Bhagavad Gita, The Voice of the Silence,* or *The Gospel According to St. John,* that are exactly relevant to what is needed. Then he will be able to intone the Word, which involves the whole of one's being and breathing, at the moment when he may joyously discard his mortal garment. It has been done, and it is being done. It can be done, and it will be done. Anyone can do it, but in these matters there is no room for chance or deception, for we live in a universe of law. Religion can be supported now by science, and to bring the two together in the psychology of self-transformation one needs true philosophy, the unconditional love of wisdom.

The crucifixion of Jesus and his subsequent resurrection had little reference to himself, any more than any breath he took during his life. Thus, in the Gospel, we read that Jesus promises that when he will be gone from the world, he will send the Paraclete. This archaic concept has exercised the pens of many scholars. What is the Paraclete? What does it mean? 'Comforter'? 'The Spirit of Truth'? Scholars still do not claim to know. The progress made in this century is in the honest recognition that they do not know, whereas in the nineteenth century they quarrelled, hurled epithets at each other out of arrogance, with a false confidence that did not impress anyone for long. The times have changed, and this is no moment for going back to the pseudo-complacency of scholasticism, because today it would be false, though at one time it might have had some understandable basis. Once it might have seemed a sign of health and could have been a pardonable and protective illusion. Today it would be a sign of sickness because it would involve insulting the intelligence of many young people, men and women, Christian, Jewish, Protestant, Catholic, but also Buddhist, Hindu, Moslem, Sikh, and every other kind of denomination. No one wants to settle for the absurdities of the past, but all nonetheless want a hope by which they may live and inherit the future, not only for themselves or their descendants, but for all living beings.

This, then, is a moment when people must ask what would comfort the whole of mankind. What did Jesus think would be a way of comforting all? Archetypally, *The Gospel According to John* is speaking in this connection of the mystery temple, where later all the sad failures of Christianity took place. This is the light and the fire that must be kept alive for the sake of all. Who, we may ask, will joyously and silently maintain it intact? Who will be able to say, as the dying Latimer said in Oxford in 1555, "We shall this day light such a candle . . . as I trust shall never be put out." Jesus was confident that among his disciples there were those who had been set afire by the flames that streamed through him. He was the *Hotri*, 'the indispensable agent' for the universal Alkahest, the elixir of life and immortality. He was the fig tree that would bear fruit, but he predicted that there would be fig trees that would bear no fruit. He was referring to the churches that have nothing to say, nothing real to offer, and above all, do not care that much for the lost Word or the world's proletariat, or the predicament and destiny of the majority of mankind.

His confidence was that which came to him, like everything in his life, from the Father, the Paraguru, the Lord of Libations, who, with boundless love for all, sustains in secret the eternal contemplation, together with the two Bodhisattvas — one whose eye sweeps over slumbering earth, and the other whose hand is extended in protecting love over the heads of his ascetics. Jesus spoke in the name of the Great Sacrifice. He spoke of the joy in the knowledge that there were a few who had become potentially like the leaven that could lift the whole lump, who had become true Guardians of the Eternal Fires. These are the vestal fires of the mystery temple which had disappeared in Egypt, from which the exodus took place. They had disappeared from Greece, though periodically there were attempts to revive them, such as those by Pythagoras at Delphi. They were then being poured into a new city called Jerusalem. In a sense, the new Comforter was the New Jerusalem, but it was not just a single city nor was it merely for people of one tribe or race.

Exoterically, the temple of Jerusalem was destroyed in 63 B.C. by Pompey and was rebuilt. Later it was razed to the ground again in 70 A.D. Since the thirteenth century no temple has been in existence there at all because that city has been for these past seven hundred years entirely in the hands of those who razed the old buildings and erected minarets and mosques. Now, people wonder if there really ever was a true Jerusalem, for everywhere is found the Babylon of confusion. Today it is not Origen who speaks to us, but Celsus, on behalf of all Epicureans. Everyone is tempted, like Lot's wife, to be turned into salt by fixing their attention upon the relics and memories of the past long after they have vanished into the limbo of dissolution and decay.

Anyone, however, who has an authentic soul-vision is El Mirador. Jesus knew that the vision, entrusted to the safekeeping of a few, would inspire them to lay the basis of what would continue, because of what they did, despite all the corruption and the ceaseless crucifixion. Even today, two thousand years later, when we hear of the miracle of the limitless love of Jesus, when we hear the words he spoke, when we read about and find comfort in what he did, we are deeply stirred. We are abundantly grateful because in us is lit the chela-light of true reverential devotion to the Christos within. This helps us to see all the Christs of history, unknown as well as renowned, as embodiments of the One and

Only — *the One without a Second,* in the cryptic language of the Upanishads. When this revelation takes place and is enjoyed inwardly, there are glad tidings, because it is on the invisible plane that the real work is done. Most people are fixated on the visible and want to wait for fruits from trees planted by other men. There are a few, however, who have realized the comfort to be derived in the true fellowship of those who seek the kingdom of God within themselves, who wish to become the better able to help and teach others, and who will be true in their faith from now until the twenty-first century. Some already have been using a forty-year calendar.

There have been such persons before us. Pythagoras called them Heroes. Buddha called them *Shravakas,* true listeners, and *Shramanas,* true learners. Then there were some who became *Srotapattis,* 'those who enter the stream,' and among them were a few *Anagamin,* 'those who need never return on earth again involuntarily.' There were also those who were *Arhans* of boundless vision, Perfected Men, Bodhisattvas, endlessly willing to re-enter the cave, having taken the pledge of Kwan-Yin to redeem every human being and all sentient life.

Nothing less than such a vow can resurrect the world today. These times are very different from the world at the time of John because in this age outward forms are going to give no clues in relation to the work of the formless. Mankind has to grow up. We find Origen saying this in the early part of the third century and Philo saying the same even in the first century. Philo, who was a Jewish scholar and a student of Plato, was an intuitive intellectual, while Origen, who had studied the Gnostics and considered various philosophical standpoints, was perhaps more of a mystic or even an ecstatic. Both knew that the Christos could only be seen by the eye of the mind. *If therefore thine eye be single,* Jesus said, *thy whole body shall be full of Light.* Those responding with the eyes of the body could never believe anything because, as Heraclitus said, "Eyes are bad witnesses to the soul." The eyes of the body must be tutored by the eye of the mind. Gupta Vidya also speaks of the eye of the heart and the eye in the forehead —

THE PLEDGE OF KWAN YIN

Never will I seek nor receive private, individual salvation; never will I enter into final peace alone; but forever and everywhere will I live and strive for the redemption of every creature throughout the world from the bonds of conditioned existence.

KWAN YIN

U nconditional affirmation of the Kwan Yin pledge can only come from the unconditional core of the human being. Words are uttered in time, and usually delimit meaning. They express thought, but they also obscure thought. To be able to use words in a manner that reaches beyond limits is to recognize prior to the utterance and to realize after the utterance, that one is participating only on the plane of that which has a beginning and an end, though in emulation and celebration of that which is beginningless and endless. Every word and each day is like an incarnation. Silence and deep sleep convey an awareness of duration that cannot be inserted into ordinary time, but indicate the return to a primal sense of being where one is neither conditioned by nor identified with external events, memories, anticipations, likes and dislikes, hopes and fears, possibilities and limitations. Common speech and ordinary wakefulness, for most individuals, are but clouded mirrors dimly reflecting the resonance and radiance of spiritual wakefulness. Any sacred pledge may be uttered by a human being with a wavering mind and a fickle heart, but it can also be authentically affirmed in the name of the larger Self that is far beyond the utterance and the formulation, yet immanent in both.

This is the time-honoured basis of religious rites, as well as the original source of civil laws. Émile Durkheim explained how early in the evolution of societies human beings learnt to transfer the potency of religious oaths to secular restraints and thereby established a high degree of reliability in human relationships. Mohandas Gandhi spoke of the sun, the planets and the mighty Himalayas as expressing the ultimate reliability of the universe, and taught that when human beings bind themselves by the power of a vow, they seek to become wholly reliable. If reliability essentially connotes a consistent standard of unqualified and unconditional success, then in taking a vow one is necessarily seeing beyond one's limitations. If one is wise one allows for the probability of failure and the possibility of forgetfulness, but somewhere deep in oneself one still wants to be measured and tested by that vow. Thereby a vow which is unconditional, which releases the spiritual will, calibrates one's highest self-respect and is vitally relevant to the mystery of self-transformation.

The Kwan Yin pledge is a Bodhisattvic vow taken on behalf of all living beings. It is closely connected with the *Bodhichitta,* wisdom-seeking mind, the seed of enlightenment. The idea that an unenlightened human being can effectively generate a seed of enlightenment is the central assumption behind the compassionate teaching of Mahatmas and Bodhisattvas, of the Buddhas and Christs. A drop of water is suggestive of an ocean; a flashing spark or single flame is analogous to an ocean of light; the miniscule mirrors the large. Herein lies the hidden strength of the Kwan Yin pledge. What may seem small from the standpoint of the personal self, when it is genuinely offered on behalf of the limitless universe of living beings and of all humanity past, present and future, can truly negate the finality of finitude, the ultimacy of what seems urgent, the immensity of what appears immediate. The human mind ceaselessly creates false valuations, giving ephemera an excessive sense of reality, to uphold itself in a world of flux. To negate this tendency in advance and to assign reality only to the whole requires a profound mental courage. It requires, while one is alive, a recognition of the connection between the moment of birth and the moment of death, of the intimate relationship between the pain of one human being and the sorrow of all humanity. But it also involves a recognition that greater beings than oneself have taken precisely such a vow, have affirmed this pledge again and again. Therefore, one can invite oneself, however frail, however feeble, into the family of those who are the self-chosen, unacknowledged but unvanquished friends of the human race.

The prospect of such a vow is naturally perplexing to the lower mind which is almost totally ignorant of the priorities of the immortal soul, and knows very little about even this life, let alone about previous lives. On what basis could the personality assume a gnostic authority in regard to its own limitations? If one simply looks at the last ten years of one's life, one will readily see that many things which looked irrelevant, remote, even impossible in the past, unexpectedly become part of one's way of thinking, ones depth of feeling. If a human being does not truly know himself, merely to be aware of himself at the personal level in terms of persisting limitations is frustrating. This does not take into account in oneself that which is ineffable and unexpressed, whatever cannot come through the confining parameters of thought, the truncating crudities of speech and the stultifying restrictions of action.

The Kwan Yin pledge can be taken by anyone at any time, but the level of thought and intensity with which it is taken will determine the degree and reliability of response of the whole of one's being. Shantideva puts this in the form of an ordination:

> When the Sugatas of former times committed themselves to the Bodhichitta, they gradually established themselves in the practice of a Bodhisattva.
>
> So, I too commit myself to the Bodhichitta for the welfare of all beings and will gradually establish myself in the practice of a Bodhisattva.
>
> Today my birth has become fruitful; my birth as a human being is justified.
>
> Today I am born in the Buddha Family; I am now a son of the Buddha.
>
> Now I am determined to perform those acts appropriate to my Family; I will not violate the purity of this faultless, noble Family.

To be able to take one's place in the glorious company of Bodhisattvas is not to assume that one can, purely on one's own, fulfil this exalted aim. But once one has truly affirmed it, no other aim has any comparable significance. This recognition would be critical to a timely taking of the mighty vow of the Buddha, the sacred pledge of Kwan Yin, the Bodhisattva ordination of Shantideva. Timeliness in this sense would mean that one simply cannot imagine an alternative. If a person were to take the pledge prematurely, lacking this sense of necessity, it would precipitate difficulties, making that person guilty, tortured with anxiety, involved even more in futile comparisons and contrasts with other human beings, more depressed, more desolate. But out of all these failures there may come some sense of timeliness at a later moment of ripeness.

Timeliness does not occur all at once. Timeliness, like all wisdom, must be the ripe fruit of time-bound experiments and time-bound errors. Because these are time-bound, they are evanescent; they are not enduring. In the same way in which one stumbled and learnt to walk, or mumbled the multiplication tables, one may rediscover something about grace in movement or the deep logic of elementary numbers. So also one may rediscover the higher stage, the fuller meaning, the larger significance for the whole of one's life, of the pledge one took. Suppose a person truly resolves to injure no human being and wishes to release love in every direction. If one is deeply attracted by this affirmation, what does it matter if there is something imperfect and inconclusive in one's repeated efforts to embody it? Mature individuals, who have done this again and again, know that soon after one has made such an affirmation one is going to be tested. One has invited the Light of the Logos to shine upon the dark corners of one's being. Through heightened awareness one sees unconscious elements in one's nature which one did not even imagine were apt to give offense, but are now discerned as obscurations of one's deepest feelings, one's finest nature, one's truest, profoundest sense of brotherhood. These discoveries are significant, but the hardest lesson at all times is the paramount

necessity of patience and persistence. This is a pledge in favour
of selfless service, and it cannot ever be premature. It will always
be timely, though compelling timeliness can only come when
there is serene insight, supported by the strength of personal
invulnerability.

It is the immemorial teaching that the pristine seed of
enlightenment, however small, may germinate far in the
future into a flowering tree of wisdom, a mighty trunk of
enlightenment. Inherent to the pure seed is a potency that
represents the complete disavowal of considerations of success
and failure for oneself, separate from the whole world. There is a
fundamental abnegation of all the earthly criteria of happiness,
power and achievement. For the immortal soul, the pledge could
never be premature. Nevertheless, every sacred utterance should
be the result of deep thought and true feeling, and should be
renewed in silence, enriched by contemplation, and carried over
from waking through dreamless sleep into the day of daily
manifestation. If a person knows this much, then that
person knows what is the essential nature of the task of self-
transformation. As the task also involves self-forgetfulness and
reaching out to all human beings, a point must surely come when
the very thought of one's own progress or lack of it in relation to
the pledge will shrink into insignificance simply because one's
consciousness becomes so occupied with the greater growth, the
larger welfare of the human race. If a person thought this out
carefully, he or she could safeguard against the greatest danger,
ignoring which is the mark of immaturity: the cold forgetfulness
that arises from the initial unwisdom or psychic heat in taking a
vow. *A vow is sacred; it must germinate in silence. It invokes sacred
speech, but it must ripen through suffering.* Where the vow involves a
recognition of the ubiquity of human suffering and where one
chooses to make one's own suffering meaningful and creative
for a larger purpose, the vow has self-correction built into it.
Those who have received this great teaching and have been
inspired by the very highest ideal, will be wise to take the Kwan
Yin pledge at some level. In the words of Buddha, "Anyone who

even hears about Kwan Yin begins the search then and there for enlightenment."

The light of daring is essential to the timely taking of the Kwan Yin pledge. In the *Kwan Yin Sutra* there is a reference to the flames of agony that consume personal consciousness. Kwan Yin in its metaphysical meaning is bound up with fire and water. Kwan Yin is connected with the primordial Light of the Logos, which is the paradigm and the pristine source of all creativity in the cosmos, of the hidden power in every human being to produce a result that is beneficent. If Kwan Yin is ontologically connected with light, but is also compared to the ocean, what then is the meaning of the textual reference to extinguishing the flames of agony? This is a metaphysical paradox. What is light on the most abstract level of undifferentiated primordial matter is the darkness of non-being, such as that which is around the pavilion of God in the Old Testament, or that which is sometimes simply referred to as "In the beginning", the Archaeus, the dark abysm of Space. Kwan Yin is rooted in Boundless Space and therefore involves noumenal existence at so high a level of attributeless compassion in Eternal Duration that it is the paradigm of all the vows and pledges taken by vast numbers of pilgrims throughout unrecorded history. It is also called *Bath-Kol*, the Daughter of the Voice, in the Hebrew tradition, that which when sought within the inmost sanctuary bestows a merciful response within the human heart. There is a latent Kwan Yin in every human being. It is the voice of conscience at the commonest level. It is the *Chitkala* of the developed disciple. At the highest level it is *Nada*, the Voice of the Silence, the Soundless Sound, that which is comprehended in initiation, and ceaselessly reverberates in the *Anahata*, the deathless centre of the human body, transformed into a divine temple.

The deeper meaning of the Kwan Yin pledge is enshrined in profound metaphysics, but at the same time, it reaches down to the level of human ignorance and pain, at all levels extinguishing the intensity of craving, the fires of nescience. This is the teaching of the *Kwan Yin Sutra*. When that which is light at the highest level descends, it becomes like unto cool water, although intrinsically it is so radiant that it would be blinding. But when it is diffused it converts its state into a fluid which is extremely soothing, sometimes compared to the cool rays of the moon. And then it is capable of giving comfort and sustenance. When a person is soothed and cooled, it is possible to let go, to relinquish the intensity of self-concern. Personal heat is intensely painful when it is experienced without any awareness of alternatives. But when one finds that it may be displaced by soothing wisdom, the cooling waters of compassion, then it is possible to ease the pain and to convert one's mind from a falsely fiery state, which is destructive, into a cooling and regenerative condition. These are all alchemical expressions of processes that are involved in making deliberate changes in states of consciousness connected with different levels of matter.

Theosophically, every level of thought corresponds to and is consubstantial with a level of differentiation of substance. Therefore, one can even discover in ordinary language certain words that tend to heat up the psycho-mental atmosphere. The very way in which one characterizes one's own condition may do a lot of violence through language. One can burn oneself or become totally suffocated by the flames, though the Hasidic mystics remind us that even if the castle is burning, there is a lord. Even while one is burning there can be some recognition of that incorruptible, inconsumable essence in oneself. This possibility is the root of all faith in one's power of spiritual survival, as well the basis of all notions of physical survival, which are only shadowy representations of this deeper urge to persist and prevail. If one has everyday experience of how certain words and shibboleths can engender a lower heat, one can also employ gentler words, healing metaphors and analogies, broader categories, that soothe and cool one's atmosphere. Even learning to do this is an art, one that can only be practised in a human being's sincere efforts at apprenticeship to the great masters of the art. Kwan Yin is the cosmic archetype of the art. She who expresses compassion in every conceivable context shows how inexhaustible are the ways of compassion of wise beings, how Initiates use every opportunity to release help. This is part of the universal inheritance of humanity. It is also mirrored in every mother or father who, despite all the lower levels of concern, somewhere knows that what he or she does cannot really be put into the language of calculation, cannot really be weighed or measured.

Gratitude cannot be compelled, but without it life would not go on. It is as if human beings impose upon what they innately know a false structure of expectations, which entangles them in mental cobwebs that are entirely self-created. If emotion becomes sufficiently intense, bitter and sour, there can be a tremendous burden, but even that burden is an act of compassion of the spirit because its weight eventually burns out the *tanha*, the persisting thirst for material sensation, for false personal life. It will dissolve at the moment of death, but this does not happen all at once. It will receive certain shocks in life, and thereby human beings come to throw off the enormous excesses of their own compulsive cerebration, a great deal of the wastage and the futility of their own emotions, the wear and tear upon the subtle vestures through their own anxieties.

What Nature does as a matter of course can be aided by conscious thought. But where it is aided by conscious thought in the name of the highest cosmic principle and in the company of a long lineage, a golden company of great exemplars of the vow and the pledge for universal enlightenment, one can truly consecrate one's life and thereby refrain from becoming too tensely involved in the process of everyday psychological alchemy. This is implicit in what Buddha taught. If one truly enjoys the very thought of what Kwan Yin is, and of what is in the Kwan Yin pledge, this enjoyment should itself help to reduce much of the agony and the anxiety, the tension and strain of daily striving. The real problem is to be wholehearted with as undivided a mind as can be brought to the pledge. This must be done without qualifications, without contradictions, but with that holy simplicity of which the mystics speak, a childlike innocence,

candour and trust. It is an act of acceptance of the universe and a
letting go of whatever comes in the way. When anything does
interfere, it must be consumed in the fires of sacrificial change
that alone will lead to true spiritual growth. Many a monk on
the Bodhisattva Path has found immense benefit through the
talismanic use of these three verses:

> *If you are unable to exchange your happiness*
> *For the suffering of other beings,*
> *You have no hope of attaining Buddhahood*
> *Or even of happiness in this lifetime.*

> *If one whom I have helped my best*
> *And from whom I expect much*
> *Harms me in an inconceivable way,*
> *May I regard that person as my best teacher.*

> *I consider all living beings*
> *More precious than 'wish-fulfilling gems',*
> *A motivation to achieve the greatest goal:*
> *So may I at all times care for them.*

THE JOY OF DEVOTION

The waters of immersion purify a man only if he is wholly immersed.

HASIDIC SAYING

True devotion is neither involuntary emotion nor gratuitous feeling, but an innate and indestructible soul-power. There is a vital difference between the surging depths of feeling and the oscillations of volatile emotion. Emotion is often compelling, but its seeming intensity is as short-lived as the cyclonic wind which howls and vanishes. Feeling is much more durable, corresponding to the unmoved silent depths of the ocean, a measureless expanse of water with a potential strength far greater than manifest energy. Every human being risks, through faulty upbringing or through grievous neglect of finer feelings — especially when the libido is awakened between fourteen and twenty-one — being scarred for life by becoming caught in one of two extremes. Either there is wasteful expenditure of emotion — excess of excitement with its inevitable shadow of disappointment, deficiency and gloom, *or* there is stern external control over emotion that induces an inability to convey authentic feeling in one's relationship to a child, in one's encounter with a stranger, or even in greeting a friend with the eyes of trust.

The term 'devotion' remains one of the more beautiful words in the language, its suggestive and sacred etymology harking back to the taking of a vow. At the popular level this may be seen in frenzied devotion to a secular cause such as that of a political party. There can be total commitment without any streak of scepticism. There is neither wavering nor weakening of such commitment, but it is focussed upon an abstract idea attached to some tangible form. Few human beings, however, can contain the vast energy of unconditional commitment within the vessel of any external organization. Attempts to do so in messianic politics merely re-enact what happened in earlier history in relation to dogmatic religion. Owing to the limitations of sectarian ideologies and organizational structures, and especially due to the difficulty of distinguishing between the impersonal, immortal individuality and the changing personal mask, ardent votaries fall prey to self-righteousness, an outburst of exaggerated emotion mistaken for deep feeling. No wonder Socrates challenged Euthyphro's claims to knowledge of piety or holiness — the relation between gods and humans — the most exalted, elusive and mysterious of subjects, wherein one's credential is the uncommon recognition that one does not really know. What was true in his day is even more evident in our own time. Many people are running away from past symbols of piety, from various forms of totalism and tokenism in churches, and from every kind of trivialized, degraded and vulgarized ritual and sacrament. But in rushing to the opposite extreme, pretending to be nihilists, they are often trapped in the tragic nihilism of having no faith in themselves, not even enough to carry on from day to day. Muddled thinking and negative emotions reinforce each other, corrupting the psyche.

Devotion is much more than wanting to be devoted. It is far more than having a euphoric feeling, however holy this may seem at the time. Devotion is a different order of consciousness from that involved in the expenditure of emotion. Its sovereign power can only flow freely from the *Atman*, the perpetual motion of transcendental light that shines upon every human soul. It is invoked through an inward prostration of the mind within the sanctuary of the heart, towards the Light of the Logos. To ask how one can prostrate before that which one does not comprehend is to ask how to be humble before the great mystery of nature, the vastitude of life, or the saga of humanity. To be humble in this sense is not merely to say to oneself that one does not know, but also means that one can thrill with the thought of the *mysterium tremendum*. Even though one does not know its destiny or destination, one may feel reverence for the whole of humanity; though one cannot fathom the breadth or depth of nature, one rejoices in one's kinship with nature; though one has no final answer to the basic questions of life, one remains open towards the life-process. Such simple devotion generates the proper mental posture, which Krishna depicts in the *Bhagavad Gita*. It is neither too high nor too low, neither so abject that one cannot generate any enthusiasm nor so lofty that one is isolated within an ivory tower of self-delusion.

True devotion comes to birth through the firm recognition of the unity of all life and the universality of the highest ideals and ideas conceived, transcending the human capacity to formulate and transmit them. When devotion continues undiminished through the trials that it necessarily brings — just as light increases the shadow — it renews itself. It must be put to the test, and it surely will be. The moment one approaches the presence of a spiritual Teacher and professes one's devotion, the jealous Lhamayin of endless space rush to taint and rupture the current of total commitment. That is always the way, illustrated in the fairy stories and myths of all peoples. One has to encounter the abyss; one has to be tried and tempted. Jesus had three great temptations, of which a beautifully perceptive account is given by Dostoevsky in the story of the Grand Inquisitor. All Initiates go through trials, and they do this deliberately because, although those who are perfected before birth really need no tests, they compassionately re-enact the archetypal story for the sake of the human race. Any person can, from small beginnings, tap the immense potential power in a vow to give birth to lasting devotion. This cannot be done even with an authentic start and a self-sustaining rhythm unless it is fortified by the fearlessness and courage that are rooted in the invulnerable truth of one's devotion. We can discover many analogies in daily life. Individuals may recognize that however much they muddied their relations with their parents, they need not be hostile toward those who gave them human bodies. Persons can look back and see that although they were dreadful in their behaviour towards their teachers, they can still cherish the feeling of gratitude to those who taught them the alphabet. Without retrospective veneration of parents and teachers, one has no right to speak or put words on paper or to enjoy the privilege of articulation. All of this is part of the universal code of human decency.

When a person is willing to put right his elementary obligations, then the more difficult problems in one's relationship to one's spouse or children, to friends, strangers, critics and so-called enemies can also be brought into the arena of rigorous self-examination. There is essentially one paramount choice for every person. Either one self-consciously tests oneself and cooperates with the process of testing by nature, or one is dragged unwillingly to life's examinations. Much as one may be afraid of failing every question, still, the only way one can calmly face the moment of death is by seeing that there is something yet to be learnt. No one can complete the probation of a lifetime without having learnt some critical lesson to be derived from each incarnation. In every age and all over the world, noble souls have taken birth for whom none of this is new. They have known from early childhood that their lives have a single sacred purpose, the golden karma of devoted service to the Brotherhood of Bodhisattvas. They faithfully nurtured the fire of devotion even before they found the sole object to which it could be fully directed. Therefore, as surely as day follows night — the long night of awakening which may seem very long indeed while it lasts — they infallibly enter the orbit of the Mahatmas who are ever at work in the world and who are compassionately concerned to extend every opportunity for the whole of humanity to benefit from the sacred circle of chelas. Disciples pledged and put through probationary trials and training become one-pointed in mind, single-hearted, and of one will in their heroic capacity to release a power stronger than the sum of its parts and truly a magnet for the highest forces in nature.

Devotion is rather like the harnessing of electrical energy. In order to be properly channelled to some end, the resistance or responsiveness of the conductor is crucial. Just as a river cannot rise above its source, the power of devotion is as great as the height upon which it is focussed. Devotion is also affected by the clarity of the mental picture of the ideal, even though that evolving picture may fall short of the ideal which, when fully realized, becomes so all-encompassing that it is beyond the possibility of formulation in words or of any expression in particular modes. As Shelley knew,

> Rome's azure sky,
> Flowers, ruins, statues, music, words, are weak
> The glory they transfuse with fitting truth to speak.

Human beings can come to learn that devotion fundamentally alters the relation and ratio between the unmanifest and the manifest: what is not said is more important than what is said; what is not shown or seen is more suggestive than what is shown and seen. Francis Thompson exclaimed —

> O world invisible, we view thee,
> O world intangible, we touch thee,
> O world unknowable, we know thee,
> Inapprehensible, we clutch thee!

This celebrates the passage from the region of maya to the realm of SAT. One of the oldest invocations in the Upanishads is: "Lead me from the unreal to the Real. Lead me from darkness to Light. Lead me from death to Immortality."

The relation between the manifest and the unmanifest is analogous to the relations between *chela* and guru, between *Manas* and the *Manasa*, and between man and mankind. Every human being is a necessary limb in the whole of humanity, a fact symbolized in the ancient and profound Jewish conception of humanity as the manifestation of Adam Kadmon, one great collective person. The same idea is found under different forms in the Renaissance, for example in Leonardo da Vinci's suggestive painting of a man within a man. Every human being is a microcosm of the macrocosm. Each is as a child in reference to the whole of humanity, a chela in reference to the sacred and mystical collective Host. But humanity is more than existing human beings. Though a difficult conception for a small minority of the world today, this is as obvious as $2 + 2 = 4$ to the vast majority. Humanity is always greater than the number of people incarnated at any given time. E.F. Schumacher pointed out that the earth could be seen as underpopulated. From the universal standpoint of global welfare, the resources of the earth are capable of supporting a larger number of people than the present population. When human beings fail in their plans — based upon false, half-true or short-term assumptions — they begin to mock Mother Nature. Nature in all her abundance and affluence has never failed the entire human race in recorded history nor earlier, and will not fail the human race in any time to come. Human beings bring upon themselves their own karma, collectively in groups and as individuals, and thereby they experience the holocaust, mentally or physically.

All human beings are fallen gods. As a thinking being with a highly complex brain that no animal possesses, with the sacred gift of speech, each human being already has the highest faculties. Each one has the sovereign powers of choice and of imagination — the king-faculty — which are both essential to the guru-chela relationship. Suppose a person suddenly awakens and affirms that to be a human being is a tremendous privilege. Even though it may be, as Thoreau said, that only one out of a thousand is a real individual with courage and strength, none the less anyone can gain access to the entire human heritage. If one is willing to rediscover what it means to be human, this brings one into the radius of the divine. One is at least on the threshold of the recognition that there are powers and principalities throughout the whole of nature, and that so far from being a blind and inanimate world moved mechanistically by collocations of atoms in random statistical patterns, this is indeed an intelligent universe with innumerable conscious centres of cosmic ideation and energy. If a person begins to see nature in this way, then it is possible to recover the richness of one's divine inheritance. Man is descended from those whom Pythagoras called the Fathers of the human race, whom the Hindus called the Agnishwatha Pitris, the givers of the solar light of self-consciousness to humanity. These spiritual ancestors were reverenced by the Chinese and the ancient Egyptians, just as the heroes of old were honoured by the Greeks and the Romans. The whole of the human story is a magnificent and mostly unrecorded saga replete with immense resources that are still accessible to individuals. By self-election and self-determination, each person must lay claim to the universal treasure of wisdom.

Mahatmas are primarily concerned with humanity as a whole, not with separate units in themselves. Their constant focus is upon universal good, and their wise efforts are directed to the humanity of tomorrow. How can a person with a restricted range of consciousness become a chela to Mahatmas, who are attuned to *Mahat* or cosmic ideation and whose compassion flows towards the entire human race, born and unborn? Although the vast gulf in awareness cannot be easily spanned by the prospective chela, it is bridgeable through true devotion. Inversion of standpoint begins with looking and judging from below above. It is like standing on a little footstool in a crowded room and formulating an exact conception of the Himalayas or of the galaxies moving through boundless space. This is futile and even perverse. Generally, the mental posture of diverse individuals towards mankind or the Mahatmas is not the same all over the world, and therefore none can really gauge the destinies of souls. How, then, may aspirants who from their own altitude cannot fathom the empyrean come any closer to the Mahatmas by devotion, determination and total dedication? This is possible only because the enlightened are generous in their shower of light and wisdom, like the rains which render the earth fragrant and fertile. One should rise mentally as far above as possible towards the most exalted conception of humanity, of Mahatmas and chelas, and then with eyes open, see everything mirrored below. Thus one can heal, correct and cure oneself.

One can become capable of showing expansiveness, generosity, magnanimity and gratitude and, above all, reverence, because without reverence one is less than human. Where there is reverence, there is growth. It is nurtured in the silence in which, from humble beginnings unseen below the soil, a plant may grow and in time become a tree that can take its place in secluded forests of towering sentinels. Primeval forests mirror something vastly more overwhelming in relation to the Mahatmas, who have been compared to the sturdy limbs of a mighty banyan tree with its roots above the firmament and its branches below on earth. The heavenly tree of wisdom has been known as *Brahma Vach*, *Bodhi Dharma*, gnosis and by many other names. The Vedas depict the Rishis and seers as of one mind, one heart, one will and one voice. It is the Voice of 'the Ancient of Days', transcending all known frontiers and concepts of human history and evolution. With the vast perspective of the accumulated wisdom of the ages, the disciple must rejoice rather than despair in the realization that he is zero. The power of the zero in mathematics depends upon where it is placed. Zero before a number has no value. If zero is the numerator of a fraction, the value is nought; if it is the denominator, the value is infinite. If zero is put after a number, its power is significant. Everything depends on where the zero is inserted. The three-dimensional sphere filled with empty space can accommodate tetrahedrons and the dodecahedron. If a human being did not have analogous empty spaces within the brain and the chambers of the heart, there would be no room for the *Akashic* fires or the *Anahata* vibration.

True joy is far from a frenetic attempt to convince oneself that one is enjoying oneself. When one continually needs convincing, nothing adequately convinces. *Ananda* has nothing to do with ephemeral pleasures or private self-satisfaction. True joy or *ananda* springs up in the heart and mind like artesian wells, and though it may overflow in appropriate words and gestures, it is always greater than the power and possibility of expression. The highest joy lights a fire that can never be put out. If the level of joy reached is unstable, it may be no more than a compensatory form of consolation. It will be temporary and intermittent. It cannot mirror the *ananda* of the Mahatmas, whose every affirmation has the accent of transcendental truth and is verifiable through self-realization. Once deep joy is aroused, it is consistent and capable of self-maintenance. It is similar to the quiet cheerfulness of mountaineers carrying little lanterns across dark, iridescent slopes, patiently climbing steep ascents, crossing abysses and caverns while heedful of the great rumblings of nature. Theirs is the peaceful joy of knowing that even if they cannot climb any further now, they could start again, that even if each is alone and without friends in a solitary spot, yet somehow something may happen and timely help may come. And if indeed it is one's lot to die then and there, death comes as a deliverer and a friend. Human beings must seek out the meaning of life and death, asking the question, "Suppose I die tonight? What reason is there for me to be joyous?" If one can find it today, then one can live differently from tonight and tomorrow. There is always joy around us, and the hidden joy suffuses the manifest gloom.

The worst of times is also the best of times. Joy sees beyond the chaotic city that has to go. It is not clinging but courageous, willing to greet the unknown and the uncertain, fearlessly and with maturity. It is capable of drawing the larger circle and enclosing myriads of unknown human beings, never confining oneself within a small circle of confused allegiance.

The ancient teaching of India declared: *He who loves lives; he who loves himself lives in hell* (the hell of loneliness and gloom); *he who loves another lives on earth; he who loves others lives in heaven; but he who silently adores and loves the Self of all creatures lives in that Self—and that is eternal peace.* The level of love determines the measure of joy. Joy flowing from the degree of love one is initially capable of generating acts as a stimulus to larger loves and greater joys that eventually will dissolve into the cosmic dance of Shiva, wherein all the elements are involved. This is enigmatic because it involves the mathematics of the soul and of the universe, the Karma of nations and the whole of humanity. The moment one reaches out beyond one's own shadow, turning towards the light that lighteth every man that cometh into the world, then there is joy flowing from the immortal soul in the realm of illimitable light. There is joy in the sure knowledge that though there is life and death, there is also immortality, which does not participate in what is called life and what is feared as death, but is greater than all the small cycles and little circles of time and space. There is joy in the awareness that there is limitlessness in the realm of cosmic ideation, eternal duration and boundless space.

This is the timeless teaching of divine wisdom, and it has always had urgency for the individual, as in the days of Jesus, when he asked, 'Whom choose ye this day?' A critical, ultimate, irreversible choice is involved. Now, when the opportunities are great for the whole of the human race, something has begun which will become in time a mighty stream that will nourish the earth. It will reflect the hidden fire of the Mysteries, known to those who have travelled far on the secret Path that leads to the invisible summits of enlightenment. At the first portal of the Path, there is the fateful inscription: "Abandon hope all who enter here." Abandon hope for the petty personality, abandon hope for ambition, pride and selfish desire. Abandon hope, above all, for one's own salvation if one would enter the Path, which leads to a galaxy of Gurus, mighty men of meditation and lovers of all humanity who are wholly dedicated to the sacred goal of universal enlightenment. They have said: "If you wish to know us, study our philosophy. If you wish to serve us, serve our humanity. If you take one step in our direction, we will take one step in yours."

INDIVIDUATION
AND INITIATION

The Daimones *are . . . the guardian spirits of the human race; 'those who dwell in the neighbourhood of the immortals, and thence watch over human affairs,' as Hermes has it. In Esoteric parlance, they are called* Chitkala, *some of which are those who have furnished man with his fourth and fifth Principles from their own essence; and others the* Pitris *so-called. . . . The root of the name is* Chiti, *'that by which the effects and consequences of actions and kinds of knowledge are selected for the use of the soul,' or conscience, the* inner Voice *in man. With the Yogis, the* Chiti *is a synonym of* Mahat, *the first and divine intellect; but in Esoteric philosophy* Mahat *is the root of Chiti, its germ; and* Chiti *is a quality of* Manas *in conjunction with Buddhi, a quality that attracts to itself by spiritual affinity a* Chitkala *when it develops sufficiently in man. This is why it is said that* Chiti *is a voice acquiring mystic life and becoming Kwan-Yin.*

The Secret Doctrine, i 288

The integral relationship between initiation and individuation can be grasped through the essential logic of the entire process of evolution. From the standpoint of matter, the logic of transformation involves increasing heterogeneity, differentiation and complexity. At the same time, there is a commensurate withdrawal of subjective and spiritual faculties which cannot function freely through limited projections or distorted reflections. The degree of spiritual volition depends upon the texture of the reflecting medium. In the collective thrust of evolution every single life-atom in all the seven kingdoms of Nature is touched by the same primal universal impulse towards self-consciousness. Within the broad perspective and purpose of evolution as a whole, the possibilities of initiation are enriched by individuation at a high level of self-consciousness. Initiation, in its most hallowed meaning, must always involve the merging of minds of Guru and chela into a state of oneness with the ineffable Source of Divine Wisdom. This mystical and magical relation of *Manas* and *Mahat* was comprehended and transmitted in secret sanctuaries. It was intimated in the enigmatic etymology of the word *Upanishad,* 'to come and sit close', so that there could be direct communion of minds and hearts. Sacred teachings are conveyed and communicated through the eyes and not merely through words, although mantramic sounds have a sacred and vital function. In the *Bhagavad Gita* Arjuna's earnest enquiries and Krishna's cosmic affirmations and psychological adjustments bring to birth within the mind of the chela the seed of *chit,* a level of consciousness which negates, transcends, and also heightens individuality. Initiation is the highest mode of individual communication, and it necessarily involves a mystic rapport between one who has gone before and one who is to come after, rather like the magnetic transference between mother and child. Such a relation is inherent in the logic of evolution because, as a result of an extremely long period of evolution, it is impossible to find any mechanical sameness between all human beings. They are identical in their inmost essence but so markedly different in the internal relations of their vestures that there cannot be complete equivalence between any two persons. Hence experience and reflection reveal both the mystery of each individual human being and the commonality of what it is to be human.

At one level of communication *The Secret Doctrine* is a metaphysical treatise on cosmic and human evolution. But at another level, for those who are Buddhic, it is not merely a book, but the initiatory presence of the compelling voice of the Verbum or Brahma Vach, reverberating in the society of sages, the Rishis who are of one mind and one lip. For the ardent seeker of Divine Wisdom, *The Secret Doctrine* is a series of stepping-stones, as the Upanishads and the great scriptures of all times have been, towards initiations into the mysteries of Selfhood. Through ever-renewed contact with the teaching, the chela begins to enact self-consciously and by degrees the realities which ordinary individuals sporadically experience at some level through deep sleep. This process comes alive through prolonged meditation for the sake of universal compassion, making one's breathing more benevolent for the purpose of elevating all beings in all the kingdoms of Nature. When a person begins to do this, it is the awakening of *Bodhichitta,* the seed of enlightenment. It is the first step in translating knowledge into wisdom, words into realities, and resolves into actions. Having turned the key of compassion in the lock of the heart, the disciple will come to realize, through inward communication with the Teacher, the fuller meaning of the Upanishads:

> *Upa-ni-shad* being a compound word meaning 'the conquest of ignorance by the revelation of *secret, spiritual* knowledge'. . . . They speak of the origin of the Universe, the nature of Deity, and of Spirit and Soul, as also of the metaphysical connection of mind and matter. In a few words: They CONTAIN *the beginning and the end of all human knowledge* . . .
>
> The Secret Doctrine, i 269-270

The practical import of the metaphysical teaching of *The Secret Doctrine* lies in the fact that the highest spiritual powers are partly used by each human being every day but without fully knowing it. Light is universal, but it makes all the difference whether one has a blurred sense of perception and merely consumes light, or whether one can take a magnifying glass and concentrate light. There are also those who are like the laser beam which can direct a concentrated shaft of light to destroy cancerous cells and produce a range of extraordinary effects upon the physical plane. There is something of *kundalini* at work in every human being. Electricity and magnetism are sevenfold and work at the highest cosmic level of *Akasha,* but they also work at the most heterogeneous and diffusive level because everything is electrical and magnetic, from the occult standpoint. The aspirant must grasp, even at a preliminary level, the moral and psychological implications of this metaphysical "power or Force which moves in a curved path" in man and Nature.

> It is the Universal life-Principle manifesting everywhere in nature. This force includes the two great forces of attraction and repulsion. Electricity and magnetism are but manifestations of it. This is the power which brings about that 'continuous adjustment of *internal relations to external relations*' which is the essence of life according to Herbert Spencer, and that '*continuous adjustment of external relations to internal relations*' which is the basis of transmigration of souls . . .
>
> *Ibid.,* i 293

The two aspects of this omnipresent power mentioned here have to be totally mastered by the initiated yogi in all their possible manifestations. Long before this stage is reached, the disciple must begin to learn to govern these internal and external relations through *Buddhi Yoga* in order to fulfil the prerequisite conditions of magnetic rapport with a true Teacher of Wisdom.

The universal process of adjustment of the external to the internal, which leads to involuntary reincarnation for human beings, must be understood in terms of karma. At the most primary level, whenever human beings entertain and succumb to emotional reactions, they establish mental deposits and astral grooves which require many lives for proper adjustment. That is why over eighteen million years so many people approach the Path again and again but stumble and lose their track just as often. They cannot make a fundamental breakthrough even when in the presence of great teaching. For those who have made the teaching an internal living power in their consciousness, this is comprehensible as essential, just as the world seems clear to a child when its eyes are directed to the light of the sun. Whilst this is true for all human souls, the philosophical recognition of how this works is important. Every emotion registers an appropriate record in the astral vesture. It is wear and tear on the *linga sharira* and is at the expense of something or someone else. Thus selfishness is increased. This is true even if the emotion is benevolent for emotion itself is a form of passivity. Emotion is quite different from deep feeling which is unmodified by cyclic change or external event and is totally independent of outward demonstration. Emotion is like cashing a check: whilst it makes money available, it depletes the account. It is a way of demanding proof. As a form of external indulgence it is a passive fantasy which weighs heavily upon the astral vesture. To that extent it obscures one's inmost feelings which are detached and compassionate. All the higher feelings are ontologically powerful and at the same time they constitute a pure negation psychologically. Though only an initial understanding of the problem, this is sufficient to explain why merely sitting down to postures and trying to control the external breath by *hatha yoga* exercises cannot make a significant difference to the inevitable adjustment of internal and external relations inherent in life itself. There is no substitute for facing oneself, asking what one is truly living for, how one is affected by likes and dislikes, and how one's temper — or *sophrosyne* — is unbalanced through various irritations.

In the ancient schools one would not be allowed to begin serious study of yoga until one had mastered one's temper. In the school of Pythagoras candidates were tested from the first day in regard to their personal vulnerability. That was the stringent standard of all schools preparing for the mysteries of initiation. The laws have not changed even though the external rules may seem to have been modified. It remains an inescapable fact of Nature and karma that if one loses one's temper even after a lifetime of spiritual development, one's progress is destroyed in a single mood. Like a city or a work of art, the time to construct is long, but destruction can be swift. One has to think out one's true internal and external state of being, even if one goes to the Tolstoyan extreme of seeing every kind of fault in oneself. Tolstoy did not do this out of pride but rather because he was so thoroughly honest that he simply could not think of a single fault in anyone else which he could not see present in himself. This sense of commonality, rooted in ethical self-awareness, leaves no room for judging anyone else or for running away from anyone because one sees that the whole army of human foibles is in oneself, and that every elemental is connected with internal propensities in one's astral form. To think this out Manasically is crucial in the Aquarian Age. The wise disciple will recognize that thoroughness, urgency and earnestness are quite different from fatuous haste and impulsiveness. Even if it takes months and years to think out and learn to apply the elementary axioms of the Science of Spirituality, it is necessary to be patient and persistent, rather than revel in fantasies that leave residues in successive lives. When something so obvious which one can test and comprehend is taught, this is an opportunity for growth which demands honesty in thought and intelligence in response. To receive the timeless teaching in this way enables the self to be the true friend of the Self. Not to do this is one of the myriad ways in which the self becomes the enemy of the Self because it is afraid of facing the facts and the laws of nature connected with relations and patterns in the vestures. Self-regeneration is a precise science and it is possible to test oneself in a manner that fosters *sophrosyne*.

This spiritual intelligence test is not a matter of making some sweeping moral judgement about oneself, because that will have no meaning for the immortal soul. It would simply not be commensurate with eighteen million years of self-conscious existence. It is really a waste of time to say "I'm no good, I'm this kind of person, I'm bound to do this." Such exclamations are absurd because they do not account for the internal complexity and psychological richness of sevenfold man, let alone the immensity of the human pilgrimage. It is more important to understand and recognize critical incipient causes, to see how the karmic process takes place, and to arrest the downward slide into fragmented consciousness. To do this firmly with compassion at the root, one has to meditate upon some fundamental idea. One might benefit from the golden example set by disciples who practise the precept: "All the time everything that comes to me I not only deserve but I desire." This form of mental asceticism is the reverse of psychic passivity and self-indulgent fatalism. It is a clear and crisp recognition that there is karmic meaning to every single event, that nothing is unnecessary even though one may not yet know what its meaning is. Ignorance of the process of adjustment of internal and external relations is merely a reflection of the limitation of one's own growth at the level of lower mind. To accept totally one's karma is like a swimmer recognizing the necessity of accepting the tidal currents of the ocean. A swimmer is not doing a favour to the ocean by accepting its sway. Deliberate and intelligent acceptance of oceanic currents is the difference between drowning and surviving.

When it comes to karma on the causal plane with reference to human consciousness and invisible forces, the same principle applies. That is why Buddha said, "Ye who suffer, know ye suffer from yourselves." Though the teaching seems obvious when stated, it must really be thought through at the core of one's being if one is going to alter the karmic tendencies of the forces at work. One must ask whether the whole of one's being is cooperating with the totality of one's karma. Unless one engages in this meditation and willingly accepts all karma even though one does not understand most of it, no regrets or resolves will make any difference. The constant task of learning, which is a matter of activating and sensitizing all the centres of perception, has an intimate bearing upon diminishing the range and reach of the irrational in one's responses to life. There is a direct connection between the *kundalini* force of adjustment of internal and external relations, which moves in a curved path, and the karmic predominance of the various elemental powers in the human constitution. In the words of Hermes Trismegistus:

> All these Genii *preside over mundane affairs,* they shake and overthrow the constitution of States and of individuals; they *imprint their likeness on our Souls,* they are present in our nerves, our marrow, our veins, our

arteries, and *our very brain-substance* . . . at the moment when each of us receives life and being, he is taken in charge by the genii (Elementals) who preside over births, and who are classed beneath the astral powers (Super-human astral Spirits). They change perpetually, not always identically, but revolving in circles.

Ibid., i 294

Throughout the cyclic development of each soul, the proportional composition of the vestures out of the five elements is continually being adjusted. Through the attraction and repulsion of their coessence to the vestures, certain elements become the dominant ruling factors in one's life. Unless one engages in noetic mental asceticism, one will invariably remain passive to the psychic sway of these irrational forces. Without ratio, harmony and proportion, one cannot employ the vestures as channels for the benevolent transmutation of life-atoms: rather one will needlessly compound the karma of selfishness. The compassionate projection of the spiritual energies of the soul requires that the genii be made subordinate to the awakened Buddhi-Manasic reason. The genii

permeate by the body two parts of the Soul, that it may receive from each the impress of his own energy. But the reasonable part of the Soul is not subject to the genii; it is designed for the reception of (the) God, who enlightens it with a sunny ray. Those who are thus illumined are few in number, and from them the genii abstain: for neither genii nor Gods have any power in the presence of a single ray of God.

Ibid., i 294-295

By the "few in number" is meant those Initiates and Adepts for whom there is no 'God' but the one universal and unconditioned Deity in boundless space and eternal duration.

The truly reasonable part of the soul is extremely important in the Aquarian Age. To think clearly, logically and incisively must be the true purpose of education. To unfold the immense powers of pure thought, the reasonable part of the soul must be given every opportunity to develop so that the irrational side is reduced. Its false coherence must be broken by seeing it causally. One must begin with a willingness to acknowledge it readily, and see that there is no gain in merely pushing it aside. The development of the reasonable part of the soul, which is not subject to the genii, culminates in the reception of the god who enlightens it with a sunny ray, the *Chitkala* that is attracted by contemplation. Clear, pure reason characterizes the immortal ray which is connected with the star that has its genii, good and evil by nature. The use of reason and clarity of perception in the spiritual and metaphysical sense involves the heart as well as the mind because they cooperate in seeing and thinking clearly. Once this is grasped, one can make a decisive difference to the amount of unnecessary karma involved in one's irrational emanations and wasteful emotions. One can begin to let go of all that and calmly cultivate the deepest feelings.

At a certain point it will become natural for the mind to move spontaneously to spiritual teachings and universal ideas whenever it has an opportunity. It would not have to be told, nor would one have to make rules, because that would be what it would enjoy. When it becomes more developed in the art of solitary contemplation, it will always see everything from the higher standpoint whilst performing duties in the lower realm, thus transforming one's whole way of living. This will make a profound difference to the conservation of energy and the clarification of one's karma. It will also strengthen the power of progressive detachment whereby one can understand what it means to say that the Sage, the *Jivanmukta,* the perfected *Yogin,* is characterized by the golden talisman of doing only what is truly necessary. He only thinks what is necessary. He only feels what is necessary. There is so powerful a sense of what is necessary in the small, but from the standpoint of the whole, that there is no other way of life that is conceivable or imaginable. This internal Buddhic logic can never be understood by reference to external rules and characteristics because one has to come to it from a high plane of meditation and total detachment from the realm of external expression.

When the disciple is sufficiently self-evolved from within without, then the further individuation of the soul through self-conscious initiations may proceed. Prepared by testing and by trials, the reasonable part of the soul may receive a sunny ray, communicated by its spiritual ancestors, themselves inseparable from the disciple's own seventh principle. The parentless progenitors of spiritual intelligence or consciousness are known at one level as Bodhisattvas, at another level as Dhyani Buddhas, at still another level as Manushi Buddhas. All of these are spiritual ancestors of what is called *Buddhi* — individually one's own intuitive principle, but in a strict philosophical sense the pure vehicle of one universal light. *Buddhi* as a principle is its emanation, a gift from a Dhyani Buddha or spiritual progenitor. Seen in this way, all the higher principles are pure emanations from spiritual instructors and parents, in the same way that until the age of seven a terrestrial parent is the spiritual and mental progenitor of the thinking of a child. The child's own intelligence is involved, and children vary in their responses because of accumulated karma. So too with the chela on the Path. The language that parents use, the ideas that they evoke, and their mode of consciousness colour the child's psyche during the day, giving a certain tone to the environment. Though most parents hardly think deliberately about what is at stake, owing to their lack of knowledge and insight, nonetheless they have the inimitable opportunity of initiating the child into the wise use of its latent powers. This is only an imperfect analogy on the lower plane of differentiated consciousness and everyday relationships between highly vulnerable personalities. It can scarcely intimate the magical privilege of communicating with Adepts and Initiates, and of participating in the compassionate ideation that permeates the magnetic field in which the chela grows. As an immortal soul, each individual is potentially an inheritor of the whole field of human consciousness over eighteen million years; as an initiated chela each may freely assume this sacred birthright as a spiritual inheritor of the parentless *Anupadaka*.

The Bodhisattva Path of self-regeneration and of initiation into the mysteries of the higher principles begins and ends with the quickening of the reverential feeling of devotion and gratitude for every single being who ever did anything for oneself. Those who are fortunate enough to perfect that power of endless, boundless gratitude and spontaneous reverence to every teacher they ever learnt from are in a better position to understand how to invoke the highest gift of self-consciousness from the greatest spiritual progenitors. In a fearless way but also in a proper posture of true devotion and reverence, one can invoke the Dhyani Buddhas in dawn meditation, during the day, in the evening and at night, whenever and how often one reaches out in consciousness to them. Before this can be done effectively, one must learn to cleanse the lunar vesture, calm the mind and purify the heart. Every thought or feeling directed against another being makes that heart unworthy to feel the hebdomadal vibration of the Dhyani Buddhas.

Self-concern pollutes rather than protects. Self-purification and self-correction strengthen the capacity to liberate oneself from the karmic accretions of lives of ignorance and foolish participation in the collective dross. Such are the laws of spiritual evolution that this purification can only proceed through the sacrificial invocation of the whole of one's karma. Then one can begin to become truly self-conscious in one's interior relationship to the Dhyani Buddhas, the Daimon, the Genius which can speak to one through the Kwan Yin, the *Chitkala*, the Inner Voice. Just as a vast portion of the world's sublimest music is only theoretically available to the average person, the finest vibrations of *Akasha-Alaya* must remain of little avail to most mortals until they fit themselves to come and sit close to the Teachers of Brahma Vach. "To live to benefit mankind is the first step."

THE TEMPEST

A MYSTERY PLAY

The more one delves into the genius of Shakespeare, the greater is the realization that, as veil after veil is lifted, there will remain "veil upon veil behind." Who was Shakespeare? What manner of man was he? What was the power behind his plays? These are questions more easily asked than answered. The vicissitudes of Shakespeare's reputation and the vagaries of critical opinion alike substantiate H.P. Blavatsky's statement that Shakespeare, like Aeschylus, "will ever remain the intellectual 'Sphinx' of the ages."

The scattered hints in Theosophical literature, though few and far between, are sufficiently suggestive to indicate the protean and profound nature of Shakespeare and his message. "My good friend — Shakespeare," wrote Mahatma K.H., quoting from him in a letter. In her editorial opening the first volume of *Lucifer*, H.P. Blavatsky declared that

> 'Shakespeare's deep and accurate science in mental philosophy' (Coleridge) has proved more beneficent to the true philosopher in the study of the human heart — therefore, in the promotion of truth — than the more accurate but certainly less deep, science of any Fellow of the Royal Institution.

Again, we know from her letter to A.P. Sinnett that she wanted a student to write out "the esoteric meaning of some of Shakespeare's plays" for inclusion in *The Secret Doctrine*. Lastly, we have W.Q. Judge's statement: "The Adepts assert that Shakespeare was, unconsciously to himself, inspired by one of their own number."

Shakespeare was a magnificent creative genius who, coming under Nirmanakayic influence, became a myriad-minded master of life and language. His amazing and expansive knowledge of the super-physical and the invisible, his penetrating and compassionate insight into human nature, his transcendent and kaleidoscopic imagination, his intuitive perception and his inspired passages — all these are at once the expression and the evidence of the deep inwardness of his plays, and of the luminous influence of Adepts.

What was the nature of Adept influence upon the mind of Shakespeare? It is not to be thought that Shakespeare was, from the first, under the special care and observation of the Great Lodge, but rather that the superior possibilities embedded within himself were what higher inspiration spurred into stronger activity. This was possible because of the largeness of his mind and the receptivity of his soul. The breadth of his Soul-Life could cause the offspring of his Fancy "to share richly in the vital Fire that burns in the higher (Image-making) Power." Above all, he possessed the power, as John Masefield has written, to touch "energy, the source of all things, the reality behind all appearance," and to partake of the storehouse of pure thought.

We will not, however, find it an easy task to unravel the mystery locked up in the allegory, symbol and character portrayal of the great plays. For, "the very fact that Shakespeare remained unconscious of the Nirmanakayic influence which his genius attracted shows that we must not expect the unadulterated expression of Divine Wisdom in all he created."

There are two possible ways of studying any of Shakespeare's plays in terms of Gupta Vidya. The first is the easier one of extracting hints of esoteric truth out of the significant lines and passages of the play. The second is the more difficult one of interpreting the entire tale and theme of the play according to one or more of the seven keys of symbolism suggested in *The Secret Doctrine*. We will use both methods, but concentrate on the second, which, if less easy, will be found more fascinating.

The group of plays to which *The Tempest* belongs and of which it is presumably the last, was written in the final period of Shakespeare's life. All these plays are romances, neither tragic nor comic but both, full of unexacting and exquisite dreams, woven within a world of mystery and marvel, of shifting visions and confusing complications, "a world in which anything may happen next." Strangely remote from 'real' life is this preternatural world of Shakespeare's final period, and the universe of his invention is peopled with many creatures more or less human, beings belonging to different orders of life. The romantic character of these plays is reflected in the richness of their style. Here we have the primary facts of poetry, suggestion, colour, imagery, together with complicated and incoherent periods, softened and accentuated rhythms, tender and evanescent beauties. These plays reach the very apex of poetic art, revealing a matured magnificence of diction and the haunting magic of the purest lyricism, altogether appealing more to the imagination than the intellect.

The fundamental feature, however, of these plays of the final period is the archetypal pattern of prosperity, destruction and re-creation which their plots follow. Virtue is not only virtuous, but also victorious, triumphant, and villainy is not only frustrated, but also forgiven. These are dramas of reconciliation between estranged kinsmen, of wrongs righted through repentance, not revenge, of pardon and of peace. Tragedy is fully merged into mysticism, and the theme is rendered in terms of myth and music, reflecting the grandeur of true immortality and spiritual conquest within apparent death and seeming defeat.

Upon the firm foundation of the accepted conclusions regarding the chronological order of the plays of Shakespeare, and of the peculiar features of the final period, modern critics have been only too eager to build their plausible and picturesque interpretations.

We have, first, the Dowden doctrine, supported in different degrees by other critics, likening Shakespeare to a ship, beaten and storm-tossed, yet entering harbour with sails full-set to anchor in Stratford-on-Avon in a state of calm content and serene self-possession. This view gives the final period of the playwright the attractive appellation of "On the Heights", and perceives in these last plays the charm of meditative romance and the peace of the highest vision. *The Tempest* is reverentially regarded as the supreme essence of Shakespeare's final benignity.

Lytton Strachey's contrary thesis, echoed partially by Granville-Barker, is that these faulty and fantastic last plays show that Shakespeare ended his days in boredom, cynicism and disillusionment. Dr. E.M.W. Tillyard and John Middleton Murry not only see no lack of vitality, no boredom with things, no poverty of versification in these later plays, but, in fact, evidences of the work of one whose poetical faculty was at its height.

The best interpretation is that of Wilson Knight in *The Crown of Life*. He regards Shakespeare as equivalent to the dynamic spiritual power manifest in his plays, and finds in the Shakespearean sequence the ring of reason, order and necessity. His plays spell the universal rhythm of the motion of the spirit of man, progressing from spiritual pain and despair through stoic acceptance and endurance to a serene and mystic joy. Whereas in the tragedies is expressed the anguish of the aspiring human soul, crying out from within its frail sepulchre of flesh against the unworthiness of the world, these last plays portray the joyous conquest of life's pain.

It is, however, important to point out the danger of stereotyping the divisions of Shakespeare's life, and the need to be wary how we apply our labels and demarcations to "so mobile a thing as the life and work of man." In the last analysis, Shakespeare was all of one piece; he developed, but in his development cast nothing away; his attitude towards life deepened, but his essential outlook always remained the same.

We could attribute the surpassing majesty of the plays of the final period to the great expansion of the creative power and dramatic skill which had first begun to show themselves in their grandeur in the tragic productions of 'the middle period.' This expansion was the product, as it is the proof, of the Adept Inspiration from which Shakespeare progressively benefited and on which he increasingly drew. Thus, we are fully prepared to regard the final period as the culmination of a spiritual odyssey which found its consummation in *The Tempest,* his last and greatest of plays. In this view, then, *The Tempest* is a broader, deeper "embodiment of the qualities drawn from the higher planes of man's being in which Imagination rules," a perfect pattern of myth and magic as of music and marvel.

The tale of *The Tempest* is well-known but we shall briefly recapitulate its salient strands. It is, primarily, the story of Prospero, rightful Duke of Milan, and his charming child, Miranda, both banished by the usurper Antonio, his brother, and living unknown on a lonely island. Here, through a long period of successful study and practice, Prospero has matured into a master-magician, and Miranda has flowered into a marriageable maiden. The play opens with a violent storm and a resulting shipwreck, caused at the bidding of Prospero by the invisible hosts of the elements, of whom Ariel is the chief. The royal party involved in the shipwreck is saved according to Prospero's plan, and is scattered on the shore, in three different parts of the island. Alonso, the King of Naples; Sebastian, his brother; Antonio, the usurper; Gonzalo, an honest old Councillor; and two Lords, Adrian and Francisco, land on one side of the island and most of them fall into an induced slumber, during which the vigilant and vile Antonio persuades the susceptible Sebastian to join in a plot to kill the King. Thanks to the intervention of the invisible Ariel, the plotters are prevented from fulfilling their purpose, and the entire party is led to look for Ferdinand, the son and successor of Alonso.

Meanwhile, Ferdinand has met Miranda and has been forced into her father's service, which he patiently undergoes until Prospero is pleased to bestow on him his daughter. At the same time, in a third part of the island, Caliban, the deformed and savage slave of Prospero, has been met first by Trinculo, the King's jester, and then by Stephano, a drunken butler, both of whom foolishly join the faithless Caliban in an abortive plot against his powerful master. These three groups are all, in the last Act, brought together near his cell by Prospero, after Antonio and Alonso and Sebastian have been made by strange and fearful sights and sounds to repent of their folly; after Ferdinand and Miranda have been treated to a visionary masque, played by spirits; and after Caliban and his companions have been brought to their senses — all of which is accomplished through the agency of Ariel. The play ends with the restoration of disturbed harmony, the recompense of the good and the repentance of the deluded, the release of Ariel from Prospero's service, and the reconciliation of one and all to the new order ushered in by Prospero, who shows himself to be a man of wisdom and a master of destiny.

Let us first briefly consider different interpretations of the underlying theme of *The Tempest*. There is, first of all, the excellent but purely artistic interpretation of Dr. Tillyard whose thesis is that the play gives us the fullest sense of the different worlds within worlds which we can inhabit, and that it is also the necessary epilogue to the incomplete theme of the great tragedies.

A more ambitious and comprehensive attempt is that of Wilson Knight, who interprets the theme of the play from various points of view — poetical, philosophical, political and historical. Poetically, he considers the play artistic autobiography, its meanings revealing a wide range of universal values. Philosophically, he maintains that *The Tempest* portrays a wrestling of flesh and spirit. Politically, he interprets the play as the betrayal of Prospero, Plato's philosopher-king and a representative of impractical idealism, by Antonio, Machiavelli's Prince, and a symbol of political villainy. Lastly, the play is regarded historically as a myth of the national soul, Prospero signifying Britain's severe, yet tolerant, religious and political instincts, Ariel typifying her inventive and poetical genius, and Caliban her colonizing spirit.

Another serious attempt at interpretation is that of Colin Still, whose study of the 'timeless theme' of *The Tempest* has not attracted the attention it deserves. He regards this 'Mystery play' as a deliberate allegorical account of those psychological experiences which constitute Initiation, its main features resembling those of every ceremonial ritual based upon the authentic mystical tradition of all mankind, but especially of the pagan world. Still takes Prospero as the Hierophant, and in one aspect, as God Himself; Ariel as the Angel of the Lord, Caliban as the Tempter or the Devil, and Miranda as the Celestial Bride.

The comedians, Stephano and Trinculo, led on by the Devil, constitute a failure to achieve Initiation; the experiences of the Court Party, which is of purgatorial status, constitute the Lesser Initiation, its attainment being self-discovery; while Ferdinand attains to Paradise, to the goal of the Greater Initiation which consists in receiving a 'second life.' The wreck is considered symbolic of the imaginary terrors of the candidate for Initiation, and the immersion in the water as symbolic of his preliminary purification. The Masque is regarded as apocalyptic in character, and the cell is taken to represent the *Sanctum Sanctorum*, only to be entered after full initiation. And so Still goes on giving every detail the status of a semi-esoteric symbol drawn mainly from pagan ritual.

Still's thesis, though basically sound, is obscured by theological terminology, and its detailed application often leads to a certain forcing of analogy. Prospero, for instance, is a man, not God, and Caliban is too clearly a thing of Nature to be called a Devil, or Satan. Still's centre of reference is altogether less in the poetry or in the philosophy than in a rigid system of pagan symbolism applied to the play.

In theosophical terms, we can approach *The Tempest* from at least three angles — the psychological, the cosmic and the occult. Of these, we shall adopt the last for detailed interpretation of the characters in the play. Before that, however, it will be worthwhile to indicate how the psychological and the cosmic keys may be applied.

The psychological key enables us to construe the theme of *The Tempest* in terms of the principles of the human constitution and the everyday experiences of the majority of mankind. In this line of interpretation, Prospero would represent *Atman*, the universal Self, which overbroods the remaining constituents of man, and allows for their rescue from all internal disequilibrium, thus producing that divine and unifying harmony which spells poise and proportion, as well as power and peace. Miranda, the daughter of Prospero, would be that specialization of *Atman* which we know as *Buddhi*, the spiritual and at present *passive* principle in man, the vehicle of *Atman*, and at once the expression and the essence of pure wisdom and of true compassion. It is in this sense that Miranda represents the fallen and Sleeping Soul of the uninitiated and deluded man. Ferdinand, the Prince who aspires to the companionship of Miranda, could be made to symbolize the higher *Manas*, the incarnated ray of the Divine in Man, while Antonio, the usurper who plans to secure personal power at the cost of his weakening conscience, could represent the *kama manas*, or the desire-mind. To complete the picture, Caliban could be taken as the *kamarupa* or the passional part of man in material form, and Ariel as the type of the assemblage of presiding deities, *devatas* or elementals, in the human personality. This, in silhouette form, would be the system of symbols that could be constructed on the basis of the psychological key — a system which, interesting as it is in its ramifying implications, it would not be difficult to develop.

The second interpretation, which we have called the cosmic, follows from a comprehensive view of the evolutionary stream in Nature, of the Great Ladder of Being. This interpretation is implied in H.P. Blavatsky's oft-quoted statement that

> the Ego begins his life-pilgrimage as a sprite, an 'Ariel', or a 'Puck'; he plays the part of a super, is a soldier, a servant, one of the chorus; rises then to 'speaking parts', plays leading roles, interspersed with insignificant parts, till he finally retires from the stage as 'Prospero', the magician.
>
> *The Key to Theosophy*, 34

In this line of interpretation, the play presents an image of the glorious supremacy of the perfected human soul over all other things and beings. At the peak of the evolutionary ascent stands Prospero, the representative of wise and compassionate god-manhood, in its true relation to the combined elements of existence — the physical powers of the external world — and the varieties of character with which it comes into contact. He is the ruling power to which the whole series is subject, from Caliban the densest to Ariel the most ethereal extreme. In Prospero we have the finest fruition of the co-ordinate development of the spiritual and the material lines of evolution.

Next to Prospero comes that charming couple, Ferdinand and Miranda, exquisite flowers of human existence that blossom forth under the benign care of their patriarch and Guru. From these we descend, by a most harmonious moral gradation, through the agency of the skilfully interposed figure of the good Gonzalo, to the representatives of the baser intellectual properties of humanity. We refer to the cunning, cruel, selfish and treacherous worldlings, who vary in their degrees of delusion from the confirmed villainy of Antonio to the folly of Alonso. Next, we have those representatives of the baser sensual attributes of the mass of humanity — the drunken, ribald, foolish retainers of the royal party, Stephano and Trinculo, whose ignorance, knavery and stupidity make them objects more of pity than of hate. Lowest in the scale of humanity comes the gross and uncouth Caliban, who represents the brutal and animal propensities of the nature of man which Prospero, the type of its noblest development, holds in lordly subjection. Lastly, below the human and the animal levels of life, in this wonderful gamut of being, comes the whole class of elementals, the subtler forces and the invisible nerves of nature, the spirits of the elements, who are represented by Ariel and the shining figures of the Masque who are alike governed by the sovereign soul of Prospero. Shakespeare obviously knew of these invisible spirits and recognized their place in the panorama of evolution.

The esoteric or occult is the highest approach to any allegorical system. *The Tempest* can be made, on this approach, to yield a subtle and complete account of the ways and workings of the Great Lodge of Adept-Gurus, and the trials and tests on the path of probationary chelaship, leading, through a series of progressive awakenings, to the attainment of the goal of conscious godhood, even amidst the irksome conditions of earth-life. This esoteric interpretation is really based on two postulates — of the probationary character of all incarnated existence, and of the ceaseless unfolding, from within outwards, of the whole of Life.

To start with, let us understand the character of Prospero. By various critics, Prospero is regarded as a magician, a superman, the spirit of Destiny and the symbol of Shakespeare himself. In our interpretation he is a perfected human soul, a god-man, an Adept, the wise master of Nature and the compassionate despot of destiny, the creator of his own circumstances, and the designer of the drama of the Shakespearean world. Above all, he is the accomplished personification of that super-state which the earlier Shakespearean characters aspire to, but never attain.

H.P. Blavatsky defines an Adept as

> a man of profound knowledge, exoteric and esoteric, especially of the latter; and one who has brought his carnal nature under subjection of the WILL; who has developed in himself both the power (Siddhi) to control the forces of nature and the capacity to probe her secrets by the help of the formerly latent but now active powers of his being.
>
> "Chelas and Lay Chelas"

More simply, she defines an Adept as "one who has reached the stage of Initiation, and become a Master in the science of Esoteric Philosophy."

In the light of these criteria, Prospero becomes for us a logical conception. We see him at the beginning of the play standing

> like a white pillar to the west, upon whose face the rising Sun of thought eternal poureth forth its first most glorious waves. His mind, like a becalmed and boundless ocean, spreadeth out in shoreless space. He holdeth life and death in his strong hand.
>
> The Voice of the Silence

He has attained this state through protracted study and effort which had begun even when he was the reigning Duke of Milan.

> The government I cast upon my brother,
> And to my state grew stranger, being transported
> And rapt in secret studies. . . .
> I, thus *neglecting worldly ends,* all dedicated
> To closeness and the bettering of my mind
> With that, which but by being so retir'd
> O'er-prized all popular rate....

This is considered by many a critic to be his 'fatal flaw' whereas actually Prospero was obeying "the inward impulse of his soul, irrespective of the prudential considerations of worldly science or sagacity." Far from having been a scholar unfitted for direct action, he was a spiritual recluse on the brink of magical power, who has spent his period of retirement on the lonely island in perfecting his adeptship. This retirement is symbolic of the mental renunciation by the chela of the material things of life. When he attains to full adeptship and complete mastery over himself and Nature, Prospero, as a member of the Great Lodge, now performs one of its two tasks to bring, in his turn, prospective members and probationary chelas to the island on which he has attained perfection. It is on this sacred mission that he is engaged throughout the play.

Personification of wisdom and compassion that he now is, he has become one with destiny, one with the purpose of the great law of Karma. His name itself is allegorical of his beneficent character. In this light, we should regard Antonio and Alonso, not as Prospero's personal enemies, but as types of humanity who, in their ignorance and delusion, disturb the divine harmony that they are then compelled by their destiny to restore, and who, in their folly, curse the aspiring chela who returns amidst them as an Adept, only to bless. Prospero uses his tempest-magic only to draw the deluded to his island, teaching them through disaster to repent of their evil doings, and then raising them through his forgiveness. He is the eternally compassionate one who redeems the society that rejects him by the dynamic spiritual power which he radiates, even in repose. Prospero's consciousness is already set beyond the horizon of ordinary men, in eternity; he is elevated above the petty, personal motives of average humanity, and he feels the profound pain of the Great Instructors at perceiving the unteachability of some of their pupils.

We must also note the true significance of his final speech, the Epilogue. Having consummated his purpose and performed his first task, Prospero, the Adept, renounces the formal robe of the magician and resumes the ceremonial appearance of a duke. He has attained to a higher degree of Adeptship. He will return to earth-life as a *Rajarishi,* or divine ruler, and now undertake the more difficult task of directing, under royal guise, large masses of men, and re-establishing righteousness on earth. When he does this, Prospero, the Adept, like Padmapani of the Buddhist legend, completely identifies himself with the sufferings of mankind and assumes the burden of helping men to find their salvation.

From Prospero we must turn to Ariel. Critics have considered Ariel as a symbol of the subtle powers of the imagination, the personification of poetry itself. Theosophically, he may be taken as belonging to the highest class of elementals, sufficiently individualized to be marked off from the Nature spirits, 'the nerves of Nature,' in the play. Ariel, stamped by his master with a Manasic impress, becomes the agent of his purpose, and his instrument in controlling the congeries of elementals to develop the action of the plot. He helps raise the tempest, being part of it; he puts some of the people to sleep, so tempting the murderers, but wakes the others just in time; he thunderously interrupts the feast, drawing the moral. He plays tricks on the drunkards, overhears their plot, and leads them to disaster. He puts the ship safely to harbour, and later releases and conducts the mariners.

All this shows the intelligence and the reason with which his master has endowed him. He is impressed, however, not merely with reason, but also with emotion. As the opening scene of the closing Act indicates, Ariel, though non-human, aspires to be human and seems to have caught a faint reflection of human feeling through Prospero's influence. His earlier imprisonment by Sycorax and his release by Prospero are both suggestive of tests undergone by elementals before they are used by the perfected Adept. Further, his instinctive impulse to become free, and the pure joy he shows when finally released by Prospero, are indicative of the higher points of evolutionary progress which he desires and deserves to reach.

All this about Ariel can be clarified by statements in Theosophical philosophy. *The Secret Doctrine* states that while the lowest elementals have no fixed form, the higher possess an intelligence of their own, though not enough to construct a thinking man. W.Q. Judge defines an elemental as

> a centre of force, without intelligence, without moral character or tendencies, but capable of being directed in its movements by human thoughts, which may, consciously or not, give it any form, and to a certain extent, intelligence.
>
> *Path*, May 1888

Ariel is a highly evolved elemental which progresses towards the human kingdom by its service of Prospero, the Adept.

Caliban has been over-philosophized by critics of the eminence of Browning and Renan. The mass of interpretation which his character has evoked is second only to that on Hamlet. In all literature, it has been contended, there is no being so mysterious as this brute, earth-born, halting on the confines of humanity. His character, according to Hazlitt, grows out of the soil, and he has the dawning of understanding, though without reason or the moral sense. The gulf between him and humanity has been proclaimed to be unbridgeable even by Prospero's influence and teaching. According to Wilson Knight, Caliban is a combination of man, savage, ape, water-beast, dragon and semi-devil, and symbolizes, among other things, all brainless revolution, the animal aspect of man, the anomalous ascent of evil within the creative order, the external quality of time itself. It has, however, been claimed by some critics that Caliban, though carnal and of the earth, earthy, is neither vulgar nor unlovely.

Coleridge, especially, has been very kind to Caliban, and considered him, in some respects, a noble being. Towards the end of the last century, Daniel Wilson put forward the proposition that Caliban is the exact missing link, connecting man and the anthropoids, the highest ape and the lowest savage.

All these interpretations of Caliban's character, though suggestive and interesting, fall far short of the Theosophical explanation. Even at the hands of Colin Still, Caliban fares badly. He makes of Caliban the Tempter, the personification of Desire. Actually, however, there is enough textual evidence to indicate that Caliban represents the material line of evolution and the lunar side of Nature. He is man in form, but not man in mind. His is the lower intelligence of the Shadow of the Barhishad or Lunar Pitris, closely connected with the earth. They are our material ancestors who give the Chayyas or 'Shadows' that must, to become self-conscious men, be lighted up by the Agnishwatta Pitris, the "Sons of the Fire," as they are called in *The Secret Doctrine*. Caliban, then, has intelligence, but not enough to make a thinking man. He may be taken to allegorize "the vanity of *physical* nature's unaided attempts to construct even a perfect *animal* — let alone man." This imperfect physical form cannot be lighted up by the Great Lodge of Adepts until it develops into a proper human shape.

In the first Act, we have Prospero saying to Caliban:

> ...Abhorred slave
> Which any print of goodness wilt not take,
> Being capable of all ill! I pitied thee,
> Took pains to make thee speak, taught thee each hour
> One thing or other: when thou didst not, savage,
> Know thine own meaning, but wouldst gabble, like
> A thing most brutish, I endow'd thy purposes
> With words that made them known: but thy vile race,
> Though thou didst learn, had that in't, which good natures
> Could not abide to be with.

Again, he is called

> A devil, a born devil, on whose nature
> Nurture can never stick. . . .

Later in the play, he is termed a "misshapen knave," a bastard "demi-devil," a "thing of darkness" which is "as disproportion'd in his manner as in his shape." And yet this same Caliban, when he shows the first signs of repentance and realization at the end of the play, unfolds the possibilities of future progress, saying

> . . . I'll be wise hereafter
> And seek for grace. . . .

In the esoteric interpretation Ferdinand is an accepted Chela, who, having successfully passed all the tests and trials set by Prospero, is then united with Miranda, the personification of wisdom, *Buddhi*, similar to the Egyptian Isis and the Gnostic Sophia. It is significant to note that Ferdinand first falls in love with Miranda, but soon realizes the importance of serving a Master before attaining to wisdom and exclaims, in the last Act, that he has received a "second life" from his gracious Guru. Again, Ferdinand is warned by Prospero in the First Scene of the Fourth Act against the dangers of falling prey to his carnal passions and thus forfeiting his right to enjoy wedded happiness. The same warning against the awful consequences, for one who has pledged himself to Occultism, of the gratification of terrestrial lusts is given by H.P. Blavatsky. Similarly, the indispensable prerequisites for psychic development which she gives — "a pure place, pure diet, pure companionship, and a pure mind" — are fulfilled by Ferdinand before he is initiated into wisdom. He has successfully undergone the discipline of ascetic diet and of arduous labours, and is therefore rewarded with the hand of Miranda.

> If I have too austerely punish'd you,
> Your compensation makes amends; for I
> Have given you here, a third of mine own life,
> Or that for which I live: who, once again,
> I tender to thy hand: all thy vexations

Were but my trials of thy love, and thou
Hast strangely stood the test; here, afore Heaven
I ratify this my rich gift.

Lastly, it is important to note that Miranda, the symbol of Wisdom, is consciously considered by Ferdinand as vastly superior to a number of sweet-tongued ladies who represent the many pleasures of the senses which hold down in bondage the winged spirit of man.

Admir'd Miranda!
Indeed the top of admiration, worth
What's dearest to the world: full many a Lady
I have ey'd with best regard, and many a time
The harmony of their tongues hath into bondage
Brought my too diligent ear:
                    . . . But you, O you,
So perfect, and so peerless, are created
Of every creature's best!

In taking Miranda as the symbol of wisdom, we are assigning her the right role in the scale of significance in the play. Had she been more weakly drawn, she would have been too insignificant to be of any interest, and had she been more strongly delineated, she would have been too dominating and individualistic to be sweetly subordinate to Prospero. As it is, however, Ferdinand and Miranda together represent, at the end of the play, a new order of things that has evolved out of destruction; they also vouch for its continuation. Having attained to Divine Wisdom, the initiated Chela can help to carry on the mission of his Master.

Having suggested the esoteric significance of the main characters, it is enough to take note of the remaining persons in the play. Antonio, the deluded and defiant villain; Sebastian, the weak-willed and cynical evildoer; Alonso, the gullible and guilty ruler, — all these represent the considerable portion of selfish and ambitious humanity which is given ample chances by the compassionate Adepts to repent of its past and to reform in the present. Stephano, the drunken and ambitious butler, and Trinculo, the stupid and cowardly jester, typify the grosser section of sensual humanity which, far from realizing its folly, rebels against the established order of things and is, therefore, for its own sake, made to suffer. Then we have the good Gonzalo, type of the loquacious and large-hearted dreamers who, for all their naïveté, are the quickest to come to a discovery of their own inward divinity. It is he who exclaims, at the end, that they have, at last, found themselves, and thus takes the first step on the path of chelaship.

Finally, we may consider the members of the crew who are immersed in a state of stupor as representing the dormant and ignorant mass of common humanity that is unaware of the probationary character of the school of life, in which they, nevertheless, continue to learn. Thus, from the highest to the lowest, everyone in the mighty march of evolution is elevated a stage higher than before, at the end of the play, through the noble efforts of Prospero.

Having considered the characters, let us notice some of the symbols in the play, and their esoteric and psychological significance. Esoterically, the tempest can be taken to stand for the tremendous thrill of Nature at the attainment by a human being of complete perfection, at the birth of an Adept. This is magnificently described in *The Voice of the Silence*:

> Know, Conqueror of Sins, once that a Sowanee hath cross'd the seventh Path, all Nature thrills with joyous awe and feels subdued. The silver star now twinkles out the news to the night-blossoms, the streamlet to the pebbles ripples out the tale; dark ocean waves will roar it to the rocks surf-bound, scent-laden breezes sing it to the vales, and stately pines mysteriously whisper: 'A Master has arisen, a MASTER OF THE DAY'.

The same rare and solemn event is wonderfully delineated

in poetic detail by Sir Edwin Arnold towards the close of the Sixth Book of *The Light of Asia*. The *raison d'être* of this disturbance and delight produced in Nature by man's attainment of perfection is to be found in a statement by Mahatma K.H.:

> Nature has linked all parts of her Empire together by subtle threads of magnetic sympathy, and, there is a mutual correlation even between a star and a man.

Further, this tempest is no awful cataclysm of Nature, but has its benedictory aspect, as is clearly seen in the play. It is a necessary prelude to the peace and calm that spell the hope and joy of the whole of creation, as it is also a blessing and a boon to the striving souls of humanity. Psychologically, the tempest may be regarded as a condition of terrible internal disequilibrium, an intense ferment of the human consciousness which stirs the turbulent soul to its divinest depths and awakens it to the austere reality of the life of the spirit.

If we understand the dual significance of the tempest, it will be easy to explain the meaning of the symbol of the sea. It would stand for the sea of samsara or the great Ocean of Life with its boisterous waves of Being, and the timeless tide of the Ever-Becoming.

> Behold the Hosts of Souls. Watch how they hover o'er the stormy sea of human life, and how, exhausted, bleeding, broken-winged, they drop one after other on the swelling waves. Tossed by the fierce winds, chased by the gale, they drift into the eddies and disappear within the first great vortex.

Psychologically, this stormy sea may be taken to signify the emotional nature of man, with its waves of varied passions, and its tide of deathless desire.

The Island is no casual creation of the poet's fancy, nor does it typify any terrestrial place known to history or guessed by geography.

It may be taken to symbolize Shamballa, the Sacred Island referred to in *Isis Unveiled* and *The Secret Doctrine*. This, once an actual island in the Central Asian Sea, is now fabled to be an oasis in the Gobi Desert. The island of *The Tempest* stands for the dwelling-place of the Divine Instructors of mankind, those mighty Maha-Yogins of whom Prospero is at once a type and a symbol. Psychologically, this island could be taken as a new dimension of awareness, a magnetic and enclosed environment of the indwelling soul of the chela, inaccessible to the thoughts and the things of the world.

Esoterically, Prospero's cell would stand for the Hall of Initiation, the *Sanctum Sanctorum*, into which Ferdinand is invited to enter only in the Fourth Act, with the close of the Masque; the Court Party is invited only to "look in" at the end of the play, in the last Act. This cell is similar to the Saptaparna cave near Mount Baibhar in Rajagriha, the ancient capital of Magadha, in which a select circle of Arhats received initiation from Gautama Buddha. The cell is a most solemn symbol, corresponding to the Christian Holy of Holies and to the Adytum "wherein were created immortal Hierophants." Psychologically, this cell may be taken to stand for the "inmost chamber, the chamber of the Heart", the *Brahma-pura* or the secret closet into which Jesus asks us to retire for prayerful meditation.

Prospero's wand is a protective and creative instrument, the same as *Vajra* or as *Dorje*, a weapon that denotes power over invisible evil influences, a talisman that protects its owner by purifying the atmosphere around him. Mystically, *Vajra* is "the *magic* sceptre of Priest-Initiates, exorcists and adepts — the symbol of the possession of *Siddhis* or superhuman powers, wielded during certain ceremonies by the priests and theurgists." Psychologically, the wand may be taken to stand for the protective purity of the heart of the chela progressing on the path of Occultism.

What about the visionary Masque, conjured up with the help of nature-spirits by Ariel at the bidding of Prospero, for the benefit of Ferdinand and Miranda? This vision of the gods, raised by magical evocation, is a part of the ceremony of initiation and is partly intended to remind the successful Chela of the existence of higher powers and potencies in the universe. We have Prospero telling Ariel:

> . . . Go bring the rabble,
> O'er whom I give thee power, here, to this place:
> Incite them to quick motion, for I must
> Bestow upon the eyes of this young couple
> Some vanity of mine Art; it is my promise
> And they expect it from me.

The purpose of this masque is, however, more than that; it is also

> A contract of true love to celebrate;
> And some donation freely to estate
> On the bless'd lovers.

The fertility, purity, chastity and virility invoked and represented by the goddesses and the daring nymphs define a particular relationship, not only between husband and wife, but also between Guru and chela. Without going into details, it is enough to state that this masque, though mechanically contrived, makes a deep impression upon Ferdinand and is proclaimed by him to be a "most majestic vision," that "makes this place Paradise." The spirits acting the parts of gods and goddesses are merely nerves of Nature or centres of force having astral forms, partaking to a distinguishing degree of the element to which they belong and also of the aether, and acting collectively as a combination of 'sublimated matter and rudimental mind.' Psychologically, the vision of the Masque may be taken as a subjective experience of the ever-varying pageantry of the invisible universe.

Having interpreted the characters and some of the symbols of *The Tempest,* let us now illustrate the other method of studying the play — to pick out passages and lines that point to the pure essence of Theosophic truth.

The first important passage we shall consider is the famous speech of Gonzalo in the First Scene of the Second Act, which is an excellent parody on the pretty Utopias that men, in their immature but charming idealism, dream about and vision forth. His rejection of all the implements of war and machinery and his reliance on Nature's abundance express an admirable yearning, while his dream of a new golden age is delightful in its universality. Yet, the bounties of Nature and freedom are not to be had on terms so easy, certainly not by sinners, nor can they be described in categories so simple. Gonzalo, like all eager and impatient revolutionaries, forgets that a perfect society is inconceivable without perfect men, that Utopias must be peopled with Prosperos, if they are to be realized on earth. The foil to his inadequate vision is to be found in Miranda's exclamation in the last Act when she sees, for the first time, a substantial slice of humanity in Alonso, Antonio, Sebastian, Gonzalo, Adrian and Francisco:

> O, wonder!
> How many goodly creatures are there here!
> How beauteous mankind is! O brave new world,
> That has such people in't!

Yet, when all is said on the side of rationalists, Gonzalo's dreams, though naïve, are both natural and necessary; they are the visions in which thousands of eager youths and high-spirited men have revelled, the visions of Coleridge and Wordsworth, Blake and Shelley, William Morris and Samuel Butler and H.G. Wells, visions which, though illusory and incomplete, have a call for the nobler souls among us. As things exist, however, such visions only invite the cynicism and the scorn of the Antonios and Sebastians of this unimaginative world.

A beautiful exposition of wisdom is in the famous speech of Prospero at the end of the Masque, which portrays the mayavic nature of all manifestation, and the changing character of all conditioned existence.

Our revels now are ended. These our actors,
As I foretold you, were all spirits, and
Are melted into air, into thin air:
And, like the baseless fabric of this vision,
The cloud-capp'd towers, the gorgeous palaces,
The solemn temples, the great globe itself,
Yea, all which it inherit, shall dissolve
And, like this insubstantial pageant faded,
Leave not a rack behind. We are such stuff
As dreams are made on, and our little life
Is rounded with a sleep.

This profoundly philosophical speech is a splendid statement
of the idealistic doctrine of maya, of Appearance and Reality.
Earth-life is proclaimed to be a short sleep, and the material world
a delusive dream. This conception is beautifully brought out and
elaborated in *The Secret Doctrine*. Maya or illusion

> is an element which enters into all finite things, for
> everything that exists has only a relative, not an absolute,
> reality, since the appearance which the hidden
> noumenon assumes for any observer depends upon his
> power of cognition. . . . Nothing is permanent except
> the one hidden absolute existence which contains in
> itself the noumena of all realities.
>
> *The Secret Doctrine*, i 39

The last long passage that we might mention is Prospero's
farewell address to the elementals, in the First Scene of the Fifth
Act, and his renunciation of the ritual (but not the knowledge)
of Magic, ending with the words:

                    . . . But this rough magic
I here abjure; and, when I have requir'd
Some heavenly music which even now I do,
To work mine end upon their senses, that
This airy charm is for, I'll break my staff,

> Bury it certain fathoms in the earth,
> And deeper than did ever plummet sound
> I'll drown my book.

This speech must be taken together with the last, in the Epilogue. These two speeches are, in a sense, self-explanatory, in the light of our interpretation of the characters and symbols of the play. It will be enough to point out that, while the first is addressed to the elementals, and delineates the type and technique of the magic that Prospero has used in the past, the second is addressed by him to humanity in general, as well as to his chelas in particular, and indicates the new and difficult future that is opening out before his prophetic gaze.

The Tempest gives us a complete view of human existence in the timeless soul of poetry. The central thought of the play is that the whole of existence is probationary and progressive, that true freedom consists in the service of one's fellow-men, that the way to the attainment of the wisdom of Adepts is untiring and selfless persistence in the effort of self-education. Music and magic meet in *The Tempest,* so wedded that none can put them asunder. The denouement is full of grace and grandeur. As Hazlitt says,

> The preternatural part has the air of reality, and almost haunts the imagination with a sense of truth, while the real characters and events partake of the wildness of a dream.

Creatures of rare loveliness are here created for us by Shakespeare who, through reconciliation, forgiveness and good-will, renews the promise of a better and more beautiful world.

Bombay
April 26, 1949

THE SOUL OF TIBET

Many souls all over the globe were deeply moved by the tragic happenings in Tibet which led to the dramatic escape and exile of the fourteenth Dalai Lama. Here was a harmless, happy people, with a distinctive culture and traditional society totally different from that existing anywhere else in the world. To some this society seemed to be an archaic survival, an anachronism in the modern age, a 'theocratic' system which Europe had rejected long before the Enlightenment and the French Revolution. And yet, in spite of all facile attempts to label Tibet, many had a feeling of deference towards a religious culture they could not claim to understand. Despite all the travellers' tales, the several volumes written by scholars and by others fascinated by Tibet, one still felt that the essential truth had not been told, that perhaps it could never be told by anybody inside that remote and close-knit community to anyone outside it. A few went so far as to follow Burke's maxim: "We must venerate where we cannot understand." But even the most insensitive of persons, willing to write off Tibet and dismiss its tradition, had somewhere deep down a sense of not knowing what one was talking about.

Most observers, ranging from the troubled sceptic to the ardent admirer and even to the true believer — most felt that there had taken place a sudden confrontation, unprecedented in history, between a way of life centered on spiritual concerns — which could be criticized in terms of modern criteria but nonetheless had a radiant integrity of its own — and the crude forces of aggression and the destructive passions of politics which are all too familiar in the outside world. It seemed as though Tibet was a test case: can a spiritual tradition survive if it does not arm itself against aggressors who are ruthless, who care nothing for the tradition they are prepared to tear apart or for the culture they are willing to destroy in the name of modernization? This is a question which still troubles many people.

The Dalai Lama is fortified by his faith that in the end Tibetan tradition, embodied in the way of life of which he is the custodian and the conscience will survive, will even eventually triumph. He is also convinced that, as time goes on, more and more people will come to see that Tibet has a profound political and spiritual significance for all humanity. Elementary human rights have been flagrantly violated by aggressors among a people who were not linked with any foreign power, who were not involved in any sense in the Cold War or giving cause for offence to any neighbouring nation.

Here, then, is a test case of the vindication of basic human rights, and the Dalai Lama pins his hopes on people everywhere who think about this, who read the reports of the International Commission of Jurists, who seriously try to get some idea of the implications, for a people such as the Tibetans, of the desecration of their monasteries and shrines, and of a stable religious and social order in need of internal reform. His Holiness feels that if men and women continue to be silent about Tibet they will be betraying their very humanity.

We find that on the political plane the issue has been so sharply and squarely stated that it ultimately touches upon those fundamental decencies which make life meaningful. But, also, the Dalai Lama is convinced that the tragedy of Tibet has a spiritual significance and a meaning even for those who are not primarily interested in the Buddhist tradition. Even for them it must appear tragic that there should have been this brutal interference with the benefits of a gentle and tolerant people. Do the virtues of tolerance and civility for which Europe fought so hard — and which were finally enshrined in the seventeenth century — do these virtues mean nothing to people who may not necessarily share in the beliefs of the Tibetans?

The Dalai Lama speaks with a faith and confidence akin to that of the Encyclopaedists, the great humanists and the religious prophets, and it would be wonderful for any of us to get something of this faith. How this could be translated into immediate political action is a question which is not a matter for casual discussion. Although nowhere more than in England was there an immediate response in the way of sympathy and material support for the Tibetans in their plight, yet already, in a short time, many people even there have begun to take the subjugation of Tibet for granted, and sometimes to talk as though the Tibetan cause were wholly lost. The Dalai Lama has spoken very warmly about England as the leading spiritual and cultural centre of the whole of Europe. He thought that the British Government, more than any other Government in the West, was aware of the historical background of Tibet and the implications of all that had happened. He also felt that the admirable work of the Tibet Society in England was a pointer to the kind of sympathy and support which could be fruitful.

It is indeed distressing that we should come across the feeling that Tibet is a lost cause, an irretrievable tragedy, and that perhaps the time has come to write Tibet's epitaph. Some of us are keen to do what we can for the refugees and to assist the Dalai Lama, while still regarding the cause of Tibet, at least in a political sense, as hopeless. This feeling of hopelessness is unwarranted but perfectly understandable in our time. Whatever we may feel about the legitimacy of the survival of the Tibetan way of life, we are all affected by the tremendous increase in historicism, determinism and fatalism in the modern world, and especially in our own century, even though we instinctively condemn these attitudes when they are couched in their crudest Marxist form. Many of us think that there is something irreversible about the process of modernization, something titanic and totally irresistible about the Industrial Revolution, the march of science and technology. We consequently feel that when any country, but especially a country with an archaic society and a simple economy, with a monastic culture and old-fashioned ideas of government, comes up against a modern aggressor, be he communist or anyone else, the traditional system must necessarily give way to the forces of modernization.

When the British entered Tibet at the time of the famous Younghusband Expedition, and even earlier — going back to the emissary sent out in the eighteenth century — there was a willing recognition that Tibet was no worse for being different. It is Britain, more than any other power that has moved out into far places, which has preserved that due respect for differing cultures and traditions which comes naturally to a people steeped in a traditional culture that has set a high value upon tolerance and the acceptance of diversity. The British failed in the assimilation of people who were racially and culturally different, but they were able to play a protective role in many areas of the world where they were in power. Even in countries where they unwittingly launched the process of modernization they had doubts and reservations; they were never too certain that this was the universal panacea.

But when a country such as Tibet comes into violent contact with fanatical believers in the gospel of material progress and ruthless modernization, can it survive? If we are convinced it cannot, then we can do no more than merely deplore the actual methods used by the Chinese, which indeed are ghastly. And here we have the cruel paradox of modernization introduced by methods which take us right back to the Middle Ages, methods which beggar description. Sickening details of the heinous things that are being done in Tibet in the name of modernization are to be found in the objective reports prepared by the International Commission of Jurists.

Are we going to be content with deploring the pace, the cost, the pains and the ruthlessness of this compulsory modernization? Has not the time come for us to reassess our high valuation of the very process of modernization? If we do this, we shall become less inclined to accept without question the notion that it is inevitable and unavoidable in every part of the world. We may even come to distrust the dogmatism or fatalism with which people declare Tibet to be a lost cause.

If we wish to appreciate the significance of Tibet, we must not merely have second thoughts about the blessings and inevitability of modernization but also discard at least one version still in vogue of the doctrine of Progress. No doubt the idea of progress is an ancient one, derived from several sources of the Western tradition, different from the cyclical views of history of the East, but it assumed a wholly new form in the last sixty years. All the early apostles of progress — Herder, Kant, Condorcet, Renouvier — regarded it mainly as a moral concept, an ethical ideal towards which modern man was moving. Renouvier clearly condemned the deterministic notion of progress. There is, after all, no religious warrant for the belief that the Kingdom of God will inevitably appear on earth in the foreseeable future. There is no scientific proof for the belief that technological and scientific developments will necessarily ensure better social relations, happier and more harmonious human relationships. There is no economic basis, either, for the belief in indefinite and automatic expansion.

But none of these doubts entered sixty years ago into the minds of those who took the permanency of their political universe for granted. Then, for the first time, as a result of the Darwinian theory of evolution, a new and specious form of the doctrine of progress came into being: the idea of inevitable, automatic, cumulative and irreversible progress achieved purely through technological inventions, economic betterment and the raising of living standards. This idea, although it was powerfully attacked and rejected by several leading thinkers and writers in Europe, still lingers on in people's minds even if they disavow it. This lingering latter-day notion of progress is a serious obstacle to our appreciation of the significance of Tibet.

If we look at Tibet with this idea in our minds, there is no chance of our really understanding it. Tibetans have lived in a land rich in mineral resources but refused to develop them because they believed that this would be an unnecessary and undesirable interference with the soil. These are people willing to spend a significant proportion of their meagre earnings upon the maintenance of a vast number of monasteries; a people completely happy to accept that the only education available to them (and it was generally available in Tibet) was an essentially religious education. It is true that those who did not wish to

become monks went to these ancient monastic universities and
got some kind of secular learning, but not what we would today
call secular learning. They might acquire a little knowledge of
elementary mathematics, indigenous medicine, traditional arts and
crafts and practical skills. But how could such people be fitted
into any scale of values we might have?

It is not going to be easy for 'progressive' people to seize
on the true significance of Tibet, and to realize that they are
confronted not just by helpless exiles pleading for sympathy but
by a moral challenge to many assumptions they normally would
not question. As the Dalai Lama has said in his book *My Land
and My People*, one cannot understand Tibet if one has no feeling
for religion.

What is religion to the Dalai Lama, to Tibetans? Religion, he
says in his book, has got everything to do with the mental
discipline, the peace of mind, the calm and poise, the inner
equanimity achieved by any human being, which is bound to
show in his daily life. The Dalai Lama says explicitly that religion
is not a matter of merely going into retreats and monasteries.
No doubt when this is done it has its value, but religion is not a
matter of outward profession or formal observance. His Holiness
does not even use the word 'Buddhism' with anything like a
sectarian sound. He is simply not interested in making claims of
any sort. Religion means for him something quite different from
what it means to almost all of us in the modern world. For him,
and for the Tibetans, religion means what it meant in Carlyle's
definition: the beliefs by which a man really lives from day to
day, not the beliefs to which he merely gives verbal or even mental
assent.

The Tibetan view of religion is indeed something totally
different from our ordinary response to religious as opposed to
secular thought. How many of us really believe that even more
important than material advancement and the utilitarian criterion
of physical pleasure, is the possession of priceless truths
concerning the numerous inhibitions and tendencies which afflict
the human psyche and of which we have hardly any definite and

exact knowledge? If we do believe this, we will be prepared to approach in a spirit of humility the thousands of Buddhist texts in Tibet that came from India, Nepal and China. Tibet is a repository of the real wisdom of the East — a much abused phrase. It has been the home of thousands upon thousands of manuscripts, scrolls, and volumes in which we have not only profound spiritual truths but also examples of a highly developed system of logic and dialectics that was primarily put to a metaphysical and a religious use but which in itself provides a unique discipline to the mind. Tibet has no parallel in this sphere. Of course, no one would admit that he does not care for logical processes. But how much thought do we give simply to perfecting the art of enquiry and disputation? How much time do we give to evolving a technique of constructive discussion? Do we really know how it is possible to resolve the apparently contrary standpoints of relative truths in religion and philosophy and our human relationships?

This technique was highly developed in Tibet. It was founded upon the doctrine of what the Dalai Lama calls the Dual Truth: the distinction between a Platonic archetype of absolute truth, which is unknown to mortal man but can always be held up as an ultimate ideal, and the relative truth every human being embodies, acquired purely by reference to his own experience. We have here the basis of an epistemology which in its higher flights enters into mysticism and metaphysics, but which at the same time is firmly grounded in undogmatic empiricism. The resulting attitude of mind enshrines the belief that a man can only speak authentically in the name of the experience he himself has had. That is why to the Dalai Lama and to the Tibetans it would be irrelevant what one calls oneself or how one is labelled, and this is as true on the political as on the religious plane.

It is simply not possible for people who rely largely on their own direct experience to make a general issue out of Communism or to generalize about the Chinese, though they have had to suffer acutely from acts of aggression performed by particular people calling themselves Communists and Chinese. This does not mean that they are 'soft' on Communism or blind to the developments in China, but it is a generally shared attitude to life in Tibet — a willing recognition of the inherent worth and true measure of any man, as well as of his stature as a soul, manifested through his acts and gestures, his face, his smile, his total self. There is also an immediate recognition of the evil, separative tendencies in all of us which cause violence, but with this recognition there is a spontaneous compassion for the evil-doer. It is quite literally possible, in the case of Tibetans, for thousands upon thousands of people to say, in their daily lives, "Lord Buddha, forgive him for he knows not what he does." The doctrine of renunciation, of universal salvation and collective welfare, a doctrine embodied in the ideal figure of the Bodhisattva, is meaningful to the ordinary man in Tibet. It is not just a mysterious truth to which a chosen few have privileged access. It is significant that the Dalai Lama in his book does not wish to make special claims on behalf of Gautama the Buddha. He casually states that the Buddha is one of a thousand Buddhas. But this makes no difference to the inward gratitude and profound reverence that he has for the Buddha as the transmitter and exemplar of truths that have become part of the way of life of millions of people in the world.

So the very idea of renunciation is absorbed into the consciousness of ordinary people: the idea that a man reveals himself by the extent to which he can shed what he has, and not by how much he acquires. This is an idea which we might put under the label of Christian charity, or Buddhist compassion, or something else — but the fact of the matter is that modern society is founded, as William Morris saw, upon the opposite principle. It is only in the modern world with its shallow moral values that the very spirit of acquisitiveness has given us a new and dominant criterion of judgment, so that we feel if a person acquires more and more of this or that — be it degrees or titles, wealth, or property shares, fame or influence — he is worthy of admiration and imitation. He may at best use his assets in the service of some exclusive cause. It is very difficult for a man to pretend that he is acquiring something for the sake of the whole of humanity; it is not so difficult to pretend that he is acquiring something for the sake of a particular nation, or group — to identify his own personal ambition with a narrow conception of collective self-interest. And we all know how easy it is indeed for us to say that we wish to get ahead for the sake of our children and our families. But once the acquisitive instinct becomes deep-rooted, there takes place a total transvaluation of values — something that is so subtly pervasive that we do not notice the resulting corruption in our natures and in the society to which we belong.

Once this happens, inevitably we begin to set up new idols and false gods. We gradually come to abandon the heroic ideal as well as the very notion of intrinsic value and merit. The heroic ideal which was precious to the Greeks and to the ancient Indians has been applied by the Tibetans to the unseen odyssey of the human soul. We cannot easily imagine what it means to live by the idea that an individual can by his self-discipline dare all, that the world is a place of probation, that he does not have to take what does not belong to him, that he can take freely from Nature and put his own talents to a use that may compel admiration and evoke emulation but dispenses with the cruder forms of competition and conflict. This heroic ideal, which even in its worldly form did so much good to Europe and to England even as late as the nineteenth century, has gone — some feel for good.

In Tibet, then, there have been large numbers of people who were shown a technique of creative thinking based upon the doctrine of the Dual Truth, a technique perfected by lamas in the great monasteries of Drepung and Sera. Among the Tibetan people the doctrine of renunciation, as opposed to the notion of personal salvation, is deeply rooted, more than anywhere else even in the East. In India, the original home of the Buddha, the doctrine of *moksha* or *mukti,* the quest for personal salvation, became so deeply rooted for centuries that it engendered a selfish individualism, a subtle kind of spiritual isolationism. As a result, most people are not wedded to a living ideal of renunciation, although it is to be found in the Indian scriptures. But this ideal did mean, and has continued to mean, a very great deal to a large mass of people in Tibet. So here is a claim to uniqueness that we may make on behalf of the Tibetans, though they have no interest in making any claims to uniqueness, unlike people less deeply rooted in their cultures and religions.

This is not the occasion to go into all the Tibetan beliefs. The moral values that flowed from their system of beliefs were richly reflected in their daily lives, despite their human failings. Many visitors to Tibet in the course of centuries were much struck by the gentleness, humility, humour and dignity of the people, such as they had not seen anywhere else. These endearing qualities were combined with the rare virtue of intense devoutness to which there is no parallel, as was freely admitted even by the missionaries who went to Tibet. Tibetans are men of quiet faith, but also men of cheerful simplicity; not men of words, not men obsessed with the idea of personal development or any activity that merely enhances the ego. These men were constantly retreating within, training themselves to meditate and to maintain peace of mind in daily life, preparing themselves for the tests that are brought to light by intense suffering. It is not then surprising that the Dalai Lama should now say in effect: "This is the hour of our trial, this is the time when we must show our faith." In his book he extols the creed of *ahimsa* or non-violence and salutes Gandhi as the greatest man of the age.

This does not mean that the Dalai Lama has no use whatever for the small but brave Tibetan army. He recognizes, as indeed any person who believes in the Dual Truth must, that while we must keep clearly before our minds the unadulterated ideal, we must also be prepared to allow others to show their courage and their integrity in differing ways — each human being in a sense being a law unto himself. This is implicit in the very notion of the doctrine that each person has to find out his own way and his own sphere of duty. In his book the Dalai Lama's plea is somewhat like this: "This is our great moment of trial; we have had such moments in our history, but more than ever before we are being tested in our capacity to endure immeasurable suffering with courage and compassion. We must show our willingness to speak the truth until men may hear it in all quarters of the globe, but at the same time preserving, with deliberate intention, freedom from hatred of the people responsible for our suffering." Almost everyone who reads the Dalai Lama's book will be deeply moved by the last paragraph, in which he clearly conveys this spirit of detachment, non-retaliation and of active compassion. At the same time he does not flinch throughout the book to state courageously what is at stake.

Mr. Hugh Richardson has pointed out, in his excellent book *Tibet and Its History*, that although one may deplore the blunder committed by the Indian Government in its handling of the entire Tibetan question in 1950 — in allowing itself to be mesmerized by the word 'suzerainty' while not laying down the full implications of the word 'autonomy' — it has at least atoned, if atonement were possible, by doing all it can, freely and generously, for the Tibetan refugees. And yet not enough could be done by any Government. Other Governments gave money — Australia and England, initially, and some assistance has also come from other countries. The scale of the problem is so vast, however, that unless we can organize effective international action to provide the material basis for the scattered community of Tibetans outside Tibet, we will not really be doing our bit for Tibet.

All this only refers to the sheer physical survival of an uprooted community. But is this all that will be left of the old Tibet? Is it not possible that ancient Tibet may rise again? In India, or perhaps elsewhere? Or will there be several little Tibets? We are here faced with large questions, and it is because these occur at the most practical level that it has been necessary to look a little at Tibetan values and beliefs. In rendering elementary assistance to these Tibetans we must not forget that it is also our duty to help them to maintain their spiritual independence and the integrity of their way of life.

Of course, the eminent monks who have come from Tibet and who represent the efflorescence of the Tibetan tradition do not need to be cushioned and protected. But what of the children? Mr. Christmas Humphreys, in two lectures which he gave in

London, spoke with very great feeling about the problem of the Tibetan children, who are now beginning to receive Tibetan education but are being approached on every side by swarms of missionaries. The very idea is repellent — of children being looked upon simply as religious cannon-fodder, and actually being approached, not because their souls are to be saved (for which of us is going to fall for that kind of self-deception?), but just so that the egotistical claims of some people may be statistically fulfilled to their own satisfaction. If the whole world were to become Catholic or Protestant or Communist, the outcome would only be that we should find the largest number of lapsed Catholics or Protestants or Communists in world history. The idea of formal conversion is absurd and even irreligious, and now there is a real danger that many of these Tibetan children would be the hapless victims.

In the past we have been given subtle distortions of Tibetan thought. The remarkable Englishmen who visited Tibet, from Bogle to Gould — men like Sir Charles Bell — wholly responded to Tibet, as they might respond to the classical culture of Europe. Lesser men who did not know any better were merely interested in stressing the oddities and peculiarities of Tibetan beliefs, without adequate understanding or spiritual insight. A great deal was written about the ritual dances, about necromancy and polyandry and other such intriguing practices. No attempt was made to distinguish the crude and the vulgar, the debased and the distorted (which exist in every religious tradition) from the pure and the sublime aspects of Tibetan religion.

In his book, the Dalai Lama draws attention to the wholly false picture often given of 'Lamaism' in Tibet, implying that Buddhist tradition in Tibet is something totally different from elsewhere. On the contrary, when they left India, the original and primeval Buddhist teachings took root in Tibet. This can be verified by reference to innumerable texts which have never left Tibetan soil until recently with the dramatic flight of the Dalai Lama. The Dalai Lama says in his book that no one today can say he really understands Buddhist philosophy unless he studies these Tibetan texts.

The Dalai Lama's book also clears up some other common misconceptions about Tibet. He readily concedes that there were social abuses in the old system, but refers to the programme of reform begun by the previous Dalai Lama and which he himself tried to continue. In any case, the existence of social abuses and pseudo-religious practices in Tibet does not lend any real justification for the Chinese conquest or for present attempts to Christianize Tibetan refugee children and alienate them from their traditional culture. If we are at all sensitive to the best in Tibetan tradition and recognize the importance of preserving its integrity intact, then we could do a real service to Tibet by raising our voices against the Westernization of Tibetan children.

Meanwhile, the Dalai Lama, characteristically, does not complain but looks ahead. For him there is still much to be done. Countless Tibetan refugees need practical assistance. The cause of Tibet must continue to be raised at the United Nations; it must secure the active support of an increasing number of people and their Governments. At the same time, he realizes that the suppression of religious life and thought in Tibet itself may result in a steady diffusion of Buddhist teaching throughout the world. In India itself, for the first time in many centuries, Hindu and Buddhist are drawing together, an event of great significance. It is as though Judaism and Christianity really drew together without people from one religion being converted to the other. It is as though for the first time Protestants were really prepared to learn from the Catholics, and Catholics prepared to learn from the Reformation. Of course, the renewal of the Hindu-Buddhist tradition is now only in its early, seminal phase, but it could eventually produce a rich harvest. The Dalai Lama himself may move about from one end of the country to the other, reaffirming once again, in the homeland of the Buddha, the simple and profound truths that he preached on Indian soil. The soul of Tibet will survive, and therefore we cannot despair of the survival of Tibet, in that ultimate sense.

But we dare not despair of the survival of Tibet even in the more worldly and ephemeral sense as long as Tibetan resistance continues and men respond to the claims of conscience, as long as we can still take a long view of history and smile at the inordinate pretensions of messianic systems, and as long as people retain their faith that truth must triumph and justice will prevail.

The Royal Society, London
June 13, 1962

THE EYE OF WISDOM

The idea of Eternal Non-Being, which is the One Being, will appear a paradox to anyone who does not remember that we limit our ideas of being to our present consciousness of existence; making it a specific instead of a generic term. An unborn infant, could it think in our acceptation of the term, would necessarily limit its conception of being, in a similar manner, to the intrauterine life which alone it knows; and were it to endeavour to express to its consciousness the idea of life after birth (death to it), it would, in the absence of data to go upon, and of faculties to comprehend such data, probably express that life as "Non-Being which is Real Being." In our case the One Being is the noumenon of all noumena which we know must underlie phenomena, and give them whatever shadow of reality they possess, but which we have not the senses or the intellect to cognize at present. . . . Alone the Initiate, rich with the lore acquired by numberless generations of his predecessors, directs the "Eye of Dangma" toward the essence of things in which no Maya can have any influence.

The Secret Doctrine, i 45

Beyond the range of all maya, and beyond all but the most exalted conceptions of the divine dialectic, lies the highest possible state of supreme noetic vision, the state of the opened Eye of Dangma, spoken of so beautifully in magnificent metaphors in the *Stanzas of Dzyan.* Beneath this level of pristine consciousness, all ideas of being reflect an inevitable limitation, owing to one's sense of present existence and awareness of specific circumstances. For us, to be a being is to be a being at a particular time and a particular place, or for a certain period of time in a certain place in this world. The all-enveloping nature of this mayavic limitation of consciousness is brought home by the metaphor of the unborn infant in the womb. Each of us is like this to a greater or lesser degree, and, like the infant in the womb, were it to express its conception of being, we are not directly able to formulate the true nature or causal ground of our being, especially with reference to the larger life of beings outside the self-limiting context of our narrow consciousness. Further, if we contemplate the possibility of being born into a larger and richer world, we can only see the process of that birth itself as equivalent to death — the end of life as we seemingly know it. For typical human beings, then, who think that they have been born once into this world of illusion, the prospect of becoming *dwijas,* or twice-born, can only be described as a passage into non-being. Nevertheless, the veil of maya is not so impenetrable to the human will and spirit that we cannot cultivate a deepening intuition that this birth — which seems death to the lower nature — is the solemn path of initiation into real Being.

In our case, and depending upon our degrees of philosophic detachment, we may be vaguely or acutely aware that all the beings we seem to know, including ourselves, are merely shadowy phenomenal representations of noumenal realities, and even of a single supreme Noumenon. Through devotion and *tapas,* we may learn to sift through the dross of phenomenal experience, thereby quickening the dormant powers of *Buddhi-Manas* which alone can bring us to the threshold of birth into true life in spirit. Having inverted what we did and knew, what we felt and were as babies, we can learn as fallen adults, like the miner looking for gold.

> The impalpable atoms of gold scattered through the substance of a ton of auriferous quartz may be imperceptible to the naked eye of the miner, yet he knows that they are not only present there, but that they alone give his quartz any appreciable value; and this relation of the gold to the quartz may faintly shadow forth that of the noumenon to the phenomenon. The miner knows what the gold will look like when extracted from quartz, whereas the common mortal can

form no conception of the reality of things separated
from the Maya which veils them, and in which they
are hidden.

Ibid., i 45

In other words, there is not only gold in the hills, but there is
gold in every grain of dust, in every atom, in every moment of
time if only we would know it. The fact that more human beings
do not know this at this point of human evolution is not primarily
because of universal ignorance, but more because of avoidable
perversity. Where human beings grow up turning their eyes away
from what is golden in other human beings — in their acts, in
their words and in their lives — it is scarcely surprising that they
should develop a peculiar and fatal fascination with dross.

Hence the vital importance of directing one's thought,
aspiration and devotion towards the ideal of the perfected Sage,
who carries with him the inheritance of countless generations of
distilled wisdom and directs the faultless Eye of Dangma towards
the essence of things where maya casts no shadows. If human
beings mired in illusion and a false sense of their own being are
to gain what *The Voice of the Silence* calls 'the right perception of
existing things' and 'the knowledge of the non-existent', then
they must seek for Him who will give them birth in the Hall of
Wisdom. It is there that the teachings of Gupta Vidya in relation
to the twelvefold chain of the *nidanas,* the chain of dependent
origination governing birth and death, and also the four Noble
Truths of Buddha have their greatest but most secret meaning.
There are secret truths contained within all uttered truths, within
the doctrine of the *nidanas,* and within the four truths. There are
secrets within secrets, worlds within worlds. If seekers of wisdom
are like miners of gold, they must have some idea what they are
looking for, but at the same time they must freely and openly
admit their ignorance, recognizing that the true teachings and
their accredited custodians are their sole saving grace.

All true wisdom comes from using the teachings given in the
best way one can, and it is virtually fruitless instead to attempt

to distill wisdom from the world of empirical unrealities. Certainly if every time divine wisdom is available, it avails little or nothing to so many human beings, even those who come into direct contact with it, it is because they have somehow convinced themselves otherwise without evidence or reason. They falsely suppose that a mere accumulation of worldly experience for its own sake, randomly gathered in the passage of events and from the opinions of others, will somehow add up to wisdom. In the totality of things that happen to a human being gripped by *avidya* — who is mostly an automaton, acting like a robot most of the time, a creature of habit at best, and moved by drives which produce guilt and repression — there is nothing remotely comparable to what may be found in consciously chosen experience as a means of testing and applying, apprehending, discovering and rediscovering one single sacred spiritual truth intimated by the authentic teachings of the Brotherhood of Sages.

The wise are those who, when they receive such teaching, become almost from the beginning deaf and blind to everything else, and see all else only in relation to that which is sacred. They make the very best experiments they can as early as possible, therefore garnering the lessons of life and become unacknowledged but self-dependent sources of inner wisdom. Tested by experience and enriched by human pain and suffering, they become endowed with the light and the lustre, the beneficence and the benediction, of true compassion in their conscious ideation in meditation, let alone in their outward utterances and external deeds. As dauntless and detached learners, they make the fields of their experience the basis of Gandhian experiments in truth. Whilst understanding that the Absolute is the ultimate basis of all life and experience, but is wholly untouched by it, they shun the false and cowardly notion all human difficulties arise merely through maya. Illusion is not really the problem, because the whole world is caught up in a transcendental divine process of which is maya is a necessary part. Maya is inseparable from Ishvara in the sum total of everything that exists in the realm of conditioned existence, and to miss this is to fall prey to a sense of pseudo-detachment that has nothing to do with true spirituality.

The real difficulty is entrenched delusion. It is the deliberate consolidation of the ephemeral and the finite at the expense of the immortal and infinite in man and Nature. Delusion, or *moha*, works through a deliberate captivity to a conditioned sense of being, through mindlessness and passivity, through appalling fear and insecurity, through a terrible obsession with success and failure, through slavery to comparative merit and external façades. In this way, illusions become delusions and after a point act as drugs that destroy the life-blood in the astral vesture. Once the circulation in the astral body is shut off from the subtler vestures, it becomes a poison that brings decay and death long before the soul is mercifully freed from the body. This is, of course, an unnatural condition, but it arises through a misuse of the mind, and it can only be corrected and cured by a fundamental *metanoia*, what Buddha called a turning around of the mind. All thinking is either from the standpoint of the real or from the standpoint of the unreal, from the standpoint of the one or from the standpoint of the many. Thinking is good and valuable, or evil and harmful, to the health of soul according to the ground, the basis, the premises and the presuppositions from which it proceeds. Even a human being who is at a loss in relation to ultimate premises or abstract presuppositions can concretely start with the question 'Who am I?' One can seek the basis of an honest concept of oneself, but not just as a bundle of habits or in terms of a series of acts and episodic reactions. One must also take into account all that has been frustrated, all that is potentially present, all that has been locked in and denied speech and denied expression — in one's eyes, in all the gateways of the human body, but above all through one's tongue in conversation and utterance. To be truly humble at least towards one's view of oneself is a starting point which can certainly give a lot of integrity to thinking. One cannot really use that as a basis and a starting point without also including other selves, without becoming concerned with general truths about the human condition, about the relationship of man to Nature, Nature to god, and therefore god to man. Deep thought upon the relationship of the very highest to the very lowest, the most abstract to the most concrete, naturally leads to a search for a principle of continuity that transcends perceptions and conceptions, events and episodic experience, memories and anticipations. Such thought reaches beyond the realm of conditioned being to the deepest ideals, the finest hopes and the most sacred longings of the human soul.

If a human being persists in thinking beyond the realm of the phenomenal and has the courage to investigate the realm of the noumenal, and even to go beyond it, then there may be some hope of a partial mirroring in the lower vestures of the remote potential of the Eye of Dangma. But, to make the Eye of Dangma a central force in human consciousness is impossible without initiation by a perfected Master of suitable pupils at the right time. But such birth without the utter death of the personal self was never part of the program of human evolution, because that would violate the most sacred laws guarding the highest treasures and mysteries which are only opened to the true Eye of Dangma. But, much below this level and even simply in the desire to synthesize and go beyond all polarities, one can look in the direction of the Eye of Dangma, even if in the world of the blind, the deaf and the dumb.

Here it is valuable to actually deeply reflect upon the joy of agnosticism and the joy of recognition of the possibility and meaningfulness of indefinite growth to all beings and to the human kingdom. Through study and through meditation one will come to understand that the only authentic posture towards the Absolute is that of reverential agnosticism, a feeling of the immense sacredness of contemplating the unknown, and the freedom that comes from sensing its fathomless depths. The more one contemplates the highest conceivable wisdom, the more one can appreciate and enjoy the dignity and place of each and every relative truth. The more one draws closer in mind and heart to the highest perfected beings, the more one loves and reveres and sees something sacred and worthy of veneration in every single human being, but also in the entire world of monads in all the kingdoms of Nature, and indeed amidst the hosts of elementals below the mineral kingdom.

To reflect in this way is to increase one's sheer joy in the process of human growth itself, as well as the unglimpsed prospects yet to be realized and the unknown plateaus yet to be scaled by humanity as a whole. In that sense, the highest humanism and the greatest hope for humanity as a species often comes more readily to agnostics and atheists than to true believers in any and all creeds, which, however grand, become in time like narrow cages and iron boxes. Therefore, the true test of what it is to be humane is to enjoy the achievements of all human beings. The achievements of the greatest human beings may look remote, but they are accessible to us in the act of adoration of all the finest, the greatest, the grandest philosophers, poets, artists, architects, seers, saviors and Sages at all levels, from the highest to the most immediate and simple in the saga of the human race. Joy at the thought of unknown human beings reaching towards the more inaccessible Mount Everests in consciousness can itself effectively enlarge the horizon of human possibility. For a lot of human beings who must linger throughout their lives in the darkness and amidst the noise of the plains, this is a true basis for being a member of the human family, for finding meaning and joy in existence. It is a firm basis for unbounded optimism and for a faith that is not only undefeated, but can never be defeated by any possible external event.

Since nothing can proceed from the unknowable Absolute, it would be ridiculous to seek some sign from it to assure oneself that one's faith is well-founded and that one is progressing in the direction that is pointed to in the teachings. What does make sense, however, is a firm inner trust in those that are pointing out the way. Further, there is at least one simple way in which one could test and discern the authenticity of one's own sense of active learning in relation to the essence of the abstract idea, ideal and fact of the absolute. One can test oneself by the criterion of what is natural to a human being, which is to look up to that which is above and beyond, to greet and to revere it, to trust it, and to try out in practice what one has learned, putting oneself to the test. Most of all, it is to deepen one's gratitude and reverence for those who are like forerunners and predecessors, pathfinders and sign-posters, pointers of the way. And any deviation from this is unnatural, self-destructive, and inimical with all growth, and the karmic reaction will quickly give one some sense of the inexorable law that governs all spiritual growth and all spiritual transmission, and which is reflected at all levels, in all spheres of human society.

Sadly, human beings are ceaselessly self-deceived, which means that they largely live to no purpose, with little or no real awareness of the Absolute or even the relative. Now, if one viewed participation in phenomena as a potentially instructive means of developing the power to perceive noumenal, formless, spiritual essences acting within the relative, this would help. In time, one would develop an increasing appreciation of the Absolute and relative, and this would tend to reduce self-deception and even help one to begin living to benefit others. Even though this is true, it is nevertheless not enough to dispel self-deception at the root, because human beings certainly do know this at some level, and yet, in fact, they are chained and enslaved through their deception and delusions. Given the versatility of the lower mind, and given the incredibly powerful and potent nature of the mahamaya, when these two combine with the tendency to deceive oneself within human consciousness, it becomes clear that one cannot make a jump to full authenticity, integrity and self-honesty. Just as in mathematics or music, or in the arts or sciences, one cannot, simply because of trying sincerely, expect to make a conceptual leap to the highest, so too in the broader arena of spiritual life. This is so because of another tendency which affects the actual quality of one's motive in learning. We may recognize it in extreme poisonous, cancerous cases, but we never or seldom detect it in its early forms in ourselves — in all our habits of thought and feeling, word, speech and deed — and that is the tendency to absolutize the relative.

In modern thought we are caught in the trap of ceaselessly

absolutizing the relative owing to our inability and difficulty in understanding unity or diversity, let alone of unity in the midst of diversity. This has given rise to shallow ethical relativism in all our relations to each other and our self-conception. In practice it leads to the appalling belief that anything goes, or, as put by Ivan in *The Brothers Karamazov,* 'If God is dead all is permitted.' One cannot cultivate a sense a moral responsibility without freeing ourselves from the trap of ethical relativism. One must begin by refusing to regard anything conditional as final or sacrosanct before the bar of one's own quiet self-contemplation. At the same time, in one's own self-study — engaged in repeatedly as often as possible, daily, weekly, monthly — one should seize upon the highest and the noblest, wherever it be in Nature, mankind, oneself or in others, and make that hold the initiative. One must keep this as that which is inviolable, that which is beyond analysis and argument, that which is the testing-ground and the touchstone. Then with its help and strength, one must turn to everything else and look, with calm detachment and a sense of proportionality — *sophrosyne* — upon all that comes as the noise of the world, despite the vast clamor and seeming majority support, spelling no doubt the decay, downfall and doom of vast number of souls at a certain climacteric moment in the history of the human race.

To do this requires the courage to individuate, and that is why to individuate and even to begin the dialectical quest, let alone to cross the barrier between being and becoming, is much more difficult than anything else. Too many people have flattered and distracted themselves by seemingly being preoccupied with the higher reaches, because of their terrible fear that they are in the grip of the very lowest forces. They have not even begun to stand up straight or to take a few steps. They must first learn to maintain a minimum continuity in the attempt to move from the realm of death to the realm of life and immortality, from the region of ignorance to the realm of wisdom. The authentic life of the dialectic is marked by degrees of progressive awakening and increasing insight into that which is essential, true and lasting, that which is universally applicable at all times, and that which must cancel all lesser truths.

The pernicious tendency to absolutize the relative is in direct proportion to one's degree of conditionality as a self-conscious participant in the pilgrimage of humanity towards universal enlightenment. Thus, the effort to become less conditional in one's willingness to serve others is a direct help in moving toward a truer conception of the unconditional Absolute. This is the root reason for vow taking on the spiritual path of the dialectic. The unconditional is in all conditions. It is in the present moment. It is both a philosophical and a mathematical puzzle that the present moment cannot lapse because it must be divisible into infinitesimals and recurring decimals, and therefore no duration of time can have an end, even if it may seem to have a beginning. If that is so, there is that which is incommensurable, that which is actually and also potentially infinite within the finite, within each moment, within each and everything, and therefore, the unconditional is the ground on which we stand. To stand knowingly upon the ground of the unconditional is to raise one's sights to the unconditional in the sky as a remote ideal, but also to apprehend it as that which touches upon our very breathing. To take one's stand in the unconditioned is to learn to distinguish, in a world of conditionalities, that which opens the door, that which is freer, that which is less conditional, and that which is more open-minded. This is an exquisitely fine art and it is enormously enhanced by taking a stand in the conviction that certain things are inviolable and supremely sacred.

That is what great souls have again and again shown, as for example Gandhi, when he was a boy, in regard to the vow he made to his mother about vegetarianism. It was shown by the vow of supreme resolve and renunciation taken by Buddha when he was a young man and he first saw the basic facts about human life. This is the archetypal vow taken by all souls, and it is the universal measure of true manhood. It is the hallmark of what it is to be truly human — to move towards the divine, and to divinize one's life by making small beginnings. Instead of treating as sacred a false view of privacy, let alone the fleeting and deceptive boundaries of personal consciousness, one must revere the light in the eyes, the flame of love in the heart, the spark of decency and empathy which enables one to reach out in universal fellowship to all beings. It is this which must be made the basis of what is inexorable, inviolable and irreversible in oneself, if one is to become an apprentice in the fine art of becoming eventually like those who have crossed that ultimate threshold where any reversal or fall is inconceivable, those who have become *achyuta*, incapable of falling, like the Absolute.

Far beyond the threshold that separates becoming from being in the Platonic dialectic lies the threshold that separates being from Non-being, which is real Being. To cross it means to become a perfected spirit, what to ordinary conception is a pure abstraction, a non-being that can have no gunas or attributes. Hence, the extreme difficulty in conceiving the true state of the highest perfected sages, those who alone realize in full the vision of the Eye of Dangma. Psychology has no conception of such a being or spirit, while metaphysics rejects entirely the possibility of the infinite having any conscious relation to the finite. Moreover, perfected spirit and the eternal principle are virtually synonyms. Hence, to speak of the existence of a perfected spirit as implying consciousness, or to speak of a non-entified presence implying unconsciousness, or absolute conscious, in the eternal principle, amount to much the same thing. The conception of a perfected spirit as a presence signifies the essential and co-extensive identity between the highest Sages and the entire plane of *Akasha*, the plane of *Mahat* or Universal Mind.

That which is Akashic is also Fohatic, always capable of mediating between mind-spirit and matter. Ultimately, spirit and matter are one, and therefore Fohat is always capable of dynamizing, through the interaction of spirit — which is matter at a sufficiently homogeneous level that it is like pure spirit, matter which is at a sufficiently heterogeneous level that it is like mere matter. This is the engine, the bridge, the dynamizing capacity of Fohat itself in *Akasha*. Both *Akasha* and Fohat at the highest and deepest level have to do with constant, ceaseless, universal, unbounded ideation. Any human being who begins to move in this direction, regardless of the boundaries and limitations that are inescapable for him at any given time, begins to enter that plane on which he or she may become capable of communing, tapping and receiving help from much greater minds and hearts, much greater men and women of meditation and compassion, who on higher planes are engaged in eternal ideation. If this were not true, there would be something irredeemable about the human condition and there would be something totally false about almost everything that we take for granted and in terms of which we live. Therefore, there is something transcendental as well as something temporal in notions like *rta*, universal harmony, and dharma, that which upholds, supports and maintains any and all living beings in this cosmos. There is also something supremely important in the endless points of Fohatic connection between the attributeless, transcendental Absolute and that which is immediately before our ordinary senses at any given time, and in any context.

What the sage realizes continuously, and what the apprentice on the path struggles to glimpse intermittently, is that the Absolute, as the source of all manifestation, is therefore also the source of the plenitude we see around us. Dwelling on this idea reminds one of the inherent generosity in all being, however we tend to approach this generous plenty through the psychological medium of relativities, light and darkness, good and evil, like and dislike, and so forth. To use these dichotomies wisely requires a recognition of them in ourselves, and then a determination to treat them as stepping stones to rectification. Rectification is a sacred concept in the Buddhist Sangha and on the Buddhist path, as also in the teachings of Confucius, who spoke of the rectification of terms in the light of the Great Extreme. Indeed, the greatest need of our time is the rectification of anything and everything at the simplest level in relation to the ABC's of human living. This is difficult, but the existence of perfected Sages tells us that it is possible. Were it not difficult enough, however, we add to it by being all too interested in the contradictions and workings of the pairs of opposites in others. In other words, we have become cowards and escapists, evading the task of confronting life directly and living autonomously, let alone individuating. So, we live vicariously through the lower perceptions of others, wandering in the twilight zone of shadows and zombies, of soulless beings and beings that have pledged themselves far back in the past to the finality of certain self-destruction and loss of soul. This is the basis of judgmentalism or fault finding. We are warned that this is the downward path, if only for the reason that it muddies karmic waters and does a lot more harm to ourselves and others besides.

Authentic meditation on the Absolute can alone purify our perception of the relative. Meditation is the greatest purifier. Like the Spiritual Sun, the purifier of purifiers, the AUM is the supreme purifier. When we meditate on the AUM and the Spiritual Sun, and on the highest beings who are the living, dynamic, omnipotent embodiments of the highest current that flows from the sacred heart of the Spiritual Sun, reverberating as the eternal AUM throughout the ages, we have an infallible and ever-accessible means of cleansing our consciousness. We can cleanse our thoughts — even the very best, cleanse our feelings — even the noblest, because they are all polluted by the lie of separateness, by the false sense of self-hood, by the fearful self-protective concern for oneself separated from all others. If we were to avail ourselves of meditation as a purifier we would soon see the irrelevancy, let alone the profanation, of judging others, and begin, therefore, to be suffused with thoughts of generosity to all.

In other words, we would begin to transform generosity and magnanimity from being fugitive and superogatory feelings in the heart, to being the firm basis in the mind of all our thoughts, word and deeds. We would learn to think generously about this world, about Nature, about all humanity, about human growth, and about all rays of the one light. We would also learn to think generously about all those individuals from whom we learned, and to whom we owe far more than we can repay in one life, and even learn to be generous to all those from whom we learned only by negative example. In time, we would become generous in the consciousness itself that we bring to waking each day and to going to rest each night, drawing from a deeper source of abundant generosity within the realm of *Akasha*, within the divine sphere around the human being, and within the immortal soul, making it flow with the dawning of light each morn, and with the diffusion of light through the day. Letting go all false sense of conditioned being, we could withdraw in meditation into the hidden darkness, the land of Silence and Non-being, wherein lies the Supernal Light that neither rises nor sets, which is the ultimate source of all that gives meaning and beauty, grace and generosity, to human life, and which is eternally witnessed by the opened Eye of Dangma.

KARMA AND

REINCARNATION

KARMA AND CHOICE

*My friend, if the whole path and movement of heaven
and all its contents are of like nature with the motion,
revolution, and calculations of wisdom, and proceed after
that kind, plainly we must say it is the supremely good soul
that takes forethought for the universe and guides it along
that path.* — Athenian Stranger

PLATO

Anyone who wishes to make practical use of the universal
principles of justice and compassion inherent in the
doctrine of karma must first grasp the idea that what we
call the karmic effect is actually inherent in the karmic cause. This
could be seen in two ways: first of all, philosophically or
metaphysically, and secondly, morally. If karma refers to the
totality of interaction of all beings in a single, unified cosmos,
then it must be the case that every single act, rooted in a thought
or an idea, already contains within itself the whole series of
manifestations which *appear* to exist as its distinct effects. That
appearance is illusory. What we call the effect of an act is already
contained in the origination of the first impulse of the first
thought and feeling constituting the act. This is very difficult to
comprehend metaphysically. But anyone could come closer to
understanding it from the moral standpoint.

Each one could look at any single act that he has done and
link it up to the state of mind in which he acted and to the quality
or colour of feeling that was present in that act. He could look
behind 'thought' and 'feeling', in the separative and specific
sense in which the words are used here, and attempt to see the
act in terms of the totality of his character, in relation to the whole
of his life, at least since he became a responsible adult, whenever
that was for the individual person. The whole of his life has led
to this particular act. On this act we have the indelible stamp of

the kind of person he is and has become in all the time since the moment of birth, but, more perceptibly, at least since he became a responsible adult. If the whole of his being is imprinted upon that act, in a universe of law he has already, in the very act, determined the consequences of that act to himself as a mind-being, as a unit-being. Therefore, any sound morality would be one that provides a self-validating, compelling and continually applicable basis for ethics, both on the plane of thought and on the plane of feeling, which together are represented in what we call external acts.

A person who is wise and fortunate enough to include a method of relative and increasing self-scrutiny into his day is engaged in what might be called 'doing one's moral arithmetic.' If he could do this, he would soon be able to work out a few simple sums. Then he would not have to wait, in an Epimethean way, for the sum totals of external effects, from which it is extremely difficult to trace back. Anyone who has studied a bit of elementary mathematics knows, if he is given the answer to a problem, that from the answer one cannot speedily work out the process that leads to the answer. In a very good teaching system, a person would be given more appreciation for grasping the process, even if the actual answer reached is only an approximation. Certainly, this would be preferable to rewarding a person who happened to hit the answer but did not have the proper sequence of steps that follow from the initial statement of the problem, using the relevant basic rules or equations or tables that are provided to him to work out this answer.

In the moral realm this is extremely difficult, and points to the difference between ignorant human beings and Adepts. An Adept is one who has mastered the mathematics of the soul. Indeed, he embodies it every moment, twenty-four hours a day, and therefore he continually acts with a seeming casualness but out of a profound deliberation based on total detachment. With this perspective, we can understand the reason why the heavenly wisdom in relation to karma should be imparted, in this day and age, with the extraordinary care that has been taken by the

Mahatmas. Those who have the good karma — even if not entirely deserved in this life — of coming into contact with *Bodhi Dharma* are given the opportunity to move from a position of muddle and irresponsibility to a gradual awakening to their responsibility as moral agents: as Manasaputras, as descendants from the divine ancestry of the great collective host that gave the fire of self-consciousness to human beings over eighteen million years ago. Those who do reasonably well render incalculable service. No one can do more than try, and even to try is to make a real choice. They are, in a sense, fortunate, because they are protected from attachment to results since they are not in a position to calculate what Adepts alone can work out precisely. They can render some benefit to the whole of the human race, to the karma of a nation, to the family in which they were born, and to their associates.

The time has come when no student of Theosophy can afford to ignore the practical moral implications of this aspect of karma, even if he is not immediately ready to grasp the profound philosophical and metaphysical basis of the idea. We have found already in this century, in the last twenty-five years, that the idea has partially come into contemporary thought. Inward responsibility is the focus of several exploratory efforts by contemporary philosophers who want to see its application to punishment. Wittgenstein raised the question whether there is any internal, rather than extrinsic, relation between an act and its reward or punishment. Philosophically, this is difficult to grasp, but deep down we must feel a profound pity and compassion for any person who is a murderer and who is now delighted, in one sense, that he does not have to be executed, but who, on the other hand, is nonetheless excruciatingly tortured by his own thoughts. In some cases, such persons may spend a whole lifetime adding to their karma by broodings that are even worse than the thoughts which led to the murder committed. In other cases, they may be able to look back upon what was done with a sense of relative bewilderment, which Simone Weil would have called a kind of "innocence through penitence."

No one could truly make a moral use of the teaching and

become a real penitent without becoming ready, before the moment of death, to have deserved the priceless privilege of coming into contact with divine wisdom. To do this seriously requires spending time reflecting upon the idea of the interpenetration of cause and effect and how it applies to each and every one. As long as there is no understanding and proper study of karma, no one will be able to introduce any order into his life relative to the disorders of our time. Nor will he be able to generate a current of true repentance or appreciate the relationship of mercy to justice that is essential to a comprehension of concepts like reward and punishment. There is the statement in *The Ocean of Theosophy* that "Karma is a beneficent law, wholly merciful, relentlessly just, for true mercy is not favor but impartial justice." Normally, we think of mercy as gratuitous or arbitrary and justice as relentless or ruthless. In terms of the universal law of karma, human appellations like 'justice' and 'mercy' are misleading. They are merely approximations arising through an inadequate understanding of connections between causes and effects applicable only over very short time spans and also modified by the gap, not merely between any legal system and the moral justice of the universe, but between the theory of that legal system and its working in practice.

Suppose a very sincere man truly wanted to find out what is due from him to every other human being on earth — let us say because he has consulted ancient wisdom or merely because he has read Godwin, or even because he thought about it. If this person then asked what could it mean for him to do justice to every human being he ever met in this life, it would be very difficult for him to make a practical response. The mathematics are too complicated. The person hardly knows anyone else. It is forbidding enough to do justice to any human being on earth. But that is what is required on the path of understanding, of *Jnana Yoga.*

Supposing, then, this person said, "To the extent to which I cannot know what is due from me to every single being, and yet that is where I want to go — though it take a very long time, even many lives — I have a firm faith that the very desire and determination to go in this direction is not only a holy one, because it is the noblest feeling I feel, but it is wholly compatible with the truth and totality of things." This makes immensely joyous the prospect of having myriads of opportunities in future lives to be able to perfect the enterprise. Such a person might also say, "Meanwhile, to the extent to which I do not know what doing justice to every single human being means, I might as well err in one direction rather than in the other." As long as one is caught up in *attavada*, the delusion of being separate from everyone else — the only conception of sin in the teachings of Buddha — then, if one is going to sin it is better to sin in the direction of exaggerated praise of others than in the opposite direction.

If this generation is to make the enormously arduous move from being the most abnormal in soul-sickness to becoming human, it would be extraordinarily important to emphasize mercy and compassion. Beyond all else, to be human is to radiate benevolence. As long as one strives to be compassionate and merciful, it will be imperatively and inevitably the case that one will come to understand justice better. Through mercy one may come closer to an appreciation of divine justice, cosmic justice, and above all learn what it means to be just to every living being, every elemental, every constituent of the seven kingdoms of nature. Every single human being has also the prerogative of doing justice to his or her true self.

Metaphysically, in relation to the three planes of the Unmanifested, there is no distinction in the Three-in-One between absolute, attributeless Compassion, absolute, dimensionless Truth, and absolute, unconditional Love. There is no difference because all three together constitute the invisible point in an ever-revolving mainspring that is the vital centre of the great wheel of universal harmony. Through the notion of harmony, a person might come to reflect upon the metaphysical relation between justice and mercy as centripetal and centrifugal forces. The starting point to gain this perspective is self-examination. Take a period in one's

life. A day might be too short for this for the average person —
you might take a week, a month, a year — and actually list out
on a sheet the number of occasions on which one either omitted
or was fortunate to be able to exemplify justice to every other
human being. Then on a separate sheet list the number of
occasions on which one tried to be merciful to other human
beings, or where through thoughtlessness and inconsideration
rooted in self-worship — which is nothing but the insecurity of
the shadow — one omitted to be merciful. Soon one will make
an amazing discovery because one will find that these are two
different aspects of a single truth. That truth is the degree to which
ignorance was the pole star of one's life centred in the personal
mind, and the extent to which one's highest ideation became
manifest in one's consciousness and conduct.

No act is performed without a thought at its root, and this
is the basis of karma for thinking beings. This is always the case.
What it implies in strict elementary logic is that even the most
apparently automatic act has a thought at its core, either at the
time of performance or as leading to it. A being who is fully self-
conscious, who has attained to universal self-consciousness, and
therefore is totally aware of the Self, is incapable of ever engaging
in any act at any time without an instantaneous and simultaneous
awareness of the intention accompanying it. Because this
idea is so sacred, a lot of harm is done by people who talk idly
of 'thought-forms' and 'vibrations.' This is the sad result of
dissemination, among the unready mass, of the delusions of the
failed students of *Philosophia Perennis*.

In ordinary language we all are aware of what it means
to say, "Oh, that's a good idea." "Oh, that's a good thought."
Everyone, at some time in his life, maybe at some season of the
year, has had a good thought for someone else. "Oh, let me do
this for someone else. Let me send this Christmas card. Let me
express this goodwill." Every human being has experienced the
most natural form of occultism — having a good thought and
seeking for it an appropriate form of expression. In this age where
it is so rare, they are very privileged who, through the magic of

the madness of love, spend a lot of time not just on the benevolent thought but on the manner and the appropriateness of the expression of the thought. Some people, by a kind of soul-intuition from previous lives, and especially when they are very young, realize that a good idea must have the total purity of privacy if it is to be preserved. There must be an insulation from uncongenial elementals in making that thought inviolate, wrapping it up within an invisible circle of secrecy and privacy, so that it becomes a point in metaphysical space and may find an appropriate form.

When we begin to see this, we are better able to know what it means to earn the privilege of hearing the teaching that men are manifested gods, creative mind-beings; Manasaputras bearing the burden of the responsibility for raising all manifested matter; carriers of the divine mandate of helping the great architect, the collective demiurge behind the manifested universe. These thrice-blessed "fortune's favoured soldiers" may suddenly begin to feel the immensity, the grandeur, the glory of the responsibility of being human, a thinking being, capable of choosing at will a thought and, by dwelling upon it and pouring over it the waters of selfless love, being able to find, out of the more subtle matrix of life-atoms which constitute the thought-vehicle, a form for its benevolent expression. In other words, a person who lives by an inner light begins to see that the real form of a true thought is wholly invisible. It has nothing to do with differentiated matter or the externalities of dependent origination in dependent relationships. He really comes to understand something about subtle matter.

Two alternatives face such a person, and both alternatives apply to different classes of cases, so that he has a constant choice problem, like the choice problem of the Demiurge mentioned in the *Timaeus*. Out of *many* worlds is patterned only *one* world. This is the dilemma which the Demiurge must overcome. The human being, too, must be ready to grasp the fundamental problem of choice facing him. On the one hand, there are certain thoughts which are of such quality — impersonal, universal, unifying, beneficent — that where they are self-consciously generated or drawn from the *Akasha*, they do not need any form. They are like sparks or like shooting stars that descend with a speed much greater than that of light and they find an appropriate way of sparking off myriads of atoms. On the other hand, there are those thoughts which need to be encased in a purified, distilled essence, but fashioned out of a purified astral form, out of something more than differentiated matter but something less than the pure, undifferentiated, universal, homogeneous essence. Such thoughts, when they are given that kind of force, are deliberately chosen mental assets. They become available for all other human beings encountered in our lives and yet may also become embodied for a very long time to come so that others could draw upon them for almost an indefinite future.

What a great privilege, then, is open to the human being who has had the good fortune to learn from Brahma Vach. No one should ignore the ideal as a fit object of meditation. Every person is equally entitled to make the attempt, and no one need fear that he is so unworthy that he cannot make it. On the other hand, he should be spared the terrible karma of the delusion that Everest may be climbed quickly. 'Climbing Everest here means choosing every single thought. That is very hard. It requires lives. But one can begin right now choosing a few thoughts, having a little less passivity in relation to most thoughts every week, a little less of that disordered, unthinking, thoughtless, machine-like activity which is lower than that of the animal kingdom, and a little more of deliberate thought. One could, within three months, make amazing discoveries about the mystery of karma — more discoveries from three months of this practice than from a lifetime of mere use of the word 'karma.'

William Q. Judge pointed out that "the weak and mediocre furnish a weak focus for karma, and in them the general result of a lifetime is limited, although they may feel it all to be very heavy. But that person who has a wide and deep-reaching character and much force will feel the operation of a greater quantity of karma than the weaker person." A character broad in vision, generous in sympathy, deep in motivation, firm in the degree of deliberation — this is the self-created product of thought ranging from calm consideration to continuous meditation. Whether a man will have "much force" will depend upon becoming one-pointed in the use of force. Kierkegaard spoke about the purity of heart that goes with a concentration of will when it is focused upon one thing at a time. This is the same idea as that expressed by Cardinal Newman in the line, "Lead kindly light, one step enough for me," which was so much a favourite of Gandhi. These steps form a very beautiful kind of dance. The great pioneers of the future choose to learn this on the physical plane and in the moral realm, but with the intention of making themselves a bridge to other human beings who want to learn to do this dance, step by step by step.

This means the will is very much involved. The will is weakened by obscurity of mind, by conflict of feelings, by lack of priorities in relation to purposes. The conservation of energy is the baseline upon which every man takes a stand. On this basis alone he determines the degree of intensity to the force that he can release. There have been many men of much force, but their vision was limited. Their motivation was not rooted in the depths of their being, and so they became like Ozymandias. They created huge thought-structures and towards the end of their lives a few wrote manuals for the benefit of others, telling them to do this, that, and the other thing. But the will was disproportionate in relation to the idea. What is most critical, then, in the formation of character is the food that a human being receives in the way of spiritual and mental diet.

Spiritual and mental diet forms the character. If a person wanted to use this teaching, he would make vast discoveries by doing a little meditation upon the Three Fundamentals of *The Secret Doctrine* in the light of the idea that their ethical bearing is universal. They enable the person, whoever, whenever, over the years, who decides to become a student of Gupta Vidya, to widen his vision and deepen his understanding. And he can do this at home, at work, in solitude, and in all spheres of life. Wherever he walks, he walks in a sphere of light and he walks as a man with an ever-widening vision. He becomes a man whose character is rock-like in its integrity. His integrity is as firm and unyielding as the spinal cord when it is a true vehicle of the divine fire, and his being is magnanimous with the fullness of his heart. He reaches outside of himself in every direction — his mind and soul compassionately encompassing every possible point of view, especially when embodied in the haunting, stumbling efforts of another human being who is trying to begin by asking, "Who am I?" To truly answer this question could be centrally important to anyone who wants to become, over the next thirty years, in the humanistic phrase of a nineteenth century writer, "A man not of property but of character."

The whole practical use of the teaching requires recognition of the distinction between the various classes of karma. If we would understand not merely when karma is expended in spite of ourselves, but when we could make a difference in relation to the expending and altering of effects of karmic influences that work in our lives, we must see the operation of the three classes within the three fields mentioned in the ancient and sacred axioms upon the subject of karma. A crucial aphorism states:

> Changes may occur in the instrument during one life so as to make it appropriate for a new class of Karma and this may take place in two ways: through intensity of thought and the power of a vow, and through natural alterations due to complete exhaustion of old causes.

The choice here relates to positive, deliberate, Promethean penances that any man could engage in — intensity of thought and the power of a vow. Intensity of a thought means that the thought is worthy of meditation, of being used for reflection. The stronger the nature, the more impersonal and intense will be the force of the meditation. The more recurrent that meditation, the more that intense thought is generated to a point where it goes into orbit.

Every time one's mind turns to meditation, there is, unfortunately, some obscuration. There are forms that arise in connection with it as in the denser part of the earth's atmosphere. Any person who thinks that with the steam engine of existing thought he is going to propel himself into outer space — and 'outer space' equals 'inner space' metaphysically — is making a mistake. But there is no reason for a person to aim to start off with reaching the moon or any planet further off from the earth. He might start, however, by hoping that he attains to sufficient intensity in his meditation to begin to become a revolving wheel, such that when it revolves, it lifts him somewhat above the grosser atmosphere of the earth, but which yet, as it revolves, smoothly comes back into earth life. This revolution is, after a point, calm and steady.

If intensity of thought is understood in this way, the power of a vow is enshrined in the ancient idea of a pilgrimage. Step by step, true pilgrims move by the power of a vow. A vow is taken by a person who, in taking it, stands looking in a certain direction, with a clear purpose in mind. Whatever minor vows we take follow from a great vow — a vow to be a good student of *Bodhi Dharma*. To bring that down into today means making many decisions, making minor vows. We should not tell anyone these vows unless there is need to do so for the sake of helping others. They should simply be carried out. To combine two analogies, even if a pilgrim comes by borrowed car and mechanical transportation, he has eventually to walk toward the doors of the mystery temple, to be received and come in on his own.

A vow has to do with an attitude of mind. Unless there is an adjustment and a purification in the attitude of mind, intensity of thought cannot be handled. Intensity of thought will boomerang and it will merely make one's karma worse. This happens to many people. One does not want it to boomerang except to the extent to which it, Shiva-like, attenuates and destroys the shadowy self-idea. On the other hand, one wants one's thought to reach out as a beneficent force to all other elementals, mixed with psychic embryos that constitute the universe in its preponderant astral light, as well as the planes above and planes below. A person who can direct such a beneficent motive will find that intensity of thought will be potent and constructive if it is accompanied by the positive and penitent attitude implicit in the taking of a vow.

To take a vow means, "I am soft, I am shaken that I live like this. If these things are representative of my mental attitudes, I will expiate them, not merely by my suffering and recognition that that is the way I was, but also in a conscious sacrifice of similar intentions upon the altar of that holy and untrodden invisible, unmentioned, intangible ground of the heart." There alone one may truly worship the causeless cause. There, the only object of worship is the universal spirit. The only priests are good thoughts and good intentions. The only sacrificial victim is the personal self, with its inimical and hostile intentions and thoughts that are incompatible with and unpurifying to the sanctity of the inner sanctuary.

Because of the great holiness of the subject of karma, and because all vows remind us of the Buddha's vow, it is appropriate to recall that any human being could learn from the example of Gautama Buddha. From his example we may appreciate the full strength that is possible from a life-binding resolve: self-generated, self-binding, self-administered, constant and consistent, focused upon one main, universal impersonal idea. Anyone who seeks the ancient Path to enlightenment can thereby earn for himself the invisible sacred bond with the Lodge of Mahatmas. He who wishes to be worthy of that association until the moment of death could, by the power of a vow to help and serve other human beings, wipe out many karmic residues. He could gain the immense privilege of accelerating, with a toughness in response and anticipation, the self-conscious purgation of personal and constrictive karma.

Even though all of this sounds so forbidding, it is like a grain of dust in relation to the voluntary sacrifice of those who descend on earth to take upon themselves the karma of all. They take upon themselves the limitations and weaknesses of all, and do what they can with that additional burden to increase the opportunities of those struggling souls who, despite their failures of yesteryear and of previous lives, warm at the moment of choice and have earned the joy of a new beginning. Such a soul could say, "I am not worried anymore about the past because I know that I am a *manasa*." Such an one will bring his questions about the mysteries of Self and karma to Brahma Vach. He can stand erect and proud as a man and walk like one, silently determined to increase his efforts on behalf of every human being caught in the overwhelming agony of ignorance. It is ignorance of the *Bodhi Dharma*, ignorance of themselves, and ignorance of the self-made windings of karma that make men suffer. It is only by the karmic force of a vow made on behalf of all our fellow men that the dawn of universal enlightenment may be hastened. Such a vow will be a living power in a man's life, making him a living embodiment of the unity of all beings.

Begin thy work, first having prayed the Gods
To accomplish it. Thou, having mastered this,
That essence of Gods and mortal men shalt know
Which all things permeates, which all obey.
And thou shalt know that Law hath established
The inner nature of all things alike;
So shalt thou hope not for what may not be,
Nor aught, that may, escape thee.
                                        PYTHAGORAS

KARMA AND DESTINY

It is the Spiritual evolution of the inner, immortal man that forms the fundamental tenet in the Occult Sciences. To realize even distantly such a process, the student has to believe (a) in the ONE *Universal Life, independent of matter (or what Science regards as matter); and (b) in the individual intelligences that animate the various manifestations of this Principle. . . .*

The ONE LIFE *is closely related to the one law which governs the World of Being —* KARMA. *Exoterically, this is simply and literally 'action', or rather an 'effect-producing cause.' Esoterically it is quite a different thing in its far-fetching moral effects. It is the unerring* LAW OF RETRIBUTION.

The Secret Doctrine, i 634

Karma is the universal law of the One Life in all its myriad manifestations from the cosmic to the atomic, spanning eternity and the present in each moment. Every evolving intelligence encapsulated in matter is unerringly subject to the ceaseless effects of Karma and must conform itself, at first unconsciously and then freely, to its inexorable decree of universal harmony. The doctrine of Karma unveils the metaphysical key to the mysteries of authentic human choice, free will and divine destiny, but it can be comprehended only when applied with Buddhic insight to the large experiences and small events of life on earth. To discern the karmic meanings of the complex details of daily life, whilst experiencing the elusive mystery of incarnation, one must begin with the vibratory rates of the simplest thoughts and feelings, words and deeds, linking them to levels of motivation, states of consciousness, fixity of mind and fidelity of heart. Each thoughtful or thoughtless impulse of the inner nature magnetizes one's environment through the activity of the organs of the outer vestures, invoking exact compensation and ethical retribution.

There is nothing mechanical in the karmic adjustment of magnetic differentials; it is an inward and moral process, an integral aspect of a continual choice between spiritualization and materialization. The distinction between distributive and collective Karma, like the difference between the raindrop and the storm, exists within a larger process of essential unity. Humanity and its units, its races, nations, tribes and individuals, embody a vital energy and share a common destiny which none may resist or repel. The eternally patient and compassionate teacher of mankind, Karma sternly instructs each and all in the supreme lesson that there is no individual enlightenment or welfare apart from sacrificial service to every sentient being, collectively constituting the One Life.

This pivotal principle, the substratum of free will and destiny, may be understood in terms of the choice between the manvantaric star of one's individuality and the personal star of a single lifetime. Throughout all possible variations in personal destiny over myriad lifetimes, this choice must be made again and again. The clarity and direction of one's choices in previous lives shape the fabric of circumstances in which one chooses in this life and future lives. That fabric might be a refined tapestry in which may be etched the mystic emblems of the pilgrimage of the soul, or a coarsely knotted cloth of confused dreams and missed opportunities. Psychologically, there is the wayward choice between two voices: one is the voice of illusion and delusion, of the senses and of the separative personal consciousness which cannot embrace a holistic perspective encompassing many lives; the other is the voice of Krishna-Christos, the voice of God in man which speaks in the universal language of the soul. There is a direct relation between one's recurrent choices in regard to these voices, and one's readiness, in the realm of action, to ally oneself with Krishna, standing luminously alone, or his innumerable adversaries. In the Mahabharatan war fought on *Kurukshetra*, the field of external encounters, individuals are constantly making, mostly unconsciously or with partial self-consciousness, fateful choices between Krishna and his armies. This archetypal choice

was offered by Krishna to the depraved Duryodhana, who rejected
Krishna in favour of the armies trained by him, reflecting short-
sighted empiricism. When Arjuna was offered the privilege of
having Krishna as his charioteer, he happily and willingly chose
Krishna, even though he did not fully fathom the invisible stature
of Krishna, let alone his cosmic splendour.

Philosophically, the Mahabharatan war is emblematic of the
inevitable ethical and spiritual struggle to which every human soul
is irreversibly committed by the fact of Manasic awareness,
traceable to the sacrificial descent and benediction of the solar
ancestors over eighteen million years ago. Each chooses, Krishna
teaches, according to his lights, whatever seems best. Thereby the
subtle threads of one's self-devised destiny are fused, and one must
pass below the throne of Necessity without looking back, like the
pilgrims in the Myth of Er, to live out and learn from the karmic
results of one's choice. Recorded by the Lipikas, engraved in one's
vestures and reflected in surrounding circumstances, this destiny
rises up to meet the soul at every turn in life. Yet, though it is
'written in the stars', destiny does not preclude the risks and
possibilities of further choice.

> Only, the closer the union between the mortal
> reflection MAN and his celestial PROTOTYPE, the less
> dangerous the external conditions and subsequent
> reincarnations — which neither Buddhas nor Christs
> can escape. This is not superstition, least of all is it
> *Fatalism.* The latter implies a blind course of some still
> blinder power, and man is a free agent during his stay
> on earth. He cannot escape his *ruling* Destiny, but he
> has the choice of two paths that lead him in that
> direction, and he can reach the goal of misery — if such
> is decreed to him, either in the snowy white robes of
> the Martyr, or in the soiled garments of a volunteer in
> the iniquitous course; for, there are *external and internal
> conditions* which affect the determination of our will
> upon our actions, and it is in our power to follow either
> of the two.
>   *The Secret Doctrine,* i 639

Even if through past actions one is destined to suffer miseries at the hands of various agencies, the power of choice remains. It is a constant factor throughout all the vagaries of karmic precipitation. As Plato taught, the gods are blameless for the inward condition of the soul in every situation, and each sufferer must choose between either preserving purity of consciousness or becoming stained by the iniquities of unthinking reaction, mental violence and a refusal to take responsibility.

Choices are not random. Collectively, they show a tonality and texture which traces the line of life's meditation, the dominant choice over a lifetime. This choice depends upon the degree of discernment of the different types of external and internal conditions surrounding the soul. Externally, there are myriads upon myriads of elemental centres of intelligence already imprinted by the thoughts, feelings and acts of individuals, past and present, embodied and disembodied. They are drawn to each person and respond to the rationalized desires of the lower self, thus giving seeming substantiality to the entrenched delusion of personal existence based upon likes and dislikes. Those who are extremely weak-willed from the standpoint of the soul and excessively self-willed in the eyes of others have fostered the deceptive notion that they are forging their own path in the world, whereas in truth they are only acquiescing through compulsive reaction in their lunar destiny. Alternatively, there are internal conditions which include the solar potency of pure ideation of the Monad, the immortal *Buddhi-Manas* which is capable of sustaining a strong current of selfless meditation. The range and richness, continuity and depth, of such meditation depend upon mental calm, unconditional compassion and spiritual fearlessness. On the noumenal plane, thought, motivation and volition are indeed inseparable. Authentic mystical states arise from the fusion of the deepest aspirations, the finest feelings and the strongest affirmations of meditation within the solemn stillness of the sanctuary of the soul. Daily renewed in deep sleep, consecrated at dawn and dusk, and invoked with humility before sleep, the inward vision of universal good may be made into a continuous current through the potency of a Vow. In time one can silence the lower mind at will, altering the polarity of the nervous system, and ponder the karmic meanings and lessons inherent in the events and opportunities of each day. Thus reaching beyond any limited sense of identity and in the oceanic calm of one's true selfhood, one may listen to the voice of God within the heart, the daimon honoured by Socrates and Gandhi. For a trained mystic who has learnt to give Nature time to speak, the inner voice can become the ever-present *Chitkala*, the benediction of Kwan Yin as a constant guardian.

For the average person, whose highest vestures are veiled by the samskaric residues of past actions and present vacillation, the inner voice cannot be heard and the pre-birth vision of the soul is forgotten. Yet, they may be mirrored dimly in the muddled personal mind as vague and chaotic recollections, as feeble and faltering notions of some essential reform to be made in life, or some sacrificial act of goodness to be offered in the service of others. Through inconstant flickerings along the invisible spinal cord, there may be sporadic resolves to renew the most precious moment one can recall from early childhood or from fleeting contact with the benevolent current of past teachers. In a variety of ways, even if only fitfully and imperfectly, every person can receive help from internal conditions which can release the spiritual will. The greater the fidelity, the selflessness and self-assurance with which one cleaves to these inner promptings of the immortal soul, the more instantaneously they light up the immediate task at hand. Above all, the more they are heeded, the less the effort needed to sustain continuity. With the same certitude, the opposite consequences follow for those who foolishly ignore or flaunt this inner guidance for the sake of enhancing the delusive sense of personal self-importance. But even the most spiritually impoverished human beings are sheltered by the invisible protection of the Divine Prototype, and therefore even amidst the muddle and froth of psychic fantasy there is a concealed thread of truth. Wise and loving friends might be able to recognize and strengthen it. A true spiritual teacher could help to sift the wheat from the chaff, quicken the inward process of alchemical transmutation, and show the pathway to Divine Wisdom.

As the One Law of spiritual evolution, Karma is more generous to each and every human soul in need of help than the niggardly thinking of the nihilistic can envisage. It is neither a doctrine that is so abstruse and remote that it cannot be related to the present moment, nor is it nearly as inflexible and hostile as claimed by those who have gratuitously declared a vote of no-confidence in themselves and in the human race. Far from precluding the idea that each human being has a unique and inherently significant mission on this earth, the Law of Karma actually ordains that every single person has a divine destiny which he or she alone can and must fulfill. There is an authentic dignity and beauty, a profound meaning, to the uniqueness of the divine presence in and around every human soul. The sacredness of individual choice was affirmed as the basis of human solidarity by the inspired forerunners of the Aquarian Age, those luminaries who initiated the Renaissance and the Enlightenment in Europe. If the prospect has not yet smiled upon all, this is because too many have laboured under the dead weight of traditional theology or secular fatalism.

> Those who believe in *Karma* have to believe in *destiny* which, from birth to death, every man is weaving thread by thread around himself, as a spider does his cobweb; and this destiny is guided either by the heavenly voice of the invisible *prototype* outside of us, or by our more intimate *astral*, or inner man, who is but too often the evil genius of the embodied entity called man.
>
> *Ibid.*

The heavenly voice of the invisible Prototype is heard and felt, without any external tokens of empirical certitude. In the life of a good and simple person, who makes a mental image of Christ or Buddha, Shiva or Krishna, that voice may seem to come in a form engendered by the ecstatic devotion of the individual who has purity of heart. Many thousands of people all over the world belong to the invisible fraternity of fortunate souls who, having made a fearless and compassionate invocation on behalf of a friend or relative in distress, suddenly heard a vibrant voice of authoritative assurance and sensed an aureole of light soon after. This voice may appear to come from outside oneself, and, paradoxically, that other voice, the voice of the intimate astral, all too often the evil genius of man, seems to originate within. When it speaks, it aggravates the confusions of the compulsive persona, inducing the hapless listener to rush into mindless activity. When the heavenly voice speaks to the depths of one's soul, it has a calming influence and allays the anxieties of *kama manas*. There is a natural soul-reticence to tell others about the heavenly voice, and a grateful concern to treasure its words in silence. However well-intentioned, anything that is allowed to pass through the matrix of the psychic nature risks distortion and generates a smoky obscuration that acts as a barrier to further guidance and profounder help from the Divine Prototype. What begins as unthinking indiscretion soon becomes delusive, and unless promptly checked, culminates in abject servitude to the astral shadow. Then, deceived by this simulacrum, the shadow of oneself outside the path of dharma, one is drawn in a direction that may be contrary to one's true destiny. This abdication from the soul's self-chosen task in the course of evolution may initially be imperceptible but the choice of destinies remains as long as the two voices can be heard.

> Both these lead on the outward man, but one of them must prevail; and from the very beginning of the invisible affray the stern and implacable *law of compensation* steps in and takes its course, faithfully following the fluctuations. When the last strand is woven, and man is seemingly enwrapped in the net-work of his own doing, then he finds himself completely under the empire of this *self-made* destiny. It then either fixes him like the inert shell against the

immovable rock, or carries him away like a feather in a
whirlwind raised by his own actions, and this is —
KARMA.

Ibid.

One cannot continue to listen to the voice of delusion until
one finds oneself trapped in the self-woven meshes of despair, and
then hope to be suddenly and vicariously saved. Recognition of
the futility of seeking vicarious salvation is no reason for inertia
or fatalism. One should never underestimate the potency of *tapas*
and true repentance. Sages alone are in a position to judge the
karmic ratios and curves of any person and they never dismiss
the hope of self-redemption for a single human being. They
understand the practical import of the Bodhisattva vow, which is
rooted not in wishful thinking but in the essential nature of the
soul. Even if only at the moment of death, when the Divine
Prototype assists in the separation of the principles, inner guidance
is available in recognizing the true meaning of one's life. Long
before the transition called death, there are precious opportunities
in times of cool reflection, and during the nightly passage into
sushupti, to strengthen the bond with the Higher Self. But these
opportunities must be used wisely if one is to take hold of the
plank of salvation — the immortal Monad — and not be carried
off by the whirlwind of worldly distractions.

By bringing Buddhic intuition to bear upon the necessary
relations of past causes and present effects in particular situations,
it is possible to extract karmic lessons from a ceaseless process of
becoming which would otherwise appear random, chaotic or even
trivial. Whilst it may seem easier to apply a general principle to a
specific situation than to derive higher meanings from lower
phenomena, it is important though difficult to show relevance,
integrity and proper timing in bringing the abstract to bear upon
concrete contexts. These interrelated aspects of Buddhic
understanding, intimately connected with the Platonic teaching
about the upward and downward dialectic, are mirrorings of
Karma operating on the mental plane through cyclic time. Both

the seemingly subjective processes of thought and the apparently objective features of its activity are instantiations of the One Law. Metaphysically, it is the inseparability of spirit from matter that accounts for the immutability of law in nature and the correspondence of modes of action between different planes of substance or matter. Nevertheless, there is a fundamental distinction between noumena and phenomena, between spiritual factors and physical forces, and this is connected with the crucial difference between the Akashic Divine Prototype and the astral form, the manvantaric star and personal constellation of each incarnated individual.

The entire teaching of Karma is an elaboration of the truth of "absolute Harmony in the world of matter as in the world of Spirit." We need to see the similitude of all things and the signature of the Divine in all the works of Nature. Anyone can appreciate the beauty of the sunrise and sunset or look at the night sky and sense the harmony of the heavens. But in the West, since the days of Pythagoras and Plato, it was already known, and commented upon by Cicero and Philo, that few could connect what they saw in the firmament with what was taking place around them on earth. For too many people spend too much time in idle gazing, without looking from above below and from below above, bridging the gap between heaven and earth. The benevolent and protective feeling towards the whole of humanity experienced by astronauts privileged to view the good earth from outer space is a poignant pointer to the future. But it is not necessary to journey into outer space to gain a feeling for global welfare. Strong and mature men and women of universal culture can serve as witnesses to the human significance of the harmony of the heavens, and become attuned to the music of the spheres. Sensing in their own hearts the majestic harmony of the metaphysical world of spirit, they may recognize its mirrorings in the world of matter.

Karma either comes as an avenging "fury or a rewarding angel." The distinction has nothing to do with externals, but rather with the inward spiritual impulse of one's actions, which by their benevolent or selfish motivation, draw back upon the doer the blessings or curses of unerring destiny.

Yea —

'Wise are they who worship Nemesis'

— as the *chorus* tells Prometheus. And as unwise they, who believe that the goddess may be propitiated by whatever sacrifices and prayers, or have her wheel diverted from the path it has once taken. 'The triform Fates and ever mindful Furies' are her attributes only on earth, and begotten by ourselves. There is no return from the paths she cycles over; yet those paths are of our own making, for it is we, collectively or individually, who prepare them.

Ibid., i 642-43

The only prayer that is consistent with the religion of responsibility is the sacrificial invocation of the Higher Self on behalf of all humanity. Through growing gratitude for the gifts already received from parents and teachers, one may gain the courage and honesty to correct one's freely chosen course. In time one can learn to insert oneself into the universal giving and receiving of that which is the heartbeat of sacrificial Karma. With greater intelligence and maturity, with more wisdom and discrimination, but above all, with a profounder benevolence for all living beings, one will enter into a richer sense of the citizenship of the world. Nourished in the silence and solitude of meditation upon the One Light, one can exemplify a detached precision and effortless transcendence as a compassionate participant in the visible cosmos of beings who are sharers in collective Karma. In time one may sense the awesome stature of the manvantaric star of each individual abiding behind and beyond the panoramic changes induced by the personal constellations which provide opportunities to participate in the samsaric stream of individual and collective self-consciousness.

KARMA AND REPENTANCE

There are two influential doctrines which could colour the attitude of the seeker of wisdom towards the concept of true repentance. Both doctrines contain a germ of truth, but in their extreme formulations they are false and pernicious, dangerous distortions. One is the fatalistic doctrine of mechanical repentance, tied to a severely formal view of punishment. We have the notion that the only way in which we can expiate our sins of omission and commission is by receiving in the future the precise penalties attached to our acts, that there can be no repentance which mitigates our penalties. We may say to a sinner, "You have done wrong; you may regret your action and you may try to learn the lesson of your failure, but you cannot avoid the consequences of your act in the future; your karma is bound to catch up with you sometime and you must be ready to receive your penalties." The other doctrine is that of sudden repentance, sometimes linked to the idea of vicarious atonement. We have here the notion that it is possible by profound regret and a dramatic act of confession and self-abasement to set aside the inexorable working of the law of Karma. We may say to a sinner, "You have sinned, yet you need not be oppressed by the thought of your future penalties; you can here and now cancel the consequences of your past sins; you can invoke the compassion of the Illustrious Beings who are the Great Guardians of the Law; you can implore the forgiveness and the blessing of the God within you." Which is worse — a too mechanical or a too lax interpretation of the Law of Karma? What is true repentance?

In order to answer these questions we could usefully turn to the story of Ajamila in Book VI of *The Bhagavatam*. By means of stories from the lives of prophets and kings, sages and devotees, this great scripture popularizes the truths contained in the Vedas. It would be easy to draw the wrong lessons from these stories or to read into them our own preconceptions. Every story must be seen as a corrective to a prevailing error or a half-truth concerning morality, salvation and the spiritual life. There are the well-known stories about Narada, Kapila, Dhruva and Prahlada and many stories about Sri Krishna. This fascinating work was composed by Vyasa, who handed it down to Suka, who in turn passed it on to King Parikshit, from whose court it was subsequently transmitted by saintly minstrels.

The story of Ajamila is briefly as follows. He was a man who married a woman of evil ways and became very dishonest, an easy prey to wicked and sinful habits. Of his ten sons, his favorite was the youngest named Narayana. One day, when Ajamila thought he was dying, he was terror-stricken by the sight of three ugly, demonlike attendants of the King of Death. He called his son Narayana, but as he uttered the name his mind became wholly concentrated on Narayana or Vishnu, the Lord of Love. While he was thus intently meditating upon God, there appeared before him the attendants of Lord Vishnu who confronted the attendants of Death. The latter asked the former why they were preventing the Law from taking its course. As a man sows, so must he reap, they said. Man is subject to the three *gunas* and his present life shows plainly his past as well as his future. His deeds leave their impressions on his subtle body and these impressions control his actions, and his future life is determined by all his present deeds. Ajamila was in his early youth, the attendants of Death reminded the attendants of Vishnu, a devout and truthful man, self-controlled, well versed in the scriptures, a friend to all beings and creatures. But one day, while in the woods gathering flowers for worship, he was aroused by the sight of a lustful couple, lost all control of himself, became greatly attached to the woman who was a wanton, forsook his lawful wife for her and gave up the pure life that he had been living. He wasted his entire fortune trying to please this woman and began to employ dishonest means to earn his living. He was now about to die in all his sins, to be taken to the King of Death who would punish him justly, and the suffering he would undergo could purify him.

The attendants of Vishnu replied that Ajamila had expiated all his sins by uttering the name of God and surrendering himself to the Lord. Wrongdoing is not eradicated or expiated, they said, if the mind continues to follow wicked desires, but when the name of God and the love of God have purified the heart all sins are completely destroyed. The mere name of God has power to save even the most depraved. On hearing all this, the attendants of Death went away and Ajamila regained his consciousness and gradually got back his health. He felt that he had received a great blessing perhaps owing to a few good deeds stored up from his past, and his whole life seemed to be transformed. He gave up his evil ways, renounced his home, practised Yoga for many years, attained self-control, and his mind became firmly fixed in the contemplation of the Divine Self. When death finally came to him, he gave up his body while chanting the sacred name of God and absorbed in meditation, thus freeing himself from the bondage of karma.

In the preamble to this story we are told that if a man commits sinful acts which he does not expiate in this life, he must pay the penalty in the next life and his suffering will be great. Expiation and repentance are of no avail to a man who continues to commit sinful acts knowing them to be harmful. All sinful thoughts and evil deeds are caused by ignorance and true expiation comes from illumination. The fire of spiritual knowledge consumes all evil and ignorance, and complete transformation of the inner life is accomplished by following and living the Truth and through the development of the love of God. Even the most sinful man is purified if he surrenders himself to the God of Love and with whole-souled devotion serves his devotees. The path of love is the simplest way by which to free ourselves from sin. Death is conquered and the fear of death is overcome by meditation upon Krishna, the God of Love. This message and the illustrative story of Ajamila seem to imply that a man can, by intense and sudden repentance, earn for himself the right to expiate his sins through prolonged meditation and devotion in this life, even freeing himself from the bonds of karma. It would also seem that such a view is contradictory to the doctrine of exact and inexorable Karmic retribution.

W.Q. Judge stated that "Karma is a doctrine too vast and complicated to be disposed of by set rules applied like balance-sheets to commercial enterprises; but one thing is certain — Karma is action viewed from every side and on each occasion." In his article entitled "Is Karma Only Punishment?" he points out that one branch of the Law of Karma deals with the vicissitudes of life, with the differing states of men, with rewards and punishments. Each state is the exact result bound to come from acts that disturb or preserve the harmony of Nature. Karmic rewards work both on the material plane and on the inner character, on the circumstances and on the tendencies of the person placed in a particular environment. We are continually fitting our arrows to the bow and shooting them forth, but it is not the arrow or the bow that counts. The important thing is the motive and the thought with which the missile is shot. Again, in his article on "Environment," Judge held that the real environment to be understood and cared about is that in which karma itself inheres in us. It is only because we see but an infinitesimal part of the long series of karmic precipitations that any apparent confusion or difficulty arises.

The third aphorism on karma points out that "Karma is an undeviating and unerring tendency in the Universe to restore equilibrium, and it operates incessantly." Aphorism No. 6 states that "Karma is not subject to time, and therefore only those who know the ultimate division of time in this Universe know Karma." Aphorism No. 13 holds that the effects of Karmic causes already set in motion "may be counteracted or mitigated by the thoughts and acts of oneself or of another." Further, we know from Aphorism No. 19 that "changes may occur in the instrument [of the Ego] during one life so as to make it appropriate for a new class of Karma," and this may take place through intensity of thought and the power of a vow and through natural alterations due to complete exhaustion of old causes. Aphorism No. 20 tells us that the soul and mind and body "have each a power of independent action," so that "any one of these may exhaust, independently of others, some Karmic causes." Aphorism No. 25

makes it clear that "birth into any sort of body and to obtain the fruits of any sort of Karma is due to the preponderance of the line of Karmic tendency." Aphorism No. 27 asserts that "measures taken by the Ego to repress tendency, eliminate defects, and to counteract by setting up different causes, will alter the sway of Karmic tendency and shorten its influence in accordance with the strength or weakness of the efforts expended in carrying out the measures adopted." Finally, Aphorism No. 28 affirms that "no man but a sage or true seer can judge another's Karma."

The section on Karma in *Light on the Path* similarly presents an occult rather than a mechanistic conception of Karma. We learn that the future is not arbitrarily formed by any separate acts of the present but that the whole of the future is in unbroken continuity with the present as the present is with the past. Even a little attention to occultism produces great results. When a man gives up the indecision of ignorance, even one definite and knowing step on the good or evil path produces great karmic results.

> He who would escape from the bondage of Karma must raise his individuality out of the shadow into the shine; must so elevate his existence that these threads do not come in contact with soiling substances, do not become so attached as to be pulled awry. He simply lifts himself out of the region in which Karma operates.

This is precisely what Ajamila did. He learned that there was no cure for desire, for the fear of death or the thought of reward and punishment save in the fixing of the sight and hearing upon that which is invisible and soundless. He freed himself from the bonds of karma only by fixing his whole attention on that which is unaffected by karma. If Ajamila was able to invoke the name and the love of God on the approach of death, this must have been because he did not allow his misdeeds to corrupt his inner consciousness or to destroy the line of his ideation in his early life and in previous lives. Ajamila's repentance may seem to us to be sudden or even easy, but this is precisely where we are mistaken. It is only a highly evolved soul who can refrain from rationalization even when he falls into a nightmare of wrongdoing, who can bring total intensity to his thought of his Higher Self and the God of Love. It is because we are not in a position to know the entire karmic sequence in the lives of Ajamila, it is because we do not see that part of his karma was working through his finer tendencies developed over a long period, that we look upon his dramatic conversion as an easy way of expiation and a setting aside of the Law of Karma.

Many people take a crudely materialistic view of karma and cannot come closer to its profoundly mysterious workings on the subjective planes of consciousness. Every human being has within himself the karma-less fount of being, the Guardian and the Divine Parent who is a spectator of karma but is untouched by it. Mere personal repentance is of no avail and cannot expiate our sins or free us from the effects of our actions. True repentance must belong to our deepest natures, must clearly reveal the root cause of our betrayal of the divine within us, the crucifixion of the God within. Spiritual conversion or resurrection is only possible if we cease to identify ourselves with our personal sheaths while assuming full responsibility for their scars, and if we wholeheartedly activate our vesture of immortality by sacrificial *tapas* and regenerative meditation. It is a mistake to isolate sinful acts or acts of repentance if we wish to grasp the working of the Law of Karma on the invisible as well as the objective planes of being.

And he said unto them:
Take heed what ye hear: with what measure ye mete,
it shall be measured to you; and unto you that hear shall
more be given. For he that hath, to him shall be given; and
he that hath not, from him shall be taken even that which
he hath.

And he said:
So is the kingdom of God as if a man should cast seed

into the ground; and should sleep, and rise night and day, and the seed should spring and grow up, he knoweth not how. For the earth bringeth forth fruit of herself; first the blade, then the ear, after that the full corn in the ear. But when the fruit is brought forth, immediately he putteth in the sickle, because the harvest is come.

And he said:

Whereunto shall we liken the kingdom of God? or with what comparison shall we compare it? It is like a grain of mustard seed, which, when it is sown in the earth, is less than all the seeds that be in the earth; but when it is sown, it groweth up, and becometh greater than all herbs, and shooteth out great branches; so that the fowls of the air may lodge under the shadow of it.

And with many such parables spake he the word unto them, as they were able to hear it.

The Gospel According to Mark 4:24-33

REINCARNATION
AND SILENCE

Every man's soul has by the law of his birth been a spectator of eternal truth, or it would never have passed into this our mortal frame, yet still it is no easy matter for all to be reminded of their past by their present existence.

PLATO

While we may know about the long and complex history of the doctrine of reincarnation, the crisis of our time is such that the response of thinking men and women is and should be, "How does it help me? What difference could it make to my life?" In the *Bhagavad Gita* Lord Krishna, speaking as the Logos in the cosmos, but also as the hidden god in every man, makes a supreme, unqualified affirmation. Like similar utterances in the great scriptures of the world, the words of Krishna have a ring of self-certification. He simply affirms for all men that there is an inexhaustible, inconsumable, incorruptible, indestructible, beginningless and endless spirit that is the sovereign ruler within the temple of the human body. Yet the same Krishna, having made this affirmation, ends his speech by asking Arjuna to recognize the honest position of the finite mind of the ordinary man by saying, "The antenatal state of beings is unknown; the middle state is evident; and their state after death is not to be discovered."

Any human being must recognize that, in so far as his mind is a bundle of borrowed conceptions — because he has grown up conditioned and circumscribed by the limiting factors of heredity, family, education and the social environment — he cannot do any more at first than come with pain to the point of declaring with profound honesty, "I really do not know. I do not know about evil. I have no idea of many things that happened to me earlier in this life. I have no idea of what will happen to me tomorrow, next year, let alone after the moment of death." This could give integrity to the quest. At the same time, when a human being begins at the level of categories and concepts, he also knows that there is something unspoken about his particular life — his tears, his thoughts, his deepest feelings, his loves and longings, his failures and frustrations, his invisible, hidden determination to hold fast in times of trial, to triumph over obstacles that seem forbidding. Beyond all of these there is that secret of his own soul which he cannot share with anyone else or even bring to the level of human speech. He knows that there is a depth and dimension to his own experience as a conscious sentient being which can participate in the transcendental wonder of the world, which can be aroused to depths and to heights and to a tremendous breadth of cosmic vision when looking at awesome vistas in nature or when surveying the great epochs of human history. But at the same time this secret cannot be conveyed. It cannot be demonstrated or fitted into the workaday categories and concepts needed to survive in a world of psychological limitation and scarcity.

The problem is one of translation. Seen philosophically, if we assume that there is something prior to be translated into something else that is shareable, it is a problem of self-discovery. It involves integrating the potential, intermittently intimated in our consciousness, with the actual which is a story that could be streamlined and which any Hollywood scriptwriter could convert into a celluloid version, a banal sequence of scenes. There must be something between our inchoate intuition of the inexhaustible and our painful recognition of the factuality of the temporally finite sequence that seems to string these events together. Memories clutter the mind. We look back with regrets or look forward with hopes, with longings that may be vain and ineffectual or may be impossible to share with anyone else.

What is self-validating for a Krishna or for the immortal spirit of man can only become a supreme and total fact for a human being when he has begun to strip away the layers and vestures of consciousness through which he is bound. In a Wordsworthian sense, every child is crowned by the aura of the divine, and has in his eyes some recognition of having lived before, some glint of an ancient wisdom distilled into the very essence of his response to the furniture of the world. Yet every human being, growing out of the child-state, loses those intimations. How are we to recover them compatibly with the integrity and self-consciousness that we must bring to every level and aspect of our human experience? This necessitates further work upon the whole of one's nature. Where we do not know, we may discard the dogmas that claim to know. There are those which insist that man is merely a fortuitous concurrence of atoms — in the name of a science which would be disowned by the greatest, most agnostic and creative scientific thinkers. There is the dogma derived from religion that man is a soul created by an anthropomorphic being at a certain point of time and consigned to eternal hell or heaven, and there are other corruptions of thought such as transmigration into animal form.

When a person discards dogmas and starts with the standpoint of genuine unknowingness, combined with a willingness to learn, he has taken a stand that is truly individual, yet within the context of all mankind. Then, as he works upon himself, he must find out what is unique and gives continuity to himself. At the same time, further growth in this quest will only be possible when he can truly dissolve the sense of separateness between himself and other beings. When the barriers fall away, his love can become almost limitless in scope. He can feel the pain in every human heart and enjoy the world through the eyes of every human being. Clearly, this cannot be done by a person except at some specific level and cannot be done totally within any short-term curve of growth. We would need a number of births to attain that degree of universalization wherein we could merge the universal and the individual and also maintain stasis throughout the different levels on which we have to communicate with widening or narrowing circles of human beings. In that sense, what is self-validating at one level could only become wholly valid and be a fully embodied truth when one's whole life revolves around it.

Many an unlettered man, in the words of the poet, is a mute, inglorious Milton, unknown, unnoticed by other men, and, like Markham's man with a hoe, conveys through his eyes the sad awareness that this is an old story that includes all beings and will persist far into the future. For the pseudo-sophisticated intellectual classes to see as much would be extremely difficult. People for whom there is very little else can sustain the awareness of some fundamental truth. To be able to do this self-consciously within a process of growth is extraordinarily elusive for a man burdened with the mental complexities of contemporary civilization, because he cannot ascend to universal brotherhood except very partially, intermittently and, alas, defensively.

To make reincarnation a vital truth in one's personal life is to treat each day as an incarnation, to greet every person as an immortal soul, inwardly and in silence, and to empathize with every human failure as a limitation — an effect with causes — comparable to all other limitations. It is the ability to see, even in the longing of the person who is almost totally lost, that spark of the Divine which could eventually be fanned into the flame of the cosmic and compassionate fire of wisdom of the Buddhas and Bodhisattvas. It is an old tradition in the East that those who truly know of the immortality of the soul can only say, "Thus have I heard."

Why is there no immortality for what we call the 'personality,' the particular mask that we wear, through which we appear to other people to be someone with a name and a form, a recognizable identity? However glorious the aggrandizement of personal selfhood may seem in a Nietzschean sense, it is still something that limits and is limited, and hence must participate in finitude and mortality. To wish immortality for that which is visibly mortal, for a mind which is like a cobweb of confusing conceptions, is at best a compensatory illusion. Ultimately, it is a sign of weakness. But the Great Teachers did not come to tell man what he already knows — that there are limitations. They came to tell him that beyond these limitations he could be free. Buddha declared: "Know ye who suffer, ye suffer from yourselves.

None else compels that ye are caught in this Wheel of Life." When Jesus spoke of the weakness of the flesh, he also intimated that the spirit is free, that it is the source of will, and that when it is truly willing, it is immortally free.

It is only by reinforcing a weaker side of our own nature that we could project from a limited view of ourselves a confused picture of personal immortality. Despite all the self-advertisements of the age, hardly any man can do full justice to himself. A man who is loudly making the case for himself is all too often belittling himself. Even the finest self-images have some illusion built into them, and to extrapolate them into the future and into the past is to limit oneself unduly. The notion of personal immortality becomes extremely degrading in a universe of law, where everything experienced by consciousness is connected, in the course of time, with everything that follows it. If a person, early or late in life, uses the doctrine of rebirth, or some notion of personal immortality, as a crutch to cling to, physical death may well be succeeded by a dreamy state of illusory happiness after a period of purgatorial separation from all the excrescences of the life just lived. Then he will have to come back, and alas, in so doing, as Plato suggests in the Myth of Er, he may choose the very opposite of what he seeks. A person who mistakes the external tokens of the good, the true and the beautiful for the transcendental *Agathon* may well find himself drawn, even propelled, into an environment where he is punished by getting what he wants.

What we need is *metanoia*, a fundamental breakthrough in consciousness. Otherwise the notion of immortality avails us naught. Many Theosophists of every sort hold to reincarnation as a dogma rather than as a basis for meditation. It cannot help unless a man can really come to see that it is a fact in Nature — a law of life in a universe of cyclic processes — and can live by that law increasingly. He can recognize mistakes, and through repeated self-correction, open new vistas. He may make existential affirmations of perfectibility — which must be on behalf of all if they are to be authentic — and give everyone he meets something of the taste of true optimism in regard to the future. Unless a person can do these things, even if he speaks the language of *impersonal* immortality, still it would be nothing but a projection of a personal conception of immortality.

The teaching of the Mahatmas is utterly uncompromising on such matters. For the personal consciousness there can be no immortality, while for the indwelling soul, for the individual ray of the overbrooding *Atman*, immortality is a fact. For the mediating mind of the middle, immortality has to be won, to be earned, and is neither a gift nor a fact. The mind must progressively detach itself from its external vestures, like a musician who goes beyond worship of his instrument or of his fingers moving on the instrument or of his own self-image, and is merged into something beyond all recorded music, into a reverence for the inaudible music of the spheres. Until a man can do this self-consciously as a soul (and he cannot do it without pain and thoroughness if he is to be honest with himself), immortality for him will be merely a compensatory myth. It will not carry that conviction with which alone he could lighten the loads of others and, through eyes of love, make many lives more meaningful.

If we trace the English term 'soul' to its Greek antecedents and equivalents, we soon find a wide variety of meanings. Even before the time of Socrates, many accretions and materializations had already gathered around the concept. It was compared to the wind. It was also supposed to mean 'that which breathes,' 'that which is alive.' And it was given many other meanings and often couched in metaphorical terms through analogy with sparks and a central fire. It became crucially significant for Plato to enrich the notion of 'soul' and to give it an existentially human meaning to do with the very act of search, the very desire to know the good, the hunger to make distinctions — not only between the good and the bad but between the good and the attractive, not only between the true and the false but between the true and the plausible. The desire to make noetic discriminations becomes the basis for a functional definition of the soul. Plato taught that, metaphysically, the soul may be seen either as perpetual motion or as a self-moving agent. In one passage he refers to a particular kind of motion which is not visible in the material realm but may be properly ascribed to the hidden Logos, the invisible deity. Elsewhere, what he identifies as the soul is connected with volition. What would it avail a man who uses the word in a Socratic sense but does not come to terms with his own will-problem, or worse still, becomes identified intellectually with his weak-willed self?

Language is very important here. The prolonged abuse of the term 'soul' in the Middle Ages resulted from a decisive shift in meaning. An active agent was replaced by something passive, something created. In a corruption of the Socratic-Platonic meaning, the 'soul' became merely something acted upon, a passive agent receiving reward or punishment. The term 'soul' almost became unusable, so that in the Renaissance humanists had to assert the dignity and divinity of man in ways that did not involve them once again in the debased coinage of the terminology of the past. In the twentieth century the term 'self' is coming into wide circulation, recovering some of the dignity of the classical conception of the soul.

A person brought up in a corrupt language system could receive tremendous help by borrowing a term from Sanskrit and trying to recognize its open texture. The compassionate Teachers of the Theosophical Movement chose to introduce from that sacred language terms like *Manas* — the root of the word 'man,' from *man*, 'to think' — into the languages of the West. When Emerson eulogizes "man thinking" he is using two English words in a manner that confirms exactly the full glory of the idea of *Manas*. Yet we also know that both the words 'man' and 'thinking' can be so degraded in everyday usage that they do not convey the glory of manhood implied by *Manas*. The term *Manas* in Sanskrit means not only 'to think,' but also 'to ideate,' 'to contemplate.' To contemplate in this classical sense is to create, to sustain a continuous and controlled act of creative imagination enveloping more and more of the whole, while retaining that core of individuality which signifies responsibility for the consequences of all thoughts, all feelings, all words, and all acts. This is a kingly conception.

It is often advantageous for a person to go outside his particular prison-house of debased language and explore classical concepts. As we grow in our awareness, we may make the beautiful discovery that even in the accents of common speech there are echoes of those pristine meanings. The literal meaning of words is less important than the tone of voice in which we use them. It is possible for a man in the street to say to another, "Hi, man" with unconscious contempt, and for a traveller in the Sierras to say, "Hi, man," in a manner that expresses genuine fellow-feeling. Miranda in *The Tempest,* seeing human beings for the first time, exclaims:

> O, wonder!
> How many goodly creatures are there here!
> How beauteous mankind is! O brave new world,
> That has such people in't!

Every word has a depth and beauty of feeling that makes ordinary English words rise like wingèd skylarks into the universal empyrean — generous, cosmic and free. Beyond all languages and concepts, the very act of articulation is of immense importance.

Perhaps the most beautiful passage on the subject of reincarnation is to be found in *The Human Situation* by Macneile Dixon. This great lover of the literatures of the world, of Plato and Shakespeare, dared to suggest:

> What a handful of dust is man to think such thoughts! Or is he, perchance, a prince in misfortune, whose speech at times betrays his birth? I like to think that, if men are machines, they are machines of a celestial pattern, which can rise above themselves, and, to the amazement of the watching gods, acquit themselves as men. I like to think that this singular race

of indomitable, philosophising, poetical beings, resolute to carry the banner of Becoming to unimaginable heights, may be as interesting to the gods as they to us, and that they will stoop to admit these creatures of promise into their divine society.

By speech a man can betray his divine birth, and just as this is true of speech in its most sacred and profound sense, it is also true of human gestures. The simple mode of salutation in the immemorial land of Aryavarta is filled with this beauty. When the two hands come together, they greet another human being in the name of that which is above both, which brings the two together, and includes all others. There is something cosmic, something that has built into it a calculation of the infinite in the expedient, even in this gesture.

But what is true of gestures could be even more true of human utterance. The surest proof of the divinity and immortality of man is that through the power of sound he can create something that is truly magical. He can release vibrations that either bless or curse, heal or hinder other beings. This is determined by motivation, intensity of inmost feeling, and the degree of individual and universal self-consciousness, nurtured and strengthened through constant meditation and self-study.

Suppose one were to ask of the gods, "Give me one of two gifts for all men. Give me first that gift which will suddenly enable all men to say that they know about reincarnation and the soul, and that they believe in immortality. Second, give me that gift which enables all men to help babies to grow with a feeling of dignity, deliberation, beauty and sanctity in regard to human speech." The wise would know that the latter gift is much more valuable than the former, because mere beliefs will not save human beings even though truly philosophical reflection upon alternatives is part of the prerogative of a Manasic being, a man in Emerson's sense. These beliefs can only be made to come alive through the exercise of conscious and deliberate speech, with a delicate sensitivity for the existence of other beings, and an immense inner compassion for all that is alive. If human speech were not constantly wasted and made into something so excessive and destructive, so mean and niggardly, we would not find so much of the self-hatred, mutual distrust, pessimism and despair that characterize our lot. We would not find ourselves in a society which is free but where, alas, the loudest voice is the most feared and tends to have the widest impact.

Anyone who can existentially restore the alchemical and healing qualities of sound, speech and silence, to some limited extent, in the smallest contexts — in relations with little children, with all he encounters even in the most trivial situations — does a great deal for the Bodhisattvas. Those Illuminated Men, by their very power of thought and ceaseless ideation, continually benefit humanity by quickening any spark of authentic aspiration in every human soul into the fire which could help others to see. The truth of reincarnation requires much more than a casual scrutiny of our external lives and our spoken language. It must be pondered upon in the very silence of our souls. It is a theme for daily meditation. In the *Bhagavad Gita* Lord Krishna tells Arjuna that true wisdom is a meditation upon birth, death, decay, sickness, and error. To meditate upon each of these and all of these together is to begin to know more about the cosmic and the human significance of the truth of reincarnation.

DEATH AND IMMORTALITY

The Soul is bound to the body by a conversion to the corporeal passions; and is again liberated by becoming impassive to the body.

That which Nature binds, Nature also dissolves; and that which the Soul binds, the Soul likewise dissolves. Nature, indeed, bound the body to the Soul; but the Soul binds herself to the body. Nature, therefore, liberates the body from the Soul; but the Soul must liberate herself from the body.

Hence there is a two-fold 'death'; the one, indeed, universally known, in which the body is liberated from the Soul; but the other, peculiar to philosophers, in which the Soul liberates herself from the body. Nor does the one entirely follow the other.

PLOTINUS

In the *Bhagavad Gita* Lord Krishna tells Arjuna that he must meditate upon birth, death, sickness, decay and error. This particular strand in the *Bhagavad Gita* is central to Buddhist thought. It is not easy for us to put ourselves in the position of a Tibetan Buddhist, to whom meditation on death is not a morbid activity, reserved for a special period in one's life, a time of deep depression owing to the fear of imminent death. It is rather part of a process of meditation which is ceaseless. To meditate on death is to meditate on life. To ask any question that is significant about the fleeting experiences that come to the ego, bringing pain as well as what appears to be happiness, to understand any of these fleeting experiences, is impossible except in the context of the total continuum. It is indeed difficult for us to understand what it means to put death in its proper place and to consider it in a wider context.

Throughout the history of European thought and of conventional Christianity, we have come to accept certain distinctions that are precious to us, a distinction between God outside the universe and the universe, between man and Nature, and ultimately between God and man. Therefore any consideration, within the context of these Western and Christian concepts of death or immortality, could only have meaning to us in terms of a relationship to be rediscovered, a lost relationship to be regained between man and God. Thus, the thought of the reabsorption of the human being into the elements of nature sounds indecent, unnatural, something that needs special explanation. We have become so identified with our own image of ourselves as detached autonomous beings — autonomous in a Cartesian sense in relation to the whole of knowledge, autonomous in a Kantian sense in relation to our moral life — that it is very difficult for us to imagine that our total standpoint is delusive, is wrong.

There is another current that has always existed as a golden stream in European thought, which is Pythagorean and Neo-Platonic and has concentrated upon a doctrine of emanations rather than a doctrine of creation. Under this scheme of things, man is intimately bound up with the universe. Man is the universe writ small. The universe is man magnified a million times. And therefore a human being only begins to be human when he understands his own relationship to Nature and the cosmos. He only begins to understand, let alone to master, the powers of Nature, when he has understood and begun to master the elements in his own nature. There is a continuous connection between man and the universe, and any conception of the divine must enter integrally into the picture that men have of the universe, and therefore it must integrally enter into one's image of oneself.

It is impossible in this view to look at Nature in a mechanistic fashion, to see it in a seventeenth-century manner. It is impossible because we are so bound up with Nature that we cannot but anthropomorphize or humanize everything in Nature. We must get rid of the great error of egoity, identification with the personal, fleeting, physical self, and begin to see that in our body, that in our personality, are material, natural elements which are the

same in all beings, and in all human beings especially. We thus
gain a sense of the wonder and the mystery, the glory, the
grandeur, the romance, the color, of the cosmic panorama, while
at the same time we need the capacity to detach ourselves from
the elements of our nature and to become therapeutic in our
whole approach to that nature.

This stream of thought is connected with the idea that man
emanates energies, that the universe itself is a continuous stream
of emanations from an unknown origin and an absolute
reality, that in every emanation something is retained of the
primordial origin of the emanation and something is transmitted
as well, and that there is a total, ceaseless, continuous process of
transformation. This idea, stressed in Pythagorean thought, is
central to the Tibetan Buddhist.

If we look at the pre-Buddhist religion of the Bonpas, we
find that it seems to us to be strange, primitive, terrifying in some
ways, an obsession with gods and demons. But in the light of what
we have just seen, it should be possible to discern that the
individual belonging to the Bonpa tradition was really seeking
his own way of gaining his citizenship in an apparently hostile
universe. The same idea becomes richer and constructive, imbued
with purpose and meaning, for the Buddhist. If we remember this
central assumption, so important to understanding death and
immortality in Tibetan thought, then we would readily recognize
that something has gone wrong in the image of Tibet that
popularly prevails in the West and in the westernized East.

A great deal has been written about the visions of the dead.
There are frescoes in many Tibetan temples depicting them,
sometimes in the form of bright and varied colors, which cannot
have any symbolic significance to the outsider, sometimes in the
form of terrifying deities stamping upon a demon and yet with a
tremendous power of beneficence and redemption. When we read
about these visions of the dead and about the Day of Judgment
in *The Tibetan Book of the Dead,* we conjure up a picture of a people
with extraordinary imagination, to whom the whole universe had
a reality which we do not see or seize. Thus we miss the universal

import of the teaching of death which was put in so many forms, vulgarly understood by some monks and laymen in Tibet but intuitively grasped by those who knew the purpose of this vast web of symbolism.

There is no easy way for us to meditate upon birth and death, decay, sickness and error in relation to Tibetan teaching simply by looking at a particular painting of the visions of the dead or even by reading *The Tibetan Book of the Dead.* These are no doubt useful, but what is really necessary is to get back to that central posture which Krishna enjoined upon Arjuna, to meditate upon all of these and to see them together. If it is possible to see birth and death as connected forms or phases of a single stream of consciousness, then we have to grasp the idea of a universe alive, ever-changing, conscious in a sense we cannot directly comprehend. Our consciousness is a reflected consciousness, distorted many times, distorted by particular tendencies and complexes or *samskaras,* by particular likes and dislikes, preconceptions, weaknesses of the will, by particular forms of illusion, so that it is very difficult for us to grasp directly this pure and total consciousness behind the ever-changing forms and phases assumed by a single substratum.

In Buddhist thought we are helped to begin to make the distinction by seeing that this entire universe is both *samsara* and *nirvana. Samsara* and *nirvana* spring from the same ultimate essence, the *Adi Buddha,* the ultimate Buddha nature; but *samsara* is the world of flux, the world of change, the world of illusion. Arising out of the sensations that we have of the very flux of *samsara,* we have *avidya,* congenital ignorance. It is more than ignorance as we normally understand it. It is not just lack of knowledge. It is a peculiar perversity of the modified consciousness available to us which prevents us from rising to the level of total universal consciousness and seeing all human and cosmic experiences as continuous events in a single stream. *Nirvana,* on the other hand, we describe by negation. *Nirvana* to us is some kind of total emptiness, nothingness; this has been the consistent interpretation of people unsympathetic to Buddhist teachings. It is very easy, of course, to conjure up a world of illusion which was manufactured by certain people because they were not able to come to terms with it, and then to suggest that they sought an escape in some imaginary and totally empty state, opposed to what we would normally call 'living', 'becoming involved' in this world of matter. But *samsara* and *nirvana* actually refer to the two tendencies of the involvement of consciousness in form and the evolution of form to the height of consciousness, form and consciousness being differentiated only by a difference of degree and not of kind. To understand this is to see that *samsara* is ultimately the veil that is cast upon the nirvanic condition of illuminated and enlightened beings.

Even the *Nirvanee* as seen by us, the moment we personify him, the moment we separate him out from the rest of humankind as a single individual who attained to a particular state in a particular manner, immediately becomes a samsaric illusion. We then conjure up our own idealized and delusive images of enlightened, immortal individuals. So it is really important to see that if life is a continuous and total process, and if it undergoes a great variety of modes in relation to the actual forms of matter, then this consciousness in the universe must always require some form of embodiment, and therefore even the enlightened man cannot be imagined in a totally disembodied state.

There are those like the Capuchin Della Penna, who in their distorted picture of Tibetan Buddhists, give the impression of a Tibetan belief in some imaginary world of *Lha*, disembodied spirits, bodiless gods, an airy, fairy world of abstract entities, with no relationship to the universe as we know it. In 1882 *The Theosophist* published an important contribution by the Chohan Lama who was the chief of the Archive-registrars of the libraries containing manuscripts on esoteric doctrines belonging to the Dalai and Panchen Lamas of Tibet. He pointed to the distortions of the pure Tibetan teaching, and explained the basic propositions which are necessary to know before we can understand the *Lha* and so-called disembodied entities. This is why we have to grasp the statement in the *Prajnaparamita* that form and void are ultimately only aspects of each other. The moment we become aware or conscious, immediately our consciousness becomes embodied in thoughts or feelings, in images which are formal or material in relation to our actual state of awareness. In this sense, pure awareness is something that we cannot possibly visualize. All our awareness is relative to the particular plane of perception on which we function. It involves the use of organs of perception that are appropriate to this plane of perception. Now if we could see this, then we could begin to consider that the human being lives not merely in a visible, physical world but in several worlds intertwined. He is in fact constantly living in six worlds, according to the Buddhist Canon. But more important than the number, whether it be six or seven or some other, it is essential to grasp the idea that the outside world, in the context of which we become aware, is entirely relative to our organ of perception.

We are all somewhat aware of this. Phenomenalists since Berkeley have recognized how very much the existence of objects is dependent upon our perceptions of them. The same idea has been elaborated by Wittgenstein in another way — that we have no grasp of reality apart from the clusters of concepts that are bound up with our habitual usage and our language-games. Anybody who reflects for a moment could see this. We have no direct, privileged access to reality. The moment we begin to think about space or time or Nature, the moment we begin to speculate about the universe, the moment we begin to theorize about it, even when we try just to gain what appears to us to be direct awareness of a particular set of objects, we have immediately allowed to come between those apparently neutral and independent objects, in a mechanistic Cartesian universe, and ourselves as privileged spectators, the veil of concepts, the concepts which we need to produce a commonsensical map or a metaphysical map. Without these we cannot attempt to isolate particulars, let alone to apprehend them, to distinguish them, to classify them.

We need to see that each human being is continually inhabiting several universes and has available to him the various organs of awareness or perception which are appropriate to these different universes. Therefore, one could come to discern that what is life to one man on one plane of perception is death to another. In the *Gita* we have Krishna's statement that what is day to the enlightened man is night to the ordinary man, and what is night to the ordinary man is day to the sage. What is day to the ordinary man is night — the night of ignorance. To generalize the idea, what to some people are significant realities are ephemeral illusions in the eyes of others. And we are all involved in this psychological relativity. No one has a privileged position. If there were perfected men, the moment they come into a physical universe and are involved in communication with physical beings, — even they cannot totally free themselves from the imprisonment that we all undergo in a physical universe. Every universe binds us.

Is it then possible, simply by grasping this idea, to conceive of the possibility of moving from one universe to another, so to speak, all within the mind, all within ourselves? Is it possible for us to study the various elements in our nature, in terms of different colors of the rainbow, in terms of different gods in Nature? Is it possible for us to see all these various facets of Nature as seemingly independent but essentially interdependent aspects of a single substratum, of a single universe? For if we can do this, then we would see that death need not be viewed as something unnatural.

It is life that seems to be unnatural. The poet Kalidasa raised this question with the help of an analogy. Why do we feel that death is unnatural and life is natural, when life is like a few drops of water in a pot. There ought to be something unnatural about this. It is this which needs explaining. And if the water is thrown back into the ocean, there is nothing unnatural about that. So death, in this view, does not require special explanation. It is life that requires explanation. Therefore we do not begin by asking why do we die. We ask why we were born. If we wish to understand what is the kind of consciousness that we are going to preserve on the eve of death, or what perhaps may be the consciousness that we will experience soon after death, we must go back to the beginning. What do we remember about our consciousness as far back as possible, near the moment of birth? What conceivably could we have felt before we were born? Now these are questions that many people would find impossible to entertain, and yet the true philosopher, the man of meditation, the man who really wishes to see life as a whole, cannot shirk them.

Buddhist philosophy explains that life in a body can be explained by the tremendous desire for bodily life that belongs to us. This we can recognize in ourselves. We can distinguish people in terms of the desire for sensation. We can distinguish the same person at different points in his life, according to the degree of his hold on life. Everything in this world of *samsara* is a conspiracy to encourage this hold on life, this hold on possessions, this hold onto the image that men form of the body, their identification with their own name and form, their *namarupa*. In this lies the seed of separateness — *ahankara*, the seed of violence — *himsa*, the seed of falsehood — *asatya*. Falsehood, violence, separateness are all rooted in the fierce craving for life, for personal existence. And when we begin to reflect upon this, we can see its significance. We can think of people who desperately wish to project their own personal existence on the stage, literal or metaphorical. We know for ourselves how very often the desire for survival or the hatred of survival is nothing but our own attitude to a continuation of our personal life. That is why, whether in the Christian or in the Buddhist tradition, all the pictures given to us of post-natal states become for us personal visions with personal prospects, awful or glorious, with immense significance for us as personalities. Whereas we are really asked by spiritual teachers to get back to the basic origin of *avidya*, or ignorance, which is *tanha*, the will to live.

This ancient Buddhist idea is not just a phrase. It is so important an aspect of this universe that Gandhi, who tried to resuscitate the teaching of Buddha, actually formulated a law.

He declared that the willingness to kill is exactly in inverse proportion to the willingness to die. Some might think that there is truth in this statement, though formulated as a law it seems extravagant and pseudo-scientific. But not at all, when we grasp the idea of *tanha*, the desire for life. The greater the desire for life, the greater the craving for personal existence, the total identification of our consciousness with that which is fleeting and transitory and perishable and personal, the more intense our awareness of ourselves as separate from others, the greater is the impulse to survive, the Hobbesian fear of death which seems so crucial to all life and to all existence in society. The greater then becomes the violence, the willingness to kill, on the plane of thought or feeling as well as on the physical plane.

On the other hand, the person who does not feel so strongly, who has deliberately come to discern that this binding force which brought him into life is itself worthy of meditation and worthy of transcendence, such a man begins to loosen up this hold of his consciousness over his body and his material instruments. He then begins to see himself as others see him, as he sees a photograph of himself ten years ago, as in fact an illusory entity, a thing of no consequence or of no more consequence than any other thing. It is not necessary that he has to go from attachment to aversion. Aversion is itself a form of attachment. The man who denies loudly that he has any desire for life is deeply attached. It is not easy to master the process of getting beyond attachment and aversion, and seeing in its proper perspective the force of cohesion inherent in matter and in the forms of consciousness we consolidate. This force draws us into separative existence and engenders an ever-growing fear of death.

Death then serves simply as an opportunity to get away, temporarily, from the craving for personal existence. This force, although it seems so intense while it lasts, is still transitory. It is an interference with the pure vision of consciousness and therefore must come to an end. A great opportunity comes to each human being at the time of death. Either he sees the significance of what is happening and begins to take the first steps toward conscious

immortality, or even after he has discarded the physical vesture
— there are many universes and there are many vestures — he
begins once again in a new form to live out his old attachments,
to sublimate them, to refine and purify them. All his old loves
may now become purer. They may become idealizations. But
nonetheless he gets involved again in his continual craving for
personal existence. And then of course his return to physical life
becomes a natural thing, something involuntary to him, inevitable
in Nature.

Therefore we are told that if we want to understand what
happens after death, we must first grasp 'death consciousness.'
What is the state of consciousness that we possess just before we
die? What is the mood in which we are prepared to receive this
new experience, to enter this new world? The more we have a
thirst for life, the more we assume that life is natural and death
unnatural, the more we are terrified of the great world of the
unknown, and the more we then put up a resistance to the natural
opportunities for the freeing of consciousness that are available
with the discarding of the mask of the physical body.

But on the other hand, the person who has the knowledge
of the *bardo* knows that he is now about to enter an intermediate
state between birth and death, a period of gestation, a period in
which there can be no Karma. The law of causality can operate
fully only on the plane of the physical universe. A person cannot
reap the results of actions generated by him in a physical body
except in a physical body on the physical plane. But he is involved
in a condition in which, because he has got out of the physical
body or because the physical vesture has fallen away, he now has
the opportunity to consider his available vestures and the other
universes consubstantial with them.

These vestures have been expounded in terms of the *Trikaya*
doctrine, the doctrine of the three bodies — the *Dharmakaya*,
the *Sambhogakaya*, and the *Nirmanakaya*. The *Dharmakaya* is the
body made up of *Dharmadhatu*, that in the universe which
constitutes the undifferentiated and ultimate Buddha nature.
The *Sambhogakaya* represents the manifested, the perfected,

embodiment of all that exists in Nature. It is the origin of the idea of an omnipresent god, worshipped by Hindus as Vishnu, the god who pervades all things, and which in other traditions has been the subject of numerous graphic visions, vivid pictures of the perfections of Deity. The *Nirmanakaya* is that body or vesture which represents the incarnation of this ultimate substance or substratum which underlies *Dharmakaya*, and which is exhibited in its glorious universal perfection in *Sambhogakaya*. The *Nirmanakaya* vesture enables an enlightened being to project itself on a material plane. In Mahayana teaching it is suggested that we, who in physical life are bound down by it and are terrified by death, can take comfort from the fact that there is a vesture perfected by beings who are not merely able to maintain their condition of pure awareness or total enlightenment in some subtle immaterial body but are also able to materialize it, and to differentiate their embodied nature into all the beings around them, consciously and deliberately. So the mere fact of having a material body is not the obstacle, but rather attachment and identification with it.

It is possible for us to introduce into this scheme of things a dualism such as we have in orthodox Christianity, which contrasts life that is transitory with the life eternal. We could contrast physical life with pain and original sin, with 'the body of resurrection', and then of course we get a simple dualistic scheme. Life becomes an episode not a state, unrelated to the future except through a particular mechanism such as the Day of Judgment. We are then launched into an eternity of a condition where, if we choose and we have chosen aright and repented at the right time, we shall get this body of resurrection. But in Tibet we do not have such a dualistic picture connected with the total dogmatism people bring to the idea that there is only one life, of which they have no proof — and the onus of proof is on them because the majority of humanity has thought in terms of rebirth. Even for people who think in this way, it is not easy to make the leap in imagination to a conception of innumerable universes, an endless chain of manifestation, and a continual transformation of consciousness which goes through life and beyond life, beyond what we call death, and back into incarnated life again.

Soon after the actual withdrawal from the physical body, the 'soul,' — a term derived from the Greeks, the Kwan Yin in every man in Tibetan tradition, the Voice of the Spirit or Conscience, the Great Word, the Great Sound of the *Adi Buddha* — this 'soul,' as we call it, this self-consciousness in us, becomes capable when physical life is discarded of perceiving, though only for a very short time, the pure body of *Dharmakaya*. Simply because of the first separation of consciousness from physical embodiment, the soul begins to have a glimmer of total undifferentiated consciousness, in the form of a vision of pure, clear, colorless light. But this is a tremendous thing for us to contemplate. We are not prepared for it before we die, and therefore it may not mean anything to us unless we begin to meditate upon it now. But if it happens, and we cannot make anything of it, and we fall into some kind of swoon or stupor before this ineffable light, then we are no better off for having had a foretaste or a vision of this great experience which is perfected by the enlightened ones who remain immortal.

We then enter the next state of the *bardo* where we begin to see this same total voidness or *tathata*, the *sunyata* state, the *Dharmakaya* body of the universe. But we see it through a mist, through a beautiful rainbow mist, and of course then we see many colors. We begin to dream and to experience ideal consciousness. Having failed to come to terms with total undifferentiated consciousness in its abstract, absolute manner, we now fall into a plane of consciousness where we begin to reflect upon idealized types, the archetypes of Plato. But these archetypes are connected with a personal life that is gone, so that we begin to look back without a clear awareness that we have left the physical body. Then, gradually, awareness of this grows, though one still continues to be conscious of one's personal self. Therefore all one's loves and all one's desires are in terms of the life that went before. One is in a dreamy condition, which may sound blissful by comparison with the burdens of earthly life, but is still delusive.

Here is another opportunity for the person to see what has really happened, to see the unreality of it, and see once again the reality of total undifferentiated consciousness. But in fact most people cannot seize this opportunity because they are not prepared for it.

What instead happens is that they are confronted with all that they are in their personal natures. They are confronted with their natures with which they had identified themselves, and which are now exteriorized out of themselves because they imagine that they are not all the bad things that they once thought they were. Suddenly we are confronted with all the elements in our nature in the form of visions, a whole array of terrifying deities holding up to ourselves all the things which are in us. It is only if there is within us a certain weakness that we are afraid of something external. It is only when we are identified with some particular attribute which is personal and separative that we then have a certain fear of what is outside. It is a common observation that an ambitious man is the first to hold out against the ambition of another man, a proud man against the pride of another, and so on. We also know about people filled with lust who love to hold forth against lust. This is exactly what happens in the *bardo* state, only here the individual is confronted with a whole array of embodied beings, symbolized in visions for the sake of understanding. We should not anthropomorphize this condition as the literalists have done. But we are confronted with innumerable formulations of elements in our nature with which we have not come to terms, which we have not seen for what they really are in their true colors.

This great opportunity is afforded to us all. It might be called consulting the Book of Judgment, the Book of Memory. Whether we quail before this great and frightening revelation of all our personal *samskaras*, our peculiar personal and divisive tendencies, whether we are re-attracted to them and are rapidly drawn back to earthly life, or whether we are able to grasp the nirvanic (as opposed to the samsaric) stream of consciousness which enables us to see the inwardness of this great panorama — that is the choice open to us. But it cannot be made then. It has to be made during life. Herein lies the importance of considering all these teachings about death. It is only now that we have the opportunity to prepare ourselves for the appropriate state of mind before departing from the physical body, or before discarding it, which would enable us fruitfully to avail ourselves of both post-natal and post-mortem consciousness and the various phases of this intermediate state of *bardo*.

Most human beings are unable to attain the seed idea of enlightenment which is fructified in the form of an imperishable vesture by those who have fully prepared before death to enter into the state of immortality. For most people, even the seed idea of immortality cannot be grasped, and therefore they are quickly drawn to all the various *samskaras* or attributes which come back to them. There is a persisting matrix made up of all these attributes, revivified by one's own newly-formed desire or attachment. Then one begins to make one's first entry into physical life through having formed a line of attachment with particular parents. Such people dream about mating couples and get so involved with the purely physical side of life that they are very soon caught in the illusory process of birth. They cannot expect to know what birth means because they did not know what death meant.

So, this whole teaching is highly significant if we can see its practical implications and various facets. By reading *The Tibetan Book of the Dead*, or by looking at Tibetan pictures of the visions of the dead, one could accumulate a vast amount of detail about the symbolic forty-nine days of the *bardo* with all its day-to-day visions. But merely accumulating a great deal of fantastic knowledge does not add anything to our meditation on death. The moment we start with ourselves and ask not why we are afraid of death but why we hold on to life, the moment we begin to see significant connections, it will be possible for us to discern that at all times we have available to us either the standpoint of *nirvana* or the standpoint of *samsara*. If we are ready to see this, we can come to understand those who have gained or can gain immortality in this scheme of things.

Ordinarily, according to Tibetan teachings, people will not incarnate immediately. When someone has died, that person will not linger or be drawn back to earth-life except in three cases. First are those Bodhisattvas, those enlightened sages who deliberately linger, having renounced *nirvana*, to assist and help other human beings to gain the knowledge that they have of the meaning of all these states. Secondly, there are those people who die with a total obsession with one line of thinking, not necessarily bad or sinful beings, but those with an *idée fixe*. These people will also linger. They will prolong the entry into the *bardo* state, and the more they prolong it, the more difficult it will be for them to pass from the swoon into the state of awakening, into a new consciousness, and benefit front it. The third class of beings who are drawn back and hover around earth-life are those who had so intense a love — like a mother's love for children — a sense of unfulfilled or uncompleted love, or a love which, however much fulfilled, is still so powerful and so personal that it binds people and draws them back to earthly life. But even these will not appear as *bhuts* or ghosts unless they are galvanized into activity by adepts in the art of necromancy, a practice strongly condemned in pure Buddhist teaching.

Such nefarious practices do go on in the name of Buddhist tradition among several Red Cap sects, especially in places like Bhutan. They have actually been put forward as Tibetan Buddhist, in the name of scholarship, by people who have quoted supposed authorities who have never even visited Lhasa, let alone had the privilege of some kind of initiation into the pure teachings of the Panchen Lama and the Dalai Lama. It is not therefore a question of considering all the various forms which possession could take that would constitute a true understanding of the Tibetan teaching of death, let alone of immortality. That there must be such demonic usurpers is not difficult to conceive. But they are unnatural. Tibetan teachings do refer to the victims of suicides and murders, people who are in the state of swoon and could be used by other beings who function freely on subtle planes of consciousness, using subtle vestures for their own foul purpose. But this is not something that need concern us.

The crucial insight that we gain from Tibetan teaching is that immortality is not something to be achieved or won, not a prize to be awarded to a favoured few. Immortality is nothing but another aspect of mortality. Even now we either live immortally or live mortally. We either die every moment or we live and thirst, depending on whether we are focused upon the nirvanic or upon the samsaric aspect of embodied consciousness. If we are constantly able to sift the meaning of experiences and to see our formal vestures for what they are and pass from one plane of perception to another, then indeed it may be possible, when blessed with the vision of clear, pure light — the great vision of *sunyata* — to enter straightaway into that vesture which enables us to remain free from the compulsion of return to earthly life. But this cannot happen unless it flows naturally out of the line of life's meditation. It cannot happen all of a sudden. It is not some kind of special dispensation. It is itself a product of the working of Karma.

Beings who have undergone this condition of final illumination have either chosen to remain immortal but in the *Dharmakaya* vesture, unrelated to manifested beings and humanity, or they have chosen the *Nirmanakaya* vesture and deliberately chosen to enter into relationships with human beings. These *Nirmanakayas* ceaselessly point to the basic truths concerning the meaning of death and the perpetual possibility of immortality. They teach people that within themselves they are Buddhas without knowing it. Now, the *Prajnaparamita* states that the Buddhas are themselves only personifications and therefore they could become illusions for us. What is it that we are going to meditate upon when we consider the immortals? Are we going to think of them as glorified physical personalities, archangels in radiant raiment, somehow idealized and more beautiful but related to our own physical conception of physical life? Or are we going to think of them as minds, a great gathering of extraordinary and powerful minds who collectively constitute the great mind of the universe? Or are we going to look upon them simply as beings who have become aware of their true Buddha nature and have therefore become instruments for the working of consciousness, instruments that will be helpful and unifying, because that is the nature of consciousness, whereas the nature of form is divisive.

Thus the whole doctrine, even of the *Lha*, those gods seemingly tucked away in a limbo, refers to beings who not merely work in relation to the world but also by their ceaseless collective ideation maintain in the world the force of the Buddha nature. The Buddha nature is not some abstract principle. It is actually embodied in the collective consciousness of such beings perpetually in the universe. We come to see that the various phases in the process of the concretization of the universe from an absolute realm, through archetypes, through individualized forms of thought, and ultimately to material forms, that this whole process is re-enacted in the *bardo* state, between death and rebirth. A great re-enactment has taken place. Who knows what re-enactment takes place within the embryo especially during the first seven months in the mother's womb? Science and medicine know almost nothing about what happens then or why. These are the great mysteries connected with the primal facts of birth and death. If we can consider that there is available in Buddhist teaching the knowledge that there is regular re-enactment of a continuous cosmic process before the eye of the soul, then we can see that enlightenment is not the great terminus to a laborious and boring process of striving, but a ceaseless opportunity which inheres in this very world of woe and delusion, which we call *samsara*, and to which we cling like blind fools, knowing not Life and afraid of death.

Caxton Hall, London
November 1963

They who are on the summit of a mountain can see all men; in like manner they who are intelligent and free from sorrow are enabled to ascend above the paradise of the Gods; and when they there have seen the subjection of man to birth and death and the sorrows by which he is afflicted, they open the doors of the immortal.

TCHED-DU BRJOD-PAI TSOMS

. . . as 'there is more courage to accept being than non-being, life than death,' there are those among the Bodhisatwas and the Lha — 'and as rare as the flower of udambara are they to meet with' — who voluntarily relinquish the blessing of the attainment of perfect freedom, and remain in their personal selves, whether in forms visible or invisible to mortal sight — to teach and help their weaker brothers.

A Gelung Of The Inner Temple

ANAMNESIS

Since, then, the soul is immortal and has been born many times, since it has seen all things both in this world and in the other, there is nothing it has not learnt. No wonder, then, that it is able to recall to mind goodness and other things, for it knew them beforehand. For, as all reality is akin and the soul has learnt all things, there is nothing to prevent a man who has recalled — or, as people say, 'learnt' — only one thing from discovering all the rest for himself, if he will pursue the search with unwearying resolution. For on this showing all inquiry or learning is nothing but recollection.

PLATO

Anamnesis is true soul-memory, intermittent access to the divine wisdom within every human being as an immortal Triad. All self-conscious monads have known over countless lifetimes a vast host of subjects and objects, modes and forms, in an ever-changing universe. Assuming a complex series of roles as an essential part of the endless process of learning, the soul becomes captive recurrently to myriad forms of *maya* and *moha*, illusion and delusion. At the same time, the soul has the innate and inward capacity to cognize that it is more than any and all of these masks. As every incarnated being manifests a poor, pale caricature of himself — a small, self-limiting and inverted reflection of one's inner and divine nature — the ancient doctrine of anamnesis is vital to comprehend human nature and its hidden possibilities. Given the fundamental truth that all human beings have lived many times, initiating diverse actions in intertwined chains of causation, it necessarily follows that everyone has the moral and material environment from birth to death which is needed for self-correction and self-education. But who is it that has this need? Not the shadowy self or false egoity which merely reacts to external stimuli. Rather, there is that eye of wisdom in every person which in deep sleep is fully awake and which has a translucent awareness of self-consciousness as pure primordial light.

We witness intimations of immortality in the pristine light in the innocent eye of every baby, as well as in the wistful eye of every person near the moment of death. It seems that the individual senses that life on earth is largely an empty masquerade, full of sound and fury, signifying nothing. Nevertheless, there is a quiet joy in the recognition that one is fully capable of gaining some apprehension not only of the storied past but also of the shrouded future by a flashing perception of his unmodified, immutable divine essence. If one has earned this through a lifetime of meditation, one may attain at the moment of withdrawal from the body a healing awareness of the reality behind the dense proscenium of the earth's drama.

Soul-memory is essentially different from what is ordinarily called memory. Most of the time the mind is clouded by a chaotic association of images and ideas that impinge upon it from outside. Very few human beings, however, are in a position to make full use of the capacity for creative thinking. They simply cannot fathom what it is like to be a thinking being, to be able to deliberate calmly and to think intently on their own. Automatic cerebration is often mistaken for primary thinking. To understand this distinction, one must look at the fundamental relation between oneself as a knower and the universe as a field of knowledge. Many souls gain fleeting glimpses of the process of self-enquiry when they are stilled by the panoramic vistas of Nature, silenced by the rhythmic ocean, or alone amidst towering mountains. Through the sudden impact of intense pain and profound suffering they may be thrown back upon themselves and be compelled to ask, "What is the meaning of all of this?" "Who am I?" "Why was I born?" "When will I die?" "Can I do that which will now lend a simple credence to my life, a minimal dignity to my death?"

Pythagoras and Plato taught the Eastern doctrine of the spontaneous unfolding from within of the wisdom of the soul.

Soul-wisdom transcends all formal properties and definable qualities, as suggested in the epistemology, ethics and science of action of the *Bhagavad Gita*. It is difficult for a person readily to generate and release an effortless balancing of the three dynamic qualities of Nature — *sattva, rajas* and *tamas* — or to see the entire cosmos as a radiant garment of the divine Self. He needs to ponder calmly upon the subtle properties of the *gunas*, their permutations and combinations. Sattvic knowledge helps the mind to meditate upon the primordial ocean of pure light, the bountiful sea of milk in the old Hindu myths. The entire universe is immersed in a single sweeping cosmic process. Even though we seem to see a moving panorama of configurations, colours and forms, sequentiality is illusory. Behind all passing forms there are innumerable constellations of minute, invisible and ultimately indivisible particles, whirling and revolving in harmonic modes of eternal circular motion. A person can learn to release anamnesis to make conscious and creative use of modes of motion governing the life-atoms that compose the variegated universe of his immortal and mortal vestures.

The timeless doctrine of spiritual self-knowledge in the fourth chapter of the *Bhagavad Gita* suggests that human beings are not in the false position of having to choose between perfect omniscience and total nescience. Human beings participate in an immense hinterland of differentiation of the absolute light reflected within modes of motion of matter. To grow up is to grasp that one cannot merely oscillate between extremes. Human thought too often involves the violence of false negation — leaping from one kind of situation to the exact opposite rather than seeing life as a fertile field for indefinite growth. This philosophical perspective requires us to think fundamentally in terms of the necessary relation between the knower and the known. Differences in the modalities of the knowable are no more and no less important than divergences in the perceptions and standpoints of knowers. The universe may be seen for what it is — a constellation of self-conscious beings and also a vast array of elemental centres of energy — *devas* and *devatas* all of which participate in a ceaseless cosmic dance that makes possible the sacrificial process of life for each and every single human being. If one learns that there are degrees within degrees of reflected light, then one sees the compelling need to gain the faculty of divine discrimination (*viveka*). That is the secret heart of the teaching of the *Bhagavad Gita*.

The *Gita* is a jewelled essay in *Buddhi Yoga*. *Yoga* derives from the root *yog*, 'to unite', and centres upon the conscious union of the individual self and the universal Self. The trinity of Nature is the lock of magic, and the trinity of Man is the sole key, and hence the grace of the Guru. This divine union may be understood at early stages in different ways. It could be approached by a true concern for *anasakti* — selfless action and joyous service, the precise performance of duties and a sacrificial involvement in the work of the world. It may also be attempted through the highest form of *bhakti* or devotion, in concentrating and purifying one's whole being so as to radiate an unconditional, constant and consistent truth, a pure, intense and selfless feeling of love. And it must also summon forth true knowledge through altruistic meditation. *Jnana* and *dhyana* do not refer to the feeble reflections of the finite and fickle mind upon the finite and shadowy objects of an ever-evolving world, but rather point to that enigmatic process of inward knowing wherein the knower and the known become one, fused in transcendent moments of compassionate revelation. The pungent but purifying commentary by Dnyaneshvari states in myriad simple metaphors the profoundest teaching of the *Gita*. In offering numerous examples from daily life, Dnyaneshvari wants to dissolve the idea that anything or any being can be known through *a priori* categories that cut up the universe into watertight compartments and thereby limit and confine consciousness. The process of true learning merges disparate elements separated only because of the looking-glass view of the inverted self which mediates between the world and ourselves in a muddled manner. The clearest perception of *sattva* involves pure ideation.

The *Gita* presents a magnificent portrait of the man of meditation who has all his senses and organs under complete control. Whatever he does, he remains seated like one unaffected and aloof (*kutastha*). He does not identify with any of the instruments musically necessary for the creative transformation of the cosmic process. The Religion of Responsibility is rooted in *Rta,* sattvic motion in unmanifested Nature, and it makes sattvic consciousness (*dharma*) accessible to imperfect individuals. A human being who valiantly journeys in consciousness behind and beyond the visible process of Nature — like a ballerina in Stravinsky's "Rite of Spring" becoming Spring itself while remaining a single character in the concordant ballet — maintains a joyous and silent awareness of the whole process while coolly functioning at various levels with deft dexterity. All human beings, insofar as they can smoothly function at diverse levels of precise control and painless transcendence, can attain to firm fixity of mind and serene steadfastness of spirit — the sacred marks of initiation through sattvic ideation in the secret heart. Sattvic knowledge is the invisible common thread transcending all apparent differences. It gives support to rhythmic activity which is simultaneously precise, liberating and intrinsically self-validating, without the creeping shadow of inconstancy.

The self of the individual who is sattvic is integrated with the Self which surveys the whole world with its congeries of forms and objects, whilst seeing all of these appearances in local time and visible space as evanescent parts of a continuous process of interconnected if conceptually discrete causes and consequences. This is like a mighty river that flows from a hidden stream issuing from a sacred source in the depths of the highest mountain ranges. Dnyaneshvari offers an apt analogy which applies both to anamnesis and to *Turiya-Sattva*. Just as when a stream becoming a river empties itself into the great ocean, so too will individual consciousness when it withdraws itself from its reflected sense of 'I-ness' within the world of insupportable illusions. When the principle of self-consciousness initiates this inner withdrawal, it quietly empties itself into the great ocean of primordial light,

Daiviprakriti, universal and self-luminous consciousness. Yet at the same time it remains active within *Hiranyagarbha*, the pristine golden egg of immortal individuality, cosmic and trans-human.

From the standpoint of the man of meditation, light and darkness are archetypal categories applicable at many levels. Philosophically and mystically, darkness at the level of inversion is chaos, and light as we understand it in nature is associated with the illumination of a field of consciousness. Psychologically, for many sad souls darkness is the deepening shadow of loneliness, and light shines as the resplendent vision of human brotherhood and the spiritual solidarity of all that lives. This can become a glorious vision of enduring hope, invulnerable faith and unwavering affirmation. Rodin's well-known simile in stone suggests that the pilgrim-soul and weary toiler is plunged in deep thought. All such persons are asking the oldest question — "Who am I?" Significant trends are emerging across the globe, and the crisis is aggravated by the breakdown of alternatives everywhere and especially in the North American continent. Light and darkness refer to every revivified conception of what is real, what is abstract and what concrete in the vast field of unilluminated objects and hazy memories, the negations and affirmations of consciousness resulting from the repeated negation of a false sense of 'I' in a fast-changing world.

The Secret Doctrine offers the ancient analogy of the Sun to the individual emerging out of the cave of *avidya* in search of Universal Good (SAT). Though difficult to exemplify, a talismanic exercise in practical instruction is conveyed. Close your eyes, and from the depths of inmost consciousness travel outward to the extremest limits in every direction. You will find equal lines or rays of perception extending evenly in all directions, so that the utmost effort of ideation will terminate in the vault of a sphere. Think of yourself as within a numinous golden egg, a divine sphere. Close your eyes, draw within, behind and beyond your own shadowy conception of yourself, behind the superficial and self-limiting images of the mind's surface, cast there by the lunar activity of the world, and eclipse your own restless lunar self.

As you withdraw behind your five senses, focus upon the point between your eyes and see that point as only a representation in the physical face of a field of consciousness where there are innumerable points, each of which is at the centre of a radiant sphere formed by a reflection of the fiery substance of the dark ocean of space.

From the standpoint of your own self-conscious ray of light, try to think outward to the extreme limits of boundless space in every direction. You will find that equal lines or rays of perception will terminate in all directions in the invisible vault of a macrocosmic sphere. The limit of the sphere will be a great circle, and the direct rays of thought in any direction must be right-line radii from a common centre in an immaterial, homogeneous medium. This is the all-embracing human conception of the manifesting aspect of the ever-hidden *Ain-Soph*, which formulates itself in the geometrical figure of a circle with elements of continuous curvature, circumference and rectilinear radii. This geometrical shape is the first recognizable link between the *Ain-Soph* and the highest intelligence of man. The rule proclaimed at the portals of the Pythagorean School and the Platonic Academy limited entry to those who had deeply reflected upon divine geometry.

According to Eastern esotericism, this great circle, which reduces to the point within the invisible boundless sphere, is Avalokiteshwara, the Logos. It is the manifested God, the Verbum of the *Gospel According to St. John,* unknown to man except through its manifested universe and the entirety of mankind. The One is intuitively known by the many, although the One is unthinkable by any mode of mere intellection. Reaching within consciousness means going behind and beyond every possible perception and conception, every possible colour and form. Form corresponds to knowledge on the lower reflected lunar plane; colour corresponds to the knower at the level of the reflected ray. The objects of knowledge are merely modifications of a single substance. These do not yield any simple triadic diagram, but involve a gradual ascent within consciousness, in a tranquil state of contemplation, towards the greatest parametric conception of the One. The Logos sleeps in the bosom of *Parabrahm* — in the Abstract Absolute — during *pralaya* or non-manifestation, just as our individual Ego is in latency during deep, dreamless sleep. We cannot cognize *Parabrahm* except as *Mulaprakriti*, the mighty expanse of undifferentiated cosmic matter. This is not merely a vesture in cosmic creation through which radiate the energy and wisdom of *Parabrahm*. It is the Divine Ground.

The Logos in its highest aspect takes no notice of history. The Logos is behind and beyond what appears important to human beings, but the Logos knows itself. That transcendent self-knowledge is the *fons et origo* of all the myriad rays of self-conscious, luminous intelligence focused at a certain level of complexity in what we call the human being, rays which, at the same time, light up the infinitude of points in space-time. As the Logos is unknown to differentiated species, and as *Parabrahm* is unknown to *Prakriti*, Eastern esotericism and the Kabbalah alike have resolved the abstract synthesis in relatively concrete images in order to bring the Logos within the range of human conception. We have images, therefore, such as that of the sun and the light, but there is freedom through concentration, abstraction and expansion, while there is bondage through consolidation, concretization and desecration. The Logos is like the sun through which light and heat radiate, but whose energy and light exist in some unknown condition in space and are diffused throughout space as visible light. If one meditates at noon on the invisible midnight sun, which sages reflect upon in a calm state of ceaseless contemplation, and if one remains still and serene, one could exercise the privilege of using the divine gift of sound. The sun itself is only the agent of the Light in *The Voice of the Silence*. This is the first triadic hypostasis. The Tetraktys is emanated by concentrating the energizing light shed by the Logos, but it subsists by itself in the Divine Darkness. A tremendous light-energy flows from the deepest thought, wherein one continuously voids every conception of the reflected ray of egoity or the individual self, all objects and universes, everything in what we call space and time. Thus the individuating mind enters subtler dimensions, through which it can approach universal cognition in a resplendent realm of noumenal reality, opening onto a shared field of total awareness in *Mahat*, wherein the self-consciousness of divine wisdom (*Vach*) is eternally enacted by self-luminous Mahatmas, the Brotherhood of Light.

The true teaching of Brahma Vach is enshrined in the secret code language of Nature. A new mode of initiation has already begun. Invisible beings in their *mayavi rupas* cherish the teaching, but no visible beings are entirely excluded. The quintessential teaching is conveyed in so many different ways that prepare for the sacred instructions in deep sleep, even for those struggling souls who seize their last chance in this life. The more any person can maintain during waking hours the self-conscious awareness of what is known deep within — even though one cannot formulate it — the more one can hold it and see it as blasphemous to speak thoughtlessly about it. Though such persons participate in all the fickle changes of the butterfly mind, the more attentively they can preserve and retain the seminal energy of thought with a conscious continuity, the more easily will every anxiety about themselves fade into a cool state of contentment. Like a shadow following the lost and stumbling seeker of the light, a true disciple will unexpectedly encounter the forgotten wisdom, the spiritual knowledge, springing up suddenly, spontaneously, within the very depths of his being. Then he may receive the crystalline waters of life-giving wisdom through the central conduit of light-energy, symbolized in the physical body by the spinal cord. One may walk in the world with deep gratitude for the sacred privilege of being a self-conscious Manasaputra within the divine temple of the universe for the sake of shedding light upon all that lives and breathes. In seeing, one can send out beneficent rays. In hearing, one can listen beyond the cacophony of the world. Whilst one is listening constantly to the music of the spheres echoing within one's head and heart, one is able to send forth thoughts and feelings that are benevolent and unconditional, extended towards all other human minds. These thoughts could become living talismans for the men and women of tomorrow in the fields of cognition wherein the war between light and darkness, the living and the dead, is now being waged.

The Philosophy of Perfection of Krishna, the Religion of Responsibility of the Buddha and the Science of Spirituality of Shankara, constitute the Pythagorean teaching of the Aquarian Age of Universal Enlightenment. There are general and interstitial relationships between the idea of perfectibility, the idea of gaining control over the mind, and the exalted conception of knowledge set forth in the eighteenth chapter of the *Gita*. To begin to apprehend these connections, one must first heed the mantramic injunction from *The Voice of the Silence:* "Strive with thy thoughts unclean before they overpower thee." Astonishingly, there was a moment in the sixties when millions became obsessed with instant enlightenment; fortunately, this is not true at present. Few people now seriously believe that they are going to die as perfected beings in this lifetime. This does not mean that the secret doctrines of the 1975 cycle are irrelevant to the ordinary man who, without false expectations, merely wants to finish his life with a modicum of fulfilment. All such seekers can benefit immensely from calmly meditating upon the *Sthitaprajna,* the Self-Governed Sage, the Buddhas of Perfection. This is the crux of Krishna's medicinal method in the *Gita.* He presents Arjuna with the highest ideal, simultaneously shows his difficulties and offers intensive therapy and compassionate counsel. This therapeutic mode continues until the ninth chapter, where Krishna says, "Unto thee who findeth no fault I will now make known this most mysterious knowledge, coupled with a realization of it, which having known thou shalt be delivered from evil." In the eighteenth chapter he conveys the great incommunicable secret — so-called because even when communicated it resides within the code language of Buddhic consciousness. The authors of all the great spiritual teachings like the *Gita, The Voice of the Silence* and *The Crest Jewel of Wisdom* knew that there is a deep mythic sense in which the golden verses can furnish only as much as a person's state of consciousness is ready to receive.

H.P. Blavatsky dedicated *The Voice of the Silence* to the few, to those who seek to become *lanoos*, true neophytes on the Path. Like Krishna, she gave a shining portrait of the man of meditation, the Teacher of Mankind. In chosen fragments from the *Book of the Golden Precepts*, the merciful warning is sounded at the very beginning: "These instructions are for those ignorant of the dangers of the lower IDDHI." In this age the consequences of misuse of psychic powers over many lives by millions of individuals have produced a holocaust — the harvest of terrible effects. Rigid justice rules the universe. Many human beings have gaping astral wounds and fear that there is only a tenuous connecting thread between their personal consciousness and the light of the higher nature. Human beings have long misused *Kriyashakti*, the power of visualization, and *Itchashakti*, the power of desire. Above all, they have misused the antipodal powers of knowledge, *Jnanashakti*, so that there is an awful abyss between men of so-called knowledge and men of so-called power. What is common to both is that their pretensions have already gone for naught, and therefore many have begun to some extent to sense the sacred orbit of the Brotherhood of Bodhisattvas. On the global plane we also witness today the tragic phenomenon of which *The Voice of the Silence* speaks. Many human beings did not strive with their unclean hobgoblin images of a cold war. The more they feared the hobgoblin, the more they became frozen in their conception of hope. Human beings can collectively engender a gigantic, oppressive elemental, like the idea of a personal God, or the Leviathan of the State, which is kept in motion by reinforcement through fear, becoming a kind of reality and producing a paralysis of the will on the global plane.

Today, for the first time in recent decades, we live at that fortunate moment when psychopathology and sociopathology have alike become boring, throwing the individual back upon his intuitions, dreams and secret intimations. Individuals cannot suddenly create refined vestures for the highest spiritual thought-energy, but they can at least desist from self-degradation. No protection a human being can devise is more potent or powerful than the arc of light around every human form. Any individual with unwavering faith in the divine is firmly linked with the ray descending into the hollow of the heart. One can totally reduce the shadowy self to a zero. The cipher may become a circle of sweetness and a sphere of light. It is imperative to keep faith with oneself in silence and secrecy, as every telling weakens the force that is generated. Krishna says, "In whatever way men approach me, in that way do I assist them." This is offered unconditionally to all. Near the end of his instruction he says, "Act as seemeth best unto thee."

Basic honesty will go far to clean out the cobwebs of delusion and confusion so that the seeds of spiritual regeneration may be salvaged. Patience is needed together with enduring trust in the healing and nurturing processes of Nature that protect the seeds silently germinating in the soil. They cannot be pulled up and scrutinized again and again, but must be allowed to sprout in the soft light of the dawn, enriched by the radiant magnetism of universal love which maintains the whole cosmos in motion. Even a little soul-memory shows that there is no need to blame history or Nature, much less the universe, for the universe is on the side of every sincere impulse. Even the most wicked and depraved man may have some hope. Even a little daily practice delivereth a man from great risk. Even a minute grain of soul-wisdom, when patiently assimilated with a proper mental posture in relation to the sacred teachings and the sacrificial Teachers, will act as a beneficent influence and an unfailing guide to the true servant of the Masters of the Verbum. This incommunicable secret of Krishna is the sweetest and most potent gift of the divine Logos of the cosmos to the awakened humanity of today and the global civilization of tomorrow.

CONTINUITY OF CONSCIOUSNESS

What does modern science know of the duration of the
ages of the World, or even of the length of geological periods?
Nothing; absolutely nothing. . . . Indeed, in the
Cimmerian darkness of the prehistoric ages, the explorers
are lost in a labyrinth, whose great corridors are doorless,
allowing no visible exit into the Archaic past. Lost in the
maze of their own conflicting speculations, rejecting, as they
have always done, the evidence of Eastern tradition, without
any clue, or one single certain milestone to guide them, what
can geologists or anthropologists do but pick up the slender
thread of Ariadne. . . . They are 'prehistoric' to the naked
eye of matter only. To the spiritual eagle eye of the seer and
the prophet of every race, Ariadne's thread stretches beyond
that 'historic period' without break or flaw, surely and
steadily, into the very night of time; and the hand which
holds it is too mighty to drop it, or even let it break.

The Secret Doctrine, ii 66-67

Ariadne's thread represents unbroken continuity of consciousness in the One Life. In relation to perception (*samvriti*) and knowledge (*prajna*), it stands for the principle of *Buddhi*, spiritual intuition, which by analogy and correspondence cuts through the maze of detail to the heart of the matter. Ariadne's thread is also the *sutratman*, the integrity of the immortal soul, the meta-psychological basis of individual awareness extending back over eighteen million years and serving as the storehouse of soul-memory (*anamnesis*). Through its capacity to tap *Akasha*, the universal empyrean upon which are recorded all the archetypal truths behind the mass of manifested projections, the immortal soul, by reference to its inherent wisdom, can recover the most illuminating continuity of consciousness. It can bridge apparent gaps on the physical plane — between days and nights, between seasons and years — and cross chasms between incarnations. Even more important, it can span the *pralayas,* the periods of obscuration between Races and Rounds. This timeless wisdom of the soul cannot be comprehended by the ratiocinative, rationalizing mind.

Through material evidence, sensory data and induction, it is possible to accumulate masses of information which may then be submitted to logical or methodological analysis. Thus one can infer conjectural estimates of the age of the sun and the moon, of the earth and man. But such inferences, however intriguing, shed no light upon the complex relationship between cosmic and human chronology. Even if one extends anthropological estimates of the age of man to a period of nearly twenty million years, as suggested in the late work of L.S.B. Leakey, one grasps no sense of what happened to humanity during those unchronicled years. And, seeing only fragments of the conscious life of humanity, it is nearly impossible to conceive of the humanity of the hoary past, and its vital relationship to the decisive lighting up of *Manas* over eighteen million years ago at the midpoint of the Fourth Round. With regard to more antique times and previous Rounds, empirical evidence that the physical earth and physical entities in space go back hundreds of millions of years reveals no helpful connections between all these enormously ancient relics and human evolution. In short, nearly nothing that is significant or definitive can be known about the primordial origins of conscious life through a reductionist methodology relying upon sensory evidence and inference from external shells and petrified astral deposits.

Instead of expecting such an unphilosophical methodology to assist in the recovery of universal continuity of consciousness, one must adopt a radically different approach, grounded in metaphysics. Employing a dialectical methodology analogous to the ontological process it seeks to apprehend, one must begin with persistent enquiry into the profound connection between the One and the many, the Logos and the Logoi. One must meditate upon phases of progressive manifestation, coming down from the most subjective level conceivable to the most objective visible level. This radical transformation of method requires introversion, a turning within the immortal soul. But, since external evidence is so incomplete and so inadequate to understanding millions of years of conscious life, and since at the same time it is immensely difficult to turn within, it may seem impossible to make much progress. Without seed thoughts for meditation, it may appear hopeless even to begin the enquiry. Yet, this is not true. It is merely a presumptive delusion arising from the protracted hubris of Western nations, which, out of habitual ignorance of other languages, simply have not seriously considered the calendars and chronologies of ancient Indian, Chinese and other cultures. As H.P. Blavatsky repeatedly and forcefully affirmed a century ago, one must revert to time-honoured Eastern sources even to make sense of what may be sporadically inferred from physical evidence.

Paradoxically, despite the pioneering efforts of intrepid thinkers in the latter part of the nineteenth century in philology and phonetics connected with the entire stock of Indo-European languages, there has been subsequently an enormous shrinkage of chronologies in reference to Eastern civilizations. The balance has been redressed somewhat, in reference to China, largely through the work of Joseph Needham over the past thirty years. More recently, Jawaharlal Nehru, in his remarkable *The Discovery of India,* observes that there are five times as many books on India in the London Library as on China. Many were written by nineteenth-century Englishmen who confidently explored such various topics as the early relationship between India and Mediterranean civilization, the parental connection between Sanskrit and other languages, and the suggestive similarities between the oldest forms of architecture in India and architectural forms which later became prominent in Gothic Europe and throughout the Middle East.

Whilst many of these authors were overwhelmed with admiration by what they discovered over a lifetime — when not blinded by religious bigotry — they nonetheless could not recognize the continuing relevance of the ancient Indian records. This resistance arose either because they did not have free access to them and also to accurate Brahminical explanations, or because they were obsessed by the supposed primacy of Greek civilization. Now, all of this has been exploded, and anyone with a lively sense of karma can appreciate the appropriateness of atonement for past ingratitude. When modern Europeans came in contact with the much older and essentially noble civilization of India, and found elements far more ancient than Egyptian relics, something went clearly wrong with xenophobic assumptions and even with regard to 'scholarly' dating. *The Discovery of India* invaluably demonstrates that many Europeans, even before the twentieth century, had traced the origins of major elements of Western civilization to ancient India. Despite their discomfort in proceeding to the fullest conclusions, they established the necessity of taking Eastern records seriously.

It is no wonder, then, that H.P. Blavatsky took the trouble in *The Secret Doctrine* to spell out certain details of ancient Indian and Brahminical calendars and chronologies. Before specifying exact figures, she remarked:

> The best and most complete of all such calendars, at present, as vouched for by the learned Brahmins of Southern India, is the . . . Tamil calendar called the 'Tirukkanda Panchanga', compiled, as we are told, from, and in full accordance with, secret fragments of Asuramaya's data. As Asuramâya is said to have been the greatest astronomer, so he is whispered to have also been the most powerful 'Sorcerer' of the 'WHITE ISLAND', which had become BLACK with sin,' *i.e.*, of the islands of Atlantis. . . . He was an Atlantean; but he was a direct descendant of the *Wise Race, the Race that never dies*. Many are the legends concerning this hero, the pupil of Surya (the Sun-God) himself, as the Indian accounts allege.
>
> *The Secret Doctrine*, ii 67

According to this calendar, 1,955,884,687 years had elapsed between the beginning of evolution on Globe A of the earth chain in the First Round and the year 1887. It also located the manvantaric period of astral evolution in the sub-human kingdoms, and distinguished it from the subsequent period after the appearance of incipient 'humanity' on the earth chain. H.P. Blavatsky cited certain puzzles connected with the internal figures in this Tamil calendar, and also contrasted it with other orthodox Hindu calendars. As she explained both here and elsewhere, these riddles develop because esoteric figures cannot be revealed outside initiation. She then proceeded to present a simpler schema computed by P. Sreenivas Row, which begins with a single mortal day and extends all the way to the Age of Brahmā. The telling significance of these figures is that they show that abundant knowledge is available, not only in the inaccessible cave libraries of the Kunlun Range, but also in calendars in common use in South India today, which could be employed as the basis of study. To understand this, one needs something more than a knowledge of mathematics: the method of analogy and correspondence.

Sanskrit and what is now called Tamil are *reliquiae* of ante-Diluvian and ante-Poseidonian languages. In them critical terms like *kalpa* and Manu have a depth of occult symbolism which can only be grasped by taking them as generic terms applicable to the large and to the small and to many diverse levels of manifestation. This plasticity of meaning affords some protection to those who made these figures available but wanted to hold back certain clues that could, in the hands of unprepared human beings, become dangerous. At the same time, because of the generic nature of these words, one can understand by analogy and correspondence that what pertains to the vast *Mahakalpa* also applies to the *kalpa* in the small. What applies to a hundred years of Brahmā applies to one day of Brahmā and also to the much smaller period of a *Mahayuga*.

All of this poses a formidable challenge to the intuition and provides a great deal of food for thought and meditation.

Working by analogy and correspondence with various sets of figures, myriad applications may be made not only on the vast scale of cosmic evolution, but equally on the minute scales of days, hours and minutes. For example, H.P. Blavatsky cited the views set forth by Dr. Laycock in *Lancet* regarding the universal applicability of septenary cycles of days and weeks to all animal life, from the ovum of an insect up to man, and affecting all their vital functions, including birth, growth, maturity, disease, decay and death.

> Dr. Laycock divides life by *three great septenary periods;* the first and last, each stretching over 21 years, and the central period or prime of life lasting 28 years, or four times seven. He subdivides the first into *seven distinct stages,* and the other two into *three* minor periods, and says that 'The fundamental unit of the greater periods is *one week of seven days, each day being twelve hours';* and that 'single and compound *multiples* of this unit, determine the length of these periods by the same ratio, as multiples of the unit of twelve hours determine the lesser periods. *This law binds all periodic vital phenomena together, and links the periods observed in the lowest annulose animals, with those of man himself, the highest of the vertebrata.'* If *Science* does this, why should the latter scorn the Occult information, namely that (speaking Dr. Laycock's language) *'one week* of the manvantaric *(lunar)* fortnight, of fourteen days (or seven manus), that fortnight of twelve hours in a day representing seven periods or seven races — is now passed'? This language of science fits our doctrine admirably.
>
> *Ibid.,* 623

Anyone who tentatively explores such mysterious connections between numbers and daily life begins to touch the Ariadne's thread of the immortal soul. Exactly how this is done and what its effect will be depends upon one's motivation and the tropism of one's soul. Some, ill at ease with the shrunken categories of modern science, yet enthralled with the sky, the planets and the galaxies, may be able to discern intuitive connections which inspire them in their dreams and activate their soul-memory. Others, who tend to think philosophically and metaphysically, may find that such enquiries arouse a hunger for meditation, which in turn helps them to see the archetypal logic of these processes. At the very least, such enquiries will yield an enormous sense of freedom from all that limits the horizons of human thought, all that constrains the reach of the human imagination. Once the imagination is freed, one can make one's own discoveries, through myth and symbol, and express them, through poetry or otherwise. The core discovery strengthened by all this enquiry is a sense of kinship, not only with all humanity and all past civilization, but also with the flora and fauna of the earth, and ultimately the living cosmos in its entirety.

The recovery of continuity of consciousness and the reawakening of soul-memory are central to *The Secret Doctrine*. These cannot emerge except through devotion and gratitude, and through preparing oneself to sit at the feet of real Gurus. Hence, H.P. Blavatsky's repeated insistence that the West must relinquish its adolescent egotism; hence, too, her constant recurrence to the figure of the Arhat, the perfected man, the Adept and Initiate. Before one can recover continuity of consciousness in the *sutratman*, one must acknowledge the existence not only of soul-memory but also of perfected sages, souls free from the illusion of time and able to witness vast periods of evolution as ordinary human beings watch moments. For the Mahatma, Ariadne's thread stretches in unbroken continuity and total wakefulness beyond the manifestation of this world and into the night of *pralaya* and beyond.

The highest ideal in the Brotherhood of Bodhisattvas is to gain a sense of continuity with the substratum of reality that persists even when there are no worlds, but only the night of non-manifestation. By plumbing the depths of that night, even beyond the night of time, Buddhas and Bodhisattvas find a freedom and detachment that enables them to see worlds and aeons through an instantaneous flash of Buddhic light. What the perfected human being can do in fullness every human being can attempt, if he or she will practise the toughest of all kinds of mental asceticism — turning a deaf ear to the conventional unwisdom of the exoteric world whilst remaining constantly attentive to every source of potential learning. To release this oceanic sense of universal continuity, one should turn to the sky and the stars, to the poets and the prophets.

To trace Ariadne's thread across incarnations, much less *pralayas* affecting Races and Rounds, requires the tremendous courage that can come only through systematic meditation. This inner discipline is not merely one activity amongst others, capriciously undertaken. It is, rather, the basis for awakening the powers of discrimination of different levels of composition or aggregation, of reduction, reabsorption and dissolution. The mastery of these processes, which takes place within the subtle vestures and is centered on the *karana sharira*, has a direct relationship with the alternation of *manvantara* and *pralaya*. Broadly, the septenary Teachings of Gupta Vidya concerning the seven planes of matter and seven states of consciousness have a general reference to all systems within the cosmos. The Teachings also have a more specific reference to the solar system and a primary focus for humanity on this earth. Humanity, circling round the seven globes, finds itself in the Fourth Round on Globe D, the most material of the terrestrial spheres. This globe is preceded by three ethereal globes and succeeded by three globes which are also ethereal but represent a more evolved state of consciousness. In the present fourth life-wave, occupying millions upon millions of years in its circuit through the seven globes, humanity finds itself evolving through a sevenfold series of vestures that are adapted to matter as it exists in this system. Having attained self-consciousness over eighteen million years ago, in the middle of the Third Root Race, and now belonging to the Fifth Sub-Race of the Fifth Root Race, it still must experience many periods of relative activity and rest before arriving at the close of the present Round.

The most immediately relevant shift in the basis of active manifestation applicable to humanity in general is the gradual transition from the Fifth to the Sixth Sub-Races of the Fifth Root Race. Because the Law of periodicity is universal, this transition cannot take place without a pralayic dissolution of aspects of the human vestures and their subsequent remanifestation in a transformed mode. Whatever the subtle consequences of this significant change on the four lower planes, the essential locus of this transmutation is in the fifth and sixth principles of human nature — *Manas* and *Buddhi*. Hence, the meaning and magnitude of the present transformation cannot be apprehended from any standpoint bound up with the lower quaternary, but only from within the Manasic principle of self-consciousness through its meditative attunement to *Buddhi*. Otherwise, the apparent *pralaya* of contemporary civilizations, as well as the promise and potential of an incipient golden age, cannot be comprehended.

The teachings of Gupta Vidya with regard to *manvantara* and *pralaya* are meant to be studied not merely out of intellectual interest or philosophic curiosity. They are intended for those who truly seek to become *yogins*: those who, by daily meditation, daily self-study and the daily renunciation of the fruits of action, seek self-consciously to bring about profound changes in their subtle vestures consonant with the present phase of evolution. Through the spiritual discipline of concentration, they aim at making the astral form coherent, and the mind controlled. In the context of such a regenerative discipline, the radical difference between psychic action — which works at the level of the molecular and the structural — and noetic action — which works at the level of the atomic — is vital. Here the term 'atomic' refers to that which is even more rudimentary than what science calls atomic or even subatomic. This cannot be apprehended unless a person experiences self-consciously the progressive refinement of magnetism, involving sub-hierarchies of colour and sound and yielding a percipient awareness of the most minute subdivisions of various classes of elementals.

The basic distinction between the psychic and the noetic applies not only to all the elements, but also to thoughts, and indeed to everything perceptible at any level of form. Through deep meditation, one may awaken the capacity to touch that golden Buddhic potency which is in everything, and thus bring about a beneficent alchemical transubstantiation. But one must first have attained to such a degree of disinterestedness that one can consciously assist and accelerate the processes of change, quickening the process of dispersion. Through meditation one must learn to cooperate intelligently with the atomic noetic potential of the higher Triad in a pralayic process of continuous dispersion and dissolution, refusing to allow any recoalescence of that which is dying, so as to sustain continuity of consciousness into that which is being born.

Unfortunately, through possessiveness, through enormous thirst for sensation, through reassertion of *ahankara* — the drives inherent in the Fourth Round, whose dominant principle is *kama* — most humans tend to solidify, to concretize the moribund residues of the past. This is analogous to the physical process, whereby creatures that lived in previous, more ethereal Rounds leave behind them fossils, concretized residues. If this process of consolidation applies to all the life-atoms that make up the astral form in its aspects linked to the physical body, it is also relevant to the subtler states of the astral vesture. To understand and assist the corresponding process of perpetual dissolution, or *nitya pralaya,* is to engage in a kind of letting go, that continual practice of dying which Plato depicts in *Phaedo* as central to the life of the true philosopher. Conscious and continuous dispersion of all the elements is inseparable from an equal sensitivity to constant and perpetual creation, or *nitya sarga,* the invisible creation at the primary causal level of Nature which continually maintains the universe in motion. Taken together, *nitya pralaya* and *nitya sarga* are complementary aspects of the Great Breath. Meditation upon *pralaya* and *manvantara,* dissolution and creation, is linked with mastering spiritual and mental breathing. This involves not only their rhythm but also their attunement to the subtlest level of cosmic breathing.

The profound Teaching regarding *nitya pralaya* and *nitya sarga*, like everything else connected with spiritual self-transformation and self-regeneration, cannot be consciously applied unless one learns to work in terms of cycles of seven and fourteen years. One must prepare for that stage by thinking out to the core who one is, why one is alive, what one truly wants, and what it is one is prepared to live for. This requires a careful preparation in detachment, as well as the courage to face and fully accept one's karmic responsibilities in the realm of dharma. These are the prerequisites of discipleship and practical occultism. Merely by thinking upon these ideas, individuals can tap soul-knowledge in relation to past lives, wherein this knowledge was direct and active. If a person is sufficiently compassionate, suffused with an authentic concern for the welfare of all that lives, determined to be vitally helpful to humanity in some future life — ten lives or a hundred lives from now — then he or she can sufficiently prepare for occult training by coming to understand now that which will come to one's aid at the moment of death. This self-conscious strengthening of the sutratmic thread will enhance the moment of birth in the next life, easing entry early in that life into the Bodhisattvic current.

In the nineteenth century H.P. Blavatsky sought to assure those who had retired from productive lives that even in old age they might prepare their mental luggage for the next life. Today many suffer from impetuosity rather than procrastination. Through weak wills, frustrated ambitions or fearful eschatologies, they are resolved to do everything quickly or not at all. This is mental laziness, as well as a futile attempt at moral blackmail directed against the universe. Instead of such self-destructive cowardice, one should strive to be fearless in the metaphysical imagination, and dwell on the highest conceptions. One should be ready to look up to the boundless sky whilst addressing one's obligations on earth. Holding fast to a serene rhythm of selfless devotion, one should develop an ethical sensitivity to others, whilst maintaining an alert attentiveness to one's own obligations. One must refine a sense of balance, soaring to the empyrean in meditation, whilst controlling the quotidian details of ethical involvement. Thus metaphysics and ethics may be brought together, to create a steady, strong current of fervent aspiration. Thus too, the process of dissolution is quickened, the potential for continuous creation increased. By letting go, one cooperates with nature's archetypal rhythms.

Beyond these cyclic transformations lies the Triad of absolute abstract Space, Duration and Motion, the metaphysical basis for all continuity of consciousness. All three may be seen as aspects of the Three-in-One, expanding the conceptions of matter, time and motion into primordial substance, boundless eternity and divine thought. It is also helpful to concentrate on absolute abstract Motion as the One Life. This has a philosophical bearing upon one's notions of relative degrees of reality and unreality, of emptiness and illusion, of dependence and causality. The One Life comprises both light and electricity in all their cosmic manifestations and is equivalent to the universal soul or Anima Mundi. In Sanskrit it is the *Jivatman*, the analogue of the Platonic *nous* or mundane cosmic intelligence, absolutely free from differentiated matter and ever-designing action. Through the invocation of the *Jivatman*, the ever-pulsating life-principle, infinite and all-transcendent, Aryan philosophy addresses itself to that perpetual motion which is beyond the distinction between consciousness and unconsciousness. Only in relation to a field of manifestation, relative to *Mahat* in *manvantara* and *pralaya*, can one speak of that which is conscious, self-conscious or unconscious. So entirely does *Jivatman* transcend all human conception that it may as well be spoken of as absolute unconsciousness as absolute consciousness.

If the One Life or *Jivatman* is beyond all these distinctions, this implies that absolute and abstract continuity of consciousness has nothing to do with the purposes and processes of manifestation. It could, for example, be confusing to speak as Hegel does of the Absolute seeking to attain self-consciousness, or, in Hindu terms, of *Parabrahm* having some motive in manifestation. The notion of pure being or absolute consciousness admits of no contrast or polarity, and can participate in no relativities whatsoever. Nor can it have anything to do with the infinite extension of any attribute of finite manifestation (even so subtle an attribute of manifestation as thought, which necessarily presupposes the differentiation of a field and its perceiver). If, then, one is going to meditate upon universal life as a boundless ocean of energy without frontier or finite purpose, one must be freed of all binding conceptions and limiting teleologies, and even all thought bound up with mental instantiation in time. One of the Rishis likened the Reality apprehended in *pralaya* to the depths of a boundless ocean of ceaseless energy.

In that fathomless divine abyss, everything is potential, but as a formless and fundamental rhythm or pulsation without reference to any worlds or to manifestation itself. It cannot be understood in relation to the absence of worlds. It is neither definable through affirmation nor through negation, neither through instantiation nor through privation. Cyclic or periodic existence, on the other hand, involves changes of form and state. Archetypally, this may be understood in terms of the potential of the seed, which gestates, then sprouts, then, as a tree with branches and limbs, bears in turn a myriad seeds. On an abstract level, this entire process contains an intrinsic reference to form and matter as it appears to minds that perceive it, and therefore, also a reference to variations of states of perceptive consciousness. These contrasts within manifested matter and consciousness are essential to cyclic existence but in no way characterize the impartite and boundless Reality beyond manifestation.

To every cycle there is a mayavic element, a veiling of that which is indestructible and entirely unaffected by transformation. The life potency that is in the seed in essence is a reflection of something on the Akashic plane unaffected by the seed's sprouting. Some beings on this plane may worry whether seeds sprout, but in terms of the essence, the sprouting is of no significance. Once this idea is grasped, one can begin to understand how it is possible, through perception of formless spiritual essences, to change one's perspective in reference to any cycle or to relate the phases of one cycle to another. One may, for example, relate the seven days of the week to the seven planets, and both to the seven phases of human life. Thus one may discern both sequence and possibility, whilst stripping certain cycles of a portion of their limitation. The ability to do this at will depends upon the extent to which one's consciousness is freed from the clutches of *kama manas,* desire, time and sensation. When the ray of the *Jivatman* is emancipated from the bondage of change, it can experience the universal pulsation of its omnipresent source. Thus it is possible to create a certain 'negative capability', in the Keatsian sense, a capacity for awareness of the unmanifest side of Nature. The greater this capacity, the more one can correct the natural tendency within incarnation of being caught up in the results and rancours of yesterday, today or tomorrow.

Authentic continuity of consciousness consists of unbroken self-conscious experience of the universality of the life-process, enjoying and relishing its unity amidst all the diversity. It is the ability to trace the Ariadne's thread of the One Life in all the seven kingdoms of nature amidst all the multitudinous forms, whilst at the same time reverencing it at its very root in a realm that is beyond manifestation, beyond the realm of form, exempt from change, undivided by subject and object. The purpose of all study of the sacred and secret science is to gain this freedom for the imagination and this depth for meditation, so that one may become better able to see to the core, and better able to discard that which obscures the Monadic spark. In practice, this means elevating, through daily discipline, one's ethical nature to the same level as one's metaphysical imagination.

One must reach a point where one's only desire or wish is on behalf of the whole, and where one's celebration of all human beings in one's own silent meditation is so real and so joyous that the boundaries of selfhood are shattered. Too often, the two wings of metaphysics and ethics are unbalanced, and spiritual aspirants find that they cannot convert metaphysics into magic. They lack the strength of mind and heart to void their sense of egoity and enclose all humanity within the vast continuity of universal self. Hence, the exercise of the metaphysical imagination must be strengthened daily through meditation, in the midst of the therapeutic practice of self-study and the cheerful performance of dharma. When ethics and metaphysics retain a durable continuity, and flow with a graceful balance, they can be synthesized, to awaken Buddhimanasic wisdom and the soul-memory of the *sutratman*. Drawing upon that wisdom and sacrificing all strivings at its universal fire, one can make the requisite changes in consciousness, in the substance of the subtle vestures, and in one's magnetic field, so as to become effortless in the continual self-conscious enactment of the AUM.

NOETIC SELF-DETERMINATION

If the general law of the conservation of energy leads modern science to the conclusion that psychic activity only represents a special form of motion, this same law, guiding the Occultists, leads them also to the same conviction — and to something else besides, which psycho-physiology leaves entirely out of all consideration. If the latter has discovered only in this century that psychic (we say even spiritual) action is subject to the same general and immutable laws of motion as any other phenomenon manifested in the objective realm of Kosmos, and that in both the organic and the inorganic (?) *worlds every manifestation, whether conscious or unconscious, represents but the result of a collectivity of causes, then in Occult philosophy this represents merely the ABC of its science. . . .*

But Occultism says more than this. While making of motion on the material plane *and of the conservation of energy two fundamental laws, or rather two aspects of the same omnipresent law — Swara — it denies point blank that these have anything to do with the* free will *of man which belongs to quite a different plane.*

"Psychic and Noetic Action"   H.P. Blavatsky

Gupta Vidya, the philosophy of perfectibility, is based upon the divine dialectic, which proceeds through progressive universalization, profound synthesis and playful integration. These primary principles are inseparably rooted in the cosmogonic archetypes and patterns of universal unity and causation. They are in sharp contrast to the expedient and evasive methodology of much contemporary thought which all too often proceeds on the basis of Aristotelian classification, statistical analysis and a sterile suspicion of intuitive insight. Whatever the karmic factors in the ancient feud between these divergent streams of thought, it is poignantly evident that their polar contrast becomes insuperable when it comes to understanding human nature. Gupta Vidya views the human situation in the light of the central conception of an immortal individuality capable of infinite perfectibility in its use of opaque and transitory vestures. The greater the degree of understanding attained of Man and Nature, the greater the effective realization of spiritual freedom and self-mastery.

In the methodology of modern thought, the more sharply its conceptions are formulated, the more inexorably it is driven to a harsh dilemma: it must either secure the comprehension of Nature at the cost of a deterministic conception of Man, or it must surrender the notions of order and causality in favour of statistical indeterminacy and randomness in Nature, thereby voiding all human action of meaning. Gupta Vidya not only dispels this dilemma, but it also explains the propensity to fall prey to it, through the arcane conception of two fundamental modes of mental activity. These were set forth by H.P. Blavatsky as "psychic" and "noetic" action. They refer to much more than 'action' in any ordinary sense, and really represent two distinct, though related, modes of self-conscious existence. They provide the prism through which the perceptive philosopher can view the complex and enigmatic relationship between human freedom and universal causality. All creative change and all dynamic activity in the universe are understood, in the perennial philosophy of Gupta Vidya, as spontaneous expressions of one abstract, pre-cosmic source symbolized as the Great Breath. In its highest ranges this is Spirit, and beneath that, it encompasses every mode of motion down to and including action on the physical plane.

> Motion as the GREAT BREATH (vide "Secret Doctrine", vol. i, sub voce) — ergo 'sound' at the same time — is the substratum of Kosmic-Motion. It is beginningless and endless, the one eternal life, the basis and genesis of the subjective and the objective universe;

> for LIFE (or Be-ness) is the *fons et origo* of existence or
> being. But molecular motion is the lowest and most
> material of its finite manifestations.
> "Psychic and Noetic Action"   H.P. BLAVATSKY

Several important consequences follow from this single origin of
both subjective and objective reality. For example, the strict unity
and universal causality implied by the conception of absolute
abstract Motion entail the basic principle transmitted from ancient
knowledge into modern science as the law of the conservation of
energy. In a world of finite manifestations, such as that of
molecular motion, this law has immense importance. The
conception of entropy is an allied principle equally crucial in
understanding the particularized motions and relationships
between objects having specific kinds of energy in the world as
we know it. Yet this does not really reveal much about the deeper
sense in which there is collection and concentration of energy,
from the highest *laya* state down through the physical plane of
manifestation. There is a sense in which enormous energy is held
waiting to be released from higher to lower planes. Potential
energy, related to the higher aspects of the ceaseless motion of
the One Life, transcends all empirical conceptions based upon
observable phenomena.

This virtually inconceivable scale of modes of subtle
manifestation of the Great Breath has immediate and evident
implications in regard to cosmogony. But it is also highly
significant when applied to the subjective side of conscious
existence. Whilst the laws of physical motion and energy are
natural modes of manifestation of that divine Breath, no merely
objective description of them can do justice to the *subjective* side
of purely physical events, much less to deeper layers of human
consciousness and noumenal reality. Every plane or octave of
manifest existence has both its subjective and objective side, even
as every plane has its own dual aspect of activity that may variously
be seen as more gross or more subtle, more concrete or more
abstract. This vertical dimension of existence is often spoken of

as the distinction between the subjective and the objective, though this is quite a different sense of these terms from the lateral distinction applied to any particular plane. The tendency to confuse or conflate these two senses of the subjective-objective distinction is in direct proportion to the grossness or concreteness of an individual's state of consciousness. Insofar as an individual's range of consciousness is limited to constellations of objects, persons and events, it will not be capable of comprehending the notions of metaphysical subjectivity or objectivity, or of metaphysical depth.

This is crucial when considering the seemingly abrupt transition from medieval to modern thought accompanying the movement away from a vastly inflated, but exceedingly particularized, conception of the subjective realm towards an almost obsessive concern with physical objectivity. As the capricious happenings and hearsay of the 'age of miracles' were gradually replaced by a rigid conception of external and mechanical order, it increasingly came to be understood that the inner life of man must also conform to universal laws. In what was a marked advance upon earlier notions of both physics and psychology, there emerged, in the nineteenth century, the explosive recognition that everything in the psychological realm is also subject to causality. This was powerfully put forward as part of a grandiose ethical scheme by George Godwin, the philosophical anarchist. Late in the nineteenth century several social scientists argued that if causality is to be applied to all phenomenal events and processes, it must also apply in some way to the world of what may be called psychic action. It must, in short, be applicable to all the states of mind experienced by human beings in bodies with brains.

It thus becomes vitally important to draw a clear-cut distinction between the mind and the brain, taking account of the subjective and objective aspects of both. In general, contemporary science has been either unwilling or unable to do this. Without this essential distinction, however, it is impossible to generate any firm basis for the notions of autonomy, self-determination, individuality, free thinking and potent ideation. Arcane philosophy begins at that precise point where an abyss has been discovered between the mind and brain. It is indeed a glaring gap, for though causality applies to both, it is difficult to discern clearly what the relationship could be between them, let alone to find exact correlates between the two parts of the distinction in terms of specific centres and elements. Without the assured ability to distinguish decisively between them, the temptation is great to deny free will altogether and succumb to a reductionistic and mechanistic view of human nature. This the occultist and theurgist must deny, in theory and in practice.

> The actual fact of man's psychic (we say *manasic* or noetic) *individuality* is a sufficient warrant against the assumption; for in the case of this conclusion being correct, or being indeed . . . the *collective hallucination of the whole mankind throughout the ages*, there would be an end also to psychic individuality. Now by 'psychic' individuality we mean that self-determining power which enables man to override circumstances.
>
> *Ibid.*

All human beings have some experience not only of a persisting sense of individuality, but also of an ineradicable sense of being able to separate themselves from an observable objective field. They have a deep sense of being able to affect it consciously, and indeed even to control it. To dismiss so vital and universal an experience would be to betray a narrow, pseudo-philosophical prejudice towards mechanistic determinism. Not even all animals have precisely the same stimuli or reactions. Certainly, human beings in very similar environments respond quite differently to external stimuli. One cannot deny, then, that a human being can make a vital difference to his environment through his calm appraisal of it, or even through simply comparing or sharply contrasting it with something else. Either through the fugitive sense of memory or through the fervent thrill of anticipation, based upon a relaxed sense of identity projected into the past and the future, or even through heightened perceptions of the unsuspected relations between one's own circumstances and those of other beings, individuals make decisive choices among newly discovered alternatives. So long as they can ask probing questions about the degree to which they can possibly alter their mental outlook, they can truly determine for themselves, through these subtle changes of attitudes, their untapped ability to alter these circumstances.

In general, such attitudes may be rather passive or defiantly resistant to circumstances. But they may also include an intelligent acceptance of circumstances rooted in a capacity for conscious cooperation with necessity. One may completely transform one's environment through rearranging elements in it, through constructive dialogue with other agents and, above all, through an inner life of daily meditation and effortless self-transcendence. Thus free will can function, and so unfold a unitary consciousness coolly capable of deft self-determination. Having understood all this, the main challenge is to come to a clear comprehension of the self-determining power in man and, more specifically, to understand the delicate operation of the diverse faculties of the mind in the compelling context of universal causality. In this regard, the shrewd argument of George T. Ladd concerning mental faculties is crucial. Having contended that the phenomena of human consciousness must require a subject in the form of a real being, manifested immediately to itself in the phenomena of consciousness, he proceeded to consider how that real being perceives its relationship to the activity of consciousness.

> To it the mental phenomena are to be attributed as showing what it *is* by what it *does*. The so-called mental 'faculties' are only the *modes of the behaviour* in consciousness of this real being. We actually find, by the only method available, that this real being called Mind believes in certain perpetually recurring modes: therefore, we attribute to it certain faculties. . . . Mental faculties are not entities that have an existence of themselves. . . . They

are the modes of the behaviour in consciousness of the
mind.

Ibid.

In other words, Ladd denied that one can comprehend the real
being, or unit consciousness, exclusively through those recurring
modes that are associated with certain 'faculties'. Just as one
would find the idea of a unit being, in this metaphysical
monadology, incompatible with crude physical behaviourism, it
is also incompatible with psycho-physical and psychological
behaviourism. Put another way, the inherent power of Manasic
'I-am-I' consciousness transcends all patterns such as those which
inhere in the volatile *skandhas*. The human being can consciously
transcend all behaviour patterns. He can readily transform
anything through tapping his inherent powers of volition and
ideation. Ladd then concluded:

> The subject of all the states of consciousness is a
> real unit-being, called Mind; which is of non-material
> nature, and acts and develops according to laws of its
> own, but is specially correlated with certain material
> molecules and masses forming the substance of the
> Brain.
>
> *Ibid.*

Full understanding of these laws, mastery over action and the
capacity to coordinate the mind and brain can come only from a
strong intention to attain these ends, together with a purgation
of one's entire field. One cannot work with incompatible mixtures,
which are inevitably explosive. One cannot infuse the potency of
the noetic mind into the polluted psyche. One must purge and
purify the psyche before it can absorb the higher current of
transformation which is alchemical and fundamentally noetic.

The question then becomes how, in practice, one can readily
recognize the subtle difference between an illusory sense of
freedom and a real and valid sense of self-determination. Insofar
as people are misled by everyday language and by fleeting sense-

perceptions, and insofar as they have an associationist picture of mixed memories and indelible images, rendering them essentially passive in relation to mental and emotional states, they may totally fail to see that all these familiar states fall under laws of causality. They may also be unable to make significant noetic connections. Based upon luminous perceptions of noetic connections, one must learn to see their causal chains and calmly project possible consequences of persisting patterns tomorrow, next year and in the future. One must then take full responsibility for the future consequences of participation in connected patterns. The moment one recognizes and perceives significant connections, one will see that at different times one could have made a distinct difference by the way in which one reacted, by the degree of sensitivity one showed, and by the degree of self-criticism one applied to these states. The moment a human being begins to ask 'why', he demands meaning from experience and rejects uncritical acceptance or mere passivity towards anything in life, including the recognizable sequence in which mental phenomena manifest.

Through this noetic capacity to question the association and the succession of events, one can decisively alter patterns. One can thus move from an initial level of passivity to a degree of free will whilst, in the act of seeing connections and making correlations, raising questions and altering patterns. Given the Buddhist doctrine of *skandhas,* or the Hindu doctrine of *samskaras,* each personality collects, over a lifetime, persisting associated tendencies. These persisting tendencies of thought and character are reinforced by appropriate emotions, desires and habits. Hence, the mere making of sporadic alterations in the inherited pattern of tendencies will be a poor example of free will, since over a longer period of time the pattern itself is conditioned by certain basic assumptions.

To take a simple example, as long as the will to live is strong and persistent, there is a sense in which free will is illusory. One lacks the fundamental capacity to make significant changes in one's *skandhas* or personality. This is an expression of *prarabdha* karma, the karma with which one has begun life. It is already reflected in one's particular body, one's mind, one's emotions, character and personality — and, indeed, in one's established relationship to a specific heredity and environment. This is part of the karma one cannot alter easily from within. Though these ideas go far beyond anything that is conceived in ordinary behaviouristic psychology, it is vital that the complex notion of free will be raised to a higher level, making greater demands and requiring more fundamental changes in one's way of life and outlook. It is precisely at this point that the distinction between psychic and noetic action becomes crucial. One must understand the locus in consciousness of the incipient power of free will, and then distinguish this from the fundamental source of will which lies entirely outside the sphere of the personality and the field of *prarabdha karma*, *skandhas* and *samskaras*. Speaking of Ladd's conception of mind as the real unit being that is the subject of all states of consciousness, H. P. Blavatsky commented:

> This 'Mind' is *manas*, or rather its lower reflection, which whenever it disconnects itself, for the time being, with *kama*, becomes the guide of the highest mental faculties, and is the organ of the free will in physical man.
>
> *Ibid.*

Whereas *Manas* itself is noetic, and signifies what could be called the spiritual individuality, there is also that which may be called the psychic individuality — this same *Manas* in association with *kama*, or desire. This projected ray of *Manas* itself has a capacity, though intermittent, for a kind of free will. Consider a human being who is completely caught up in chaotic desires and who is extremely uncritical in relation to his experiences, his tastes, his likes — in short, to his self-image. Even that kind of person will have moments of disengagement from emotion and a relative freedom from desire. In such moments of limited objectivity the person may see what is otherwise invisible. He may see alternatives, recognize degrees, glimpse similarities and differences from other human beings in similar situations; gradually, he may sense the potential for self-determination. Even lower *Manas*, when it is disconnected from *kama*, can exercise free will, giving guidance to the mental faculties that make up the personality. This limited application of free will, however, is obviously quite different from full self-determination. The projected ray of *Manas* is the basis of the psychic nature and potentially the organ of free will in physical man. *Manas* itself is the basis of the higher self-conscious will, which has no special organ, but is capable, independent of the brain and personality, of functioning on its own. This noetic individuality is distinct from the projected ray of lower *Manas*, which is its organ, and distinct too from the physical brain and body, which are the organs of the psychic lower *Manas*. This source of spiritual will is characterized in the *Bhagavad Gita* as the *kshetrajna*, higher *Manas*, the silent Spectator, which is the voluntary sacrificial victim of all the mistakes and misperceptions of its projected ray.

The contrast between the silent Spectator and the despotic lower *Manas* explains the difference between the psychic and the noetic. Wherever there is an assertion of the egotistic will, there is an exaggeration of the astral shadow and an intensification of *kama manas*. When the projected ray of *Manas* becomes hard and cold, it tends to become parasitic upon others, taking without returning, claiming without thanking, continuously scheming without scruples. Ultimately, this not only produces a powerful *kamarupa*, but also puts one on the path towards becoming an apprentice *dugpa* or black magician. The *dugpa* or sorcerer works through coercive imposition of combative will. It accommodates nothing compassionate or sacrificial, no hint or suggestion of the supreme state of calm. This suggests a practical test in one's self-study. If one is becoming more wilful, one is becoming more and more caught up in lower psychic action. One's astral body is becoming inflamed, fattened and polluted, and one is losing one's flickering connection with the divine and silent Spectator. This is a poor way of living and ageing, a pathetic condition. If, on the other hand, one is becoming humbler and more responsive to others, more non-violent, less assertive and more open to entering into the relative reality of other beings, loosening and letting go the sense of separateness, one is becoming a true apprentice upon the path of renunciation, the path of benevolent magic. The altruistic use of noetic wisdom, true theurgy, is the teaching of Gupta Vidya.

The silent Spectator is capable of thinking and ideating on its own. It is capable of disengaging altogether from lower *Manas*, just as lower *Manas* can disengage from *kama*. This skilful process of disengagement is similar to what Plato conveys through Socrates in *Phaedo* and also in the *Apology*. It is a process of consciously dying, which the philosopher practises every moment, every day. By dying unto this world, one can increasingly disengage from the will to live, the *tanha* of the astral and physical body. It is possible by conscious spiritual exercises for the individual progressively to free higher *Manas* from its lower Manasic limitations, projections, excuses, evasions and habits. It can come into its own, realizing in its higher states what Patanjali calls the state of a Spectator without a spectacle. This requires repeated entry into the Void. Even to those who have not deeply meditated upon it, the idea of supreme Voidness *(shunyata)* is challenging; it appeals to an intrinsic sense of sovereign spiritual freedom that exists in every human soul as a Manasic being. As a thinking, self-conscious agent and spectator, every individual is, in principle, capable of appreciating and understanding, at some preliminary level, the possibility of universalizing self-consciousness. But actually to expand consciousness and gain emancipation from all fetters requires a life of deep and regular meditation.

This majestic movement in consciousness towards metaphysical subjectivity is directly connected with the capacity to contact in consciousness the noetic and noumenal realm behind the proscenium of objective physical existence. It is evident, for example, that the solar system is a complex causal realm involving planetary rotation around the sun according to definite laws. From the standpoint of Gupta Vidya, everything is sevenfold.

This is as true of planets and constellations as of human beings. The solar system also involves seven planes, and each of its planets has seven globes. The physical sun is, then, the centre of revolutionary motion by the planets on the physical plane. This regulated activity is no different from anything else seen on the phenomenal plane in the manifested world. It is a representation in physical space of invisible principles. All such physical entities have correlates on the invisible plane, both subjective and objective.

Starting with the fundamental principle of universal unity and radical identity of all motion and activity in the Great Breath, there are close connections between the metaphysical aspects of all beings. Hence, there are metaphysical correlations between the subtle principles in human nature and the subtle principles of the sun and planets. Thus, there are invisible aspects of the moon which correspond to the lower principles in man, the psychic nature of the human being. There are also higher principles which correspond to *Atma-Buddhi* and to the noetic capacity of higher *Manas*. Depending upon whether a human being is mired in psychic consciousness or rises to the noetic realm, he or she will have more or less self-conscious affinities with these different aspects of the solar system. When they look to the sky at night, their responses will differ not only on the physical plane but also on these invisible planes. One person may simply be impressed by the brightness of Venus in relation to the moon, being entranced by the physical beauty of the phenomenon. Another person might be interested to think in terms of the recondite activities and functions known even to contemporary astronomy. Still another, who is deeply rooted in the philosophy of Gupta Vidya, and a practitioner of regular meditation, would see something quite different in the heavens.

It is a common observation that different people see different things and derive different meanings from the same phenomena. Different people embody different degrees and balances of psychic perception and noetic apprehension of psycho-physical phenomena. To be able to see noetically one must begin by focussing upon the Spiritual Sun. This means that one must embark upon a programme of meditation and mental discipline directed to making conscious and consistent a secure sense of immortality. True immortality belongs to the *Atma-Buddhi-Manas*, the noetic individuality, and must be made real as an active principle of selection in reference to the lower principles. A person who does this will be able, like the Vedic *hotri*, to draw upon the highest aspects of the lunar hierarchies around the full moon and also the sublime energies and hidden potencies of the Spiritual Sun.

To perceive and connect the noetic in oneself with the noetic in the cosmos requires a synthetic and serene understanding. Such understanding is the crystalline reflection of the ineffable light of *Buddhi* into the focusing field of higher *Manas*. *Buddhi*, seen from its own subjective side, is inseparable from the motion of the Great Breath, whilst its objective side is the radiant light of higher understanding. Noetic understanding is, therefore, rooted in universal unity. Its modes are markedly different from the analytical method of the lower reason, which tends to break up wholes into parts, losing all sight of integrity and meaning. No matter what the object of one's understanding, the fundamental distinction between psychic and noetic implies a subtle and vital difference between the set of properties that belongs to an assemblage of parts and the set of properties that belongs only to the whole, which is greater than the sum of its parts.

If one is going to use an analytic method, one must begin by recognizing that there are different levels of analysis requiring different categories and concepts. Merely by breaking up a phenomenon, one may not necessarily understand it. The *yogin*, according to Patanjali, does the opposite. He meditates upon each object of concentration as a whole, becomes one with it, apprehending the *Atma-Buddhi* of that phenomenon through his own *Atma-Buddhi*. He draws meanings and produces effects that would never be accessible to the analytic methods of lower *Manas*. Others, for example, may decompose sound into its component elements of vibration, yet fail to hear in them any harmony or special melody; they may talk glibly about motion and vibration, yet be deaf to the harmony produced through vibrations. A musically tone-deaf physicist may know quite a lot about the theory of sound and yet may lack the experience or ability to enjoy the experience of masters of music. Conversely, those who are masters of music, and who may know something about the analytic theory of sound, may know nothing about what the *yogin* knows who has gone beyond all audible sounds to the metaphysical meaning of vibrations.

Thus there are levels upon levels of harmony within the cosmos spanning the great octave of Spirit-Matter. Gupta Vidya, which is always concerned with vibration and harmony, provides the only secure basis for acquiring the freedom to move from plane to plane of subjective and objective existence. The arcane standpoint is integrative, and always sees the One in the many. It develops that intuitive faculty which detects what is in common to a class of objects, and at the same time, in the light of that commonality, it enjoys what is unique to each object. It is this powerful faculty of mind that the theurgist perfects. Through it, he quickly moves away from the phenomenal and even from manifest notions of harmony. And through noetic understanding he can experience the inaudible harmony and intangible resonances that exist in all manifestation. A person attentive to the great tone throughout Nature will readily appreciate the music of the spheres. Such a person can hear the sound produced by breath, not only in animals and human beings, but also in stars and planets. Such a hierophant becomes a Walker of the Skies, a Master of Compassion, in whom the power of the Great Breath has become liberated. All ordered Nature resonates and responds to the Word and Voice of such a hierophant, who lives and breathes in That which breathes beyond the cosmos, breathless.

CONTINUITY AND CHOICE

Suffering arises out of exaggerated involvement in a world of colour, forms and objects, maintained by a false sense of personal identity. As long as people persist in this pseudo-continuum of existence, they necessarily forfeit the exercise of their inner creative capacities and cannot fully seize the opportunities of self-conscious evolution. Human beings produce a false sense of self out of a series of intense particularizations of will, thought and feeling, all of which become the tokens of selfhood. As a result, in the very process of fragmenting oneself into a diversity of desires and conflicting and colliding aims, or of limiting oneself by conceptions which must be concretized in some narrow programme in space and time, suffering is built into one's life. All exaggerations of the void and illusory ego, all failures to recognize the overarching One, all attempts to live as if one were the centre of the world and without any self-conscious awareness of the beyond, mean that one can only gain happiness, pleasure or fulfilment at a cost. An obscuring shadow follows all pleasure — a compulsive feedback, a necessary negation, an unavoidable depression. When people do not detach themselves and negate excessive involvement in advance of every thought, the negation must come from outside, and after a point people lose their hold over the central thread of unifying or synthesizing awareness.

Suffering is the obscuration of the light of universal understanding. As long as we live in terms of narrow conceptions of ourselves, shrunken conceptions of space and of time, and with an exaggerated intensity that will necessarily be followed by an external negation, suffering is built into our life. It is coeval with that ignorance of the real which makes what we call human life possible. Human life is a passing shadow-play in which human beings identify with roles and, like candles, are eventually snuffed out. It is a play with a brief intensity focused upon a paltry role and based upon identifications with name and form. One who experiences great suffering, or who reflects deeply upon the relationships at the very root of this process, may come to see that the world and oneself are not apart.

The world is at least partly of one's own making but it is also made by the limiting conceptions of other human beings. They have become involved in the creation of a world in which limitation is a necessary part, and they too have forgotten what they innately knew. All human beings begin life by sounding the OM. They all have a cool awareness of the ineffable when they are little children, before they begin to lisp and to speak. In the youth of their sense-organs they experience wonder in relation to the whole of life. In the process of growing up, however, they take on the illusions of others — of parents, elders, teachers, and a variety of people around them — and then they become forgetful of what they already knew. We may reawaken awareness only by self-conscious self-renewal. Awareness is like a colourless universal light for which there are as many focusing media as there are metaphysical points in abstract space. Each human being is a ray of that light. To the extent to which that ray projects out into a world of differentiated light and shade, and limitations of form and colour, it is tinctured by the colouring that comes to it from a mental environment. Philosophically, the mental environment is far more important than the external physical environment.

When one sees this process archetypally, one recognizes that there is no separation between oneself and the world except in language, reactive gestures, and in certain uncriticized assumptions. Most importantly, there is no separation of oneself from other human beings as centres of consciousness. The notions of 'mine' and 'thine', attached to pleasure and pain, to joy and suffering, are arbitrary and false. Is that which gives one great joy exclusively one's own? And, on what grounds do we assume that the suffering of human beings in numerous states of acute self-limitation is purely theirs? Does each one have his own exclusive property rights in collective human suffering and thereby have nothing to do with us? Suffering is intrinsic to the universal stream of conditioned existence. Most living is a kind of pseudo-participation in what seem to be events, but which are merely arbitrary constructions of space-time, and are largely non-events. When a human being comes to see that involvement of a single universal consciousness in a single homogeneous material medium, the very notion of the individual 'I' has dissolved.

We are all aware when we go to the dentist and submit ourselves to something that seems physically painful, through our very awareness of what is happening and our deliberate attempt to think away from our identified involvement with the part of the physical body which is suffering, we can control our sensations to some extent rather than being wholly controlled by them. If this insight could be extended, we might see that the stream of universal consciousness is like an ever-flowing river — in which all conceptions of 'I' and 'you' and 'this' and 'that' are mere superimpositions — and then we could begin to stand consciously at some remove from the process of life. Suppose a person came to listen to a discourse of the Buddha with petty expectations, because somebody said it would be quite good, or worth hearing, or fairly interesting. Someone else might have come with a deeper idea because he or she was awake as a soul and had the thought that it is a tremendous privilege to be in the magnanimous presence of a Mahatma, and hence he or she might be lit up. If one is truly lit up, one's wakefulness makes the greatest difference to the whole of one's life. It could be gathered up self-consciously at the moment of death. But even a person who comes with so profound a thought into a collective orbit where there are many souls in states of only relative wakefulness and caught up in residual illusions, may forget the original moment.

The suffering of human life is a jolt which the whole gives the part, the individual ray, to re-awaken in it a memory and awareness of the original moment. Here we can see the significance of certain meditations undertaken by Bhikshus. In Buddhist philosophy there are references to meditations on the moment of birth. Yet how are we to meditate on it when it is an event that has no sense of reality for us? It is simply a certain date on the calendar. The mystery of individuality lies in the privilege and the possibility of making one's own connections within what otherwise would be a vast, fragmented chaos of events. One could make these connections simply by habit, in terms of one's first thoughts, or in terms of the reactions of the world and the opinions of others. Or one could make them self-consciously from the standpoint of the whole. This, of course, is very difficult to experience immediately, but every human being can begin to grow in this direction.

A fearless and dispassionate examination of the past shows that a lot of what once seemed extremely important was utterly insignificant and a lot of what looked impossible to go through was relatively easy. One could take stock of one's awareness independent of external events and focus it upon intense periods in the past which seemed to be especially painful, meaningless, or terrifying, but which one came through. Then one can ask whether, just as one now feels a kind of remoteness from past events, so too at the very moment of birth, did one feel a kind of remoteness from future events? Was one really involved, or only involved in one part of oneself? Then one can shift to the moment of death and raise the difficult question whether one can see oneself dying. Can one actually see a certain moment where there is an abandonment of a corpse which, through the natural processes of life, must decay and disintegrate and, while seeing this, still hold to an immense awareness of the whole? A person who is able to imagine what it would have been like to stand at a distance from the foetus that became the baby boy or girl can also imagine being at a distance from the corpse which is being discarded. He or she can also see that there is a thread that links these moments, and that the succession is no more arbitrary than the pattern of a necklace when seen from the standpoint of the whole.

The One Life comes into a world of differentiation through prismatically differentiated rays. We can sense in the gentle quality of dawn light something that does not participate in the opalescent colours of the day, something removed from what we call heat and light, cold and shade — a quality of virginal light that is a reminder of states of matter appropriate to states of consciousness which are created and held as potential by beings in general. Then we can begin to see that the whole point of human suffering in its collective meaning is to overcome pain and the false sense of separation. This is the point in consciousness where human beings as individuals could maintain a noetic and complete wakefulness — *turiya,* a profound awareness from a standpoint which transcends the greatest magnitudes of space-time. It goes beyond solar systems and intimates that the depths of space represent in the very core of apparently nothing, a subtle creative gestation of matter. If one can see the whole world in terms of its plastic potency, as radiant material for a single universal spiritual sun, then one gains the dignity and the divinity of being a self-conscious individuating instrument of the universal Logos.

This is the sacred teaching of all Initiates. It is the teaching of Jesus in the *Gospel According to John,* the teaching of Buddha in the *Heart Sutra,* and the teaching of Krishna in the *Bhagavad Gita* and in the *Shrimad Bhagavatam.* These beings, fully awake, see that all human life, including human suffering, is a projection of a false involvement in a false sense of self. They bear witness to the reality of universal consciousness, not as something potential but as that which can be used as plastic material for new forms of spiritual creation. Creative imagination is not an abstract immaterial force, but the most rarefied and subtle form of material energy that exists. It can be tapped by concentration. By repeated and regular attempts at concentration upon this conception of the One, negating the false sense of the self, one builds and gives coherence to one's subtler vehicles, shaping what is now chaotic matter and forming a temple, a worthy vesture for a self-conscious being aware of the divinity of all beings and capable of maintaining that awareness through waking, dreaming and deep sleep. Having entered into the void, having entered into the light beyond these states of consciousness, the awakened soul remains in it by choice, while giving the impetus to other human beings to make the same attempt. Suffering and ignorance are collective; enlightenment and spiritual creativity are universal. This is the great hope of the timeless teaching concerning true continuity of consciousness.

Within the limits of time, however, which is an illusion produced by the succession of states of consciousness, there is only a before and an after, and no full scope for creativity. Consider, for example, a moment of love. Suppose you suddenly come into contact with someone of whom you could say, like the poet Yeats, "I loved the pilgrim-soul in you." There is a magical, intense flow between two pairs of eyes, and in one instant, a taste of eternity. If two individuals later tried to understand this in terms of what was there the day before and what was there the day after, they would have simply slipped onto another plane. If two people who have such a golden moment of co-awareness later on forget it or identify it with passing and contemporary illusions, then of course they might see it simply as a date in a calendar to be remembered by ceremonial tokens. That is not the same as re-enactment, because the essential quality of that moment was the absence of before and after, or any noticeable succession of states of consciousness. It was not as if they met calculatingly with anticipations and fears, and it was not as though soon after they thought of it as a memory of an event. They simply experienced in a moment of fusion of consciousness a freedom from the false division of eternal duration into a past, a present and a future. It was as if they stood not in one city, not in one street, not in one place, but in eternal space. This is an experience which by its very nature is so profound and beautiful that many people desperately look for it. This may be where the critical mistake is made. In the very attempt to look for it, one might overlook opportunities and arenas where it is more likely to happen. The very notion of seeking it, or wanting it, of maneuvering it, is stifling.

Our experience of time involves craving and memory. Time is bound up with fragmented consciousness in a universe of change and a constantly moving world of process. At best, it is a deceptive device of convenience for gaining a sense of control in eternal duration, to serve purposes arising from the standpoint of the narrow needs of some particularized self in relation to other particularized selves, where it is useful to talk in terms of a before and an after. Consider a good physician who has seen you at different times and to whom you are more than a file. When receiving an examination, it is as if you are both friends looking together at a common medium which is the physical body you inhabit and which has certain cycles and a history. Two minds looking together at the same body can suddenly see connections between before and after. Patterns emerge and a serial view of time has practical convenience.

We have, however, another view of time which allows us to discover other types of patterns and connections. If all patterns and connections had to be discovered exclusively by individual human beings, then the human predicament would be even more grave than it now seems. Because many patterns are already given, it is a case of looking for them with a deep detachment, so that one does not cut up and fragment the process. Suddenly one may see that there is a certain moment here and another point, tendency or characteristic there with which it connects. E.M. Forster employed this idea in his novels and expressed it as a mantram — "Let us connect." To him, in pre-1914 England, the whole difference between human beings moving from the sheltered world of 1914 into the increasingly stormy and socially disordered world of Europe after the First World War, was in the extent to which they could survive the collapse of inherited identities and self-consciously create their own connections. Either human beings forge their own connections or connections will be made for them, but then they will sound arbitrary or malignant, suggesting that some dark, hostile Fate as in Thomas Hardy's novels, is causing everything. When human beings can self-consciously make these connections, they begin to live with an increasing sense of freedom from time. Time may be seen in terms of eternal duration, which is prior to it, and hence there are golden moments. Time may also be seen in terms of mere convenience, according to a calendar, to help facilitate a limited involvement between human beings, in limited roles and contexts, to take place in a reliable manner. This mode of time may even be made to approximate some broader concept of distributive justice. Time must be seen as an illusion, must be seen for what it is, if a person is to gain the real continuity of consciousness connected with true creativity.

Today there are various fascinating studies of creativity, which cite examples such as Kekule's dream that was critical in biology. Kekule dreamt one night of a serpent eating its tail and when he woke up, he got a flashing insight into the circular rather than linear nature of certain processes of growth which are fundamental in molecular biology. The more one looks at such cases, the more one comes to see that truly creative beings cannot be programmed. Even in a society fearfully hostile to creativity, creative minds can still use available resources compassionately. Typically, creativity is difficult to attain because there is too much desire to have it programmed and delivered according to a schedule set by personal consciousness. This comes out in capitalist society in its most extreme form when people feel that there must be a kind of pre-established, controlled, and mechanistic way in which one could have creativity by numbers. By emphasizing substitutability and measurability, by regarding human beings as labour-units who are convertible terms, one can evolve an aggregated view of output and product which is truly dead for the creative artist. A great potter has no sense of excitement in looking at a pot. It is already dead. What was alive was the process of visualization and the process of taking that mental image, while the potter's wheel was moving, and seeing the shape emerging. The magical moment of emergence is real. Human beings in general have a parasitic attachment to the products of creativity but the vital process of creativity eludes them because it defies ordinary modes of division of time.

Here, then, is the most critical point, both in relation to continuity of consciousness and in relation to the Demiurge. The Demiurge in the old myths and in many a rustic Hindu painting, is like Vishnu asleep, from whose navel a lotus emerges which is the universe. Mahavishnu is floating upon the great blue waters of space. Around the serpent on which this Great Being rests there is a circle within which a whitish milky curdling is taking place. Intense activity surrounds the periphery of the great wheel of eternity, on which is resting in a state of supreme, pure inactivity, the divine Demiurge, itself only an aspect of the Logos. The great Rig Vedic hymn states, "The One breathed breathless." It was alone and there was no second. Alone it breathed breathless. There is a transcending sense of boundless space, in relation to which all the notions of space that we have — of an expanding universe, of a closed universe, of solar systems, and galaxies — all of these are like maps and diagrams relating points that are already conceptually separated out and which have boundaries, but are merely partial representations or surface appearances upon the depths of a space which has no boundaries or contours, and which is never delineated in diagrams.

If continuity of consciousness is to be seen not as something individual but rather universal, embedded in the very process of the manifestation of the One in and through the many, then it is necessary to think away from conceptions of time that are arbitrary and to a view of space which is boundless. Metaphysically, the reason why the Demiurge can both be involved in space fashioning many systems, and also witness all of these like bubbles upon a surface, is because space is not empty. After three hundred years of thought and experiment, modern science is catching up with ancient wisdom and is beginning to see that there is no such thing as empty space, that the content of space is not dependent on other categories of measurement or upon other standpoints of perception. What looks like pitch-black darkness could in fact be enormously full from another and more profound understanding. In one of the great passages in the early part of *The Secret Doctrine*, the commentary upon the *Stanzas of Dzyan* says that what to the Initiate is full is very different from what appears full to the ordinary man. The more human beings self-consciously expand awareness, the more they can free their deeply felt conceptions of the world, of reality, and of themselves from the notions of part and limit, from future anticipations and a present cut up into separate particular events, and the more they can bring a conscious sense of reality to their own mental awareness of space as a void — what the Buddha called *sunyata*, Emptiness — and the more they can replace the ordinary conception of form by the Platonic, which is not bound up with anything fixed.

Archetypal forms are like flashes of light. We may represent them by external coatings or by geometrical figures, but that is to imply that they are fixed, whereas in fact they are in a ceaseless, fluid interconnection. A constant transformation is taking place in the Divine Mind from one into another appearance of a geometrical form. There is a profound statement of this conception, which has great application to the individual who wishes to meditate upon it and use it in daily life: "The world is a living arithmetic in its development and a realized geometry in its repose." Every human being is involved in that arithmetic, and therefore growth is possible for the individual. Further, beyond and above that which changes, grows and develops, each is also consubstantial with the One that breathes breathless. Therefore, for the deeper Self, the whole universe is a realized geometry in repose.

If one went to sleep with a self-conscious awareness, using such profound images to extend the conception of the very reality of the world that one will enter into when going to sleep, and if on waking up one could greet the world in terms of these great divine images, then the whole world would become a vast playground for creativity and the freely created expression of a dancing intelligence that is involved in everything. One can suddenly find immense joy, a kind of eros or love, surging within. Then of course one would not identify love with a deficiency need. Creativity has nothing to do with a sense of incompletion, except in the sense in which the whole of manifestation is necessarily incomplete. It has to do with a sense of something tremendous welling up from within. There is a necessarily unprogrammed, unpredictable nature to the creative artist in every man. A human being could look towards every context and situation, and self-consciously greet the world as a creative being, but to do this requires the courage to break with one's sniggering, supercilious, paranoid self. One must wake up and be unafraid of the divine inheritance that belongs to everyman. This, however, can never be done collectively. Individuals can only do this by choosing to strike out on their own. We have an excellent definition given in the very first essay of H.P. Blavatsky on "What is Theosophy?": 'The true Theosophist is one who independently strikes out and godward finds a path.' All create their own paths back to the original source, based upon original inspirations, unique and priceless opportunities out of each one's particular stock of experience of making reason come alive as the embodiment of beneficent forces, the eternal verities, the quintessential truths of all history.

Even though such decisions cannot be made collectively, none the less the whole of humanity is now coming closer to what is called the moment of choice, the time where consciousness must either move forward or vacate vestures because it cannot maintain the patterns of the past. This follows directly from the principle that the whole universe is continuously implicated in involution and evolution. In a universe of ceaseless motion there is a breathing in and a breathing out: one universal homogeneous spirit breaks into rays just as at dawn rays emerge out of the light. They get involved in what become in time separate forms of differentiated matter. Having become involved, they must eventually reach a point where matter has descended to the level of maximum differentiation. Then spirit is withdrawn from its involvement in the most heterogeneous matter back into its original source. This is what is symbolized in the serpent eating its tail. It led to Hegel's metaphysical theory of evolution, because it makes of every man's journey an integral part, while at the same time only a partial and to some extent apparently separate expression of one collective universal process. How can we move from this scheme to the concepts of choosing and a moment of choice, which are bound up with the notion of individual responsibility?

We may, as some have done, compare the earlier systems of philosophy to the developing states of consciousness of a child. After birth every baby resides in a state of awareness that is so bound up with the mother that it has no sense of being separate. There follows a second stage when an awareness of particularity, detail and multiplicity emerge together with a sense of being not separate but simply someone who is resting, so to speak, in the bosom of the mother, of the whole, of space. Then comes a third stage when the little child becomes enormously fascinated with its conception of itself, a kind of solipsistic or even narcissistic stage where it becomes very interested in its own feelings. It gives a kind of definition and clarity to its own desires, taking hold of itself in terms of its own wants and needs. A point surely does come, without tracing the whole process in detail, where a person begins to experience something of the joy and the thrill of having to make a decision, of taking a stand, of having to choose.

By analogy and correspondence, what seems thrilling at the time of puberty — being able to choose — may be applied on the plane of the mind to being able to choose an idea, a system of ideas, or a philosophical system. This is not merely selecting a series of particularizations, but choosing a whole way of thinking out and giving shape, direction and authentic continuity to one's mental development. All of this has become difficult to understand because of the operation of an evolutionary paradox: the necessary homogenization of the psyche is accompanied by the increasing necessity for responsible choice free of psychic influence. This may be the historical destiny of America — to foster a hazardous jelling of people from all parts of the world, producing a huge, homogenized, psychic amorphism. Everything is kept in a fluidic state so that as wise beings enter into it, they will, in taking on this plastic material and using the enormous power released by mixing and mingling, give that energy an ennobling sense of direction. This means a moment of choice is emerging for a whole race or a nation. Many people are aware of this in America today. There was a time when glamour was attached to being decadent, but much of that nonsense has been swept away. Today the pre-packaged tins of glamour have become so boringly or pathologically familiar that there is no novelty any more attached to them. It is as if human consciousness has drained the last drop of false involvement in all of these soulless dregs of matter that are being spewed forth. This is happening because there is a complex convergence of forces and Karma is working very fast in giving people their precise allocations. There is a tremendous opportunity also for those who can work with the Promethean solar forces of the future, which at this time are extremely subtle, imperceptible yet causally crucial.

We are at a new point in history where persons cannot, as in older days, merely go by labels. Individuals have become much more sophisticated and a significant increase in self-consciousness, in regard to the eclecticism of the human mind, has emerged. The moment of choice takes a variety of forms, but in the end all the choices come back to one basic choice: living in terms of a false conception of psychic identity caught passively in a series of events happening to oneself, or living self-consciously with awareness as a noetic being. Put in a starkly simple way, one is either going to be a psychic being and behave more childishly as one grows older, or one is going to be noetic and actually grow up. To behave noetically is to reawaken something of the pristine, beautiful awareness of a baby but while one is grown up. One may be in one's forties or fifties and still have self-consciously something of the thrill found in a baby's face looking out on the world with eyes of complete truth, accepting the wonder of life.

This must be deliberately and individually chosen. The insidious legacy of vicarious atonement makes people think that this can happen to them without their having to do anything, simply by being on the side of the correct doctrine or on the side of God. Buddha came to destroy the false idea that simply by making one dramatic and tearful choice, all the rest will automatically happen. No doubt there is much wisdom in what Jesus said: "Seek ye first the kingdom of God and all else will be added unto you," but to seek the kingdom of God is to seize the critical moment of choice. "Whom choose ye this day, God or Mammon?" This formulation by itself is too narrow because its interpretations limit the magnitude of the choice to the sphere of the false self. In the presence of the light one either has to live in and for the light or one has to live like a vampire in fear of the light. Human beings have to become self-conscious, creative beings who can continuously release creativity, the light of understanding, and true sympathy, and who can thereby gain contentment and joy in a more collective sense of human welfare and a more universal sense of progress. Otherwise, they must lapse back into their habits and then, lacking responsibility, they cannot help plunging into a pattern which is one of vampirization or mere mechanical, automaton-like living.

There is a stern logic to this choice because it is not taken at any one point of time alone. Once we grasp the choice in its full sense, it is one that is taking place at every moment in time. Hence Buddha said that no moment of carelessness in relation to continuity of consciousness is possible. Eternal vigilance is the price, not only of political liberty, but even more of spiritual freedom. This is because eventually human beings who understand the logic of this choice and have made a critical choice, accept the consequences, connecting in turn to other choices, thereby creating a cumulative cycle. They also connect that cycle of ascent to various tokens of memory, objects in their lives, friends, or their contact with the Lodge where they rekindle regularly their spiritual impulses. Eventually they reach a point where they can understand the inexplicable joy, as well as the burden, of choosing a thought. Functionally, the definition of an enlightened being, of an Initiate, is a being who chooses every thought. Things do not happen to Initiates; thoughts do not come to them. They choose them. To be able to get to the ultimate capacity not only to choose every thought but to make it a living reality by mastering the power of *Kriyashakti*, totally purified creative imagination, is an exalted ideal truly inspiring and relevant to every human being. By renewing one's sense of the reality of this ideal, one can reach a point where one can give up altogether the false notion of personal or individual spiritual progress. It is replaced by a beautiful awareness that whatever happens is a kind of resignation to the universal flow of light working through one self-consciously. It is like swimming on the ocean. We appreciate that the collective pull of the ocean is divine harmony, in terms of which one cannot lose.

If good karma is that which is pleasing to the real man, to the Ishwara, the divine within, then good karma is universal harmony. None can lose if they really are unafraid of anything coming to them in terms of universal divine harmony. Fear arises only for those who would somehow like everything programmed and arranged for them, so that if things go wrong, they can blame it on the people who arranged it, and if things go right, they could forget to say thanks and take the credit. Fortunately, this small-minded view of the world cannot be supported any longer. We have reached a point where it is really the same for all. It is a matter of choosing consciously the divine harmony and saying that whatever eventually comes is not merely what I deserve but what I desire. We must come to that point in life where we are ready for everything and anything, and see the whole of life as being on the side of that in us which alone is capable of surviving. Then we shall be happy to let go that which cannot be supported by a living person who is willing self-consciously to die. At the same time we shall be assured, in a cool, relaxed and totally conscious way, of the universal currents of divine harmony within us. Then we could say that we are human beings who have chosen rightly and fundamentally. This is not once-and-for-all. We shall have to reinforce and renew it many times a day, not in the old sense of ritual but simply by becoming aware of our thinking processes. One day it could have meaning for us to say that we actually choose our thoughts and life-atoms, that we have not one reaction which is not submitted by us to the process of deliberation. Then many more shall be worthy of the most sacred of all titles in collective evolution, of being what Emerson called Man Thinking, a Manasaputra, a trustee of the sacred fire of individual and universal self-consciousness, with "the priceless boon of learning truth, the right perception of existing things, the knowledge of the non-existent."

SELF-TRANSFORMATION

'The worlds, to the profane,' says a Commentary, 'are built up of the known Elements. To the conception of an Arhat, these Elements are themselves collectively a divine Life; distributively, on the plane of manifestations, the numberless and countless crores of lives. Fire alone is ONE, on the plane of the One Reality: on that of manifested, hence illusive, being, its particles are fiery lives which live and have their being at the expense of every other life that they consume. Therefore they are named the "DEVOURERS."'
. . . 'Every visible thing in this Universe was built by such LIVES, from conscious and divine primordial man down to the unconscious agents that construct matter.' . . . 'From the ONE LIFE formless and Uncreate, proceeds the Universe of lives. First was manifested from the Deep (Chaos) cold luminous fire (gaseous light?) which formed the curds in Space.'

The Secret Doctrine, i 249-50

Matter distributed in space manifests a series of dimensions or characteristics correlated with the different Rounds of cosmic and human evolution on earth. Just as shared perceptions of extension, colour, motion, taste and smell have developed through the persistent use of five familiar sense-organs, so too emerging humanity will experience through the sixth sense of normal clairvoyance the corresponding characteristic of matter which has been called permeability. The three so-called dimensions of length, breadth and thickness are merely the triple aspects of extension, marked out by measurements made through customary devices. To restrict the common conception of Space, as Locke did, to what is simply a single characteristic of Matter is severely to limit perception, to confine and condition it by a perspective that is not even fully three-dimensional. In order to free everyday consciousness from this narrow focus, one must sense a new dimension of depth, which is related to suffering rather than to length, breadth and thickness. Depth, which is sometimes termed height, in mystical parlance, is crucial to a person who is truly skilled in regular meditations, withdrawing the wayward mind to a still centre while visualizing an ever-extending circumference around that motionless point. Through conscientious practice this regenerative activity of consciousness can purify, elevate and intensify one's interior life. Lateral expansion can fuse with depth of concentration to generate the vibrant awareness of the vault of the luminous sphere of mystic meditation. A profounder sense of non-being can enrich the quality and range of all astral perceptions in the course of time. One becomes a modest master of one's own orchestra.

In general, a person largely sees what one expects to see, owing to an enormous routinization in sensory responses. This has been fully confirmed in contemporary experiments. Any person who perceives an unfamiliar object is apt to experience a proportionally greater variation in the retinal image than when watching a familiar object as it is removed and receding into the distance. The human organism is always adapting, through its sense-organs, all pre-existing sensations and memories of stimuli, to what is recurrent and what is unfamiliar and unexpected. Hence, physical pain and mental suffering often come through the compassion of maya, which induces fleeting shocks to the sensory apparatus lest out of a false sense of familiarity, the mechanical observer takes too much for granted, thus making the creative faculties atrophy and the brain-centres sluggish. When suddenly one is confronted with what is strangely unfamiliar, one is compelled to think and contemplate. The immortal Triad overbrooding every human being is aware, like a Pythagorean spectator, that its reflected ray is continually tempted to abdicate its responsibility — as a thinker and chooser. It becomes like a mindless robot mired in automatic responses. The more these compulsive reactions are moralized in terms of good habits and the spurious semblance of virtue, the more subtle and insidious they become, enmeshing noetic consciousness, substituting passivity for plasticity, and destroying flexibility in discriminative response to the flux of events. When restless beings encounter individuals with a very different pace of life, or who live in greater closeness to the good earth, they are forced to recognize a richer way of life, a greater awareness of depth.

In modern society, there is a constant risk of awareness being reduced to a mechanical series of automatic responses which preclude true thinking and inhibit self-examination. When reflex responses in chaotic cerebration are reinforced through familiar clusters of tawdry images and shallow emotions, perverse thoughts invade one's sphere. This is a pervasive problem in our time of accelerated change and decisive sifting. Consider a person who attempts to become attentive while reading a text but who is not used to it and whose consciousness is shackled to the wandering mind, weak sensory responses and a general lack of attention and order in daily life. Such hapless persons cannot really read exactly what is in the text and cannot focus on it, let alone see around it and probe into profound suggestions buried within and between the lines of the text. To be able to shake the system out of this false familiarity, breeding a banal contempt for the supposedly stable world outside, the greatest teacher is suffering.

In the Aquarian Age in which many see the life-process as the continually enacted and essentially hidden interplay of harmony and disharmony, suffering always comes as a benevolent teacher of wisdom. Pain serves as a shock to one's sense of identity, illusory self-image and acquired or ancestral habits. It challenges one's pride and perversity. It compels one to pause for thought and radically reappraise the meaning of life, obligations, and potentials in oneself and others. When suffering comes, it plumbs below the surface of the psyche, touching depths of untrammeled consciousness. Noumenal and noetic awareness enters into everyday experience, and is saluted by remarkable constellations of poets, singers and seers. Incidents of life once taken for granted suddenly look very different, because one's sensibility has been sharpened. Were this not so, there would be little meaning to the mere succession of events and the mere recurrence of mechanical responses to the sensory stream of consciousness.

There is constant learning, and there is the ever-present possibility of deepening the cognitive basis of awareness, the operative level of self-actualization. This is part of the evolutionary and unending process of etherealization and refinement of life in the cycle of rapid descent and painful ascent. This is an exceedingly slow and subtle process — there is nothing automatic about it — but it is ubiquitous. Such a process of refinement must involve first of all an altered mode of awareness, which for most human beings means the conscious adoption of a radically different perspective on human life and cosmic evolution. But it must also transform the range and reach of one's sense-perceptions, through a better and finer use of the sensory powers of touch, taste, smell, sight and hearing. Further, this process of etherealization and refinement must proceed through a harmonious commingling of centres in the brain-mind and spiritual heart, through inward surrender to the Sovereign Self and the silent invocation of the Light of the Logos.

One may imagine the immortal Triad as overbrooding the head, though incompletely incarnated because its reflected intelligence must consciously ascend towards the level of proper harmonization. This could be expressed in terms of metaphysical truths about consciousness which operates under laws of expansion and contraction, implying continuous creation, preservation and regeneration through destruction. These archetypal modes have been traditionally symbolized in the Hindu pantheon by Nara-Nari, Agni, Varuna and Surya, and also by Brahmā, Vishnu and Shiva. This sacred teaching about cosmic and human consciousness could also be conveyed from the standpoint of matter. The essential axiom of Gupta Vidya is the affirmation that spirit and matter are really two facets of one and the same Substance-Principle. Objectivity and subjectivity are wholly relative to centres of perception, to degrees of differentiation, and to the coadunition and consubstantiality of objects with subjects upon overlapping planes of substance.

Put entirely in terms of matter, this would imply that a person whose consciousness is deepened would experience a richer awareness of the invisible aspects and mathematical points of visible matter. There would be a heightened sensitivity to the gamut of invisible relations between life-atoms, corresponding to subtle colours and rarefied sounds.

One would also be replacing an angular view by a rounded view: the greater the depth, the greater the roundedness. The price people pay for the settled three-dimensionality of their conception of the world of phenomena is that the brain-mind becomes captive to angular views. If people are not truly self-conscious, they become extremely obtuse or are hopelessly caught within narrow angles and restricted orbits of perception. Whereas a person who can intensify the depth of perception and feeling, through private pain and unspoken suffering merged in effortless awareness of the vast suffering of all humanity, gains greater depth as a human being. This is continuously enriched by meditative experience of the Silence that surrounds the mystery of *Sat* and *Asat,* Being and Non-Being. The more this becomes a way of life, the more it is possible to have a profoundly balanced view of the world and a well-rounded conception of selfhood, alchemizing and elevating personal awareness and individual sensibility to the height and breadth of universal self-consciousness and the depths of boundless space, eternal motion and endless duration.

This process of self-transformation may be illustrated by an initially shadowy circle, a very narrow segment of which seems to be lit up. There is a seemingly central focus, but it is only central to that visible segment, whilst the centre of the whole circle, most of which is obscured, remains hidden. This is analogous to the relationship between the personal ego and the individual Self. A human being with a narrow sense of identity is living only segmentally, existing only at one sensory level with reference to an unduly restricted horizon of human experience. Such a person is not properly centering, not really trying to get as full and rounded a view of himself and the world as possible. Out of this roundedness he could begin to sense a sphere of light surrounding himself in which he lives, moves and has his being. This will loosen a great deal of the fixity of categories of thought and emotional responses which, if seen clairvoyantly, reveal a sad mutilated shadow of the true Self of a human being. Herein lies the rationale for recovery through meditation of that pristine and rounded conception of the Self which is more in harmony with the music of the spheres and the Golden Egg of Brahmā in the ocean of SPACE. This transformation is indeed the psychological equivalent to the Copernican revolution, in which the sun of the *Atman* is central to the solar system. For the *Atman* to become the centre of a luminous sphere of selfhood would require a firm displacement of the false centering of consciousness, through *kama manas*, within a distorting segment of separative identity which is trapped in a fragmented view of space, time and secondary causation. The dwarfing of one's true selfhood is the crucifixion of Christos, the obscuration of the light, the plenitude, the potential and the richness within every human being on earth.

To convey this as a criterion of human stature, the greater the depth of one's inwardness, the broader, the vaster, the wider the range of one's sympathies, and the more one is able to appreciate a wider variety of experiences, situations, contexts and human beings. The more secure one's depth of consciousness, the more one is able to exercise the synthesizing gift of the Monad, capable of seeing in terms of any of the specific sub-colours, and also able to penetrate to the very centre of the white light, seeing beyond it, and benevolently using the entire range of the spectrum. What is true of colours applies equally to sounds, and ultimately to consciousness itself. This is the sacred prerogative of a human being. It is because human beings fall, owing to shared and inherited limitations, but also owing to self-created limitations, they forfeit or forget altogether this sovereign prerogative and fail to mend themselves through meditation and self-study. Hence, the healing and restorative property of sleep which Shakespeare so suggestively describes as Nature's second feast, man's great restorer. The average human being deprived of the benefit of *sushupti* or sleep would simply not survive for long. Sleep and death are Nature's modes of restoration of balance. In order to take full advantage of sleep, the seeker must initially experience the pain of forcing the mind to return to a point on which it is placed, to a chosen idea, bringing the heart back to the deepest, purest and most pristine feeling of devotion, warmth and love. If one did this again and again, then certainly one would not only become more deep in response to life but one would also become more of a spiritual benefactor to the human race, drawing freely from the infinite resources of Divine Thought and the Light of the Logos, Brahma Vach.

> Just as milliards of bright sparks dance on the waters of an ocean above which one and the same moon is shining, so our evanescent personalities — the illusive envelopes of the immortal MONAD-EGO — twinkle and dance on the waves of Maya. They last and appear, as the thousands of sparks produced by the moon-beams, only so long as the Queen of the Night radiates her lustre on the running waters of life: the period of a Manvantara; and then they disappear, the beams — symbols of our eternal Spiritual Egos — alone surviving, re-merged in, and being, as they were before, one with the Mother-Source.
>
> *The Secret Doctrine*, i 237

The Monad-Ego is the three-tongued flame, the *Atma-Buddhi-Manas* which overbroods throughout the *manvantara* myriads upon myriads of personalities, instruments and vehicles through which the great work of evolution proceeds. This is made possible by the fact that the three-tongued flame of the four wicks is connected with the myriads of sparks. Although in each life these sparks seemingly become entangled through the four derivative principles into a shallow sense of separative identity as a personal man or woman in that life, this is really an illusion. All the elements in all the personal lives throughout the *manvantara* represent the diffused intelligence which is here ascribed to a single source — the Queen of the Night — radiating her lustre on the running waters of life. Between the hidden source of the flames throughout evolution — the Central Spiritual Sun — and the manifest source of all the myriad sparks involved in the evanescent phenomena witnessed by personal consciousness in incarnated existence, there would be a causal relationship. One is like a necessary reflection of the other. This is true cosmically. It is also true of every single human being. The astral form is like a lunar reflection of a solar light-energy that belongs to the *Atma-Buddhi-Manas* which is like the sun overbrooding every single human temple. The profoundly mysterious relation between the two is intimated by the symbol of the thread of Fohat. A very fine thread connects the solar activity of the higher principles and the lunar activity involving the reflected and parasitic intelligence of personal consciousness.

Everything can be seen, as in the Platonic scheme, as a reflection of what is higher on a more homogeneous plane. The relative reality of every single entity and event in life is a shadowy reality that presupposes something more primordial and more homogeneous. In this way, all life would trace back to the one single field of homogeneous ideation, homogeneous substance. If this is what makes the universe a cosmos — a single system — then the solemn task of the human being is to integrate life consciously and cheerfully; to do this, one must first negate the false sense of identity that belongs on the lunar plane. One must perceive in depth all the elements of being that contribute to the seeming continuity of consciousness in and through the astral form, and then reach further inwards through deep meditation to the sacred source of all consciousness and life. This alchemical work is represented in many myths as the separation of what is food for the soul from what is not, before and during after-death states. This sifting takes place through all Nature and is the deliberate undertaking of those who are pledged to self-regeneration in the service of humanity. " 'Great Sifter' is the name of the 'Heart Doctrine', O Disciple."

The subtlety of this alchemical art arises from the fact that the pseudo-identity of the lunar plane involves not only the flux of fleeting emotional states but also a bewildering array of ghostly mental constructions. At a fundamental level of conceptualization, we have the tangled roots of the Ashwatha tree of samsaric illusion. This endemic tendency to hypostatize the emanations of cosmic mind was ably diagnosed by Professor Bain.

> The giving reality to abstractions is the error of Realism. Space and Time are frequently viewed as separated from all the concrete experiences of the mind, instead of being generalizations of these in certain aspects.
>
> *The Secret Doctrine,* i 251

Here Bain is referring to a long-standing tendency to reification, the cardinal error of classical realism which eventually produced a welter of conflicting interpretations of what were designated as 'universals'. These universals were abstract entities and were wholly sundered from the wealth of particulars in the world of phenomena. This generated insuperable theoretical difficulties. When the universals are applied to Space and Time, independent of all concrete experiences of the mind, they give rise to the false impression that the archetypes are remote from and unconnected with the activity of *kama manas* in the everyday world of subjects and objects. Strictly, one should recognize that at any point of time, relative to the succession of states of consciousness, there is simultaneously a non-linear clustering of conceptual frameworks that presuppose a spatio-temporal field. Bain is stating at a simple level what is crucial to the macrocosmic process at its pregenetic level. Space and Time are suffused and conceptually bound up with cosmic and human consciousness. We cannot truly separate anything from conscious life.

Every single point in space is animated by intelligence and the indwelling light of living awareness. There is nothing inanimate, nothing inert, nothing dead in the entire universe of matter and motion in Space and Time. In seeking through a series of philosophical negations to blank out all psychological

concretions, and then embark upon mystic meditation in the
Divine Dark, the great Night, one will view it not as an inane
void but rather as intense absolute light which is also absolute
darkness. All limited and limiting concepts of the contraries are
derived from everyday experience of heterogeneity, in terms of
which therefore, when one enters into the realm of the
homogeneous, one becomes hypnotized by the contrast between
the homogeneous and the heterogeneous. There is, however, a
further stage of enlightenment wherein one begins to enjoy so
strong, continuous and intense an awareness of the homogeneous
that one cognizes the homogeneous in the heterogeneous, sees
infinity in a grain of sand, eternity in an hour, the large in
the small. This is the hidden message of the *Bhagavad Gita*:
The cosmos is in the atom and the whole of the cosmos is like an
atom. Commenting upon the mysterious fohatic thread
connecting all of life, H.P. Blavatsky states:

> This relates to the greatest problem of philosophy
> — the physical and substantial nature of life, the
> independent nature of which is denied by modern
> science because that science is unable to comprehend
> it. The reincarnationists and believers in Karma alone
> dimly perceive that the whole secret of Life is in the
> unbroken series of its manifestations: whether in, or
> apart from, the physical body. Because if —
>
> *Life, like a dome of many coloured glass,*
> *Stains the white radiance of Eternity —*
>
> yet it is itself part and parcel of that Eternity; for life
> alone can understand life.
>
> *The Secret Doctrine,* i 238

When one is willing to gain a dynamic perception of the
macrocosmic depth within microcosmic life, then one may
develop a radically new mode of apprehending the world. In
connection with restoring this vital continuity between all the

aspects and phases of life, one must take up the difficult but important exercise of treating each day as an incarnation. It is hardly easy to grasp what this means at first. To understand truly, one can initially take four broad divisions, thus seeing a day in terms of the archetypal *process* of childhood, adolescence, adulthood and old age. One can make further and finer distinctions, once one has gained insight into the fourfold division of human life, thus transcending lumpy categories which ineffectually mediate between the atomic and the cosmic. One can gain a more mobile sense of reality, capable of reaching to the infinitesimal in consciousness, capable of rising to the transfinite. As this process becomes continuous, it inevitably affects all one's centres of perception, altering the flows of energy within the nervous system. This is why meditation must at some point give rise to a whole new set of sensory responses to the world and prepare one also for that level of cosmic consciousness where one becomes vividly conscious of the magical power of concentrated thought. When idea, image and intent are all fused in a noetic, dynamic energy which ignites the spiritual will, one gains precision and control, and can ultimately become a self-conscious agent in the transmutation of matter, the alchemical transformation of the vestures through the *tapas* and *yajna* of self-regeneration. Through calm reflection, one can begin to give a sense of reality to what are otherwise like metaphorical or vapidly abstract instances of universal consciousness, far removed from the prison-house of personal consciousness. But when one begins to enter into the activity of *Lila* itself, one can gain great strength, steadiness and spiritual sustenance, drawing apart from all forms, and gathering oneself into the mysterious interior intelligent centre of one's original spiritual consciousness.

It is a MYSTERY, truly but only to him who is prepared to reject the existence of intellectual and conscious spiritual Beings in the Universe, limiting full Consciousness to man alone, and that only as a 'function of the Brain'. Many are those among the

Spiritual Entities, who have incarnated bodily in man, since the beginning of his appearance, and who, for all that, still exist as independently as they did before, in the infinitudes of Space.

The Secret Doctrine, i 233

One must relocate oneself within the depths of this vast general perspective of a host of Dhyani Buddhas and Bodhisattvas, exalted beings of different degrees of consciousness ranging from the most universal consciousness that even transcends the solar system to very high consciousness in this solar world and in lunar bodies. This boundless and beatific panorama is presented in many different ways in all the great mystical texts, and given *par excellence* in the universal vision of the eleventh chapter of the *Bhagavad Gita.* Through it, one may begin to see that the world as ordinarily known is but a surface revealing only pale reflections in an immense shadow-play. One can begin to apprehend the initially discomforting, but ultimately revolutionary, thought that what is going on in oneself is not even guessed by one's lower mind. Many of the problems of human beings arise because the inefficient, insecure and fear-ridden lower mind — lamed in childhood and competitive hot-houses — claims to reveal all, although it is only a small part of the whole. In truth, most of what is really going on inside a human being occurs during deep sleep, or scattered moments of awareness in waking life, which do not register at all in *kama manas.* They cannot be recorded, still less reported. Hence, the paradox known to many mystics arises — what is called life is a form of death from the standpoint of the immortal soul.

As Krishna says in the *Gita,* to the spiritually wise what men call day is the night of ignorance. It is a mere shadow-play of elemental interaction imperfectly edited by a lower mind which is naturally a helpless prisoner of its own particular perceptions, expectations and memories. This "tale told by an idiot" is independent of the true life of the immortal soul, which is well characterized as silent (since the immortal soul cannot find in the languages that belong to the heterogeneous realm any vocabulary for its own spiritual knowledge and cognition). It can, however, be reflected in the proper use of the sacred power of speech and the mystical potency of sound. The invisible entity may be bodily present on earth without abandoning its status and functions in supersensuous regions. If the overbrooding Spirit were not connected, like a daimon or indwelling tutelary genius, with personal consciousness, there would be no possibility of awareness and of learning for the soul with all its misfirings and mistakes. Even then, that learning itself is partial because what is truly happening within the real Self, the invisible entity and the immortal daimon, cannot really be summoned by the uninitiated without bringing the instruments in line with the spiritual will of the *Atma-Buddhi-Manas*.

What happens involuntarily and naturally in deep sleep must be done consciously in waking life through philosophical negation, deep meditation, calm reflection and Pythagorean self-examination. If done daily, in time it will be possible to bring closer the astral vesture and the true divine Self that otherwise is only partially involved or only inadequately incarnated. Taking this as a general truth about humanity, it connects with the complex doctrines of Rounds, Globes and Races and the eventual development that will take place in the Rounds far in the future. There will be much fuller incarnation possible, because of the radical change that would have taken place in the plasticity and resilience of the material vestures. Matter will be so markedly different that it can readily reflect Spirit with a pristine purity which is virtually independent of the entire stream of monadic and material evolution. To move self-consciously in this direction of depth perception is the willing contribution of the true pilgrim who enters the Path and takes vows for lives, vows that involve the ceaseless process of self-transformation for the sake of universal enlightenment. True disciples will consecrate each day to Hermes-Budha, to the Manasaputras, the descending luminous beings that make human self-consciousness possible. All Lanoos will strengthen the centre of silence within themselves until it can be used for the calm release of a new current of energy, a new line of life's meditation, which fuses thought, will and feeling in daily life for the sake of the larger whole. Wise men and women will take full advantage of this teaching to bring forth the greatest strength and sacrifice that can be released in their own lives for the sake of Universal Good, the Agathon on earth as in Heaven (*Akasha*), the *summum bonum* which flows from *Saguna Brahman* but is gestated within the bosom of *Nirguna Brahman*, boundless Space in eternal Duration.

MEDITATION
AND SELF-STUDY

METAPHYSICS AND ETHICS

Tat tvam asi

It is natural for us to make a firm distinction between our study and our application of Gupta Vidya, between theory and practice. As a result, we contrast the capacities of the head and the heart, and assume that we seek and secure different kinds of nourishment from *The Secret Doctrine* and *The Voice of the Silence*. At the same time, we also know that Gupta Vidya is essentially the Heart Doctrine, distinct from the head-learning with which our world abounds. What is more, the whole purpose of spiritual discipline is to blend the head and the heart, to broaden our mental sympathies and to awaken and direct the intelligence of the heart. Does this simply mean that we need for conceptual clarity the dualistic view of the spiritual life as long as we remain as inwardly divided as we are, and that this dichotomy is made only so that it may be destroyed as we become rooted in the holiness that reflects an inner wholeness? It is certainly convenient to regard all conceptual distinctions and classifications as mere scaffoldings and to choose the best available at any particular stage of our growth. But, in order to appreciate the distinctive significance of philosophical classifications, we cannot merely regard them like the maps of early mariners, whose explorations needed as well as corrected their initial cartographical knowledge. We need, in fact, to acquire an entirely new and original view of the relation between true metaphysics and enduring ethics and to appreciate the profound epistemological nature and the peculiar therapeutic value of Theosophical statements, as indicated in the First Item of *The Secret Doctrine*.

Metaphysics, as normally understood, is speculative rather than gnostic and is often the product of the propensity to subsume existing knowledge under a complete system, an imposing pattern that is then ascribed to reality with a dogmatism that pretends to a certainty that it cannot possibly possess. It is in accord with cyclic law that this kind of metaphysical system-building is suspect today and has even led to an extremist and naïvely positivistic reaction among die-hard empiricists. Similarly, ethics, in the everyday sense, consists of injunctions and imperatives that are rarely susceptible of rational inquiry and are either endowed with a spurious absoluteness or are regarded as relativist and subjectivist preferences, from which we choose as from a menu. Given the pretentious nature of ordinary metaphysics and conventional ethics, we can understand the insistence of Hume, the sceptical Scot of the 18th century, that metaphysical statements are *a priori* assertions that are incapable of verification, that we cannot logically derive any ethical imperatives either from them or from statements of fact, and that our ethical preferences cannot possess certainty or universality or freedom from arbitrariness. The metaphysical assertion that "X is true or must be true" cannot help us to answer the question, "Why ought I to do Y?" It is indeed not surprising that the speculations of most metaphysicians do not give us a basis for moral conduct and moral growth, and that the injunctions of many conventional ethical codes do not have their basis in the moral and spiritual order of our law-governed cosmos.

In the literature of Gupta Vidya, however, every metaphysical statement has an ethical corollary and connotation, and every ethical injunction has a distinct metaphysical basis. It is impossible to grasp the force of any of the seven *Paramitas* of *The Voice of the Silence* without a comprehension of the Three Fundamental Propositions regarding God, Nature and Man that underlie the order of reality intimated by the Stanzas of the *Book of Dzyan*, on which *The Secret Doctrine* is closely based. Theosophical literature assumes, as shown especially by *Light on the Path*, the truth and validity of the Socratic axiom, "Knowledge is virtue." For example, to know, with the heart as well as the head, and to be fully aware that the sin and the shame of the world are verily our own, must totally transform our actions as well as our attitudes in relation to all our fellow men and also to our own sins and lower self. We cannot rely on that which is not real, in an ultimate and philosophical sense. The ethics of Gupta Vidya teaches the only possible reliance — on the Divine Ground of all Being and beyond — that is available to those who become aware of the degrees of reality in an ever-evolving universe that is itself only a relatively real emanation from the Eternal Reality. Our conduct consists of emanations that cannot but harm us and others if they are not emanated in the creative and impersonal manner and with the conscious control that marks the ceaseless process of cosmic emanations from a single source — "Life of our life, Force of our force." Until we are free from the dire heresy of separateness (*attavada*), we cannot claim to have grasped the doctrine of *Samvritti* or of the *Nidanas*, that teaches us about the origins of delusions and chains of causation. To know is to become, and to become is truly to know.

In an illuminating passage in *The Secret Doctrine* on the "Causes of Existence" and on the Buddhist concept of *Nidana* and the Hindu concept of maya, H.P. Blavatsky states that science and religion, in trying to trace back the chain of causes and effects, jump to a condition of mental blankness much more quickly than is necessary,

> for they ignore the metaphysical abstractions which are the only conceivable cause of physical concretions. These abstractions become more and more concrete as they approach our plane of existence, until finally they phenomenalise in the form of the material Universe, by a process of conversion of metaphysics into physics. . . .
>
> *The Secret Doctrine*, i 45

If we consider this even as a logical possibility, then clearly the knowledge of these metaphysical abstractions gained and given by trained Initiates is epistemologically prior to the external order of reality in the material universe. Such metaphysics, the product of intuitive apprehension and capable of patient verification by the extrasensory experiences of independently acting individuals, is different in kind from the speculative metaphysics of the ordinary variety and is more analogous to the methods of investigation of the greatest natural scientists. This is why we are told that

> it is difficult to find a single speculation in Western metaphysics which has not been anticipated by Archaic Eastern philosophy. From Kant to Herbert Spencer, it is all a more or less distorted echo of the Dwaita, Adwaita, and Vedantic doctrines generally.
>
> *Ibid.*, 79 fn.

The very nature of the metaphysics of Gupta Vidya is such that we cannot approach it merely with the head, independently of the heart. The purely ratiocinative and intellectualist approach to ordinary metaphysics is itself the result of "the inadequate distinctions made by the Jews, and now by our Western metaphysicians," so that "the philosophy of psychic, spiritual, and mental relations with man's physical functions is in almost inextricable confusion." Our metaphysical conceptions are clearly conditioned by our own mental development and cannot have the absolute validity that we claim for them. This is especially true of the evolution of the GOD-IDEA. Hence, for every thinker there will be a "Thus far shalt thou go and no farther," mapped out by his intellectual capacity.

> Outside of initiation, the ideals of contemporary religious thought must always have their wings clipped and remain unable to soar higher; for idealistic as well as realistic thinkers, and even free-thinkers, are but the outcome and the natural product of their respective environments and periods.
>
> *Ibid.*, i 326

Not merely does modern metaphysics fall far short of the truth, but even its basic concepts and usages of terms like 'Absolute', 'Nature' and 'matter' are shallower and cruder than their corresponding concepts propounded by the Lodge of Adepts.

Initiation into the metaphysics of Gupta Vidya is more than an intellectual or moral enterprise; it is a continuous spiritual exercise in the development of intuitive and cognitive capacities that are the highest available to men, a process that includes from the first a blending of the head and the heart through the interaction of *Viveka* and *Vairagya*, discrimination and detachment. Even our initial apprehension of a statement of arcane metaphysics involves an ethical as well as mental effort, just as even the smallest application of a scriptural injunction to our moral life requires some degree of mental control and the deeper awareness, universal and impersonal in nature, that comes from our higher cognitive capacities. Moral growth presupposes "the silent worship of abstract or *noumenal* Nature, the only divine manifestation," that is "the one ennobling religion of Humanity."

Despite its contempt for metaphysics and for ontology, materialistic science is honeycombed with metaphysical and contradictory implications, and even its 'atoms' are 'entified abstractions.' "To make of Science an integral *whole* necessitates, indeed, the study of spiritual and psychic, as well as physical Nature." But, although *real* science is inadmissible without metaphysics, and those scientists who trespass on the forbidden grounds of metaphysics, who lift the veil of matter and strain their eyes to see beyond, are "wise in their generation," H.P. Blavatsky declares towards the end of *The Secret Doctrine* that the man of exact science must realize that

> he has no right to trespass on the grounds of meta-
> physics and psychology. His duty is to verify and to
> rectify all the facts that *fall under his direct* observation;
> to profit by the experiences and mistakes of the Past in
> endeavouring to trace the working of a certain
> concatenation of cause and effects, which, but only by
> its constant and unvarying repetition, may be called A
> LAW.... Any sideway path from this royal road
> becomes *speculation*.
>
> *Ibid.*, ii 664

It is a sign of advance that scientists today are less given than their predecessors in the latter half of the nineteenth century to "metaphysical flights of fancy". Bad metaphysics is clearly worse than none. On the other hand, as modern psychology becomes less materialistic and as race-evolution proceeds, a greater appreciation of the higher intuitive and cognitive capacities will emerge and may enable the most intuitive scientists to venture more effectively into metaphysics.

It is, therefore, necessary for students of Theosophy to see the fundamental difference between what goes by the name of metaphysics and has rightly become suspect today, and the "metaphysics, pure and simple", with which *The Secret Doctrine* is concerned. We cannot, however, grasp the metaphysics given in Theosophical teachings unless we perceive its close and inseparable connection with Theosophical ethics. We are told in *The Secret Doctrine* that the "highly philosophical and metaphysical Aryans" were the authors of "the most perfect philosophical systems of transcendental psychology" and of "a moral code (Buddhism), proclaimed by Max Müller the most perfect on earth." Without a proper understanding of Theosophical psychology and the teachings regarding the nature and constitution of man and the working of Karmic law, we cannot appreciate the metaphysical basis of Theosophical ethics or the ethical significance of Theosophical metaphysics. Hence the importance of a careful study and application, from the first, of the Ten Items from *Isis Unveiled* or the Propositions of Oriental Psychology, and of the Aphorisms on Karma by W.Q. Judge. Until this is done, we cannot begin to see the ethical import of the statements in *The Secret Doctrine* or the metaphysical basis of the statements in *The Voice of the Silence* and *Light on the Path*.

We are told explicitly in *The Secret Doctrine* that "to make the workings of Karma, in the periodical renovations of the Universe, more evident and intelligible to the student when he arrives at the origin and evolution of man, he has now to examine with us the esoteric bearing of the Karmic Cycles upon Universal Ethics". Our ethical progress depends on an increasing awareness of the "cycles of matter" and the "cycles of spiritual evolution", and of racial, national and individual cycles. The kernel of Theosophical ethics is contained in the statement that "there are *external and internal conditions* which affect the determination of our will upon our actions, and it is in our power to follow either of the two."

This contains a great metaphysical and psychological truth, which is illuminated by the seminal article on "Psychic and Noetic Action", written, late in life, by H.P. Blavatsky, the Magus-Teacher of the 1875 cycle. Theosophical ethics is in the end no easier to understand properly than Theosophical metaphysics. It can no more be grasped by the mentally lazy than Theosophical metaphysics can be comprehended by the morally obtuse. There is nothing namby-pamby about Theosophical ethics and it is as fundamentally different from conventional ethics as Theosophical metaphysics is from conventional metaphysics. Just as modern metaphysics is a shadowy distortion of archaic metaphysics, modern ethics is a sad vulgarization of the archaic ethics taught by the early religious Teachers of humanity. It is to be welcomed that more and more questioning people today are less and less prepared to accept blindly conventional ethical codes merely because they are traced back to so-called scriptural revelations, just as they have little use for the metaphysical speculations of even the formidable minds of the past. If the ethical nihilism of today is even more repugnant to the Theosophist than sterile positivism, he would do well to regard both as the Karmic price we have to pay for the moral and metaphysical dogmatism of the past.

Although we may talk of Theosophical metaphysics and Theosophical ethics, and classify texts broadly under these heads, we must get beyond the conventional distinction between metaphysical and ethical statements and grasp central concepts, such as Dharma and Karma, which are protean in scope and profound in content, and incapable of being regarded as purely metaphysical or exclusively ethical. It is significant that the supposedly anti-metaphysical and superbly moral teaching of the Buddha was centred in the complex concept of Dharma rather than in *Brahman* or *moksha,* in the stern law of moral compensation and universal causality, rather than in a conception of infinite Deity constructed by the finite mind of man or in any notion of salvation or redemption which caters to the spiritual selfishness of the individual.

In the European tradition, a natural reaction to theocentric systems of thought was the Cartesian affirmation of the autonomy of the individual in relation to knowledge and the later Kantian proclamation of the autonomy of the individual in relation to morality. The Theosophist, however, holds to the Pythagorean and ancient Eastern maxim that man is the mirror and microcosm of the macrocosm. It is in this context that he must evolve from egoism to egoity, from personal self-love to individual self-consciousness, which is impossible without a heart-understanding of the Law of Universal Unity and Moral Retribution. The close connection between metaphysics and ethics in Theosophy is ultimately based on the workings of Universal Law, which affects the exact and occult correspondences between the constituents of man and of the cosmos. This ancient doctrine of correspondences has been ignored by modern metaphysicians and moralists, but it was known to modern mystics and poets from Boehme to Swedenborg, Blake to Baudelaire.

MEDITATION
AND SELF-STUDY

Atmanam atmana pasya

M editation and self-study are of immeasurable
importance to every single person. They concern the
longest journey of the soul, the divine discontent in
human life. The quest for true meditation and the yearning for
real self-knowledge are as old as thinking man. Today, more
than ever before in recorded history, there is a widespread hunger
for teaching and instruction concerning meditation
and concentration. Some seek even more, longing for a way of
life irradiated by the inward peace and joyous strength of
contemplation. Ours is an age of acute, almost obsessive, self-
consciousness. Everyone is oppressed by the ego-games endemic
to contemporary culture, the thought-forms and speech habits,
the paranoid, loveless and competitive modes seemingly required
merely to keep body and soul together. We are tempted to think
that there is some inescapable necessity to assert ourselves to
survive, to protect ourselves from being exploited, engulfed or
drowned. At the same time, we look in many directions, to ancient
and modern as well as to new-fangled schools of psychological
health, hoping to enhance our capacity for self-analysis, mental
clarification, and minimum control over our personal lives.

The hunger for authentic knowledge and reliable techniques
of meditation, and the poignant concern for self-definition, are
paramount needs of our time. They are more fundamental, more
lasting and more bewildering than all other clamorous claims.
But they appear to move in opposite directions. The impulse
toward meditation seems to be towards opting out of the world —
the world of illusion — or at least the decaying structure of any
society. It suggests liberation, an escape from the great wheel of

birth and death and the whole life-process. It involves the desire
for an equivalent to the conventional concepts of heaven. Images
of eternal, nirvanic and absolute self-transcendence are often
analogous to the perpetual and perfect release which men
desperately seek and fail to find on the physical plane of the lower
eros. On the other hand, the entire concern for self-analysis and
self-understanding is bound up with the need to improve our
relation to our fellow men, our capacity for survival, the abject
dependence on acceptance and love. It is so much directed to a
re-entry into the world that self-study and meditation seem to
represent poles that fly off in opposite directions. And in both
cases there are more teachers than disciples. There are so many
schools, so many sects, such a vast range of panaceas that there is
something absurd and also deeply sad about the ferment on the
threshold of the 1975 cycle.

If we think for a moment of another age, a distant time
in which men sought for supreme wisdom concerning the
immortality of the Self and the ultimate joys of contemplation,
we may discern that there were men and women who gave their
whole lives to a sustained and desperate search. They consecrated
everything they had for the sake of finding some answer by
which they could live, and from which they could gain a more
fundamental insight, a more permanent solution, not only for
themselves, but also in relation to the intense human predicament,
the malaise of mankind. Today we certainly do not find anything
comparable to the exacting demands and the aristocratic sense
in which many are called, few persist, fewer are chosen, and very
few succeed. There is a tantalizing statistic in the *Bhagavad Gita*
suggesting that one in a million succeeds in the quest for
immortality. When we think of that exalted perspective upon
the journey, in an age where there is an almost universal concern,
and if we consider it in impersonal terms, for the sake of all and
not only for ourselves, we are bound to feel deeply puzzled.
Something is going wrong. Yet there must be a legitimacy in
what is happening. How can one understand this? Where can
one find the true wisdom and teaching? Where are the real

teachers? Where are those authentic men of meditation who can by their compassion consecrate the whole endeavour, showing not only discrimination in the choice of deserving disciples, but also a supreme justice befitting the total need of the world as a whole? The more we ask questions of this kind, the more we must retreat, if we are honest, into a cleansing confession of complete ignorance.

We do not know whether there is in the world any knowledge, of which there are external signs that are absolutely certain, in relation to a sovereign method. The conditions, the requirements and the object of the quest are obscure to us. Viewing the immense need of our age, we are uncertain whether there is anything that could adequately serve the diverse needs of vast numbers of varied kinds of human agony, sickness and pain. We might think we are in the Dark Ages, that the Mahatmas have gone, and that there is no longer access to the highest conception of wisdom in relation to meditation or self-knowledge. This answer would come naturally to a humble and honest seeker in the context of the immemorial tradition of the East. In the West one might be inclined either to argue that having no way of knowing whether the whole thing is a distraction, it is better not to look in any direction, or, to see our plight in terms of the messianic religious traditions of the Piscean Age.

Thus there is a restless intensity to the search for a technique or formula, which is not merely a surefire method of meditation or of self-study, but which is in fact a panacea for salvation. Those who are not only concerned for themselves, but share a sense of awareness of the common needs of humanity, think less in terms of a mere panacea than of a mandate for universal salvation. They seek what is not only supremely valid, decisive and certain, but what could also be made available to all and is capable of ready use by human beings as they are — with all their fallibilities, limitations and imperfections — whether as apprentices and beginners, or merely for the sake of avoiding the slide into self-destruction. They are looking for what can in fact be widely marketed and made available. Put in another language, the idea of a mandate for salvation becomes more understandable and can be lent a certain minimal dignity. It is as if one says that one wants, for any ordinary person in the street, not the knowledge he needs for him to become a saint or a sage, or a man of meditation perfected in self-knowledge, but simply the knowledge that would enable him to have what he cannot find in any pill or potion, and cannot get from any physician or psychiatrist.

It is the knowledge that will help him to balance his life and to gain, in a chaotic time, enough calm and sufficient continuity of will-energy, to be able to survive without succumbing to the constant threat and danger of disintegration, ever looming large like a nightmare. What is needed is the ability to avoid the dreadful decline along an inclined slope tending towards an awful abyss of annihilation and nothingness. On that inclined slope are steps that are very painful and readily recognisable, not only by oneself but by each other. They represent the weakening of the will and the progressive inability to reinforce the will, especially amidst the breakdown of all those collectivised goals of societies and men in terms of which one was once able to generate a kind of extraordinary will-energy. In our Promethean or Faustian culture individuals simply do not have the will-energy required for the most minimal notions of survival. When we put the subject in this agonizing contemporary context, and not in a classical context seemingly removed from our time, we are entitled to ask whether there is any ancient text on meditation and self-study worthy of scrutiny and deeply relevant in one's life, which is in principle capable of universalization and could have the widest relevance to our contemporary condition.

Here one may turn to the meticulous and enigmatic wisdom of that immensely compassionate and extraordinary human being whom we know as Helena Petrovna Blavatsky. She chose, though only at the very end of her life, to give to the world and yet dedicate to the few, a translation from unknown Tibetan sources of stanzas, chanted in monasteries and sanctuaries of initiation, which she called *The Voice of the Silence*. This beautiful book was blessed in her time by the man whose karmic privilege it was to assume the custodianship of all the orders and schools in Tibet, the Dalai Lama of her day. Early in this century it was published in a Peking edition that had a preface from the Panchen Lama. It is a book that has been blessed by the visible representatives of the authentic tradition of Tibet. For those who have read the book and compared it to the *Bhagavad Gita,* and to the classical Indian texts on meditation and the Self, either going back to Patanjali or Shankaracharya or coming down to modern representatives of the old tradition — to those who have done this at even some elementary level, it is clear that the book is extremely difficult but also that it is an invitation and a challenge.

There are those who have actually taken very seriously, on trust, the words of H.P. Blavatsky on the very first page of the book — "Chosen Fragments from the Book of the Golden Precepts, for the Daily Use of Lanoos." Only wishing to become a *lanoo* or a disciple, they aspire to a discipline that is divine but which must be practised every single day. Those who are simple enough, like God's fools, to have this kind of response to the book, and who use it, soon find themselves in the position of asking whether they really understand what is being taught and whether these instructions are living and relevant realities in their lives. No doubt there may be moods in which the text may seem to be empty words, but over a period does it honestly make a difference to one's consciousness, one's daily life, one's capacity for calm self-control and growth in self-knowledge? When a person applies these tests to himself, all that can be said in advance is that people who have so used the book have found it of sufficient help to them to become immeasurably grateful to those responsible for giving the world this version of an old and traditional discipline. Indeed, there must surely be a few for whom the book ultimately ceases to be a book, and for whom the very pathway of ascent through portals becomes a supreme reality in their lives. For them the problem becomes not one of questioning this reality, but one of relating it to the so-called realities of the world in which we live. How do we live this life, not in some secluded and protected spot on earth, but here and now? In crowded cities, among lowly human beings, everything seems to drown and crowd out the message of this book. Anyone who wishes may consider meditation and self-study in the context of the teaching in *The Voice of the Silence*. It seems only appropriate that seekers of wisdom should avail themselves of the privilege of doing this, not only for their own increasing benefit, but also out of a genuine wish to share with those who may not have had the opportunity to give themselves a chance to use this teaching and this book. Minimally, one could say that this would be no worse than anything else they could think of. But each one must decide on his own.

If we do approach the subject in this context, we might ask how this book, even what one knows of it, helps to link up the contemporary agony with the supreme flights of meditation of the classical past. Astonishingly, both are in the book — at the beginning and at the end. Early in the book we are told about the immense tragedy of the human condition:

> Behold the Hosts of Souls. Watch how they hover o'er the stormy sea of human life, and how, exhausted, bleeding, broken-winged, they drop one after other on the swelling waves. Tossed by the fierce winds, chased by the gale, they drift into the eddies and disappear within the first great vortex.

The crisis of identity, the psychological terror, the desperate struggle for survival and for a minimum meaning to be attached to one's life — these are all around us. At best we can only imagine the boundless compassion of beings so much greater than ourselves who are capable of comprehending the enormity of the anguish. At the same time, the book tells us what the ideal man of meditation would be like. It gives us a moving and compelling picture, a vibrant image of the man of meditation. It shows how he is mightier than the gods, that he is so strong that he "holdeth life and death in his strong hand." His mind, "like a becalmed and boundless ocean, spreadeth out in shoreless space." So great is the emergence of such a Being, at any time or place hidden in the obscurity of the secret history of mankind, that it is known and recorded and receives a symphonic celebration in all the kingdoms of Nature. The whole of Nature "thrills with joyous awe and feels subdued."

The text evokes in us memories of a forgotten past, of mythic conceptions, of golden ages that are gone, when men, like children, sat in an atmosphere of trust and peace, with abundant leisure, under the shade of trees. While some came for shelter, some to fall asleep, some to sit and learn, and some to sit and chat about everything ranging from the most metaphysical to the most practical, still others came for the sake of the existential embodiment of the discipline of a life of contemplation. Images of this kind come into our minds, while at the same time we perhaps see that there is a continuity within the agony of mankind throughout history. There is a deeper anguish, a divine discontent at the very core of the human condition, which is as old as man and which is as strikingly pertinent as all the accounts of the needs of our age. Somewhere there is a connection between the tremendous consummation of the Supreme Master of meditation and light — he who has become one with the universe, who has become a living mirror of the glory of the garment of God, of the universe as a whole, of the Self of all creatures — somewhere there is a connection between that Being, if he is a part of the family of man, and all those who are on the verge of disintegration.

There is in every single human being the embryo of this ideal man of meditation, and we can at least imagine what it would be like for such a being to be present somewhere in our midst, if not in ourselves. We also can recognize that we have our own share in the desperate demand for psychological survival. In this way we restore an integrity to our own quest and are somewhat deserving of that illumination which will take hold in our consciousness in relation to the great and priceless teaching. We might begin to wonder whether perhaps there is a golden chord that connects the golden sphere of a man of meditation and the complex intermediary realms in which he must, by pain and anguish and awakening, by knitting together minute golden moments rescued from a great deal of froth and self-deception, come to know himself. If there were not a fundamental connection between meditation and self-study, something of the uniquely precious wisdom in this great text would be lost to us. When we begin to realize this in our lives, we come to appreciate that, while we may not be in a position to make judgments about teachers and schools in a vast and largely unrecorded history or in our own time, nonetheless we do know that there is something profoundly important in stressing *both* meditation and self-study, in bringing the two together. We must reconcile what looked like a pair of opposites and get beyond despair to something else which allows an existential and dynamic balance between meditation and self-study. This is the quality of compassion. It is in the heart of every human being in his response to human pain, and brings him truly into the fellowship of those Beings of Boundless Compassion.

A man is a Buddha before he seeks to become a Buddha. He is a Buddha potentially. The Buddha at one time must have had a desire to become a Buddha, to understand human pain. The Buddha vow is holy because it is a vow taken on behalf of all. There is in everyone the capacity to want something for the sake of all, and also honestly to want it for oneself. In this there is an authentic mirroring, in every human heart, of the highest, the holiest and the most pregnant of beginnings of the quest. There are many beginnings, many failures, and many seeming endings. The quest itself, since it applies to all beings and not only to any one man, is beginningless and endless. It is universal, since any individual quest in this direction becomes at some point merged into the collective quest. Put in poetical form, or recognized in the simplest feelings, there is something metaphysically important and philosophically fundamental to the connection between meditation or self-transcendence, and the kind of self-study which makes true self-actualization possible. There is a way in which a man can both be out of this world and in this world, can forget himself and yet be more truly himself. These paradoxes of language are difficult to explain at one level and yet we all know them to be the paradoxes of our very lives. In our moments of greatest loneliness we suddenly find a surprising capacity to come closer to beings far removed from us, men of different races and alienated groups in pain. Then we come to feel a brotherhood that is so profound that it could never be secured in any other way. These are part of the everyday experience of mankind.

Here we touch on a crucial emphasis, maintained sedulously by the Gelukpa tradition of Tibet, which affirms that unless you spend sufficient time in refining, studying and purifying your motive, in using compassion as fuel to generate the energy needed to take off and land, you should not begin to rush into meditation. It is a slow school, but it greets the aspirant in the name of all. It scorns powers and the notion of one man becoming a superman in isolation from the quest of other men. Making no promises or claims, it does not insult our intelligence by promising us something to be attained without effort.

Are we not old enough in history to be somewhat apprehensive of schools that promise too much and too soon, when we know that this does not work in any sphere of life? Would we go to some local, loud-talking musician who tells us that he could make us as good as Casals in a week? Would we even take him seriously? We might go to him out of fun or sympathy or curiosity. Why in the most sacred of all realms should we be misled? Is it because of our impatience, our feeling of unworthiness, an advance fear of failure? These questions throw us back upon ourselves. In raising them, in probing our own standpoint at the original moment of the beginning of the quest, we make discoveries about ourselves. They are very profound and important, as they may sum up for us a great deal of the past. They would also be crucial in the future where we may come to sense the supreme relevance all along the way, when it is hard and rough, of what Merlin said to Arthur: "Go back to the original moment." If one could understand the fullness of what is anticipated in that original moment of our quest, one could trace the whole curve of our growth that is likely to emerge, with its ups and downs. Yet it cannot tell all as long as there are unknown depths of potentiality and free will in a human being.

A statement in *The Morning of the Magicians* suggests that so long as men want something for nothing, money without work, knowledge without study, power without knowledge, virtue without some form of asceticism, so long will a thousand pseudo-initiatory societies flourish, imitating the truly secret language of the 'technicians of the sacred.' There must be some reason why the integrity of the quest requires that no false flattery be made to the weaker side in every man. *The Voice of the Silence* tells us early on: "Give up thy life, if thou would'st live." That side of you which is afraid, which wants to be cajoled and flattered and promised, which would like an insurance policy, must go, must die. It is only in that dying that you will discover yourself. We all limit ourselves. We engage in a collective act of daily self-denigration of mankind. We impose, in addition to our tangible problems, imaginary and insurmountable difficulties owing to our dogmatic insistence on the finality of our limitations.

The Wisdom-Religion is transmitted so as to restore in the human being, and collectively in the world, the reality of the perfectibility of man, the assurance that men are gods, that any man is capable of reaching the apex, and that the difference between a Buddha or a Christ and any one of us is a difference of degree and not of kind. At the same time it shows that the slaying of the dragon, the putting of the demon under the foot, the command of the sovereign will of the Adept, "Get thee behind me, Satan," are heroic deeds every one of us could accomplish. Potential gods could also become kings. Every man could be a king in his own republic, but he can only become a king and eventually a god if he first experiences the thrill of affirming what it is to be a man — man *qua* man, one who partakes of the glory, the potentiality, the promise and the excellence of human nature, one who shares points of contact with the mightiest man of meditation. He must understand what the power of his thought can do, and discern a connection between the imagination of children and the disciplined imagination of perfected teachers.

With this exalted view of the individual embodiment of the collective potentialities of man, a person can say, "I'm proud to be a man and man enough to give myself a minimum of dignity. I'm willing to be tried, to be tough, to go through a discipline. I'm willing to become a disciple, and dissipate that portion of myself which is pretentious, but which is also my problem and my burden — like the donkey the man carries on his back in the Japanese fable — instead of making it an ever-lengthening shadow by walking away from the sun. I can make that shadow shrink by walking towards the sun, the Logos reflected in the great teachers, which is real and in me and every single living being." This is a great affirmation. To make it is profoundly important. It is to affirm in this day and age that it is meaningful for a man to give up lesser pretensions and engage in what may look like presumption, but is really an assertion in his life that he can appreciate the prerogative of what it is to be a *manushya,* a man, a self-conscious being. That is a great step on the path of progressive steps in meditation and self-study.

So far all that has been said is about beginnings, but this really is an arena where the first step seems to be the most difficult. Also, it is a matter of how you define the first step. An analogy may be made here with our experience in the engineering of flying machines. The designs were there; the diagrams were there; the equations were there; the knowledge of what is involved in maintaining a jet engine at high altitudes was there. The tough part was the take-off and landing problem. We now know more widely, in an age when people turn in desperation to a variety of drugs, that it is very difficult to have control over entry into the higher states of consciousness in a manner that will assure a smooth re-entry into ordinary life. It is because of the take-off and landing problem that we need both to be very clear about our beginnings and also to see the whole quest as a re-sharpening of the integrity of the beginning, in relation to meditation and self-study.

In the Gelukpa schools one would be told to spend a lot of time expanding compassion but also meditating on meditation. What is one going to meditate on? Meditate on meditation itself. Meditate on men of meditation. In other words, the more you try to meditate, the more you realize that meditation is elusive. But this is an insight that protects you from self-deception. Ultimately, the entire universe is an embodiment of collective mind. Meditation in its fullness is that creative power of the Platonic Demiurge, of the Hindu Visvakarman, of the Logos of the Gnostics, which could initiate a whole world. That initiation or inauguration of a world is a representation of the mighty power of meditation. You can become, says *The Voice of the Silence,* one with the power of All-Thought, but you cannot do so until you have expelled every particular thought from your mind-soul. Here is the philosophical and cosmic basis of meditation in its fullness. All meditations can only be stepping stones towards a larger meditation. What will give us a gauge of the quality, strength and meaningfulness of our power to meditate, and of our particular meditations, is our ability to harvest in the realm of self-knowledge that which can be tested in our knowledge and understanding of all other selves. To put this in another way, if to love one person unconditionally is so difficult for us, how extraordinarily remote from us seems to be the conception of those beings who can unconditionally love *all* living beings. We cannot do it even with one. Now someone might say, "No, but I can do it with one or a few sufficiently to understand in principle what it would be like to do it for all." Someone else might say, "Oh, when I look at my life I find that I don't know what it is fully to love any one, but I do know that somewhere in my loneliness and pain I feel the closeness of anonymous faces, a silent bond of brotherhood between myself and many others."

There are different ways by which we could see in ourselves the embryo of that boundless love and compassion which is the fruit of self-knowledge at its height, where a man becomes self-consciously a universal embodiment of the Logos, having no sense of identity except in the very act of mirroring universal light.

There must be a tremendous integrity to a teaching and discipline which says that every step counts, that every failure can be used, and that the ashes of your failures will be useful in regrafting and rejuvenating what is like a frail tree that has to be replanted again and again. But the tree one is planting is the tree of immortality. One is trying to bring down into the lesser vehicles of the more differentiated planes of matter the glorious vesture of immortality, which showed more clearly when one was a baby, which one saluted in the first cry of birth, and of which one becomes somewhat aware at the moment of death.

There is a hint at the moments of birth and death, something like an intimation of the hidden glory of man, but during life one is not so awake. This becomes a problem of memory and forgetfulness. The chain of decline is started. It was classically stated in the second chapter of the *Gita*: "He who attendeth to the inclinations of the senses, in them hath a concern; from this concern is created passion, from passion anger, from anger is produced delusion, from delusion a loss of the memory, from the loss of memory loss of discrimination, and from loss of discrimination loss of all!" Every man is fragmenting himself, spending himself, limiting himself, finitizing himself, localizing himself, to such a degree, with such an intensity and irregularity, and such a frenetic, feverish restlessness, that he is consuming himself. Physiologically, we know that we cannot beat the clocktime processes of the changes in the physical body. Therefore we cannot expect to find the elixir of immortality on the physical plane. But we all know that by attending to the very process of growth and change, and by awareness of what happens to us in sickness, that we do have some control and can make a difference by our very attitude and acceptance of the process. If you are very ill, by worrying about it you are going to make yourself worse, but there are people who are really quite ill, who by acceptance have gained something of the aroma of well-being.

These are everyday facts having analogues and roots in a causal realm of ideation and creative imagination which gives shape and form to the subtle vehicle, through which a transmission could take place of the immortal, indestructible and inexhaustible light of the Logos which is in every man and came into the world with every child. It is the radiance of Shekinah, the *nur* of Allah, the light of *St. John*. It is a light that looks like darkness and is not to be mistaken for those things that have a glamour on the sensory plane. To bring it down or make it transmit through the causal realm and become a living *tejas* or light-energy issuing forth from the fingers and all the windows and apertures of the human body is, of course, asking for a great deal. But what one is asking is meaningful, and we have got to try to understand.

It is so important in this quest to keep asking questions, both about apprenticeship in meditation and the repeated attempts and failures at gaining self-knowledge, that this in itself brings about a great discovery. There is a critical factor or determining role that may be assigned to what *The Voice of the Silence* calls the principle of sifting. " 'Great Sifter' is the name of the 'Heart Doctrine'." The ratio between meaning and experience, which in Plato's definition of insight is the learning capacity of the human soul, is that which enables one man to learn from one experience what another man will not learn in a lifetime. We see this all around us. We often see ourselves repeating the same mistakes and at other points we are relieved that we finally learnt something sufficiently well. That is the x-factor, the mystery of each human being, the capacity to be a learner when it is tough, to say, "I don't want to kid myself." In this way a man builds a raised platform of confidence that is authentic and stable because the man at the height of the quest is a man of such supreme confidence that it is no longer personal. It is the confidence of the universe, and he embodies it. He becomes a conscious agent of the collective and creative will in the universe. What this means in another sense is spontaneous forgetfulness of self. He is so assured that he doesn't have to claim anything. He can forget name and form. He can totally afford not to think of the small self, the little 'me', because he has accepted and inherited, come to embody, renounce and enjoy, the entirety of a universe of infinite possibilities. He acquires the psychological capacity to maintain a meaningful relationship between a universe of ontological plenty, analogous to a realm of illimitable light where giving does not deplete, and a universe of scarcity, a region of finite matter where there are hard choices to be made and where to move in one direction is to negate another, to take one thing is to give up something else, and to use time or energy in one way is to deny their use in other ways. Not to see the latter is to be a fool. Not to see the former is to deny oneself the opportunity to enjoy and actualize the potentiality and plenty of the universe in every man.

Instead of being depressed that we cannot really do more than meditate in small ways and that we are liable again and again to get into the cuckoo cloud of fantasy which we have to give up, we must say, "I will persist." What is important in meditation is continuity of consciousness. All attempts at meditation are merely fumbling attempts at building a line of life's meditation. A being who does this fully, like the Buddha, could say when asked whether he was a man or a god, "I am awake." To be fully awake is difficult. We are partly awake and partly asleep. One only fully meditates when one is fully awake and one cannot be fully awake except in relation to the One which is hidden, the supreme reality which has no form, which will never show its face, and yet which can include all faces and assume all forms. One is fully awake only when one can know proportionality, and accurately assign relative reality to everything. One must be able to say, "Yes, that's true. I can understand Eichmann. I know there is that in me which can be the embryo of a Hitler. I also know there is that in me which makes me feel close to Christ." A man can then expand his conception of the Self, so that nothing outside annoys or attracts him of which he cannot see in himself exact and genuine analogues. He can also say, "Somewhere I understand, at the very root of my nature, what it would be like to visualize the Golden Age where all men are consciously and continually bathing in the noon-day glory of the Divine." As Paul Hazard said: "As long as there are children, there will be a Golden Age." All of us can attempt to make mental images of the Golden Age, and to do so is deeply therapeutic, individually and collectively.

The Gelukpa tradition, which seems so demanding, has points of contact for all of us with our daily lives. One could say that to meditate is to remove hindrances to continuity of consciousness caused by the modifications of the mind. We do have to go on doing this again and again. You do it much better when you sit down to it and prepare for it properly, but above all you do it best when you meditate on universal good, as Plato taught. When you sit down to meditate on universal good — which you cannot conceptualize and which includes and transcends all conceptions of welfare and particular goods — you can free yourself from a great deal of tension. But you cannot stay there very long without the danger of falling asleep, of becoming passive, of fantasizing. You have to pull out at the right time. You do not want to dilly-dally, least of all to be anxious and settle for imitations. You want the real thing even if for a moment. The more you do this, the more it becomes like breathing. You do not have control over breathing, but fortunately most of the time your breathing can take care of itself.

What about mental breathing? That is where discipline is needed in regard to meditation. You can do something about the disordered, unregulated mental breathing, the way in which you receive the world of objects and in which you forget that awareness which you do have of the One that is hidden. Unless you can regulate this mental breathing, you cannot authentically laugh at and look at the absurdities and weaknesses of your lower self and make it genuinely meaningful for you to say, "I am more than you think. I am more than anyone else understands. And so is everyone else." Not only that, but this can be extended. One can be convinced in one's darkest hour, like men in concentration camps, that there is something profoundly precious to one's own individual sense of being human. One can be proud of what one somewhere knows one has to give to the world, which can be an authentic gift to the whole of mankind. When one can legitimately be proud of that, and increase the content of that knowledge, it ceases to be a feeling. Then one is not afraid of anything in oneself. Then one can understand and rejoice in the statement in *Light on the Path*: ". . . no man is your enemy: no man is your friend. All alike are your teachers."

Life is a school. There is an eternal learning and at any given time you alone can determine how much improved you are as a learner. One comes to see that while the whole of life is a teacher of concentration, that the whole of life also makes it difficult for you to retain the power needed to become continuous in your consciousness. This means that you are both immortal and mortal. To recover immortality while you are aware that you are mortal is not easy. You can do it at one level in one way at one time. You can feel it at some other time in a certain mood. To really do it, however, you have to know it in the classical sense defined by Plotinus — by reason, by experience, and by illumination, independently and by each. You have only half-knowledge otherwise. Knowing it mentally is not enough, though it is important. Knowing it in terms of a peak experience, though very grand, is not adequate to the demands of life. That we may fail to know independently by an appeal to illumination, reason and experience is to say that we know nothing. Yet, what we seek potentially includes all knowledge. These are paradoxes which become realities, truths about consciousness, because consciousness knows no limitations. The power of identification, the power of projection, the power of making yourself, of self-analyzing reflection or *svasamvedana*, is immense. You can play roles and if you can play every role, you can also play the role of the Christ. You can play the role of the Buddha. But you cannot begin to understand what this means unless you can also recognize what it is to play the role of a Hitler, and furthermore, what it means to be the *Kutastha*, he who plays no role whatsoever.

There is an integrity to this quest which is coeval with the whole of life. No one can reduce it to a technique. It is a very beautiful teaching. There never could be enough time, nor could there be any meaningfulness in assuming that anyone could ever fully tell anyone else what is involved. In the end each has to plunge into the stream. Every attempt at meditation within the context of universal meditation, and every attempt at self-knowledge within the context of the fullest concept of self-knowledge, is a meaningful stepping-stone. It can be carried forward in a ceaseless process of alchemy. Once we decide not to settle for the easier way out, once we taste the joy of the toughness of the Path, then we also find it is fun. It is enjoyable. One can truly say that he even enjoys knowing his failures. Then one may fall into another trap. One may too much enjoy being aware, but if one does, life will correct. We will suddenly look and find that we are ready to plunge into the abyss again.

All of these are representations of what in reality is a process of building, out of the repeated dyings of our vehicles, that fabric of stable, subtle, radiant matter which can be inhabited by ceaseless ideation and universal contemplation, so that one can be a man of meditation who can live as and for every other being. You are a Bodhisattva. You can become a Buddha. It is not possible for any of us to say this to ourselves except in the context of some genuine understanding. Otherwise it is false. Hence, of course, we need teachers. The best teachers give us the confidence that we have access, each uniquely but within ourselves, to that triadic sanctuary within, which becomes the gateway to the cosmic triad. We can then say, as did the ancient Aryans, *Atmanam atmana pasya*: — "See the universal self through your own immortal self." The issue is one of reaffirmation but it is a reaffirmation we can receive only from those who, as they affirm it, can make us believe. Of this we could never be judges, because we would never know whether the problem was in us or in them. But if we are sufficiently in earnest we will know, even though we will make mistakes. We will say, "This is real. This not only speaks *to* me; this speaks *within* me. I am hearing a voice which is the voice of my own Self." When this becomes real for a man, then indeed he is blessed. He enters that kind of initiation and reaches that threshold beyond which the quest will be extremely challenging, but from which he cannot fall back.

There is such a point. To reach that point is possible. This is the great priceless boon of learning the truth about meditation and the Self that all the great texts give, which was for long periods of time used as the basis of a discipline in secret sanctuaries of initiation, and which we have in *The Voice of the Silence,* the voice of Brahma Vach. It is possible for any person to make the wisdom of this book a living power in his life. Then he does not have to be wasting energy and time as to what he thinks of someone else, because that no longer matters, since there is no longer any 'someone else'. He has become the One. The seeker has become the object of his quest. There is no gap between himself as a knower and the known and the knowledge. The three are in one. They are all in one at the beginning, but unconsciously to him. Self-consciously they become one again. Until he reaches that point, or until he makes a proper beginning, let him not waste time running around in circles, expending energy, asking all those kinds of questions which are really the questions of the man who is never going to climb mountains, who is never going to swim, who is never going to walk. The lame cannot be made to walk unless they want to walk upon this path. The sick cannot be healed unless they wish to be healed. Therefore we are profoundly grateful to all those teachers of Gupta Vidya who once again gave us the knowledge and the assurance, the faith and the conviction, that we are the Path, that we can heal ourselves, and that we can become what we may now think is impossible. We can become that, not for our own sake, but for the sake of all and thereby become guides and exemplars to those who need our help.

Toronto
October 9, 1971

MENTAL POSTURE

Seek this wisdom by doing service, by strong search, by questions, and by humility; the wise who see the truth will communicate it unto thee . . .

SHRI KRISHNA

Lord Krishna strings the sacred teachings of the *Bhagavad Gita* on the golden thread of mental posture, the relation between the spiritual seeker and the Divine Wisdom embodied as the Light of the Logos in lustrous beings. Mental posture refers primarily to an attitude of mind, and constitutes the sacred trust between chela and Guru. Those who wish to become sincere and true servants of all mankind with its immense suffering, and of the Great Masters of Wisdom with their inexhaustible light, must prepare themselves by a process of purgation whereby they negate the false conceptions of themselves derived from the world into which they are born, from their heredity, upbringing, environment and education. This is done by a method of intense self-questioning. Platonic thought is essentially a dialogue with oneself. When people really begin to ask questions of themselves, and also attempt to apply the principles involved in formulating questions in a multiplicity of contexts, then they gradually begin to glimpse the dynamic, albeit mysterious, relation between manifest and unmanifest.

We could compare wisdom to light — the ineffable light of the Invisible Sun. Is this light obscured in a solar eclipse? Actually, it is then even more accessible to men of meditation. Is this light inaccessible during an eclipse of the moon? Not to men of meditation. But, alas, most human beings are not men of meditation. They have never really thought seriously, hungered sufficiently, wanted with enough intensity of one-pointed devotion, the great Teaching in relation to the immortality of the soul. Divine wisdom can come alive through the *Manas-Taijasi,* the thinking principle irradiated by the Buddhic fire of the divine dialectic. Before *Buddhi* can become one with *Manas*, before Truth and Love can be brought together in a mystic marriage, there is a preliminary betrothal. The thinking principle sunders its false allegiance to the shadowy self or the astral body, and then draws towards the hidden light of the sun, the light of *Buddhi* which is fully lit in Buddha.

If wisdom may be compared to light, method may be compared to a lens. We have different lenses for a microscope and a telescope. We need one lens for looking at that which is so invisibly small as to become visible only through a powerful magnifier. When looking closer at the stars, we need a lens suitable to a telescope, with specific refractive powers and made of particular kinds of glass. In all searching instruments, through which we wish to focus light for the sake of understanding and making discoveries in relation to the mysteries of matter at all levels, we also need to know something about the angle at which the refraction of light may affect the intensity, clarity, purity and stability of the images formed.

All human beings, every day of their lives, are involved unconsciously in the quest for wisdom. When they become postulants or neophytes, they are put on a preliminary probation and can be received as disciples only after they have completed preliminary qualifications. All of these involve a re-orientation of their life outlook in relation to who they are, why they were born, their attitude to the moment of death, where they are going, the nature of their every relationship, and above all whether they are ready to pledge themselves *irreversibly* towards that which they find irresistible — the great thrill that accompanies the light of daring lit up in the heart, the thrill of compassionate service to the whole of suffering humanity.

At the very beginning of the fourth chapter of the *Bhagavad Gita* there is an extraordinary statement. Having first established the inexhaustible nature of this yoga, Krishna states that the Secret Doctrine was first communicated to Vivasvat — the primordial manifestation of the divine Wisdom within the vast cosmic depths, understood in the Kabbalah as 'the ancient of Days', and in the New Testament as 'That which was in the beginning.' It is eternal and yet a reflection of itself is the first light in every great period of manifestation. It was transmitted through Vaivasvata Manu, the essential root-type of the mankind in existence for at least a million years. Then it was communicated to Ikshvaku, the mighty Brotherhood of Mahatmas. Their compassion is boundless and their concern is profound for the primary needs of every epoch. They make allowances for the errors of thought that became magnified over the last two thousand years and more. They recognize the mathematical accuracy of the law of cycles under which there may be permitted from age to age — for the preservation of the just, the destruction of the demoniac and the re-establishment of righteousness — the timely promulgation of divine wisdom by the Avatars who come as the Great Teachers of Humanity.

Any human being in any part of the world who retires at night with a true feeling of responsiveness to the travails of suffering humanity, receives help in deep sleep, if his inmost self turns towards Ishwara. The intensity of desire, the propriety of motive, and the devotion of the heart will necessarily determine the infallible beneficent response that comes from within deep sleep, and also enables one to tap the pristine vibrations brought down by earnest sacrificial meditations from the peaks of universal ideation into the surrounding magnetosphere of the globe. Therefore, after Krishna says that the sacred teaching was communicated to Vivasvat and to Manu and also to Ikshvaku, and then to the Raja Rishis, the royal sages behind the chief dynasties of all the ancient kingdoms which witnessed the forgotten renaissances of antiquity, he says to Arjuna, "All of this I now make known to you." Why? Because "Thou art my devotee and my friend."

Mental posture is critical and crucial, and everyone can at any time alter his or her standpoint. One way to do it at all levels is to emulate the wise Rishis of the *Rig Veda*. Having given the great *Hymn of Creation,* raising questions about why, when, how it all began, they said, "Who knows?" The gods, the sages? Perhaps not even they. When people gain the thrill of true agnosticism then they liberate themselves from the thraldom of strain and from self-concern in its negative, destructive, wasteful sense. They begin to release the living power of the continuity of the divine spirit within the temple and the tenement of the reflected ray, so that the solar light activates all latent centres and cells within the body. Therefore, they know at each step the preparation needed for the next. Each step shows the way, as in mountain climbing. A point is eventually reached where, out of enormous compassion for the multitudes in the plains, a stout fearlessness amidst the raging storms, with a steady, sure-footed stance, carrying a lantern that sheds the light hidden in the divine darkness, a person suffuses his pilgrimage with purity, strength, and immense joy. He recognizes that the universe is vast, boundless and beautiful, and is constantly willing to release beneficent thought-streams for the good of all, thereby deserving the grace of the Guru.

Recognition of the light and rectification of mental posture begin in the ability to ask real questions. A real question must itself be rooted in one's life. We have magnificent examples of this among little children, who initially find the universe so wonderful that they are constantly raising real questions. Why is it human beings lose child-like trust and cease to show the pure joy of questioning? The twentieth century will one day come to be known not only for concentration camps, not only for the horrors of all the killings in the world, but also for the massacre of minds under an educational system where children are treated as objects. Children are labeled and graded, and encouraged to pretend they know instead of honestly saying, "I don't know." The strain is too much. If one receives such instruction, one tends to be instantly threatened wherever there is real knowledge. After a point it starts to have its effect on the face, on lacklustre eyes which become either self-destructive or replete with the "jealous *Lhamayin* of endless space."

Could all these people start all over again? They can — because the *Gita* teaches that unknown to themselves, they are making sacrifices. Some make sacrifices to the god of work; others make sacrifices to the god of self-worship; still others make sacrifices to what they think to be knowledge. Consider the whole of humanity and those souls that did not like making sacrifices in previous lives. Where will they be reborn? Those who wanted opportunities life after life — complaining in villages, "If only I had education"; rebelling against arranged marriages, "If only I could choose freely"; restlessly looking for excitement, "The countryside is boring. I want to go to the big town" — such people generated a line of life's meditation. All of these are the world's discontented from all classes.

To sense this is to ask questions about meaning, rooted in experience. But questions about meaning become real only when they are rooted in experience of pain. Where one's experience of pain is inserted into the pain of humanity, there is universality in the quality of the suffering, in the myriad dimensions of experience, and in the hunger for meaning. Thus it is that Krishna endorses indifference to the multitude of differences abounding in the world. The offerings are the Supreme Spirit. The sacrificial butter is the Supreme Spirit. All is the Supreme Spirit. All comes back into the One, but in coming back into the One, the great choice for man is in relation to the whole or the part, the living or the dying, the future or the past; That which is unchanging or that which is ever changing; That which is indestructible, though invisible, or that which is both perishable and visible. One may choose That which is the eternal witness, the inmost sanctuary, the protective power within the immortal soul of every man. This soul-power can be released by any human being, despite all the confusions, muddles, mistakes, self-deceptions, rationalizations and wanderings in the dark. Somewhere the wonderings in relation to the light persist and all else drifts away as autumnal leaves.

What is hidden in the root systems of the trees that are so many human beings? It is the Real. As long as the waters of life below are mingled with the waters of wisdom above, then everyone is able, out of the moisture of the suffering of the heart and the sincerity of persistent attempts, to become rooted within the great hidden underground. It is possible to take a proper mental posture in relation to That which is spaceless and timeless, dateless and deathless, That which existed before birth and That which will exist after the moment of death. To do this within oneself is to find that the whole universe is a magnificent unbound encyclopedia of answers, and that the whole of life is a series of questions. One starts to walk in the world with the light of questioning in one's eyes. When one starts to move in the world with questioning in the heart; when one starts to see all others in terms of those fundamental and enduring questions that concern all human beings; and where the questioning becomes a quest, then life is a single question that cannot be answered without meditation upon birth, death, decay, sickness, but above all, upon error. When one meditates on all of these, in time one's life is not only a quest, but a beatific, ceaseless contemplation. Then a person comes closer to the great mystery of the fourth chapter of the *Gita*, which teaches: "That man who sees inaction in action and action in inaction is wise among men." There is action during deep sleep. There is inaction amidst the daily round and the common task, the milling crowds, lost and confined, cribbed and cabined, within the cast-iron cage of their shadowy selves and vociferating on behalf, not of the universal good, but of their own little selves.

Behind this masquerade there is the Soundless Sound. The *Mandukya Upanishad* says that eventually we truly come to recognize, to revere, and to renounce everything for the sake of the One — *OM TAT SAT* — That which is beyond all colours and forms, all limitations, all labels, all distinctions, all beginnings, changes and endings. We see beyond all conditions and conditionality itself when we feel that the unconditional is not distant but closer to us than our own heart. We become that which all beings are, at different degrees of knowledge and forgetfulness, but which we can self-consciously embody. Though there are many things we remember and also many that we forget, we are that which could never be remembered and could never be forgotten because it is beyond and behind memory. It is beyond and behind the limbos and the Lethe of delusive forgetfulness. It is that primordial pulse that precedes all manifestation and what we call recorded history. It is older than billions of years and is vaster than outer space. Behind and beyond all the labels which humanity hugs there is a boundless ocean and an eternal river. Like Hesse's Siddhartha, we may learn from the ferryman the great secret. All those who come to the river ask all kinds of questions, but most are questions about money or time, questions about all the other people who come, questions on behalf of themselves. But he who has watched it all, this Vasudeva, knows that there are great sounds of every kind in the river. Because he has seen behind and beyond all the ripples on the surface of the river, he has seen a tremendous compassion in the very depths of the waters.

When a man senses the living reality of the energy of the compassion of wisdom, then he begins to become a free man. For him the answer of the ancients is the start of his life. The Many come from the One because compassion first arose in It. That same compassion ensures the return of each and every one of the Many back into the One. When this teaching has been learnt, has been burnt into the brain and into the very heart and soul, then, as the *Mandukya* urges, we abandon all other questions. We cleave unto the truth of the Soundless Sound. When one comes to that point, then life is a question mark and each of us is the answer.

All questions are rafts that can transport a person part of the way and no further. In the end, the passenger plunges off the raft; this must be done again and again. No one can swim in mid-ocean without taking a small canoe or a small raft to the waters. When watching ships on the ocean, we may see that all of these are like human beings on a boundless voyage. We experience that transcendental feeling common to all. It could be lit and re-lit, purifying our motives, redeeming us from our own small-minded thoughts and self-defeating patterns, freeing us from our bondage to our limited conception of this world. We could move with the glory and the dignity of those who know that within every human heart is the possibility of sensing the immortal spirit.

The beginnings of all are protected by the Law. Wisdom, method and practice are fused in a dialectical inter-relationship. At the start, wisdom could be put at the apex of a triangle, and method at the midpoint of the base. At a later stage, the points could be varied. Then a time comes when one sees that the very separation between the knower, the known and the knowing is only a conventional one, and that the three are a union within the universe and a union within every man. In the end we always return to the same point. Man can gain self-knowledge only if he makes his soul-gaze centre on "the One Pure Light, the Light that is free from affection." Then and only then can he use the Golden Key of method to unlock and throw open the radiant portals of Wisdom.

THE SENSE OF SELF

Feeling, while going about, that he is a wave of the ocean of self; while sitting, that he is a bead strung on the thread of universal consciousness; while perceiving objects of sense, that he is realizing himself by perceiving the self; and, while sleeping, that he is drowned in the ocean of bliss; — he who, inwardly constant, spends his whole life thus is, among all men, the real seeker of liberation.

SHANKARACHARYA

All the varied vestures of the incarnated human being are distinct sheaths on adjoining planes of consciousness, each with its own rates of vibration, all participating in the potency of ideation and mirroring archetypal relations. What is implied in the Vedantin association of the lower vestures with unwisdom is the false sense of separateness, the illusory stability and entitative existence that we ascribe to a form. What is the significance of the seven orifices in the human face and the thirty-three vertebrae of the spine? What is to be understood from the varying textures of the different layers of skin? Is the physical body to be analysed in terms of its constituent elements, or is it to be viewed in relation to the pulsating rhythmic movement in the heart? Such questions are rarely asked. Most human beings take for granted a haphazardly acquired and habitually retained assemblage of sensory perceptions and residues identified with a name and form which is really a static mind-image of the body. Individuals deny themselves the possibility of direct experience without the mediation of routinized anticipations or of frozen images projected upon objects. Anyone may learn to discern and comprehend the recurring patterns, resistances and responses of the body. Even more, a person may come to view the body, as the *Gita* depicts, as a nine-gated city. A person can learn to use the body as a musician wields a musical instrument, self-consciously impressing energy upon its myriad life-atoms caught up in chains of interconnected intelligence.

The body is a vast and complex matrix of interdependent centres of energy, each of which puts a human being in touch potentially, and therefore in many cases unconsciously, with everything else that exists on the physical plane. The body exists at a certain level of material density, with a biological entropy built into it, as well as a degree of homeostatic resistance to the atmosphere around. This level of resistance in the physical body enables it to maintain itself and is the basis of physical survival. Those who truly reflect upon this could make a significant difference by the deliberate and creative interaction of their own ideas and feelings. For example, while eating food, a person's thoughts, emotional states, magnetic field and inward reverence to the invisible elements of food can make a fundamental difference to the qualitative osmosis of energies transmitted to the organism. The body can be seen as a sacred instrument in rethinking one's entire relationship with the world. There is reflective intelligence at the lunar level and the astral and physical vestures are subject to various cycles and different rates of motion. These cycles are mathematical equations and patterns at the cellular level. The mathematics of the complex system that is the physical body, with all its cycles, corresponds closely to the mathematics of the galaxies and the vast cosmos. One could come to learn from the natural cycles and then from the particular bent given to them by one's own emanations, thus gaining some grasp of one's dominant anticipations and typical responses. Whoever engages in daily self-study could come to discern the distinct ways in which the body affects the mind during different portions of the day and the week, as well as the succeeding phases of the lunar month.

Shankaracharya lived at a time when ritualistic practices were widely prevalent, and many had become blindly dependent upon detailed and complex knowledge of what to do, when, during each of the many subdivisions of the day. All of this knowledge would not enable a person to get to the core of the causal body — the delusive identification through an 'I' with limiting conceptions of space and time, together with the persisting notion of oneself as the actor. Shankara taught that one must get to the root of the 'I-making' tendency — the illusory sense in which one is separate from the world which is supposed to exist as clay material for one's purpose. This false conception of selfhood becomes deeply rooted because it is pleasurable, owing to passive identification with those sensations that have pleasing responses in different parts of the body. It is reinforced in the language and the milieu of those valuations of segmented aspects of conduct which tend to routinize, making a person take experience totally for granted, just as the physical senses can lead an unthinking person to take for granted that the more solid a thing seems to the tactile sense, the more it is solid in reality. There is a radical failure to understand that the whole visible world is like a screen, hiding a vast mathematical activity, and that for all its bewildering complexity, this phenomenal realm may be reduced to certain primary relationships that archetypally correspond to the numbers between zero and ten.

By rethinking much of what one took for granted before, one could come to conceive of an exalted state such as Shankara conveyed in *The Crest Jewel of Wisdom*. In this serene state an individual would be devoid of all sense of psychological involvement in any of the desires and aims, any of the obsessions, passions, infatuations and concerns of the world, in any of the criteria of success and failure or pseudo-valuations of people generally. Furthermore, having no sense of tightness, of excessive anxious-ridden involvement in the activities of the body, such a person begins to experience a tremendous exhilaration, a rhythmic breathing and a profound peace. It is like seeing a part of oneself carry out its natural functions, and yet remaining totally outside every kind of manifestation in which any single portion of oneself is involved. A person who reaches this stage can combine with this detachment a deep gratitude, a joyous affirmation that there is a certain value to the body as a pristine vesture. At the causal level — in what is called the *karana sarira* or causal body —

fundamental ideas prevail which are often hidden to most human beings but which, if they were examined, would wipe out whole chains of thinking, complex patterns of activity over many years. They would all be eradicated by getting to the core of a fundamental idea. A person who steadily works on the plane of ideation so renovates the thought-body that it becomes possible to release self-consciously the inexhaustible potentiality of divine energy. The entry points between the causal body and the astral vesture are made more porous and, in time, the physical body may reflect and transmit the radiant joy of universal ideation.

A person may learn to live in attunement to the plane of those enlightened free men who are not captive even to the vast conceptions of space and time associated with the universe as a whole. Such a person will be ever engaged in intense meditation upon the Unmanifest, which increasingly becomes the only reality. A person who begins to see through the eyes and with the help of the illumination of the Guru finds that the physical body is only a dim reflector of light-energy and also provides a means of shielding the divine radiance. By extending the possibilities of human excellence to the uttermost heights of control, purification, refinement and plasticity that can be brought about by the deliberate impact of disciplined thought upon gross matter, one can revolutionize one's conception of matter. Einstein pointed out in the twenties that a lot of what is called matter simply dissolves into a prior, primordial notion of space. The body can become an architectonic pattern in space which has within its own intricate symmetry an inherent intelligence that is not transparent at the level of image and form. It has the capacity of holding, releasing and reflecting the highest elemental associations that accompany the profoundest thoughts. Nature is the great magician and alchemist. The wise man is an effortless master of lunar forces, correlations, patterns and potencies.

The critical fact for any human being as a self-conscious agent is the capacity of objectivizing, of putting upon a mental screen as an object of reflection anything, in principle, that one wishes. A human being recognizes the range of self-consciousness through a process of progressive abstraction. This includes familiarization with what looks initially like mental blankness — like pitch-black night, where there are no conventional signs, no contours or landmarks, no north or south, east or west. A person who begins to sense the depths of subtle matter will discover that what seems to be a void or darkness is in fact a rich, pulsating light-substance that is porous to the profoundest thought. Then one realizes what initially was simply a bald fact about human beings — taken for granted and therefore forgotten — that all things are mutually and vitally interrelated. Human beings are generally so conditioned by mechanical responses to the ordinary calendar and clock-time that they can hardly apprehend the immensity of the doctrine of relationality, which presupposes that the visible world is a vast psychological field of awareness. The universe exists because there are minds capable of generating conceptions that have points of common contact and thereby an outwardness and extension sustaining an entire field of consciousness. As one cannot set any limit in advance to the range and development, the potency and the scope of all the minds that exist, one cannot readily imagine what it is like to negate everything that exists, to stand totally outside it.

Initially, it is extremely difficult to imagine all of this, so the whole world is at first apprehended as so unfathomably mysterious as to engender a feeling of alienation and fear. But why should moving into more expanded states of consciousness make one afraid? Who is afraid, and afraid for what? At any given time there is a film or shadowy image that is one's false self between one's inherent capacity to make a vaster state of consciousness come alive and one's captivity to the familiar array of objects and opinions. One is like the fabled monkey which, in trying to collect nuts from a jar, held onto them so tightly that he was not able to open his hands and get any. There is an impersonal, impartial sweep to the mental vision of a Man of Meditation that simply cannot correlate and connect with, or take at face value, the common concerns of the world. It is necessary to grasp the strength and richness of viewing the universe as an interior object of intense thought which could be expanded indefinitely, eliminating self-imposed and narrow notions of identity and embracing vaster conceptions of the Self. The significance of this standpoint lies in that continuity is upheld but not formulated. Herein is the basis of indefinite expansion, of growth without hindrance. Existing frontiers of knowledge cannot provide the basis of judgement of the potential realm of the knowable. What is now known is meagre in relation to the immensity of the unknown. It is meaningful to relinquish the delusive sense of certainty to which so many people cling at the expense of an ever-deepening apprehension of relationality.

In general, human beings seem to need the illusions that sustain them. There is something self-protective in relation to all illusions. At least people are thereby helped from becoming fixated on obsessional delusions. There is even something enigmatic about why particular persons are going through whatever they endure. A great deal of human frustration, pain and anxiety, fear and uncertainty, arises from the desperate attempt to keep alive a puny sense of self in an alien world. Individuality arises only through the act of making oneself responsible for the consequences of choices, of seeing the world as capable of being affected by one's attitudes and, above all, as an opportunity for knowing and rejoicing in wisdom and for rising to the levels of awareness of higher beings. The plane of consciousness on which such beings exist is accessible to all those who are willing to stretch themselves, patiently persist in going through the abyss of gloom, and endure all trials. Infallibly, they can enter those exalted planes and experience a strong sense of fellowship with beings who at one time would have seemed inaccessible. This ancient teaching is worthy of deep reflection. Its abstract meaning pertains to the elastic relation between subject and object, subjectivity and objectivity, and their mutual relativity as illustrated in one's daily experience. A vast freedom is implicit in this no-ownership theory of selfhood. It is helpful to break up one's life into periods and patterns, to note one's most persistent ideas, ambitions and illusions, as well as those points on which one's greatest personal sensitivity lies, and to make of these an object of calm and dispassionate study, to be able to see by questioning and tracing back what would be the assumptions which would have to be true for all of these to exist. To do this is to engage in what Plato calls *dianoia*, 'thinking things through', whereby in one day a person could wipe out what otherwise would hang like a fog over many lives. There is a fusion of philosophical penetration and oceanic devotion which is characteristic of high states of consciousness. There is no separation between thought and feeling — between *Manas* and *Buddhi* — such as is ordinarily experienced.

At one time a natural reverence existed in all cultures in ritual forms which eventually became empty of significance or could no longer be made meaningful when languages were lost or philosophical conceptions were neglected. Individuals today cannot force themselves to be able to feel any of the traditional emotional responses to any single system or ritual. Human beings should creatively find their own ways of making sacred whatever it is that comes naturally to them. What is sacred as an external object to one person need not be to another. The forms of ritualization have all become less important than they were, and that is not only due to the rapid pace of change but also because of the volatile mixture of concepts and of peoples all over the world, together with a growing awareness of the psychological dimension of seemingly objective conceptions of reality. But even though there is a pervasive desacralization of outward forms, the deepest feelings of souls are unsullied by doubt. It is only by arousing the profoundest heart-feelings that one can open the door to active spiritual consciousness. There is in the heart of every person the light of true devotion, the spontaneous capacity to show true recognition and reverence. To do this demands a greater effort for some people than for others. When human beings come to understand the law of interdependence that governs all states of consciousness, their impersonal reason as well as their intense feelings will point in the same direction. It is only this single-minded and whole-hearted mode of devotion which will endure, but its focus must be upon universal well-being.

> It is not the individual and determined purpose of attaining Nirvana — the culmination of all Knowledge and wisdom, which is after all only an exalted and glorious selfishness — but the self-sacrificing pursuit of the best means to lead on the right path our neighbour, to cause to benefit by it as many of our fellow creatures as we possibly can, which constitutes the true Theosophist.

THE MYSTERY
OF THE EGO

*If we feel not our spiritual death, how should we dream
of invoking life?*

CLAUDE DE ST. MARTIN

The sure test that individuals have begun to ascend to higher planes of consciousness is that they find an increasing fusion of their ideas and their sympathies. Breadth of mental vision is supported by the depth of inmost feeling. Words are inadequate to convey these modes of awareness. Mystics cannot readily communicate the ineffable union of head and heart which has sometimes been called a mystic marriage. Such veiled metaphorical language may often refer to specific centres of consciousness in the human body. If the body is the living temple of an imprisoned divine intelligence, the metaphorical language of the mystics points to a tuning and activation of interrelated centres in the body. There is a mystical heart that is different in location and function from the physical heart. There is also a seed of higher intellection, "the place between thine eyes", which is distinct from those centres of the brain that are involved in ordinary cerebration. The more a person is able to hold consciousness on a plane that is vaster in relation to time and space, subtler in relation to cause and motion, than normal sensory awareness, the more these higher centres are activated. Since this cannot take place without also arousing deeper feelings, the original meaning of the term 'philosophy' — 'love of wisdom' — is suggestive and significant. There is a level of energy released by love that is conjoined with a profound reverence for truth *per se.* This energy releases a greater capacity to experience self-conscious attunement to what is behind the visible phantasmagoria of the whole of life, drawing one closer to what is gestating under the soil in the hidden roots of being, and closer to the unarticulated longings of all other human beings. Everyone senses this kinship at critical moments. Sometimes, in the context of a shared tragedy or at a time of crisis caused by a sudden catastrophe, many people experience an authentic oneness with each other despite the absence of any tokens of tangible expression.

To bring the disciplined and developed creative imagination into full play is to do much more than merely to have a passive awareness of sporadic moments of human solidarity. These moments are only intermittent, imperfect and partial expressions of vaster capacities in the realms of thought and feeling. To draw out these capacities fully requires that we withdraw support from everything that is restrictive. The higher Eros presupposes a kind of negative Eros, a withdrawal of exaggerated emotional involvement in the things of this world, in sensations and sense-objects, in name and form and in ever-changing personalities. This withdrawal is based upon a recognition that there is a lie involved in superficial emotion, and a calm awareness of a noumenal reality which is unmanifest. To realize this is to prepare for the potential release of the higher Eros, but this is truly difficult because to negate means to come to a void. There is no way to withdraw from the froth of psychic emotion and the tangles of discursive reasoning without experiencing a haunting loneliness and immense void wherein everything appears meaningless. Though painful and even terrifying, this is the necessary condition through which the seeker must pass if he is to die so that he may be reborn. *The Voice of the Silence* teaches that "the mind needs breadth and depth and points to draw it towards the Diamond Soul". It must actively generate these mental linkages through deep meditation upon the suffering of humanity, seeing all individual strivings as part of a collective quest for enlightenment, focusing with compassion upon the universal suffering that transcends yet includes all the pains and agonies of all living beings.

When a person can connect and coordinate these periods of deliberate meditation and conscious cultivation of universal compassion, and experiences ordinary life through these contacts with the realm of non-being, then the purification and renovation of the temple has begun. There is a starving out of entire clusters of elementals, minute constellations of matter that have been given a murky colouring and destructive impress, and which make up the astral vesture. These matrices of frustration, limitation, anger and self-hatred are gradually replaced by new clusters of life-energy — readily available throughout nature — which are more attuned to the highest abstract conceptions of space, time and motion. Thus there is a greater incarnation of the indwelling divine nature. Every human body may be seen as a mystic cross upon which the Christos within is being crucified. To nurture radical renovations in the vestures through the concentrated mind and disciplined imagination, by forging connections between points touched in meditation and in everyday life, is to make possible, after the Gethsemane necessitated by collective karma, a fuller manifestation of the Christos, the god within. This long journey is coeval and coequal with the whole of life and the entirety of mankind. When individuals discern in their own quest a cosmic dimension, impersonality and selflessness in their endeavours become an authentic affirmation of what is potentially within all. It is impossible to grow in awareness of what one truly is without finding that the barrier between oneself and other beings weakens. There is an internal integrity to this quest, and, therefore, it is pointless to pretend that all at once, simply by words, gestures and rituals, one can suddenly come to a universal love of all mankind. Of course, some desperate people, through drugs or other adventitious aids, experience enthralling intimations of the wonder of life or of its unity. These are the result of temporarily loosening the screws in the complex psychophysical organism called the human body and should not be mistaken for true wisdom. The crucial difference lies in continuity.

The more consciously one is able to sense the universal presence of the true Self, the more one can maintain continuity. The more one can see the moment of death and its connection with the present moment, the more one can participate in the unmanifest core of the universal quest. While the mystical capacity for sensing cosmic Eros grows, the desire to express it declines. Those who are caught up in external appearances crave messianic miracles and want to treat the universe as if they could manipulate it. This is a stumbling block to the quest. The real quest has an integrity that can be tested continuously because it must release an energy of commitment to the whole. Just as it is only through the cessation of the repetitive revolutions of the lower mind that higher thought is released, it is only by the cessation of limiting desires on the heterogeneous plane of perception that the true Eros may be released.

The Voice of the Silence teaches:

> Shun ignorance, and likewise shun illusion. Avert thy face from world deceptions: mistrust thy senses; they are false. But within thy body — the shrine of thy sensations, seek in the Impersonal for the 'Eternal Man'; and having sought him out, look inward: thou art Buddha.

Tragically, the divine origin of human consciousness is all too often forgotten by individuals who permit themselves to become entrapped in "world deceptions". Just as people in a room with artificial light forget the light of the sun, consciousness, when it is focused through a lucid zone that points in the realm of externals in one direction, is in the very activity of awareness shutting off a larger consciousness. Human beings reinforce each other in assigning reality to the visible tip of the whole of life, to that which is maintained and activated by words, names and desires which have public criteria of recognition that can be fulfilled on the plane of external events. On the other hand, an individual who senses the rays of the Spiritual Sun, enfolded in the blackness of the midnight sky, comes closer to wisdom, participating in the reflections of lesser lights, while retaining an inward reverence for the cosmic ocean of light, is living within the moment with a calm awareness of eternity. *The Secret Doctrine* suggests that what is called light is a shadowy illusion and that beyond what are normally called light and darkness there is noumenal Darkness which is eternally radiant.

In the focusing of consciousness on the plane of differentiation, the process is broken into forms and colours, moments of time, fields of space. In the breaking up of consciousness, something gets caught, causing mental inertia. Cosmic spirit can only manifest in and through a material matrix, but it cannot manifest without mind, or without the energy that brings about the fusion of the matrix and what is potentially present in spirit. This is why, in all spiritual disciplines, the battleground is the mind. The fact that the mind becomes dual is the price paid for self-consciousness and this price involves both self-limitation and the limiting of other selves. This limitation is reinforced by religious beliefs that foreshorten the age of man and the earth, and also by constricting fears of death and decay, whether applied to human lives or collectively to a culture. There is a consequent increase in the inability of consciousness to free itself from its frozen identification with a particular aspect of the differentiated field which is at best only a veil cast over the greater life process. At the very core of the life process all worlds are potentially present. In addition to a particular differentiated field, an infinite number of potentially differentiated fields lie latent in a pregenetically differentiated state. This is the core of reality in the realm of divine thought called *Mahat*, the realm in which Mahatmas abide. It is also at the heart of cosmic Eros or Fohat.

Whether one examines the collective structure of society or an individual in a nuclear family, one will find myriad ways in which human beings transfer anxiety and limitations to each other. Not all human beings are equally trapped, nor are they all prey to the same kinds of illusions. Some individuals are perpetually subject to delusive expectations of worldly success. Their experience is painful and it seems they never truly learn. There are others who experience violent reactions, and just because there is so much violence in their reaction, they are bound equally at the extreme points in the oscillation between optimism and pessimism. Still others seem to be shrewd and subtle in leaving possibilities open by negating their involvements intuitively and unconsciously, even though they may not have any metaphysical map to guide them. There are always a few everywhere who are reminiscent of the great galaxy of beings who are awake during the long night of non-manifestation. They self-consciously begin with a certain thread of awareness, and those who know them from an early age may sense how calmly they are going to lay aside their mortal vestures in the end. Theirs is a beautiful, self-conscious reflection, though guarded and veiled, within the lesser vehicles and ordinary orbits of profane existence. While other human beings are cursing life and themselves, these heroic pioneers move as if they are constantly making an inward advance towards that which they knew early in life, and to which they will be true until the end.

The difference between human beings has to do with previous lives, and with the sad fact that many human beings seem to gravitate again and again in the same direction in which they had formerly been trapped. Given a sufficiently vast period of evolution, all human beings require in some sense to be where they are and need their illusions. This is true metaphysically and in regard to evolution as a whole. But under the law of cycles, in certain periods of history and at crucial moments in the present, people come to a parting of the ways, a moment of choice. It is as if they sense that if they do not do something, they are going to be left behind. One cannot hold down high souls who have work to do in regard to human evolution, who are going to sow the seeds for the harvest of tomorrow. One cannot expect them to be held back by those who are born then under karma, even though unwilling or unready to put themselves in that posture where they confidently affirm their right to belong to a larger life. This is part of the complex process of the dying of a civilization or an epoch, and of the coming to birth of a new order through a long and painful gestation. Ultimately, then, fragmentation and entrapment of consciousness cannot be understood solely in terms of the interdependence between human beings, or the differences between people bound up with the same illusions and those with the courage to break them. The missing term in such an account is the confrontation between self-consciousness and the void.

If life after life every time one starts to negate and encounters the void, one flees back into the world, a pattern is established which cannot be sustained indefinitely. Suppose that such an individual comes into contact with beings who have gone through the void and see no difference between the void, themselves and all other beings. Such Men of Meditation do not entertain any emotions below the level of cosmic Eros, and they do not engender any thought-currents except those in the context of *Mahat*, the universal mind. Contact with such beings is an immense opportunity but also an immense challenge, an instrument of precipitation. The entire riddle of the entrapment of consciousness, when moved from the general plane to a particular person, can only be solved by the individual. The perspective can be given, the metaphysical maps provided, but each person must examine why he or she is in a particular condition in terms of memories, feelings or ideas. By keeping in the forefront of awareness a conception that is larger than any habitual view of self, and with the assurance that there are those who have been able to resolve for all what individuals find so difficult to resolve for themselves, each will be helped. In the end, each must plunge into the stream. All must engage in individual self-study, asking again and again, "What is important to me? What am I prepared to let go? Have I the courage to die and be reborn?" A person who is in earnest will, without losing a sense of proportion and humour, set aside periods in which to take specific steps in the direction towards the Path. This centres upon what H.P. Blavatsky called the mystery of the human ego, the mystery of each human being.

The need for self-study bears directly upon the discovery of the thread of individual continuity, the *sutratman*. This thread of consciousness in every person is only an aspect of the monadic essence of which one is a ray. It is what makes of a person a monad, a particular being or an individual, separate only in the functional capacity to reflect the universal. Every human being is a unique lens capable of self-consciously reflecting universal light. If that is what all individuals are in essence, when they are manifesting through personalities bound up with name and form and involved in the world of differentiated matter, they become caught up in a psychic fog that obscures the clarity of the monadic vision of the true meaning and purpose of the pilgrimage of life. Nevertheless, in that fog there remains a residual reflection of what the monad in its fullness knows. This is what may be called the golden sutratmic thread within every human being. The thread is activated during deep sleep, but during waking life it cannot very easily be activated. It is involved in the baby's first cry at birth, and is glimpsed at the moment of death. It can be self-consciously activated in meditation.

The true, sacrificial meaning of the Theosophical Movement is to give human beings in waking life points of contact with what they truly know themselves to be in deep sleep, and to do this in a manner that can give to each the strength of a collective affirmation. "To live and reap experience, the mind needs breadth and depth and points to draw it towards the Diamond Soul. Seek not those points in *Maya's* realm." The golden thread can only be lit up as a constant basis of light by each one individually. Every person must clean out the mirror-like mind which gathers dust while it reflects. Each person by self-study and self-examination helps to mitigate the obscuration of the golden thread-light which is broken up into details, lost in the externals, caught up in particular events, through memories looking backwards and through wish-fulfilment producing unreal psychic states. All must banish this obscuration on their own.

In the end, however, one cannot activate that golden cord, as Plato called it, without the exhilaration of self-transcendence. Paradoxically, when you are truly yourself, you forget yourself. To be calmly engaged in the manifestation of the golden thread is to increase awareness of all other beings and the whole of life. Self-study, then, has further depths of meaning. When a person in a period of true contemplation has a vision of the sutratmic Self, brought down from above and enriching consciousness through the activation of divine thought, then suddenly there will be a kickback arising from the resistance of the lesser self. One will painfully discover that the mind cannot stay for very long on a sufficiently abstract and impersonal level, and that the heart cannot continuously hold that which is the collective misery of mankind and bear love to all beings. It falls back to lesser concerns. Self-study becomes a way of studying the lesser self with firmness and honesty, together with a sense of humour towards the ridiculousness of the lesser self, the impostor that shuts out the richness and potentiality of the Self. True self-study takes the form of studying those periods of waking life where there is a forgetting and therefore a denial of the Self. Self-study is a way of minimizing the propensity to forget and the need for too many reminders, and above all, safeguarding against the need to have one's knuckles rapped by admonitions that come from the life process. To choose one's reminders rather than have them come from outside is to adjust the ratios of moments of time that are well spent to those that are wasted through being caught in forgetfulness of the golden thread. These wasted moments constitute the tragedy of the crucifixion of the Christos. The more one finds this happening, the greater the necessity to get to the root of the problem. Self-study can never be made the object of schemata because it must vary for every individual, and any person may find that repeated efforts yield only limited results. There may be particular moments when there is a brilliant flash, and one sees through so much in the masquerade that one is freed. But this is something about which no general rules can be made because it involves the interaction of complex variables and the emanations of consciousness in the life of every man, and so it constitutes part of the mystery of the ego itself.

As taught and exemplified by Socrates, philosophic self-study during life is an integral part of a continual preparation for the moment of death. A fruitful source for study and reflection is the *Bhagavad Gita*. Robert Crosbie suggests, in his remarks on the eighth chapter, that there is a real danger that fruits of effort will not carry over to the next life. The measure of difficulty in truly availing oneself of the teaching is identical to that involved in becoming immortal. Those for whom the teaching becomes a reality are able to reverse the false image given by the maya of the life process and by the moulds of interaction of men in terms of the reality they assign to the finite, the ever-fleeting and the false. They are able to reverse it so completely that they see with the eyes of pity and participate in the illusions of men with a constant inward awareness of *Mahat* and cosmic Eros. Such men display an existential consciousness of immortality which goes beyond external tokens and marks, beyond forms, words and concepts. It is that consciousness which ultimately must become the basis by which one thinks, and therefore by which one lives, and each one must cultivate this independently. Few individuals will reach that point in life before the moment of death where they have gained the power to slay their lunar form at will. After death every human being has to linger in a state in which there is a purgatorial dissipation of the lunar form made up of illusions, fears and anxieties engendered during life. All of these constitute the substance of what people call 'living' and 'the self', and to dissipate them in life means to have periods where one can see right through oneself. Most human beings are blocked in this because they have developed the tendency of seeing through others more than they see through themselves.

On the Path, one is not concerned to see through anything in anyone else without an appropriate compassion that can only be real if based upon knowledge gained by having broken through comparable illusions in oneself. One must first build into daily life an awareness that negates illusions, sifting and selecting between what is quintessential and what is not in every experience. Until this becomes a steady current, one is not going to be able to dissipate the lunar form at will before death, but for those who have done this, dying is like the discarding of clothes. Life in the ordinary sense has no hold over them and therefore their coming into the world is not involuntary. This is very difficult for most human beings to understand. As they go through a painful process of acting in one direction, reacting in another direction, they may suddenly hope that by some confession or ritual they can wipe out the past, but since that is impossible, the wheel of life is extraordinarily painful, monotonous and meaningless for them. They keep being propelled back into life, repeating the same oscillations of illusion. This is graphically described by Plato in the Myth of Er. There is a sense in which conventionally good people choose the life that they envied. If their goodness is caught up in appearances, they are going to be misled by external trappings. To be above the realm of appearances is to see to the very core of life, to see the essential justice of all things; and to be able to handle such insight one will need true compassion. To exemplify this authentically and continuously is in fact to be able to ceaselessly negate one's own self and to see that self as being ultimately linked up with every other being on every plane. At its root it is no-thing; it is not conditioned, it is not in the process, it is beyond.

This is a long and difficult process, but given the mystery of the ego, people do not really know why they failed in the past when they made such attempts and they have no right to despair in advance. They do not know, through what seem to be small steps taken with integrity, that great results might accrue to them. Sometimes the first earnest steps may be taken very late in life. Fortunate is the man who begins this very early in life. But whether early or late, it can be tested in relation to reduction of fears and an elevation of all encounters with other beings. The Theosophical Movement seeks to maximize the opportunity for human beings to gain strength, support, inspiration and instruction in working upon the maintenance of conscious continuity of awareness. That awareness helps them to develop an eye for essentials in daily life, enabling them to distinguish the everlasting from the ever-fleeting and not to mistake the ephemeral for the enduring, not to mistake appearances and forms for archetypal realities. To do this again and again and to make it ultimately a line of life's meditation is the only constructive way in which a person can prepare for the moment of death. This is to put the issue in psychological terms. It could also be put in terms of the sound that a human being can utter at the moment of death. That sound can be chosen only in a limited sense, because the whole of life is going to determine a dominant thought and feeling, and these will determine what sound is uttered at the moment of death. The line of life's meditation is reflected in the particular aperture in the human body through which the life-current withdraws. A very wise being who looks at a corpse will see straightaway through which orifice life departed, and hence will know a great deal about the consciousness of the soul.

The wisest beings during life gather up all their energies, like the shy and watchful tortoise, into that which is within and above them. At the moment of death they will have a sublime gnostic experience which is an affirmation of immortality, a joyous discarding of all awareness of conditions. Having put themselves beyond conditions, they are able to experience not only immortal longings, but through the continuity of unconditioned cosmic Eros and through the continuity of an unconditional awareness of *Mahat*, they experience spiritual freedom. This detachment may look at times austere, but it is combined with an inexhaustible compassion and immense vitality. If they live right, without being caught in the process, every burden lies lightly upon them. They are constantly stripping away even as other men are draining themselves in the gardens of illusion. They constantly affirm on behalf of all the Upanishadic invocation:

> *Lead me from the unreal to the real.*
> *Lead me from darkness into light.*
> *Lead me from death to immortality.*

When one can make a positive inner affirmation of the Divine within, this becomes a potent current of thought and feeling, energy and life. Without words, all one's actions will convey to others a sense that behind the games of life there is a deeper reality of pure joy in which there is dignity to every individual. As a preliminary training in making this invocation, every night before going to sleep one should renounce all identification with the body and the brain, with form, with all likes and dislikes, with all memories and anticipations. One should invoke the same affirmation upon rising, as well as at other chosen times and spontaneously whenever possible. If it is to be meaningful in the context of a universe governed by the boundless ideation of *Mahat* and suffused by the beneficence of cosmic Eros, this invocation must be made not only for oneself, but for all.

THOUGHTFULNESS

Man is the sole being in the natural order who is not compelled to pursue the same road invariably.
CLAUDE DE ST. MARTIN

The *Mundaka Upanishad* provides the archetypal image of the spiritual archer. His is the unremitting quest for divine wisdom, seeking complete unison with *Brahman*, the ultimate Reality. In this quest there must be no thoughtlessness. Lack of thought is a serious impediment to the cultivation of skill in the art of creative action. At the same time, *The Voice of the Silence* enjoins disciples to free themselves from all particular thoughts and be attuned to All-Thought.

> Thou hast to reach that fixity of mind in which no breeze, however strong, can waft an earthly thought within. Thus purified, the shrine must of all action, sound, or earthly light be void; e'en as the butterfly, o'ertaken by the frost, falls lifeless at the threshold — so must all earthly thoughts fall dead before the fane.

Wherein lies the difference between thoughtlessness and that state of transcendence which is rooted in a serene identification with the Divine Mind?

There are myriad paradoxes in relation to the spiritual path, as everyone knows who makes a strenuous attempt to incarnate in daily life the immeasurable wisdom of Brahma Vach. These paradoxes are pertinent for anyone who is in earnest, who is not merely ready to plunge into the stream, but who has already entered the stream as a *srotapatti* and laved in its rushing waters. There are those who delay this crucial step for lifetimes, even after the privilege of coming into the orbit of great Teachers from the Lodge of Mahatmas. They are afraid to take the first step into the stream. But those who have soaked in the struggle know that the recurring paradoxes are far from being instantly resolved, especially by the ratiocinative mind with its obsessive craving for certitude. Mystical paradoxes deepen as veil upon veil lifts and one finds veil upon veil behind. This must be so, for otherwise we would live in a static universe and Mahatmas would be but icons to be worshipped, like the discarded archangels of the past, periodically placated out of fear or the wish for favours. There is none of this in the vast philosophical cosmogony of *The Secret Doctrine*. It postulates one universal stream of consciousness which, at its source, is unconditioned and beyond all forms, qualities, colours and representations, beyond every finite locus in space-time. But equally, within this immense stream of encompassing and transcending consciousness, everything counts. Every being is significant and every single error has its consequence. It is difficult to accommodate so awesome a conception within one's mind and to insert one's own odyssey into the vaster odyssey of all. There is nothing in our upbringing, nothing in the limiting language of common conversation and trivial talk, that can sufficiently prepare one for the grandeur of the enterprise, so that one may feel the authentic joy of comradeship with the mightiest men of meditation. They are the immortal embodiments of universal *Mahat* who can, with a casual, relaxed and joyful sense of proportionality hit the mark amidst the limitations of collective Karma. This means, paradoxically, that they cannot hit the mark every single time either, and this too is involved in hitting the mark.

The root of these paradoxes in relation to thoughtfulness and transcendence lies in the insuperable problem of formulating the aim. The aim cannot be anything less than *Brahman*. That is the eternal hope. Every single act can have that aim because each act focuses upon a specific target in time and space which is *Brahman*. That is, at one level, the joy and the absurdity of it. In every act of manifestation — bathing, walking, mailing a message — the Logos is present. There is a sense in which the aim — the transcendental *Brahman* — is present in each moment of time as well as in every act at each point of space and in every thought. What, then, obscures the aim of a manifold human being of becoming totally one and remaining constantly attuned to *Brahman*? Why does a person need the sacred OM as the bow and to be continually tuning all one's instruments? Can one ever receive in a world of shadowy knowledge any real teaching concerning the inward meaning of the Soundless Sound? Who will teach the true intonation of the OM and everything to which it corresponds in thought, motive, act and feeling? As the mystery deepens, one must come to recognize that even in the largest perspectives of life, one can discern something that is false and which obscures still greater realities.

The correction that needs to be made in the lesser perspective is archetypally related to the correction needed in the larger perspective. Whenever one has a sense of self-encouraging exaggeration — not only verbally or in terms of external expression, but in the feeling-content and motivational coloration of particular thoughts — there is falsity and distortion. *Brahman* could not be in everything if each single thing does not appropriately mirror *Brahman* and, in an ever-changing universe, recede into non-being. There is an intrinsic illusoriness in the shadowy self that emerges like a smoky haze. In Platonic language, this temporary excess necessarily implies temporal deficiency and therefore imbalance. This may become obsessional — like infatuation — and all cognate thoughts are thereby tainted. The condition is even worse for a person lacking in mental steadiness. One discovers this speedily when one really wants to concentrate on something and even more painfully when one sits down to meditation. The moment one tries to meditate on that which is above and beyond and includes all, one confronts limitations in one's conception of selfhood. There is no way even to ponder the profoundest of vows, the holiest motive of the Bodhisattvas, in relation to the ceaseless quest for the sake of every sentient being. One will encounter a multitude of hindrances. Most thoughts are premature, feeble and abortive. One is not truly awake, but is rather in a dizzy phantasmagoria in which distorted shadows flit.

Through an illusory sense of self, one is attached to a misshapen bundle of memories and identified with a form, an image and a name. Persisting thoughtlessness means that one has fallen into a state of fragmented consciousness, and this is not only owing to the imperfections shared with all other human beings, but also through an irreverent attitude to the vestures brought over from previous lives. Such are the scars of failures from former times of opportunity to strengthen and perfect the spiritual will for the sake of universal good. Myriad are the ways in which many souls have frequently failed over an immense period of evolution.

Thoughtlessness is indeed the foremost obstacle. In a philosophical sense and in relation to the enormous Manasic capacity of the highest beings, even the well-meant thoughts of most people reflect some sort of thoughtlessness, a large measure of unconscious inconsiderateness. When one considers the most elaborate schemes of reform, the astute strategies of clever planners, one comes to see that even those models and scenarios which are the product of great ingenuity and attempt to take so much into account, still leave out a lot which is evident to persons with common sense. In every case, they also leave out whatever is hard to reckon, especially the good of the unborn and of all beings on invisible planes. As long as one does not think about such considerations, they will recede from the horizon of human concern. Even if one thinks about them, it is difficult to discern how they are immediately relevant to any particular decision, however crucial. There is a deep philosophical sense in which what is tolerated at the beginning as unavoidable thoughtlessness is painfully costly in the long run. A Master wrote with characteristic casualness to one of his disciples that an Adept, when distracted, is fallible. Adepts put themselves on the same plane as vulnerable people. They want their pupils to understand the laws at work and the logic behind their acts, and not become prisoners of false assumptions or facile expectations. One can never fully fathom the spiritual archer, perfected in the capacity to control all vestures, to move freely from plane to plane, and to draw forth dialectically from the cosmic empyrean the laser beam of the Buddhic ray into the here and now. This precludes any attachment to perfection in the realm of time. Especially pertinent in Kali Yuga, it is always true as long as Mahatmas must take into account all imperfect beings in a universe of law. Hence the compassionate casualness and wise detachment of the sages, exemplified by the way in which Buddha in the *Diamond Sutra* dialectically negated the teachings of a lifetime. There is a symmetry and roundedness to the exalted vision of spiritual Teachers for which there is no substitute in any systematized teachings.

Unless one engages in repeated exercises in the effort to learn spiritual archery through meditation, it is impossible to comprehend the injunction: *"Thou hast to feel thyself* ALL-THOUGHT, *and yet exile all thoughts from out thy Soul."* To be one with All-Thought is not at all like a hypnotic or drug-induced euphoria. Nor is it like the fleeting sense of self-transcendence experienced through the lesser mysteries on the plane of physical eros or ordinary love. It is not even captured in that beatific union of a babe in the arms of its mother. These are incomplete and even deceptive intimations. There is something incommensurable in the joys of higher meditation, wherein one discovers an effortless emancipation from boundaries, not only of space and time but of ordinary language and conventional distinctions of aim, activity and result. There is a complete exemption from all dichotomies and also an assured knowledge of ontological plenty on the plane of profound meditation. Any person who picks up Patanjali's *Yoga Sutras* and reads that the sage, just by meditating on this or that, can do amazing things, may view this as metaphorical or miraculous. Noetic magic is extremely difficult for the mundane mind to comprehend. It may be partly understood, however, through one's efforts to loosen the hold of particular thoughts, what Patanjali called self-reproductive chains of thought. Thought-images recur repeatedly, and even though one may seem to be choosing one of several thoughts, one is rapidly drawn into a determinate series of thoughts enmeshed in unconscious likes and dislikes, memories and fears, other people's opinions and prejudices — indeed in everything floating in the astral light and numberless borrowed notions. There is also a sense in which one ceases to choose thoughts even when attempting to select a train of thought.

Evidently there is no easy way of getting rid of inconsideration and thoughtlessness, much less of gaining an understanding of what *The Voice of the Silence* means by becoming one with All-Thought. To become one with All-Thought implies the capacity to see all possible worlds, to see one's own world simply as one of many, and furthermore, to sense the reality of coexisting worlds. The idea of Be-ness has nothing to do with existence on the physical plane in the realm of form. How, then, can a person truly accommodate what it means for a human being to have many possible conceptions of the good for one's family, for one's community and for the whole of humanity? Each manasic being is so rich in the potential capacity for seeing possible good that, upon descending from the plane of ideation into the realm of action and pursuing the best possible way to move oneself and others towards the larger good in a given karmic context, one must be extremely flexible. The richness of the realm of pure ideation is virtually incommunicable. Therefore, it is hard for a person even to conceive what it would be like to be a Mahatma, a radiant mirror of *Mahat*, and to see the galaxies and the solar system in visible space as manifested representations that hide many real though invisible existences. Although this is difficult, every attempt can be meaningful. The critical point is how honest one is prepared to be in making discoveries of one's limitations in one's daily efforts in the direction of meditation and spiritual archery. If a person is trying to learn *T'ai chi* or dancing and finds after a few months that he or she is not tough enough to take a teacher's honest report, someone else might see that this person is never going to learn *T'ai chi* or dancing.

In the spiritual life no one truly wise is going to be a censor or a judge. Nonetheless, a true guru, with knowledge of a person's strength and limitations, may show the delicate art of adjusting the chela. In doing that it would be impossible for him to break the laws governing the processes of spiritual growth by telling somebody in advance about his prospects. A person has to discern this for himself. He has to make his own critical progress report upon himself, and the more tough he is, the more he will see the need to relax, because he discovers so much that is painful. He either must escape, bluff or cheat or, if he can see that this is all part of what he is trying to be honest about, he must relax and resolve to move steadily and never give up. When a person vows never to give up and at the same time is clear-sighted in regard to difficulties, then that person is truly in earnest. Each sincere effort will be sacred. It will be witnessed by those mighty beings of compassion who, unknown to the aspirant, are on his side and see him as a friend. The Theosophical Movement exists in the world to show human beings that if they can make that critical breakthrough, take the first crucial step, then they will infallibly receive help, not as a favour, but because in trying to be on the side of the universe, the universe will be on their side. By rooting themselves in eternity, they could come to know, in a para-historical sense, that time is on their side. It is not on the side of any one person or of any one class, but of all. They could be assured that the future will triumph over the past, and that the circle will become ever larger. One may even come to understand why one's higher life has some sort of underpinning in the bedrock of the universe. Such assurances cannot be translated into the pseudo-certainties of the wandering mind with its daily thoughtlessness, but they arise in the consciousness of those who have touched the tranquil waters of All-Thought.

TO BE AND NOT TO BE

Guarding the nest beneath through the life-breath, the
Spirit of man rises immortal above the nest.
Brihad Aranyaka Upanishad

In earlier eras death and regeneration were often no more than remote subjects of philosophical curiosity or idle speculation. In contemporary history, however, this is increasingly the burning issue in the daily lives of innumerable individuals. Many people are afraid to formulate the central concern, but somehow they sadly acknowledge to themselves that Hamlet's question — "To be or not to be" — no longer has for them the literary flavour of a formal soliloquy. It is an anguished question so acutely pertinent at any moment that many people approaching the moment of death, as well as half-alive hosts of young men and women, are anxiously asking what is the meaning of modern life, and the possibilities of sustaining a clear, firm hope for the future. At a time of critical transition from obsolete formulae and shallow answers to a stark future without familiar guarantees, the very idea of survival takes on a strange and awesome meaning. In the early nineteenth century, when Prince Talleyrand was asked what he did during the French Revolution, he simply replied, "I survived." This is poignantly true of millions of people today. The mere fact of existing through one day from morning to evening, one week, one month, seems like a singular achievement. Is this because, as some rashly assert, a malign historical fate in the form of some tyrannical and frightening monster or ever-resourceful and vindictive scapegoat is responsible? Or does the explanation lie hidden in a new intensity of psychological pain of vast numbers of people nurtured by an inexplicable convergence of individual insights? People sense something about each other because of what they partly know about themselves. They recognize that many of the illusions that made modern life a spectacular caravan of glittering progress have become insupportable. These illusions are seen to be either deliberately manufactured lies or pathetically ineffectual forms of perception.

A person who really does believe that "God's in his heaven, all's right with the world", may either have had an inexplicable stroke of good fortune or some apparent reason for smug satisfaction in personal or professional life measured in terms of status or achievement. Even if such a person senses the grandeur of the world, he can no longer expect other men and women to concur with him. If they are tolerant and good-humoured in the way so many young people were for a golden moment in 1967, they might concede, "If it makes you feel good, go ahead." But such indulgence is now a luxury that few people apparently can afford. A person dare not admit to himself that he is enjoying himself. To do so seems somehow to hurl a blasphemous curse upon the social scene. Is this really because the sufferings of men are visible tokens of physical torment, or rather because there is a profound and pervasive soul-frustration? Behind the restlessness of vast ill-directed energy are haunting questions. Human beings do not find time for thought or contemplation. They do not sit down and calmly question where they are going, who they are, why they are doing what they are doing, why they share with many other human beings a seeming paralysis of will. Those who have been fortunate, owing to their early upbringing in easier times, to build up an infrastructure of habits which enable them to get up early and to greet the dawn, or to smile after breakfast and to have a sense that they had planned the day, at least have a sense of being able to cope at some level with life. But their sense of coping with it is wholly parasitic upon the acceptance of an excessive valuation placed upon something which is sacred only so long as no one questions it. The same people, late in the evening or around the time of twilight, or over the dulling effect of mixed drinks, suddenly only too readily admit the emptiness of their day. They willingly plunge in the opposite direction into a malaise which they dare not acknowledge during the day.

The rare opportunity at this moment lies in an increasing recognition by many that the time is past for diagnosis, patter and endless stating of the obvious. It is time to find out what one can do to make a difference in one's own life. The difference is, at heart, between the living and the dead. One might deliberately assume a critical distance from the contemporary scene and ask why the original impulse behind the technological culture with its staggering vitality — unprecedented in recorded history — seems to have run down. One might ask even more fundamental questions in terms of essential categories of apprehension that transcend history as a chronicle of events. That history is a tedious catalogue of sins, crimes and misfortunes is no new discovery. Gibbon came to this conclusion when examining the Roman Empire. Hegel held that the only lesson learnt from history is that nothing is learnt. Far more is needed than a feeble explanation of the contemporary hiatus with its anomie in terms of any rationalist philosophy of history. The relationship between propositions about collectivities and their fate and the individual's inability to give credible meaning to his own life is difficult to establish. Psychologically, the problem manifests as the apparent need for constant reinforcement. This has taken such an acute psychophysiological form that most human beings today manage to cope with the enormous flux of sensory stimuli only by attenuating or toning down the impact of external stimuli. If they attempted the opposite, magnifying auditory and visual responses, intensifying sense-perceptions in general, they would be utterly lost. They would be smoked out amidst the blazing chaos of the surrounding world. So they take the opposite path — though seldom choosing it consciously — and it consolidates into a habitual pattern. They tone down, turn off, maintain a seemingly safe standpoint of passivity in relation to the world. They purchase magazines they do not read, see pictures they cannot grasp, greet people they do not truly notice. They deal with seemingly diverse objects of interest with minimal involvement. In a short time, this inevitably becomes self-defeating.

The more one reduces the impact of external stimuli upon one's sensorium, the more one needs more intense inputs of the same kind to sustain any residual capacity for assimilation. Therefore, it is not just metaphorically true that the U.S.A. is now a nation in which vast numbers of people suffer from spiritual hypoglycemia, an inability to distil the essence of experience into a form that could meaningfully channel energy, nurture creativity and sustain commitments. It is deeply threatening to many on the Pacific Coast that the sun shines, suspended like a blazing jewel over the ocean. Nature's abundant intimations may remind some of Athens, Alexandria and Knossos, of places far apart in historical time but where seminal impulses from a tempestuous intellectual and psychic ferment led in time to a tidal wave of creative energy, a renaissance of the human spirit. Though many may have a dim awareness that something like this seems to be imminent, they cannot in any meaningful manner connect themselves with what they see around them. The sense of the emptiness of all, the voidness of one's life, the meaninglessness of everything into which one is tempted to throw oneself with a false intensity, is intensifying so rapidly that all words seem irrelevant mutterings. Promises of golden citadels in the future resemble the unsecured promissory notes of a defunct company. Vision has no point of contact with anything in daily experience which all can use, to feel that they are truly affecting the world. It provides no basis for growth, no stimulus to the acceptance of pain, denial and death. The physical body, owing to its homeostatic metabolism and the involuntary processes of Nature, functions as a system which can continually restore equilibrium. This is hard to achieve on the psychological plane in relation to the arbitrary fabrication of *namarupa*, name and form.

Brahma Vach speaks directly to any human being willing to get to the root of his own self-questioning. One has to ask fundamental questions. Is one willing to grant that this vast universe is a macrocosm, a single system, beyond comprehension and cataloguing, dateless yet with a future history which is unknown? If Nature exhibits processes that seem to move in opposing directions — expansion and contraction, withdrawal and involvement, separation and integration, aggregation and disintegration — can these be seen as the warp and woof of a single texture, interdependent aspects of an intelligent life-force? If this is true, why is it that human life has become so detached from the ordering principle in the cosmos? Why is the hazy conception of organic growth in Nature, man-made conceptions, human lives and plans and notions of success and failure, satisfaction and misery, so inadequate to resolve fundamental questions about wholeness and disease? Is the individual prepared to concede that the physical body is fighting a constant and futile battle against inevitable disintegration, without which the organism could not even maintain itself? It surely seems like a losing battle. One is dying every moment. But is a person psychologically prepared to welcome this inescapable truth? Is one prepared to create for oneself, at least as an abstraction, a viable sense of identity that has no relationship to heredity and environment, to past events and future hopes, anticipations and regrets, fears, muddles and neuroses? Is one willing to see oneself not as a static sum of psycho-social conditions but as a dynamic series of states of mind over which one has little control, especially over their unavoidable shadows?

Could a person place his or her sense of selfhood beyond the proscenium of the theatre in which there are disordered scenes, a chaotic flux of deranged events with no inner connection? Is it perhaps meaningful for a person to say that to be a human being lies in the very act of seeking connections? If so, in discovering connections between events, past, present and future, between different elements in oneself, between elements in oneself and in others, why is it that one is such a cocksure coward? Why is one so willing to edit perceptions and memories to a degree that shuts out intermediary facts? Why is it that one will refuse to face what is readily confirmable by statistics concerning the untoward consequences of certain lines of activity? Human beings have become clever at avoiding the cancelling of their illusions to a point where they could not live. They have become adroit in avoiding those extreme conclusions that in concentration camps, in arenas of acute suffering, individuals in our own time have been forced to consider. The stark language of existentialism can be purchased so easily that anyone may quote Sartre or discourse in romantic terms about the promethean agony and the burden of living. It is too easy to entertain the deceptive feeling of sharing in the poignant experience of Camus' *The Stranger* or of some piteous character in Sartre's *No Exit*.

In a deep sense human beings are afraid that neither the past nor the present contains clues to the future, collectively, historically or individually. The recognition that the restless intensity of men and women in pursuit of so-called progress was achieved only by making a Faustian deal with the devil, with some illicit external authority, is sufficient to show that the deal can no longer be made. Human beings cannot go back in the same direction; least of all can they do this if they inherit more opportunities for choice and greater psychological and social mobility than has ever been available to so many. All the games are over. Suddenly people are discovering the full implications of what it is to live in a society without moorings, charts or maps. Many are not even concerned to destroy the pathetic delusions of others because they feel that merely by ignoring them, these illusions are shown to be the more brittle. If a person consults the wisdom of the ancients, he will come to recognize that there is something true of nature as a whole which is also fundamentally significant to the human psyche.

Two contraries are simultaneously true of every person. First of all, at all times and in all contexts, any person can only live by making some unchallenged assumptions — that he is the centre of the world, that the world exists for his benefit, that his parents lived to bring him into the world, his teachers laboured to help him to get on in the world, his friends exist to support him in the world, that the vast panorama of visible nature exists for his enjoyment. Evil exists for his own moral education; he can recognize his assured detachment from evil by readily

condemning it. The whole world for every man is seemingly a
spectacle of which he is the central actor, the hero in a drama
which, though private, can extend in every direction and become
coterminous with as much of the social scene, of contemporary
history and of the cosmos as he chooses to make it. At the same
time, however, the contrary proposition is also true: the universe
is indifferent to him. He is a very small affair in relation not only
to the whole universe, to humanity or his nation, but even in
relation to his immediate neighbourhood. For a man to feel fully
conscious of both propositions at the same time is extraordinarily
difficult — like telling a man who pleads, "To be or not to be,
that is the question", that the unavoidable answer is "To be and
not to be". This has little meaning unless one begins to ask what
it means to say that one is or one is not. What is the very basis,
the cash value, the logical foundation, the *raison d'être*, the
psychological significance of existing in a world unless one can
understand what it is to exist in a world, to be anything at all?
Why do men and women assume that because their categories,
utterances and theories limit human consciousness, any difference
is made to the vast energy-fields in the universe?

Consciousness is prior to form. Consciousness defies
categorization. Consciousness is indefinable. All states of mind
are only arbitrarily connected with an apparent succession of
moments in time. Time is only an illusion produced by the
succession of our states of consciousness as we travel through
eternal duration. It does not exist where no consciousness exists
in which the illusion can be produced. There could not be a world
of objects perceived by human beings unless it were a kaleidoscope
of forms which had the illusion of stasis. Yet this is a universe of
perpetual motion in which the appearance of stasis in form is a
psychological trap resulting from an optical illusion. This
persistent illusion becomes inescapable because one has a
magnified sense of one's own existence. One's ego-sickness thus
becomes a form of health. The excess of exaggerated valuation
becomes normal because it can neither be contradicted nor
falsified. When a boy first meets a girl and says he loves her,

thinking that his love for her is infinite and inexhaustible, that she is infinitely worth loving and his love is the greatest thing on earth, this is really a truth about himself. If he believes in it, he is the only one who can verify or falsify that belief. No one else can deny it to him, and no one can confirm it. If a person gets into the habit of excessive valuation of seemingly separate objects which are apparently static in a universe of motion, he must do this as a conscious participant or as an unconscious agent in the illusion. He could do so as a conscious negator who has to use the language of stasis in the discourse of daily life and in the ritual responses of everyday human encounter. He has to be many selves. But at any given time, only that self is alive and relevant to him which he can actualize and maintain in a collective context. This means that the self which engenders his deepest thoughts and feelings, woven from the fabric of his private meditation and secret heart, that self which has no assignable name or date, which has no reference to events, is a self that simply cannot be rendered in language. Only by a systematic and deliberate process of inverting the naming game can a person become self-conscious of that which is fundamental to life itself — the ceaseless motion at the very core of life which cannot be subsumed under any pair of opposites, even life and death.

At this point, mythic images and archetypal analogies are more helpful than the tortured language of discursive reason. The greatest living image of antiquity is the cosmic dance of Shiva. Brahmā — from *brih*, 'to expand' — is the creative expansive force that nurtures the universe of differentiated life. Vishnu is the preserving and sustaining continuity in the field of consciousness which enables a world to maintain itself. Death and regeneration may summon that supremely enigmatic god Shiva, engaged in a spectacular cosmic dance which effortlessly negates all ephemeral expectations. Shiva's magically fluidic movement in the sublime cosmic dance *(Tandava Nritya)* re-enacts the continual victory of immortality over death, of consciousness over form, of the ever-existent over the necessarily limited and evanescent. And yet Shiva has the appearance of being immobile. It is an overwhelming image. Anyone who has seen a statue of Shiva Nataraja could recognize that it is full of a burgeoning potential energy, immeasurable yet motionless. It is a glorious presentment in a divinely human form of the universe as a whole — a rhythmic, harmonious, ceaseless motion. While there are sporadic staccato movements, while there are dense shadows and great empty spaces in contrast to the dramatic intensity of movement, at the same time it is like a blank screen. From one standpoint one sees form and nothingness, lights and shadows; from another point of view one senses something deeper which relativates light and shadow and makes both equally unreal in relation to primordial, ever-existent darkness pregnant with infinite possibility. There is inconceivably more light than could ever be shown by visual contrast with darkness. Metaphysically, a profound and purifying theme for deep meditation is the Void or Darkness, the *Mysterium Tremendum*, beyond all light and darkness.

As an aid to understanding, one might think of the mystical analogy of the midnight sun. Most human beings under the sun cannot transcend the awareness of what the sun does for all, beyond complimenting the sun by saying that it is gorgeous or great. To be able to visualize the reality of the sun without form or visible representation is an act of philosophical re-creation, metaphysically and magically enshrined in the great myth of Shiva. There is the glorious prospect of self-conscious godhood in man which accepts, enjoys and celebrates; of continuity of consciousness which looks forward to recurrent psychological death as a necessary step in a subtle process of invisible growth; of cancellation and negation, voluntarily chosen or compelled by Nature, which makes possible endless re-creation. There is only one ultimate choice for the human being. He must either void his puny plans, his absurdly narrow impositions upon the world and the great fluid process of life, or it will be done for him in a universe of constant interaction and total interdependence. There is a tremendous difference between taking the standpoint of a being who is unconditioned, who sees beyond form, who stands behind the veil of appearance and yet participates in the flux and thereby cooperates with the negations of his own externalizations, and the personal stance of someone who lives as if he dare not know what other people think of him. He sadly dwells in a protected cocoon of self-spun illusion from which he will never emerge, hiding from everything which threatens the false stasis and equilibrium derived from a premature cohesion that he imposes, preserves and reinforces in his plausible identifications. In the words of Plotinus:

> The Soul is bound to the body by a conversion to the corporeal passions; and is again liberated by becoming impassive to the body. That which Nature binds, Nature also dissolves; and that which the Soul binds, the Soul likewise dissolves. Nature, indeed, bound the body to the Soul; but the Soul binds herself to the body. Nature, therefore, liberates the body from the Soul; but the Soul must liberate herself from the body. Hence there is a two-fold 'death'; the one, indeed, universally known, in which the body is liberated from the Soul; but the other, peculiar to philosophers, in which the Soul liberates herself from the body. Nor does the one entirely follow the other.

Although this esoteric doctrine is far-reaching and fundamental, it is meaningless for a person who does not seriously use it in daily life in alert "care of the soul", as Plato taught. This is also true of the whole of *Brahma Vidya*. Buddha taught the doctrine of *anatta*, 'non-self', and Buddhist monks insisted on the idea that there is no personal entity or separate existence. One finds similar utterances by Krishna, Shankaracharya and Christ, and by all true Teachers, showing the supreme need for self-transcendence and second birth. Being alive in a world where the common denominator of illusions constantly throws a shadow upon the screen of time compels even those who know better to drink the muddy waters of collective delusion. Everyone has ample experience of this dross. One may generate a sense of what one is going to do this week, of premeditation and deliberation, allowing quiet spaces between moments and events, being alone, determining what one wants to do, deciding how much value to put upon each engagement in the week. Taking mental stock in advance of every week is a talismanic act of courage, and it must be repeatedly tested. How else will one know that one is aligned with any realistic thinking about the future, about the coming season or decade? Having resolved to live one's own life as well as possible for an entire week, one enters into one or another institution replete with the drugged — doped on alcohol, amphetamines, or one or another illusion — wandering around like psychic automata, heavy with fatigue, uttering words without meaning and making gestures without faith. One is going to fall prey to the collective psychic *turba* and one is going to forget. According to the Buddhist texts on meditation, if a person truly meditates upon *tathata,* he soon comes to comprehend the wheel of births and deaths. He will begin to see why people cling to those few oases in their spiritually desolate lives where they enjoy a sense of the timeless, states of mind unconcerned with the succession of events, where they can appreciate a natural flow. These periods have become rare, and so that which takes place unconsciously during sleep or in the trance state cannot be made relevant to the conscious self. A person must put these aside and accept the fact that life is one tedious thing after another. Being able to live from within, meaningfully and creatively, to live without illusion by negating without suspicion and distrust, is extraordinarily difficult to understand. Yet it is this mystical paradox which is the secret of immortality represented by the ceaseless outpouring of life and light from the sun. There is a rhythmic solar breathing in and breathing out, recapitulated for each human being in the heartbeat — the systole and diastole, the contraction and expansion that maintains in continuity a living process that sustains itself. The process is not wholly self-generating because there is no such thing in the realm of differentiated gross matter; nonetheless, even in the realm of matter, the process of life assumes a certain rhythm of self-replenishment.

Great spiritual teachers know that the only way to overcome time is through the untapped wisdom of the soul, which is immutable and immortal in relation to all its vehicles. By returning to the very root of consciousness, it is possible on the plane of thought or ideation to create around oneself a self-sustaining field, at a certain critical distance from form, out of a living awareness which is always deeper than that needed to maintain and sustain activity in existence. Self-consciousness at its very beginning is like the *1* that commences the arithmetical series. Form at its root is geometrical and assumes the primary geometrical expression — that of a sphere. Thus, every human being must think of the Self as the One that is pre-existent to all the manifestations of one's own personal self, one's own states of mind and emotion, one's ties through time to the past and the future through memory, anticipation and regret, through destructive and wasteful re-enactment of what has gone, reliving in advance what cannot therefore be truly experienced. For a person to do all this is continually to restore the full awareness that, as the *Katha Upanishad* teaches,

> Higher than the impulses, higher than the bodily powers and the emotions is the soul, and higher still is the Self. Higher than this is the unmanifest and higher than the unmanifest is the Spirit.

This is the hidden SELF. It is prior to all manifestation. What is unmanifested in that SELF is ontologically prior to and psychologically more potent than all that is manifested. To use a simple analogy, a truly creative architect is absorbed in the intrinsic activity of creation out of the alembic of his imagination, against the plastic and fluidic energy of the materials with which he works. For him to visit a building that he has planned and built is really to see something with which he has very little concern. He does not involve himself in that which shows itself, for it is lost in the limbo of the past. There are human beings in life who can relate in this way to other human beings, situations and events by self-consciously managing minimal involvement sufficiently well to make the involvement meaningful for others. This requires a conscious training of the 'I', an increasing ability to invoke that which is beyond all the actors present. Every good actor knows what is meant by the Shakespearean utterance, "The play's the thing." So too with every walk of life.

Reflective human beings find that there is something that maintains and sustains systems, industries and institutions, something impersonal, unaffected by who comes and goes, arising out of collective need, articulation and incarnation, maintained in existence and given life by collective wills, minds and imaginations. When a person asks himself what in him is dying and relinquishes what is already passing, he releases a golden opportunity to re-create himself. *When a person balances out in one's own daily equations what is dying against what is opening out from within, one becomes a free human being who existentially discovers in time the secret of immortality.* One also discerns that the secret of immortality is merely a puzzling phrase in ordinary language. But where a person gains self-awareness through intensive self-knowledge of all the variables and sub-sets that constitute one's emotional and psychic natures, one's mind-being and one's own sense of physical and mental selfhood, one may become a magician. By abstracting oneself away from all that in which one had contained one's sense of self, one can attain an amazing capacity to see an expansive Self that has no relationship to events, persons or places, to yesterday and tomorrow, to bits and pieces of oneself emotionally, psychically or mentally. One begins to live with a new awareness actuated from deep within one's consciousness. One begins to activate the Buddha-body of the Buddhist tradition, the light-body of mystical texts, the resurrection-body in Christian mysticism. This subtlest of all vestures is gestated by the primordial root causes which are ontologically prior to all the constellations of secondary and superficial causes. One's critical decisions arise out of basic desires, ultimately rooted in a fundamental willingness to endorse a limited sense of reality.

Between the unmanifested world and the SELF we find the truly 'real'. What is real is prior both to what is latent and to what is active, and yet it is posterior to SELF. That SELF has nothing to do with what is usually called the self, collective or individual, wholly parasitic upon the process of manifestation. Everyone knows the differences among human beings arising from how they see themselves. To flee every intimation of one's deeper Self out of fear for the manifesting and ever-dying self is not to live at all. This is the toughest aspect of the immemorial teaching of *Theosophia* — the ever-present beginning. The Theosophical Movement since 1875 seems to have made a relatively small difference to the scene of recorded history in modern civilization, and it even appears at times as if Krishna, Buddha, Shankara, Pythagoras, Plato and Christ came in vain. There is an essential sense in which they all came in vain in the midst of unregenerate humanity. The first step of initial detachment is the most difficult and threatening for disciples. It is a detachment in which a person is willing to put one's entire sense of self upon the dissecting table and to renounce it while doing this with no promise, no guarantee, nothing to comfort one in relation to the great venture, a dark and unknown journey. It is a deeply private journey, and it is a journey where the first step is the most difficult. In recent years many people have been playing an intolerable game of talking ignorantly about this sacred journey, but suddenly they discover something painful about each other — that there is a new breed of cowards who lack the will of those with older illusions who put their frothy energies to practical use. These are weak-willed men and women wanting to be saved, dramatically and messianically, and they unconsciously engender a nefarious vampirism, stealing energy from those more vulnerable and susceptible. It is a ghoulish game of those who cannot go back to the old illusions and yet do not have the courage to commence the spiritual path in earnest.

Brahma Vidya is exacting because it instructs the individual who is truly serious about apprehending the meaning of death and discovering the secret of immortality — "Give up thy life, if thou would'st live." Give up everything associated with so-called living. See it for what it is. Only after a sufficient period of courageous persistence can one begin to live. This painful recognition might well have the dignity and the power of a vow. It could summon a fresh release of creative energy from the inexhaustible, indescribable Self within, which has been repeatedly denied but which is relentlessly chasing one like the Hound of Heaven. It is oneself, one's only friend, one's best ally and invisible escort, one's own priest and authentic prophet, the guru and the guide, the radiant Christos within. To hold firmly to this sovereign truth is to make a new beginning and a radical change in consciousness. A person cannot move from the first part of the injunction, "Give up thy life", to the second, "if thou would'st live", on individualistic and separative terms, because no personal life means anything to the passionless and ever-revolving universe. New life may be found only by those who can find some meaning in the lives of others, can throw themselves into a vaster vision of life which is universifiable, in which others can share and participate. It is elementary wisdom and commonsense that makes a human being recognize that the larger circle must prevail.

Each and every person must go along with the ever-expanding circle or be left behind in the great pilgrimage of humanity. Many men and women cling to their own contracting circles of confining allegiances, limiting ideas, base and petty plans, prating about absurd delusions of self-importance — all because they are terrified of the uncharted Void which is the creative abyss from which tomorrow must spring. And for such people necessarily there is a Gotterdammerung: they are doomed through avoidable selfishness and there is no providential or accidental escape. But when, from the very intensity of one's own concern with the *Götterdämmerung*, a human being really begins to extend out the radius of selfhood, then one suddenly begins to find that one lives in a radically new sense. In such a totally different way of life, one is apparently wholly involved, but only because one is always laughing, always voiding, always seeing through, without hurting the feelings of others, without denying to oneself the unsought opportunity of participating in the play.

One gradually becomes a person for whom it is true that in giving up life, one begins to live. One has learned that it is possible to be and not to be — to be in space-time and yet not to be in space-time. This is to live infinitely, eternally, and immortally. It is to live the sovereign life of the king with the inward light of indissoluble consciousness focused through a continuous golden thread of mystic meditation, upon which could be strung, like so many beads, everything that is meaningful within the great reservoir of experience. This tremendous vista restores to life its fundamentally joyous optimism, its core of creativity. They are wise who say, even at the level of a slogan, that the person of tomorrow is mature in some sense that was not true of the people of the past. It requires a new kind of adult hope, a new kind of maturity, to live coolly in this new dimension in a manner that transcends past societies. To live is to maintain that kind of coolness which is sustained by an ever-expanding, living warmth for all beings on earth. One can only inherit the kingdom by claiming it. Hence the Biblical saying that the kingdom of God must be taken by force — the force of courage. This is the courage to be alone, to be a *raja* within one's own realm, and to re-establish order among the insurgents that masquerade as unavoidable drives, basic necessities and necessary patterns. To restore order in the kingdom of one's life is to attain the sovereignty of a truly free human being who is at once determining the value to put upon things and voiding them as well. One is living and not living, dying and not dying. One is constantly reclaiming the virgin nature of a boundless consciousness that flows through one in a stream, reclaiming it from the necessary process of disintegration that must characterize all forms and finitude.

One finds out for oneself that immortality can have no meaning except in reference to a recognition and acceptance of mortality. Though the language is paradoxical, the experience is possible. Alas, many men and women fail to come closer to experiencing it because they are excessively afraid to die. Ascribing mortality to parts, one can consciously do what Nature does with organisms, thereby maintaining one's individuality in the whole. Through letting go of particular things, one keeps the core of one's identity beyond time and space, beyond flux and cessation, beyond form, colour and limitation. A person who attains to this point moves naturally in embodied consciousness into a condition of something like serenity, obeisance and discipleship. Such an individual is sufficiently on the threshold to want the full incarnation of the Triad that is above him, to seek it with the whole of his being. One makes room for it (because Nature abhors a vacuum) by expelling all lesser energies and persisting in silent mental obeisance to the god within. The Triad has begun to mirror itself. It has not yet fully incarnated in the disciple, but the Triad overbroods and its mirroring shows in the calm of one's nature.

The peace that passeth all understanding is like the calm of the depths of an infinite ocean. It is beyond description, but once experienced or realized, it can never be confounded with what the self-deluded call pleasure. There can be no ego-satisfaction, for this calm involves self-forgetfulness. It is a calm where there is no awareness of being calm. It is a flow that is not aware of itself as separate in the great process of life. The Triad can incarnate gradually. Every time it enters the soul there will be a kickback in the shadowy self. When it fully descends, it can maintain itself only by a self-conscious union with the Brahmā-Vishnu-Shiva Triad — pure creativity, patient preservation of the essential and meaningful, and passionless elimination of the redundant and irrelevant. When this is attained, it becomes a rhythmic process coeval with the whole of one's life. Then it becomes as natural as breathing. As the *Brihad Aranyaka* intimates:

> Then the point of the heart grows luminous, and when it has grown luminous, it lights the soul upon its way: from the head or from the eye or from other parts of the body. And as the soul rises upwards the life-breath rises upwards with it; and as the life-breath rises upwards with it, the powers rise up with the

life-breath. The soul becomes conscious and enters into Consciousness.

Then his wisdom and works take him by the hand, and the knowledge gained of old. Then as a caterpillar when it comes to the end of a leaf, reaching forth to another foothold, draws itself over to it, so the soul, leaving the body, and putting off unwisdom, reaching another foothold there, draws itself over to it.

As a worker in gold, taking an ornament, moulds it to another form newer and fairer; so in truth the soul, leaving the body here, and putting off unwisdom, makes for itself another form newer and fairer: a form like the forms of departed souls, or of the seraphs, or of the gods, or of the creators, or of the Eternal, or of other beings.

The soul of man is the Eternal. It is made of consciousness, it is made of feeling, it is made of life, it is made of vision, it is made of hearing; it is made of the earth, it is made of the waters, it is made of the air, it is made of the ether, it is made of the radiance and what is beyond the radiance; it is made of desire and what is beyond desire, it is made of wrath and what is beyond wrath, it is made of the law and what is beyond the law; it is made of the All. The soul is made of this world and of the other world . . .

As they said of old: Man verily is formed of desire; as his desire is, so is his will; as his will is, so he works; and whatever work he does, in the likeness of it he grows.

NEGATION AND
TRANSCENDENCE

Having stripped off the rags of perishability, He put on imperishability which none can take away.
Evangelium Veritatis

And when thou sendest thy free soul thro' heaven,
Nor understandest bound nor boundlessness,
Thou seest the Nameless of the hundred names.
ALFRED, LORD TENNYSON

To see clearly is poetry, prophecy, and religion — all in one.
JOHN RUSKIN

We are now living our immortal lives.
EDWARD BELLAMY

The term 'Absolute' in ancient and modern metaphysics refers to that which transcends all manifestations, differentiations and distinctions. When the terms 'absolute' and 'relative' are used together as correlatives, each is dependent on the other for its meaning. There is evidently a significant difference between the term 'absolute' *per se* and when it is used as a correlative term. The philosophical connection between these two uses of the term 'absolute' has a mystical and ethical importance, which is crucial to our understanding. The Absolute is transcendent, in relation to both Being and non-Being. At the same time, it is a well-tested maxim that *to be* is *to be intelligible*. This standpoint is truly Platonic and is the primary root of absolute idealism. Plato himself was an objective idealist, unlike subjective idealists of the Berkeleian or the later Yogachara schools, which deny that the world has any reality apart from the thoughts and conceptions of beings. For the objective idealist the world, though deeply rooted in ideal forms, archetypal thoughts and a hidden realm of noumenal reality, also mirrors that fecund reality in the entire vast assemblage of variegated forms moving in the panoramic region of particulars.

For Plato, anything that exists can, in principle, become an object of thought, of cognition and, therefore, of what we call shareable knowledge, at different degrees of individual apprehension. The other tradition, which is also old, but which has come to dominate in the last three centuries with monopolistic pretensions, is that of empiricism, wherein *to be* is *to be experienced*. There is a significant difference between *intelligibility in thought* and what we may call *experience*, which inevitably has an element that is common and concrete among all beings. It customarily pertains to the prosaic sensory world of external objects and all the complex connections between them. 'Experience', in this sense, is central to the empirical conception of the known yet shifting boundaries of reality and causality, of identity and inter-connection.

Regardless of each of these standpoints, if the transcendental Absolute is by its very nature both beyond and also within every atom in the worlds of relativity, the use of 'absolute' and 'relative' as correlative, contrasting terms becomes comprehensible, reliable and meaningful. It is reliable as a means of measurement in science and mathematics. It is meaningful as a basis of appraisal in ethics and aesthetics and, in general, comprehensible as a basis of grading in regard to all finite objects and subjects, contexts, conditions and states. In other words, as long as we can speak of more or less, greater or lesser, more true, more beautiful and more good, or, less true, less beautiful and less good, as long as we can make all these discriminations in the world of particulars, it is indeed possible for us to use consistently as a pair of opposites the terms 'absolute' and 'relative'. An example from science immediately comes to mind, the notion of absolute temperature, which in fact is not based upon any ultimate zero point, but conventionally and sensibly upon a certain degree which has become the effective standard of measurement because, below that temperature, gases cease to coalesce. The entire concept of absolute temperature is related to the known laws of thermodynamics and, in this sense, there is something conventional about it. All measurements of temperature gauged by it are meaningful in relation to a norm that has been taken as fixed because it is both conceptually and practically convenient. That is, it is operationally convenient in understanding the behavior of gases.

When we use the term 'absolute' in regard to any limited context, as for example when we say, "This is absolutely true", we mean 'without qualification'. We implicitly draw a contrast with a whole lot of other things which will need qualifications, or which have a lesser sphere of reference, or which refer with much less degree of relevance and intensity to that situation. We are perfectly familiar with using these terms 'absolute' and 'relative' as correlates. And yet, neither of these has anything to do with the intrinsic transcendence of what we call the Absolute. But because it is immanent in every atom, the most transcendental is also the most immanent, though hidden to the gaze of the physical eye and hidden also to the purview of the perceiving mind as it normally functions. Therefore, it is not surprising that what is so supremely transcendental also enters always and everywhere as an often overlooked element in our agreed appraisals in a world of relativities.

Philosophically, the Absolute is "unthinkable and unknowable", in the words of the *Mandukya Upanishad*, and yet partially apprehensible and cognizable by contrast with what we can know or apprehend of the relative. To say that it is unthinkable and unknowable is merely to say that all thinking and all knowing must fall far short of the very reality, the very nature, the very essence of the Absolute. But to say that it is apprehensible and knowable by contrast with what we know of the relative simply means that we may know something, may have some apprehension, even of what is indefinitely large, extremely remote, or conceptually transcendental such as when we talk of an ideal number or an ideal point, or when we talk of the ideal of perpetual motion. All of these are perfectly meaningful because they serve as standards of reference or as means of negation and transcendence of all that is on a lesser scale by some implicit standard of commensuration. Such a standard is implicit because commensuration may pertain to a vast array of particulars, and then take a big jump — what is sometimes called a conceptual shift or quantum leap — to the notion of an ideal or an absolute level. Yet this is intelligible and manageable. Indeed, it is also widely relevant because of the mathematical notion of the actual infinite, which is a concrete notion in applied science, in mechanics and in some of the influential geometries of the last hundred years.

To say this is to lend meaningfulness as well as a due measure of agnosticism to all modes of knowing. It is to give limit and value to all levels of being and reality, but, at the same time, recognize the relative illusoriness of all states and conditions. This noetic standpoint is somewhat difficult to sustain today even in theory, let alone in practice. And yet, it is truly challenging to intellectual indolence and mental passivity, to non-exertion and non-trying, as well as to the deep-seated incurable craving in human beings for certainty and finality in a world of ever-changing phenomena. Above all, it is a helpful corrective to the unconscious but sometimes explicit obsessional tendency to absolutize the relative, as well as implicitly to settle for some frozen image or stipulated relativation of the Absolute.

What every human being perceives at any given time is deeply real, having a vital immediacy and relative importance that is essentially non-transferable, and cannot be effectively conveyed to another human being who does not independently have the same feeling at that moment of time. So, there is something incommunicably authentic about a 'peak experience', springing from a deep sense of self-transcendence in a human being. The danger lies in making that subjective experience the chief yardstick for all objective comparison, not only of actual but of past, present and future states, and even of all possible states of experience. Ethically the failure to recognize the transcendental and the immanent, the unique as well as the universal, as primary pairs of opposites in constant interaction, can consolidate moral backsliding, as well as become an obdurate obstruction to moral growth and refinement. Even worse, one may settle, as many do, for a convenient dualistic contrast between the ideal and the existent, the distant and the immediate, the ineffable and the tangible. This can only intensify rajasic restlessness and tamasic abdication, as well as notoriously aggravate sattvic self-righteousness, which in turn reacts upon *tamas* and *rajas*.

Furthermore, any canonical dualism alienates a human being from the rich diversity and minute degrees of human striving, imperfection and attainment, from the highest possibilities as well as souls in distress. One is alienated from the highest possible beings who exist at any given time on earth or elsewhere, and also from human beings who are at the lowest levels of striving for subjective reasons that are all too difficult to ascertain. The tension of the subject-object dichotomy confines one's perspective, perceptual range and capacity, as well as one's circle of affinities and one's degree of empathy. At the worst, it consolidates the absolutization of the relative. That is what conventional external religion does, and also popular, over-simplified science. All knowledge, in fact, which is packaged and pedantically transmitted through mass education, consolidates the absolutization of the relative, the limitations of human beings and the human condition, the narrowing of the horizon of human experience even in the sensory realm and certainly beyond it, and also hardens one's judgments and reactions concerning other human beings, both as subjects and even as objects. Altogether, it narrows the base of one's awareness and the capacity to extend and alter, enlarge and deepen, one's sympathies, ideals and psychological states. It produces the smug boundedness as well as the false finality of one's perceptions, concepts and perspectives. Above all, and this is extremely crucial, it limits the inherent focus of one's motivation and the force of the inward stimulus in oneself to self-correction, to self-realization, to self-striving and to self-transcendence.

Given an initial grasp of the distinction between the term 'absolute' by itself and the term 'absolute' as contrasted to the 'relative' the various meanings and uses of these terms may be rightly understood.

First of all, consider the Basic Proposition that the Absolute is out of all relation to conditioned existence and is, therefore, inconceivable and indescribable. This means that nothing can be logically predicated of it in words and signs, owing to the limits of logic and of language. The Basic Proposition concerns the meaningfulness and legitimacy of predication as well as the incommensurability and ineffability of the Absolute as an object of cognition or comprehension, apprehension or awareness. But, it does not rule out, either in principle or in practice, a consubstantiality between the core of one's own being and the intrinsic self-existent nature of the Absolute. Not does it in the least vitiate the meaningfulness of meditation, the bliss of contemplation, or the potency of philosophical negation in the realm of particulars, wholes and worlds.

Secondly, the terms 'absolute' and 'relative', as a pair of predicates, convey a vital sense of opposition or contrast. But, since nothing can be predicated of the Absolute, whatever the sense of the term 'absolute' as a predicate opposite to the sense of the term 'relative', this sense cannot properly be predicated of the Absolute. That is, the very contrast between 'absolute' and 'relative' cannot be turned back as a basis for attributing anything to the Absolute. Similarly, whatever sense the term 'relative' has as a predicate, this cannot properly be taken to establish or convey the idea of something related to the Absolute by opposition. That is why one cannot possibly maintain that the Absolute thinks or feels, in any sense that embodied beings can grasp. Any of the verbs we use in relation to our consciousness, in relation to ordinary human cognition, feeling or conduct, cannot be applied to the Absolute simply because all these everyday words have built-in limits and limitations that arise not only out of their customary use but even out of their conceivable use. Even the greatest conceivable thought or feeling cannot by itself limit or characterize the attributeless Absolute.

The most primitive relational predicates, such as 'the same as' and 'other than', are inherently inapplicable to the Absolute. The Absolute is peerless and incomparable. There is nothing outside the Absolute which could in any respect resemble it. Nor can anyone truly say that anything or everything is other than the Absolute, or that, in relation to the Absolute, all else is unreal. To attempt to do so is to oppose everything else to the Absolute, which is actually to limit it and to overlook its omnipresence. We should discern the latter truth just as clearly as we can recognize the former. The intrinsic relativity of all attributions and predicates sharpens our meditative awareness of the supreme transcendence of the Absolute. It also deepens our mystical apprehension of the most pristine metaphors given by the sages, especially Absolute Space, dimensionless and unbounded, or Absolute Motion and Consciousness, or Absolute Duration. These pregnant analogies point to the all-inclusiveness of the Absolute, to the omnipresence, omniscience and omnipotence of the Absolute, as mirrored in time, in space, and in all contexts. But all cognitive identifications of similars and contrasts, equivalences and opposites can apply only to our increasing if inevitably incomplete apprehension of the Absolute.

It would be perfectly legitimate for two people to say that their tentative conceptions of the Absolute are similar to each other. But for them to agree that these cognitive conceptions are similar to the Absolute would be saying too much. And equally, for two people to find in a third statement something which they say is incompatible with the Absolute would also be saying too much, even if it were incompatible with what they recognize as the reasonable similarity of their recondite conceptions of the Absolute. Yet, while such intellectual identifications of similars and contrasts can only dimly contribute to our imperfect cognition of the Absolute, they can nonetheless enable the individual to transcend effectively the conceptual and imaginative horizons of the human mind and human heart. Thereby, they could release a deeper, a more assured and abiding, sense of unitary Being in the Self of All. Often we fall short of this profound possibility, because we are so conscious of how much more sensitive we are in feeling than someone else, or how much sharper we are in cognition than others. Hence, we do not push our own capacity for cognition or feeling to the limit, to the point where it empties itself and leaves us in a luminous state which transcends the mind and the heart.

It is a state of sublime effortless silence, but powerful and potent. It is most sacred because it is our moment of silent awareness of the awesome Presence of the One Self, the unitary Being, within the fragmented selves and inmost sanctuaries, of all men, women and children. This is what is meant by the poetic saying that "deep calls unto the deep" — an expression truly meaningful to great mystics and great lovers who are, alas, rare to find in this loveless and prosaic world. The object and goal of love, its source and stimulus, must ever cancel and exceed all comparisons and contrasts. Such *bhakti* is incomprehensible to many and is indeed beyond the duality of division or the arena of comparison and conflict, or even the closeness and joy of communion.

Thirdly, the contrasting terms, 'absolute' and 'relative' cannot tell us anything about the Absolute, either directly through the term 'absolute' or indirectly through the term 'relative' — through the back door so to speak. Therefore, we need to go wholly beyond words like 'within and without', 'above and below', 'before and behind', in relation to the Absolute. However, in regard to our individual and collective cognition of the Absolute, all authentic approximations, all creditable attempts, may be compared to the six directions — North, South, East, West, Above and Below — so as to generate a conceptual tree of paradigmatic standpoints. Like the *saddarshana*, the six schools of philosophy in classical Indian thought, we may find room for idealism, both subjective and objective, on the one hand, and for materialism, on the other. If, in a Leibnizian sense, every windowless monad has a distinct, unique and original standpoint, our authentic approaches to the Absolute must embrace and enjoy multiple standpoints. This is as meaningful as holding an apple or an orange, seeing it and feeling it from every standpoint, and in every possible way. Even sense perceptions involve a degree of Buddhic synthesis, and if so it is vital that we make our minds more rounded and less angular in their apprehension of worlds, objects, subjects and selves. Whilst it is always meaningful to focus our concentration upon a single point — what is called *ekagrata* or one-pointedness — there is room for the rounded point of view. This is rare, especially in the realm of the mind or in the rhythm of the heart. There is also room for single-mindedness and single-heartedness. This is what is meant in mathematics by the topological similarity between the transfinite and the infinitesimal, or by Plato's stress on the concordance between the two poles of his thought — creative mathematics and rapturous self-knowledge, the Eternal Forms and the immortal soul (as in *Phaedo*).

Fourthly, as a pair of contrasting terms properly predictable of things 'absolute' and 'relative' do seem to have an intelligible meaning. But we must always recognize that when we speak of that which is relative in some regard, it is only relatively relative and not absolutely relative. Similarly when we speak of that which is absolute in some respect, we must recognize that it is only relatively absolute. Even if it were shown and known to be absolute in relation to a specific world, we cannot rule out all possible worlds and therefore we have no basis for absolutizing what is absolutely true in our world. In language and in logic, as indeed in our progressive apprehension and changing cognition of the world and of ourselves, it is always meaningful to talk in terms of degrees of reality, or of what is relatively real and relatively absolute. This is relevant not only to levels of awareness corresponding to states of consciousness and planes of substance, but also to the way time, space and circumscribed causality enter into our perception and modes of cognition, as well as modify and affect the contents of our cognition.

Furthermore, and at the highest level of what hardly three or four eminent yet exoteric minds in an entire century have even come to see, all statements and systems have temporal limits, that is, a beginning and an end. Even the most general statements or the most comprehensive closed, logical and axiomatic systems must contain inclusions as well as omissions, or have rules of relevance and reference as well as implicit, if not explicit, rules of exclusion. In contemporary mathematical logic, this is associated with the great work of Kurt Gödel in the 1930. Given this truth, if Man is a unitary being, his finite awareness must have a fluidity and elasticity, a mobility and a resilience, which protects the future — both his own and, inseparably, the future of other beings. It must also acknowledge all past attempts of apprehension, which is why one has to do proper justice to all one's predecessors known and unknown, as well as the integrity of all starting points and termini of apprehension. No one can be blamed for being where he or she is conceptually or empirically, or for being where she or he alone can start, or indeed, for being where he or he must end a certain process of enquiry.

This was partly glimpsed by Kant when he stated that there are, in principle, as many points of view and systems of thought as there are states of awareness at different moments of time and in different spatial and conceptual, as well as empirical, contexts. What is true in principle can only become meaningful in practice if human monads or minds train themselves to become more multidimensional in thinking, more tentative in regard to limits and boundaries, and more hospitable to modes of apprehension which demand a higher level of synthesizing and a greater degree of inclusiveness than we normally need or use in our everyday encounters and our common discourse. In fact, this may be taken as the crucial yardstick of any advanced civilization, and therefore, it is vital to the emerging global civilization of the future — to its lifelong education, its new social institutions, its range and richness of discourse, and its quest for that which is greater and that which is beyond.

Fifthly, the ready recognition that we can only speak of that which is relatively absolute is important to preserving a pristine sense of the non-dual immanence of the Absolute. However, the same problem is repeated when speaking of the transcendent and the immanent. What is transcendent to one person may be immanent to another, or what is transcendent at one time or place, or in one state of mind, maybe be immanent at another time or place, or in another state of mind. This is a simple truism, but it is crucial to the deliberate, disciplined attempt to meditate daily by dissolving distinctions and boundaries, by progressively removing all hindrances and limits. It is central to the attempt to contemplate continuously, however briefly, in a manner that alters our sense of what is real, or of what is really immanent and what is truly transcendent. At the same time, it is also necessary to recognize that the notion of degrees of apprehension, or levels of awareness, must be seen as preserving intact the *difference in kind*, not of degree, signified by our fundamental conception of the Absolute as indivisible, unitary, all-transcendent, as well as wholly and continuously immanent everywhere and always. This difference in kind of the Absolute from all else, including human conceptions of deity, makes the arcane conception of the Absolute distinct from that of everything else that exists, as well as from the Absolute of medieval theologies and modern philosophies.

At this point, one can raise one's sights beyond *epistemology* to the level of *ontology*, but the ontology of meditative metaphysicians and genuine mystics. Here, we will need to focus upon the primeval differentiation in the Absolute.

First of all, the difference between the Absolute and the relative arises even at the highest level, the plane of the Unmanifested Logos. There is a primary ontological distinction between the Absolute — the *Parabrahman* or SAT of the Vedantins, the One Reality, which Hegel characterized in the nineteenth century as both Absolute Being and Non-Being — and, the first manifestation — the impersonal and, philosophically, Unmanifested Logos, which is the precursor of all the manifested Logoi of every sacred tradition. The Absolute is sometimes mistakenly called the 'First Cause', as Aristotle did, but since this implies the inappropriate conception of an ordinal series, the term is better reserved for that first impersonal manifestation, which is the second element in this distinction. The First Logos exists as that which is, was and will be, or the uncreate power, the *Atman,* and from it is generated in the dark waters of Space — Chaos or undifferentiated substance, or in our human case what we call *Buddhi* — from or through the image of the Absolute reflected in those waters, the image of Him or It which moves on them.

It is a fundamental axiom that the Absolute is the One without a second, wholly beyond and even inherently incapable of all relations, inclusive of absence and presence, Being and non-Being, but beyond both. It is the ubiquitous and immaculate SAT or Be-ness, the source of all worlds and epochs of manifestation. It is never capable of being brought into the realm of manifestation, of comparison and contrast, of modalities and relativities, even noumenally, let alone phenomenally. If this is so, the Absolute is beyond both the actual and the potential infinities of mathematics and of motion. It is essentially different from any linear extrapolation into infinitude in space and time, motion and duration. The Absolute must, therefore, never be identified or confused with the First Cause of pantheistic philosophies; or even with the primal dawn and differentiation which is the Unmanifested Logos — that which is, was and will be; or with the uncreate *Paramatman* gestated in the dark waters of space — of *Aditi,* Primordial Chaos; or with the ever-existent *Mulaprakriti,* the Veil upon the Absolute.

Put more simply, the unending is not the Endless Ever Self-Existent. The indefinite, the indescribably large, or the conceptual, potential infinite, is still not the same as the inherently boundless or the inconceivably eternal, or the all-inclusive transcendence of all possible sum totals in the realms of the unmanifested, as well as the manifesting and the manifested. This important, fundamental and rather abstruse truth is sometimes suggested by the difference between zero and one, taken as symbolic of the distinction between the Absolute and the First

Logos. At other times it is also suggested as a difference between the indivisible One and the number series including real numbers, imaginary numbers and negative numbers, as well as the entire host of what we call natural numbers, though this difference is strictly more appropriate as symbolizing the distinction between the First Logos and its successive emanations.

Secondly, the subsequent genesis of gods and human Monads takes its rise in and from one and the same point, which is the one universal, immutable, eternal and Absolute Unity. The forever concealed, primal triune differentiation, not from, but in the one Absolute, is symbolized by the *Sacred Four* or the *Divine Tetractys*. In the metaphysical world it is the unit ray or *Atman*. It is *Atman*, the highest spirit in man which, in conjunction with *Buddhi* and *Manas*, is called the upper Triad or Trinity. We must carefully distinguish between, on the one hand, the forever concealed primal triune differentiation in the Absolute — *Sat-Chit-Ananda*, Truth-Intellection-Bliss in the metaphysical world beyond the unmanifest and the manifest, symbolized, since Pythagoras, by the Divine Tetractys, unthinkable and unspeakable, the Holiest of the Holy, and, on the other hand, the Unit Ray which is contained in the One point — the universal, immutable, eternal and Absolute Unity. There is No-thing, and there is primordial unity which is different, the latter being merely a reflection of the former in the dawn of differentiation. You can only talk of unity where there are many things to be brought into that unity. But, before things emerge at all, even at the highest noumenal level of the unmanifest, there is No-thing and it ever exists. So unity is merely a reflection of No-thing in the dawn of differentiation, and also the *fons et origo* — the fountain head and origin, the One Source of All.

The Divine Ground, another phrase sometimes used of the Absolute, the *Urgrund*, is beyond the primeval radiation of the Unit Ray, and yet there is nothing which we can ascribe to the former that we cannot also, and even more meaningfully, ascribe to the latter. Every time we try to characterize the Absolute, what we are really doing, but in a muddled way, is to characterize the unit ray, which is That which was, is, and ever will be, and which is the pristine mirroring of the Absolute. The Godhead is beyond the One God who gives rise to all gods, Monads and atoms, as well as all the seven kingdoms of Nature. In this sense, the *Atman*, the eternal breath, the light of eternal motion, the omnipresent *Aum*, is indistinguishable from the primeval, all transcendence, ever-existent AUM, the Soundless Sound which ceaselessly reverberates throughout the ages of worlds, gods and mortals and of all immortal beings in *mahapralaya* and *mahamanvantara*.

Thirdly, the way to approach this abstruse, and yet sublimely sacred, mystery is nearer to all human beings than even the tips of their own fingers. It is hidden in every atom and every heart. The true follower of the Gupta Vidya worships it in spirit, within the Absolute Unity — the ever-pulsating great heart beating throughout, as in, every atom of Nature. Each such atom contains the germ from which he may raise the Tree of Knowledge whose fruits give Life Eternal. To the true man or woman of constant meditation who ceaselessly adores in his or her inmost being the Absolute Unity — the eternal heartbeat of the hidden cosmic heart or divine hebdomad — every atom and its nucleus are sacred and all-potent. Each is capable of gestating from within without its pristine germ, the sacred Tree of Knowledge or Life Eternal, which is the concealed soul of the glorious Tree of Life omnipresent.

The Tree of Knowledge is the immortal soul of the Tree of Life. This then is the Sacred Heart of the Divine Mysteries, the true basis of spiritual growth and conscious involution back to the One Source. It is the logic behind the language of silent unuttered prayer or worship, inward communion and ceaseless contemplation, bringing the ardent seeker closer, even if only a little, to the Men of the Word, the Knowers of *Vach*, the Adorers of the *Verbum*. The Rishis and Mahatmas, Buddhas and Bodhisattvas, the Watchers of the Night, constitute the Banyan Tree of Initiation, the eternal embodiments and perennial transmitters of Brahma Vach, Gupta Vidya, the *Philosophia Perennis*.

> Ah! The Wonder of the Banyan Tree!
> The disciples are elders; the Guru is a youth;
> The Teaching of the Guru is SILENCE.
> The doubts of disciples are all dispelled.
>
> ADI SHANKARACHARYA

THE INMOST SANCTUARY

The 'Master' in the sanctuary of our souls is 'the Higher Self' — the divine spirit whose consciousness is based upon and derived solely (at any rate during the mortal life of the man in whom it is captive) from the Mind, which we have agreed to call the Human Soul (the 'spiritual soul' being the vehicle of the Spirit). In its turn the former (the personal or human soul) is a compound in its highest form, of spiritual aspirations, volitions, and divine love; and in its lower aspect, of animal desires and terrestrial passions imparted to it by its associations with its vehicle, the seat of all these.

H.P. BLAVATSKY

Restoration of the right relationship between the Master in the inmost sanctuary and the incarnated consciousness is gained only through a sacrificial process of self-purification. Obscuring and polluting tendencies nurtured in the mind through its misuse over many lives must be removed by a self-chosen and self-administered therapy. Like the Pandava brothers exiled from their kingdom through their own folly, or like the master held prisoner in his own house by those who should be his servants in the parable of Jesus, the pristine divine ray of the Logos in man is trapped and stripped of its sovereign place in human life unless consciously sought by the aspirant. This invocation of wisdom through the supplication of the mind to the spirit was seen by the ancient Greeks as the cultivation of *sophrosyne* — the subordination of the inferior element to the superior. It is shown in *The Voice of the Silence* as the *shila* virtue — the attunement of thought, will and feeling to the pulsation of divine harmony, *Alaya-Akasha*. The mind stands as the critical link between the divine and the animal nature. The recovery and right use of the privilege of human existence depend upon the subordination of the elements of the lower *rupa* existence to the spiritual ideation of *Arupa Manas*.

The sacrificial posture and selfless motive required for this self-purification can be readily grasped through a telling analogy. There is not a modern metropolis which does not maintain the equipment needed to neutralize the effluvia of human waste and thereby reduce the danger of infection to its population. Similarly, a large number of devices are available, both to cities and to individuals, for the purpose of removing sediments and impurities from drinking water, through distillation, filtration and osmosis, to make it available in a purer and fresher form. With the human mind the same principles of public health and civic responsibility would require that each individual and every society strive to purify the muddy stream of human passions which pollute those coming into contact with it. Every human being has received the crystalline waters of life in a pure and unsullied condition, and therefore everyone has the karmic responsibility for every failure to return these waters to the ocean of life in a pristine condition. Insofar as this responsibility has been neglected by individuals, under karma in successive lives they are self-condemned to immersion in the waters they themselves have poisoned. Under the laws of karma affecting the processes of reincarnation and the transmigration of life-atoms, individuals owe it to their neighbours and their descendants, as well as to themselves, to purify their mental emanations.

In practice, this implies a continuous cleansing of one's thoughts, one's words and one's actions; these in turn fundamentally depend upon the purification of the will. Unfortunately, purification of the will, which is vital to the spiritual regeneration of humanity, is itself seriously misunderstood as a consequence of the process of pollution of consciousness and magnetism. Mired in the morbid obscuration of higher consciousness, too many people suppose that a bolstering of the lower will is a means to survival. Nothing could be farther from the truth. The higher spiritual will does not itself need to be strengthened, but it may be released through the removal of obscurations and hindrances. So long as the will is activated by the individual only on behalf of passions and the illusion of the persona, that will is not worth having. Hence, many people have discovered that the will cannot be released on behalf of lesser purposes. This predicament is conspicuous in those diseased societies which place an inordinate emphasis upon the personal will. Will itself is a pure colourless principle which cannot be dissociated from the energy of the *Atman* released through breathing. Thus when human beings breathe benevolently, blessing others with every breath, they can release the beneficent will-energy of the *Atman*. As soon as the will is released on behalf of the personal ego, however, against other human beings, it is blunted. This inevitable paralysis of the antagonistic lower will is indeed a beneficent and therapeutic aspect of karma.

Viewed from a collective standpoint, many human beings can be seen as having been weakened because they have absorbed life-atoms from others who have misused spiritual knowledge and the potency of the higher will. Throughout the world perhaps one in ten persons has insistently used the will against other human beings in this or previous lives. This may have been for the sake of bolstering the insecure identity of the *persona* or, worse, through the misuse of spiritual knowledge connected with false meditation, indulgence in drugs and mediumistic practices. Since 1966 contemporary society has witnessed the emergence of a number of centres of pseudo-spiritual activity; now it is witnessing the inevitable psychological breakdown of many who were responsible for this moral pollution. The waves of spiritual influence initiated by the descent of Krishna offer golden opportunities to all souls, including those inverted natures self-blocked from inward growth by their own failures on the Path in previous lives. Amongst these there were some too cowardly to make a new beginning, who sought instead to compensate for their own weakness and delusion by cashing in on the currents of the 1975 Cycle. Having forfeited timely opportunities offered through compassion, they are self-destroyed when Krishna takes a firm stand on behalf of the entire human family because they are unable to generate a genuine concern for others. Never having generated an interest in the welfare of the vast majority of mankind, they are self-condemned. Sadly, they cast a long shadow over a much larger class of weaker souls who are affected by them, no doubt through their own delusions and vulnerabilities.

Persons are sometimes drawn into dangerous orbits of misused knowledge through loose talk about such sacred subjects as *kundalini, kriyashakti* and the activation of the higher spiritual centres in man. Ordinary people who enjoy a normal measure of spiritual health wisely avoid those places where they are likely to hear profane chatter. Through a natural sense of spiritual good taste they simply shun those places where self-deluded con men congregate to make a living off the gullible. Today, because the moral and spiritual requirements for participation in the humanity of the future have become more evident to many people, the market for such deceptive opportunism has begun to diminish. The America of P.T. Barnum, who said that a sucker is born every moment, has been replaced to a large extent by the America of Abraham Lincoln, where, as is well known, one cannot fool all the people all the time. Although many souls have to travel a great distance along the path of self-integration, they have learnt enough not to be duped by pseudo-spiritual blandishments. Just as they have learnt not to believe everything conveyed by the mass media and not to leap at every free offer or supermarket discount, they have also learnt to pass up invitations for instant development of *kundalini* and every facile promise of spiritual development that dispenses with the judicious control of the emotions and passions.

Even in the difficult area of sexuality the idea of strength through celibacy (e.g. Gabrielle Brown, *The New Celibacy*, 1980) has gained some currency amongst many people, young and old, who find the burden of ego-games and unequal experimentation intolerable. There is nothing wrong with the sacred act of communion and procreation, and as the ancient Jews believed, God is pleased when a man and a woman come together in true unison. Nor need this issue be obscured by pseudo-arguments concerning the Malthusian spectre of over-population. As the economist E.F. Schumacher pointed out, even if the entire population of the globe were concentrated in America, this would result in a population density no greater than that of Great Britain, a nation long noted for the spaciousness and greenery of its countryside. North America itself, over its ancient and almost entirely unwritten history, has supported many varied civilizations, some of which displayed a much greater spiritual maturity than is evidenced in its recent history. Broadly, one cannot understand the physical facts of life on earth, much less the spiritual facts of life, through a language of conflicting claims and counter-claims, rationalizations and compensatory illusions, or pseudo-sophisticated statistical arguments based upon a selfish and shallow view of the nature of the human psyche.

The purification and release of the will must be comprehended in terms of human individuality, and therefore must be considered in the light of the mystery of every human soul. Since this mystery encompasses an entire series of reincarnations extending over eighteen million years, it can only begin to be appreciated through careful consideration of the motley evidence offered by one's participation in varied states of consciousness in the present life. Any individual concerned to recover the spontaneity and benevolence of the spiritual will must be willing to examine courageously the manner and extent to which he or she has become the servant not of the divine Ego, but rather of the lower astral form and its attendant incubi and succubi.

> For this 'Astral' — the shadowy 'double' (in the animal as in man) is not the companion of the *divine* Ego but of the *earthly body*. It is the link between the personal SELF, the lower consciousness of *Manas* and the Body, and is the vehicle of *transitory, not of immortal life*. Like the shadow projected by man, it follows his movements and impulses slavishly and mechanically, and leans therefore to matter without ever ascending to Spirit.
>
> H.P. BLAVATSKY

Plato explains, in a myth in the *Timaeus*, that when the Demiurge was fashioning the form of man, he endowed the human body with a stomach. This was done, according to the myth, out of compassion because otherwise man, unlike the animal, would be in danger of eating continually. Not only would this be disastrous for human health, but it would needlessly preoccupy consciousness with the intake and elimination of physical food. If human consciousness is to mature fully, it cannot be preoccupied with the *persona*, with the stomach and the libido, with physical space, time and motion. Consciousness must be freed to contemplate eternal motion, boundless space and infinite duration. This liberation from the bonds of the *persona* cannot be accomplished all at once but must be attempted again and again, through persistent efforts over a lifetime of meditation.

The radical reorientation of consciousness, away from the *persona* and towards the Divine, requires ceaseless striving and unremitting patience. Such continuity cannot be sustained over a lifetime unless it can be sustained for a year or even a week. In this arena, where clean beginnings and steadiness of application are crucial, one may gain great help from the example of the good gardener, who comes again and again to tend seedlings and plants, and yet allows nature time to work its magic. In fact, people who actually do some planting can gain considerable benefit through the restoration of their contact with the earth and by gaining an organic sense of growth. They can learn that all life is sacred, including the human body, and that every form of life can and should be treated with due respect. To recover this lost sense of the inviolable integrity of nature, however, one must be able to insert oneself into the whole, gaining intimations of what it is like to be a single blade of grass in a field or a single tree in a vast forest. As a modest experiment one might go to a nursery and purchase a seed, a pot and some soil. If one asks properly, the clerk will give whatever instructions are necessary and then one can take these materials home, carefully and with respect. Then after planting the seed in the soil with humility and love, treating it not as a symbol but as life, one can set the pot firmly upright in a place prepared for it. Each day one can give to the growing plant what it requires by way of water and nourishment, but it is important to do this with an assurance and confidence that comes with humility before nature. Forgetting oneself and without anxiety, one can observe the process of organic growth. In doing this properly, one will also be sowing in oneself the seeds of a new confidence rooted not in fear, not in deceit, but rather in fearlessness and truth, the source of authentic humility.

As one spends a few moments each day noting the growth of the plant, one may see this as linked magnetically to the seed of the new astral form which one seeks to gestate within oneself out of the soil of the old astral. This old astral is chiefly composed of patterns of selective memories, which are instinctual, habitual and compulsive, as well as somewhat inefficient and so unreliable that they would be unacceptable in any court of law. Having no firm basis in either fact or truth, they are primarily externalizations based upon misconceptions and predilections directed against those to whom we owe so much. Rather than remaining captive to an appalling burden of memories and an attendant tendency to judgmentalism towards parents, grandparents and ancestors — of whose trials and difficulties one knows little or nothing — one should mainly concentrate the mind upon the nurturing of the new astral form to which one is attempting to give birth. Indeed, one's motive in doing this should be to benefit all those who have come before and to whom one should be grateful. One is aiming at the attainment of an active state, where one has energy, but in which one is not bound to one's *persona* and irrational self through the forces of *kama*, *krodha* and *lobha* — desire, anger and greed. Speaking of the purifying and benevolent energy of the spiritual will, H.P. Blavatsky pointed to the fundamental requirements of spiritual regeneration and their connection with the discovery of one's true immortality.

> It is only when the power of the passions is dead altogether, and when they have been crushed and annihilated in the retort of an unflinching will; when

not only all the lusts and longings of the flesh are dead, but also the recognition of the personal Self is killed out and the 'astral' has been reduced in consequence to a cipher, that the Union with the 'Higher Self' can take place.

H.P. BLAVATSKY

The path of inner gestation and self-regeneration depends critically upon the recovery of the capacity to think clearly, freely and creatively. This prerogative, guaranteed to every human being by the cosmos, which never has been (and nor can it ever be) abridged by any terrestrial institution, is the sacred and sacrificial birthright of every Monad blessed with the fire of *Manas*. Whilst true thinking may be rare, this is not the fault of any society or governments and it is irresponsible and immature in the extreme to blame one's lack of thoughtfulness upon anything outside oneself. Thinking, in fact, has nothing to do with blame; the more one thinks, the less one will be involved with blaming altogether. As Merlin exhorted Arthur, "Think! Think! THINK!" It is extraordinary how rare true thinking is, but as soon as one does begin to think, thinking things through — *dianoia* — then one begins to concentrate and gains the ability to go back to an original moment. Those who have completed this training, true disciples who have gained effortless mastery over their astral forms at will, can instantly summon the moment of birth or of death. Herein lies the authenticity and integrity of the true spiritual Path. If ever one hears someone speak of astral travel who is unable to say what his thoughts were before the moment of birth, one should know immediately that such a person is deluded, or a dupe. It is too late to be taken in by such twaddle, much less participate in it.

One should begin by trying to think through what is essential in one's life, seeking to recover, if not one's moment of birth, then one's moment of spiritual awakening in this life. What were one's dreams as a child before seven? Was there any moment of awakening then, when one realized that one was worth more than all of one's toys and trinkets? Was there any moment of awakening between the ages of seven and fourteen, when bright possibilities of the future were glimpsed and was there a moment around the age of puberty, when one was filled with hopes and ideals in relation to human brotherhood? Did the possibilities of human growth, beauty, fulfillment and promise fire one's imagination? What were the secret dreams and longings for the good that one whispered to one's closest friend in school but did not mention to adults? Were there certain withdrawn and sensitive moments in one's life which one did not mention to another living soul, but rather honoured in the heart? Each person must self-consciously recover these golden moments for himself or herself because no one else can do this for another. Each person must discover the seeds of goodness within himself or herself and nurture them. If one is to take into account one's failures, mistakes and errors, then it is only fair that one should also note in one's life-ledger one's golden dreams and finest thoughts. One should learn to accentuate the positive and not become preoccupied with the negative. The best means to do this is not to speak very much about oneself to others. Be silent for awhile. Learn to talk less and think more. Then, as one takes note of the truest things in one's life, one will begin gradually to see connections within, and one will no longer be a slave to connections imposed from outside by others.

Ultimately, one's life is one's own. It does not belong to parents or friends or spouse or any other. In one's spiritual life one cannot come closer to the Guru until one has become worthy of the blessing, and this can only be done by voluntarily putting oneself through vows within a period of probation. During that period of probation there will be a tremendous testing brought on by no one else but oneself. By putting oneself as oil in a refinery, or as a jewel in a cleansing solvent, one chooses precisely which trials and tests are to be brought upon oneself by oneself. Through the power of one's resolve one enters upon an alchemical process of removal and burning out of impurities in one's nature. If, for example, one pronounces a sacred word like *Atman*, then one both blesses and curses oneself. One curses oneself in that the darkness will be drawn out; one blesses oneself in that the Light of the *Atman* will be shed upon one's nature. One can choose to stand in the Light of the *Atman*, but then there will be war — war between that part of oneself which loves and is one with the Light, and that part which is incompatible with the Light. It is impossible to cling to Light and darkness at the same time. One cannot worship both God and Mammon. One must choose, and even though one cannot choose all at once, each choice on behalf of the Light increases self-respect. Every time one chooses to meditate instead of cerebrate, every time one chooses to contemplate instead of chit-chat, every time one chooses to learn from other human beings instead of becoming judgmental, one gains dignity and a measure of self-respect. And unless one respects oneself, one cannot earn the respect of others. This does not mean that one should work at this anxiously and with strain. Rather, one should accept and recognize one's unimportance, seeing oneself as only one amongst billions of human beings, treating this not as an excuse but as one of the primary facts of life.

Human beings must find out for themselves individually the meaning and purpose of their life. Each human soul in incarnation has a sacred mission and goal. One must have the courage to discover what one has come to earth to do. If one has come to work for the City of Man, then one must train oneself. One must come out of the Necropolis, the city of the dead. One cannot work for the City of Man whilst remaining captive to the city of the dead. One must learn compassion for the morally and mentally crippled, the blind and lame, the victims of crime and ignorance, as well as the criminals themselves. One must become a person of strong nerves capable of loving more and more people, and along with this one must become aware of what one can handle and what one cannot. Each individual is different, and it is necessary to learn something about the plastic potency of one's own astral vesture. What are its capabilities and what its limitations? There is also great meaning and value in meditating upon a vast and general promise which is the glorious goal of universal human evolution. It is good to envisage in the mind, not merely for oneself but on behalf of all, the prospect of that sacred moment far along the Path when, as H.P. Blavatsky said:

> the 'Astral' reflects only the conquered man, the still living but no more the longing selfish personality, then the brilliant *Augoeides*, the divine SELF, can vibrate in conscious harmony with both the poles of the human Entity — the man of matter purified, and the ever pure Spiritual Soul — and stand in the presence of the MASTER SELF, the Christos of the mystic Gnostic, blended, merged into, and one with IT forever.

Mahatma K. H., commenting upon the Tibetan proverb that everyone is master of his own wisdom, states that each is at liberty either to honour or degrade the slave. He then goes on to link this with the eternal process of evolving subjective matter into objective atoms. This intimates that one must, through the power of meditation upon extremely abstract and subjective thoughts, evolve new life-atoms. It is these fresh and pure life-atoms which will push out the old life-atoms of one's astral body. This is analogous to taking a purgative medicine to clean out unhealthy and unwanted residues in the body. It is even more analogous to the taking of an antibiotic, such as penicillin which was discovered in bread mould by Sir Alexander Fleming. One must, so to speak, extract out of the fungus of one's chaotic mind a purifying idea capable of cleansing one's entire mental field. One must directly and deliberately intervene in the war between creators and the destroyers within one's astral frame. Like an antibiotic medicine derived from life itself, yet capable of destroying harmful bacteria, one's heartfelt ideals, distilled and clarified through meditation, have the power to release the purifying and benevolent energy of the spiritual will. This is only an analogy pointing to the process of mental self-purification through sacrificial meditation, which is a vital part of the sacred science of spirituality. That science is mathematically exact and precise in its laws and is therefore not possessed by human beings who are captive to the illusions of terrestrial existence. It is an arcane science which combines meta-chemistry with meta-biology, and it is rooted in a metaphysics which only becomes dynamized and activated when it is rendered into meta-psychology — that wisdom which is used and applied in daily life. When it is properly used, and this has nothing to do with mere words — though it has a great deal to do with the use of the tongue — it is extremely powerful and is equivalent to the release of the spiritual will flowing from the *Atman*.

For the neophyte, the initial step is to become a true pragmatist by putting to use the idealism which is within the soul and which is consubstantial with the plane of Mahat-mic ideation in the cosmos. It will then become possible to bring into the unreal world of time, which ordinary human beings mistake for reality, the fruit of meditation, the flower of contemplation and the fragrance of self-study and self-correction. When one is filled with the milk of human kindness, it will become possible to extract from the depths of one's divine nature the ambrosia of immortality. In deep sleep, when one is far from the *persona*, when the personal nature is reduced to a cipher, one may receive the gift of Krishna, a drop of the divine elixir. The personal nature will know nothing of this secret gift, and when one awakens, it matters little what the personality makes of the change. What is important is that one honour and treasure it and go forth into the day, sifting and selecting that which is of value, that which is good and true and beautiful. One should not do this strenuously, but rather with a lightness and relaxation consistent with one's own sense of unimportance in relation to the entirety of mankind.

All forms of over-exertion and strain are signs of a sense of personal self-importance and a desire for attention incompatible with spiritual maturity. Karma cannot condone an abnormal desire for attention for oneself at the expense of the human race, because karma cannot shelter the propensity to indulge in attention to the shadowy *persona*. Therefore, one must learn and enjoy a new set of rules wherein one does not ask for more ego space than one is entitled to. But if one understands what it is to be only one amongst billions of human beings upon the earth and only one of a smaller though extensive class of beings who have come into the Avataric orbit, then one will know how to do this. Instead of yielding to the backward tendency to impose one's personality and problems upon others, one will learn to do *tapas* in silence, so as to prepare oneself for the opportunity to serve which comes with being in the presence of other human souls.

If one would become worthy of being in the presence of Krishna, then one must begin by attempting to understand what Krishna meant when he said that he established this entire universe with but a single portion of himself and yet remains separate from it. Whatever be the percentage of that portion of himself, and that would vary with the needs of the era, his essential nature remains *Kutastha* — He who standeth apart. The sense in which Krishna is separate from the universe is mystical and metaphysical, but one cannot hope to begin to understand this if one remains subject to the delusion that one can understand oneself by understanding Krishna. This is a typically Western misconception. One must understand oneself through understanding other human beings; when one has understood oneself through all other human beings, then one may begin to understand Krishna. Through love and devotion one can cross the barriers of the mind and the heart and the self, and prepare oneself for *Mahasmashana* — the burning of the corpse of the *persona*. There one is consumed by the fire of devotion so as to be reborn to live purely for the sake of others and not at all for oneself. Only those who have crossed that sacred threshold, difficult of approach, can participate in the conscious creation of their lower self. Very few have heard of this mystical threshold, and of these, even fewer have been able to approach it. Fewer still are those who have made a burning-ground of their hearts for the sake of the Guru, and thereby truly entered his service. Yet such is the great teaching and rich promise given by Krishna to his devotees, to all those heroic souls who would become willing servants of the City of Man.

THEURGY AND TRANSMUTATION

*To those who knew that there was more than one key
to theogonic symbolism, it was a mistake to have expressed
it in a language so crude and misleading. For if the educated
and learned philosopher could discern the kernel of wisdom
under the coarse rind of the fruit, and knew that the latter
concealed the greatest laws and truths of psychic and physical
nature, as well as the origin of all things — not so with the
uninitiated profane. For him the dead letter was religion;
the interpretation — sacrilege. And this dead letter could
neither edify nor make him more perfect, seeing that such
an example was given him by his gods. . . . Now all the gods
of Olympus, as well as those of the Hindu Pantheon and
the Rishis, were the septiform personations (1) of the
noumena of the intelligent Powers of nature; (2) of Cosmic
Forces; (3) of celestial bodies; (4) of gods or Dhyan Chohans;
(5) of psychic and spiritual powers; (6) of divine kings on
earth (or the incarnations of the gods); and (7) of terrestrial
heroes or men. The knowledge how to discern among these
seven forms the one that is meant, belonged at all times to
the Initiates, whose earliest predecessors had created this
symbolical and allegorical system.*

The Secret Doctrine, ii 764 - 65

It is, according to Gautama Buddha, a greater feat to govern
oneself than to command all the elements in Nature. All
Nature and its powers bend heavenwards before the gentle,
irresistible theurgy of the perfected Bodhisattva, the pilgrim-soul
who has reached the summit of the Path and become the son of
the Dhyanis, compassionator of the triple worlds, greater than all
gods. The potential of pure *swaraj* or self-rule is latent in every
Monad, and is quickened by the fiery ray of the Manasa Dhyanis.
When first the dark fire of their formless intelligence ignited

self-consciousness in the evolved forms of terrestrial humanity over eighteen million years ago, man became a living link between heaven and earth. Conscious of the divine presence within his preceptors, his companions and himself, he was governed by a natural impulse towards gratitude, devotion and benevolence He lived in effortless sympathy with the hosts of bright *devas* and *devatas* that he found in and around himself and throughout the entire realm of Nature. Reflecting the Akashic ideation infused into him by the *Manasa*, his actions radiated a benign and spontaneous magic.

Although the impress of that primordial time is ineradicable, human beings have descended so low in consciousness that they can scarcely believe, much less recall, their original estate. Emerson's charitable characterization of man as God playing the fool cannot account for the awful process by which man has become spiritually self-orphaned and blinded, becoming a burden to himself and a parasite on Nature. What, one might ask, are the strange gods and alien altars towards which human beings have directed their pristine powers in degrading themselves? Since there is no power greater than that which made Monads self-conscious, one need not look beyond oneself to find the cause of one's own impoverishment. Nor need one look anywhere but within to find the means whereby one may embody the divine impulsion towards its transcendent end. The regeneration and restoration of humanity requires individuals to heed the wisdom of Krishna's teaching that all beings go to the gods they worship, and thereby awaken to self-conscious immortality in unison with the unmanifest godhead.

Such an awakening can be neither metaphysically cheap nor psychologically simple; one must skillfully navigate between the Scylla of desperate salvationism and the Charybdis of cynical materialism. If man is potentially a self-conscious link between heaven and earth, one might ask how man is specifically connected with the earth and with heaven. The elements constituting the human vestures are indeed consubstantial with the fabric of Nature outside the human form. Thus, man is linked to the earth through the five sense-organs, each of which has its astral analogue, and also through a variety of classes of elementals. Through each of the astro-physical senses, and especially the sense of inner touch, man is continuously involved in complex processes of interaction with the elemental kingdoms. On the other side, he is connected with the Dhyanis and the *devas* through daimons, which are the invisible essences of the elements, elastic, ethereal and semi-corporeal, in Nature. These daimons are made up of a much more subtle matter than that which composes the astral form of the average human being. By consciously drawing upon them, one can bring about the progressive etherealization of one's vestures. Just as the crucifixion of Jesus symbolizes the bondage of spirit on the cross of matter, so too the Eucharist signifies the spiritualization of material vestures and the liberation of the spirit. This process must be initiated through meditation, intensified through refinement in consciousness, through reverence, renunciation and compassion. If one can suffuse one's whole being with benevolent and elevated thoughts and feelings, it is possible, over a period of seven years, to reform the life-atoms that constitute the astro-physical form. Such a radical renewal will be apparent in one's hands, face, toes and tongue — indeed at every point in the body.

This in itself is only one small application of the vast body of arcane and exact knowledge regarding the hosts and hierarchies of beings involved in human evolution. In neo-Platonic thought these beings were divided into three broad classes:

> According to the doctrine of Proclus, the uppermost regions from the Zenith of the Universe to the Moon belonged to the Gods or Planetary Spirits, according to their hierarchies and classes. The highest among them were the twelve Huperouranioi, or Supercelestial Gods, with whole legions of subordinate Daimons at their command. They are followed next in rank and power by the Egkosmioi, the Inter-cosmic Gods, each of these presiding over a great number of Daimons, to whom they impart their power and change

it from one to another at will. These are evidently the personified forces of nature in their mutual correlation, the latter being represented by the third class, or the Elementals.

H.P. BLAVATSKY

In every aspect of life, human beings are intimately and immediately engaged with these ordered ranks and legions of daimons or elementals. The elementals are neither immortal spirits nor tangible bodies; they are merely astral forms of the celestial and super-celestial ideas that move them. They are a combination of sublimated matter and rudimentary mind, centres of force with instinctive desires but no consciousness in the human sense. Acting collectively, they are the nature-spirits — the gnomes and sylphs, salamanders and undines of alchemical tradition.

All these daimons, together with the higher gods, are connected with the seven sacred elements. At the highest metaphysical level, these elements have nothing to do with what we call fire, air, earth and water. For, in essence, these elements are not material, nor may they be understood in terms of visible functions on the physical plane. Just as the hosts of celestial and super-celestial gods are guided from within by the power of formless spiritual essences, and act outwardly in their dominion over the daimons of the elements, so these daimons themselves preside directly over the elements of the four kingdoms of organic life, ensouling them and giving them their outward capacities of action. Thus, when human beings arouse *Buddhi* in *kama*, the reflection of the sixth principle in the fourth, *Buddhi* will transmute the lower *Manas*. In the *antaskarana*, in the channel of aspiration, the force of *Buddhi* in *Manas* will actually become manifest in the fingers, nostrils and lungs. *Buddhi* will be aroused in all the centres of the brain and the heart. It will then be possible to invite or invoke the chief controllers of the many classes of daimons. When this takes place, the teaching that man is a living link between heaven and earth takes on a concrete meaning in benevolent magic based upon arcane science.

Unless, however, one draws a basic distinction between the spirit and the soul of man, any effort to practise theurgy will be inverted and turn into psychism or even sorcery. Despite the Pauline classification of spirit, soul and body, Christian theology obscured the distinction between spirit and soul. Even the philosophic doctrines of the medieval Kabbalists, though they paralleled the teachings of the neo-Platonists, were not fully in accord with ancient wisdom. The neo-Platonists were, however, well aware of the dangers and seductions of all theurgy; they knew that would-be neophytes could be caught in the clutches of treacherous daimons. Those who cannot clearly distinguish between spirit and soul, cannot firmly distinguish between higher and lower daimons and theurgy will drift into thaumaturgy. As a result, they are likely to form alliances with lower hosts, worship secondary or even tertiary emanations.

> The most substantial difference consisted in the location of the immortal or divine spirit of man. While the ancient Neoplatonists held that the Augoeides never descends hypostatically into the living man, but only more or less sheds its radiance on the inner man — the astral soul — the Kabalists of the middle ages maintained that the spirit, detaching itself from the ocean of light and spirit, entered into man's soul, where it remained through life imprisoned in the astral capsule. This difference was the result of the belief of Christian Kabalists, more or less, in the dead letter of the allegory of the fall of man.
>
> H.P. BLAVATSKY

The sad consequence of this concretized view of the Fall of man was twofold. First, by ontologically drawing spirit down to the level of soul, it made possible a dependence of spirit upon a third-degree anthropomorphic deity, Jehovah. Secondly, by repudiating the body as representing the Fall through intrinsic sinfulness, one was left with a passive conception of the soul, concerned only with salvation and damnation. The neo-Platonists, however, who viewed the soul as quite distinct from the transcendental spirit, saw no grounds for such an ontological or devotional subordination to lower daimons. They took an active view of the process whereby the soul seeks to link itself to the transcendent spirit. With regard to the spirit,

> they allowed its presence in the astral capsule only so far as the spiritual emanations or rays of the 'shining one' were concerned. Man and his spiritual soul or the monad — *i.e.*, spirit and its vehicle — had to conquer their immortality by ascending toward the unity with which, if successful, they were finally linked, and into which they were absorbed, so to say. The individualization of man after death depended on the spirit, not on his astral or human soul — Manas and *its* vehicle Kama Rupa — and body.
>
> H.P. BLAVATASKY

From this one may see the central importance of the connection between *Atma-Buddhi* and *Manas.* One may also grasp the fundamental importance of devotion to the Brotherhood of Bodhisattvas, for without devotion it is impossible to tap the energies of *Atma-Buddhi. Manas* is only as luminous as its capacity to focus consciously and radiate the Atma-Buddhic light. If it can do that, then *Manas* can displace and control *kama manas,* disengaging the lower *Manas* from *kama,* which means freeing the mind from excesses, excuses and evasions. All such errors arise out of the lower manas through its fearful attachment to the body and identification with class, status and property. All of these taints erode the confidence of the soul through the inherent capriciousness of the daimons and elementals within the lower vestures. They are based upon a misguided belief in some entity which holds together all these elementals; in truth, there is only a derived or borrowed sense of entitativeness which is appropriated by the quaternary. This temporary coherence is due to its link with *Manas.* The lower quaternary is like an image or reflection of the light occurring through an appropriate medium.

If the reflective principle of the mind confuses its own image with the authentic source of its illumination, then the polarity of self-consciousness is inverted and the powers of the soul subverted. Fragmentation precludes integration.

All efforts towards spiritual self-regeneration depend upon strengthening awareness of the shining thread which connects *Atma-Buddhi* to *Manas*, and by reflection, *Atma-Buddhi-Manas* to the quaternary. If this thread is not nurtured in meditation, one will not be able to alter the quality of sleep and so gain continuity of consciousness between day and night and through different states of consciousness. If one cannot do that, one will not be able to generate a strong sense of individuality and 'I-am-I' consciousness. One will not realize one's Self-Being as a reflected ray of the overbrooding Dhyani, linked to the Spiritual Sun. If one cannot do this, one will always identify with one's name and form, and spiraling downwards, fall into the midst of hosts of secondary and tertiary daimons. When the vision of the soul is deflected downward, it will look only upon that which is dark relative to the invisible radiance of spirit. Fixed by the immortal soul's energy, this false identification with *namarupa* will be accompanied by a continuous exaggeration and intensification. As this misuse of divine energy is indefinitely prolonged, the immortal soul will, in time, be estranged from its ray. By assigning an exaggerated sense of reality to that which belongs to physical life, to eating, drinking, working at a job — one is generating a false sense of life, limiting both time and consciousness. This remains essentially true even if one generates a strong attachment to the concept of moral probity in connection with this incarnation. Owing to the diversion of divine energies, all identification with name and form ultimately produces dark emanations which accumulate in *kamaloka*, where they must be confronted soon after death.

It is possible, however, to cooperate with the processes of individualization after death. It is possible to live in a manner that dispenses altogether with *kamaloka* and dispels the karmic accumulations of past attachments. But such a life requires a recognition of total responsibility. It means learning to live with no attachment to name or form. One must ask oneself who is responsible for one's personality and body, who is responsible for one's every thought and feeling? Who is responsible for the condition of every life-atom that enters into and emanates from one's visible and invisible vestures? In asking these questions, one begins to withdraw identification from the instruments, to see oneself as a Monad, and to approach the state of total responsibility from above below. This responsibility extends to the entire field of one's manifest and unmanifest interactions with all life-atoms. It extends far beyond face and form, to one's ultimate status as a true Pythagorean spectator. Only by generating a profound sense of critical distance from all names and forms may one learn to exemplify the entirety of one's dharma in this world.

Forswearing all anxiety and attachment, all immodesty and false pride, one must learn to put to work in the best possible manner all the instruments and all the energies affecting all the hosts of daimons and devas involved in the human sphere. This can only be done if one develops, retains and strengthens a sense of being changeless and immortal, as Krishna taught Arjuna in the second chapter of the *Bhagavad Gita*. One must withdraw from all false ideas of vicarious atonement and salvation which are, as Plato taught in *Laws,* extremely harmful to the vigilant life of the spirit. Every temptation to cut corners through selfish propitiations and degrading rituals is indeed expensive karmically. The very attempt blinds the eye of wisdom, cuts the soul off from its source of light and leaves the wandering pilgrim a wretched and ridiculed victim of its false gods.

This, in epitome, is the odyssey of the fall of the human soul since its pristine golden age in the Third Root Race. Just as the divine spiritual instruction of that period retains its impress upon the imperishable centres of the soul to this day, so too does this long karmic history lie like a series of encrustations around humanity and the earth. Because man is linked with hosts of elementals within his vestures and with hosts of daimons without, this karmic inheritance is inscribed in the spatial arena of collective human evolution. It may be discerned in the mystical and sacred geography of the globe itself. Gupta Vidya suggests that when the sevenfold host of divine preceptors descended upon earth to initiate and instruct infant humanity, they descended from Sveta Dwipa, a division of Mount Meru. They established seven divine dynasties reigning over seven divisions of the earth or globe. During the Lemurian and Atlantean ages, some of these divisions changed; others have not.

The eternal and transcendental geography of Mount Meru is partially mirrored in divisions of the earth connected with the polar regions. Hence, northern Asia is termed the eternal or perpetual land and the Antarctic is called the ever-living and the concealed. The freedom of the polar regions from the vicissitudes of racial evolution and geological change is a reflection of the permanence of the *axis mundi* of Mount Meru. The association of the North Pole with Sveta Dwipa, however, should not be thought of merely in terms of a terrestrial region. It would be more helpful to think of a Fohatic magnetic field associated with ice and snow. It is to be found both in snow-capped mountains and in desert oases, such as the Gobi Desert of Central Asia. The poles of the earth are likened in Gupta Vidya to valves regulating the ingress and egress of the solar-selenic radiance affecting the earth. They are intimately connected, through Fohatic arteries girdling the globe, with the circulations of daimons in the atmosphere. By correspondence, within the human form they are analogous to the circulation of the blood and other fluids with their invisible elemental constituents.

To connect this meta-geography with the inward life of the soul, one must connect the idea of pilgrimage to the idea of the restoration of the obscured flows of spiritual energies within the human temple. As Shankara and others taught, the sacred places of pilgrimage in the world mirror centres within the human body. Thus, there is a deep meaning behind the saying of the Puranas that even the incarnated gods themselves rejoiced to be born in the condition of men in Bharata Varsha in the Third Root Race. In one sense, Bharata Varsha is India, the original chosen land

and the best division of Jambhu Dwipa. More essentially, Bharata Varsha is the land of active spiritual works *par excellence,* the land of initiation and divine knowledge. Hence H.P. Blavatsky's remark that one who visits India in a proper state of mind can find more blessings and more lessons than anywhere else on this earth.

Evidently, this must not be understood in an external mechanistic or physical sense, since there are millions upon millions of souls on the Indian subcontinent who have nothing to do with this eternal current. Just as thousands of people might never show Buddhic perception, even though they saw Sir Richard Attenborough's powerful film on Gandhi, so too, numerous individuals could either visit or be born in India without developing Buddhic insight. Rather, H.P. Blavatsky's comment must be understood in the light of Christ's statement that whenever two or three are gathered in his name, he was present amongst them. Again, one could think of the meaning of *Dharmakshetra* in *Kurukshetra,* the invisible and omnipresent field of dharma wherein all human beings ceaselessly live and move. Hence the teaching of the eighteenth chapter of the *Gita:* "Wherever Krishna, the supreme Master of devotion, and wherever the son of Pritha, the mighty archer, may be, there with certainty are fortune, victory, wealth, and wise action."

The awakening of *Buddhi* depends upon soul refinement and soul sensitivity, which can only emerge from a noetic understanding of the noumenal language of the soul. That language is experienced by every human being during deep sleep, but it can only be developed when significant connections are made between what transpires in deep sleep and in waking life. One must learn to understand arcane symbols at many levels. One must, for example, become receptive to the idea that the Sveta Dwipa of the *Puranas* is one with the Shamballa of Buddhist tradition, and that both are identical with the abode of the Builders, the luminous Sons of Manvantaric Dawn. All such mystical names pertain to a plane of consciousness accessible to human beings within. Mount Meru and the mystical descent of the Ganges can be correlated with critical points within the spiritual spinal cord and the invisible brain. Yogic meditation transports one to inner centres, wherein dwell the gods of light. In this Sveta Dwipa, the luminous Sons of Manvantaric Dawn are eternally present during the *mahamanvantara*. Though they came out of the Unknown Darkness, according to mythic chronology, they are still ever present on that plane as the root of the world, as timeless spectators in the bliss of non-being. Man links heaven and earth so fully that no mode of incarnation can entirely erase the alchemical signature of one's origin.

The lessons of mythic chronology and mystical geography must be applied by each individual to his or her own incarnation. All human beings are always involved with the cycles of the gods and daimons, the *devas, devata* and elementals. Every child is basically an Atma-Buddhic spark with a ray of lower *Manas* which becomes active in the seventh month in the mother's womb. Typically, the ray of *Manas* does not become active until the age of seven, around which time it brings with it the power to choose and to take responsibility. In some it may be retarded, in others it may come too soon, before there is adequate moral preparation. But the parent who would follow the wise practices of the oldest cultures will only do the minimum that is needed for the baby. That parent will leave the baby alone to bathe in its own state of consciousness. At the same time, adults should listen to a baby's sounds and address it as an immortal soul, as a human being capable of controlling and commanding the elementals. In so doing, an adult can arouse in the elementals that gather round a child those which are benevolent as well as those which are strong but not possessive. That everything essential to human life is capable of universalization and capable of becoming an object of responsibility may be imparted to a child before it learns to walk, or certainly when it learns to talk. Then it is crucial to draw out a baby's innate intuition in *Atma-Buddhi* by explaining and guiding it through the incarnation of *Manas*.

By the age of seven, the child should have learnt to sit still and to receive wisdom, and be prepared to inhabit Bharata Varsha. This is nothing but a recapitulation of human evolution up until the midpoint of the Third Root Race, when the Manasa Dhyanis descended into the waiting human forms. Between the ages of seven and fourteen, a child must be very still, calm and deliberate. It can be taught deliberation by deliberate parents; anxious parents find, to their shock, their own neuroses reflected in their children. A child who is given enough basis for self-respect and self-consciousness without verbalization, before the age of seven, can, after *Manas* awakens it, engage in proper dialogue with a respect for alternatives and a freedom of thought. This combination of discernment and discipline is crucial if the child is to resist the chaos of companions in junior high and high school. Here both parents and children alike should closely observe and follow the best examples they can find. They should withdraw attention from negative examples, abstaining from needless analysis. In this way, the parent may help a child overcome the tendency, prevalent since Atlantis, of fascination with evil.

All this preparation encourages a balance between the centrifugal and centripetal forces which engage the incarnated ray more fully by the age of fourteen. The centrifugal power of spirit or *Buddhi* is capable of diffusing from a single point in every direction within a sphere. This omnidirectional diffusion mirrors the ceaseless motion of the *Atman*. In *Manas*, the capacity to hold, to focus and to concentrate these energies is associated with the centripetal energies. A helpful example in the balancing of these energies may be gleaned from those older cultures which never allowed people to speak when they were confused or excited until they had sat down. Adolescents must learn to collect themselves, to draw their energies together in calmness, if they are to avoid the rush, the tension and the anxiety endemic to the cycle between fourteen and twenty-one. Once they have developed some mature calmness, depth and strength, they can release the potential of the higher energies of *Atma-Buddhi-Manas*. In a sense, all humanity is presently engaged in this adolescent phase.

In the Aquarian Age a dynamic principle of balance is needed. Whilst this has its analogues on the physical plane, and even in the astral vesture, it must not be approached on this level, lest there be a degradation of the idea into Hatha Yoga. Instead, one must begin with the Buddhi-Manasic, with the emotional and mental nature, and find on the physical plane appropriate means of expressing that creative balance. Thus one can produce a rhythmic flow and a light ease in one's sphere of influence which reflects a life of deep meditation. The ultimate aim is a fusion of love and wisdom, which then becomes Wisdom-Compassion, the fusion of *Buddhi* and *Manas*. The fusion of *Buddhi* and *Manas* at the highest level is inseparable from the path of adeptship.

Because of the inherent pacing and cycle of soul-evolution, and because of the karmic encrustations human beings have produced in themselves through associations with secondary and tertiary hosts of daimons, no one can be expected to accomplish all of this in a single lifetime, or indeed in any immediate future series of lives. But each being can make a beginning, and, at some level, fuse *Buddhi* and *Manas*. Although overactive in *kama manas*, most human beings are mediumistic, yet in the *antaskarana* there are authentic longings for the higher. Such longings must first be purified and made manasic through universalization. This requires sifting finer thoughts and higher impulses from the dross of *kama manas*, then releasing them for the welfare of humanity as a whole. This means ignoring statistical portraits of humanity given by mass media and developing an inward sense of one's intimate relationship on the plane of ideation and aspiration with millions upon millions of immortal souls.

The more one can change the ratios of one's thought about oneself, one's thought about Bodhisattvas, and one's thought about humanity, the better. As these ratios change, the patterns of one's associations of daimons and elementals will shift, progressively transmuting one's vestures and refining one's capacity for benevolence. Gradually, as one thinks more and more in the direction of Bodhisattvas and of humanity, one will come to see oneself as someone who has the confidence and capacity to control elementals at home, at work and in the world. Thus, one can help oneself and so help others to recover the lost link with the Manasa Dhyanis. One may learn to become a being of true meditation and compassion, capable of serving as a self-conscious living link between heaven and earth.

THE NACHIKETAS FLAME

*A hundred and one are the heart's channels; of these
one passes to the crown. Going up by this, he comes to the
immortal.*

Katha Upanishad

Viraga — indifference to pleasure and pain, illusion
conquered, truth alone perceived — marks the beginning
of the razor-edged Path. For reasons connected with the
cosmogony of Gupta Vidya, human beings find the first step on
the Path most difficult. They must come to an initial standpoint
of detachment from the world, with its false values, its fickle
glamour and attractions, its febrile nightmares and anguish.
Indifference simply means perceiving no essential difference
between pleasure and pain because both arise from compulsive
cerebral reactions to sensory stimuli. They are alike devoid of
intrinsic meaning for that impartite Self which sustains its own
transcendent conception of spiritual growth. Two individuals,
from seemingly identical experiences of pleasure or pain, may
come to contrasting conclusions and derive radically different
implications. Consider two persons who enjoyed identical
dinners, containing ingredients guaranteed to produce an acute
stomach-ache, such that both suffered severe gastric pains the
next day. Similar facts yield no insights into the diverse
meanings that persons might ascribe to their experiences. This
points towards the philosophical basis for self-reference and
voluntary action. Man is a reality-assigning, value-assessing and
meaning-ascribing agent, who needs minimal freedom from
titillation and disturbance induced by pleasurable or painful
experiences. Once this initial standpoint of philosophical
detachment is established even to a small extent, one will
soon find out for oneself that it shows the spiral Path of inward
growth.

When one averts attention from the chaos of external events, through the dawning realization that ascribing meaning and assessing value is one's own task *(svadharma)*, one rapidly confronts a host of unresolved elements (unappeased *devas* and *devatas*) — repressed longings, fears and fantasies — within what is often wrongly called the 'unconscious'. Once they are set in motion, one risks slipping into alternating euphoric and terrifying states of mind, losing hold over the real world of supernal light one seeks as well as the public domain of shared sensory impressions. To dare to face oneself fully is difficult, if only because the more illusions one strips away, the more illusions crop up, like a hydra-headed monster. The protracted and painful, self-reinforcing nature of mundane illusions is boringly familiar, but they must be firmly cut through. Sufficient detachment helps one to glimpse the central but undiscovered truth of transcendental Selfhood, shining behind and beyond the world of maya. This truth about the hidden SELF is also the truth about the secret Path, which must be trodden in solitude. Only by taking each step is the next revealed. Like a winding mountain path which cannot be discerned from a hazy distance, it cannot be traced without treading it.

One must foster steadiness, determination and constancy, remaining fixed in the recognition of the spiritual insignificance of the passing panorama of the lunar subconscious and the supreme value of the single truth one now partly sees and wholly seeks. When a willing resignation *(vairagya)* is sustained at this level, one is ready to experience greater fearlessness *(abhaya)* and penetrating insight *(prajna)*. Viraga is 'the Gate of Balance'. Repeatedly, at different levels of inward growth, through daunting trials at successive stages of spiritual life, one needs to establish a stable fulcrum in consciousness, reflecting a mentally renewed standpoint of calm steadiness and cheerful balance. Though seemingly complicated, this is not unlike walking, or balancing on a bicycle, or standing on a tightrope. One only knows for oneself that it is possible to maintain balance, or that it is necessary to preserve absolute faith in one's strength of mind and soul-wisdom. A tightrope walker cannot mechanically teach a doubter how to balance and perform delicate maneuvers upon a very thin, taut wire. The experienced acrobat can take all the appropriate security measures in regard to the wire, but it is the apprentice learner who must not move one iota from an absolute, immovable conviction that he can both maintain and restore balance, and that even if he experiences a sudden loss of balance, he can still bring himself back to a steady state of balance. Existential equilibrium cannot be taught to someone who is not whole-heartedly engaged in the elusive quest for balance amidst ceaselessly shifting variables and parameters. Yet, the more one gains proficiency in the practice of *viraga*, the more it becomes as natural as breathing.

One must be yoked through raja yoga, by regular meditation (*dhyana*), deep self-study (*svadhyaya*), unconditional devotion (*bhakti*), sustained reflection (*dianoia*) and sagacious equanimity (*sophrosyne*) to the universal and indwelling Self (Avalokiteshvara) of Krishna-Christos. That Self is veiled rather than revealed by compulsive speech and chaotic thought-vibrations. One must sustain in the daily round of duties a secret spiritual discipline which no one else can discern from peering at perfunctory externals. This 'divine discipline' has to do with fidelity to that sovereign standpoint which steadily sees the unmanifest Self behind the mental furniture of the world and manifest selves. What is at first a simple exercise in repeated restraint and resilient balancing can become, after a while, a rhythmic mental breathing as natural as physical breathing, leading to a state of inmost tranquillity. *The Voice of the Silence* enjoins the lanoo or disciple to be ready to find "thy body agitated, thy mind tranquil, thy Soul as limpid as a mountain lake". It is certainly feasible to realize this fully within oneself, to abide constantly in those depths of spiritual self-awareness (*svasamvedana*), wherein there are no waves or ripples, but rather a sublime experience of serene limpidity, crystalline clarity and radiant translucence, which are all intrinsic to *Alaya*, the universal *Paramatman*. This state of self-awareness must be brought down into the realm of the higher mind in a manner that makes for steady self-tranquillization and self-regeneration, which is compatible with vigorous incarnation in the sphere of active duty. Like all subtle delineations of spiritual detachment, these helpful lines from *The Voice of the Silence* have a hallowed, archetypal significance. These are vitally relevant at the very start, but they presage the sweet efflorescence at the end, and they have crucial applications all along the ancient Path.

The *Katha Upanishad* teaches that once one hears of the secret Path to enlightenment and conscious immortality, one cannot pretend life will be the same again. Once the flashing insight has torn away 'the loathsome mask', the blazing words of truth cannot be set aside as if they were never heard. All who enter the sacred orbit of Great Teachers and true gurus are self-condemned: they will never again be able to nestle in the soft folds of delusion, for the 'Hound of Heaven' will pursue them to the bitter end. Not to recognize this is either naïve ignorance about oneself and the cosmos, or bovine perversity in the face of the precarious incarnation of supernal light within the imperfect vestures and inherent limitations of the deceptive world of samsara. Since supple balance in motion requires both vision and verve, when one is in right earnest about treading the Path, one will find that one cannot keep one's feet on that arduous Path without the sustained practice of spiritual archery, taught in the *Mundaka Upanishad*. This requires the repeated realignment of mental vision, symbolized in archery by the correct relation of eyesight to the distant target, allowing for the trajectory of the arrow, the texture of the bow, wind and weather. AUM is the sacred bow, the arrow is spiritual resolve, and the fixed target is the indestructible, invisible, formless, supreme Self (*Paramatman*), mirrored in the embodied Self (*Jivatman*), the divine Triad within and beyond one's manifest identity.

As Gautama Buddha taught, one soon realizes upon entering the Path that it is impossible to fall back with impunity into thoughtlessness and heedlessness. Eternal vigilance is the price of spiritual freedom, and is constantly stressed in the training of *srotapattis* and would-be Bodhisattvas. On the razor-edged Path,

as it is called in the *Katha Upanishad,* everything is finely balanced
and highly energized. The greater the knowledge, the greater must
be the responsibility and courage to accept the consequences of
all thoughts, images, emotions and acts. More and more, one must
feel a profound and cool heart-awareness of one's kinship with
all those whose self-created fetters have become, through
ignorance and cupidity, like the entwining coils of a venomous
snake. Unconditional compassion (karuna) and wise action
(upaya) cannot come without the moral stamina to stay on the
Path, despite seductive distractions, insidious rationalizations and
specious excuses for sluggishness and backsliding. The sacred
lineages of true Teachers (the Guruparampara) vivify the
immemorial teachings by the light of measureless love and
wisdom-compassion, effortlessly exemplified in their celebration
of universal unity and human solidarity, and the supreme
transcendence of the sovereign Self in the temporal realm of maya.

It is only through the Guru that the chela has the golden
opportunity of lighting up 'the Nachiketas flame' of discernment
and daring. Once lit, it must be sedulously guarded and tended
by the chela, and eventually fanned into the fire of wisdom-
sacrifice *(jnana yajna)* which gives light to all and takes from none.
Established on this hoary Path, a stage will definitely come when
all indifference to earthly reward will be natural and easy. In the
Katha Upanishad Nachiketas simply could not see the point of the
glittering gifts Yama, the god of death, offered him: riches,
kingship, kingdoms and earthly happiness. All these had no
meaning for Nachiketas because he knew too well the deceptive
trappings of a life he had long since outgrown. He sought only
the secret of immortality, and was unreservedly willing to
honour the privilege of receiving the secret and retaining it with
constant gratitude. Every skill and faculty is needed while
climbing the steep mountain precipices of the secret Path.
It must never be forgotten that all the needed resources are
within oneself, and they will all have to be summoned and
utilized, on this razor-edged Path. Having heard about the Path
and having grasped that one cannot evade this recognition,

however partial or fleeting, one must see the profound sense in which the Path is difficult to tread.

The powerful metaphors — indeed the entire parable — of the *Katha Upanishad* have manifold layers and levels of meaning, all pointing to the secret spiritual heart. In *The Voice of the Silence* the Paramita Path is connected with *antaskarana*, the inward bridge between the impersonal and personal selves. The time will come when the seeker must choose between the two, for either must prevail. One cannot both be upon the Path and also maintain the absurd but prevalent misconception that there is a personal entity inside oneself, a 'ghost in the machine', to whom things are happening and who is holding the reins in life's journey. This is the root illusion in the eyes of enlightened seers; no such entity really exists; there is only a bundle of propensities and reflexes, images and fantasies. The concatenation of elemental entities comprising the shadowy self are engaged in their own activity, propelled by the gunas expounded in the closing chapters of the *Bhagavad Gita*. The evanescent and ever-changing personality may cling to the illusory misconception that it is acting freely, but it is no more than a congeries of numerous life-atoms pursuing their own predetermined proclivities. The celebrated metaphor of the chariot, also deployed in Plato's *Phaedrus*, is given a vast extension in the *Katha Upanishad* as it is applicable to cosmic as well as to human activity. The *Katha Upanishad* may be seen not only as a philosophical dialogue, but also as an alchemical text, replete with deeply evocative, enigmatic and magical mantrams.

At some point one must mentally let go of the route by which one has come, what Gautama Buddha called the Raft and *The Voice of the Silence* terms the *antaskarana* bridge. This letting go is depicted in the image of the complete sacrifice (*mahasmashana*) of the 'assemblage of sins' and the *namarupa* (name and form) to the impersonal, immortal Self upon the altar of the secret heart. For a *Manasa* to be engaged in embodied existence means that an impersonal cosmos has made an immense sacrifice. This is symbolized physically by the sacrifice of the father giving of his life-essence, and mentally by the magnanimous sacrifice of a great being giving freely of his spiritual essence so that evolution may go on. It is also evident in the noble sacrifice of the mother who, over a period of painful gestation, gives everything to the astral body (*linga sharira*) of the soul coming into the world, just as the maternal matrix of *Akasha* nourishes the embryo of the globe. The impersonal has sacrificed for the sake of manifestation on the personal plane. This must be deliberately reversed through an intense awareness of what one owes to one's father, mother, and all one's teachers, especially to one's spiritual parents and preceptors. The conscious reversal involves taking everything one has, with all one's powers and limitations, and readily sacrificing it for the sake of the self-conscious re-emergence on the plane of manifestation of the inward god, the inner sovereign, who otherwise would remain the silent Self. One must allow that Self within, who is no different from the Self of all, to assume divine kingship within the human estate.

No one can tap the highest resources without becoming secure enough to want nothing for the puny, shadowy self. Moved solely by desires that elevate the whole of humanity and the entirety of creation, and established in that proper mental posture, one can abandon the *antaskarana* bridge, because one can re-create it at will. Seeing one's personal self as no different from other personal selves, one can do the bidding of the divine through the instrumentality of anything in Nature, including, therefore, the use of one's *persona,* in which one has renounced absolutely all proprietary interest. Becoming aware of the life-atoms in one's vesture, one realizes that there is no such thing as the 'personal self' save in a metaphorical sense. Life-atoms are constantly streaming in and out as part of the ceaseless spiritual transmutation of matter on seven planes and the awesome law of sacrifice within the seven kingdoms of Nature. The true *hotri* or hierophant is an initiated alchemist able to send forth beneficent emanations through a mighty current of concentrated thought, mystic meditation, noetic vision and unconditional compassion, consciously quickening the upward movement of all the available life-atoms. To such a sage or magus, the *antaskarana* Path does not have its former significance, except as a drawbridge to be extended at will in the service of universal welfare.

All seekers must seize the teaching which refers to taking the first crucial step on the Path. One may begin with a genuine feeling of gratitude for all one's gifts and advantages in life. Every limitation and setback could be seen as an invaluable opportunity for learning the lessons of life as well as the mysterious workings of karma. Such an attitude of mind is assuredly helpful for any person trying to gain an initial self-understanding before treading the Path. At another level, it is even more important to realize what *The Voice of the Silence* calls the 'priceless boon of learning truth, the right perception of existing things, the knowledge of the non-existent'. Nachiketas is an archetypal seeker, a Golden Age figure who lived at a time when many people were aware that nothing was more precious than the sacred teaching about immortality and the Supreme Self. Men and women searched all their lives and went through many trials and tribulations simply for the sake of coming closer to anyone who served the secret Brotherhood of Bodhisattvas, Rishis and Mahatmas. Now, in Kali Yuga, the Iron Age of Darkness, only those who have devoted many lives to the Path can know the magnitude of what has already been given to mankind. It would be a sad mistake not to take full advantage and make the best possible use, within one's own situation and spiritual limitations, of the golden opportunity to respond gratefully and reverentially to real teachers of Divine Wisdom, Brahma Vach. This can only be authentically achieved through honest attempts to live by and for the sacred teachings. Though the initial responses may be faltering and even fearful, the moment a seeker begins to nurture a holy resolve whereby one will neither remit nor run away from the sacred task to one's last breath, even a modest effort at the start will be charged with meaning and depth by the unconditional nature of the soul's affirmation.

The value of the first step is much enhanced when a person, instead of starting off with a shrunken conception of individual success and personal failure, thinks instead of human need, human pain and ignorance. The stakes are high for multitudes of souls in our time, and immense could be the harvest from seeds sown in the right places with a wise detachment toward results. Souls, galvanized by spontaneous love of their fellows in dire need, can be sustained till the last breath by a steadfast determination to persist and never abandon the quest. When the seeker truly wakes up and stands firm, then he or she may seek spiritual instruction from those who bear witness to the Master-soul within. The neophyte can thus increase the possibilities of conscious, constant access to *Sat* (truth), *Chit* (ideation) and *Ananda* (bliss), which abide as a luminous triadic force and feeling within the still depths of the spiritual heart. Even if one may feel, in times of stress, that one can never be wholly attuned to the Krishna-Christos within, one must continually seek and yearn, keeping alive the Nachiketas flame of devotion.

To comprehend this teaching in terms of the spiritual heart, one must start from the cosmic and descend to the human. The pulsating rhythm of noumenal life can never be perceived until a person begins to inhabit those higher planes which permit a conscious and compassionate use of subtle supersensuous substance, in relation to which the physical body is like a coat of skin or a garment of gross matter. The Upanishads teach that for a wise man death is not an event. No one would think that the shadow is alive in the same sense in which the body is. For the sage, the body is like a shadow of that which is subtler and which it dimly reflects. The subtle body in turn is a shadow in relation to something still more supple which it partially mirrors. The dialectical method of the Hermetic fragments and the neo-Platonic mystics requires us to keep rethinking our view of light and shadow at many levels as we travel inwards and upwards. One may approach the vast mystery of life by sensing the visible sun as a great heart which is constantly beating. There is a systole and diastole to the cosmic heart of the invisible sun, without which no single heart could beat. The thrill of life in every atom and mineral, in every plant and animal, and in every human heart, is merely a derivative expression of perpetual motion in the ceaseless, rhythmic breathing of the hebdomadic heart of the invisible cosmos.

Everything is sevenfold and acts upon seven planes. Descending by analogy and correspondence to that miniature solar system which is the individual human being, one discerns an outwardly disordered and harmonious system. But this is only true apparently, not fundamentally. Each and every person consists of a multi-faceted hierarchy of dynamic and complex systems, among which the most invisible are the most ordered and harmonious. What is most visible is the most disordered, being the most heterogeneous and entropic. On the external plane there are many obscurations and many violent, discordant movements. It is thus difficult to grasp the majesty and grandeur of the proposition that every human being is a microcosm, a miniature universe. But the core of the teaching of *Buddhi Yoga* is that each human soul is capable, out of the region of the disordered and disharmonious, of coming closer through a series of progressive awakenings to that realm wherein one spontaneously affirms the mantram of Jesus Christ, "I and my Father are one." Manifested consciousness may be yoked to the unmanifest consciousness of the unembodied Self — the miniature Spiritual Sun in the heart of each and all, ever abiding in a proper relationship to every planet and to the subtlest vestures of the soul.

Anyone may begin by releasing the highest feelings of which he or she is capable. This unravels the paradox, for Gupta Vidya is the only key by which souls may unlock the sacred chamber of the deepest wisdom, which by definition must be secret, as suggested in the Upanishads and their best commentaries. The word *upanishad* itself implies secret, direct teaching from Guru to chela, Master to pupil. Gupta Vidya or the Heart Doctrine must be felt before one will be ready to use freely the sacred teachings about the inner analogues — in the realms of ideation, emotion and vital energy or volition — of the circulatory, respiratory and other systems and sub-systems in the human frame. A beautiful Sanskrit word for the heart occurs in the Upanishads: — *guhya*, 'that which is hidden, that which is in secret'. It is like the sanctum sanctorum of an old Hindu cave temple, with its suggestive analogies to the human body. Even if one goes into the temple, and even if one is admitted into the sanctum sanctorum, there is nevertheless a mystery beyond that which is seen and heard, tasted and smelt and touched. There is a sixth sense of supersensuous touch, sound and hearing, and a seventh sense, analogous to the mathematical concept of limit, whereby one senses that one will never quite arrive at the end, the sense of the ineffable and infinite, invisible, inaudible and intangible.

The wise know that this is the deepest symbolism of the temple: even if one presses into the darkest place in the sanctum sanctorum of the temple, it is only a point of entry into subtler states of consciousness and beyond, to the deepest depths of eternal duration and perpetual motion and boundless space. The term *guhya* refers to what anyone who grows self-consciously in regard to the various subtle sheaths of the human constitution is going to discover — the astral brain and astral heart, and beyond them their noumenal antetypes. There are subtle senses, and those who develop them can experience their tremendous range and reach, along with appropriate problems which would not be intelligible in terms of the physical plane. So too with the brain and the heart. There would be a progressive series of discoveries of correspondences at different levels in the different sheaths of the Supreme Self, in an ascending order of closeness to their cosmic analogues.

Anyone who feels that there is a divine spark in every human soul, about which one could silently think and with which one could inwardly commune, taps the potential wisdom of the hidden fire within the spiritual heart. Those who at some level begin to live this truth in every thought and feeling-impulse that they generate, deepen their inmost feeling for the sacred cause of the spiritual elevation of the human race, the deliberate pursuit of self-knowledge for the sake of all souls. The more they can light up and rekindle, deepen and sustain this heart-feeling as a constant flame of devotion, the more they can take what might look like thin, frail candles and light up their hearts. In time, the Nachiketas flame blazes up and is established on the square platform of the altar in the sanctuary of the spiritual heart. There it can shine in its resplendent glory as a hidden regenerator of the sacred temple in which the immortal soul abides, and which is its share in the seven kingdoms of Nature. Thus the true beginning is in the sphere of soul-feelings. Until and unless one's inmost heart can vibrate with the generosity and compassion, even a fraction of the immense heart-pulsation behind invisible Nature and the mighty host of hierophants — those Rishis and Mahatmas who recorded the Vedas and bequeathed the Upanishads — one will not be able to light up one's own pathway to conscious immortality. This heart-light can take the persistent and patient seeker from the broad plains to the entrance to the secret Path, of which it has always been true that 'many are called, but few are chosen'.

DHYANA MARGA

Ere thou canst settle in Dhyana-Marga and call it thine,
thy Soul has to become as the ripe mango fruit: as soft and
sweet as its bright golden pulp for others' woes, as hard as
that fruit's stone for thine own throes and sorrows, O
Conqueror of Weal and Woe.
Make hard thy Soul against the snares of Self; deserve
for it the name of 'Diamond Soul'. For, as the diamond
buried deep within the throbbing heart of earth can never
mirror back the earthly lights, so are thy mind and Soul;
plunged in Dhyana-Marga, these must mirror nought of
Maya's realm illusive.

The Voice of the Silence

Every authentic system of spiritual discipline indicates different stages upon the path of progressive mastery over the mind. The path of progressive awakening to supreme unconditional universal Truth is an arduous course of intensified practice leading to serene contemplation. *Dhyana Marga* — the Path of Meditation — is an inward fusion of mentality and morality that releases the mystical energies of enlightenment. Transcending ratiocinative analysis and ethical endeavour, though yielding to the full fruition of both, *dhyana* is the mysterious catalyst spoken of by Jesus which "leavens the whole". It is the living presence of the *Dhyani* energies vital to any lasting nucleus of universal brotherhood formed by sincere aspirants and neophytes on the Path. Like the fabulous wish-fulfilling gem or the pearl of great price, *dhyana* is one of the priceless treasures of the Path which must, at a certain stage of development, be earned by the disciple before there can be any further advance. If this is true of the cyclic process of individual growth, it is even more true of the evolutionary stream of humanity.

From the beginning of the 1975 Cycle emphasis has been laid upon reaching beyond discursive reasoning and analytic study.

Though skilful analysis can be helpful, it is no more efficacious than one wing of a bird in flight. The other wing is ethical practice, purification of motive and steadfastness in reference to one's deepest integrity and fidelity of commitment. The balance between these two aspects of development has been stressed from the start, but as in the life of a bird a definite stage comes at which further development of the wings is neither possible nor desirable, so too in the growth of a committed group of sincere individuals, many of whom have bound themselves by commitments to the spirit of the Pledge of Kwan-Yin. Touched by the potent vibration of the Cycle, a strong nucleus of seekers has persisted, despite ups and downs, in creating a distinct current of direction in their lives. In ways known and unknown to themselves, they have resonated to the current Seventh Cycle of the Theosophical Movement, the last of the series initiated by Tsong-Kha-Pa in the fifteenth century in Tibet. It is deeply fitting that all aspirants upon the path of *The Voice of the Silence* should now seek to become more firm and steadfast with regard to *dhyana* or meditation.

True meditation begins with intense concentration or *dharana* — bringing the mind to a clear focus, which then gives way to the uninterrupted contemplation that is the beginning of *dhyana*. In its full unfoldment it can lead to true wisdom — *prajna* — complete absorption in one's higher consciousness with universal self-consciousness, a state of being marked by the attunement of *Atma-Buddhi-Manas* to the Cosmic Triad. The actual level of attainment reached by anyone attempting this meditation and the pace of his or her development are relatively unimportant. Whatever doubts, anxieties or ambitions some may bring to such attempts are largely irrelevant. What is significant is that a definite and increasing number of human beings should make an attempt, at whatever pace, to learn the practice of true meditation. The simple fact that a number of human beings recognize this common undertaking and obligation, sensing the common joy in the quest for gaining greater proficiency in *dhyana*, is propitious and encouraging to the alchemical work of the

Theosophical Movement. It is a positive contribution to the profound impact of the 1975 Cycle, to the elevation of human consciousness in the world as a whole, and to the careful preparation of the ground for the Mystery Temples of the future.

The apprentice on the path of *Dhyana Marga* must learn that the senses are liars; it is precisely at that moment when one seems outwardly to be most alone and engaged in the difficult task of acquiring mental concentration that one is in fact most directly related to humanity. Once one sees this clearly, it becomes possible to insert one's honest and humble efforts in the practice of *dhyana* into a larger effort by a number of people. If they bind themselves together by invisible threads spun through firmness and contemplation and by a continuous current of meditation, they can leaven up the world, in the metaphor of Jesus. This has nothing to do with any individualistic accomplishment. Rather, through their meditation, they can create a magnetic field into which can be focused the wisdom of Avalokiteshvara, the wisdom of the collective Hosts of Dhyani Buddhas, Mahatmas and Bodhisattvas. Metaphysically, it is the totality of actual and invisible wisdom behind the whole of this system of worlds, which is itself a partial emanation of the primal Adi-Buddha. The aggregate sum-total of actual and potential wisdom forming the radiant core of the system of worlds is nothing but a spark of that absolute and infinite ocean of purely transcendental Wisdom from which arises the possibility of all worlds and all periods of manifestation.

Wisdom is neither created nor destroyed, neither increased nor decreased, but is universal, inexhaustible and vast. It is already self-existent on a primordial plane and is in fact the very ground of the possibility of existence. It may be represented in thought and in collective manifestation as a Host of beings called the Army of the Voice. This is merely a metaphor to intimate something of the virtually inconceivable grandeur and precision of the array of divine elements and beings that constitute the living cosmos. It is possible to focus that light of universal wisdom, continual contemplation and eternal ideation within a matrix created by the love, unity and joint heroic efforts of a nucleus of human beings formed over a period of time. Thus, it is possible to bring down onto the plane of mundane human existence glimpses and rays, sparks and flashes, of that divine light of wisdom that is all-potent on its own plane but is otherwise latent and unavailable. Collectively, a group of human beings can become like a great lens for the drawing down of the light of unmanifest wisdom into our globe to meet the cries of pain, the hungers and the longings of myriads of minds and hearts.

To begin to become an apprentice of eternal wisdom in time, one must gain some minimal understanding of cycles. There can be no practice of concentration and meditation, *dharana* and *dhyana*, unless one can rise above the sequence of alternating states of consciousness involved in the breath, the pulse, sleeping and waking, the passage of seasons, septenates of years, life and death and rebirth. Whilst it would be a false and self-imposed burden to expect to comprehend complex evolutionary cycles, one may, nonetheless, bring a minimal sense of the marriage of continuity and detachment to one's understanding of the collective human pilgrimage. The 1975 Cycle of the Theosophical Movement, its Seventh Impulsion, marks its anniversary on November 17, a date that is significant not only in the nineteenth and twentieth centuries of the Christian era, but in relation to human consciousness on this earth in general. According to Clement of Alexandria, it was the true birthday of Jesus. Historically, it was the birthday of Pico della Mirandola, the light of the Renaissance. It is also the anniversary of many extraordinary events in history, both recorded and unrecorded. It is one of a series of occult points in the year that may be thought of as birthdays of the Dhyanis, points of intersection in cyclic time of aspects of Avalokiteshvara with manifested humanity. Thus, whilst the Seventh Impulsion of the Theosophical Movement is directly linked to this particular aspect of the manifestation of Avalokiteshvara, it cannot be separated from the other manifestations of the Logos present at other cyclic intervals.

The present period is one of those watersheds in human evolution that represent the end of a complex series of events in recorded history. It involves the end of the old monastic orders, including the Hindu, Tibetan, Chaldean, Egyptian, Jewish and Christian. All of these will disappear in their older forms. If one is attached to these forms, this will seem to be a great loss, a sort of spiritual discontinuity in human affairs. If, on the other hand, one is detached and therefore able to penetrate to the core of the cycle, one will understand the continuity of the transition and sense that which will tap the quintessence of these old orders and yet transcend them. At the end of every long epoch of human evolution, at the dawning of a new epoch, there is inevitably a night of disintegration. Even if one is able to overcome one's doubts, fears and anxieties in the face of the necessary dissolution of forms, it is still difficult to envisage in advance which of the inexhaustible possibilities of Divine Wisdom will be realized in a subsequent period of development. The wisest of beings are truly agnostic about the future. All neophytes would be wise in their turn not to attempt to extrapolate on the basis of what they think they know about recorded history and the tragedies of the twentieth century. Most human beings are so self-absorbed in their petty personal concerns that they know almost nothing even of the little story called recorded history over three thousand years, much less the broader global developments that have taken place in the first five thousand years of the Kali Yuga.

So long as one is worried about what has happened, is happening and will happen — so long as one is caught up in the illusions of the past, present and future — one cannot hope to understand or assimilate the perspective of meta-history. It is possible, nonetheless, in golden moments to glimpse the presence of the powerful vibration that was predominant in the golden age of humanity a million years ago at the dawn of the Fifth Root Race, an epoch hearkening back to that which existed eighteen and three-quarters million years ago in the Third Root Race. Manifestation itself is a complex-seeming superimposition of derivative vibrations upon the primal Soundless Sound. Moments in history such as the present should not be understood in terms of the seemingly static, though exceedingly ephemeral, images that waver on the surface of space but rather in terms of the vibrant impulsions behind these transitory forms. Thus, at present, the vibration of the Third Root Race may be felt as superimposed upon the process in which there is an inevitable end of all that has become degraded in recorded history. Everything in historical time eventually becomes unusable to the spirit, becomes warped and distorted, attracts lower elementals — forces bound up with human failure, greed, exploitation, self-righteousness, moralism and also universal human ignorance. Buddha put this simply in saying that existence is suffering. Put in another way, most human beings would agree that whatever specific form of happiness they might envisage, they will find it a torment to be condemned to the eternal experience of this form of happiness. Bondage to form is inconsistent with the freedom and immortality of the spirit; it is not in the order of Nature.

The vibration of the Logos associated with Hermes-Mercury-Budha which rejoices in the void anticipates, encompasses and transcends all historical parameters. This vibration represents the reverberation of Brahma Vach, unaffected and unmodified by the great vicissitudes of the historical process and the cycles of manifestation. It is archetypally and magnificently summed up in the figure of Sage Bhusunda in Valmiki's *Yoga Vasishtha*. When asked by Sage Vasishtha how he had remained untouched by the dissolution of worlds, Bhusunda replied:

> When at the end of a *kalpa* age the order of the world and the laws of Nature are broken and dissolved, we are compelled to forsake our abode, like a man departing from his best friend.
>
> We then remain in the air, freed from all mundane conceptions, the members of our bodies becoming devoid of their natural functions, and our minds released from all volitions.
>
> When the zodiacal suns blaze forth in their full vigour, melting down the mountains by their intense heat, I remain with intellect fixed in the Varuna *mantram*.

When the diluvian winds burst with full force, shattering and scattering the huge mountains all around, it is by attending to the Parvati *mantram* that I remain as stable as a rock.

When the earth with its mountains is dissolved into the waters, presenting the face of a universal ocean, it is by the volatile power of the Vayu *mantram* that I bear myself aloft.

I then convey myself beyond this perceptible world and rest in the holy ground of Pure Spirit. I remain as if in profound sleep, unagitated in body or mind.

I abide in this quiescence until the lotus-born Brahmā is again employed in his work of creation, and then I re-enter the confine of the re-created world.

Yoga Vasishtha Maharamayana
Nirvana Prakarana XXI

Surveying vast worlds, epochs, civilizations and historical eras, Bhusunda stood apart, rooted in *dharana* and *dhyana*. He represents the eternal spectator, unaffected and unmodified by the vicissitudes of the process of history. It is this supreme detachment rooted in meditation that may be called the Hermes current. When that Logoic current is self-consciously sounded at the level of SAT — Truth-Wisdom — it becomes the mirroring in time, on the lower planes of manifested existence, of the eternal vibration of Brahma Vach. To understand this is to see that everything emerging from that Hermes current is a preparation for *dhyana* — irreversible and boundless meditation. Thus there is already in the rich resources of the 1975 Cycle nourishment available for earnest souls eager to learn how to engage in deep, strong and firm meditation, so as to become lenses for the light of Divine Wisdom.

If this is the nature of the great undertaking of *dhyana,* and if some individuals confront many difficulties in rising to meet the opportunities of the Cycle, it ultimately must be due to a lack of sufficient motivation. No explanation of deficiency in meditation owing to this or that circumstance can ever be adequate. It is illogical to attempt to explain an inability to maintain continuity of consciousness in the formless realm by pointing to any collection of circumstances in the derivative regions of form. Hence there is strong emphasis in every authentic spiritual tradition upon the purification and cleansing of the heart. Before one can really master the mind, one must cleanse the heart. It is necessary to see all the distorted, complex and awkward elements in one's feeling nature. And yet there is hardly a human being alive who does not know what it is to care for another, who does not know what it is to suffer, and who does not want to relieve the suffering of others. In fact, the very sense of the hideousness of the deformities of one's feeling nature is nothing but a reflection of the soul's awareness of its intrinsic beauty and purity. Like a craftsman with the highest standard of excellence, the soul surveys its self-evolved vestures with an objective eye.

Rather than becoming fascinated with that in oneself, much less in others, which must be let go because it does not measure up to the best in oneself, one must learn to hold fast to those authentic elements that represent, in every human heart, the vibration of a minute point of universal life, light and love. This *dharma*-energy can be used to purify the heart so that one can bring not just part of oneself but the whole of one's being into line with a single strong motivation so as to be of help to all living beings. One may release the will to be of service in the relief of human ignorance and the alleviation of the deeper cause of all human pain that is the false notion of the self. One may begin to learn the positive joy of bringing down the light of wisdom and letting that light diffuse into as many beings as it possibly can. When such motivation begins to pervade one's being, becoming strong and firm, it gives a buoyancy and lightness, an incentive and resolve to keep going.

Once this current is established, one sees that one's past failures stemmed from either the inability to commit oneself completely and irrevocably to the quest, or a neglect of the detailed and difficult task of burning out every impure element in the heart. In any event, through the release of heart energy, one is prepared to begin burning out all the corrosive motivations that arise from fear, self-protection, body identification, identification with the astral form, with *tanha* — the clinging to forms in general. Clinging to the realm of sensations is at the root of the hardness and impermeability of the lower mind. Once one begins to understand how much pain obscurity of the mind produces within and without, one can bring a greater honesty and maturity, a greater intensity, to the task of self-purification. One will find it easier if one lets go of the notions of personal salvation, progress and enlightenment, discarding all elements of fascination with the ups and downs of the personal nature. All these represent only the outer rind of human life; they are of little consequence at the moment of death.

One must be willing to become fearless in the spirit of *virya*, the dauntless energy and unwavering courage to enter into the realm of unconditional Truth — SAT. The root teaching of voidness has to do with the emptiness of the notion of self-sufficiency and independence, the falsity of the notion that there is anything that is disconnected from the entire chain. All of this has got to be negated. It is a delusion that arises from linguistic tricks and convention, lax mental habits, refusal to confront the fact of death, unwillingness to confront the life process as it works in Nature. Ultimately, it is a refusal to recognize that conscious immortality means entering the light beyond all forms and conditions. It is, as *The Secret Doctrine* shows, a fundamental abrogation of one's destiny as an evolving human being:

> . . . as long as we enjoy our five senses and no more, and do not know how to divorce our all-perceiving *Ego* (the Higher Self) from the thraldom of these senses — so long will it be impossible for the *personal* Ego to break through the barrier which separates it from a knowledge of *things in themselves (or Substance)*. That Ego, progressing in an arc of ascending subjectivity, must exhaust the experience of every plane. But not till the Unit is merged in the ALL, whether on this or any other plane, and Subject and Object alike vanish in the

absolute negation of the Nirvanic State (negation, again, only *from our plane*), is scaled that peak of Omniscience — the Knowledge of things-in-themselves; and the solution of the yet more awful riddle approached, before which even the highest Dhyan Chohan must bow in silence and ignorance — the unspeakable mystery of that which is called by the Vedantins, the PARABRAHMAM.

The Secret Doctrine, i 329-330

Only when one can prepare oneself through degrees of *dhyana* rooted in supreme detachment — *vairagya* — can one enter the light of unconditioned Truth or SAT and remain there in ceaseless contemplation. Wherever there is conditionality, there is the inevitability of discontinuity. Conditionality and discontinuity go together. Instead of becoming disturbed by them, however, one should rejoice in the lesson. The more one becomes unconditional, the more one can confront latent conditionality. Thus, one may begin to discern the persistent origins and causes of distortion, discontinuity and tension. The neophyte should understand at the outset that even when one attains to *dhyana* in its true sense, as a confirmed chela on the Path, there are still seven lives of the most vigorous self-training yet ahead. Once one understands this, one can let go of all the tension that comes from taking on false burdens. Instead of cluttering the mind with mere words and shadows, the undigested cuds of unchewed ideas, one should learn how to take a phrase, a sentence, an idea from the teaching, and chew on it as thoroughly as possible. In every ancient tradition of *dhyana*, it is impossible to dispense with higher analysis. Skill lies in striking the right balance — neither too much nor too little. As one engages in the process of *dhyana*, various hard knots will emerge. It is necessary to stand back and subject them to analysis. One must see the components, the causes, the combinations that form the knot. Along Dhyana Marga there will be a periodic need for such analysis — a kind of self-administered open mind and open heart surgery. It can be done when the need arises if one has prepared adequately and honestly and if one is surcharged by a tremendous love of one's fellow beings and an ardent desire to become a meditator.

In time, one will begin to generate a continuous rhythm of meditation, broken occasionally by passing thoughts, but fundamentally flowing as ceaselessly as a current in the heart. When it is interrupted in a more serious way, one will immediately strive to repair one's foundations through some detailed analysis of the problem so that one may be purged and freed of a particular impediment. Once a momentum of meditation is established, these interruptions become a much rarer occurrence than expected. Depending upon one's earnestness in meditation, which can only be understood in relation to love of the whole human race, one's own so-called pain and difficulties will become trifling in relation to the world's pain. Unless one gets these balances right early on, one will have a distorted importance of the preparatory phase of one's own quest. That could stall the whole voyage. But once one is truly moved by that fire of universal feeling that exists in everyone, one will find the courage needed to maintain the quest. Taking advantage of the rhythms of the seasons, of Nature, of the teachings of the Cycle, one will become more assured and so more able to stay, for longer periods, in an uninterrupted state of meditation.

One will probably not attain the higher stages of *dhyana* in waking meditation for quite a while, perhaps a lifetime. Nonetheless, one is invited to think about these stages, to visualize and resonate to them. This is extremely important and has to do with the release of the powers of the soul. One should completely forget about whether one can or cannot do some particular thing right now. One should not be afraid to contemplate any of the glorious possibilities of the very greatest human beings and Masters of meditation. One should take every opportunity to adore perfected human beings; in adoring them one will give life to the seeds and germs of *dhyana* in oneself. This does not amount to some mechanical and harsh doctrine of pseudo-equality. Rather, it depends upon recognizing that every human being has an exact karmic degree in relation to *dhyana* and *prajna*. Paradoxically, it is only by recognizing this that one can truly understand what it means to say that all human beings stand in the same sacred unmanifest ground of the unmodified, impartite Divine Spirit. Thus, as one grows in understanding of these soul powers, one may enjoy reflecting upon higher states of meditation, as represented by the portraits of perfected beings in the sacred texts and scriptures of all traditions. It is irrelevant and counterproductive to be bothered by the inevitable fact that one will not immediately experience these high states of consciousness.

One may, for example, reflect upon that state of *dhyana* likened to the calm depths of the ocean, recognizing in the metaphor the freedom of the universal Self. To abide in that is like remaining in the Egg of Brahmā. Though this high state of true self-government may seem very distant, one may nevertheless deeply reflect upon it. One may ask what it would be like to have a mind that is so oceanic and so cosmic, so profoundly expansive and inclusive of all things in all minds, that it is capable of reverberating to everything in the mind of Nature. Certainly one should include such lofty thoughts in one's horizon. In this way, one will come to recognize that what at first seemed a burdensome and laborious task is in fact a joyous working out, stage by stage, of clusters of karma. It is also a lightening and a loosening, in each context, so that there may be a flow from the subtler ethereal vestures into the grosser vestures. How this will actually affect the visible vesture in this life will vary from one individual to the next. Many meditators become wizened, but they have no regrets because they have no attachment to the external skin and shell. Instead, they rejoice in the inner purification that has taken place. Even one's perspective changes in regard to what is truly helpful to the immortal soul and what is harmful. Once one touches the current of this supreme detachment and begins to enter the light of the void through efforts at *dhyana*, one may begin to make one's own honest and yet heroic, courageous and cheerful way towards gaining greater continuity, control and proficiency in meditation. Blending the mind and heart, one may enter the way that leads to the *dhyana* haven:

The Dhyana gate is like an alabaster vase, white and transparent; within there burns a steady golden fire, the flame of Prajna that radiates from Atma.

Thou art that vase.

The Voice of the Silence

What is it the aspirant of Yoga Vidya *strives after if not to gain* Mukti *by transferring himself gradually from the grosser to the next more ethereal body, until all the veils of* Maya *being successively removed his* Atma *becomes one with* Paramatma? *Does he suppose that this grand result can be achieved by a two or four hours' contemplation? For the remaining twenty or twenty-two hours that the devotee does not shut himself up in his room for meditation — is the process of the emission of atoms and their replacement by others stopped? If not, then how does he mean to attract all this time — only those suited to his end? From the above remarks it is evident that just as the physical body requires incessant attention to prevent the entrance of a disease, so also the* inner man *requires an unremitting watch, so that no conscious or unconscious thought may attract atoms unsuited to its progress. This is the real meaning of contemplation. The prime factor in the guidance of the thought is* WILL.

D.K. MAVALANKAR

THE MAHAMUDRA
OF VOIDNESS

*Thou hast to study the voidness of the seeming full,
the fullness of the seeming void. O fearless Aspirant, look
deep within the well of thine own heart, and answer.
Knowest thou of Self the powers, O thou perceiver of external
shadows?*

If thou dost not — then art thou lost.

*For, on Path fourth, the lightest breeze of passion or
desire will stir the steady light upon the pure white walls of
Soul. The smallest wave of longing or regret for Maya's gifts
illusive, along Antaskarana — the path that lies between
thy Spirit and thy self, the highway of sensations, the rude
arousers of Ahankara — a thought as fleeting as the
lightning flash will make thee thy three prizes forfeit — the
prizes thou hast won.*

For know, that the ETERNAL knows no change.

The Voice of the Silence

True meditation upon emptiness depends upon a fullness
of preparation through a series of stages of moral practice.
Without proper preparation, authentic insight into the
nature of voidness (*shunyata*) is impossible. It matters not how
long this preparation takes; it must be honest and genuine, devised
by each human being according to his or her own individual
karmic agenda. Otherwise it is impossible to launch seriously into
meditation, to enter into it with an inward assurance that one
will never abandon it. Even after one has entered the Path leading
to *dhyana* one will, inevitably, experience difficulties. Yet one's
very presence upon that Path must be based upon an immutable
resolve. One's preparation for deep meditation upon emptiness
must be rooted in a commitment that is irreversible, inalienable
and irrevocable.

In Tibetan Buddhism this arduous course of preparation is understood as a necessary precondition for a further and even more fundamental transformation of consciousness that is the fruition of meditation upon emptiness. This quintessential transformation of consciousness is conveyed in a text composed by the First Panchen Lama as a *mahamudra*. His teaching, first written down in the sixteenth century, derives from a series of oral instructions transmitted by Tsong-Kha-Pa, the founder of the Gelukpa Order in the fourteenth century. These teachings are said to have been received by Tsong-Kha-Pa ultimately from Manjushri, one of the Dhyani Bodhisattvas and an emanation from one of the Dhyani Buddhas. The First Panchen Lama crystallized an oral tradition around a central teaching which he called a *mahamudra*.

According to a contemporary commentary upon this teaching delivered by Geshe Rabten, a religious counsellor to the present Dalai Lama, a *mahamudra* may be understood as a great seal symbolizing an immutable realization of voidness. When one enters into a formal agreement, as in signing a contract, one puts down one's name or seals a document. Everyone knows what this means in statutory law. It is sacred and irrevocable. It is firm and binding. So, too, in a deeper and spiritual sense, one may seal one's entire consciousness irreversibly upon the Path of *dhyana* — meditation. Ultimately, this is a direct subjective experience of voidness. Yet as Geshe Rabten's commentary points out, this fundamental transformation of consciousness cannot come about except as the sequel to a long and difficult period of preparation through moral practice, mental development and preliminary exercises in meditation. Even these, as set forth in the *Sutra Yana* teachings of Tibetan Buddhism, require resolves, vows and the development of an unshakeable determination that once one has begun upon this Path, no matter what the difficulties, one will seek to become increasingly honest with oneself and strive ever harder to overcome them.

One must be committed in advance not to become infatuated with one's own difficulties, but rather to see beyond them and to persevere in one's course of self-induced and self-devised inner growth. As in all of Buddha's teachings, the only authentic basis of such resolve is a motivation to heal the suffering of humanity. Every time one is inclined to falter upon this Path, one should think of the pain of human beings and the misery of human ignorance. Thinking of one's own share in the world's pain, one may realize one's obligation to lessen the burden of the world. To think about this deeply and in detail is to find the motivation necessary to carry on and to persist in a heroic search for deep meditation and the realization of truth or *satya*.

The primary means of preparation for the *mahamudra* meditation is taking refuge in the Buddha, the Dhamma and the Sangha. As soon as one directs one's mind towards the supreme compassion and enormous sacrifice of Gautama Buddha and the entire Host of Bodhisattvas, one is filled with a tremendous purifying strength. By thinking of these beings, who have attained to the state of supreme enlightenment solely for the sake of humanity, one can gain the energy and strength to form an irreversible resolve. Thus all efforts at meditation should begin with an adoration of predecessors, a rejoicing in their very existence and in the reality of their deeds and their living presence. To this joyous practice each individual may bring devotion and an undivided seriousness entirely of his or her own choice. Thinking of the meaning of one's own life in relationship to the meaning of the lives of all, and in relation to the world's pain and need, one may contemplate the great work of the Bodhisattvas, inserting one's own resolve into the broader mission of building a rainbow bridge between the Host of Dhyanis and the world of Myalba. Taking refuge in the triple gem, one can find the courage in oneself to try to aid the earth with all its plight and pain, caused ultimately by a fundamental alienation from the true Self, an ignorance of the true destiny of humanity.

It is not possible to take refuge in the Buddha, the Dhamma and the Sangha without prostrating oneself before their clearly visualized presence. In his commentary on the *mahamudra*, Geshe Rabten recommends performing one hundred thousand such prostrations, and acknowledges that even these may not be enough to bring about the necessary purification. In the East, physical prostration before objects of veneration comes naturally because of a pervasive sense of the sacred and heartfelt sentiments of gratitude towards ancestors and benefactors of every kind. But in the West, physical prostration is not something that everybody can readily undertake. It may come naturally, but one had better not simulate it, force it or fake it. Nonetheless, mental prostrations, an inward humility, and the surrendering of the personal will and the judgmental mind can be of great benefit. Nothing but good can come to a human being through the surrender of a divided and treacherous heart. The total prostration of one's being, as enjoined by Krishna in the fourth chapter of the *Bhagavad Gita*, is an essential mental posture preparatory for true meditation.

The Tibetan texts lay down for monks a series of mantrams to be chanted. As Geshe Rabten explains, the set of recitations and visualizations revolving around *vajrasattva* is intended to assist in the elimination of negative tendencies. This aspect of the *mahamudra* preparation is of particular significance to individuals who have yet to master the discipline and momentum of a mendicant. *Vajrasattva* represents the embodiment of the power of purification of all the Buddhas. Whilst Tibetan tradition lays down for monks specific modes for visualizing *vajrasattva* and specific *mantrams* to be chanted, these details are inappropriate and unnecessary for lay individuals outside the tradition. What is of crucial importance is to bring to bear from within oneself the purifying power of the Buddha-nature upon the whole assemblage of one's unholy modes of thought, feeling and will. There are, in every human being, a myriad such elements in a state of interconnection. These negative tendencies no doubt arose in former lives, and if they are not extinguished in this life, they will have their fruition in future lives of pain and suffering. The entire assemblage should be acknowledged so as to create a mental posture of total honesty.

To enter the Path, one must be free of all self-deception. Otherwise, as the Sutras teach, one will be arrested from further progress and thrown back from further growth. Such devices as prostration and chanting are intended to help one confront all one's errors, especially those that may have caused pain to other beings and which were avoidable, occasions when one knew better and yet acted wickedly. Purification in preparation for the Path leading to meditation requires that all of these must be confronted. They must be collected together, brought to the forefront of one's attention, and then burnt out at the very root. Their force of persistence must be destroyed through a resolve in relation to the future and an honest recognition of their effects upon others.

This is, no doubt, a difficult practice and must be repeated again and again. Whichever purificatory chants one selects — whether it be from *The Voice of the Silence*, the *Bhagavad Gita* or *The Jewel in the Lotus* — these must all be taken as means that are helpful in confronting what is called the *papapurusha*, the assemblage of sins. It is this hideous aggregate of negative tendencies that forms the basis, at the moment of death, of the *kamarupa*. On average, it will take some one hundred and fifty years for this form to disintegrate. But if it is more tenacious, owing to a life of self-deception, dishonesty and spiritual pretension, it can last much longer, emitting a foul odour and precipitating crimes and even murders, recognized and unrecognized, on this earth. After-death consequences involving the *kamarupa* pertain to a plane of effects, but what one does in life pertains to the causal plane of human consciousness. If one is not vigilant, one may be gestating the energies that become powerfully coagulated into a tenacious *kamarupa*. All such entities are based, in Buddhist theory, upon the force of self-grasping, bound up with the false imputation of inherent existence to the personal ego. Naturally, the presence of such entities putrefying and disintegrating over many centuries throws an oppressive pall over humanity that puts a tremendous brake upon the aspirations of every single human being. Yet this should not be allowed to become a subject of fascination or speculation. Rather, one should recognize one's own liability to contribute to astral pollution and so one should resolve to purify oneself and one's emanations.

In describing the preparation for *mahamudra* meditation,

Geshe Rabten compares these negative tendencies to seeds. It is as if one wished to build a beautiful building, but could not do so without preparing clean ground for its foundations. Before laying the foundations, one must clear away rocks and weeds, cleansing the ground of all obstructions and removing seeds that spring up and interfere with the building. At the same time, this work of purification must be coupled with the collection of materials that will be helpful in setting up the foundations. In the long run, one's fundamental attention must be directed towards the constructive end of serving universal enlightenment. There is little or no essential interest in the obstructions and tendencies that come in the way of the release of this higher motivation. All these tendencies can be classified into certain broad types which are, in the end, both banal and boring. Most of them have to do with attraction and aversion, anger and pride, greed and delusion, and, above all, a false conception of the self. Owing to this false conception of a fake ego, reinforcing it through unconscious habit and semi-conscious patterns of reaction, a persistent aggregate of tendencies has originated.

Instead of becoming preoccupied with the melodramatic history of this aggregate of tendencies, one should merely note them as they arise and mark them for elimination. They will inevitably appear when one starts to engage in meditation, and one should note them only with a view to removing them through the setting up of counter-tendencies drawn from positive efforts to visualize spiritual strengths. Hence the connection, in the Tibetan practice, between the visualization of *vajrasattva* and the elimination of negative tendencies. Each individual must learn to select the appropriate counter-forces necessary to negate the particular strong negative tendencies that arise. In drawing upon these counter-forces from within, one will discover that one can bring to one's aid many an element in one's own being that can serve to one's spiritual advantage. Every human being has a number of elements which represent a certain ease, naturalness, decency and honesty as a human being. Sometimes there is a debilitating tendency to overlook these or take them for granted.

The spiritual Path requires a progressively heightened degree of self-awareness. One should give oneself full credit for whatever positive tendencies one has, whether they have to do with outward energies on the physical plane, mental energies, moral tenacity or metaphysical insight. In order to find that in oneself which can work in one's favour, and can help in counteracting negative tendencies, one should engage in regular recitation and frequent reflection upon sacred scriptures. Thus one will discover points of resonance in one's individual karmic inheritance that can help release purifying energies flowing from the ideation of Buddhas and Bodhisattvas.

If this practice is going to prosper, one must bring to it a moral insight rooted in an understanding of metaphysics. The mind must be focused upon general ideas. One must reflect upon the relationship of insight and compassion. Insight is not merely intellectual, but rather arises through the recognition of what skill in action means in specific contexts. Insight involves a perception of how wisdom is reflected within action, and which can come about only through a deep reflection upon the process of how such insight is released. On the other side, before one can truly generate a conscious current of compassion, one must create a state of calm abiding. One must find out one's resources and potentials for calmness and for generating the maximum field of patience, peacefulness, gentleness and steadfastness. Then one must combine in practice one's capacity for calmness with one's capacity for discerning what is essential. Inevitably, this will involve a protracted study lasting over lifetimes, and include enquiry into the fundamental propositions of Gupta Vidya, the study of karma and the study of what Buddhist thought refers to as the chain of dependent origination.

In essence, this entire course of study is aimed at bringing about a meta-psychological encounter with a false view of the self that must be confronted and dispelled. Ultimately, this complex matter goes to the core of the *mahamudra* meditation. But at a preliminary level and in the course of preparation for that meditation, one must come to grips with the confused notion of oneself that is identified with bodily desire, proclivities towards pleasure and avoidance of pain. At subtler levels one must confront one's conception of oneself that is bound up with the entire chaotic series of thoughts, all of which have particular histories and form associative chains of memory that have been built up over lifetimes of indulgence. All take a variety of forms and leave discernible tracks, all are connected with certain fantasies, wishes, hopes and expectations. They are designated in various ways in different analytic traditions, but always at the root there is the protean force of self-grasping. It is not easy either to confront or to abandon, and hence *The Voice of the Silence* warns that even when one is very close to attaining *dhyana*, one may be completely disrupted by a sudden eruption of self-grasping.

> 'Ere the gold flame can burn with steady light, the lamp must stand well guarded in a spot free from all wind.' Exposed to shifting breeze, the jet will flicker and the quivering flame cast shades deceptive, dark and ever-changing, on the Soul's white shrine.
>
> And then, O thou pursuer of the truth, thy Mind-Soul will become as a mad elephant, that rages in the jungle. Mistaking forest trees for living foes, he perishes in his attempts to kill the ever-shifting shadows dancing on the wall of sunlit rocks.
>
> Beware, lest in the care of Self thy Soul should lose her foothold on the soil of Deva-knowledge.
>
> Beware, lest in forgetting SELF, thy Soul lose o'er its trembling mind control, and forfeit thus the due fruition of its conquests.
>
> Beware of change! For change is thy great foe. This change will fight thee off, and throw thee back, out of the Path thou treadest, deep into viscous swamps of doubt.
>
> *The Voice of the Silence*

This passage from *The Voice of the Silence* refers primarily to an extremely high state of consciousness and an advanced stage along the Path. It refers to a point at which the very core of self-grasping must be let go. Long before one has earned the privilege of such an archetypal confrontation with the false self, one will have to win many minor skirmishes with the force of self-grasping. For this purpose, *The Voice of the Silence* gives a specific recipe that is indispensable. It is emphasized in every authentic spiritual tradition and it is central to the 1975 Cycle and the Aryanization of the West. It is put in terms of the metaphor of the mango fruit. One must become as tender as the pulp of the mango towards the faults of others, feeling with them their suffering and pain. Yet one must also learn to be as hard as the mango stone towards one's own faults. One must give no quarter to excuse-making or shilly-shallying. Instead, one must fully accept what one thinks to be one's own particular pain, while recognizing that it is, at its core, nothing but a manifestation of delusive self-grasping.

The mango metaphor sums up all the elements involved in the preparation for deep *dhyana* — continuous uninterrupted meditation. Geshe Rabten points to a specific preparatory exercise called "taking and giving", which is a beautiful and profound instantiation of the mango metaphor. One begins by visualizing all the ignorance and all the suffering of the world. Then one must consciously take in with every inhalation of breath everything that is ugly, unsatisfactory, violent and disturbing. For the purpose of understanding and contemplation, the world's mess may be thought of as sticks of fuel burning with a thick black smoke. One must inhale this dense black smoke and let it flow through one's body, permeating every nerve and cell, penetrating to the centre of one's heart, where it destroys all traces of self-concern. Then as one exhales, one should visualize sending out light-energy towards all beings, acting through one's positive tendencies and serving to eliminate their sufferings.

This exercise of taking and giving should be conjoined with one's adoration and prostration before the Buddhas and before one's *Ishtaguru*. Indeed, *Guru Yoga* is the fifth and quintessential element of the preparation for *mahamudra* meditation. One may, at first, contemplate the *Ishtaguru* as a drop of light, or, at a

more advanced stage, one may actually contemplate the essential
form of the *Ishtaguru* in the space before one's mind. It is implicit
in the very conception of the *Ishtaguru* that the individual must
choose whichever form of contemplation will be most
beneficial. Once a choice is made, however, it is crucial that one
persistently and with full fidelity bring the distracted mind back,
again and again, to the object of its contemplation. The test of
this devotion is that one will find a deepening, and yet
spontaneous, longing to be of service to others. More and more,
one's motivation will be that the black smoke of human ignorance
and suffering should pass through oneself and become converted,
through persistence in *dhyana,* into a healing light that will radiate,
brightening and helping the lives of others. In other words, one
will become an instrument through which a great sacrifice is made
consciously, a channel through which a great redemptive force
can proceed. At that point, of course, there can be no separative
self.

One must have become like an alabaster vase, pure and
radiant, a translucent sphere mirroring the Dhyanis through
dhyana. In the act of choosing one's *Ishtaguru* or *Ishtadevata* —
whether it be under the form of Buddha or Krishna or some other
Avatar — one will in fact have entered the ray of a particular
Dhyani. One will have activated the potentiality of a Fohatic
circuit through which may be drawn the beneficent energies of
the entire Host of Dhyanis. One will infallibly recognize this
because one's body and mind will be greatly lightened. So free
does one become from any dependence upon anything outside
that one can subsist upon the food of meditation. This is an
extremely high stage which cannot be attained and maintained
except by individuals who have early made the great renunciation
spoken of in *The Voice of the Silence.*

Every neophyte can approach the threshold of that path and
gain an intuition of that exalted condition. The entire practice of
the *paramitas* at every level — cycling from *dana* through *virya*
to *dhyana* and gaining a glimpse of *prajna* and coming back to
the foundation of boundless charity in *dana* — will bring about

an inevitable loosening and lightening of the tendency to grasp, to crave and even to think of oneself as separate from other beings. The entire preparatory course of the *paramitas* is summed up in Mahatma Gandhi's mantramic phrase: one reduces oneself to a zero. In mystical terms, one becomes a sphere of light.

As one treads the difficult path towards the *dhyana* haven of pure, uninterrupted meditation, one is sure to encounter distractions. According to Geshe Rabten, these may be broadly classified into two types that always work in one or another of two directions. On the one hand, distractions may work as a kind of excitement. On the other, they may operate as a kind of sinking or blackening. With either type, one is liable to become over-active and therefore agitated, and so lose concentration through exaltation in one's happiness or joy or sense of release, or one is likely to get sluggish, drowsy, enfeebled, and thereby lose the power of concentration. These two dangers will combine, recurring again and again. Everyone, therefore, must find out where his or her propensities lie. Different individuals at different times will be more or less liable to become distracted from a current of meditation by excitement or by sluggishness. If one tends to get distracted by excitement, it is suggested that one not close one's eyes during the practice of meditation, but rather keep them open and focused upon a form that is representative of the object of meditation. Yet, if one is liable to get sluggish and fall prey to sinking, then one may benefit by focusing attention on the navel and taking one's breath from below. Different suggestions will be applicable to different people; in the end, propensities towards distractions are only significant in relation to a process of learning by trial and error.

As with all efforts to purify one's moral practice, the effort to establish a non-distracted mind must begin with a contemplation of the possibilities of a state of perfected meditation. In Tibetan tradition the state of mental quiescence needed for true meditation is represented by myriad analogies. Thus, for example, the clear cognitive nature of the mind may be represented by the image of the sun ablaze in a cloudless sky.

There is light and luminosity throughout the field of the mind, giving a supreme clarity to all its operations. There is a simultaneous omnidirectional transmission of light, and, in relation to concentration on any specific object, there is a sharpening of the contours of existence and a heightened alertness to details in the phenomenal world. The cloudlessness signifies an absence of obstruction and confusion of the cognitive nature of the mind, but also a total suffusion of the mind by the overarching, refulgent light of the sun. As Geshe Rabten explains, this analogy represents the nature of the mind as clear cognition, and though it is not to be confused with a realization of the mind's ultimate nature as voidness, it is an authentic intimation of the future course of the *mahamudra* meditation.

Another analogy, perhaps more applicable to the situation of aspirants who are just beginning the practices leading to *dhyana*, is the sureness of the eagle soaring through the sky. The eagle glides gracefully through the sky, ascending without apparent effort, and only periodically flapping its wings. The gliding state represents the absorption of the mind in the object of meditation. The flapping of the wings represents the use of the analytic faculty to dispel a temporary distraction. Whilst it will be necessary in the initial stages to employ the analytic mind to confront and dispel a great variety of distractions, one should steadily move towards the ideal of an eagle's soaring flight. One must advance from a state that is essentially one of great distraction to a steady state, in which one may remain undistracted for relatively long periods of time. Then, when distracting thought currents arise, whether they involve excitation or sinking, they may be noticed, confronted and mastered without breaking the course of meditation any more than the eagle's flight is broken by a single flapping of its wings. In meditation one's basic concern is with the graceful glide, the smooth ascent, movement towards the One.

If one is able to take the standpoint that all human history is a series of successes and failures in preparation for meditation and for initiation into the Mysteries, one may understand that the seemingly burdensome accumulation of history is nothing but the collective residues of a series of over-reactions to distractions in meditation. Confronted honestly, the entire pseudo-drama of history is nothing but a mass of excuses for the inability to maintain concentration. Thus, if one truly wants to effect a fundamental transformation in consciousness so that one becomes incapable of falling back from the true Path of *dhyana*, one must be willing to carry out the full course of preparation for that transformation. One must begin by honestly taking stock of oneself and learning to engage in a sufficient degree of self-surrender of the will, through humility, devotion, adoration and prostration, so that one may begin to attune oneself to the higher chords of one's being. Once one begins seriously to meditate, one may begin to visualize the meaning of a harmonic balance within oneself. Whether one pictures oneself as a fish swimming in the ocean of wisdom or as an eagle soaring in the heavens of light, one's emphasis must be upon developing a continuous current of meditative practice. One must develop those spontaneous reflexes whereby one confronts and dispels distracting thoughts without fascination or excess, bringing the mind back again to the main focus of attention. This must be done again and again at first, and one should never underestimate the tremendous effort involved in the beginning.

Every honest student of the path intimated in *The Voice of the Silence* will understand these difficulties. But a point must come in the practice of *dhyana* when there is a taste of the flow of uninterrupted contemplation, when there is a lightening of the load, when tension disappears — including the tension of striving — and when it becomes easier, subtler and more discriminating. Losing preoccupation with oneself, one begins to forget even the meditating self, and so becomes more aware of the vast, boundless expanse into which one proceeds. One will still be far from the summits of meditation and the accomplishment of the true *mahamudra*, whereby one permanently sets aside the bonds of delusion, but one will have embarked upon the authentic preparation for real meditation and sensed thereby the boundlessly buoyant life of the spirit.

KALAHANSA AND
KALACHAKRA

Saith the Great Law: "In order to become the
KNOWER *of* ALL SELF, *thou hast first of* SELF *to be the*
knower." To reach the knowledge of that SELF, *thou hast*
to give up Self to Non-Self, Being to Non-Being, and then
thou canst repose between the wings of the GREAT BIRD.
Aye, sweet is rest between the wings of that which is not
born, nor dies, but is the AUM *throughout eternal ages.*
Bestride the Bird of Life if thou would'st know.
Give up thy life, if thou would'st live.

The Voice of the Silence

The pregenetic logic of the cosmos which initiates the dawn
of differentiation in each *manvantara* is inseparable from
the omnipresence of *daiviprakriti*, the Light of the Logos,
at every single point in space. This must first be grasped through
the metaphysical imagination, and then through mystical
meditation upon Kalahansa, the Dark Swan of Everlasting
Duration which manifests as the White Swan of Eternity in Time.
The Great Bird of Life is the primordial and sacred bridge
between *kala* and *khandakala*, the unconditionally Timeless and
conditioned Time. The Ineffable Light hidden in Divine Darkness
in boundless space becomes, in the dawn of differentiation, the
rainbow bridge which displays the one colourless Light of the
Spiritual Sun in its beatific dance with seven veils, suggesting the
seven primordial rays in splendid unison as the *fons et origo*
of the dazzling and incalculable multiplicity of manifestation.
In this way, the Unknowable Deity assumes the pristine,
illusive appearance of Ishvara, the Manifested Logos of the
cosmos, which is the origin of the *mahamaya* that makes all
evolution and involution possible over immense periods of cyclic
recurrence.

To say that Deity is unthinkable and unspeakable is an act of honest supplication whereby we acknowledge, as well as seek to transcend, the limits of thought, individual volition and feeling, and all conceptions of being which are conditioned by finite time and bounded space. This truly requires us to raise our sights and calculations beyond the horizon of everything perceptible or imaginable in the ever-changing world of subjects and objects, acts and events, arenas and epochs, states of mind and planes of matter. We must learn to look beyond the panoramic flux of perpetually succeeding as well as simultaneously present appearances, behind and beyond all permutations of substance-matter, which are mental projections of seemingly separate minds, participating in a common field of unitary consciousness. Even the enticing notions of myriad beings and myriad objects, as well as the entire gamut of conditioned and variegated consciousness, must be transcended. In sum, any and every notion of Deity is wholly inadequate to convey the infinite transcendence, immanent omnipresence and inexhaustible plenitude of THAT (*OM TAT SAT*) which far surpasses and supercedes everything that exists, and all possible worlds, all conceivable sum-totals of actualities and actualizations. Hence the awe-inspiring agnosticism in the magnificent and incomparable Rig Vedic hymn about divine creation.

The greatest sages and the most eloquent seers can merely convey through mantrams and metaphors, analogies and chants, the inscrutable and unfathomable nature of Deity. Even the most ardent mystics can merely intimate the ineffable and incomplete nature of their numinous experience of the divine. It is beyond everything that is manifested, manifesting and even potentially capable of manifestation. The divine eludes all possible human conceptions of cosmic plenitude and potential invoked by such metaphors as the limitless sky or endless space, the boundless ocean or ceaseless motion. Beyond a point, all metaphors fail and break down, and even the mathematics of the transfinite is dependent upon limiting assumptions or unprovable axioms. There is no expanse of land or sea, desert or empyrean that can give a sufficient taste or adequate sense of boundless space, eternal duration, or perpetual motion, let alone the absolute silence and supreme stillness, the *maunam*, commended by Rishi Sanatsujatiya as comparable to the AUM, the *paramatman*, conscious immortality, supreme gnosis, and ceaseless meditation.

The greater the level of gnosis, the profounder the agnostic reverence for the Unknowable, the Unfathomable, the Inexhaustible and the Inexpressible. This has been appreciated by the profoundest thinkers in pure mathematics, theoretical astronomy, quantum physics, and microbiology. In 1927 Sir Arthur Eddington spoke for the wisest scientists of our time when he said:

> It has become doubtful whether it will ever be possible to construct a physical world out of the knowable — the guiding principle in our macroscopic theories. If it is possible, it involves a great upheaval of the present foundations. It seems more likely that we must be content to admit a mixture of the knowable and the unknowable. This means a denial of determinism, because the data required for a prediction of the future will include the unknowable elements of the past. I think it was Heisenberg who said, 'The question whether from a complete knowledge of the past we can predict the future, does not arise because a complete knowledge of the past involves a self-contradiction.'. . .
>
> A quantum action may be the means of revealing to us some fact about Nature, but simultaneously a fresh unknown is implanted in the womb of Time. An addition to knowledge is won at the expense of an addition to ignorance. It is hard to empty the well of Truth with a leaky bucket.

This metaphor is reminiscent of the tale told in Plato's *Gorgias* about the leaky jars of souls that are not only lacking in the powers of assimilation and retentiveness, but also in the dialectical ability and philosophical persistence to pursue learning beyond the boundaries of the known and the knowable. Even the best minds with the greatest capacity for lifelong learning, with the highest powers of concentration, absorption and abstraction, are marked by their wise recognition of the limits of thought and language, cognition and comprehension. Rising beyond the regions of Becoming to the realms of Being, the true philosopher or lover of wisdom goes beyond the completest models and broadest hypostases to the calm contemplation of the supreme, ineffable *Agathon*.

Whether we think in terms of boundless space, endless duration or ceaseless motion, we have an intrinsic incapacity to capture, to confine, even to mirror — much less give a local habitation and name to — the formless and nameless, omnipresent and omnipotent Deity. At the same time, the transcendence of Deity, which cannot logically have any relation whatsoever with the world of time and change, must be discernible, however dimly, in the world of Becoming. This raises a profound philosophical challenge, one which was directly confronted by classical thinkers, especially in Vedic India and pre-Socratic Greece. They recognized that the One without a second cannot, if it is unconditioned, relationless and attributeless, originate the world of the many — the world of form, colour and limitation, together with what Buddha called the "chain of dependent origination." Instead of postulating an extra-cosmic, anthropomorphic Creator, and at the risk of remaining agnostic or appearing atheistic, they spoke of pre-cosmic ideation and pre-cosmic substance as interrelated aspects of a single ever-existent Reality, or a primordial and homogeneous substance-principle. Phrases like *Sat-Chit-Ananda, chidakasham* and *chinmatra*, or *svabhavat* and *shunyata*, refer to a state of BE-NESS rather than Being, as we know it. In it lies latent the all-comprehensive set inclusive of all sets and sum-totals, the entire range of conceivable possibilities of all awareness, all matter and all energy, or force in its most primordial, pregenetic sense.

In the Divine Darkness of the night of non-manifestation, there is limitless subjectivity, omnipresent objectivity and inexhaustible energy, all existing *in potentia* and yet inseparable from each other. They are three aspects or hypostases of a primordial Pythagorean *monas* or Kosmic Monad, which is latent like a divine germ in the Divine Ground, the one indivisible substance-principle, the one supreme Reality which is the omnipresent substratum of all noumenal and phenomenal existence. Within that Divine Ground, which is often called TAT, there is an all-potent stirring or swelling, pulsation or gestation which makes possible a pristine reflection of Deity in the "waters of Space". This initiates the world of time and space, of *kala, kalakhanda* and *mahamaya,* though at an extremely subtle, ineffable and macrocosmic level, on a plane which is so homogeneous and impartite that it is the realm of non-manifestation, which can never be manifested in any region wherein there is a progressive differentiation into subjects and objects.

This is, nonetheless, the transcendent origin of all noumenal manifestation, but since this first Point originates proemally in the realm of the unmanifest, it is sometimes called the Unmanifest Logos. The Unmanifest Logos radiates, emanates and issues forth — these are all inadequate terms for a mysterious transcendental process — the manifested Logos, *parameshvara,* the all-pervasive sovereign Intelligence, divine will and supreme life-force in a vast system of worlds that subsists for an immense period of manifestation, or *mahamanvantara.* By analogy and correspondence, this can also be applied to the commencement of *manvantaras* and *kalpas,* the lesser epochs of manifestation of the solar system, the planets with their respective seven globes, and the earth chain.

When one goes back in the deepest meditation beyond all beginnings and all endings, and does this daily with the whole of one's being — emptying out all categories, conceptions and feelings of selfhood, name and form (*namarupa*), not only in relation to the body and its seeming identity, but also in relation to the subtler vestures and all possible notions of objectivity, and even in terms of all conceivable notions of subjectivity — then one comes closer to the Ever-Existent SELF. Yet, owing to the 'emergence' of the Unmanifested Logos — in a manner which led metaphysicians like Shankaracharya to speak of the world as constituted of *Ishvara* and *maya* — it is as if there are myriads of beings in myriads of worlds interacting with myriads of objects and expressing their subjectivity, thereby gathering and dispersing myriads of energies and forces. These are all permutations and combinations on successive planes of differentiation of a single Force, with seven primary manifestations.

At every point of space in every single form — in every leaf, flower or fruit — there is the fullness of Deity. That is why the ancient sacred texts often use the potent metaphor of the lotus to refer both to the Cosmos and Man, to the vast macrocosm and the crystalline microcosm. The lotus is a consecrated aid to contemplation because of its suggestive botanical characteristics, especially the fact that it contains a complete replica of itself in miniature within its seed. This theurgic and organic metaphor reveals upon reflection that everything is sacred and nothing is profane to the enlightened seer or *yogin*. At every point of space there is the ever-present possibility of arousing, activating, sensing and breathing Deity itself. From the most transcendental intimations of Deity, such as in the Vedic hymns, the esoteric Upanishads, the Chaldean or Hermetic fragments, the incantatory Kabbalistic chant of Solomon Ben Gabirol, one may derive the most omnipresent and immanent view of God.

If one meditates, commencing with a metaphysical or mathematical centre and inscribing a circle around it, and then imagines a series of concentric circles expanding in every direction, that circle becomes a swelling sphere until it ultimately dissolves into the boundless empyrean encompassing and receding beyond the entire cosmos. At the same time, it will still have its stable centre in human consciousness, at greater and greater levels of abstraction. Such is the extraordinary power of metaphysical imagination, or truly deep meditation, which can be made the

assured basis of altruistic, noetic magic. Though one may try
to apprehend this and seek to abstract one's mind by using
this evocative language, and even though one may also attempt
sanyama, the instantaneous fusion of *dharana* or concentration,
dhyana or deep meditation, and *samadhi* or total, ecstatic
absorption, there are obstacles one repeatedly encounters.

For a start, many people most of the time cannot readily
sustain this rarefied level of abstraction any more than we can
easily breathe the rarefied air high up in the mountain ranges.
On the physical plane one cannot breathe at great elevations
without assiduous practice and progressive acclimatization. When
it comes to acclimatizing the mind to that awesome degree of
abstraction required by *sanyama*, the systematic spiritual training
involved is difficult indeed. No wonder Nicholas of Cusa
remarked that unless a person has really grasped the mathematics
of the infinite, he cannot make any meaningful pronouncement
upon God. This was a wise and compassionate corrective to check
all those who were dogmatizing and unduly verbalizing in terms
of concrete images, limiting conceptions and empty words about
the Godhead.

Nonetheless, infinity is actually mirrored in the infinitesimal.
One can get a sense of depth, not merely by expansion or by
elevation of consciousness, but also by intense concentration upon
what is near at hand. Hence in yogic practices such as those given
in the *Bhagavad Gita*, emphasis is given to concentration upon
the point between the eyes as a starting point for meditation. In
the thirteenth chapter, Shri Krishna points out that Deity, which
seems so far away, is also closer than anything else. This sense of
the closeness of Deity is something one can experience in human
life when one is privileged to be present either at the birth of a
baby or at the deathbed of a human soul who is leaving the body.
At such moments and at other times in life — at solemn
ceremonies, joyous festivals, and sometimes in fleeting moments
in human relationships — one can experience a depth of feeling,
of self-transcendence and self-forgetfulness, of pure joy and
serenity, which is healing, calming and soothing to the soul.

The influence of these intimations of immanent immortality is so real that in such moments one can feel the touch of the divine.

All of this is expressed in the great metaphor of Kalahansa, sometimes translated as 'the Swan in and out of time'. Kalahansa is black, representing Divine Darkness, the plenum of all potentiality. Imagine a mighty cosmic bird with black wings which correspond to infinity and eternity. Although at rest, that same bird emanates or emerges as a white bird in space and time. Kalahansa in eternity is behind Kalahansa in time. This powerful metaphor represents the descent of Dhyanis from Divine Darkness — from what seems to be motionless absolute stillness — into the world of Becoming, where there is rhythmic motion amidst burgeoning life, growth, decay and death, but also endless regeneration. Kalahansa stands for all the endless cycles (*Kalachakra*): the cycles of the seasons, the cycles of the year, the cycles represented by the revolutions of the planets, but also the cycles of day and night and the cycles that human beings experience — in sleeping and waking, in living and dying, in birth and death and rebirth.

In all the vast cycles of time and manifestation, there is a representation of a certain rhythm which itself is a reflection of the inbreathing and the outbreathing of the Great Bird. Even when still and motionless, it is breathing in and breathing out. This means that there is an analogue to physical breathing in mental breathing, in the breathing of the organs and centres of the subtle vestures, and even a kind of spiritual breathing. There is also a diastolic and systolic movement in the spiritual heart that is only dimly reflected in the diastole and systole of the physical heart, beautiful and wondrous as it is. Therefore, in the very act of being alive there is a gratitude for life itself. There is in life itself an ultimate form of worship, piety and prayer, of celebration and reverence for the divine. This is the basis of all folk cultures, as well as all the festive gatherings of human beings over thousands upon thousands of years, where the birth or death of one being is greeted as relevant to all. There is a recognition, but also a transcendence, an insertion and immersion, of what is deeply significant and sacred in the lives of individuals into the great stream of collective life, and ultimately into the unending stream of the universal pilgrimage of humanity.

Nature is full of reminders and representations of the reality of the collective life process pointing to the significance of the great collective breathing in and breathing out of the Great Bird. The metaphor of the Kalahansa also gives beautiful emphasis to soaring and sinking in the air, reminding one of Gandhi's trenchant statement, "Human nature is such that it must either soar or sink." There is no middle, lukewarm, Lockean position, no moral stasis in human life. Every moment a human being is either soaring — and for Gandhi one of the yardsticks was becoming more non-violent — or every moment a human being is becoming more violent, more self-destructive, more deceitful. If human nature is constantly either soaring or sinking, then one could see why, as in Plato's *Symposium,* the growing of wings is taken as an archetypal image of growth.

In the *Symposium* this growth is movement upon the ladder of love. Diotima, the great prophetess of whom Socrates speaks, characterizes love as the mediating term between mortality and immortality. Love is neither human nor divine, but mediates between them. It is beyond all growth, and behind all discontent. It is behind all longings and frustrations, but above all, it is behind every effort to look up and begin all over again in a new direction. Most people start with little loves and may come to find in them mere projections of self-love. Through illusory expectations, they have concretized and over-romanticized their conception of love, trying to reduce what cannot be captured into time and space, into bonds and ties, thereby ensuring the inevitability of pain and disillusionment. Nonetheless, by persisting, human beings can come to recognize that there are many different instances and levels of beauty. They can also recognize that to apprehend Beauty itself they need the impersonal intellect. They need the power of meditation, abstract visualization and creative imagination. There is a beauty to effort and not only to achievement. There is a beauty even in failure. There is a beauty in the struggle of the human soul through pain and torment. There is also a beauty in rules and laws, even though they are imperfect representations of the ineffable beauty that is much more archetypally mirrored in the celestial patterns and the great laws pertaining to the movements of heavenly bodies. In other words, one can extend and deepen one's conception of beauty through love of truth and the truth of love.

This is a kind of sprouting of wings, because it cannot be done without releasing a divine enthusiasm and divine afflatus, without becoming more capable of being creative in new ways. It is not as if one goes through these things without their acting upon the will and desire. Indeed, they do. But above all, they act upon one's fundamental sense of life, transmuting one's image of the world in which one lives, and one's image of all humanity. Such growth may be called the sprouting of wings, and these wings help one to ascend to a higher plane of consciousness. After a point — to take the ideal case of the Adept, the perfected man who has mastered the capacity to move between planes, who has freed himself from the illusions making up the lunar body and the lunar mind, and who has totally transmuted the energy of desire — the perfected individual is not only able to move consciously between planes. On any one plane, he is able to arouse and activate a sense of the multi-dimensional nature of the cosmos in other human beings. Everything he does is unique and inimitable. Each act is an original. Yet in every act and gesture there is a capacity to turn human beings back upon themselves, arousing in them latent potentialities and forgotten soul memories and melodies of long, long ago.

In the Adept, wisdom, compassion and sacrifice come alive as living links between Deity, Nature and Man. Adeptship is the fulfillment of the Path of striving and woe, but it is essentially the spiritual efflorescence of an age, not of any isolated being. It has redemptive meaning for all human beings and the whole of Nature. Understood in this light, every human being who reflects deeply upon the quest for wisdom will see that wisdom is beyond the limits of manifestation and all limits of human knowledge. At its highest level wisdom is beyond the capacity of utterance or formulation, beyond all signs and symbols, beyond all tokens and icons. Therefore, it is transcendental and divine. At the same time, one can also see that wisdom must include the intelligence suffused throughout Nature, which works through the intricate impulses in every cell, atom and molecule. Because there is intelligence in every single speck of space, Nature itself is intelligible in principle, and Deity represents this principle of intelligibility in Nature. Thus the gift of God to Man is the power of making intelligible that which is intelligible in Nature. The ancients saw reason as the quintessential human mode of participation in the Divine. It is one of the great wings with which the human being can ascend, going beyond all discursive thought couched in terms of comparison and contrast. In its original meaning rationality had to do with *ratio* — cognition of the mathematics of the cosmos through ratios and proportions of numbers and rates of movement.

The fourth principle completing and dynamizing the triad of wisdom, compassion and sacrifice is the principle of metaphysical continuity between the highest and the lowest. "The highest sees through the eyes of the lowest" is an ancient Hermetic axiom. Therefore, God sees through an ant. The divine mind is related to the mind of an ant. There is a continuity not only across the entire spectrum and total gamut of all human existence, intellection and ideation, but also a continuity that embraces all the seven kingdoms of Nature, encompassing everything in the three elemental domains, the mineral, vegetable, animal and human kingdoms. This profound, all-ramifying principle of continuity can be understood with the help of language only up to a certain point. Beyond this, one has to experience it. If Nature is intelligible to the human mind, in principle, then man is intended to inquire into the inscrutable.

Man is most wise when he questions, but must begin by questioning himself. From this self-questioning there must arise a whole state of mind where everything is questioned and nothing is taken for granted. Because one cannot do this all the time, either through noisy speech or through favoured times of dialogue, one mostly has to do it in silence. Every baby does so openly, asking more "Why?" questions than its mother, father or teachers can either answer or have the patience for. If a child is to learn to persist within itself, it has also to learn something more — that everything cannot be told and everything cannot be talked about. Though public schools may follow the 'show and tell' method, for inward growth one must also learn the 'do not show and do not tell' method. Modern society has lost this art of quiet self-questioning, and therefore its members are mediumistically prone and sporadically subject to all the limited views of human nature and the world that make up the ephemera of bourgeois pseudo-culture. This does not merely happen accidentally; it is part of the suggestibility of the *psyche* to mass hypnosis in the twentieth century.

The dangers of this mass hypnosis were pointed out early in the century by the dying Tolstoy to the young Gandhi, and also by Robert Crosbie. Now that humanity is in the thick of this age of mass hypnosis, suggestibility and bombardment through images, it has become much harder and tougher to individuate. It is much more difficult to release a compassion that can bridge Nature and Man, and even mirror something of the Divine. Paradoxically, somewhere in human beings — especially when they are totally down and out, when they are totally friendless and all alone with no one having a single interest in them, when it is extremely difficult for them to generate any faith in themselves for the future — there is in that terribly lonely state some sense of the divine love of Buddha, the compassion of Christ. This is the secret force in the unrecorded history of man. It is the compassion of the Logos in the cosmos. Hence the meaning of *Om Mani Padme Hum*, the Jewel in the Lotus, the God in Man.

It is a constant salutation and a continuous affirmation of the ever-existent reality of a wisdom and compassion which are divine, but which can also be seen in human beings at times, and, depending upon their power of penetrating the veil of the visible, in Nature itself. To do so is the perpetual challenge that has faced all mystics and seekers in every era. Today it is an overwhelming challenge because this is an age of unprecedented discontinuity and fragmentation of consciousness. People say things in the morning they do not remember in the evening, and make promises this week they do not remember next week. It is extremely difficult to overcome the bombardment of the sensorium and brain by a mass of disparate, disconnected and useless information. That is why most people talk compulsively. With this kind of compulsive communication, the bombardment of the sensorium and brain by a mass of inputs is amazing.

It is a tremendous task to maintain continuity of universal, impersonal self-consciousness, continuity in the *Atman*, continuity in the *Brahman*, continuity in the AUM. Since it is so difficult, strong measures have to be taken. Instead of setting oneself impossible targets, one must start with honest, small targets. Can one take a single *shloka* from a sacred text and keep it in mind during the day, bringing the mind back to it from time to time, and using it to give significance and meaning to different moments in life in different contexts? Can one take a keynote for a week and think about it daily, coming back to the main theme so that one can see a continuous thread of meaning running through the week? These are aids to continuity on a small scale, but if a person truly uses them, they can help to reveal the logic behind the seasons. In time, one can learn to cooperate with the vibrations of the solstices and the equinoxes, the cycles of the sun, moon and planets, and above all, the sacred festivals and observances that mark the descents of the Logos into terrestrial and human life, associated with Rama, Krishna, Buddha or Christ. If one can work with the seasons and the timetables of Nature and the spiritual history of man, one can make the principle of continuity active, joyous and self-sustaining. One should honour whatever one can use in one's daily reflections upon life, making as many connections as possible with the great stream of history, with the spiritual pilgrimage of all humanity, and with the Promethean current of the present historical moment.

By strengthening one's capacity for continuity in these ways, one can bring wisdom, compassion and sacrifice together. The whole of life is a sacrifice. All beings are all the time ceaselessly partakers of the sacrifice of others. There is not a human being who does not owe, at any given time, more to more people than he or she has had time to pay back. How many people really think about this? Over a thousand years each human being has had a million ancestors. Whatever the incredible significance of this ancestry on the lunar and the physical plane, the ultimate spiritual ancestry of humanity is a myriad times more magnificent. It traces back to all the Fathers and Teachers of the human race, the Elder Brothers and the Saviours of humanity. When one thinks in this way, the principle of sacrifice becomes the perfect basis for rooting out the poison of self-concern and personal injustice. Through heartfelt gratitude one can root out the appalling asuric tendency to insult the universe and the Law of Karma merely because they do not coincide with one's stupid likes and dislikes. Just because one had a spoilt childhood in junior high school and never learnt to come to terms with controlling these likes and dislikes, it is terrible to make them the yardstick of life. Like a court of law without any rules or any proper defence counsel, it is an inefficient way to reach decisions.

One really does not want to encourage this raucous voice, the sound of rebellious, discontented lower *Manas* stridently proclaiming its pseudo-independence: "No one can tell me anything. I can look after myself. I am going to be independent." If any of this were true, one would not have to talk about it. One would quietly live it. The moment one feels compelled to say it, one should know that it is false. There is no harm in reminding oneself quietly and seriously of the need for self-reliance and responsibility, but, because people cannot do this, most human conversation becomes a kind of inefficient psychoanalysis, a poor, distorted form of therapy. One is talking to oneself but in the name of talking to others, which is certainly confusing to other people, and this leads to a general failure of communication. In other words, there is a high noise-to-signal ratio, and hence one cannot really listen to the deepest voice in oneself, the Voice of the Silence. One cannot listen to the music of the spheres.

Occult healing of soul deafness can come through the Great Bird, the AUM throughout eternal ages, the synthesis of Deity, Nature and Man as well as of wisdom, compassion and sacrifice. The most incredible achievement of the human race — never mind how many millions of years ago it happened — is that men and women in the most ancient civilizations of the earth recognized the archetypal nature of the most sacred of sounds. The first sound that the human mouth can utter when it opens is *A*. The sound which closes the mouth is *M*. *A* stands for all beginnings, and *M* stands for all endings, but these endings are not final, and these beginnings are not unprecedented. To go from *A* to *M* one needs a *U*, and that is the process of Becoming. Therefore AUM is the archetypal Sound of sounds. It is the origin of Amen, and it is the sound that every baby makes at the moment of birth. Very few human beings, alas, also make it their last sound at the moment of death.

AUM stands for Brahma, Vishnu and Shiva — the creative, preservative and destructive-regenerative aspects of Deity, Nature and Humanity — and therefore it applies to everything. Yet, it also goes beyond anything and everything. It is more than a sound, and points beyond itself to the Soundless Sound. The mysterious *ardhamatra*, the half meter inscribed as a dot, or *bindu*, above the crescent in the ideogram of the AUM, has been compared to the head of that Sound. It stands for the capacity to bring the threefold AUM into the realm of time, to hold it, and to make it the basis in consciousness of that which can be associated with everything in one's life — with breathing, with sounding words, and with all one's activities. Obviously, one cannot often do this loudly without drawing attention and profaning the sound. But one can keep it in the mind, and if this is done again and again, one's whole being becomes attuned to that Sound, and one can renew and refresh oneself continuously. Drawing the energy needed for the next task at hand, and at the same time remaining detached, one does not have to be caught in the process or lost in the cacophony of the world. Then one can meditate as if one were at the moment of death, about to leave this tenement and temple, which is also a worn-out instrument, and give the soul an opportunity to take wings in its subtler vestures.

AUM is an ideogram applying to the whole of Nature, which is a vast elaboration of the AUM. Every human being too is an expression of the AUM. When a human being, through the power of self-consciousness, by deliberation and detachment, concentration and compassion, out of altruism, is able to insert himself into the whole of the human family, and on behalf of all living beings is able to intone the AUM and to keep it reverberating, then one has a sense of the still, sad music of humanity. One has some sense of the invisible depths in the cosmos. One is able to see in this way that Deity is not only being daily crucified, but that Deity is also being daily vindicated. One can see, therefore, that just as Deity is indifferent to its crucifixion, it is at the same time indifferent to its vindication, though it is on the side of every being that breathes. The AUM, the Great Bird, represents that which is beyond all processes of change. It is also the changeless within the realm of change, immortality in the realm of mortality, and the ineffable light within the darkness — the darkness of human pain and ignorance, estrangement and loneliness, and also the darkness of human misdeeds, violence, degradation and self-destruction.

AUM more than embraces the entire gamut of human experience. Transcending the limits of human existence, AUM points to the potentialities and possibilities of universal self-consciousness exemplified by the greatest sages and *yogins*, Mahatmas and Bodhisattvas. In every human being — however fallible and imperfect, however tortured and tyrannized by the categories of time and desire, however torn by mental confusion and emotional conflict — there is the inaudible sounding of the AUM, even if it is not known. If it stops sounding, which it does sometime before the moment of death, death is imminent, and the wise man can actually recognize the ceasing of that sound in a human being who comes close to the end.

Owing to this ceaseless reverberation of the Soundless Sound within the *anahata*, the indestructible centre in the spiritual heart, to be human is to be potentially divine. But to be human in this sense is to be insufficiently divine, for one is only divine to the extent that one knows this truth. To know it is to live it, and one can only know and live it if one can simultaneously see it as true for each and every human being. It takes lives of self-training to become able to greet the AUM in every pair of human eyes and in everything that breathes, keeping that as the constant thought in one's consciousness. Somewhere deep down, every human being already knows this, but to be able to hold it involves a refining, a selection and a sifting on the planes of the lesser principles, the brain mind, the heart and the emotions, ultimately affecting all the life-atoms. In the light of this, one can begin to understand the archetypal mantram, *Om Mani Padme Hum* — the Jewel in the Lotus, God in Man — as the great affirmation of the indissoluble bridge between the entire human family and the whole host of Dhyani Buddhas. It is the living bond between every human being and the Dhyani Buddha that overbroods each and every human being. That basis of true hierarchy already exists in the cosmos, and one can no more wish it away than one can wish away the colours of the spectrum, the number series, or the simple fact that there are three hundred and sixty degrees in the circle of the zodiac. Every one of them gives rise to vast numbers of permutations and combinations that ultimately fix with mathematical exactness the degree of what is true for every moment of every human being.

This is much vaster than any hierarchy one can readily recognize through the finite intellect. Yet, it is simply a reflection in the human family of the divine logic of the Logos which must work through seven rays, and ultimately these must ramify through myriad subsets and subsystems. One will quickly find, even without knowing too much about mathematics, that it is staggering how much precision there is to this cosmos. Everyone is exactly where he or she is for a very good reason. In other words, if one wants Divine Wisdom, one must mature beyond the pseudo-democratic myth that everybody has a right to ask the universe to convince him that he is there because he is meant to be there. The universe is silent. The universe has no interest in convincing any human being. At this point in evolution, human beings are grown. They have been through all of this in other lives, and therefore every human being is accountable to himself. Each must release by self-questioning real self-knowledge. There is no short-cut to this, and only in this way will one discover 'the lie in the soul', that deep spiritual blockage coming from other lives which makes one so defiant of the logic of the cosmos.

All human souls have at times fallen by the wayside, and some have indeed made bad mistakes in recent lives, but every human soul has exactly the same prerogative to make a difference in the present. But, to make a difference one must first take full responsibility for oneself. Once this is done, one will begin to recognize those who know more than oneself, and from whom one can learn, as well as those who may depend on oneself, and to whom one may offer help. In this process one should learn to set one's sights as high as possible. This means that one must salute the entire hierarchy of perfected beings — Mahatmas, Buddhas, Rishis and Bodhisattvas — because, in the act of adoration of that Host of Illuminated and Enlightened Beings, one salutes the whole human race with its resplendent future. At the same time, one also gives the truest hope to oneself in the years and lives to come.

OM

APPENDICES

THE BEACON LIGHT
OF THE UNKNOWN

It is written in an old book upon the Occult Sciences: "Gupta Vidya (Secret Science) is an attractive sea, but stormy and full of rocks. The navigator who risks himself thereon, if he be not wise and full of experience,* will be swallowed up, wrecked upon one of the thousand submerged reefs. Great billows, in colour like sapphires, rubies and emeralds, billows full of beauty and mystery will overtake him, ready to bear the voyager away towards other and numberless lights that burn in every direction. But these are will-o-the-wisps, lighted by the sons of Kaliya† for the destruction of those who thirst for life. Happy are they who remain blind to these false deceivers; more happy still those who never turn their eyes from the only true Beacon-light whose eternal flame burns in solitude in the depths of the water of the Sacred Science. Numberless are the pilgrims that desire to enter those waters; very few are the strong swimmers who reach the Light. He who gets there must have ceased to be a number, and have become all numbers. He must have forgotten the illusion of separation, and accept only the truth of collective individuality.‡ He must "see with the ears, hear with the eyes,§ understand the language of the rainbow, and have concentrated his six senses in

* Acquired under a Guru.

† The great serpent conquered by Krishna and driven from the river Yanuma into the sea, where the Serpent Kaliya took for wife a kind of Siren, by whom he had a numerous family.

‡ The illusion of the personality of the Ego, placed by our egotism in the first rank. In a word, it is necessary to assimilate the whole of humanity, live by it, for it, and in it; in other terms, cease to be "one," and become "all" or the *total*.

§ A Vedic expression. The senses, counting in the two mystic senses, are seven in Occultism; but an Initiate does not separate these senses from each other, any more than he separates his unity from Humanity. Every sense contains all the others.

his seventh sense." *

The Beacon-light of Truth is Nature without the veil of the senses. It can be reached only when the adept has become absolute master of his personal self, able to control all his physical and psychic senses by the aid of his "seventh sense," through which he is gifted also with the true wisdom of the gods — *Theosophia.* . . .

True Magic, the theurgy of Iamblicus, is in its turn identical with the gnosis of Pythagoras, the γνῶσις τῶν ὄντῶν, the *science of things* which are, and with the divine ecstacy of the Philaletheans, "the lovers of Truth." But, one can judge of the tree only by its fruits. Who are those who have witnessed to the divine character and the reality of that ecstacy which is called Samadhi in India? †

A long series of men, who, had they been Christians, would have been canonized, — not by the decision of the Church, which has its partialities and predilections, but by that of whole nations, and by the *vox populi,* which is hardly ever wrong in its judgments. There is, for instance, Ammonius Saccas, called the *Theodidaktos,* "God-instructed"; the great master whose life was so chaste and so pure, that Plotinus, his pupil, had not the slightest hope of ever seeing any mortal comparable to him. Then there is this same Plotinus who was for Ammonius what Plato was for Socrates — a disciple worthy of his illustrious master. Then there is Porphyry,

---

* Symbology of colours. The Language of the prism, of which "the seven mother colours have each seven sons," that is to say, forty-nine shades or "sons" between the seven, which graduated tints are so many letters or alphabetical characters. The language of colours has, therefore, fifty-six letters for the Initiate. Of these letters each septenary is absorbed by the mother colour, as each of the seven mother colours is absorbed finally in the white ray, Divine Unity symbolized by these colours.

† Samadhi is a state of abstract contemplation, defined in Sanskrit terms that each require a whole sentence to explain them. It is a mental, or, rather, spiritual state, which is not dependent upon any perceptible object, and during which the *subject,* absorbed in the region of pure spirit, lives *in the Divinity.*

the pupil of Plotinus,* the author of the biography of Pythagoras. Under the shadow of this divine gnosis, whose beneficent influence has extended to our own days, all the celebrated mystics of the later centuries have been developed, such as Jacob Boehme, Emanuel Swedenborg, and so many others. Madame Guyon is the feminine counterpart of Iamblicus. The Christian Quietists, the Mussulman Soufis, the Rosicrucians of all countries, drink the waters of that inexhaustible fountain — the Theosophy of the Neo-Platonists of the first centuries of the Christian Era. The gnosis preceded that era, for it was the direct continuation of the *Gupta Vidya* and of the Brahmā-Vidya ("secret knowledge" and "knowledge of Brahmā") of ancient India, transmitted through Egypt; just as the theurgy of the Philaletheans was the continuation of the Egyptian mysteries. In any case, the point from which this "diabolic" magic starts, is the Supreme Divinity; its end and aim, the union of the divine spark which animates man with the parent-flame, which is the Divine ALL.

This consummation is the *ultima thule* of those Theosophists, who devote themselves entirely to the service of humanity. Apart from these, others, who are not yet ready to sacrifice everything, may occupy themselves with the transcendental sciences, such as Mesmerism, and the modern phenomena under all their forms. They have the right to do so according to the clause which specifies as one of the objects of the Theosophical Society "the investigation of unexplained laws of nature and the psychic powers latent in man.". . .

II

What does the world know of true Theosophy? How can it distinguish between that of a Plotinus, and that of the false brothers? And of the latter the Society possesses more than its

---

* He lived in Rome for 28 years, and was so virtuous a man that it was considered an honour to have him as guardian for the orphans of the highest patricians. He died without having made an enemy during those 28 years.

share. The egoism, vanity and self-sufficiency of the majority of mortals is incredible. There are some for whom their little personality constitutes the whole universe, beyond which there is no salvation. Suggest to one of these that the alpha and omega of wisdom are not limited by the circumference of his or her head, that his or her judgment could not be considered quite equal to that of Solomon, and straight away he or she accuses you of *anti-theosophy*. You have been guilty of blasphemy against the spirit, which will not be pardoned in this century, nor in the next. These people say, "I am Theosophy," as Louis XIV said "I am the State." They speak of fraternity and of altruism and only care in reality for that for which no one else cares — themselves — in other words their little "me." Their egoism makes them fancy that it is they only who represent the temple of Theosophy, and that in proclaiming themselves to the world they are proclaiming Theosophy. Alas! the doors and windows of that "temple" are no better than so many channels through which enter, but very seldom depart, the vices and illusions characteristic of egoistical mediocrities.

These people are the white ants of the Theosophical Society, which eat away its foundations, and are a perpetual menace to it. It is only when they leave it that it is possible to breathe freely.

It is not such as these that can ever give a correct idea of practical Theosophy, still less of the transcendental Theosophy which occupies the minds of a little group of the elect. Every one of us possesses the faculty, the interior sense, that is known by the name of *intuition*, but how rare are those who know how to develop it! It is, however, only by the aid of this faculty that men can ever see things in their true colours. It is an *instinct of the soul*, which grows in us in proportion to the employment we give it, and which helps us to perceive and understand the realities of things with far more certainty than can the simple use of our senses and exercise of our reason. What are called good sense and logic enable us to see only the appearances of things, that which is evident to every one. The *instinct* of which I speak, being a projection of our perceptive consciousness, a projection which acts from the subjective to the objective, and not *vice versa*, awakens in us spiritual senses and power to act; these senses assimilate to themselves the essence of the object or of the action under examination, and represent it to us as it really is, not as it appears to our physical senses and to our cold reason. "We begin with *instinct*, we end with omniscience" says Professor A. Wilder, our oldest colleague. Iamblicus has described this faculty, and certain Theosophists have been able to appreciate the truth of his description.

"There exists," he says, "a faculty in the human mind which is immeasurably superior to all those which are grafted or engendered in us. By it we can attain to union with superior intelligences, finding ourselves raised above the scenes of this earthly life, and partaking of the higher existence and superhuman powers of the inhabitants of the celestial spheres. By this faculty we find ourselves liberated finally from the dominion of destiny (Karma), and we become, as it were, the arbiters of our own fates. For, when the most excellent parts in us find themselves filled with energy; and when our soul is lifted up towards essences higher than science, it can separate itself from the conditions which hold it in the bondage of every-day life; it exchanges its ordinary existence for another one, it renounces the conventional habits which belong to the external order of things, to give itself up to and mix itself with another order of things which reigns in that most elevated state of existence."

Plato has expressed the same idea in two lines: "The light and spirit of the Divinity are the wings of the soul. They raise it to communion with the gods, above this earth, with which the spirit of man is too ready to soil itself. . . . To become like the gods, is to become holy, just and wise. That is the end for which man was created, and that ought to be his aim in the acquisition of knowledge."

This is true Theosophy, inner Theosophy, that of the soul. But followed with a selfish aim Theosophy changes its nature and becomes *demonosophy*. That is why Oriental wisdom teaches us that the Hindu Yogi who isolates himself in an impenetrable forest, like the Christian hermit who, as was common in former times, retires to the desert, are both of them nothing but accomplished egoists. The one acts with the sole idea of finding a nirvanic refuge against reincarnation; the other acts with the unique idea of saving his soul, — both of them think only of themselves. Their motive is altogether personal; for, even supposing they attain their end, are they not like cowardly soldiers, who desert from their regiment when it is going into action, in order to keep out of the way of the bullets? . . .

Gautama, the Buddha, only remained in solitude long enough to enable him to arrive at the truth, which he devoted himself from that time on to promulgate, begging his bread, and living for humanity. Jesus retired to the desert only for forty days, and died for this same humanity. Apollonius of Tyana, Plotinus, Iamblicus, while leading lives of singular abstinence, almost of asceticism, lived in the world and *for* the world. The greatest ascetics and *saints* of our days are not those who retire into inaccessible places, but those who pass their lives in travelling from place to place, doing good and trying to raise mankind; although, indeed, they may avoid Europe, and those civilized countries where no one has any eyes or ears except for himself, countries divided into two camps — of Cains and Abels.

Those who regard the human soul as an emanation of the Deity, as a particle or ray of the universal and ABSOLUTE soul, understand the parable of the *Talents* better than do the Christians. He who hides in the earth the *talent* which has been given him by his "Lord," will lose that talent, as the ascetic loses it, who takes it into his head to "save his soul" in egoistical solitude. The "good and faithful servant" who doubles his capital, by harvesting for *him who has not sown*, because he had not the means of doing so, and who reaps for the poor who have not scattered the grain, acts like a true altruist. He will receive his recompense, just because he has worked for another, without any idea of remuneration or reward. That man is the altruistic Theosophist, while the other is an egoist and a coward.

The Beacon-light upon which the eyes of all real Theosophists are fixed is the same towards which in all ages the imprisoned human soul has struggled. This Beacon, whose light shines upon no earthly seas, but which has mirrored itself in the sombre depths of the primordial waters of infinite space, is called by us, as by the earliest Theosophists, "Divine Wisdom." That is the last word of the esoteric doctrine; and, in antiquity, where was the country, having the right to call itself civilized, that did not possess a double system of WISDOM, of which one part was for the masses, and the other for the few, — the exoteric and the esoteric? This name, WISDOM, or, as we say sometimes, the "Wisdom Religion" or *Theosophy*, is as old as the human mind. The title of *Sages* — the priests of this worship of truth — was its first derivative. These names were afterwards transformed into *philosophy*, and *philosophers* — the "lovers of science" or of wisdom. It is to Pythagoras that we owe that name, as also that of *gnosis*, the system of ἡ γνῶσις τῶν ὄντων "the knowledge of things as they are," or of the essence that is hidden beneath the external appearances. Under that name, so noble and so correct in its definition, all the masters of antiquity designated the aggregate of our knowledge of things human and divine. The sages and *Brachmanes* of India, the magi of Chaldea and Persia, the hierophants of Egypt and Arabia, the prophets or *Nabi* of Judea and of Israel, as well as the philosophers of Greece and Rome, have always classified that science in two divisions — the *esoteric*, or the true, and the *exoteric*, disguised in symbols. To this day the Jewish Rabbis give the name of *Mercabah* to the body or vehicle of their religious system, that which contains within it the higher knowledge, accessible only to the initiates, and of which higher knowledge it is only the husk.

We are accused of mystery, and we are reproached with making a secret of the higher Theosophy. We confess that the doctrine which we call *gupta vidya* (secret science) is only for the few. But where were the masters in ancient times who did not keep their teachings secret, for fear they would be profaned? From Orpheus and Zoroaster, Pythagoras and Plato, down to the

Rosicrucians, and to the more modern Free-Masons, it has been the invariable rule that the disciple must gain the confidence of the master before receiving from him the supreme and final word. The most ancient religions have always had their greater and lesser mysteries. The neophytes and catechumens took an inviolable oath before they were accepted. The Essenes of Judea and Mount Carmel required the same thing. The *Nabi* and the *Nazars* (the "separated ones" of Israel), like the lay *Chelas* and the *Brahmacharyas* of India, differed greatly from each other. The former could, and can, be married and remain in the world, while they are studying the sacred writings up to a certain point; the latter, the Nazars and the Brahmacharyas, have always been entirely vowed to the mysteries of initiation. The great schools of Esotericism were international, although exclusive, as is proved by the fact that Plato, Herodotus and others, went to Egypt to be initiated; while Pythagoras, after visiting the Brahmins of India, stopped at an Egyptian sanctuary, and finally was received, according to Iamblicus, at Mount Carmel. Jesus followed the traditional custom, and justified his reticence by quoting the well known precept:

> Give not the sacred things to the dogs,
> Cast not your pearls before the swine,
> Lest these tread them under their feet,
> And lest the dogs turn and rend you.

Certain ancient writings — known, for that matter, to the bibliophiles — personify WISDOM; which they represent as emanating from *Ain-Soph*, the Parabrahm of the Jewish Kabbalists, and make it the associate and companion of the manifested Deity. Thence its sacred character with every people. Wisdom is inseparable from divinity. Thus we have the Vedas coming from the mouth of the Hindu "Brahmā" (the *logos*); the name Buddha comes from Budha, "Wisdom," divine intelligence; the Babylonian *Nebo*, the *Thot* of Memphis, *Hermes* of the Greeks, were all gods of esoteric wisdom.

The Greek Athena, Metis and Neitha of the Egyptians, are the prototypes of Sophia-Achamoth, the feminine wisdom of the Gnostics. The Samaritan *Pentateuch* calls the book of Genesis *Akamauth*, or "Wisdom," as also two fragments of very ancient manuscripts, "the Wisdom of Solomon," and "the Wisdom of *Iasous* (Jesus)." The book called *Mashalim* or "Sayings and Proverbs of Solomon," personifies Wisdom by calling it "the helper of the (Logos) creator," in the following terms, (literally translated):

I (*a*) HV (*e*) H* possessed me from the beginning.
But the first emanation in the eternities,
I appeared from all antiquity, the primordial.-
From the first day of the earth;
I was born before the great abyss.
And when there were neither springs nor waters,
When he traced the circle on the face of the deep,
I was with him Amun.
I was his delight, day by day.

This is exoteric, like all that has reference to the personal gods of the nations. The INFINITE cannot be known to our reason, which can only distinguish and define; — but we can always conceive the abstract idea thereof, thanks to that faculty higher than our reason, — *intuition*, or the spiritual instinct of which I have spoken. Only the great initiates, who have the rare power of throwing themselves into the state of Samadhi, — which can be but imperfectly translated by the word *ecstacy*, a state in which one ceases to be the conditioned and personal "I," and becomes one with the ALL, — only those can boast of having been in contact with the *infinite*: but no more than other mortals can they describe that state in words....

* JHVH, or Jahveh (Jehovah) is the *Tetragrammaton*, consequently the Emanated Logos and the creator; the ALL, without beginning or end, — AIN-SOPH — not being able to create, nor wishing to create, in its quality of the ABSOLUTE.

III

Do our benevolent critics always know what they are laughing at? Have they the smallest idea of the work which is being performed in the world and the mental changes that are being brought about by that Theosophy at which they smile? The progress already due to our literature is evident, and, thanks to the untiring labours of a certain number of Theosophists, it is becoming recognized even by the blindest. There are not a few who are persuaded that Theosophy will be the philosophy and the law, if not the religion of the future. The party of reaction, captivated by the *dolce far niente* of conservatism, feel all this, hence come the hatred and persecution which call in criticism to their aid. But criticism, inaugurated by Aristotle, has fallen far away from its primitive standard. The ancient philosophers, those sublime ignoramuses as regards modern civilization, when they criticised a system or a work, did so with impartiality, and with the sole object of amending and improving that with which they found fault. First they studied the subject, and then they analyzed it. It was a service rendered, and was recognized and accepted as such by both parties. Does modern criticism always conform to that golden rule? It is very evident that it does not. . . .

The metaphysicians who for centuries have studied the phenomena of being in their first principles, and who smile pityingly when they listen to the wanderings of Theosophy, would be greatly embarrassed to explain to us the philosophy or even the cause of dreams. Which of them can tell us why all the mental operations, — except reasoning, which faculty alone finds itself suspended and paralysed, — go on while we dream with as much activity and energy as when we are awake? The disciple of Herbert Spencer would send anyone to the biologist who squarely asked him that question. But he, for whom digestion is the *alpha* and *omega* of every dream, — like hysteria, that great Proteus with a thousand forms, which is present in every psychic phenomenon — can by no means satisfy us. Indigestion and hysteria are, in fact, twin sisters, two goddesses, to whom the modern psychologist has raised an altar at which he has constituted himself the officiating priest. But this is his business so long as he does not meddle with the gods of his neighbours. . . .

Dead-letter and theocracy have, however, had their day. The world must move and advance under penalty of stagnation and death. Mental evolution progresses *pari passu* with physical evolution, and both advance towards the ONE TRUTH, — which is the heart of the system of Humanity, as evolution is the blood. Let the circulation stop for one moment and the heart stops at the same time, and it is all up with the human machine! And it is the servants of Christ who wish to kill, or at least paralyze, the Truth by the blows of a club which is called "the letter that kills!" But the end is nigh. That which Coleridge said of political despotism applies also to religious. The Church, unless she withdraws her heavy hand, which weighs like a nightmare on the oppressed bosoms of millions of believers whether they resent it or not, and whose reason remains paralyzed in the clutch of superstition, the ritualistic Church is sentenced *to give up its place to Religion* and — to die. Soon it will have but a choice. For once the people become enlightened about the truth which it hides with so much care, one of two things will happen, the Church will either perish *by* the people; or else, if the masses are left in ignorance and in slavery to the dead letter, it will perish *with* the people. . . .

I say it again; it is only theosophy, well understood, that can save the world from despair, by reproducing social and religious reform — a task once before accomplished in history, by Gautama, the Buddha: a peaceful reform, without one drop of blood spilt, each one remaining in the faith of his fathers if he so chooses. To do this he will only have to reject the parasitic plants of human fabrication, which at the present moment are choking all religions and churches in the world. Let him accept but the essence, which is the same in all: that is to say, the spirit which gives life to man in whom it resides, and renders him immortal. Let every man inclined to go on find his ideal, — a star before him to guide him. Let him follow it, without ever deviating from his path; and he is almost certain to reach the Beacon-light of life — the TRUTH: no matter whether he seeks for and finds it at the bottom of a cradle or of a well.

IV

Theosophy, we say, comes to us from the extreme East, as did the Theosophy of Plotinus and Iamblicus and even the mysteries of ancient Egypt. Do not Homer and Herodotus tell us, in fact, that the ancient Egyptians were "Ethiopians of the East," *who came from Lanka or Ceylon,* according to their descriptions? For it is generally acknowledged that the people whom those two authors call *Ethiopians of the East* were no other than a colony of very dark skinned Aryans, the Dravidians of Southern India, who took an already existing civilization with them to Egypt. This migration occurred during the prehistoric ages which Baron Bunson calls *pre-Menite* (before Menes) but which ages have a history of their own, to be found in the ancient annals of Kalouka Batta. Besides, and apart from the esoteric teachings, which are not divulged to a mocking public, the historical researches of Colonel Vans Kennedy, the great rival in India of Dr. Wilson as a Sanskritist, show us that pre-Assyrian Babylonia was the home of Brahmanism, and of the Sanskrit as a sacerdotal language. We know also, if Exodus is to be believed, that Egypt had, long before the time of Moses, its diviner, its hierophants and its magicians, that is to say, before the XIX dynasty. Finally Brugsh Bey sees in many of the gods of Egypt, immigrants from beyond the Red Sea — and the great waters of the Indian Ocean.

Whether that be so or not, Theosophy is a descendant in direct line of the great tree of universal GNOSIS, a tree the luxuriant branches of which, spreading over the whole earth like a great canopy, gave shelter at one epoch — which biblical chronology is pleased to call "antediluvian" — to all the temples and to all the nations of the earth. That gnosis represents the aggregate of all the sciences, the accumulated wisdom *(savoir)* of all the gods and demi-gods incarnated in former times upon the earth. There are some who would like to see in these, the fallen angels and the enemy of mankind; these sons of God who, seeing that the daughters of men were beautiful, took them for wives and imparted to them the secrets of heaven and earth. Let them think so. We believe in Avatars and in divine dynasties, in the epoch when there were, in fact, "giants upon the earth," but we altogether repudiate the idea of "fallen angels" and of Satan and his army.

"What then is your religion or your belief?" we are asked. "What is your favourite study?"

"The TRUTH," we reply. The truth wherever we can find it; for, like Ammonius Saccas, our greatest ambition would be to reconcile the different religious systems, to help each one to find the truth in his own religion, while obliging him to recognize it in that of his neighbour. What does the name signify if the thing itself is essentially the same? Plotinus, Iamblicus and Apollonius of Tyana, had all three, it is said, the wonderful gifts of prophecy, of clairvoyance, and of healing, although belonging to three different schools. Prophecy was an art that was cultivated by the Essenes and the *B'ni Nebim* among the Jews, as well as by the priests of the pagan oracles. Plotinus's disciples attributed miraculous powers to their master; Philostratus has claimed the same for Apollonius while Iamblicus had the reputation of surpassing all the other Eclectics in Theosophic theurgy. Ammonius declared that all moral and practical WISDOM was contained in the books of Thoth or Hermes Trismegistus. But Thoth means "a college," school or assembly, and the works of that name, according to the *Theodidactos*, were identical with the doctrines of the sages of the extreme East. If Pythagoras acquired his knowledge in India (when even now he is mentioned in old manuscripts under the name of Yavanacharya,* the Greek Master), Plato gained his from the books of Thoth-Hermes. How it happened that the younger Hermes, the god of the shepherds,

---

* A term which comes from the words *Yavana* or "the Ionian." And *acharya*, "professor or master."

surnamed "the good shepherd," who presided over divination and clairvoyance became identical with Thoth (or Thot) the deified sage, and the author of the *Book of the Dead,* — the esoteric doctrine only can reveal to Orientalists.

Every country has had its saviours. He who dissipates the darkness of ignorance by the help of the torch of science, thus discovering to us the truth, deserves that title as a mark of our gratitude quite as much as he who saves us from death by healing our bodies. Such an one awakens in our benumbed souls the faculty of distinguishing the true from the false, by kindling a divine flame, hitherto absent, and he has the right to our grateful worship, for he has become our creator. What matters the name or the symbol that personifies the abstract idea, if that idea is always the same and is true! Whether the concrete symbol bears one title or another, whether the saviour in whom we believe has for an earthly name Krishna, Buddha, Jesus or Aesculapius, — also called "the saviour god" Σώτηρ, — we have but to remember one thing: symbols of divine truths were not invented for the amusement of the ignorant; they are the *alpha* and *omega* of philosophic thought.

Theosophy being the way that leads to truth, in every religion, as in every science, occultism is, so to say, the touchstone and universal solvent. It is the thread of Ariadne given by the master to the disciple who ventures into the labyrinth of the mysteries of being; the torch that lights him through the dangerous maze of life, for ever the enigma of the Sphinx. But the light thrown by this torch can be discerned only by the eye of the awakened soul — by our spiritual senses; it blinds the eye of the materialist as the sun blinds that of the owl.

Having neither dogma nor ritual, — these two being but fetters, the material body which suffocates the soul, — we do not employ the "ceremonial magic" of the Western Kabalists; we know its dangers too well to have anything to do with it. . . . The occult sciences are dangerous for him who understands them imperfectly. Any one who gave himself up to their practice by himself, would run the risk of becoming insane; and those who study them would do well to unite in little groups of from three to seven. These groups ought to be uneven in numbers in order to have more power; a group, however little cohesion it possesses, forming a single united body, wherein the senses and perceptions of those who work together complement and mutually help each other, one member supplying to another the quality in which he is wanting, — such a group will always end by becoming a perfect and invincible body. "Union is strength." The moral of the fable of the old man bequeathing to his sons a bundle of sticks which were never to be separated is a truth which will forever remain axiomatic.

V

"The disciples (Lanous) of the law of the Heart of Diamant (magic) will help each other in their lessons. The grammarian will be at the service of him who looks for the soul of the metals (chemist)" etc. — (Catechism of the *Gupta-Vidya*).

The ignorant would laugh if they were told that in the Occult sciences, the alchemist can be useful to the philologist and *vice versa*. They would understand the matter better, perhaps, if they were told that by this substantive (grammarian or philologist), we mean to designate one who makes a study of the universal language of corresponding symbols. . . . All things in nature have correspondences and are mutually interdependent. In its abstract sense, Theosophy is the white ray, from which arise the seven colours of the solar spectrum, each human being assimilating one of these rays to a greater degree than the other six. It follows that seven persons, each imbued with his special ray, can help each other mutually. Having at their service the septenary bundle of rays, they have the seven forces of nature at their command. But it follows also that, to reach that end, the choosing of the seven persons who are to form a group, should be left to an expert, — to an initiate in the science of occult rays. . . .

For, let it be well understood, theosophy has this in common with ordinary science, that it examines the reverse side of every apparent truth. It tests and analyses every fact put forward by physical science, looking only for the essence and the ultimate and occult constitution in every cosmical or physical manifestation, whether in the domain of ethics, intellect, or matter. In a word, Theosophy begins its researches where materialists finish theirs.

"It is then metaphysics that you offer us!" it may be objected, "Why not say so at once."

No, it is not metaphysics, as that term is generally understood, although it plays that part sometimes. The speculations of Kant, of Leibnitz, and of Schopenhauer belong to the domain of metaphysics, as also those of Herbert Spencer. Still, when one studies the latter, one cannot help dreaming of Dame Metaphysics figuring at a *bal masqué* of the Academical Sciences, adorned with a false nose. The metaphysics of Kant and of Leibnitz — as proved by his monads — is above the metaphysics of our days, as a balloon in the clouds is above a pumpkin in the field below. Nevertheless this balloon, however much better it may be than the pumpkin, is too artificial to serve as a vehicle for the truth of the occult sciences. The latter is, perhaps, a goddess too freely uncovered to suit the taste of our savants, so modest. The metaphysics of Kant taught its author, without the help of the present methods or perfected instruments, the identity of the constitution and essence of the sun and the planets; and Kant *affirmed,* when the best astronomers, even during the first half of this century, still *denied.* But this same metaphysics did not succeed in proving to him the true nature of that essence, any more than it has helped modern physics, notwithstanding its noisy hypotheses, to discover that true nature.

Theosophy, therefore, or rather the occult sciences it studies, is something more than simple metaphysics. It is, if I may be allowed to use the double terms, *meta*-metaphysics, *meta*-geometry, etc., etc., or a universal transcendentalism. Theosophy rejects the testimony of the physical senses entirely, if the latter be not based upon that afforded by the psychic and spiritual perceptions. Even in the case of the most highly developed clairvoyance and clairaudience, the *final* testimony of both must be rejected, unless by those terms is signified the φωτός of Iamblicus, or the ecstatic illumination, the ἀγωγή μαντεία of Plotinus and of Porphyry. The same holds good for the physical sciences; the evidence of the reason upon the terrestrial plane, like that of our five senses, should receive the imprimatur of the sixth and seventh senses of the divine ego, before a fact can be accepted by the true occultist. . . .

VI

Theosophy is synonymous with *Gnana-Vidya,* and with the *Brahmā-Vidya** of the Hindus, and again with the *Dzyan* of the trans-Himalayan adepts, the science of the *true* Raj-Yogas, who are much more accessible than one thinks. This science has many schools in the East. But its offshoots are still more numerous, each one having ended by separating itself from the parent stem, — the true Archaic Wisdom, — and varying in its form.

But, while these forms varied, departing further with each generation from the light of truth, the basis of initiatory truths remained always the same. The symbols used to express the same idea may differ, but in their hidden sense they always do express the same idea. Ragon, the most erudite mason of all the "Widow's sons," has said the same. There exists a sacerdotal language, the "mystery language," and unless one knows it well, he cannot go far in the occult sciences. According to Ragon "to build or found a town" meant the same thing as to "found a religion"; therefore, that phrase when it occurs in Homer is equivalent to the expression in the Brahmins, to distribute the "Soma juice."

To learn thoroughly requires a teacher, a *guru*; to succeed by oneself needs more than genius: it demands inspiration like that of Ammonius Saccas. Encouraged in the Church by Clement

---

* The meaning of the word *Vidya* can only be rendered by the Greek term *Gnosis,* the knowledge of hidden and spiritual things; or again, the knowledge of Brahm, that is to say, of the God that contains all the gods.

of Alexandria and by Athenagoras, protected by the learned men of the synagogue and of the academy, and adored by the Gentiles, "he learned the *language of the mysteries* by teaching the common origin of all religions, and a common religion." To do this, he had only to teach according to the ancient canons of Hermes which Plato and Pythagoras had studied so well, and from which they drew their respective philosophies. Can we be surprised if, finding in the first verses of the gospel according to St. John the same doctrines that are contained in the three systems of philosophy above mentioned, he concluded with every show of reason that the intention of the great Nazarene was to restore the sublime science of ancient wisdom in all its primitive integrity? We think as did Ammonius. The biblical narrations and the histories of the gods have only two possible explanations: either they are great and profound allegories, illustrating universal truths, or else they are fables of no use but to put the ignorant to sleep.

Therefore the allegories, — Jewish as well as Pagan, — contain all the truths that can only be understood by him who knows the mystical language of antiquity. Let us see what is said on this subject by one of our most distinguished Theosophists, a fervent Platonist and a Hebraist, who knows his Greek and Latin like his mother tongue, Professor Alexander Wilder,* of New York:

> The root idea of the Neo-Platonists was the existence of one only and supreme Essence. This was the Diu, or 'Lord of the Heavens' of the Aryan nations, identical with the *Iaω (Iao)* of the Chaldeans and Hebrews, the *Iabe* of the Samaritans, the *Tiu* or *Tuiseo* of the Norwegians, the *Duw* of the ancient tribes of Britain, the *Zeus* of those of Thrace, and the *Jupiter* of the Romans. It was the *Being* — (non-Being), the *Facit,* one and supreme. It is from it that all other beings proceeded *by emanation.* The moderns have, it seems, substituted for this their theory of *evolution.* Perchance

---

* The first Vice-President of the Theosophical Society when it was founded.

some day a wiser man than they will combine these systems in a single one. The names of these different divinities seem often to have been invented with little or no regard to their etymological meaning, but chiefly on account of some particular mystical signification attached to the numerical value of the letters employed in their orthography.

This *numerical* signification is one of the branches of the *mystery language,* or the ancient sacerdotal language. This was taught in the "Lesser Mysteries," but the language itself was reserved for the high initiates alone. The candidate must have come victorious out of the terrible trials of the Greater Mysteries before receiving instruction in it. That is why Ammonius Saccas, like Pythagoras, obliged his disciples to take an oath never to divulge the higher doctrines to any one to whom the preliminary ones had not already been imparted, and who, therefore, was not ready for initiation. Another sage, who preceded him by three centuries, did the same by his disciples, in saying to them that he spoke "in similes" (or parables) "because to you it is given to know the mysteries of the kingdom of Heaven, but to them it is not given . . . because in seeing they see not, and in hearing they hear not, neither do they understand." . . .

"Le Phare de L'Inconnu"   H. P. BLAVATSKY
La Revue Theosophique, May, 1885

THINGS COMMON TO CHRISTIANITY AND THEOSOPHY

That the Theosophical Society is not opposed to Christianity in either its dogmatic or pure form is easily demonstrated. Our constitution forbids it and the second object of the Society does also. The laws of our body say that there shall be no crusade against any religion, tacitly excepting, of course, the few degraded and bestial religions now in the world; the second object provides for a full and free study of all religions without bias and without hatred or sectarianism. And our history also, offering to view branch societies all over the world composed of Christians, refutes the charge that the Society as such is opposed to Christianity. One instance is enough, that of the well-known Scottish Lodge, which states in its printed Transactions No. IX, "Theosophists who are Christians (and such are the majority of the Scottish Lodge) . . . Therefore Christians who are sincere and who know what Theosophy means must be Theosophists. . . ." If members of this Society have said to the contrary it has been from ignorance and a careless thinking, for on the same ground we should also be opposed to all other religions which have any forms, and both Brahmanism and Buddhism have as much of formalism, as has Christianity. Generally speaking, then, the Society is not and cannot be opposed to Christianity, while it may lead to a denial of some of the men-made theories of that Church.

But that is no more than branches of Christianity have always been doing, nor is it as much a danger to formal Christianity as the new standards of criticism which have crept into the Church.

Nor can it be either that Theosophy as a whole is opposed to Christianity, inasmuch as Theosophy is and must be the one truth underlying all religions that have ever been among men. A calm and sincere examination of all the world's religions reveals the fact that in respect to ethics, in respect to laws, in respect to cosmogony and cosmology, the other religious books of the world are the same in most respects as those of the Christians, and that the distinguishing difference between the latter's religion and the others is that it asserts an exclusiveness for itself and a species of doctrinal intolerance not found in the rest.

If we take the words and the example of Jesus as the founder of Christianity, it is at once seen that there is no opposition at all between that form of religion and Theosophy. Indeed, there is the completest agreement. New ethics are not brought forward by Theosophy, nor can they be, as ethics of the right sort must always be the same. In his sermons and sayings are to be found the ethics given out by Buddha and by all other great teachers of all time. These cannot be altered, even though they hold up to weak mortals an ideal that is very difficult to live up to and sometimes impossible to realize in daily life. That these rules of conduct laid down by Jesus are admittedly hard to follow is shown in the behavior of Christian states toward each other and in the declarations of their high prelates that the religion of Jesus cannot be the basis for diplomatic relations nor for the state government. Hence we find that the refuge from all this adopted by the theologian is in the statement that, although other and older religions had moral truth and similar ethics to those of Jesus, the Christian religion is the only one wherein the founder asserted that he was not merely a teacher from God but was also at the same time God himself; that is, that prior to Jesus a great deal of good was taught, but God did not see fit until the time of Jesus to come down among men into incarnation. Necessarily such a declaration would seem to have the effect of breeding intolerance from the high and exclusive nature of the claim made. But an examination of Brahmanism shows that Rama was also God incarnate among men, though there the doctrine did not arouse the same sum of intolerance among its believers. So it must be true that it is not always a necessary consequence of such a belief that aggressive and exclusive intolerance will grow up.

The beliefs and teachings of Christianity are not all supportable by the words of Jesus, but his doctrines are at all times in accord with Theosophy. There is certainly a wide difference between the command of Jesus to be poor and have neither staff nor money and the fact of the possession by the Church of vast sums of money and immense masses of property, and with the drawing of high salaries by prelates, and with the sitting of prelates among the rulers of the earth upon thrones, and in the going to war and the levying of taxes by the Pope and by other religious heads. The gathering of tithes and enforcement of them by law and by imprisonment at the instance of the Protestant clergy are not at all consistent with the words of Jesus. But all of the foregoing inconsistent matters are a part of present Christianity, and if in those respects a difference from or opposition to them should seem to arise from Theosophical teachings we must admit it, but cannot be blamed. If we go back to the times of the early Christians and compare that Christianity with the present form, we see that opposition by Theosophy could hardly be charged, but that the real opposition then would be between that early form of the religion and its present complexion. It has been altered so much that the two are scarcely recognizable as the same. This is so much so that there exists a Christian sect today called "Early Christian."

Every one has at all times a right to object to theological interpretations if they are wrong, or if they distort the original teaching or introduce new notions. In this respect there is a criticism by Theosophy and Theosophists. But thinkers in the world not members of this Society and not leaning to Theosophy do the same thing. Huxley and Tyndall and Darwin and hosts of others took ground that by mere force of truth and fact went against theological views. Galileo also, seeing that the earth was round and moved, said so, but the theologian, thinking that such belief tended to destroy the power of the church and to upset biblical theories, made him recant at the risk of his liberty and life. If the old views of theology were still in force with the state behind them, the triumphs of science would have been few and we might still be imagining the earth to be flat and square and the sun revolving about it.

Theosophical investigation discloses to the student's view the fact that in all ages there have appeared great teachers of religion and that they all had two methods of instruction. One, or that for the masses of people, was plain and easy to understand; it was of ethics, of this life and of the next, of immortality and love; it always gave out the Golden Rule. Such a teacher was Buddha, and there can be no controversy on the fact that he died centuries before the birth of Jesus. He declared his religion to be that of love. Others did the same. Jesus came and taught ethics and love, with the prominent exception of his prophecy that he came to bring a sword and division as recorded in the Gospels. There is also an incident which accents a great difference between him and Buddha; it is the feast where he drank wine and also made some for others to drink. In regard to this matter, Buddha always taught that all intoxicating liquors were to be rigidly abstained from. The second method was the secret or Esoteric one, and that Jesus also used. We find his disciples asking him why he always used easy parables with the people, and he replied that to the disciples he taught the mysteries, or the more recondite matters of religion. This is the same as prevailed with the older saints. Buddha also had his private teachings to certain disciples. He even made a distinction among his personal followers, making classes in their ranks, to one of which he gave the simplest of rules, to the other the complex and difficult. So he must have pursued the ancient practise of having two sets of teachings, and this must have been a consequence of his education.

At twelve years of age he came to the temple and disputed with the learned rabbis on matters of law. Thus he must have known the law; and what that law was and is it is necessary to ask. It was the law of Moses, full of the most technical and abstruse things, and not all to be found in the simple words of the books. The Hebrew books are a vast mine of cypher designedly so constructed, and that should be borne in mind by all students. It ought to be known to Christians, but is not, as they prefer not to go into the mysteries of the Jews. But Jesus knew it. His remark that "not one jot or tittle of the law would pass" shows this.

Most people read this simply as rhetoric, but it is not so. The jots and tittles are a part of the books and go to make up the cypher of the Cabala or the hidden meaning of the law. This is a vast system of itself, and was not invented after the time of Jesus. Each letter is also a number, and thus every word can be and is, according to a well-known rule, turned into some other word or into a number. Thus one name will be a part of a supposed historical story, but when read by the cypher it becomes a number of some cycle or event or a sign of the Zodiac or something else quite different from the mere letters. Thus the name of Adam is composed of three consonants, A, D, and M. These mean by the system of the cypher respectively, "Adam, David, and Messiah." The Jews also held that Adam for his first sin would have to and did reincarnate as David and would later come as Messiah. Turning to Revelations we find traces of the same system in the remarks about the numbers of the beast and the man. The Cabala or hidden law is of the highest importance, and as the Christian religion is a Hebraic one it cannot be properly studied or understood without the aid given by the secret teaching. And the Cabala is not dead nor unknown, but has many treatises written on it in different languages. By using it, we will find in the Old Testament and in the records of Jesus a complete and singular agreement with Theosophy.

Examine for instance, the Theosophical teachings that there is a secret or esoteric doctrine, and the doctrine of inability of man to comprehend God. This is the Brahmanical doctrine of the unapproachableness of Parabrahm. In Exodus there is a story which to the profane is absurd, of God telling Moses that he could not see Him. It is in Exodus xxxiii, 20, where God says Moses could see him from behind only. Treat this by the rule of the Cabala and it is plain, but read it on the surface and you have nonsense. In Exodus iii, 14, God says that his name is "I am that I am." This is AHYH ASHR AHYH, which has to be turned into its numerical value, as each letter is also a number. Thus A is 1, H is 5, Y is 10, H is 5. There being two words the same, they add up 42. The second word is A, 1; SH, 300; R, 200 making 501,

which added to 42 gives 543 as the number of "I am that I am."
Now Moses by the same system makes 345 or the reverse of the
other, by which the Cabala shows God meant Moses to know
God by his reverse or Moses himself. To some this may appear
fanciful, but as it is the method on which these old books are
constructed it must be known in order to understand what is not
clear and to remove from the Christian books the well-sustained
charge of absurdity and sometimes injustice and cruelty shown
on their face. So instead of God's being made ridiculous by
attributing to him such a remark as that Moses could only "see
his hinder parts," we perceive that under the words is a deep
philosophical tenet corresponding to those of Theosophy, that
Parabrahm is not to be known and that Man is a small copy of
God through which in some sense or in the reverse we may see
God.

For the purposes of this discussion along the line of
comparison we will have to place Christianity on one side and
put on the other as representing the whole body of Theosophy,
so far as revealed, the other various religions of the world, and
see what, if anything, is common between them. First we see
that Christianity, being the younger, has borrowed its doctrines
from other religions. It is now too enlightened an age to say,
as the Church did when Abbé Huc brought back his account of
Buddhism from Tibet, that either the devil or wicked men
invented the old religions so as to confuse and confute the
Christian. Evidently, no matter how done, the system of the
Christian is mixed Aryan and Jewish. This could not be otherwise,
since Jesus was a Jew, and his best disciples and the others who
came after like Paul were of the same race and faith. The early
Fathers also, living as they did in Eastern lands, got their ideas
from what they found about them.

Next a very slight examination will disclose the fact that the
ritual of the Christian Church is also borrowed. Taken from all
nations and religions, not one part of it is either of this age or of
the Western hemisphere. The Brahmans have an extensive and

elaborate ritual, and so have the Buddhists. The rosary, long supposed by Catholics to be a thing of their own, has existed in Japan for uncounted years, and much before the West had any civilization the Brahman had his form of rosary. The Roman Catholic Christian sees the priest ring the bell at a certain part of the Mass, and the old Brahman knows that when he is praying to God he must also ring a bell to be found in every house as well as in the temple. This is very like what Jesus commanded. He said that prayer must be in secret, that is, where no one can hear; the Brahman rings the small bell so that even if ears be near they shall not hear any words but only the sound of the bell. The Christian has images of virgin and child; the same thing is to be found in Egyptian papyri and in carved statues of India made before the Christian came into existence. Indeed, all the ritual and observance of the Christian churches may be found in the mass of other religions with which for the moment we are making a rough comparison.

Turning now to doctrine, we find again complete agreement with the dogmatic part of Christianity in these older religions. Salvation by faith is taught by some priests. That is the old Brahmanical theory, but with the difference that the Brahman one calls for faith in God as the means, the end, and the object of faith. The Christian adds faith in the son of God. A form of Japanese Buddhism said to be due to Amitabha says that one may be saved by complete faith in Amita Buddha, and that even if one prays but three times to Amita he will be saved in accordance with a vow made by that teacher. Immortality of soul has ever been taught by the Brahmans. Their whole system of religion and of cosmogony is founded on the idea of soul and of the spiritual nature of the universe. Jesus and St. Paul taught the unity of spiritual beings — or men — when they said that heaven and the spirit of God were in us, and the doctrine of Unity is one of the oldest and most important of the Brahmanical scheme. The possibility of arriving at perfection by means of religion and science combined so that a man becomes godlike — or the doctrine of Adepts and Mahatmas as found in Theosophy — is common to Buddhism and Brahmanism, and is not contrary to the teachings of Jesus. He said to his disciples that they could if they would do even greater works — or "miracles" — than he did. To do these works one has to have great knowledge and power. The doctrine assumes the perfectibility of humanity and destroys the theory of original sin; but far from being out of concordance with the religion of Jesus, it is in perfect accord. He directed his followers to be perfect even as the Father in heaven is. They could not come up to that command by any possibility unless man has the power to reach to that high state. The command is the same as is found in the ancient Aryan system. Hence, then, whether we look broadly over the field at mere ritual dogma or at ethics, we find the most complete accord between Theosophy and true Christianity.

But now taking up some important doctrines put forward by members of the Theosophical Society under their right of free investigation and free speech, what do we discover? Novelty, it is true, to the mind of the western man half-taught about his own religion, but nothing that is uncommon to Christianity. Those doctrines may be, for the present, such as Reincarnation or rebirth over and over again for the purpose of discipline and gain, for reward, for punishment, and for enlargement of character; next Karma, or exact justice or compensation for all thoughts and acts. These two are a part of Christianity, and may be found in the Bible.

Reincarnation has been regarded by some Christian ministers as essential to the Christian religion. Dr. Edward Beecher said he saw its necessity, and the Rev. Wm. Alger has recorded his view to the same effect. If a Christian insists upon belief in Jesus, who came only eighteen centuries ago after millenniums had passed and men had died out of the faith by millions, it will be unjust for them to be condemned for a failure to believe a doctrine they never heard of; hence the Christian may well say that under the law of reincarnation, which was upheld by Jesus, all those who never heard of Jesus will be reborn after his coming in A.D. I, so as to accept the plan of salvation.

In the Gospels we find Jesus referring to this doctrine as if a well established one. When it was broached by the disciples as the possible reason for the punishment by blindness from birth of a man of the time, Jesus did not controvert the doctrine, as he would have done did he see in his wisdom as Son of God that it was pernicious. But at another time he asserted that John the Baptist was the reincarnation of Elias the ancient prophet. This cannot be wiped out of the books, and is a doctrine as firmly fixed in Christianity, though just now out of favor, as is any other. The paper by Prof. Landsberg shows you what Origen, one of the greatest of the Christian Fathers, taught on preëxistence of souls. This theory naturally suggests reincarnation on this earth, for it is more natural to suppose the soul's wanderings to be here until all that life can give has been gained, rather than that the soul should wander among other planets or simply fall to this abruptly, to be as suddenly raised up to heaven or thrown down to hell.

The next great doctrine is Karma. This is the religion of salvation by works as opposed to faith devoid of works. It is one of the prime doctrines of Jesus. By "by their works ye shall know them," he must have meant that faith without works is dead. The meaning of *Karma* literally is "works," and the Hindus apply it not only to the operations of nature and of the great laws of nature in connection with man's reward and punishment, but also to all the different works that man can perform. St. James insists on the religion of works. He says that true religion is to visit the fatherless and the widows and to keep oneself unspotted from the world. St. Matthew says we shall be judged for every act, word, and thought. This alone is possible under the doctrine of Karma. The command of Jesus to refrain from judgment or we should ourselves be judged is a plain statement of Karma, as is, too, the rest of the verse saying that what we mete out shall be given back to us. St. Paul, following this, distinctly states the doctrine thus: "Brethren, be not deceived; God is not mocked; for whatsoever a man soweth, that also shall he reap." The word "whatsoever" includes every act and thought, and permits no escape from the consequences of any act. A clearer statement of the law of Karma as applied to daily life could hardly be made. Again, going to Revelations, the last words in the Christian book, we read all through it that the last judgment proceeds on the works — in other words, on the Karma — of men. It distinctly asserts that in the vision, as well as in the messages to the Churches, judgment passes for works.

We therefore must conclude that the religion of Jesus is in complete accord with the chief doctrines of Theosophy; it is fair to assume that even the most recondite of theosophical theories would not have been opposed by him. Our discussion must have led us to the conclusion that the religion of Karma, the practise of good works, is that in which the religion of Jesus agrees with Theosophy, and that alone thereby will arrive the longed-for day when the great ideal of Universal Brotherhood will be realized, and will furnish the common ground on which all faiths may stand and from which every nation may work for the good and the perfection of the human family.

Paper read before   WILLIAM QUAN JUDGE
Aryan (New York)
Theosophical Society
1894

THE HERO IN MAN

There sometimes comes on us a mood of strange reverence for people and things which in less contemplative hours we hold to be unworthy; and in such moments we may set side by side the head of the Christ and the head of an outcast, and there is an equal radiance around each, which makes of the darker face a shadow and is itself a shadow around the head of light. We feel a fundamental unity of purpose in their presence here, and would as willingly pay homage to the one who has fallen as to him who has become a master of life. I know that immemorial order decrees that the laurel crown be given only to the victor, but in these moments I speak of a profound intuition changes the decree and sets the aureole on both alike.

We feel such deep pity for the fallen that there must needs be a justice in it, for these diviner feelings are wiser in themselves and do not vaguely arise. They are lights from the Father. A justice lies in uttermost pity and forgiveness, even when we seem to ourselves to be most deeply wronged, or why is it that the awakening of resentment or hate brings such swift contrition?

We are ever self-condemned, and the dark thought which went forth in us brooding revenge, when suddenly smitten by the light, withdraws and hides within itself in awful penitence. In asking myself why is it that the meanest are safe from our condemnation when we sit on the true seat of judgment in the heart, it seemed to me that their shield was the sense we have of a nobility hidden in them under the cover of ignoble things; that their present darkness was the result of some too weighty heroic labor undertaken long ago by the human spirit, that it was the consecration of past purpose which played with such a tender light about their ruined lives, and it was more pathetic because this nobleness was all unknown to the fallen, and the heroic cause of so much pain was forgotten in life's prison-house.

While feeling the service to us of the great ethical ideals which have been formulated by men, I think that the idea of justice intellectually conceived tends to beget a certain hardness of heart. It is true that men have done wrong — hence their pain; but back of all this there is something infinitely soothing, a light that does not wound, which says no harsh thing, even although the darkest of the spirits turns to it in its agony, for the darkest of human spirits has still around him this first glory which shines from a deeper being within, whose history may be told as the legend of the Hero in Man.

Among the many immortals with whom ancient myth peopled the spiritual spheres of humanity are some figures which draw to themselves a more profound tenderness than the rest. Not Aphrodite rising in beauty from the faery foam of the first seas, not Apollo with sweetest singing, laughter, and youth, not the wielder of the lightning could exact the reverence accorded to the lonely Titan chained on the mountain, or to that bowed figure heavy with the burden of the sins of the world; for the brighter divinities had no part in the labour of man, no such intimate relation with the wherefore of his own existence so full of struggle. The more radiant figures are prophecies to him of his destiny, but the Titan and the Christ are a revelation of his more immediate state; their giant sorrows companion his own, and in contemplating them he awakens what is noblest in his own nature; or, in other words, in understanding their divine heroism he understands himself. For this in truth it seems to me to mean: all knowledge is a revelation of the self to the self, and our deepest comprehension of the seemingly apart divine is also our farthest inroad to self-knowledge; Prometheus, Christ, are in every heart; the story of one is the story of all; the Titan and the Crucified are humanity.

If, then, we consider them as representing the human spirit and disentangle from the myths their meaning, we shall find that whatever reverence is due to that heroic love, which descended from heaven for the redeeming of a lower nature, must be paid to every human being. Christ is incarnate in all humanity. Prometheus is bound for ever within us. They are the same. They are a host, and the divine incarnation was not spoken of one, but of all those who, descending into the lower world, tried to change it into the divine image, and to wrest out of chaos a kingdom for the empire of light. The angels saw below them in chaos a senseless rout blind with elemental passion, for ever warring with discordant cries which broke in upon the world of divine beauty; and that the pain might depart, they grew rebellious in the Master's peace, and descending to earth the angelic lights were crucified in men; leaving so radiant worlds, such a light of beauty, for earth's gray twilight filled with tears, that through this elemental life might breathe the starry music brought from Him. If the "Foreseer" be a true name for the Titan, it follows that in the host which he represents was a light which well foreknew all the dark paths of its journey; foreseeing the bitter struggle with a hostile nature, but foreseeing perhaps a gain, a distant glory o'er the hills of sorrow, and that chaos, divine and transformed, with only gentle breathing, lit up by the Christ-soul of the universe. There is a transforming power in the thought itself: we can no longer condemn the fallen, they who laid aside their thrones of ancient power, their spirit ecstasy and beauty on such a mission. Perhaps those who sank lowest did so to raise a greater burden, and of these most fallen it may in the hour of their resurrection be said, "The last shall be first."

So, placing side by side the head of the outcast with the head of Christ, it has this equal beauty — with as bright a glory it sped from the Father in ages past on its redeeming labour. Of his present darkness what shall we say? "He is altogether dead in sin?" Nay, rather with tenderness forbear, and think the foreseeing spirit has taken its own dread path to mastery; that that which foresaw the sorrow foresaw also beyond it a greater joy and a mightier existence, when it would rise again in a new robe, woven out of the treasure hidden in the deep of its submergence, and shine at last like the stars of the morning triumphant among the sons of God.

II

Our deepest life is when we are alone. We think most truly, love best, when isolated from the outer world in that mystic abyss we call soul. Nothing external can equal the fullness of these moments. We may sit in the blue twilight with a friend, or bend together by the hearth, half whispering, or in a silence populous with loving thoughts mutually understood; then we may feel happy and at peace, but it is only because we are lulled by a semblance to deeper intimacies. When we think of a friend and the loved one draws nigh, we sometimes feel half-pained, for we touched something in our solitude which the living presence shut out; we seem more apart, and would fain wave them away and cry, "Call me not forth from this; I am no more a spirit if I leave my throne." But these moods, though lit up by intuitions of the true, are too partial, they belong too much to the twilight of the heart, they have too dreamy a temper to serve us well in life. We would wish rather for our thoughts a directness such as belongs to the messengers of the gods, swift, beautiful, flashing presences bent on purposes well understood.

What we need is that this interior tenderness shall be elevated into seership, that what in most is only yearning or blind love shall see clearly its way and hope. To this end we have to observe more intently the nature of the interior life. We find, indeed, that it is not a solitude at all, but dense with multitudinous being: instead of being alone we are in the thronged highways of existence. For our guidance when entering here many words of warning have been uttered, laws have been outlined, and beings full of wonder, terror, and beauty described. Yet there is a spirit in us deeper than our intellectual being which I think of as the Hero in man, who feels the nobility of its place in the midst of all this, and who would fain equal the greatness of perception with deeds as great. The weariness and sense of futility which often falls upon the mystic after much thought is due to this, that he has not recognized that he must be worker as well as seer, that here he has duties demanding a more sustained endurance, just as the inner life is so much vaster and more intense than the life he has left behind.

Now the duties which can be taken up by the soul are exactly those which it feels most inadequate to perform when acting as an embodied being. What shall be done to quiet the heart-cry of the world: how answer the dumb appeal for help we so often divine below eyes that laugh? It is the saddest of all sorrows to think that pity with no hands to heal, that love without a voice to speak should helplessly heap their pain upon pain while earth shall endure. But there is a truth about sorrow which I think may make it seem not so hopeless. There are fewer barriers than we think: there is, in truth, an inner alliance between the soul who would fain give and the soul who is in need. Nature has well provided that not one golden ray of all our thoughts is sped ineffective through the dark; not one drop of the magical elixirs love distils is wasted. Let us consider how this may be. There is a habit we nearly all have indulged in. We weave little stories in our minds, expending love and pity upon the imaginary beings we have created, and I have been led to think that many of these are not imaginary, that somewhere in the world beings are living just in that way, and we merely reform and live over again in our life the story of another life. Sometimes these far-away intimates assume so vivid a shape, they come so near with their appeal for sympathy that the pictures are unforgettable; and the more I ponder over them the more it seems to me that they often convey the actual need of some soul whose cry for comfort has gone out into the vast, perhaps to meet with an answer, perhaps to hear only silence. I will supply an instance. I see a child, a curious, delicate little thing, seated on the doorstep of a house. It is an alley in some great city, and there is a gloom of evening and vapor over the sky. I see the child is bending over the path; he is picking cinders and arranging them, and as I ponder I become aware that he is laying down in gritty lines the walls of a house, the mansion of his dream. Here spread along the pavement are large rooms, these for his friends, and a tiny room in the centre, that is his own. So his thought plays. Just then I catch a glimpse of the corduroy trousers of a passing workman, and a heavy boot crushes through the cinders. I feel the pain in the child's heart as he shrinks back, his little lovelit house of dreams all rudely shattered. Ah, poor child, building the City Beautiful out of a few cinders, yet nigher, truer in intent than many a stately, gold-rich palace reared by princes, thou wert not forgotten by that mighty spirit who lives through the falling of empires, whose home has been in many a ruined heart. Surely it was to bring comfort to hearts like thine that that most noble of all meditations was ordained by the Buddha.

> *He lets his mind pervade one quarter of the world with thoughts of Love, and so the second, and so the third, and so the fourth. And thus the whole wide world, above, below, around, and everywhere, does he continue to pervade with heart of Love far-reaching, grown great and beyond measure.*

That love, though the very fairy breath of life, should by itself, and so imparted have a sustaining power some may question, not those who have felt the sunlight fall from distant friends who think of them; but, to make clearer how it seems to me to act, I say that love, Eros, is a being. It is more than a power of the soul, though it is that also; it has universal life of its own, and just as the dark heaving waters do not know what jewel lights they reflect with blinding radiance, so the soul, partially absorbing and feeling the ray of Eros within it, does not know that often a part of its nature nearer to the sun of love shines with a brilliant light to other eyes than its own. Many people move unconscious of their own charm, unknowing of the beauty and power they seem to others to impart. It is some past attainment of the soul, a jewel won in some old battle which it may have forgotten, but none the less this gleams on its tiara, and the star-flame inspires others to hope and victory.

If it is true here that many exert a spiritual influence they are unconscious of, it is still truer of the spheres within. Once the soul has attained to any possession like love, or persistent will, or faith, or a power of thought, it comes into spiritual contact with others who are struggling for these very powers. The attainment of any of these means that the soul is able to absorb and radiate some of the diviner elements of being. The soul may or may not be aware of the position it is placed in or its new duties, but yet that Living Light, having found a way into the being of any one person, does not rest there, but sends its rays and extends its influence on and on to illumine the darkness of another nature. So it comes that there are ties which bind us to people other than those whom we meet in our everyday life. I think they are most real ties, most important to understand, for if we let our lamp go out, some far away who had reached out in the dark and felt a steady will, a persistent hope, a compassionate love, may reach out once again in an hour of need, and finding no support may give way and fold the hands in despair. Often we allow gloom to overcome us and so hinder the bright rays in their passage; but would we do it so often if we thought that perhaps a sadness which besets us, we do not know why, was caused by some one drawing nigh to us for comfort, whom our lethargy might make feel still more his helplessness, while our courage, our faith might cause "our light to shine in some other heart which as yet has no light of its own"?

III

The night was wet: and, as I was moving down the streets, my mind was also journeying on a way of its own, and the things which were bodily present before me were no less with me in my unseen traveling. Every now and then a transfer would take place, and some of the moving shadows in the street would begin walking about in the clear interior light. The children of the city, crouched in the doorways or racing through the hurrying multitude and flashing lights, began their elfin play again in my heart; and that was because I had heard these tiny outcasts shouting with glee. I wondered if the glitter and shadow of such sordid things were thronged with magnificence and mystery for those who were unaware of a greater light and deeper shade which made up the romance and fascination of my own life. In imagination I narrowed myself to their ignorance, littleness, and youth, and seemed for a moment to flit amid great uncomprehended beings and a dim wonderful city of palaces.

Then another transfer took place, and I was pondering anew, for a face I had seen flickering through the warm wet mist haunted me; it entered into the realm of the interpreter, and I was made aware by the pale cheeks and by the close-shut lips of pain, and by some inward knowledge, that there the Tree of Life was beginning to grow, and I wondered why it is that it always springs up through a heart in ashes; I wondered also if that which springs up, which in itself is an immortal joy, has knowledge that its shoots are piercing through such anguish; or, again, if it was the piercing of the shoots which caused the pain, and if every throb of the beautiful flame darting upward to blossom meant the perishing of some more earthly growth which had kept the heart in shadow.

Seeing too how many thoughts spring up from such a simple thing, I questioned whether that which started the impulse had any share in the outcome, and if these musings of mine in any way affected their subject. I then began thinking about those secret ties on which I have speculated before, and in the darkness my heart grew suddenly warm and glowing, for I had chanced upon one of these shining imaginations which are the wealth of those who travel upon the hidden ways. In describing that which comes to us all at once, there is a difficulty in choosing between what is first and what is last to say; but, interpreting as best I can, I seemed to behold the onward movement of a Light, one among many lights, all living, throbbing, now dim with perturbations and now again clear, and all subtly woven together, outwardly in some more shadowy shining, and inwardly in a greater fire, which, though it was invisible, I knew to be the Lamp of the World. This Light which I beheld I felt to be a human soul, and these perturbations which dimmed it were its struggles and passionate longing for something, and that was for a more brilliant shining of the light within itself. It was in love with its own beauty, enraptured by its own lucidity; and I saw that as these things were more beloved they grew paler, for this light is the light which the Mighty Mother has in her heart for her children, and she means that it shall go through each one unto all, and whoever restrains it in himself is himself shut out; not that the great heart has ceased in its love for that soul, but that the soul has shut itself off from influx, for every imagination of man is the opening or the closing of a door to the divine world; now he is solitary, cut off, and, seemingly to himself, on the desert and distant verge of things; and then his thought throws open the swift portals, he hears the chant of the seraphs in his heart, and he is made luminous by the lighting of a sudden aureole. This soul which I watched seemed to have learned at last the secret love; for, in the anguish begotten by its loss, it followed the departing glory in penitence to the inmost shrine, where it ceased altogether; and because it seemed utterly lost and hopeless of attainment and capriciously denied to the seeker, a profound pity arose in the soul for those who, like it, were seeking, but still in hope, for they had not come to the vain end of their endeavors. I understood that such pity is the last of the precious essences which make up the elixir of immortality, and when it is poured into the cup it is ready for drinking. And so it was with this soul which grew brilliant with the passage of the eternal light through its new purity of self-oblivion, and joyful in the comprehension of the mystery of the secret love, which, though it has been declared many times by the greatest of teachers among men, is yet never known truly unless the Mighty Mother has herself breathed it in the heart.

And now that the soul had divined this secret, the shadowy shining which was woven in bonds of union between it and its fellow-lights grew clearer; and a multitude of these strands were, so it seemed, strengthened and placed in its keeping: along these it was to send the message of the wisdom and the love which were the secret sweetness of its own being. Then a spiritual tragedy began, infinitely more pathetic than the old desolation, because it was brought about by the very nobility of the spirit. This soul, shedding its love like rays of glory, seemed itself the centre of a ring of wounding spears: it sent forth love, and the arrowy response came hate-impelled: it whispered peace, and was answered by the clash of rebellion: and to all this for defense it could only bare more openly its heart that a profounder love from the Mother Nature might pass through upon the rest. I knew this was what a teacher, who wrote long ago, meant when he said: "Put on the whole armor of God," which is love and endurance, for the truly divine children of the Flame are not armed otherwise: and of those protests, sent up in ignorance or rebellion against the whisper of the wisdom, I saw that some melted in the fierce and tender heat of the heart, and there came in their stead a golden response which made closer the ties, and drew these souls upward to an understanding and to share in the overshadowing nature. And this is part of the plan of the Great Alchemist, whereby the red ruby of the heart is transmuted into the tender light of the opal; for the beholding of love made bare acts like the flame of the furnace: and the dissolving passions, through an anguish of remorse, the lightnings of pain, and through an adoring pity, are changed into the image they contemplate, and melt in the ecstasy of self-forgetful love, the spirit which lit the thorn-crowned brows, which perceived only in its last agony the retribution due to its tormentors, and cried out, "Father, forgive them, for they know not what they do."

Now although the love of the few may alleviate the hurt due to the ignorance of the mass, it is not in the power of any one to withstand for ever this warfare; for by the perpetual wounding of the inner nature it is so wearied that the spirit must withdraw from a tabernacle grown too frail to support the increase of light within and the jarring of the demoniac nature without; and at length comes the call which means, for a while, release, and a deep rest in regions beyond the paradise of lesser souls. So, withdrawn into the Divine Darkness, vanished the Light of my dream. And now it seemed as if this wonderful weft of souls intertwining as one being must come to naught; and all those who through the gloom had nourished a longing for the light would stretch out hands in vain for guidance; but that I did not understand the love of the Mother, and that although few, there is no decaying of her heroic brood; for, as the seer of old caught at the mantle of him who went up in the fiery chariot, so another took up the burden and gathered the shining strands together: and to this sequence of spiritual guides there is no ending.

Here I may say that the love of the Mother, which, acting through the burnished will of the hero, is wrought to its highest uses, is in reality everywhere, and pervades with profoundest tenderness the homeliest circumstance of daily life, and there is not lacking, even among the humblest, an understanding of the spiritual tragedy which follows upon every effort of the divine nature bowing itself down in pity to our shadowy sphere; an understanding where the nature of the love is gauged through the extent of the sacrifice and the pain which is overcome. I recall the instance of an old Irish peasant, who, as he lay in hospital wakeful from a grinding pain in the leg, forgot himself in making drawings, rude yet reverently done, of incidents in the life of the Galilean Teacher. One of these which he showed me was a crucifixion, where, amidst much grotesque symbolism, were some tracings which indicated a purely beautiful intuition; the heart of this crucified figure, no less than the brow, was wreathed about with thorns and radiant with light: "For that," said he, "was where he really suffered." When I think of this old man, bringing forgetfulness of his own bodily pain through contemplation of the spiritual suffering of his Master, my memory of him shines with something of the transcendent light he himself perceived, for I feel that some suffering of his own, nobly undergone, had given him understanding, and he had laid his heart in love against the Heart of Many Sorrows, seeing it wounded by unnumbered spears, yet burning with undying love.

Though much may be learned by observance of the superficial life and actions of a spiritual teacher, it is only in the deeper life of meditation and imagination that it can be truly realised; for the soul is a midnight blossom which opens its leaves in dream, and its perfect bloom is unfolded only where another sun shines in another heaven; there it feels what celestial dews descend on it and what influences draw it up to its divine archetype: here in the shadow of earth root intercoils with root, and the finer distinctions of the blossom are not perceived. If we knew also who they really are, who sometimes in silence, and sometimes with the eyes of the world at gaze, take upon them the mantle of teacher, an unutterable awe would prevail: for underneath a bodily presence not in any sense beautiful may burn the glory of some ancient divinity, some hero who has laid aside his sceptre in the enchanted land to rescue old-time comrades fallen into oblivion: or, again, if we had the insight of the simple old peasant into the nature of this enduring love, out of the exquisite and poignant emotions kindled would arise the flame of a passionate love which would endure long aeons of anguish that it might shield, though but for a little, the kingly hearts who may not shield themselves.

But I, too, who write, have launched the rebellious spear, or in lethargy have oft times gone down the great drift numbering myself among those who not being with must needs be against: Therefore I make no appeal; they only may call who stand upon the lofty mountains; but I reveal the thought which arose like a star in my soul with such bright and pathetic meaning, leaving it to you who read to approve and apply it.

The Irish Theosophist   GEORGE WILLIAM RUSSELL
March & July 1897

CHANTS FOR CONTEMPLATION

FROM THE ADI GRANTH

GURU NANAK

THE JAPJI: MEDITATION
(Morning Prayer)

Proem

God is One,
His Name is Truth;
Fashioner of all things,
Fearless and without enmity,
Timeless is His Image;
Unbegotten, Self-existent;
Shown by the grace of the Guru.

Jap: The Meditation

As in the Beginning:
The Truth throughout the Ages,
Ever Existent as Truth,
Even now immanent as Truth,
Forevermore He shall be Truth Eternal.

I

Not through thought is He apprehended,
Though we strive a hundred thousand times to
    grasp Him;
Not by outer silence or long contemplation
Can the inner Silence be attained;
Nor can man's hunger for God be appeased
By amassing the world's riches.

All the countless tricks of earthly wisdom
Leave a man disconsolate; nothing avails.

How then shall we find the Truth?
How indeed shall we rend the veils of untruth?
Abide by His Will and make your own
His Will, O Nanak, written in your Heart.

II

Through His Will He engenders all forms,
But who can express the form of His Will?
All life is shaped by His design,
He determines the high and the low;
His Writ ordains all pleasure and pain.

Through His Will some are rewarded with grace,
Whilst others grope through births and deaths;
Nothing at all remains outside His Will.
O Nanak, he who senses the Supreme Will
Never egotistically boasts "It is I"

III

Those who think of might
Sing of His might;
Others speak of His gifts
As His tokens and signs.
Some sing of His exaltation
And His acts of grace;
Some sing of His wisdom,
Hard to fathom.
Some sing of Him as the fashioner of the body.
Destroying what He has fashioned;
Others extol Him for removing life
And restoring it anew.

Some declare His Existence
To be remote, desperately so, from us;
Others sing of Him
As a Presence here or there,
Confronting us face to face.

Truly to sing of the transcendent Lord
Would deplete all speech, all powers of expression;
So many have sung of Him in myriad strains.
His gifts flow in such abundance,
That man tires of getting all He gives;
Age upon endless age, man lives off His bounty.
O Nanak, the Glorious Lord smiles carefree.

IV

The Lord is Absolute Truth,
True is His Name.
His language is boundless love.
His creatures ever beseech Him:
"Give us more, O Lord, give more";
He, the Bounteous, gives untiringly.

What then should we give
So that we may see His Kingdom?
With what words
Could we gain His Love?
In the ambrosial hours of fragrant dawn,
Meditate upon and glorify
His Name and magnificence.
Our own past conduct
Has put this cloak upon us;
Yet redemption solely comes through His grace.

O Nanak, this alone we need to know:
God is Truth, the One Light of all.

V

He cannot be set up like an idol,
Nor can His likeness be shaped by man.
He begot Himself and sustains Himself,
On His heights forever unstained.
Honoured are those in His shrine
Who meditate on Him.

Sing thou, O Nanak, the hymns
Of God as the repository
Of virtues sublime:
If a man sings of God and hears of Him,
Letting love of God sprout within,
All sorrow shall vanish.
Within the soul God shall create peace everlasting.

The Word of the Guru is the inward music;
The Word of the Guru is the supreme scripture;
The Word of the Guru is omnipresent.
The Guru is Shiva, Vishnu and Brahmā;
The Guru is the Mother Goddess.

If I knew Him as He truly is,
What words could convey my knowledge?
Enlightened by God, the Guru disclosed this
        mystery:
"There is One Truth, One Giver of Life;
May I forget Him never."

VI

I would bathe in holy rivers
If I could so gain His love and grace;
But of what avail is the pilgrimage
If this pleases Him not?
What creature gets anything here,

Save through former good works?
Yet heed the Word of the Guru,
And his hints within thy soul
Will shine like a precious jewel.

The divine illumination of the Guru
Has disclosed this mystery:
"There is but one Giver of Life;
May I forget Him never."

VII

If a man lived through the four ages,
Or even ten times longer,
Though his fame spread across nine shores,
Though the whole world followed in his train,
Though he were to be universally celebrated,
Yet lacking the grace of God,
Such a man would be disowned before God,
As merely a worm amidst vermin,
His sins lying at his own door.
On the fallible who repent, 0 Nanak, God confers
     virtue,
On the virtuously striving He bestows growth in
     blessedness.
But I cannot conceive of anyone so virtuous
That he can give any goodness to God.

VIII

Hearkening to the Name,
The disciple becomes a Master,
A guide, a saint, a seraph.
Hearkening to the Name,
The earth and its bearer, the bull,
And the Heavens are unveiled.

Hearkening to the Name,
Man's vision may uncover
Planets, continents, nether regions.
Death cannot bewilder
Those that hearken to the Name;
They are beyond the grasp of Death.

Nanak says the saints are ever joyous;
Hearkening to the Name,
Sorrow and sin are extinct.

IX

Hearkening to the Name,
Mortals gain the godliness
Of Shiva, Brahmā and Indra;
Hearkening to the Name,
The lips of the lowly Extol His splendour.

Hearkening to the Name,
The art of Yoga and all secrets
Of body and mind are revealed.
Hearkening to the Name,
Vedic wisdom manifests,
And the sacred lore of shastras and smritis.

Nanak says saints are ever joyous;
Hearkening to the Name,
Sorrow and sin are extinct.

X

Hearkening to the Name confers
Truth, Divine Wisdom and contentment.
To soak in the rapture of the Name
Is to bathe in holy places.

Hearing the Name and uttering It,
A man finds honour;
Hearkening, the mind may gain
The greatest rapturous peace
Meditating on God.

Nanak says saints are ever joyous;
Hearkening to the Name,
Sorrow and sin are extinct.

XI

Hearkening to the Name,
Man dives deep in an ocean of virtue;
Hearkening to the Name,
The seeker becomes an apostle,
A minister and ruler of souls.

Hearkening to the Name,
The blind find the path;
Hearkening to the Name,
Impassable streams are crossed.

Nanak says the saints are ever joyous;
Hearkening to the Name,
Sorrow and sin are extinct.

XII

For him with deep devotion to the Name,
Words fail to convey his condition;
He himself will come to regret
If he ever sought to describe it;
Neither pen nor paper nor literary skill
Can anywhere approach it.

Such is the potency of His pure Name.
He who truly avows It knows It.

XIII
Through faith in the Name,
The mind soars into sublime enlightenment.
The entire cosmos is self-disclosed.
Through inward faith in the Name,
One avoids foolish fumbling;
With the light of such faith,
Fear of death is dispelled.

Such is the potency of His pure Name.
He who truly avows It knows It.

XIV
Nothing can obstruct or obscure the path
Of those with deep devotion to the Name;
They depart with dignity,
They lose not the right direction.
The spirit of those suffused with faith
Is wedded to the revelation of truth.

Such is the potency of His pure Name.
He who truly avows It knows It.

XV
Those with deep devotion to the Name
Ever attain to emancipation;
Their kith and kin are also redeemed.
Guided by the Guru's light
The seeker moves safely,

And many more he redeems;
Those enriched with inward faith
Do not drift like beggars.

Such is the potency of His pure Name.
He who truly avows It knows It.

XVI

His chosen are His saints, splendrous are they.
Esteemed are saints in the court of God;
Saints add lustre to the Lord's realm,
With minds focussed upon the Guru alone.

All they utter is wisdom, but by what measure
Can we count the Lord's works?
Dharma is the mythic bull: the progeny of
    Compassion,
Which holds the thread that binds all creation.

Even meagre common sense makes one grasp this:
How could a bull's shoulders support the globe?
There are so many globes, planets galore,
What indeed bears these burdens?

One prodigal pen engraved the names
Of all creatures with varied forms and hues;
But who amongst us would inscribe that record,
Or if we could, how massive the scroll would be.

How can any convey Thy beauty and Thy mighty
    works?
Who indeed has the power to reckon Thy bounty,
    O Lord?
All creation issuing from Thy single Word
Flowing outward like myriad rivers.

How can a poor creature like myself
Convey the vastitude and glory of Thy creation?
I am too petty to offer anything to Thee;
I cannot even ever sacrifice unto Thee.

To obey Thy Will, O Formless One, is man's greatest
    gift,
Thou who eternally reposes in Thy Peace.

XVII

There is no reckoning of the prayers of men,
There is no reckoning their modes of adoration.
Thy lovers are countless, O Lord;
Countless are they who intone the Vedas;
Countless are the Yogis who remain aloof from this
    world.

Countless are Thy contemplating saints,
Thy graces and Thy wisdom;
Countless are the benevolent, lovers of their
    fellowmen.

Countless Thy heroes and martyrs
Confronting the weapons of the hostile;
Countless are those who in stillness
Focus their deepest thought upon Thee.

How can a poor creature like myself
Convey the vastitude and glory of Thy Creation?
I am too petty to offer anything to Thee;
I cannot even ever sacrifice unto Thee.
To obey Thy Will, O Lord, is man's greatest gift,
Thou who eternally reposes in Thy Peace.

XVIII

There is no reckoning fools, the morally purblind;
No reckoning thieves and the crooked;
No reckoning the spillers of innocent blood;
No reckoning the sinners who keep sinning.

No reckoning the liars who revel in lies;
No reckoning the dirty wretches who live on dross;
No reckoning the traducers,
Whose heads are heaped with loads of sin.

Thus says Nanak, lowliest of the low:
I am too petty to offer anything to Thee;
I cannot even ever sacrifice unto Thee.
To obey Thy Will, O Lord, is man's greatest gift,
Thou who eternally reposes in Thy Peace.

XIX

Countless are Thy Names and Thine abodes;
Wholly beyond the reach of the imagination
Are Thy prolific realms;
Even to call them prolific is presumptuous.

Yet by words and letters
Thy Name is uttered and Thy praise conveyed;
By words we extol Thee,
By words we chant Thy graces.

In the words we write and utter about Thee,
In words on the forehead of man,
Is inscribed the destiny of man;
Yet God who inscribes that destiny
Is free from the limits of language.

As God ordains, so man obtains.
His Word makes manifest all creation;

Without the Light of His Word
Nothing is possible.

How can a poor creature as I
Convey the vastitude and glory of Thy creation?
I am too petty to offer anything to Thee;
I cannot even ever sacrifice unto Thee.
To obey Thy Will, O Lord, is man's greatest gift,
Thou who eternally reposes in Thy Peace.

XX

When hands, feet and other limbs
Of the body are besmirched with filth,
They are purified by water;
When a garment is polluted,
It is cleansed with soapsuds;
So when the mind is polluted with filth,
We must scrub it with love of the Name.

We do not become sinners or saints
Merely by making claims;
All actions are recorded;
As is the seed we sow, so is the fruit we reap.
By God's Will, O Nanak,
Man must be saved or suffer more births.

XXI

Pilgrimages, penances, mercy and charity
Secure some merit, the size of sesame seed.
But he who heeds and avows and adores the Name
Shall wash and be cleansed
In his inmost sanctuary.

All goodness is Thine, O Lord, I have none;
Though without doing good deeds,
None can hope to honour Thee;

Blessed art Thou, Creator and Creation;
Thou art the Word, primordial Truth and Beauty,
And Thou art the heart's delight and desire.

At what time, in which age, in which day of the
    month or week,
In what season and in which month did Thou
    create this world?

Pundits know not or their Puranas would tell us;
Qazis know not or the Qur'an would have recorded
    it;
Nor do Yogis know the time of day,
Nor the day of the month, the week, the month or
    the season.
God alone knows when He created this world.

How indeed, O Lord, may I approach Thee?
With what words can I extol Thee?
How can I know Thee?
With what words shall I speak of Thee?
O Nanak, all speak of Him, and each would be
    wiser than the next;
Great is the Lord, glorious is His Name;
What He decrees, that prevails.
Nanak, he who is swollen with pride in his
    wisdom
Will be humbled by God in his next birth.

XXII

Hundreds of thousands of worlds abide below and
    above our own,
And scholars tire of looking for God's boundaries.
The Vedas declare with one voice that He is
    boundless;

The Semitic scriptures cite eighteen hundred
　　worlds;
Yet the Reality behind everything is One Principle.

If it could be inscribed, it would have been,
But men have worn themselves out in the attempt;
O Nanak, proclaim the greatness of God.
None but He knows the measure of His greatness.

XXIII
Thy extollers extol Thee,
Yet know not Thy grandeur;
As rivers and streams flow into the sea,
But know not its immensity.

Kings who hold dominions vast as the sea,
With riches heaped high as the mountain,
Are not equal to the tiny worm
That forgets not God in its heart.

XXIV
His Goodness is limitless and so is its praise;
His works and His gifts are limitless;
Where are the limits of His seeing or His hearing?
Fathomless is the expanse of His Mind;
There are no limits even to His Creation.

How many vex their hearts to fix His limits,
Though seeking to fathom Infinity can find no
　　bounds;
The more we utter, the more there is still to say.
Exalted is our Lord and His throne is very exalted;
His Holy Name is beyond the most exalted.

He who would know His height must be of the
    same height;
Only the Lord knoweth the grandeur of the Lord.
Nanak says, only by God's grace and generosity
Are His gifts given to man.

XXV

Of His riches one cannot write enough;
He is the Great Giver who craves nothing;
How many proud warriors prostrate at His door;
How many others, in hosts beyond measure.

Many squander His gifts in indolent indulgences,
Many obtain His gifts and yet overlook Him;
Many the foolish who merely eat,
Many are ever weeping and wanting;
Misery and hunger are also Thy gifts.

Freedom from bondage comes through Thy Will;
No one can take it for granted.
Even a fool who seeks
Can find wisdom through suffering.

The Lord knows what to bestow and He bestows;
Few appreciate this. Those on whom He bestows,
O Nanak, the gift of extolling Him and adoring
    Him,
Are truly Kings of Kings.

XXVI

Priceless are His graces,
Priceless His doings;
Priceless the treasure of His stories,
Priceless the purveyors of them;

Priceless those who seek these gifts,
Priceless those who receive these gifts.

Precious beyond price is devotion to Thee,
Precious beyond price is absorption in Thee;
Priceless His Law and Spirit of Righteousness,
Priceless His Mansions of Dispensation;
Priceless His Scales of Judgement,
Priceless His Weights for measurement.

Priceless His boons,
Priceless His signs upon them;
Priceless His Compassion and Will;
How beyond price He remains is inexpressible.
Those who seek to convey it
Are wordless in wonder.

The Vedas venerate Him,
And so do those who read from Puranas;
The learned extol Him in myriad discourses.
Brahmā and Indra extol Him,
Shivas extol Him, Siddhas extol Him,
The Buddhas He has wrought venerate Him.
Demons and gods extol Him,
Demigods, men, sages and devotees,
All seek to speak of Him;
Many have sought and still seek to speak of Him,
Many have extolled Him and expired.

If as many people as existed in the entire past
Were now to speak of Him, each in His own way,
Even then He would not be wholly conveyed.
The Lord becomes as glorious as He wants to be.
If anyone dares to claim he can depict Him,
Note him down as the grandest fool on earth.

XXVII

Where is the gate, where the mansion
From which Thou oversees all creation,
Where sounds of musical melodies,
Of instruments vibrating, and singing minstrels,
Are fused in divine harmony?
In diverse tones heavenly singers extol Thee.

There blow breezes, waters run and fires burn,
There Dharmraj, the lord of death, presides with
        authority;
There Chitra and Gupta, the recording angels,
        inscribe
For Dharmraj to see and judge;
There are the gods Ishvara and Brahmā,
The goddess Parvati decked with divine beauty;
There Indra reposes on his heavenly throne,
And lesser gods, each in place;
One and all extol Thee.

There yogins in rapt contemplation,
Holy men of meditation,
The pure of heart, the chaste,
Men of peace and contentment,
Intrepid warriors never ceasing from
Chanting Thy glories.

From age to age, the scholar and the sage
Extol Thee in their works;
There fair maidens with hearts entranced,
Inhabiting the earth, the upper and lower regions,
Chanting Thy glories.

With gems Thou didst provide
In sixty-eight places of pilgrimage,
Thy Name is extolled;

By warriors strong and brave in battle,
By the four sources of life,
Egg or womb, sweat or seed,
Thy Name is glorified.

The earth's regions, the celestial realm and the
    cosmos
That Thou created and maintain,
Chant of Thee and extol Thy Name.
Only those Thou lovest and with Thy grace
Can extol Thee and wholly adore Thee.
Others there are who also extol Thee;
I have no recollection of them,
Nor, O Nanak, can I claim to know.
He alone is the true Master, Lord of the Word,
    constant and consistent,
He who authored creation is, shall be and will
    ever abide;
He who authored diverse species, shapes and
    colours
Sees His Work mirror His grandeur.

What He decrees, He determines;
To Him none can dictate,
For He, O Nanak, is the King of Kings.
As He ordains, so must we live.

XXVIII
Moving as a supplicant,
May contentment be thy earrings,
Modesty thy begging-bowl;
Adorn thy body with the ashes of meditation;
May contemplation of death be thy clothing.

May thy body be chaste, virginal and pure,
May faith in God be the staff which supports you;

May brotherhood with every man on earth
Be the highest longing of your Holy Order.
Know that to conquer the mind
Is to conquer the world.

Hail, all hail unto Him,
May your greetings go to the Primal God;
Pure, beginningless and changeless,
Constant from age to age.

XXIX

May knowledge of God be your food,
May mercy sustain your store,
And heed the Divine Music
Which beats in every heart.

He is the Supreme Master,
He holds the nose-string of all creation;
In arcane potencies and tricks
There is no real remedy.

Union with God and alienation from Him
Are according to His Will;
Each obtains his deserts.

Hail, all hail unto Him,
May your greetings go to the Primal Lord;
Pure, beginningless and changeless,
Constant from age to age.

XXX

Maya, the mythic goddess,
Came from the One, and her womb conceived
Three worthy votaries of the One:

Brahmā, Vishnu and Shiva.
Brahmā, it is said, brings forth the
        world,
Vishnu it is who preserves it,
Shiva the Destroyer who absorbs;
He commands death and judgement.

God makes them work as He wills,
He ever sees them, they see Him not:
That, above all, is the greatest puzzle.

Hail, all hail unto Him,
May your greetings go to the Primal Lord;
Pure, beginningless and changeless,
Constant from age to age.

XXXI

God has His seat everywhere,
His treasure stores are in all places.
Whatever a man's lot is,
God at the creation
Apportioned him his share once and for
        all.
What He has designed
The Lord forever watches.
O Nanak, His works are true,
As He Himself is the True.

Hail, all hail unto Him,
May your greetings go to the Primal Lord;
Pure, beginningless and changeless,
Constant from age to age.

XXXII

May my tongue become a hundred thousand,
May the hundred thousand be magnified
  twentyfold,
With each tongue many hundred thousands of
  times
I utter the Lord's Holy Name.
Thus may the soul take each step,
Mounting the stairs to the Bridegroom,
And become one with Him.

On hearing of celestial matters,
He who can only crawl also craves to fly.
By God's grace alone, says Nanak, is God to be
  grasped;
All else is fraud, all else is empty.

XXXIII

You have no strength to speak or in silence listen,
To seek or to renounce;
You have no power to live or die,
You have no power to gain riches or dominion and
  be vain,
You have no power to direct the mind to thought
  or reason.
He who hath the power, He designs and watches;
O Nanak, before the Lord there is no high or low
  rank.

XXXIV

God ushered the night and the day,
The days of the week and the months,
And He created the seasons;
He made winds blow and water flow,

He gave fire, He produced the nether regions;
Amidst all this he raised the earth as a temple,
Upon it He placed diverse creatures,
Varied in kind and hue,
Endless in number their names.

All these lives are reckoned by their acts.
God is True and in His Court Truth is dispensed;
Therein the elect are accepted by Him,
And by His grace and His compassion,
Esteemed in His presence.
In that Court the bad shall be sorted from the good;
When we find His Court, O Nanak,
We discover this to be true.

XXXV

I have depicted the realm of Dharma,
Now I shall depict the realm of Knowledge.

How many are the winds, the fires and waters,
How many the Krishnas and Shivas,
How many the Brahmās planning the worlds
Of many kinds and shapes and hues;
How many worlds like our own are there
Wherein acts generate consequences.

How many holy summits to be reached
With how many sages, like Narada, teacher of
    Dhruva,
On top of them.
How many adepts, Buddhas and Yogis are there,
How many goddesses and how many images of
    goddesses;
How many gods and demons and how many sages.
How many hidden jewels in how many oceans,

How many the springs of life,
How many the modes and varieties of speech;
How many the kings, rulers and guides of men;
How many devotees are there who cherish this
    Divine Wisdom.
His votaries are innumerable, says Nanak.

XXXVI

As in the realm of Knowledge shines wisdom
And Music is heard from which myriad joys flow,
So in the realm of spiritual search
Beauty is the presiding deity.
All things are shaped there peerlessly;
The beauty of the place defies description.

And whoever even tries to convey it
Will indeed later feel remorse;
Understanding, discrimination, the deepest wisdom
    is distilled there.
There are gestated the gifts of sages and seers.

XXXVII

In the realm of Grace, spiritual might is supreme,
Nothing else suffices;
There reside bold warriors, valiant and strong,
In whom is the Spirit of the Lord,
And who by His favour are fused with Him.
Their beauty is beyond utterance,
In their hearts the Lord resides,
They are deathless and undeceived.
There abide also the congregations of the blesséd;
In bliss they repose, with the True in their hearts.

In the realm of Truth
Resides the Formless One,

Who, having created, oversees His creation,
And where He watches over them with Grace;
And His creatures are joyous.

All continents, globes and universes
Are contained in this supreme realm;
Were one to try to render an account of all,
There would be no limit to the count.

World upon world is there, form upon form,
And all have their functions as ordained by God's
    Will;
The Lord sees His Creation and seeing it,
He rejoices.
O Nanak, the telling is tough, as iron is hard to
    handle.

XXXVIII

In the forge of continence,
May patience be the goldsmith;
Upon the anvil of understanding,
May he strike with the hammer of knowledge;

May the fear of God be the bellows,
May austerities be the fire;
May the love of God serve as the crucible,
May the nectar of life melt in it.

Thus in the mint of Truth
A man can coin the Word;
This is the conduct of those
Upon whom God shows favour.
Nanak, our gracious Lord
With a glance gives us joy.

Epilogue

Air, like the Word of the Guru, brings the breath
    of life,
Water nurtures us, earth is our mother.
Day and night are the two nurses
Who watch over the world
And in whose bosom we frolic.

Upon good as well as bad deeds
Shall His Judgement be made;
As we have acted,
Some of us shall be close to God,
Some shall be far away.

Those that have meditated
Upon the Holy Name,
And have departed, their task consummated,
Their faces are those of shining ones and, O Nanak,
How many they lead to liberty in their train.

SODAR REHIRAS
(Evening Prayer)

I

*(The First Hymn of the Evening Prayer is the same as
the Twenty-Seventh Hymn of the Japji)*

II

Guru Nanak Spoke:

Hearing of the Lord,
All men speak of His splendour;
He alone that has seen Him
Can conceive how splendid is He.
Who can imagine His worth,
Or who can depict Him?
Those who seek to depict Thee
Are lost in Thy depths.

O Great Lord, whose depth is unfathomable,
Ocean of graces,
Who knows the extent of Thy shores?
All the ascetics
Have encountered and tried to encompass Thee;
All reckoners of worth
Have thought and tried to weigh Thy worth;
All the pundits and mystics,
All the preachers and their mentors,
Have not been able to fathom
One tittle of Thy splendour.

All truths, all ardent austerities, every exemplary act,
Every sublime attainment of adepts
Are Thy blessings, O Lord: without Thee

No man could reach perfection.
When Thou hast given Thy grace to anyone,
Nothing can come in his way.

How empty are the words of those who seek to
      extol Thee,
Thy treasuries are already replete with Thy praises;
He upon whom Thou bestows freely,
What should he do but extol Thee?
Says Nanak: The True One is He
From whom all perfection flows.

III

Guru Nanak Spoke:

If I recall Him I endure,
If I forget Him I perish;
Difficult, truly so is it,
To meditate upon His Name.
If a man longs after His Name,
With that holy longing
He consumes all His cares.
True is the Lord,
True is His Name.
O Mother, how can He be overlooked?

Even in extolling a tiny portion of His Name
Men grow tired, but His true worth is not
      measured;
If all men were to congregate and seek to extol Him,
He would grow neither more nor less by their
      homage.
He does not die, He does not struggle and suffer;
Ever He gives and never His resources diminish.
This is the supreme wonder around Him,
That there never was nor will there ever be

Another like unto the Lord.
As exalted as Thou art, O Lord,
So exalted are Thy gifts; as Thou created the day,
So Thou created the night.
He who forgets Thee is low born.
O Nanak, without His Name
Man resembles the lowest of outcasts.

IV

Guru Ram Das Spoke:

O Servant of God, True Guru, Truth's authentic
    exemplar,
We who are poor worms seek refuge in Thee;
Mercifully show us the lustre of the True Name.

O my Friend, my Divine Guru, light up His Name
    within me;
The Name shown by my Guru is my soul's succour;
The praise of the Lord is my profession.
Joyous, truly so, are the Lord's people
Who are devoted to the Lord, who long for Him,
And with the blessing of His name their longing is
    fulfilled.
Then in the congregation of the blessèd they extol
    His graces.

Miserable, most miserable are they
To whom is not given the sweet taste of His Name;
Death is their lot
Who have not tried to take refuge
With the True Guru,
Nor have come to the congregation of the pious.
Hapless be their lives,
Hapless be their expectations from life.

The blesséd who have found the comradeship
Of the True Guru are those on whose foreheads,
    from the very first,
This blesséd fate was inscribed.
Hail, hail to the holy congregation
Amidst whom is the exquisite fragrance of the Lord;
In the company of the pious, O Nanak,
The Lord sheds the true Light of His Name.

V

Guru Arjan Spoke:

O my soul, why art thou rushed and restless,
When thou knows the Lord will protect?
In the rocks and stones He hath placed living
    creatures,
He puts their food before them.

Beloved Lord, they who choose the company of the
    blesséd
Shall secure emancipation.
By the Guru's grace
They shall reach the supreme state;
Yea, though they resemble the parched tree,
They shall become green again.

Not on thy father or mother,
Not on the friends of thy family,
Not on thy wife or thy son
Darest thou depend for daily bread;
The Lord provides everything.
Why hoard fears in the mind?
Migrating cranes fly hundreds of miles,
Leaving their young behind them.
Think, O Man: Who feeds the young birds?

God holds as in His palm
All the riches of the world
And all the eighteen arcane powers;
O Nanak, forever and always,
Make thy heart an altar unto Him.
There is no end or limit to His Being.

VI

Guru Ram Das Spoke:

His Being is pure and stainless;
He is Infinite and far beyond all grasp;
All worship Thee, all prostrate before Thee:
Thou who art Truth and the Source.
All creatures are Thine, for all Thou provides;
O Saint, contemplate the Lord who causes sorrow
    to vanish.
He Himself is the Lord, He Himself is the votary;
O Nanak, how puny is man.

Thou, O Lord, the One Supreme Being,
Thou art in all hearts and souls,
Thou encompasses everything;
Some men plead for alms, some proffer them,
All this is the great game Thou enacts.
It is Thou who gives and relishes gifts,
I know of none other than Thee.
Thou art the wholly Transcendent:
Infinite are Thou! Infinite are Thou!
How can I depict Thy graces?
Unto those who serve and sanctify Thee truly,
Nanak is a modest sacrifice.

They who contemplate Thee, they who meditate on
    Thee

In this Dark Age find serenity.
They who contemplate Thee, they are saved and
        freed;
For them the noose of death is shattered.

Those who meditate on the One who is Fearless
Will lose all fear;
Those who have sanctified the Lord
Into the Lord are now absorbed.
Blesséd and indeed blesséd are those
Who have fixed their thought on the Lord.
Humble Nanak is a sacrifice unto them.

O Lord, Thy boundless treasure
Is replete and refilled with Thy glorification.
O many and countless are the saints who adore
        Thee,
Manifold are their devotions;
They perform austerities and ceaselessly chant Thy
        Name.
How many study the smritis and shastras,
Enact the six Hindu observances?
But only those are saints truly
Who have gained the love of my Lord.
Thou art the Primal Being, the Source.
None places bounds on Thee, there is no other
        so exalted;
From age to age one and the same,
Forever Thou are the same, Immovable Source.
Whatever Thou ordains, obtains,
As Thou dost, so Thy doings endure.
It is Thou who issues all things,
And by whose edict all things expire.
Nanak sings the praises of the Maker, the
        All-knowing.

VII

Guru Ram Das Spoke:

Lord, the Source and the Truth,
As Thy Will, so it is done; as Thou gives, so I receive.
All that exists is Thine: all men adore Thee.
Those whom Thou cherishes have gained the jewel
    of Thy Name.
The enlightened have looked for it; the self-willed
    have lost it;
It is Thou who sets apart and Thou who draws
    together.

You are the Ocean: all things abide within Thee,
There is none other than Thee;
All the living are part of the game Thou plays.
By Thee, having fallen away, one is set apart;
By Thee, abiding in union, one is united.

He whom Thou helps to know Thee, he knows Thee,
And his mouth shall be forever full of Thy praise;
He who has truly served the Lord is joyous
And is easily absorbed into the Divine Name.

Thou art the Source: all that exists is Thy handiwork;
There is none other than Thee;
What Thou creates, Thou sees and knows.
Through the Guru, says Nanak,
Thou art revealed in Thy Truth.

VIII

Guru Nanak Spoke:

Man, thou residest in the world which is like unto
    a pool
Whose waters God made as hot as fire.

Transfixed in the mire of worldly love, thy feet
    cannot move forward;
I have seen people sinking in this swamp.
O heart, O foolish heart, why not contemplate
    the One?
By forgetting thy Lord, thy virtues have vanished.

I am not chaste nor honest, I am not even a pundit;
Foolish and ignorant I came into the world.
O Lord, Nanak ever prays to find
The sanctuary of their company,
Those who have not forgotten Thee.

IX

Guru Arjan Spoke:

You have gained this human frame,
This is your opportunity to be one with God;
All other labours are worthless.
Seek the company of the holy and glorify His
    Name.
Earnestly prepare to cross this terrible ocean;
Your life is indeed wasted
In love of the world's illusions.

I have not chanted His Name,
Nor done penance, performed austerities nor been
    pious;
I have not served my Lord's saints nor pondered
    Him.
Nanak says, my acts have been lowly:
Save me from shame, O Lord,
Since I take shelter in Thee.

SOHILA ARTI
(Bedtime Prayer)

I

Guru Nanak Spoke:

In the house in which men chant the Lord's
    glories
And meditate upon Him,
In that house chant the hymns of praise
And cherish the Creator.
Chant the hymn of praise of your fearless Lord.
Let me be a sacrifice unto that singing
Through which we gain endless peace.

Day by day, and forever,
He oversees His living creatures;
The Bountiful Giver protects one and all.
Who can put a price on His gifts,
Or say how splendid is He?

The year and the auspicious day for the wedding is
    fixed,
Friends shower oil at the door to greet the bride.
Grant me your blessings, O friends,
I depart for absorption into God.

The summons is sent to every home,
To each soul, every day, it is sent;
Recall, O Nanak, Him who sends the summons,
The day is not far when you too may get it.

II

Guru Nanak Spoke:

The systems are six, their teachers are six,
And six their divergent doctrines;
The Lord of all is the One,
Varied though His facets.
O brother, choose that system
That chants the Lord's glories:
Therein is thy true exaltation.

Seconds, minutes, hours, quarters of a day;
Lunar and solar days compose a month,
Yet there are so many times and so many
        seasons;
One single sun moves through all of them.
O Nanak, Thy Lord is One,
Though varied are His facets.

III

Guru Nanak Spoke:

The sky is Thy tray,
The sun and the moon Thy lamps;
The galaxy of stars are as scattered pearls,
The woods of sandal are Thy incense.
Breezes blow Thy regal fan;
Flowers of the forests
Are as oblations at Thy feet.
What wondrous worship with lamps is this,
O Thou, Destroyer of fear.
Silent Music is the sound of Thy temple
        drums.

Thousands are Thine eyes
And yet Thou has none;

Thousands are Thy shapes
And yet Thou has none;
Thousands are Thy pure feet
And yet Thou has none;
Thousands are Thy noses
And yet Thou has none.

All this is Thy play and captivates me.
In each heart there is light:
That light Thou art.
By the Light that comes from God
Every soul is illumined:
But this divine Light becomes visible
Only through the Guru's Teaching.
What is acceptable to Thee, O Lord,
Is the best *arti:* worship with lamps.

O Lord, my mind longs for Thy lotus feet
As the honey-bee for the nectar of flowers.
Night and day, Lord, I thirst for Thee,
Bestow water by Thy mercy to Nanak.
He is like the sarang, the hawk-cuckoo that
    drinks only drops of rain,
So that he may ever abide in the peace of
    Thy Name.

IV

Guru Ram Das Spoke:

With lust and wrath,
The city that is thy body
Is replete to the brim.
Confront as saint and conquer
That lust and wrath.
By God's command I have found my Guru,

And my soul is rapt
In the love of My Lord.
Prostrate meekly to the saint,
That is a pious deed;
Prostrate to the ground before him,
That is verily devotion.

The faithless find not
The bliss of love of the Lord;
In their hearts
Is the thorn of self-adoration;
And with each step they take,
It pierces deeper and deeper,
And they suffer pain and misery
Till they draw death upon their heads.

The Lord's chosen are yoked to the Lord's
    Name.
The pain of birth and the fear of death are
    shattered.
They have reached the deathless Lord;
They are greatly esteemed in all regions.

I am poor and miserable,
But I am Thine, O Lord:
Save me, O save me,
Thou greatest of the great.
Thy Name, to Thy slave Nanak,
Is as his staff and his shield.
Only in the Name of the Lord
Have I found my refuge.

V

Guru Arjan Spoke:

I entreat thee, my friend, to heed me,
Here and now is the time to serve the saints;
Here, in this world, attain the grace of godliness,
Thou shalt have enough ease in the world to come.
Each day and night the sum of days diminishes:
Find the True Guru and balance your ledger.

The world is awry, is alluring. The man
Who knows God, the *Brahmajnani,* is emancipated.
Whom God awakens to drink the elixir of His
    Name,
He knows the Unknowable, whose story transcends
    all telling.

Strive to find that
For which thou has come into this world;
And through the grace of the Guru
God will abide in thy heart.
Thou shalt abide in His Presence
In comfort and peace,
And not ever return
To be born and to die again.

O God, Searcher of hearts,
O God, who gives to each of us
The fruits of our acts,
Satisfy the wish of my heart:
Nanak, thy slave, craves
The boon that he may be made
The dust that clings to the soles
Of the feet, O Lord, of the saints.

DIVINE WISDOM IN THE
WORD OF ADAM

Al-Hikmat al-Ilahiyah

The Real, *al-haqq*, wished to perceive the essences of His Most Beautiful Names, *al-asma al-husna*, infinite in number, or put another way, to see His own Essence in a universal medium encompassing the Divine Order, which, being qualified by existence, could reveal His mystery, *sirr*, to Himself. For the vision, *ru'ya*, of a thing unto itself is not the same as seeing itself in another, as in a mirror; for it appears to itself in a form that arises from the locus of the vision. That would only appear to it owing to the existence of the locus and its reflection shown therein.

The Real first gave existence to the entire Cosmos as homogeneity without Spirit in it, being like an unpolished mirror. The nature of Divine Creativity necessitates that no locus be prepared, save to receive a divine spirit, which is also called *the breathing into him*. The latter is nothing other than the awakening of the undifferentiated form's predisposition to receive the inexhaustible afflatus, *al-fayd*, of Self-unveiling, *at-tajalli*, which has always been and will ever be. There is only the pure receptacle, *qabil*, and the receptacle comes from the Holy Afflatus, for all Order, *amr*, derives from Him, even as it returns to Him. Thus the Divine Order required the pure reflectivity of the mirror of the Cosmos, and Adam became the light of that mirror and the spirit of the form, whilst the angels represent certain potencies of that which is the form of the Cosmos, called in the language of the Sufis, *al-insan al-kabir*, the Great Man. The angels are to it as the psychic and physical properties are to the human form. Each of these cosmic potencies is veiled by its own nature so that it cannot know anything superior to itself. Each claims that it is worthy of an exalted position and ultimate closeness to God by virtue of its participation in *al-jam-'iyat al-ilahiyah*, the Divine Synthesis, deriving both from the Sphere of Divinity and *haqiqat al-haqaiq*, the Reality of Realities, and again, with respect to the form assuming these characteristics, from the exigencies of *tabi'at al-kull*, the Universal Nature, which embraces all the receptacles of the Cosmos, higher and lower.

This cannot be comprehended by discursive logic, for this type of knowledge comes only through Divine Intuition. Through it alone one knows the origin of the forms of the Cosmos to the degree they receive the spirits. This form is called *insan* and *khalifah*, Man and the Representative of God. The first quality stems from the universality of his nature and the fact that he embraces all the realities. Man is to the Real as the pupil is to the eye through which the act of seeing takes place. Thus he is called *insan*, meaning both Man and pupil, for it is through Man that the Real contemplates His creation and bestows mercy. Thus is Man transient and eternal, perpetual, everlasting, the discriminating and unifying Word. Through his existence the Cosmos subsists. He is, in relation to the Cosmos, as the seal is to the ring, for the seal is the place where the token is engraved with which the king seals his treasure. So he is called the Representative, for through him God preserves creation, as the seal preserves the king's treasure. So long as the king's seal is on it, no one dares to open it except by permission, the seal being the safeguard of the kingdom. Even so is the Cosmos preserved so long as *al-insan al-kamil*, the Universal Man, abides in it. You see that when he shall cease to be and when the seal of the lower world is broken, nothing of what the Real preserved will persist and all of it will disperse, each part returning to its source, and the whole will be translated to the Final Abode where the Universal Man will be the seal forever.

All the Names constituting the Divine Form are manifest in the human constitution so that it encompasses and integrates all existence. From this fact comes the argument that God condemned the angels. Remember that God warns you by the example of another, and consider carefully from whence the arraigned one is judged. The angels did not grasp the meaning of the establishment of God's Representative, nor did they apprehend the essential servitude implied by the Plane of Reality. For none knows anything of the Real save that of Himself which is implicit in the Essence. The angels do not enjoy the integral nature of Adam, and they comprehend only those Divine Names peculiar to them by which they glorify and sanctify the Real; nor do they know that God has Names of which they are ignorant and by which they cannot glorify Him. They are unable to sanctify Him with the sanctification of Adam. Their nature and limitation being such, they said, concerning Adam's constitution, *Will You put in it one who will work mischief in it?* They meant his rebellion, which is precisely what they themselves manifest, for what they say of Adam applies equally to their own attitude towards the Real. But for the fact that rebellion is in their own constitution, they would not have thus spoken concerning Adam; but they are not aware of this. If they indeed knew themselves, they would know their limitation, and if that were so, they would have restrained their speech. They would not have followed their challenge by calling attention to their own glorification of God or their sanctification. Adam partakes of Divine Names the angels have no part in, and they are not able to glorify Him to exalt His transcendence, as Adam does.

God explains this to us so that we might be careful and learn from it the right attitude towards Him, lest we become pretentious because of the individually restricted insight or understanding we might have realized. How can we possess something, the reality of which we have not experienced and concerning which we have no knowledge? This Divine Instruction is one of the ways by which the Real teaches His most trusted servants, His Representatives.

Let us now return to this Wisdom. Know that the universal ideas, *al-umar al-kulliyah*, have no tangible, individual existence in themselves. Nevertheless, they are present and known in the mind. They are always unmanifest with respect to individual existence, yet impose their effects on all such existence. In truth, individual existence is nothing other than universal ideas, though in themselves they are purely intelligible. They are manifest as individual beings, and they are unmanifest as intelligibles. Every individual existence emanates from universal ideas which can never be dissociated from the intellect, nor can universal ideas manifest individually in such a way that they would cease to be intelligible. Whether the individual being is determined in or out of time, its relationship to the universal idea remains the same. The universal idea and the individual being may share a common determining principle if the essential realities of the individual beings demand, as, for example, in the relationship between knowledge and the knower, or life and the living. Life and knowledge are intelligible realities, distinct from one another. Thus, concerning the Real, we say that He has life and knowledge and also that He is Living and Knowing. This we also say of Man and the angels. The reality of knowledge is one, and the reality of life is also one, and the relationship of each respectively to the knower and the living is always the same.

We say that knowledge of the Real is eternal, but that man's knowledge is ephemeral. Attachment to the determinant renders something in the intelligible reality contingent. Now consider the interdependence of universal ideas and individual existences. For, even as knowledge constitutes one who uses it as being a knower, so also does the knower constitute knowledge as being ephemeral in the case of the ephemeral knower, and as eternal in the case of the Eternal, each constituting and being constituted in turn. Universal ideas are intelligible, but have no real existence except insofar as they determine existing beings, just as they themselves are determined in any relationship with individual existence. As manifest in individual existence, they may admit of being determined, but it is impossible for them to admit of particularization or division. They are essentially present in each thing they qualify, just as humanity is present in every human being, whilst not being subject to particularization or division by the number of individual beings, but remaining purely intelligible.

Since there is a mutual dependence between that which has individual existence and that which has not, being but an unmanifested relationship, the interconnection between one individual being and another is the more comprehensible because they have, at least, individual existence in common, whereas in the former instance there is no common denominator. Without doubt, the ephemeral is utterly dependent for its possibility on that which brings it about. Its existence is derived from something other than itself, the connection in this case being one of dependence. It is therefore necessary that that which is the principle of ephemeral existence should be essentially and necessarily subsistent, self-sufficient and independent of all else. This principle bestows existence from its own essential being on ephemeral existence and in this way becomes related to it. Furthermore, since the principle, because of its essence, requires the ephemeral, the latter has a kind of necessary being. And since its dependence on that from which it was manifested is implicit in its own essence, it follows that the ephemeral should conform to all the Names and attributes of the origin except that of Self-sufficient Being, which does not belong to ephemeral existence, since even what necessary being it has comes from other than itself.

If the ephemeral manifests the form of the Eternal, then it is clear that God draws our contemplation towards what is ephemeral as an aid to knowledge of Him. He says that He shows forth His signs in the ephemeral. Knowledge of Him is inferred from knowledge of ourselves. Whatever quality we ascribe to Him, we ourselves represent that quality, except the quality of Self-sufficient Being. Since we know Him through ourselves and from ourselves, we attribute to Him all we attribute to ourselves, and for this reason the revelation comes to us through the mouths of the Interpreters (the prophets). He depicts Himself to us through ourselves. If we contemplate Him we contemplate ourselves, and when He contemplates us He contemplates Himself.

Obviously, as individuals and types, we are multitudinous, though representatives of a single reality. But we also know that there is a factor distinguishing one individual from another, without which there would be no multiplicity in the One. In the same way, even if descriptions of ourselves apply equally to Him in every respect, there is nevertheless a fundamental difference — we are originated in conformity to Him, and He is Being, free from all dependence. Thus, we should understand the One without beginning, *al-azal*, the Ancient of Days, *al-qidam*, denying Divine Primacy, in the sense of existence coming from non-existence. For although He is the First, *al-awwal*, no temporality may be attributed to Him, and thus He is called also the Last, *al-akhir*. If He were the First in the sense of being the first in time, He would also be called the Last in this sense, but manifestation has no end, being inexhaustible. He is called the Last only in the sense that all reality, though reality is attributed to us, returns to Him. His Finality is essentially His Primacy, and His Primacy is essentially His Finality. Know also that the Real has depicted Himself as being the Outer, *al-zahir*, and the Inner, *al-batin*, Manifest and Unmanifest. He brought the Cosmos into being as an unseen realm and a sensory realm so that we might perceive the Inner through our own interior and the Outer through our own sensory aspect.

He has also attributed to Himself mercy and wrath, having manifested the Cosmos as a place of fear and hope, where we fear His wrath and hope for His mercy. He has also depicted Himself as being possessed of majesty and beauty, having endowed us with reverent awe, *al-haybah*, and intimacy, *al-uns*, and so on with all His attributes and Names. He has expressed this polarity of qualities as being His two Hands devoted to the creation of the Universal Man, who integrates in himself all cosmic realities and their individual manifestations.*

* Mercy and fear are the two poles of the Qabbalistic Tree of Life, named after the fourth and fifth Sephiroth, Chesed (mercy) and Geburah (fear). Mercy is connected with Chokhmah (wisdom), and fear derives from Binah (intelligence). They are balanced in Malkhuth (the kingdom) and in Kether (the crown), the grossest and most subtle extremities of manifestation. The polarities are synthesized in Adam Kadmon, the Cosmic Man, whose embodiment is the visible Cosmos and whose symbol is the caduceus. Ibn al-'Arabi was born and grew up in regions that nurtured the Qabbalistic *Zohar* to full flower.

The Cosmos is the sensory realm, and the Representative is unseen. For this reason the Ruler is veiled, since the Real has described Himself as being hidden behind veils of darkness, which are the natural forms, and behind veils of light, which are the subtle spirits.* The Cosmos consists of *kathif* and *latif*, gross and subtle matter. It is therefore the veil covering its own reality. For the Cosmos does not perceive the Real as He perceives Himself, nor can it ever unveil itself, even though knowing itself to be distinct from its Creator, *al-khaliq*, and dependent on Him. Indeed, the Cosmos has no share in the essential Self-sufficiency of the Real, nor will it ever attain to that. In this sense the Real remains ever unknown in every way, since ephemeral being has no grasp of the Eternal.

God unites the polarity of qualities only in Adam, to confer a distinction upon him. He says to Iblis,† *What prevents you from prostrating to one whom I have created with my two hands?* What prevents Iblis is the very fact that man unites in himself the two forms, the ephemeral Cosmos and the Real, which are His two Hands. As for Iblis, he is only a fragment of the Cosmos and has no share in this Synthesis, by virtue of which Adam is the Representative. Were Adam not manifest in the form of Him whom he represents, he would not be the Representative, and were he not to contain all that his flock needs or were he unable to meet all the requirements of the other creatures, he would not be the Representative. Such Representation is suitable only for the Universal Man. The outer form of Universal Man is composed of all cosmic realities and forms, whilst his inner form is composed to correspond to the form of the Real. Thus He says in the Sacred Tradition (*hadith*), *I am his hearing and his sight*, and not, "I am his eye and his ear", in order to show the distinction between these two forms. The reality in every being in the Cosmos is in

* Muhammad the Prophet said, "God hides Himself in seventy thousand veils of light and darkness. If He lifted them, the brilliance of His Visage would consume whomsoever looked upon It."

† Iblis, the Islamic tempter, Satan.

accordance with the requirements of the essence of each being, but it must be understood that no other being enjoys the Synthesis possessed by the Representative. It is by virtue of this Synthesis that he surpasses all other beings.

If the Real did not pervade all beings as form, and if there were no universal ideas, there would be no manifestation of individual beings. Thus in truth, the Cosmos depends on the Real for its existence.

> All is dependent, naught is independent,
> This is pure truth, plainly and without metaphors.
> If I mention One, Self-sufficient, Independent,
> You know I refer to the Real.
> Each is bound up with the other without break.
> Consider carefully this which I tell thee.

You are now acquainted with the Wisdom involved in the bodily form of Adam, his ephemeral form, and you are acquainted with the spiritual form of Adam, his inner form. Adam is, then, the Real, and he is a creature. You have also learnt to know his rank as the Synthesis by virtue of which he is the Representative.

Adam is that single soul, that single spiritual essence, *an-nafs al-wahidah*, from which humankind was created, as the Real proclaims in the Qur'an: *O Men, fear your Lord who created you from a single soul and created from it its mate, so that from them both there issued forth many men and women.* The words *Fear your Lord* mean, make your ephemeral selves a safeguard for your Lord and make your inner reality, which is your Lord, a safeguard for your ephemeral selves. The Divine Order, *amr,* involves blame and praise, negation and affirmation; so be His shield in censure and make Him your safeguard in praise, so that you belong to those who act justly and are possessed of knowledge.* The Most High and Glorious caused Adam to look on all He had placed in him and

---

* The Qur'an (IV, 81) says: "Whatsoever good befalleth thee is from God; whatsoever evil comes to thee is from thyself."

held it in His Hands, the Cosmos in one Hand and in the other Adam and his seed, expounding their degrees in the inner Adam.

When God unveiled to me, in my innermost centre, what He had placed in our primordial ancestor, I set down in this volume only that which was shown to me, though not all I was given, since no book could hold it all, nor could the Cosmos as it presently exists. The seal of each Wisdom is the Word unveiled in it. I have transcribed faithfully according as was vouchsafed to me. Even if I wished to add to it, I would not be able to do so, since the plane from which it came prevents saying more.

MUHYIDDIN IBN AL-'ARABI

THE WITNESS

Bhusunda said: This *Kalpa* tree whereon we dwell stands firm and unshaken amidst the revolutions of ages and the all-destroying blasts of tempests and conflagrations.

This great arbour is inaccessible to beings who dwell in other worlds; therefore we reside here in perfect peace and bliss, apart from all disturbance.

When Hiranyaksha, the giant demon of the antediluvian race, strove to hurl this earth with all its seven continents into the lowest abyss, even then did this tree stand firm on its roots at the summit of this mountain.

And then, when this mountainous abode of the gods stood trembling, with all the other mountains of the earth, upon Varaha's tusk, this tree remained unshaken.

When Narayana supported this seat of the gods with two arms, and uplifted the Mandara Mountain with the other two, even then was this tree unmoved.

When the orbs of the sun and moon shook with fear at the terrible warfare of the gods and demons, and the whole earth was plunged in commotion and chaos, still this tree stood firm on its root.

When the mountains were uprooted by hail storms raging with terrific violence, rending away the huge forest trees of this Mount Meru, this tree was unshaken by the blast.

When the Mandara Mountain rolled into the milky ocean and gales of wind filled its caverns, bearing it afloat on the water's surface, and the great masses of diluvian clouds rolled about the vault of heaven, this tree stood steadfast as a rock.

When this Mount Meru was clenched in the grip of Kalanemi, and he was going to crush it by his gigantic might, even then this tree was steady on its root.

When the *Siddhas* were blown away by the flapping wings of Garuda, the king of birds, in their strife to obtain the ambrosia, this tree was unmoved by the wind.

When the serpent which upholds the earth was assailed by Rudra in the form of Garuda, and the world shook from the blast of his wings, this tree was still.

When the flame of the last conflagration threatened to consume the world with all its seas and mountains, making the serpent, which supports the earth on its hoods, throw out living fire from all his many mouths, even then this tree was neither shaken nor burnt down by the awesome and all-devouring fire.

So stable is this tree that there is no danger, O Sage, that can betake us here, just as there is no evil that can betide the inhabitants of heaven. How can we, O Great Sage, ever be exposed to any danger, abiding in this tree which defies all calamities? We are beyond all fears and dangers, like those who dwell in heaven.

Vasishtha asked: Tell me, O Wise One who has borne the blast of dissolution, how you have remained unharmed and undisturbed while many a sun and moon and hosts of stars have fallen and faded away.

Bhusunda replied: When at the end of a *Kalpa* age the order of the world and the laws of nature are broken and dissolved, we are compelled to forsake our abode, like a man departing from his best friend.

We then remain in the air, freed from all mundane conceptions, the members of our bodies becoming devoid of their natural functions, and our minds released from all volitions.

When the zodiacal suns blaze forth in their full vigour, melting down the mountains by their intense heat, I remain with intellect fixed in the Varuna mantram.

When the diluvian winds burst with full force, shattering and scattering the huge mountains all around, it is by attending to the Parvati mantram that I remain as stable as a rock.

When the earth with its mountains is dissolved into the waters, presenting the face of a universal ocean, it is by the volatile power of the Vayu mantram that I bear myself aloft.

I then convey myself beyond this perceptible world and rest in the holy ground of Pure Spirit. I remain as if in profound sleep, unagitated in body or mind.

I abide in this quiescence until the lotus-born Brahmā is again employed in his work of creation, and then I re-enter the confines of the re-created world, where I settle again on this tree.

Vasishtha said: Tell me, O Lord, why other Yogis do not remain as steadfast as you do through your power of *dharana*.

Bhusunda replied: O Venerable One, it is by the inseparable and supreme power of destiny, which none may prevent or set aside, that I live in this way, and others live in theirs.

None may oppose or alter that which must come to pass for them. It is nature's law that all things must be as they are ordained.

It is by the firmness of my intent that things are so fixed and allotted as my share, that they must so come to pass in each *Kalpa* age, again and again, and that this tree must grow on the summit of this mountain and I have my abode in its hollow.

Vasishtha said: Lord, you are as enduring as our salvation is long lasting, and are able to guide us in the paths of truth because established in true wisdom and steady in the intent of *Yoga*.

You, who have seen the many changes of the world and experienced all things through the repeated course of creations, are best able to tell of the wonders to be witnessed during the revolutions of the ages.

Bhusunda replied: I remember, O Great Sage, the earth beneath this Mount Meru to have once been a desolate land, having no hills, rocks, trees, plants, or even grasses upon it.

I remember also this earth under me to have been full of ashes for a period of myriads of centuries of mortal years.

I remember a time when the lord of the day — the sun — was unproduced, and when the orb of the moon was not yet known, and when the earth under me was not divided by day and night but was lighted by the light of this Mount Meru.

I remember this mountain casting the light of its gems upon one side of the valley below, leaving the other in utter darkness, like the Lokaloka Mountain which presents its light and dark sides to people on the two sides of the horizon.

I recall seeing the war between the gods and demons rage high, and the flight and slaughter of people in all the quarters of the earth.

I remember witnessing the revolution of the four *yugas*, and the revolt of the proud and vaunting *asuras*. I have seen the Daitya demons driven back to the wall.

I remember the seed of the earth being borne away beyond the bounds of the universal flood. I recollect the mansion of the world when only the Uncreated Triad remained in it.

I remember seeing no life on earth except for the vegetable creation through the duration of one-half the four *yuga* ages.

I also recall this earth to have been full of mountains and mountainous tracts for the space of full four *yugas*, when no men peopled the earth and human customs and usages had gained no ground on it.

I remember seeing this earth filled with the bones of dead Daityas and other fossil remains, rising in heaps like mountains, and continuing in their dilapidated and crumbling state for myriads of years.

I remember that formless state of the world when darkness reigned over the face of the deep, when the serpentine support of the earth fled in fear, the celestials left their ethereal courses, and no treetop or bird touched the sky.

I remember the time when the northern and southern divisions of India both lay under the one Himalayan boundary mountain. I recall when the proud Vindhyan Mountain strove to equal great Meru.

These and many other things I remember, which would take too long to relate. But what is the use of long narrations? Attend, and I will tell you the main substance in brief.

I have beheld innumerable *Munis* and *Manvantaras* pass away before me, and I have witnessed hundreds of quadruple *yugas* glide away, one after the other, all filled with great deeds and events, but now buried in oblivion.

I remember the creation of one sole body in this world, named Virat, when the earth was devoid of men and *asuras*.

I remember that age of the world when Brahmins were addicted to wine and drunkenness, when the Sudras were outcasted by the Suras, and when women were involved in polyandry.

I also remember when the surface of the earth presented the sight of one great sheet of water and was entirely devoid of all vegetation, when people were produced without cohabitation of man and woman.

I recall that age when the world was a void and there was no earth or sky nor any of their inhabitants. Neither men nor mountains existed, nor was there sun or moon to divide day and night.

I remember the sphere of heaven shrouded under a sheet of darkness, when there was neither Indra nor king to rule in heaven or earth, and there were no high, low or middle classes of men.

It was after this that Brahmā thought of creating the worlds, and divided them into the spheres of the high, low and intermediate regions. He then established the boundary mountains and distinguished Jambudvipa from the rest.

The earth was not divided then into different nations and provinces, nor were there distinctions of caste, creed or organization for the various orders of its people. There was then no name for the starry frame, nor any denomination for the pole star or its circle.

It was then that the sun and moon had their birth, and the gods Indra and Upendra had their dominions. After this occurred the slaughter of Hiranyakasipu and the restoration of the earth by the great Varaha, the boar Avatar of Vishnu.

Then came the establishment of kings over the peoples of the earth and the revelation of the Vedas was given to mankind. After this the Mandara Mountain was uprooted from the earth and the ocean was churned by the gods and the giant races of men.

I have seen the unfledged Garuda, the bird of heaven which bore Vishnu on its back; and I have seen the seas breaking up into bays and gulfs. All these events are remembered by me like the latest occurrences in the course of the world. Surely they must be within the memory of my children and of yourself as well.

I have witnessed in former ages Vishnu, with his *vahan* Garuda, become Brahmā with his *vahan* Kalahansa, and witnessed the same transformed into Shiva with the Nandi bull as his bearer.

Nirvana Prakarana Purvardha, XXI

THE UNIVERSAL PROTEUS

The great and peaceful ones live regenerating the world like the coming of spring; having crossed the ocean of embodied existence themselves, they freely aid all others who seek to cross it. The very essence and inherent will of Mahatmas is to remove the suffering of others, just as the ambrosia-rayed moon of itself cools the earth heated by the intense rays of the sun.

SHANKARACHARYA

To comprehend my answers you will have first of all to view the eternal *Essence*, the *Svabhavat* not as a compound element you call spirit-matter, but as the one element for which the English has no name. It is both passive and active, pure *Spirit Essence* in its absoluteness and repose, pure matter in its finite and conditioned state — even as an imponderable gas or that great unknown which science has pleased to call *Force*. When poets talk of the "shoreless ocean of immutability" we must regard the term but as a jocular parodox, since we maintain that there is no such thing as immutability — not in our Solar system at least. Immutability, say the theists and Christians, "is an attribute of God", and forthwith they endow that God with every mutable and variable quality and attribute, knowable as unknowable, and believe that they have solved the unsolvable and squared the circle. To this we reply, if *that* which the theists call God, and science *"Force"* and *"Potential Energy,"* were to become immutable but for one instant even during the mahapralaya, a period when even Brahm the creative architect of the world is said to have merged into non-being, then there could be no *manvantara*, and space alone would reign unconscious and supreme in the eternity of time.

Nevertheless, Theism when speaking of mutable immutability is no more absurd than materialistic science talking of *"latent* potential energy," and the indestructibility of matter and force. What are we to believe as indestructible? Is it the invisible something that moves matter or the energy of moving bodies! What does modern science know of force proper, or say the forces, — the cause or causes of motion? How can there be such a thing as *potential energy*, i.e., an energy having latent *inactive* power since it is energy *only while it is moving matter*, and that *if it ever ceased to move matter it would cease to be*, and with it matter itself would disappear? Is force any happier term? Some thirty-five years back a Dr. Mayer offered the hypothesis now accepted as an axiom that force, in the sense given it by modern science, like matter, is *indestructible;* namely, when it ceases to be manifest in one form it still exists and has only *passed into some other form*. And yet your men of science have not found a single instance where one *force* is transformed into another, and Mr. Tyndall tells his opponents that "in no case is the force producing the motion annihilated or changed into anything else."

Moreover we are indebted to modern science for the novel discovery that there exists a quantitative relation between the dynamic energy producing something and the 'something' produced. Undoubtedly there exists a quantitative relation between cause and effect, between the amount of energy used in breaking one's neighbour's nose, and the damage done to that nose, but this does not solve one bit more the mystery of what they are pleased to call correlations, since it can be easily proved (and that on the authority of that same science) that neither motion nor energy is indestructible and that the physical forces are in no way or manner convertible one into another. I will cross-examine them in their own phraseology and we will see whether their theories are calculated to serve as a barrier to our "astounding doctrines." Preparing as I do to propound a teaching diametrically opposed to their own it is but just that I should clear the ground of scientific rubbish lest what I have to say should fall on a too encumbered soil and only bring forth weeds.

"This potential and imaginary *materia prima* cannot exist without form," says Raleigh, and he is right in so far that the *materia prima* of science exists but in their imagination. Can they say the same quantity of energy has always been moving the matter of the Universe? Certainly not so long as they teach that when the elements of the material cosmos, elements which had first to manifest themselves in their uncombined gaseous state, were uniting, the quantity of matter-moving energy was a million times greater than it is now when *our globe is cooling off.* For where did the heat that was generated by this tremendous process of building up a universe go to? To the unoccupied chambers of space, they say. Very well, but if it is gone for ever from the *material universe* and the energy operative on earth has never and at no time been the same, then how can they try to maintain the "unchangeable quantity of energy", that potential energy which a body may sometimes exert, the FORCE which passes from one body to another producing motion and which is not yet "annihilated or changed into anything else"? "Aye," we are answered, "but we still hold to its indestructibility; while it remains *connected with matter,* it can never cease to be, or less or more." Let us see whether it is so.

I throw a brick up to a mason who is busy building the roof of a temple. He catches it and cements it in the roof. Gravity overcame the propelling energy which started the upward motion of the brick, and the dynamic energy of the ascending brick until it *ceased to ascend.* At that moment it was caught and fastened to the roof. No natural force could now move it, therefore it possesses no longer potential energy. The motion and the dynamic energy of the ascending brick are absolutely *annihilated.* Another example from their own text books. You fire a gun upward from the foot of a hill and the ball lodges in a crevice of the rock *on* that hill. No natural force can, for an indefinite period, move it, so the ball as much as the brick has lost its potential energy. "All the motion and energy which was taken from the ascending ball by gravity is absolutely annihilated, no other motion or energy succeeds and gravity has received no increase of energy." Is it not true then that energy is indestructible! How then is it that your great authority teaches the world that "in no case is the force producing the motion annihilated or changed into anything else"?

I am perfectly aware of your answer and give you these illustrations but to show how misleading are the terms used by scientists, how vacillating and uncertain their theories and finally how *incomplete* all their teachings. One more objection and I have done. They teach that all the physical forces rejoicing in specific names such as gravity, inertia, cohesion, light, heat, electricity, magnetism, chemical affinity, are convertible one into another? If so the force producing must cease to be as the force produced becomes manifest. "A flying cannon ball moves only from its own inherent force of inertia." When it strikes it produces heat and other effects but its force of inertia is not the least diminished. It will require as much energy to start it again at the same velocity as it did at first. We may repeat the process a thousand times and as long as the quantity of matter remains the same its force of inertia will remain the same in quantity. The same in the case of gravity.

A meteor falls and produces heat. Gravity is to be held to account for this, but the force of gravity upon the fallen body is not diminished. *Chemical attraction* draws and holds the particles of matter together, their collision producing heat. Has the former passed into the latter? Not in the least, since drawing the particles again together whenever these are separated, it proves that it, the chemical affinity, is *not* decreased, for it will hold them as strongly as ever together. Heat they say generates and produces electricity yet they find no decrease in the heat in the process. Electricity produces heat we are told? Electrometers show that the electrical current passes through some poor conductor, a platinum wire say, and heats the latter. Precisely the same quantity of electricity, there being no loss of electricity, *no decrease*. What then has been converted into heat? Again, electricity is said to produce magnetism.

I have on the table before me primitive electrometers in whose vicinity chelas come the whole day to recuperate their nascent powers. I do not find the slightest decrease in the electricity stored. The chelas are magnetized, but their magnetism or rather that of *their rods* is not *that* electricity under a new mask. No more than the flame of a thousand tapers lit at the flame of the *Fo* lamp is the flame of the latter. Therefore if by the uncertain twilight of modern science it is an axiomatic truth "that during vital processes the *conversion* only and never the *creation* of matter or force occurs" (Dr. J. R. Mayer's organic motion in its connection with nutrition) — it is for us but half a truth. It is neither *conversion* nor *creation*, but something for which science has yet no name.

Perhaps now you will be prepared to better understand the difficulty with which we will have to contend. Modern science is our best ally. Yet it is generally that same science which is made the weapon to break our heads with. However, you will have to bear in mind (*a*) that we recognize but *one* element in Nature (whether spiritual or physical) outside which there can be no Nature since it is *Nature* itself,* and which as the *Akasha* pervades our solar system, every atom being part of itself, pervades throughout *space* and *is* space in fact, which pulsates as in profound sleep during the *pralayas*, and [is] the universal Proteus, the ever active Nature during the *manvantaras*; (*b*) that consequently spirit and matter are *one*, being but a differentiation of states not *essences*, and that the Greek philosopher who maintained that the Universe was a huge animal penetrated the symbolical significance of the Pythagorean monad (which becomes two, then three △ and finally, having become the tetraktis or the perfect square, thus evolving out of itself *four* and involuting three △, forms the sacred seven — and thus was far in advance of all the scientific men of the present time; (*c*) that our notions of "cosmic matter" are diametrically opposed to those of western science. Perchance if you remember all this we will succeed in imparting to you at least the elementary axioms of our esoteric philosophy more correctly than heretofore....

---

* Not in the sense of Natus 'born', but Nature as the sum total of everything visible and invisible, of forms and minds, the aggregate of the known (and unknown) causes and effects, the universe, in short, infinite and uncreated and endless, as it is without a beginning.

I will have to remain silent as to the Dyan Chohans nor can I impart to you the secrets concerning the men of the seventh round. The recognition of the higher phases of man's being on this planet is not to be attained by mere acquirement of knowledge. Volumes of the most perfectly constructed information cannot reveal to man life in the higher regions. One has to get a knowledge of spiritual facts by personal experience and from actual observation, for as Tyndall puts it, "facts looked directly at are vital, when they pass into words half the sap is taken out of them". . . .

Men seek after knowledge until they weary themselves to death, but even they do not feel very impatient to help their neighbour with their knowledge; hence there arises a coldness, a mutual indifference which renders him *who knows* inconsistent with himself and inharmonious with his surroundings. Viewed from our standpoint the evil is far greater on the spiritual than on the material side of man: hence my sincere thanks to you and desire to urge your attention to such a course as shall aid a true progression and achieve wider results by turning your knowledge into a permanent teaching in the form of articles and pamphlets.

But for the attainment of your proposed object, viz. — for a clearer comprehension of the extremely abstruse and at first incomprehensible theories of our occult doctrine, never allow the serenity of your mind to be disturbed during your hours of literary labour, nor before you set to work. It is upon the serene and placid surface of the unruffled mind that the visions gathered from the invisible find a representation in the visible world. Otherwise you would vainly seek those visions, those flashes of sudden light which have already helped to solve so many of the minor problems and which alone can bring the truth before the eye of the soul. It is with jealous care that we have to guard our mind-plane from all the adverse influences which daily arise in our passage through earth-life. . . .

Such a development of your psychical powers of hearing, as you name — the *siddhi* of hearing occult sounds — would not be at all the easy matter you imagine. It was never done to any one of us, for the iron rule is that what powers one gets *he must himself acquire.* And when acquired and ready for use the powers lie dumb and dormant in their potentiality like the wheels and clockwork inside a musical box; and only then does it become easy to wind up the key and set them in motion. . . . Yet every earnestly disposed man *may* acquire such powers practically. That is the finality of it; there are no more distinctions of persons in this than there are as to whom the sun shall shine upon or the air give vitality to. There are the powers of all Nature before you; *take what you can. . . .*

I have asked H. P. B. to send you a number of philosophical letters from a Dutch Theosophist at Penang — one in whom I take an interest: you ask for more work and here is some. They are translations, originals of those portions of Schoppenhauer which are most in affinity with our *Arhat* doctrines. The English is not idiomatic but the material is valuable. Should you be disposed to utilise any portion of it, I would recommend your opening a direct correspondence with Mr. Sanders, F.T.S. — the translator. Schoppenhauer's philosophical value is so well known in the western countries that a comparison or connotation of his teachings upon will, etc., with those you have received from ourselves might be instructive. . . .

Simla, *circa* June 30, 1882   MAHATMA K. H.

GLOSSARY

abhyasa	Constant practice; exertion
Adhibhuta	Primordial element
Adhidaivata	Substratum of divine intelligences
Adhiyajna	Primordial sacrifice; region of sacrifice
Aditi	Vedic name for *Mulaprakriti*; the abstract aspect of *Parabrahman*, though both manifested and unknowable
Agnishwatha Pitris	*Also* Solar Pitris. A class of dhyanis who lit up the principle of manas in the third race; our solar ancestors
ahankara	Egoism; the sense of 'I', self-identity
Ain-Soph	The Absolute, Endless, No-Thing; "Boundless" or Limitless Deity
Akasha	Space, universal solvent, spiritual substance, the *upadhi* of Divine Thought
Alaya	Universal Soul; identical with *Akasha* in its mystic sense, and with *Mulaprakriti* in its essence, as it is the basis or root of all things
Amitabha	Cosmic Buddha, the "Boundless Age," the Dhyani Buddha of Gautama Buddha
ananda	Bliss, joy
Anima Mundi	The seven-fold Universal Soul and material source of all life, the divine essence which permeates, animates and informs all, the essence of seven planes of sentience, consciousness and differentiation; *Alaya*
antaskarana	The bridge between the lower mind (head) and the higher mind (heart), between the divine Ego and the personal soul of man
Anupadaka	Parent-less, self-existing
Ashwatha	Sacred tree used to kindle the sacrificial fire: the Bo tree; the Tree of Knowledge, *ficus religiosa*
asuras	Class of celestial beings born from the breath —*Asu*— of Brahmā-Prajapati; the spiritual and divine ancestors of Manasic humanity
Atma	The Universal Spirit, the divine Monad, the seventh Principle in the septenary constitution of man; the Supreme Soul
Atman	SELF; divine breath; the universal Self
AUM	The sacred syllable, eternal vibration
avidya	Fundamental ignorance, any failure to discern the truth

Barhishad Pitris	*Also* Lunar Pitris. Lunar Gods, those who evolved astral prototypes of the human form; called in India the Fathers, "Pitris" or the lunar ancestors, and subdivided into seven classes or hierarchies
bhakti	Devotion
Bodhi	Wisdom
bodhichitta	*Lit.* 'seed of enlightenment'; embryo of spiritual man
Bodhisattva	*Lit.* 'he whose essence *(sattva)* has become Wisdom *(Bodhi)*'; enlightened being who remains in *samsara* to serve and help humanity
Book of Dzyan, The	*Also 'The Stanzas of Dzyan'.* An ancient, esoteric text written in an unknown language upon which *The Secret Doctrine* and *The Voice of the Silence* are based; *see* Dzyan
Brahmā	The creative Logos; the creator of the manifest universe in the Indian pantheon, the first of the Trimurti (three forms) of Brahmā, Vishnu and Shiva (creator, sustainer and destroyer/regenerator) existing periodically in manifestation then returning to *pralaya* (dissolving into non-manifestation) at the end of this cycle
Brahma	*Also Brahman.* The impersonal, supreme and incognizable principle of the universe; the Ultimate Reality; the attributeless Absolute
Brahma Vach	Divine wisdom; divine speech
Buddhi	Intellection, intuitive discernment, direct perception, resolute conviction, wisdom; the Universal Soul; the spiritual soul in man (the sixth principle), vehicle of *Atman;* divine discernment; Universal Intelligence
chakra	Wheel, discus; cycle; sphere; plexus or nerve center
chela	Disciple, especially the initiated disciple
chit	Thought, ideation, intellect
chitta	Consciousness; sometimes used generically for 'mind'
daimon	Inner voice of conscience and intuition; an aspect of the human soul
Daiviprakriti	Divine Nature; primordial, homogeneous light; the Light of the Logos
dana	Charity; the act of giving; alms-giving; generosity in thought, word and deed; the first *paramita*
deva	God, celestial being, resplendent deity
devachan	A post-mortem state of heavenly bliss wherein the Ego assimilates and enjoys the fruition of the good karma and harvest of the universal thought and intuition of the last life
Dhamma, the	*See* dharma
dharana	Concentration; steadiness in focus; mental firmness

dharma	Duty, moral law; social and personal morality; natural law, natural obligation; teaching, essence
Dhyan Chohan	*Lit.* 'Lord of Light'; one of the the highest gods; *pl.* the primordial divine intelligences and agents of divine law through which *Mahat* manifests and guides the Kosmos
dhyana	Contemplation, meditation; state of abstraction; the fifth *paramita*
Dhyani	Divine embodiment of ideation; man of meditation
Dzyan	*Lit.* 'to reform one's self by meditation and knowledge'; *see* The Book of Dzyan
Ego, the higher	SELF; the consciousness in man of "I am I" or the feeling of "I-am-ship"; Esoteric philosophy teaches the existence of two Egos in man, the mortal or personal, and the Higher, the Divine and the Impersonal, calling the former "personality" and the latter "Individuality."
Epimethean	Of Epimetheus: Greek Titan. *Lit.*, 'Afterthought'; brother to Prometheus ('Forethought')
Eros	The third personage of the Hellenic primordial trinity of Ouranos, Gaea and Eros; the abstract and universally beneficent creative force in nature, degraded by later attributions; *see also kama*
Fohat	The active (male) potency of the *Sakti* (female power) in nature; Higher Eros or *Kamadeva*, the essence of cosmic force or electricity; *Daiviprakriti*; the link between spirit and matter
Gelukpa	*Lit.* 'Yellow Caps', the highest and most orthodox Buddhist sect in Tibet. The Dalai Lama, responsible for all Tibetan Buddhist traditions, is a Gelukpa.
gnosis	Spiritual, sacred Knowledge; the technical term used by the schools of religious philosophy before and during early Christianity
Great Breath	Symbolizing eternal ceaseless Motion; the One Life, eternal yet periodic in its regular manifestations; Absolute, omnipresent Consciousness
Grihastha Ashrama	The householder stage of life
guna	Propensity; quality; constituent
Gupta Vidya	Secret Wisdom, highest knowledge
guru	Venerable teacher; religious preceptor; spiritual teacher
Guruparampara	Sacred lineage of teachers
Hatha yoga	The practice of the lower form of Yoga, in which physical means for purposes of spiritual development are used; the opposite of Raja Yoga
Hermes-Thot	(Often written Hermes-Thoth) The archetype of Initiators; God of Wisdom with the Ancients, who, according to Plato, whether as Egyptian god Thot or Greek god Hermes, 'discovered number, geometry, astronomy and letters'

Hermes Trismegistus	A lineage of Initiators in ancient Egypt, ultimately traceable to Shiva as Dakshinamurti, Initiator of Initiates; Initiates who transferred from latent to active potency a precise and comprehensive knowledge of the complex laws governing the seven kingdoms of Nature, constituting a divine gnosis
Hiranyagarbha	The radiant or golden egg or womb; esoterically, the luminous 'fire mist' or ethereal stuff from which the universe was formed
Hotri	A priest who recites the hymns from the Rig Veda, and makes oblations to the fire
Ishtaguru	One's chosen teacher
Ishwara	The sovereign Lord; the omnipresent Spirit; the controller of maya
Itchashakti	The divine power of the will; one of the seven powers in nature and the human being
jnana	Wisdom; knowledge
jnana yajna	Wisdom-sacrifice
jnana yoga	Yoga of knowledge; communion through wisdom
Kali Yuga	The dark age; the fourth age; the iron age that began in 3102 B.C.
kalpa	Cosmic cycle, day of Brahmā
kama	Desire, attraction, passion; cleaving to existence; creative impetus and longing; *see also* Eros
kama manas	The desire mind, the lower *Manas* or human animal soul, the reflection of the higher *Manas*
kamaloka	The semi-material plane, to us subjective and invisible, where the disembodied "personalities" or human astral remains gradually disintegrate
kamarupa	The form of desire; the assemblage of cravings
karana	Instrument of action; basis of causation
karana sharira	The causal body; the inmost sheath
karma	Act, action; the law of ethical equilibrium
kosha	Sheath; body
Krishna	The eighth Avatar of Vishnu
Kriyashakti	Creative imagination; a cosmic and human power
kshetra	Field, soil; portion of space; sphere of action; Nature
Kundalini-shakti	The power of life; one of the forces of Nature; a power known only to those who practice concentration and Yoga
Kwan Yin	The female logos, the "Mother of Mercy"
lanoo	A disciple; *see also* chela

laya	Absorption, dissolution, repose; resting place; motionless point, still center; zero point
linga sharira	Astral body, aerial vesture, prototypal, vital body; *eidolon*; doppelgänger
Logos	The 'Verbum'; the 'Word'; the manifested Deity, the outward expression of the ever-concealed Cause
Lunar Pitris	*See* Barhishad Pitris
Maha Chohan	The chief of a spiritual Hierarchy, or of a school of Occultism; the head of the trans-Himalayan mystics
Mahakalpa	Great age
mahamanvantara	The manifestation of cosmos from *mahapralaya;* out-breathing of the Great Breath
Mahapurusha	Equivalent term for *Paramatman*, the Supreme Spirit
Mahat	The first principle of universal intelligence and consciousness; the primal basis of individuation; cosmic ideation; the cosmic Mind behind manifested Nature and the great hebdomadal Heart of all humanity
Mahatma	Great soul; exalted exemplar of self-mastery and human perfection
Manas	Mind; the faculty of cognition, choice and self-awareness
Manasa	"The efflux of the divine mind"; the divine sons of Brahmā-Viraj, identical with the Kumara, the Manasaputra, and are identified with the human "Egos"
Manasaputras	The sons of (universal) Mind; human "Egos"; spiritual individuality of each human being
manomaya kosha	Mental sheath; one of five sheaths of the human constitution
manvantara	Cosmic cycle of manifestation
maya	Illusion, appearance; the cosmic power behind phenomenal existence
moksha	Deliverance, emancipation
Monad	The Unity, the One; the unified triad *(Atma-Buddhi-Manas)*, or the duad *(Atma-Buddhi)*; the immortal part of man
Mulaprakriti	Root Nature; undifferentiated primordial substance; unmanifested matrix of all forms
namarupa	The fourth link in the chain of twelve *nidanas; nama* or mind, and *rupa* or form; *see nidana*
nidana	The twelve links in the chain of dependent origination, a concatenation of causes and effects; the cycle of birth, life, death and rebirth
nirguna	Without attributes; devoid of relations and qualities; un-modified; unbound
Nirguna Brahman	Brahma without attributes; Brahma (neuter); *see nirguna*

nirvana	Unalloyed bliss; the entire 'blowing out' of separateness; absolute consciousness
nitya pralaya	One of four kinds of *pralaya*, the stage of chronic change and dissolution, of growth and decay; the constant and imperceptible changes undergone by the atoms which last as long as a *mahamanvantara*, a whole age of Brahmā
nous	A Platonic term for the Higher *Manas* or Soul; Spirit as distinct from animal soul or psyche; divine consciousness or mind in man
OM	The mystic monosyllable; the soundless sound; the Word
OM TAT SAT	The triple designation of *Brahman*
para	*Lit.* 'beyond' or 'above'
Parabrahman	Supreme *Brahman;* the attributeless Absolute
paramitas	Transcendental virtues that lead to enlightenment
Philosophia Perennis	The perennial philosophy; the source of all true religions and philosophies; sometimes equated with the Secret Doctrine
Pitris	The ancestors or creators of mankind, of seven classes, three incorporeal *(arupa)*, and four corporeal; *see* Solar Pitris and Lunar Pitris
prajna	A synonym of *Mahat*, the Universal Mind; the capacity for perception; Consciousness; wisdom; the sixth paramita
prakriti	Nature in general; spiritual nature, as distinct from *purusha*, Spirit; together the two primeval aspects of the One Unknown Deity
pralaya	A period of obscuration or repose—planetary, cosmic or universal—the opposite of *manvantara*
prana	Life-Principle; the breath of life
Pranava	The sacred Word, OM
Purusha	Spirit; the primeval man; the supreme being; the animating principle in all beings
Raja Yoga	System of developing spiritual powers through union with the Supreme Spirit; regulation and concentration of thought
rajas	One of the three *gunas* which constitute the qualities or divisions of matter; activity and change
Ṛg Veda, Rig Veda	The first and most important of the four Vedas; recorded in Occultism as having been delivered by great sages on Lake Manasarovar beyond the Himalayas
Root Race	The human Race has been compared to a tree—the main stem may be compared to the Root-Race, its larger limbs to seven Sub-Races
Ṛta, rita	Cosmic order, divine law; righteousness

Saguna Brahman	With attributes and all perfections; Brahman
samadhi	*Lit.* 'self-possession'; the highest state of yoga; ecstatic meditation; supreme self-control
samsara	Conditionality, as contrasted with *nirvana*; realm of becoming, in contrast to Being; birth and death; conditioned existence; illusion
Sanatana Dharma	The eternal doctrine; the perennial philosophy; immemorial codes
Sangha, the	order of monks; assembly; community; preservers, transmitters and teachers of the dharma
SAT	The ever-present Reality, absoluteness, Be-ness
Sat-Chit-Ananda	Abstract reality, consciousness and bliss
sattva	One of the three *gunas* which constitute the qualities or divisions of matter; the quality of goodness or purity; *see gunas*
satya	Supreme truth
Shankaracharya	The great religious teacher and legendary reformer of India, the founder of Advaita Vedanta philosophy; *also* Shankara
Shantideva	685-763 A.D. Indian Buddhist monk and scholar at Nalanda, an adherent of the Madhyamika philosophy of Nagarjuna
sharira	Body
shila	Harmony in action; virtue, morality; an internally enforced ethical outlook; the second *paramita*
Shiva	Third god of the Hindu *Trimurti* Brahma-Vishnu-Shiva; in his character of Destroyer, he destroys only to regenerate on a higher plane
Solar Pitris	*See* Agnishwatha Pitris
Sophia	Wisdom; the female Logos of the Gnostics; the Universal Mind
Sophrosyne	Ancient Greek concept of self-control, restraint, soundness of mind, prudence and temperance
srotapatti	One who has entered the stream leading to enlightenment
sthula sharira	In metaphysics, the physical body
sunyata	'Void' or 'nothingness', but not a mere negation: the ineffable non-dual Reality that transcends all limitations and dualities, including *nirvana* and *samsara*
suras	Gods, *devas*
sushupti	Deep sleep consciousness
sutratman	Thread soul; reincarnating individuality

Svabhavat	The spirit and essence of Substance; from the root word *Subhava: su* — good, perfect; *sva* — self, and *bhava* — being or state of being; the "Father-Mother"
svadharma	One's own duty; natural calling; self-chosen responsibility
svasamvedana	*Lit.* the 'reflection which analyses itself'; *see paramartha*
swaraj	Freedom; self-rule, disciplined rule from within; political independence
tamas	The lowest of the three *gunas* which constitute the qualities or divisions of matter; the quality of darkness, foulness, inertia, and ignorance
tanha	The thirst for life; desire to live; clinging to life on this earth which causes rebirth or reincarnation; *also trishna*
tapas	Moral fervor; self-suffering; specific austerities and prolonged contemplation; that which burns up impurities
TAT	*Lit.* 'That'; *Brahman;* beyond the three worlds; the pre-existent
Tathagata	Nature of a Buddha; one who has followed in the steps of his predecessors
tathata	Real nature, ultimate nature; attributelessness
Tetraktys	The sacred Quaternion; the Number of numbers; the Source of Nature; manifest Deity; the creative principle, represented by the triangle containing ten points in four rows, symbolizing the creative triad, the manifesting tetrad and the basic integers $(1 + 2 + 3 + 4 = 10)$, as well as the point (1), line (2), figure (triangle, 3) and solid (tetrahedron, 4)
Theosophia	"Divine Wisdom", the substratum of truth and knowledge which underlies the universe, from which of all the great world-religions and philosophies were derived; pure divine ethics. While *Theosophia* cannot be put entirely in words, Theosophy is what can be expressed at this time.
Theosophy	The maximal expression of *Theosophia* at this time in history; *See Theosophia*
Thot-Hermes	*See* Hermes-Thot
trishna	*Lit.* 'thirst' or 'craving', the cause of suffering; *also tanha*
Tsong-Kha-Pa	1357-1419 A.D. The 'model of virtue': Tibetan Buddhist founder of a new reformed order, the Gelugpa, to which all Dalai Lamas belong; stated by H.P. Blavatsky to have initiated a Seven Century Plan to infuse the Wisdom current into Western consciousness through various agents of the Society of Sages
turiya	Spiritual wakefulness; the fourth or highest state of the soul
Upanishads	Esoteric doctrines; interpretations of the Vedas by the methods of Vedanta

upaya	*Lit.* 'skill in means' or 'skilful device', the means by which difficult teachings are made comprehensible to persons of differing mental capacities
vahan	vehicle
Vak	From *vach, vacha:* voice, word, speech
Vedas	The most ancient and sacred Sanskrit works: the *Rig, Atharva, Sama, Yajur Vedas;* from the root *vid* 'to know' or 'divine knowledge'
Verbum	The Word; the manifested Deity, the outward expression of the ever-concealed Cause; *see* Logos
viraga	Detachment; indifference to pleasure and pain, illusion conquered, truth alone perceived; in certain trans-Himalayan schools, an additional *paramita* inserted as the fourth in the series
virya	Energy directed towards truth; vigour; courage; the fourth *paramita*
Word, the	*See* Verbum
Wu-Wei	*Lit.*, 'inexertion' or 'inaction'; action through nonaction
Yang	The masculine active principle in nature that in Chinese cosmology is exhibited in light, heat, or dryness
Yin	The feminine passive principle in nature that in Chinese cosmology is exhibited in darkness, cold, or wetness
yoga	Unswerving concentration; fusion, integration; union with the divine; skill in action
yogin	Practitioner of yoga; proficient in yoga
Zoroaster	The Greek rendition of Zarathustra—*Lit.* 'the star who sacrifices to the Sun', the founder of Zoroastrianism; a title which some traditions give to thirteen Magus-Teachers

BIBLIOGRAPHY

Arnold, Sir Edwin. *The Light of Asia.* David McKay Co.,
Philadelphia 1932.

Bellamy, Edward. *The Religion of Solidarity.* Concord Grove
Press, Santa Barbara 1977. Originally published
in 1874.

Blavatsky, Helena Petrovna. *Isis Unveiled.* Theosophy Co., Los
Angeles 1982. Originally published in 1877.

———— *The Key To Theosophy.* Theosophy Co., Los Angeles 1987.
Originally published in 1889.

———— *Lucifer,* 1887-1890. H.P. Blavatsky and Mabel Collins,
London.

———— *The Secret Doctrine.* Theosophy Co., Los Angeles 1947.
Originally published in 1888.

———— *Theosophical Articles, Vols. I - III.* Theosophy Co., Los
Angeles 1981. Originally published in 1886-96.

———— *The Theosophical Glossary.* Theosophy Co., Los Angeles
1973. Originally published in 1892.

———— *Transactions of the Blavatsky Lodge.* Theosophy Co., Los
Angeles 1987. Originally published in
1890-91.

———— *The Voice of the Silence.* Concord Grove Press, Santa
Barbara 1989. Originally published in 1889.

Collins, Mabel. *The Gates of Gold.* Concord Grove Press, Santa
Barbara 1982. Combined volume: *Through the
Gates of Gold* (1887) and *Light on the Path* (1885).

Crosbie, Robert. *The Friendly Philosopher.* Theosophy Co., Los
Angeles 1934.

———— *The Language of the Soul.* Concord Grove Press, Santa
Barbara 1982. Originally published in 1919.

Iyer, Raghavan, ed. *In the Beginning (Zohar)*. Concord Grove Press, Santa Barbara 1979.

———— *The Golden Verses of Pythagoras*. Concord Grove Press, Santa Barbara 1980.

———— *The Gospel According to Thomas*. Concord Grove Press, Santa Barbara 1976.

———— *Hermes, 1975 - 1989*. Concord Grove Press, Santa Barbara.

———— *Return to Shiva (Yoga Vasishtha)*. Concord Grove Press, Santa Barbara 1977.

———— *Tao Te Ching*. Concord Grove Press, Santa Barbara 1978.

———— *The Jewel in the Lotus*. Concord Grove Press, Santa Barbara 1983.

Judge, William Quan. *The Bhagavad Gita: The Book of Devotion*. Theosophy Co., Los Angeles 1971. Originally published in 1890.

————*"Forum" Answers by William Q. Judge*. Theosophy Co., Los Angeles 1982. Originally published 1889-96.

———— *The Ocean of Theosophy*. Theosophy Co., Los Angeles 1962. Originally published in 1893.

———— *Theosophical Articles*. Theosophy Co., Los Angeles 1980.

Mavalankar, Damodar K. *The Service of Humanity*. Concord Grove Press, Santa Barbara 1982. Originally published in 1884.

Patanjali. *Yoga Aphorisms*. Theosophy Co., Los Angeles 1951.

Plato. *The Banquet*. Translation by P.B. Shelley, Concord Grove Press, Santa Barbara 1981.

Plotinus. *The Enneads*. Translation by S. Mackenna. Faber and Faber, London 1966.

Russell, George William. *The Descent of the Gods, The Mystical Writings of A.E.* Ed. by Raghavan and Nandini Iyer. Colin Smythe, London 1983.

Shankar, Bhavani. *The Doctrine of the Bhagavad Gita.* Concord
Grove Press, Santa Barbara 1984. Originally
published in 1966.

Shankaracharya, Shri. Shankara's *Crest-Jewel of Discrimination:
Timeless Teachings on Nonduality — The Viveka-
chudamani.* Translated by Christopher
Isherwood and Swami Prabhavananda. Vedanta
Press, UK 1978.

Taimni, I.K. *The Gayatri.* The Theosophical Publishing House,
Madras 1974.

Wadia, B.P. *The Grihastha Ashrama.* Concord Grove Press,
Santa Barbara, 1981. Originally published in
1941.

———— *The Law of Sacrifice.* Concord Grove Press, Santa Barbara,
1981. Originally published in 1961.

INDEX

NOTES

NOTES

NOTES

NOTES

NOTES

NOTES